CONTRIBUTORS

FRANK DAWES worked as a reporter on Fleet Street and later for the BBC, where he specialized in travel programs. He lives in Sussex and is the author of *Not in Front of the Servants*. He is the editorial consultant for this guidebook.

CHARLOTTE ATKINS is the author of several guidebooks and now Travel Editor of *Woman's Own* magazine in London.

ANTHONY BURTON has written several books on the industrial history of England—and one on the history of beer and pubs—and has written and presented several television series about England's industrial heritage for the BBC.

BRYN FRANK is the author of *Everyman's England* and *Short Walks in English Towns*. He contributed to National Geographic's *Discovering Britain and Ireland* and has written for a number of other magazines and newspapers. He is the principal researcher for Swallow Press's annual *Good Holiday Cottage Guide*.

SUSAN GROSSMAN was born in and lives in London. Formerly Travel Editor of *The Telegraph Sunday Magazine* and research officer on *Holiday Which?*, she has presented a program on food for the BBC, and was the editor of *What Hotel?* magazine.

ALEX HAMILTON is the author of seven works of fiction and a travel book on the Trans-Siberian railway. He is a winner of the Fitzgerald Award for travel writing, and Travel Editor of the British national daily, *The Guardian*.

KATIE LUCAS, the author of a best-selling book on walking tours of London, has lived in Suffolk for many years and runs a London-based specialized British tours company.

ANGELA MURPHY is a free-lance journalist who has contributed to a number of guidebooks, including the *Shell Weekend Guide Book* to England and *Hachette's Guide to Britain*.

KEN THOMPSON, journalist and broadcaster, has lived in the Devon/Cornwall area for 29 years. He edited the famous *Falmouth Packet* newspaper and was, for 12 years until 1987, Cornwall's Chief Tourist Officer.

DAVID WICKERS contributes regularly to several major British publications, is Travel Editor of *Marie Claire* magazine and Travel Correspondent of the London *Sunday Times*.

THE PENGUIN TRAVEL GUIDES

AUSTRALIA

CANADA

THE CARIBBEAN

ENGLAND & WALES

FRANCE

GERMANY

GREECE

HAWAII

IRELAND

ITALY

MEXICO

NEW YORK CITY

PORTUGAL

SAN FRANCISCO &
NORTHERN CALIFORNIA

SPAIN

THE PENGUIN GUIDE TO ENGLAND & WALES 1991

ALAN TUCKER

General Editor

PENGUIN BOOKS

PENGUIN BOOKS

Published by the Penguin Group
Viking Penguin, a division of Penguin Books USA Inc.,
375 Hudson Street, New York, New York 10014, U.S.A.
Penguin Books Ltd, 27 Wrights Lane,
London W8 5TZ, England
Penguin Books Australia Ltd, Ringwood,
Victoria, Australia
Penguin Books Canada Ltd, 2801 John Street,
Markham, Ontario, Canada L3R 1B4
Penguin Books (N.Z.) Ltd, 182-190 Wairau Road,
Auckland 10, New Zealand

Penguin Books Ltd, Registered Offices:
Harmondsworth, Middlesex, England

First published in Penguin Books 1989
First revised edition published 1990
This second revised edition published 1991

1 3 5 7 9 10 8 6 4 2

Copyright © Viking Penguin,
a division of Penguin Books USA Inc., 1989, 1990, 1991
All rights reserved

ISBN 0 14 019.927 6
ISSN 0897-6864

Printed in the United States of America

Set in ITC Garamond Light
Designed by Beth Tondreau Design
Maps by Mark Stein Studios
Illustrations by Bill Russell
Fact-checked in London by Patricia Bayer
Edited by Susan Shook

THIS GUIDEBOOK

The Penguin Travel Guides are designed for people who are experienced travellers in search of exceptional information that will help them sharpen and deepen their enjoyment of the trips they take.

Where, for example, are the interesting, isolated, fun, charming, or romantic places within your budget to stay? The hotels described by our writers (each of whom is an experienced travel writer who either lives in or regularly tours the city or region of England and Wales he or she covers) are some of the special places, in all price ranges except for the lowest—not the run-of-the-mill, heavily marketed places on every travel agent's CRT display and in advertised airline and travel-agency packages. We indicate the approximate price level of each accommodation in our descriptions of it (no indication means it is moderate), and at the end of every chapter we supply contact information so that you can get precise, up-to-the-minute rates and make reservations.

The Penguin Guide to England & Wales 1991 highlights the more rewarding parts of the country so that you can quickly and efficiently home in on a good itinerary.

Of course, the guides do far more than just help you choose a hotel and plan your trip. *The Penguin Guide to England & Wales 1991* is designed for use *in* England and Wales. Our Penguin writers tell you what you really need to know, what you can't find out so easily on your own. They identify and describe the truly out-of-the-ordinary restaurants, shops, activities, and sights, and tell you the best way to "do" your destination.

Our writers are highly selective. They bring out the significance of the places they cover, capturing the personality and the underlying cultural and historical resonances of a city or region—making clear its special appeal. For exhaustive, detailed coverage of cultural attractions, we suggest that you also use a supplementary reference-type guidebook, such as a Blue Guide or a Michelin Green Guide, along with the Penguin Guide.

The Penguin Guide to England & Wales 1991 is full of reliable and timely information, revised each year. We would like to know if you think we've left out some very special place.

ALAN TUCKER
General Editor
Penguin Travel Guides

375 Hudson Street
New York, NY 10014
or
27 Wrights Lane
London W8 5TZ

CONTENTS

MAPS

THE
PENGUIN
GUIDE
TO
ENGLAND
& WALES
1991

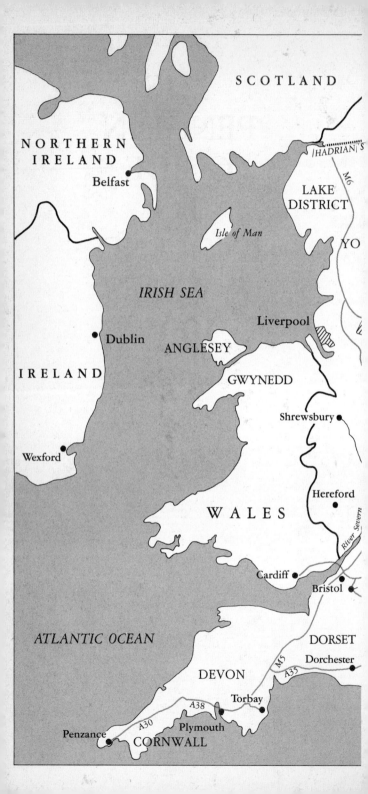

England and Wales

	miles	40
0		
0	kilometers	50

- Berwick-upon-Tweed
- Newcastle-upon-Tyne
- *WALL*
- Durham
- *A1*

NORTH SEA

NORTH YORK MOORS

RKSHIRE DALES

N

- Leeds
- York
- *M6*
- Manchester
- *A46*
- Lincoln

E N G L A N D

- Norwich
- *A1*

EAST ANGLIA

- Birmingham
- *M5*
- *A11*
- Stratford-upon-Avon
- Cambridge
- *M1*
- Cheltenham
- Oxford
- *M11*
- *M40*
- London
- Windsor
- *Thames River*
- Bath
- *M4*
- *M2*
- SURREY
- *M3*
- Canterbury
- Salisbury
- Dover
- Winchester
- SUSSEX
- KENT
- *A36*
- Southampton
- Brighton
- Calais
- *A31*
- Portsmouth
- Isle of Wight
- F R A N C E

ENGLISH CHANNEL

OVERVIEW

By Frank Dawes

Frank Dawes has worked as a reporter on Fleet Street and for the BBC, where he specialized in travel programs. He lives in Sussex and is the author of Not in Front of the Servants. *He is a member of the British Guild of Travel Writers.*

History, pageantry, and landscape are what bring tourists to Britain by the millions. Many of the English-speaking visitors are coming to the mother country of a mighty empire that no longer exists, to the "Old Country" some of them have never set eyes on before. England is still a constitutional monarchy, "Shakespeare's royal throne of kings, this sceptered isle," with an innate sense of theater that shows itself as much in the daily rituals of changing the guard at Buckingham Palace and Windsor Castle and the Beefeaters' ceremony of the keys at the Tower of London as in the larger pageantry of royal weddings, funerals, and coronations, Trooping the Colour, or the State Opening of Parliament. The love of pomp and pageantry flourishes in the age of video and television, and the British love dressing up for Medieval fairs and performing festivals in Dickensian costume.

The British royal family, apparently a never-ending subject of fascination to republicans around the world, are sometimes likened to characters in a soap opera. This does them less than justice. **Windsor Castle**, the place they call home, where Prince Albert set up the first Christmas tree to be seen in England and from which the Queen sends out her annual message to the nation and the Commonwealth, is a castle with nine centuries of monarchic history, set in a park of 4,800 acres—an easy

5

day trip to the west of London. Even Cecil B. De Mille never envisaged an epic of *that* scale.

As well as being a home, Windsor Castle is a museum, and museums in Britain are enjoying a renaissance. No longer are they seen as musty, silent places filled with rows of glass cases and stuffed animals. With all the resources of new technology, the stories of York, Canterbury, and Oxford are being retold graphically. At the same time, the history of Britain's steam-age industries is being promoted as the industries themselves wither away and die. The open-air museum at Beamish in Durham, once a great coalfield, and the new museum complex at Wigan Pier (to which George Orwell took his road) in Wigan are outstanding examples of these exciting techniques.

Great Britain's maritime heritage is being given its due not just in the national museum at Greenwich but also in such seafaring cities as Bristol, where the S.S. *Great Britain,* the first steam-powered iron ship, has been rescued from the scrapyard, and Plymouth, where the Pilgrims set sail in the *Mayflower.* Portsmouth ("Pompey" to the Royal Navy for centuries) has achieved a remarkable hat trick in setting up Henry VIII's warship *Mary Rose,* Nelson's flagship *Victory,* and the Victorian ironclad *Warrior* as walk-through dockside exhibits. (To get an idea of just how many museums there are in Britain that celebrate the nation's industrial and maritime past, see the Industrial Heritage chapter.)

Profound resistance to new ways and new ideas while adapting superficially is characteristic of an island race, and Great Britain has a longer past than most countries. But it has a present, too, and has been forced by circumstances to change rapidly in the last few years. Britain is not a museum or some kind of stage set but a small, highly developed country with a population in excess of 60 million. The fact that its people are extremely mobile, in addition to the influx of tourists, has led to an insatiable demand for more and more motorways; Britain's two major airports, Heathrow and Gatwick, have become the busiest in the world, bar none. As for the future, by 1992 the European Community will have become a single trading market, and by 1993 a railroad across Kent, the "Garden of England," will be funneling greatly increased traffic into the new Eurotunnel that, after two centuries of dreams and false starts, will finally do away with the moat that for so long has guarded England "against the envy of less happier lands," as Shakespeare put it. "This blessed plot, this earth, this realm, this England" will then be attached to Europe firmly and irrevocably. Trains will speed from London to Brussels or Paris through twin tunnels 30 miles long as easily as they now go to Manchester or Newcastle.

The British capital is gearing up for a faster pace—too fast for some people. Prince Charles has expressed concern about the effect of the accelerating development of characterless new office buildings on the familiar and much-loved skyline of the old City. The dome of Christopher Wren's St. Paul's Cathedral has been obscured by this explosion of high-rises, which is spreading eastward from Aldgate Pump into what used to be the docklands of the East End. All in all, **London** is witnessing its greatest rebuilding since the Great Fire of 1666.

London's eight square miles of waterfront, for 150 years the world's foremost seagoing port, had become a wasteland with the decline of the docks. Now from the dereliction a new city is arising between the Norman Tower of London and the stately front of Greenwich, which still looks as it did when Canaletto painted it in the mid-18th century. A London City Airport for STOL flights to Paris, Brussels, and Plymouth has been built on the site of the Royal Docks. Computer-driven overhead trains run every few minutes from Tower Bridge along the length of the Isle of Dogs, where King Henry VIII kept his hunting dogs, surrounded by a wide loop of the River Thames. The river is about to become again the great highway it was in Tudor times.

And on marshy bankside, south of the Thames, redevelopment has uncovered the remains of Tudor theaters: the Rose and the Globe—the "Wooden O"—where many of Shakespeare's plays, including *Hamlet,* were first performed. After 20 years of negotiation and planning, Sam Wanamaker's reconstruction of the Globe Theatre in timber, wattle, and daub under a tiled roof has been erected on the far side of the old bear garden adjoining the original theater sites.

Yet for all the new building of offices, shopping precincts, and leisure centers, hotels, concert halls, sports arenas, marinas, and museums, London remains a city of villages. It is a mistake to concentrate on the familiar sights of Westminster and the City and to miss out on Hampstead, Richmond, and Chelsea. London, like some other parts of Britain today, is a rich ethnic mix. In the East End, Soho, Notting Hill, and Camden Town, the customs and cuisine are worth exploring.

Nor is London by any means Britain. Castles and cathedrals, ancient churches and cottages, ruined abbeys and stately homes are scattered the length and breadth of Shakespeare's sceptered isle, its High Streets displaying a millennium of architectural styles—Norman churches, Tudor half-timbered affairs, Georgian terraces, Victorian Gothic buildings—alongside modern supermarkets. The green and pleasant landscape bears the traces of earlier conquerors and civilizations—a Roman road and villa here, a Viking place name there, Celtic barrows and tumuli and mysterious circles of Neolithic stones, such as Stonehenge on Salisbury Plain. Stratford-upon-Avon has Shakespeare; Ayot St. Lawrence has Shaw; Bradford has the Brontës, J. B. Priestley, and a whole new Muslim culture.

It is all very well to follow the beaten tourist track to Scotland via Stratford and the Lake District or York, but it is just as rewarding to make the odd detour, perhaps to seek out the rural retreat of Virginia Woolf and the rest of the Bloomsbury set in deepest **Sussex** (only an hour from London)—and rediscover Kipling at the same time—as we suggest in the Literary Southeast chapter. There are literally hundreds of **historic houses and properties** open to visitors, and only a few of them remain in private hands. The majority are run by two major organizations, each of which publishes its own guide and list of opening times, which vary enormously, and admission charges. Contact the National Trust at 36 Queen Anne's Gate, London SW1H 9AS, or English Heritage at Keysign House, 429 Oxford Street, London W1R 2HD, for details.

The Great British Heritage Pass, which can be bought in advance at travel agents around the world or, on showing a passport, at tourist information offices in England, gives unlimited access to 600 castles, stately homes and gardens, and other places of interest all over the country. The pass comes with a map-folder listing all the properties, opening times, and locations.

If you want to tread in the footsteps of Chaucer's pilgrims to Canterbury, the North Downs Way will point you there and beyond to Shakespeare Cliff, the highest point of the wall of chalk fronting the English Channel. This is but one of several **long-distance walking paths** in England and Wales—the South Downs Way, Cotswold Way,

Pennine Way, Offa's Dyke Path, and the Pembrokeshire Coast Path are just some of the others. (Guidebooks on these walks can be obtained in England from Her Majesty's Stationery Office, P.O. Box 276, London SW8 5DT, and in the United States from HMSO Books, Bernan-Unipub, 4611-F Assembly Drive, Lanham, MD 20706-4391.)

Villages and small towns whose peace was rudely disturbed by the coming of the railways in the 19th century were returned to rural slumber in the 1960s:

> When Dr Beeching took his axe
> And gave BR [British Rail] those mighty whacks
> A wondrous gift came free of tax
> For all who love to walk the tracks

Thus Hunter Davies opens his book *A Walk Along the Tracks,* in which he explores former railway cuttings and embankments now given back to wildlife, dog roses, and blackberries, including Three Bridges to East Grinstead in Sussex, York to Market Weighton, Cockermouth to Penrith, the Wirral Way, the Wye Valley, and the Somerset and Dorset. There are 8,000 miles of disused railway in Britain. Here and there the bygone age is lovingly preserved by steam enthusiasts on short stretches of track—the Watercress Line in Hampshire, the Bluebell Railway in Sussex, the North Norfolk, and the North Yorkshire Moors, to name but a few. Special steam excursions are run during the summer to Stratford-upon-Avon from Marylebone Station in London, with roast-beef lunch and afternoon tea served to each passenger.

Indeed, **rail travel** in England is enjoying a renaissance with the expansion of "Land Cruises" in special trains with sleeper cars and day trips from London. The elegant umber-and-cream carriages of the Venice Simplon Orient-Express re-create the inter-Wars heyday of the Brighton and Bournemouth Belles with trips to historic castles in Kent, Sussex, and Hampshire, to the seaside at Bournemouth, and to Georgian Bath. There are excursions by Orient-Express to the highlights of the social season—Royal Ascot, Glorious Goodwood, Newmarket, Henley Regatta—and to the parvenu Suntory World Matchplay Golf Championship.

An even earlier legacy of the Industrial Revolution—the network of **canals** carved across England two centuries ago to carry freight in narrowboats drawn by horses—is also finding a new lease on life in tourism. Nearly 2,000 miles of navigable inland waterways remain, and they offer a fascinating inside view of countryside, old villages, and market towns, sometimes off the beaten track. The choice is between renting a self-skippered narrowboat (probably painted in traditional style with roses and castles but powered by a diesel engine and comfortably heated, furnished, and equipped) and taking a cruise on a hotel boat. One of the most luxurious examples of the latter is *Le Sans Egal,* a two-decked barge that carries eight guests on the River Thames between Windsor and Oxford, with shore excursions to places of interest such as Blenheim Palace (the birthplace of Sir Winston Churchill) and special packages for Royal Ascot and Henley Regatta. The *Actief* operates a similar schedule with room for 12 passengers. A retired Royal Navy captain and his wife operate the twin barges *Barkis* and *Peggotty* through the East Anglian canals with a two-day visit to Cambridge. Contact UK Waterways Holidays, Welton Hythe, Daventry NN11 5LG, for details. Several U.S. travel agents handle bookings direct.

Britain is good **motoring** country once the visitor has adapted to driving on the left. There is a network of toll-free motorways and trunk roads that has cut travelling time considerably, and the main car-rental companies have hundreds of branches in all the larger towns and at ports and airports. The completion of the M 25, which orbits London at a radius of 12 to 21 miles, with 32 junctions connecting with motorways and major routes to other parts of the country, has added to the ease of road communications. But England *is* a small and overcrowded island, and at peak times traffic can be very heavy indeed.

"A" roads, usually marked in red on maps, are main routes. "B" roads are secondary two-lane routes, usually of reasonable standard. Motorways (expressways) are designated by the letter M. For those with the time, the "B" roads provide an alternative way of getting around the country and are often surprisingly free of traffic. However, unlike the motorways, they wander this way and that, with frequent junctions and crossroads, and road signs are not always all they might be. An Ordnance Survey or Automobile Association road map will pay dividends in any exploration of Britain's byways.

If you use the motorways to travel from center to center and "A" and "B" roads for an in-depth look at a particular area, ten days is an optimum amount of time for a tour of England and Wales. A couple of days is usually enough time to explore any one area. The British

Tourist Association's *Motoring Itineraries in Britain* is available free from its overseas offices (see the Useful Facts section following). It details 15 suggested routes, ranging from five to 15 days, and three theme tours covering writers, gardens, and Norman England. There are tourist information centers in all regions and at certain service areas on the motorways, and exits to major historical and heritage sites are clearly marked.

Nowhere is the impact of tourism on Britain more apparent than in its hotels and restaurants. The multinational companies have not only built new hotels but also restored many old coaching inns to their former glory, adding all the facilities that travellers now demand. Another development has been in country-house hotels—offering the highest standards of comfort and cuisine—often privately run by young entrepreneurs trained in the great hotels of Europe.

The standards of the smaller family-run hotels and guesthouses have improved beyond recognition, though we all still enjoy laughing at "Fawlty Towers." Fresh local meat, fish, and vegetables are featured on most menus, and good wine, properly served, is now the rule rather than the exception. No longer are overcooked cabbage and warm beer inescapable penalties for travelling in Britain, any more than freezing bathrooms or lumpy beds are. No more do the British consider discomfort to be a virtue.

The pubs of England and Wales are now allowed to remain open from 11:00 A.M. to 11:00 P.M., Mondays through Saturdays, thanks to an overdue change in a law introduced during the First World War that aimed to keep munitions factory workers sober by shutting pubs in the afternoons. Sunday closing time is now 3:00 P.M. instead of 2:00 P.M., when they may close until 7:00 P.M. and then reopen until 10:30 P.M. It is up to individual pub owners whether to stay open or to call "Time, Gentlemen, please!" as usual. Most of those in London's West End and in tourist resorts have opted for all-day opening and have increased their range of food service (pub lunches are excellent value). Some even offer morning coffee and afternoon tea in addition to alcohol.

Your choices of areas to tour in England and Wales are wide, and our book is intended to help you make your choice. A day trip south from London takes you to **Brighton**, a town by the sea, built on misbehavior following the bad example of an extravagant and debauched monarch, George IV, and to the northwest and north respectively are the ancient university cities of **Oxford** and **Cambridge**. They are miles apart geographically but always paired, with Oxford first, even when the names are merged in "Oxbridge." Each strives to outdo the other in style as well as in their annual boat race on the Thames.

Many tourists venture no farther than Oxford or **Stratford-upon-Avon**, which is a pity because beyond these two much-visited centers are virtually undiscovered tracts of countryside and unspoiled towns. We describe many such places in our chapters The Coltswolds to Winchester and The Heart of England.

To go west from London? **Wessex**, the ancient kingdom of Arthur and the knights of the Round Table, no longer exists on the map, but its legends live on in the region extending from the Avon to the beautiful South Coast of Hampshire and Dorset, where in 1944 the Allied armies were marshaled for D-Day. This is Thomas Hardy country, too, where literary tourists may identify places described under fictional names in his novels, such as Bournemouth, which appears as "Sandbourne." The New Forest, hunting ground of kings of ages past, lies just outside Southampton on this coast overlooking the Isle of Wight, where the Americas Cup was inaugurated at the Cowes Regatta. Besides **Winchester**, **the Cotswolds**, and **Stonehenge**, **Bath**, of course, with the newly renovated Pump Room and memories of Regency foppishness as well as its Roman baths, is firmly on the tourist track. Farther west yet is Plymouth, where Sir Francis Drake set sail to beat the Spanish Armada—but not before he had finished his game of bowls on the Hoe. It's a handy base for exploring **Cornwall** and **Devon**, the former a place apart that has always attracted poets and painters.

Beyond the Welsh border is another country, albeit a tiny one, with its own language and its own fierce national pride, expressed in heavenly choral singing and uninhibited rugby football. The Welsh will tell you in English that their tongue is older, indeed that it is the original language of Britain. The Welsh number fewer than three million, and there are twice as many sheep grazing on the wild and lonely hills. Although the capital, Cardiff, is less than two hours from London by high-speed train, **Wales** is still a mountain stronghold ringed with ancient castles, one of which is the official seat of the

Prince of Wales. It also has the industrial heritage of the coal-mining valleys of South Wales and the slate mines of North Wales, celebrated in marvelous museums at Blaenavon and Blaenau Ffestiniog. Every July the town of Llangollen attracts a gathering of singers, dancers, musicians, and poets for the *Eisteddfod,* or music festival. They come not just from Wales but from all over the world.

In effect, the North of England is another country, too. The decline of its traditional heavy industries of coal, textiles, steel, and shipbuilding, and the consequent high levels of unemployment, have widened what is known as the North–South Divide. The barrier is emphasized by the fact that although the **North Country** does not have its own language, as Wales does, it does have a variety of dialects. The accents of the Liverpool Scouser or the Geordies of the Northeast might well sound foreign to the uninitiated, and since the war, Muslim immigrant communities in the old mill towns have added even more strands to an already colorful tapestry.

The black slag heaps that once disfigured so much of the landscape are now for the most part grassed over. Cities like Bradford, Leeds, and Manchester, which in the past offered little but fish and chips, now welcome travellers with fine hotels and restaurants, including some that serve the ethnic cuisines of Asia. Northerners are less reserved and standoffish than Southerners, more outgoing, easier to talk to. It does rain often, but no more often than anywhere else in Britain, and just as unpredictably. The weather is the opening gambit in almost every casual conversation.

The North Country's **Lake District** has been attracting tourists ever since the English Romantics, led by William Wordsworth, made rugged scenery fashionable at a time when war in Europe made the Alps inaccessible. The scenery *is* spellbinding, but no more so than areas of Northumberland, the **North Yorkshire Moors**, and the **Yorkshire Dales**, all also national parks. Spectacular stretches of heather-covered hillside and craggy fells, wooded valleys, rushing rivers and waterfalls, gray stone country towns, and immense red-brick viaducts and bridges characterize the North Country. And the **Northumberland Coast** from Newcastle to the Scottish border is among the finest to be found anywhere in Great Britain, its long sandy beaches fringed with ancient castles that are often all but deserted.

Tourists throng the great cathedrals of **Canterbury** southeast of London and, in the North, **York**, and justifiably so, but sometimes a small village church can provide just as much of a spiritual experience. In the depths of what was once the Durham coalfield, at Escomb, is the oldest Saxon church in Britain, built with stones from a ruined Roman fort nearby when, as Bishop Lightfoot points out, "England was not yet England, when Saxons had recently settled in the island, and Danes were beginning to harry the coasts and Normans were still undreaded, because unknown."

Another part of Britain that is all too often neglected by the visitor lies between Cambridge and the North Sea and up to the Wash, the **East Anglia** that Constable loved to paint. Inland from Aldeburgh, at the navigable limit of the River Alde, are the red-brick Victorian buildings erected to process barley and now famous throughout the world: Snape Maltings, where music is taught and an annual festival is held. Yet this is a secret coast of shingle and sand dunes, marshes and salt creeks, where fishing vessels and sailing barges bask at low tide. Its spacious landscape stretches from the Stour to the Wash, changing from wooded hills and lush meadows to the watery network of the Norfolk Broads, thronged with cruisers and yachts, to the fens and flat, fertile farmlands won back from the sea with dykes and embankments.

"This precious stone set in the silver sea," this England, has many facets and other smaller islands strung about it like a necklace, from the **Scillies**, 28 miles southwest of Land's End in Cornwall, to the **Farnes**, just off the northeast coast, where gray seals breed and seabirds fill the skies with their cries. There is a rare music from these unsung isles that calls people from the mainland.

Britain's historical, literary, and cultural heritage is so diverse that it would be impossible to include everything worth seeing in one book. We have reluctantly passed over **Bristol**, the city of explorers such as John Cabot and his son Sebastian, who founded the Merchant Adventurers of London; **Lincoln** and its historic cathedral; the isolated Channel Islands of **Guernsey** and **Jersey**; and the semi-independent **Isle of Man**, off the northwestern coast of England. The fact that we are obliged to omit such gems is a measure of the "sceptred isle" 's richness. Our aim has been to select *some* of the rarer delights of "this other Eden, demi-paradise," as well as to guide you along the favorite and, by definition, more crowded paths.

USEFUL FACTS

When to Go

There is never an off-season for Britain. Although many people might prefer to come in May, when the azaleas and rhododendrons in some of the lovely gardens are in full bloom, other people might prefer year-end holiday time, when they can enjoy a typically English Christmas, with all its connotations of log fires and pantomimes.

Britain's major tourist season is July and August, and as a result hotels, restaurants, and theaters are often booked then. The stately homes and gardens also have their full share of the tourist torrent. Spring and autumn are much better times to visit.

The weather in Britain is entirely unpredictable, but these two seasons are also often the nicest. Spring can be wonderful, with mild, sunny weather and the trees coming into leaf. Autumn, with its glorious, hazy-sunny days, often goes on until Christmas. But England is, after all, an island, with an oceanic climate subject to the winds and weather of the Atlantic.

What to Wear

If you come loaded with Burberry and thick sweaters, you may have three weeks in the 80s; of course, the reverse can also happen. The answer is to bring a little bit of everything. You are unlikely to need very dressy evening clothes, because, except for grand balls, the English tend not to dress up much; they underdress rather than overdress and will go, for example, to the theater and even the opera in the clothes they wear to the office.

Getting In

Most international airlines serving Britain use London's Heathrow or Gatwick airports. Increasingly, a number of international carriers are also using the airports in Manchester and Birmingham, providing direct access to the Midlands. From North America, there are now direct flights to London from Atlanta, Boston, Chicago, Dallas/Fort Worth, Los Angeles, Montreal, New York, San Francisco, Toronto, and other cities. Just some of the many major airlines flying the North America–Britain route are Air Canada, Air India, American, British Airways, British Caledonia, Pan Am, TWA, Virgin Atlantic, and World. Qantas and British Airways fly the long route between Britain and Australia.

The London airports are well connected to the central city by public transportation. Heathrow is on the Underground (Piccadilly line; 45 minutes from the airport to Piccadilly Circus), which is very convenient. However, if you are taking the Underground from the city center to Heathrow, it is essential that you know from which terminal you are departing. One Underground stop serves terminals 1, 2, and 3; another serves terminal 4—and if you get off at the wrong stop, you will walk miles with your baggage. You can also take a Green Line bus from Heathrow to Victoria Coach Station, or Carline buses and vans to Victoria Coach Station and Waterloo, King's Cross, Euston, Paddington, and Victoria railway stations. London Transport's Express Airbus makes stops throughout central London, ending at Euston, Paddington, and Victoria stations. The bus trip from Heathrow to central London takes about 45 minutes. Taxis make the trip from Heathrow to central London in about the same time and charge about £30.

The best way to get from Gatwick to London is by train. This extremely efficient service runs directly from the main terminal every 15 minutes, and trains reach Victoria Station in just 30 minutes. Carts are available so you can push your luggage from customs to the entrance to the train platform. Hourly Green Line buses also connect Gatwick with Victoria Coach Station.

Ferries link Britain with dozens of ports on the Continent and in Ireland. The two major Continental lines are P and O, which serves Dover–Boulogne, Dover–Calais, Dover–Zeebrugge, Felixstowe–Zeebrugge, Portsmouth–Cherbourg, and Portsmouth–Le Havre (Tel: 0304-20-33-88), and Sealink British Ferries, which serves Dover–Calais, Folkestone–Boulogne, Harwich–Hook of Holland, Portsmouth–Cherbourg, and Weymouth–Cherbourg (Tel: 071-834-8122). The trip across the Channel can take anywhere from a few hours to a full day or night, depending on your destination. The fastest crossing is to be had on one of the crafts of Hoverspeed, which make the trip from Dover to Calais or Boulogne in just 35 minutes (Tel: 0304-24-02-41). P and O and Sealink, along with several other companies, also connect western England (Liverpool is the major port) with Ireland.

For those who enjoy a longer sea voyage, the Cunard line's *Queen Elizabeth II* makes the transatlantic crossing from New York to Southampton in style, from April through December.

Entry Documents

A passport is required of all travellers entering Britain, with the exception of citizens of other EC countries, who must present only an identity card. Citizens of the U.S., Commonwealth nations (Canada, Australia, and New Zealand), South Africa, and many other countries do not need a visa. Britain imposes strict anti-rabies measures, and all pets entering the country must be quarantined for a minimum of six months; unless you are moving to Britain, leave the pets at home.

Getting Around

British Rail, the national railroad network, serves some 2,500 stations throughout Britain. Major cities are connected by the extremely rapid (up to 125 MPH) InterCity trains, and overnight trains (equipped with sleeping cars) run from London to the North of England, Wales, the west, and Scotland.

If you are travelling from London, be forewarned that there are eight different train stations, each serving a different part of the country: Charing Cross serves southern England; Euston, northern Wales, the western Midlands, northwestern England and Scotland; Kings Cross, the eastern Midlands, northeastern England, and eastern Scotland; Liverpool Street, East Anglia; Paddington, western England and southern Wales; St. Pancras, the southern Midlands; Victoria, southern England; and Waterloo, southwestern England.

Several discount passes for train travel are available. The most popular is the BritRail Pass, available for both first-class and second-class travel, which allows holders unlimited travel through England, Scotland, and Wales for periods of 8, 15, or 22 days or for one month.

National Express is Britain's nationwide bus network. Of special interest to overseas visitors is the Tourist Trail, which runs from mid-May through October and links London with major tourist spots—Stratford-upon-Avon, York, etc.—around the country. Travellers can follow the entire 14-day-long itinerary or make daily forays from London. The BritExpress Card is available only at overseas British Rail offices and offers a 33 percent discount on all bus travel in Britain for one month.

Among the airlines connecting British cities are British Airways, British Caledonia, British Midlands, and Dan-Air.

Most major car-rental agencies have offices at airports and train stations in sizable cities. You must be 21 years of age (25 with some firms) and present a valid driver's license; an international driver's license is not required. Driving is on the left, and drivers from the United States and other countries where driving is on the right may have difficulty adjusting to this orientation. Be extremely careful. The same holds for pedestrians—remember to look both ways when stepping into a street.

Barge trips along the canals of the Industrial Revolution are becoming another popular way to see the English countryside. For booking details see Overview, above.

Local Time

Britain observes Greenwich Mean Time (GMT), five hours ahead of the East Coast of North America (excluding the Canadian Atlantic Provinces) and nine hours behind Sydney, Australia.

Telephoning

The country code for Britain is 44. When dialing from outside Britain, do not include the initial 0 in city codes. The London area has been split into two area codes: (071) for inner London and (081) for outer London.

Currency

The unit of currency in Britain is the pound sterling (denoted as £), which is divided into units of 100 pence. There are coins for 1 p, 2 p, 5 p, 10 p, 20 p, and 50 p, and notes in denominations of £5, £10, £20, and £50. The rate of exchange fluctuates. Check postings in banks and in daily newspapers for the current rate of exchange.

In the main hall at most airports there is a bank where you can change foreign currency into pounds and pence. Outside airports, banks are open Mondays through Fridays between 9:30 and 3:30. There are many Bureaux de Change around London, and most hotels will change money. However, both charge a higher rate than the banks do, so if at all possible, remember to change your money during banking hours.

Business Hours

Most businesses in England are closed on Sundays. This is a day for strolling in the parks and going to church. Very few shops are open, many restaurants are closed, and even museums don't open until 2:00 P.M. During the week most pubs now stay open from 11:00 A.M. to 11:00 P.M. On Sundays they open at noon and close from 3:00 to 7:00, then open until the 10:30 P.M. closing.

Shops open at 9:00 and close at 5:30, except for the one evening a week when shops in most districts of London stay open until 8:00 P.M.—Wednesdays in Knightsbridge and Kensington and Thursdays in Oxford Street. Shops and most banks are closed for bank holidays.

Holidays

Bank holidays are Christmas Day and Boxing Day (December 26), New Year's Day, Good Friday and Easter Monday, May Day (the first Monday in May), Whit Bank Holiday (the last Monday in May), and August Bank Holiday (the last Monday in August).

Electric Current

Voltage in Britain is 220/240, 50 HZ, which means that an adapter or converter is necessary for North American appliances.

Information

Offices of the British Tourist Authority provide maps, booklets on sights and travel itineraries, accommodations listings, tips on travel passes and tourist discount passes, and a wealth of other information and are located in cities and towns across Britain. BTA offices abroad are extremely helpful when you are planning a trip. Major offices are located at: 40 West 57th Street, New York, NY 10019 (Tel: 212-581-4700); Suite 600, 94 Cumberland Street, Toronto, Ontario M5R 3N3 (Tel: 416-961-8124 or 416-925-6326); and Associated Midland House, 171 Clarence Street, Sydney, NSW 2000 (Tel: 61-29-8627).

—*Katie Lucas*

BIBLIOGRAPHY

PETER ACKROYD, *Dickens' London*. Ackroyd sets the scene and then leaves it to Dickens's writings and to excellent photographs to bring Victorian London alive.

ALISDAIR AIRD, *The Good Pub Guide*. A Consumers' Association annual, this guide to the pub, that most British of institutions, gives clear descriptions of pubs and, where applicable, also describes the food they offer.

THE AUTOMOBILE ASSOCIATION, *2000 Days Out in Britain*. A complete listing of places open to the public, with opening times and admission charges.

THE AUTOMOBILE ASSOCIATION AND THE WALES TOURIST BOARD, *Castles in Wales*. This guide to Welsh castles contains 15 round-trip tours.

JOHN H. BARRETT, *The Pembrokeshire Coast Path*. Part of the HMSO walking series.

JAMES BISHOP, ED., *The Illustrated Counties of England*. Well-known writers describe their favorite counties. This is a book for those who appreciate quirky, personal views.

JANET AND COLIN BORD, *Ancient Mysteries of Britain*. Where standard guides offer strictly factual descriptions of ancient sites, the Bords explore them in terms of prehistoric religions and mystical forces.

EDITH BRILL, *Life and Tradition on the Cotswolds*. This book serves as a reminder that there is more to the Cotswolds than pretty scenery and picturesque villages. The area's sights are related to centuries of working life.

THE BRITISH TOURIST AUTHORITY, *Wales: Where to Go and What to See*. The title sums up what this guide offers.

ANTHONY BURTON, *Cityscapes*. A fully illustrated guide to 18 British cities.

————, *The National Trust Guide to Our Industrial Past*. A fully illustrated survey of industry from Neolithic flint mines to steam locomotives, including a complete gazetteer of sites open to the public.

PETER CLAYTON, *Archaeological Sites of Britain*. This illustrated guide lists and describes all the principal archaeological sites in the country. It is written as a continuous narrative and organized by region.

HUNTER DAVIES, *The Good Guide to the Lakes* and *A Walk Along the Wall*. Good companions for anyone who likes exploring the countryside on foot rather than on wheels.

FRANK VICTOR DAWES, *Not in Front of the Servants*. The definitive history of upstairs-downstairs life in England, from the early 19th century on. This book provides a fascinating view of stately homes and country houses where the vanished order of domestic service once flourished. Now a National Trust Classic.

DANIEL DEFOE, *A Tour Thro' the Whole Island of Great Britain*. A fascinating glimpse of England before the Steam Age. Published in 1724 and recently reprinted in Penguin paperback.

MARGARET DRABBLE, *A Writer's Britain*. This is no mere catalog of places visited and described by famous writers but rather a survey of how authors have viewed the land. The photographs by Jorge Lewinski are excellent.

DAPHNE DU MAURIER, *Vanishing Cornwall*. The novelist used Cornish settings for much of her work, and this book is a personal view of all she loved in the county. Although it is vanishing, happily it has not yet vanished.

MARK GIROUARD, *Life in the English Country House*. Stately homes appear on most visitor itineraries, and this brilliant and hugely enjoyable book links the architecture of the great houses to their social history.

ELIZABETH GUNDREY, *England by the Sea*. Where most guidebooks concentrate on the beaches, this guide explores virtually everything else, from old ships to bus tours of the coast.

JACQUETTA HAWKES, *The Shell Guide to British Archaeology*. This is a comprehensive guide to ancient sites throughout Britain with excellent photographs by Jorge Lewinski.

JOHN HAYDEN AND DAVID WICKERS, *The Good Holiday Cottage Guide*. A popular annual collection of the best cottages and apartments to rent for vacations in Britain.

SUSAN HILL, *Shakespeare's Country*. The country of the title is the area around Stratford-upon-Avon. This book explores the landscape of the Bard's works, rather than merely listing places known to be associated with Shakespeare.

W. G. HOSKINS, *The Making of the English Landscape*. A classic work that traces how the English have shaped the landscape, both town and country, from ancient times to the present day.

GLYN HUGHES, *Millstone Grit*. A description of life on the Pennine hills and among the mill towns of Yorkshire and Lancashire.

TOM JAINE, ED., *The Good Food Guide*. An annual review of over 1,000 of the best restaurants in Britain, produced by the Consumers' Association.

EDGAR JOHNSON, *Charles Dickens, His Tragedy and Triumph*. The definitive biography of Dickens, with evocative descriptions of the Medway towns and Broadstairs as Dickens knew them.

RUDYARD KIPLING, *Puck of Pook's Hill*. A eulogy of England and the English, especially those in Sussex.

RICHARD LLEWELLYN, *How Green Was My Valley*; *Up, into the Singing Mountain*; *Down Where the Moon Is Small;* and *Green, Green My Valley Now*. A charming series of novels set in Wales.

DAVID W. LLOYD, *Historic Towns of South-East England*. The author describes more than 60 towns, from the obviously attractive (such as Brighton) to the relatively unknown. He traces their history and explores their character with the help of excellent illustrations.

KENNETH O. MORGAN, ED., *The Oxford Illustrated History of Britain*. This is a single-volume history of Britain, from the first Roman invasion to the present day, written by a team of experts who combine erudition with readability.

JAN MORRIS, *Oxford*. This is one of those rare books that has become a classic, a description of the city that combines a wealth of information with acute personal observation.

JAN MORRIS AND PAUL WAKEFIELD, *Wales, The First Place*. This beautiful book is a celebration of Wales that strikes a perfect balance between Morris's words and Wakefield's photographs.

IAN NAIRN, *Nairn's London*. The classic guidebook revised by Peter Gasson in a new Penguin edition.

Nicholson Guides to London. A series of slim guides, including Pubs, Night Life, and a London Shopping Guide and Streetfinder.

NORMAN NICHOLSON, *Portrait of the Lakes*. The author is a poet and a native Lakelander. He provides beautiful descriptions of England's most romantic region, yet never loses sight of the area's working, everyday life.

V. S. PRITCHETT, *London Perceived*. This is London as seen by an author who has lived in the city since the days of hansom cabs and gas lights. The theme is historical, but it is history firmly tied to the London of today.

J. M. RICHARDS, *The National Trust Book of English Architecture*. This fully illustrated guide is arranged chronologically and written by a most distinguished architect.

CHARLES ROBERTSON, *Bath*. This illustrated guide explores the city's architecture but manages to work in a good deal of history as well.

EGON RONAY, *Guide to Healthy Eating Out*. As the name suggests, a restaurant guide aimed primarily at the vegetarian, although it also lists places that cater to the carnivore.

———, *Just a Bite*. This is essential reading for those looking for good, cheap meals, with the accent on "good." It is particularly useful for finding specialties, such as a genuine afternoon tea or a decent fish-and-chip shop.

EDWARD STOREY, *Spirit of the Fens*. This is an evocative study of an area that the author has known and loved all his life—an area that does not always easily reveal its charms to the casual visitor.

DYLAN THOMAS, *Under Milk Wood*. A joyful celebration of Welsh life by the country's most famous writer.

THE WALES TOURIST BOARD, *A Glimpse of the Past*. A tourist's guide to industrial trails, slate quarries, mines, and mills. Also from the Tourist Board is *Castles and Historic Places in Wales*.

———, *Walking*. Available from bookshops or Tourist Information Centres, this book lists more than 211 marked trails and paths, as well as 351 unmarked walks throughout Wales.

ELIZABETH WEST, *Kitchen/Garden/Hovel in the Hills.* Three accounts of a simple life in rural Wales.

WILLIAM WORDSWORTH, *Guide Through the District of the Lakes.* First published in 1810, this is *the* Romantic view of the Lakes.

KENNETH A. WRIGHT, *Gentle Are Its Songs.* A complete history of the Welsh *Eisteddfod* festival of song.

—Anthony Burton

LONDON

By David Wickers

David Wickers, a longtime resident of London, is Travel Correspondent for the Sunday Times *of London, Travel Editor of* Marie Claire *magazine, and a regular contributor to several other magazines and newspapers in the United Kingdom He is a member of the British Guild of Travel Writers.*

Few writers on London manage to resist the temptation to bring the good Dr. Johnson into their prose. But an up-to-date version of his most famous and flattering compliment would soften the drastic course of action for men or women tired of London. Rather than giving up on life, as Dr. Johnson suggested, they can merely shift their point of reference. When tired of one part of London, they can, nowadays, simply find another part more suited to their mood or circumstances.

Two hundred years ago, when Johnson was writing, "London" meant a condensed commercial core huddled along the northern flanks of the Thames, a sordid ghetto defined by rows of unsanitary buildings fighting for light and breath. Beyond a scatter of surrounding villages lay folds of open countryside. London today is a motley urban patchwork of places. Unlike the majority of the world's capitals, whether or not they choose to use the particular word, London does not have an obvious downtown. Ask a Londoner to put you on the right bus or train for this mythical epicenter of urban activity and you will still be none the wiser about just where you want to go.

If you, the lost cause, happen to be dressed in a smart but dreary suit and carry a briefcase, you'll probably be pointed toward the City, the hub of banking and other financial dealings centered on the Stock Exchange and the Bank of England. Wear an elegant dress with chic accessories, and you'll be politely directed toward Knightsbridge. Sport the most stylish of designer "uniforms," and the finger will point to the slickest route to Covent Garden. Look a shade less trendy, and you'll be dispatched to the West End, which geographically (just to further the confusion) refers to the streets that radiate from Oxford Circus, right in the center of town.

To broaden the idea of London's self-image, let us, for the moment, reverse the roles. Ask half a dozen residents when they are abroad to tell you where they live, and they will simply say London. Ask the same question when they are back in London, and you would expect to hear a street or a numbered district. But that's not the way it is. Londoners live in Notting Hill, Highgate, Mayfair, Chelsea, Fulham, Greenwich, and umpteen other destinations whose pedigrees are often rooted in the very villages that lay outside the London of Dr. Johnson's time. It is the differences among these districts that account for the capital's enormously rich diversity. It is not the city's museums, its parks, or the endlessly abundant evidences of yesteryear that make it special, but its lack of obvious definition. When a man is tired of London he jumps on a bus to Richmond, on a tube to Camden Town, or into a taxi to Soho.

There are several contenders for our opening pages, but we begin with London's river, "Old Father" Thames, and let the current carry us east to the City, the hub of finance, and its fringing areas. Then we leap back into the center of town to feel the pulse of Covent Garden with its historic roots but distinctly contemporary flavors. Nearby is Bloomsbury with its museums and literary associations, cosmopolitan Soho and the West End's major stores. Mayfair, its neighbor, could be dubbed American London, being home to the American Embassy, but Westminster, the seat of the British Parliament and various government offices, is undiluted U.K.

Moving west, we take a turn upmarket to Belgravia and Knightsbridge, among the city's most affluent sections. Nearby Chelsea also means wealthy residents, although the style is a shade more avant garde. But this is just as well; otherwise the culture shock between Knightsbridge and Notting Hill, northwest across Hyde Park, famous for its annual carnival when its largely black population takes to the streets in a pageant of calypso and reggae, would be hard to digest. Farther west, both Richmond and Hampton Court, famous for the palace of King Henry VIII, are green gems. Not that the west enjoys a monopoly of urban greenery. In the north, Regent's Park, with its zoo, is one exception; it's close to both Madame Tussaud's wax museum and Camden Lock's weekend market, both major tourist pulls. Islington and Hampstead, farther north, are great places for a saunter around interesting small shops (Islington for antiques, Hampstead for clothes, though neither exclusively so). Hampstead also has the bonus of the best of London's open spaces, the rural landscapes of the Heath.

Back toward the east is the epicenter of Cockney London, the East End, with its deep Jewish and, more recently, Indian and Pakistani ways of living. Back on the river is the new city of London, the Docklands area, a vast horizon of disused docklands that have been, and are still being, transformed into both residential and commercial properties. From the very latest neighborhoods in London you can walk through a tunnel under the River Thames that will bring you face to face with Greenwich, one of the most historic.

MAJOR INTEREST

Thames
Boat ride on the Thames
Tower of London
South Bank Arts Centre

The City
St. Paul's Cathedral
Museum of London
Fleet Street
The Strand
Inns of Court

Covent Garden
Royal Opera House
Shopping
Courtauld Institute

Bloomsbury
British Museum

Soho
Chinatown

Jazz
Ethnic restaurants

West End
Oxford Street and Regent Street for shopping
Piccadilly Circus
Royal Academy
The Wallace Collection

Mayfair
Grosvenor and Berkeley squares

Westminster
Buckingham Palace (Changing of the Guard)
Churchill's bunker
Houses of Parliament
Westminster Abbey
St. James's Park
National Gallery
Tate Gallery

Knightsbridge–Belgravia
Harrods and other shops
Hyde Park

Notting Hill
Annual Caribbean Carnival

Chelsea–South Kensington
Shopping on King's Road
Old houses of literary greats
Victoria and Albert Museum and other National
    Museums

Richmond
Walks along the Thames
Kew Gardens

Hampton Court

Camden Town
Camden Lock weekend market
Regent's Park and London Zoo
Nash terraces
Regent's Canal

Marylebone Road
Madame Tussaud's waxworks
Planetarium

Islington
Antiques shops and markets
Sadler's Wells Theatre

Hampstead
Hampstead Heath

East End
Cockney atmosphere
Petticoat Lane market
Kosher and Indian food

Docklands
Historic ships and buildings
New development

Greenwich
Observatory
Greenwich Park

The Thames

Although there is no single London, there is a significant single divide between the north and the south: the River Thames. Moving upstream (west) from Tower Bridge, there are more than a dozen bridges that link its northern and southern banks. Despite the ease of transition, though, the emotional divide between north and south London is deeply rooted. While the south has always had its pockets of affluence in such places as Dulwich Village and Blackheath, joined now by Battersea, Greenwich, Clapham, and a block of other recently gentrified boroughs, the north has long enjoyed the monopoly on affluence. But more to the point, as far as the traveller is concerned, south London has relatively little to offer the tourist compared with the wealth of attractions—from stylish shops to seasoned sights—north of the river.

London happened because of its river. Its commercial significance was the city's raison d'être. Today, although the forest of masts and rigging, vibrant warehouses, cranes, and general state of economic frenzy that dominated the area in the past have all but disappeared from the scene, the Thames is still the most essential element in London's chemistry.

Among the world's great rivers the Thames ranks very low. Its entire length runs only a little more than 200 miles, making it a mere stream in contrast to, say, the 4,000 miles of the Amazon or even Europe's 1,000-mile-

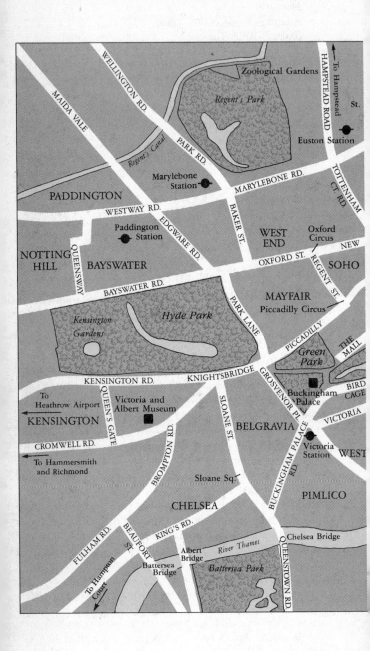

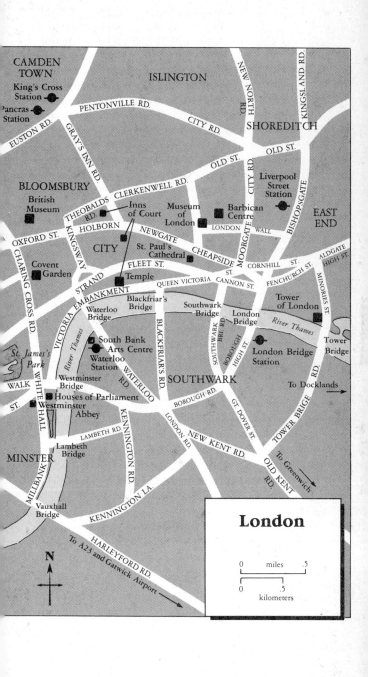

long Rhine. And it is not always a pretty sight, especially at low tide when its muddy banks are exposed. But while a boat ride along the Seine may be hard to beat when it comes to romance, Paris's river cannot hold a candle to the Thames for the sheer interest sustained by the passing panorama. In the 1950s the Thames was so filthy that anyone who had the misfortune to fall in was rushed off to have his stomach pumped. Today, perch, trout, and even the occasional salmon have been fished from its waters. The Thames has been granted a new lease on life, one in which leisure has taken the place of commerce, and its importance as a focal point for the visitor is of greater significance now than it has ever been.

A boat ride is the best way to enjoy the Thames. Starting from **Westminster Pier**, right beside Westminster Bridge on the opposite side of the road from the Houses of Parliament, you can travel on a regular number of sailings in either direction. You'll drift past several of the most important sights in the city, and while most will cry out for far closer scrutiny than from the rails of a passing launch, at least the ride—backed by a commentary—is an apt introduction to the London scenario.

The most historically important riverside sight is the **Tower of London**. First built of wood by William the Conqueror in 1067, then converted to stone a decade later, it protected the King's capital both from the invaders sailing upstream from the Channel and from conquered Londoners who might challenge his authority. Perhaps the tower's most famous historical role was as a prison to a score of leading figures, including the Little Princes (both allegedly murdered in the so-called Bloody Tower), Thomas More, Anne Boleyn, Sir Walter Raleigh, Guy Fawkes, and, the last in the line, Rudolf Hess. Many were to pass through Traitor's Gate, the main entrance, never to see the daylight again.

Although the tower is one of those "obvious" sights that the majority of Londoners probably haven't visited since their childhood, its popularity with visitors is enormous. Apart from the impressive antiquity of the place, there are two other aspects of the tower visit that will linger in the memory long after the knowledge of the date of its foundations has faded. First is the **Crown Jewels**, which include the five-pound crown said to have been worn by all British monarchs, including Queen Elizabeth II, since Charles II (and maybe even earlier), and the crown of the Queen Mother, which incorporates the enormous Koh-i-

Noor diamond (a name now associated with thousands of mostly insignificant Indian restaurants scattered throughout the city).

The second memory will be of the **Beefeaters**—more officially, the Yeoman Warders—whose history dates from their role as bodyguards to Henry VII in the 15th century. They parade every morning at 11:00 in the Inner Ward, but you can see them at their most spectacular—though you need to make a written application to the Resident Governor of the Tower to do so—at the Ceremony of the Keys, the closing of the main gates of the tower every evening at 10:00. Before you leave the tower, be sure to count the ravens. There are six, and legend dictates that when they no longer flap about the place, the tower will fall.

Immediately in front of the tower is **Tower Bridge**, probably the single most widely recognized landmark in the entire city. Though your visit may not coincide with the impressive opening yawn of its road section—or bascules—as it only occurs roughly three times a week, the bridge nevertheless makes a stunning picture. It took eight years to build and was opened in 1894 with great pomp and ceremony by the Prince of Wales, later King Edward VII. At the time it was hailed as one of the great engineering wonders of the world. In its heyday, the bridge would open for passing business some 50 times a day and required a permanent staff of more than 100, including a few whose sole role was to collect the horse droppings (presumably so they wouldn't cascade down the opening bascules onto waiting traffic).

The bridge cost £1 million to build, and in the early 1980s £2.5 million was the price of converting it into a tourist attraction. Today you can make acquaintance with the bridge from the walkway, the topmost, latticed structure that links the two great Gothic towers. The walkway and several tower rooms constitute a museum, with exhibits illustrating the history of the bridge (including, for those who miss it, pictures of the bridge with its jaws wide open for passing ships; one photograph shows a bus that failed to stop and was caught straddling the gap). Best of all, the museum affords one of the best views of the Thames to be had.

The place in central London, however, that offers the most intimate relationship with the Thames is the **South Bank Arts Centre**, by Waterloo Bridge. In front of the Royal Festival Hall, built for the Festival of Britain in 1951, there is a broad promenade along which to stroll, lean, and watch the passing barge traffic or gaze at the Houses of Parliament. The Royal Festival Hall is an architectural triumph of its time, but you may not feel that the same accolades can be applied to its neighbors. You will no doubt form a strong opinion about the newer buildings in the complex—stark, highly radical concrete presences that house the Queen Elizabeth Hall, the Purcell Room, the Hayward Gallery, the National Theatre, and the National Film Theatre. The newest attraction, opened in September 1988, is the **Museum of the Moving Image**, the largest museum in the world devoted to cinema and television. It traces the history of film from the Chinese shadow plays of 2000 B.C. to the latest in optical disc technology. Another new development is Gabriel's Wharf, next to the National Theatre, which features a colorful food market on Fridays, with some stalls open on Sundays.

The City

Unmistakably, **St. Paul's Cathedral** *is* London. Designed by Sir Christopher Wren, Britain's most highly regarded architect, the great church now sits rather uncomfortably in its surroundings, not unlike an aging, rent-controlled tenant who occupies a prime parcel of fast-appreciating real estate. Look at a selection of old paintings of London, and St. Paul's, with its curvaceous dome and squat twin towers, reigns magnificently over the skyline. Even in pictures taken during the Blitz, the wartime bombing inflicted by the Luftwaffe, the cathedral's environs lie around its ankles.

Today, the cathedral has been both hidden and dwarfed by clusters of uninspired office buildings, all fed by revenues from the City's commerce. Prince Charles has even gone on record as decrying such works as "carbuncles." Poor old St. Paul's looks pitiably ill at ease in this setting, and, architectural gem though it is, it no longer works the way Wren intended it to.

When you do occasionally catch a glimpse of the cathedral riding above the skyline of modern London—from the southern bank of the Thames, near Blackfriars Bridge, for example, or looking along from Fleet Street—it is superb. The dome, a giant pewter tureen from the outside, ornately painted within, is one of the cathedral's most impressive features. Depending on whether you are looking from within or without, the size varies; the interior of the dome is actually a false ceiling. The inside is best appreciated from a less neck-craning perspective afforded by the famous Whispering Gallery, named after its unique acoustics, which allow a *sotto voce* murmur on the far side of the dome to be carried around the circumference and heard by an ear held beside the opposite wall.

St. Paul's is arguably more a symbol of the City of London than of London the city, a confusing matter for first-time visitors but a double identity that is easy to explain. The **City of London** is both the oldest section of town and, as London's financial heart, the place that bore the brunt of 1987's Black October, when share prices plummeted. It is an official city-within-a-city. Its foundation was laid by the Romans in A.D. 43, when they built the first bridge over the Thames and declared the existence of Londinium, defending their new outpost with a wall. Fragments of their protective perimeter can still be seen today (next to the Museum of London, for example), while the names Ludgate, Aldgate, and Bishopsgate remain as testimony to the wall's existence.

Visitors with more than a slight curiosity about precontemporary London should first stop by the **Museum of London** on the London Wall, which explains the capital's story from prehistoric times. One of London's newest museums, it is an unprepossessing, modern building at first sight, its entrance opening directly onto the pedestrian walkway that connects the Barbican Centre (see below) with the rest of the City. But the building's youth lends itself to exciting, contemporary displays and light, airy galleries.

Pity the unfortunate person whose task it was to whittle down a potentially mammoth collection into a few choice exhibits that would best portray London's history. The galleries are open-plan and chronologically ordered, so it makes sense to start on the upper floor with The Thames in Prehistory, followed by Roman, Saxon and Medieval, Tudor, and Early Stuart London. Downstairs, mock shop fronts, transport exhibits, and video screens display Late Stuart, Georgian, early 19th-century, Imperial, 20th-century, and Ceremonial London (the latter includes the Lord Mayor's State Coach, built in 1757 and still used in the annual Lord Mayor's Show). Other galleries specialize in prints, drawings, and paintings of London, and costumes and textiles. Now move on to roam the streets.

In Medieval times the City expanded to roughly a square mile (677 acres). Today, British and other major

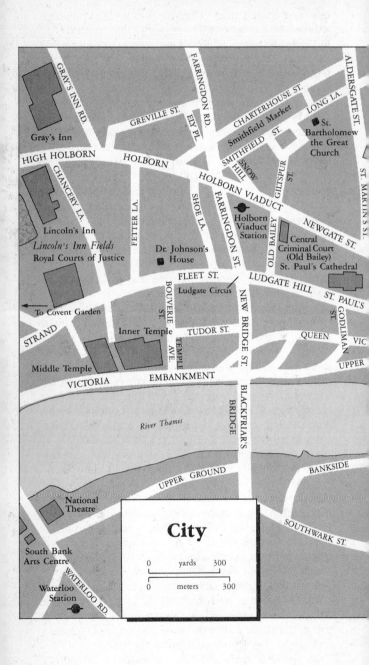

City

| 0 | yards | 300 |

| 0 | meters | 300 |

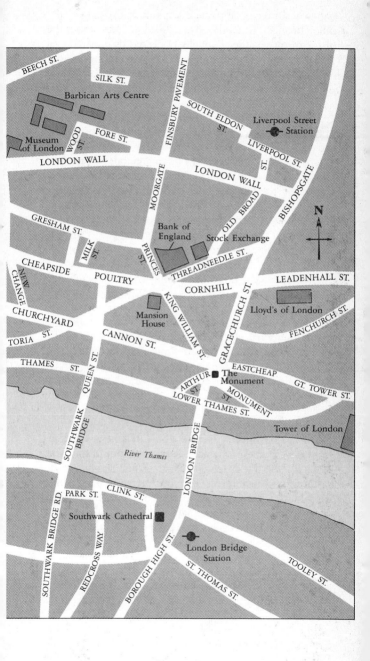

banks, insurance companies, commodity exchanges, and other financial firms have their headquarters within the historic Square Mile originally bordered by the Medieval wall. Nearly five million people pour in during the day from suburbia, but walk these streets on weekends or at night and you will hardly meet a soul.

The Great Fire of 1666 (described so vividly in Samuel Pepys's *Diaries*), the wartime Blitz, and postwar redevelopment have proved to be in the worst interests of conservation. Evidences of old London are thin on the ground. If you're blessed with a sense of imagination, though, you can get a feel of the City's past from present-day names. Cheapside was the site of a market in the Middle Ages, while nearby Poultry and Milk streets had more specific retail functions. And within the contemporary fabric of City life you will still find constant references to sheriffs, aldermen, and early trade guilds.

Signs that the City is a separate entity include the uniforms of local policemen, similar but not quite the same as those worn in the rest of London (they have red and white armbands, for a start), and various unique ceremonies, culminating in the Lord Mayor's Show to mark the annual election of the new top man. Even the Queen is traditionally escorted into the City by the Lord Mayor. And each December, the Worshipful Company of Butchers presents a boar's head to the Lord Mayor in thanks for the City's giving the butchers access to the Fleet, a tributary of the Thames, where they could clean the "entrails of beasts."

The **Barbican Arts Centre**, the City's newest grand-scale development on Silk Street, grew out of an enormous hole in the ground, a 60-acre bomb site just to the east of the Museum of London. As well as its trade exhibitions, concerts (it's home to the London Symphony Orchestra), stage plays (many by the resident Royal Shakespeare Company), conferences, and art exhibitions, the Barbican is a place where some 5,000 mostly wealthy people live. It is also a place that visitors love to hate not only for its out-of-the-way location and overpoweringly harsh design but also for the confusion that any simple movement within its labyrinthine confines seems to involve.

Of course, there are other City sights to see, including the Stock Exchange, the Bank of England, the Mansion House (the official residence of the Lord Mayor), and the futuristic Lloyd's insurance building (built like the Centre

Georges Pompidou in Paris with its insides on the out-side). Many of the buildings here will be of little interest to anyone whose working life is not plugged into the wheels and deals of commerce. The **Monument**, which commemorates the Great Fire (it started in a bakery that was situated as far from the base of the monument as it is tall), is a notable exception. It was designed by Wren, who, were he to climb to the top today, might well be tempted to leap to the bottom after seeing the clutter around his more famous edifice.

Before the development of London's Docklands, you would have found the office of nearly every national newspaper somewhere along **Fleet Street**. Although the high-tech machinations of Wapping have milked Fleet Street of some of her most successful sons (*The Times, The Sunday Times, The Daily Telegraph,* and the *News of the World* among them), a large number of the buildings are still devoted to churning out newsprint. Don't ignore the offshoots, either; Shoe Lane, for example, is home to the International Press Centre. One of Fleet Street's most beautiful landmarks is the old Art Deco Daily Express building at number 121, a world of glass and polished chromium. If Fleet Street ever loses its media connota-tions, that will be a momentous day; the printing trade has been linked with it since the beginning of the 16th century.

St. Paul's, towering above Ludgate Circus, forms an impressive eastern tail to Fleet Street. Start walking the length of the street and, between the media giants, you'll come across traditional tobacconists, topsy-turvy Tudor gabled buildings, **Dr. Johnson's House** in Gough Square (open to the public daily except Sundays and holidays), where the famous dictionary was written between 1749 and 1759, and several large outdoor clothing and sports stores. At its western end the road takes another sharp upturn in class as it becomes the Strand.

The Strand (or simply Strand) deserves a brief detour. It parallels the river (although pedestrians cannot see it), thus adding immense value to the buildings along its southern flank, most of which back onto the water. The **Savoy Hotel** is without doubt the grandest (try to have a breakfast in its delightful **River Room**), though its neigh-bor on Tavistock Street, **Somerset House**, is a close com-petitor. Built in white Portland stone, it used to be the headquarters of the Registrar General of Births, Deaths, and Marriages but now houses the less popular Board of

Inland Revenue and the Probate Registry and the very popular **Courtauld Galleries Institute**, which recently moved into new quarters here. Other worthy sights include the Wren-designed St. Clement Danes church (the bells ring out the "Oranges and Lemons" nursery rhyme at 9:00 A.M., noon, 3:00 P.M., and 6:00 P.M. Mondays through Fridays), the Royal Courts of Justice (see below), the semicircular, traffic-ridden one-way street known as the Aldwych, with the BBC's Bush House, the **London School of Economics**, and the Roman Bath—an important source of cleanliness in its heyday, now owned by the National Trust.

The Inns of Court

Apart from its literary associations, Fleet Street (along with its offshoot, Chancery Lane) cuts through the heart of legal London. Any tour of the area should begin with the **Temple**, accessible down one of the tiny side streets off Fleet Street, Middle Temple Lane. Apart from containing the 12th-century Temple church, one of England's last four round churches, the Temple is divided into the Inner, Middle, and Outer Temples. The last has long since disappeared, but the other two were developed into the Inns of Court when the church reverted to the crown.

Although the innocent outside world rarely punctures the privacy of London's Inns of Court (except as victims of some heinous deed), a stroll through the cloistered courtyards of the core of the country's legal community will reveal a uniquely tranquil world of fine stone buildings, manicured gardens, and elegant quadrangles. In a few steps you can leave the traffic hubbub of Chancery Lane and find yourself in an atmosphere more like the colleges of Oxford or Cambridge than like the City.

The "Big Four," all a short stroll from one another, are the four Inns of Court: Gray's Inn, Lincoln's Inn, Middle Temple, and Inner Temple. They have been the linchpins of Britain's closely knit legal community since the 14th century.

In 1292 King Edward I declared that the country's legal system was a mass of shortcomings. Until then all matters of justice had been dealt with by members of the clergy. They were undoubtedly the most literate members of society, but they were still laymen as far as law was concerned. Edward's desire to professionalize the legal system led to the recruitment of top students from the aristocracy. At first the students were scattered around the country, but within 100 years all barrister pupils were brought to London and accommodated in hostels, or "inns."

A note of explanation is called for before delving into the inns' hallowed territory. In Britain, unlike in the United States and most other countries, there are two distinct types of lawyer. Barristers represent the prosecution or defense in the high-ranking courts, whereas solicitors—who are forbidden to stand and be heard in these places—handle the nuts-and-bolts paperwork on a case and deal directly with clients. The barrister may never even meet those he subsequently represents in court. But the laws governing the law are beginning to change; in the near future solicitors are likely to be permitted to represent clients.

Today, each inn is a self-contained, autonomous entity with its own chapel, library, and dining hall. The latter, a richly decorated room, has always been the focal point; Queen Elizabeth I and her courtiers, for example, were wined and dined in the Tudor-style **Gray's Inn** on so many occasions that today's inmates still toast "Good Queen Bess" in a room adorned with relics of a vessel captured during the rout of the Spanish Armada. Shakespeare's plays were also acted at the inns; Gray's Inn members saw the first performance of *The Comedy of Errors* in 1594, while the magnificent Middle Temple Hall can claim the same honor for *Twelfth Night* in 1602. On sunny summer evenings you can still catch the occasional performance in the forecourt.

The college-like buildings of the Temple, just off Fleet Street, are home to the two older inns: the **Middle Temple** and the **Inner Temple**. Originally home of the Knights Templar, a military order founded in Jerusalem in 1118, the Temple was built when, weary of fighting the Holy Crusades, the knights arrived in London and needed a home. At the same time that Edward I was reshuffling the legal system, the order was disbanded and the Temple was let out to students.

While the blustering pomposity of the TV character Rumpole of the Bailey is an exaggerated impression of British barristers, there is a great deal of snobbishness attached to the inns, and the members of each one adhere to a strict hierarchy. Their interiors are sacrosanct, as they contain the offices (or "chambers") of practicing barristers, whose names are listed beside each doorway.

Over the years these lists have read like the pages of *Who's Who*. Sir Thomas More and several other Lord Chancellors were members of **Lincoln's Inn**, the place where rival Prime Ministers Disraeli and Gladstone also qualified as barristers. Sir Francis Bacon, Sir Winston Churchill, and Franklin Roosevelt belonged to Gray's Inn, and Charles Dickens was apprenticed to one of its lawyers at age 15. Sir Walter Raleigh and Sir Francis Drake were both members of the Middle Temple (it's even rumored that a serving table is made of timber from Drake's ship *Golden Hind*). John Dickinson, a Middle Templar, was the man who coined the phrase "no taxation without representation"; when the U.S. Declaration of Independence was drawn up, five Middle Templars signed the final document. Many prominent North Americans are still honorary members of the inns.

You will undoubtedly catch sight of barristers rushing to and from court in twos and threes, each clutching a bundle of "briefs." By tradition, they cannot use briefcases; all documents must be carried openly and bound by a red ribbon (hence the bureaucratic expression "red tape"). One of the rare occasions when the pace slows is at the beginning of October, when the legal year officially begins; it is marked by a procession of the wigged and robed judiciary from Westminster Abbey to the Palace of Westminster, where they stop for breakfast and then, in the afternoon, parade at the Royal Courts.

Having prepared their cases, barristers have only a short walk to work. The neo-Gothic **Royal Courts of Justice** on the Strand, home of the High Court and the Court of Appeal of England and Wales, pass judgment on the most important civil cases. The vaulted, cathedral-like Great Hall, supported by granite pillars and hung with oil paintings of former judges and coats of arms, echoes the hushed activity. Barristers, ticking on White Rabbit schedules, their black gowns bloated like galleons in a gale-force wind and frizzes (wigs) askew, emerge from one corridor, zip across the hall, and disappear into another. Don't even attempt to follow them; five and a half miles of corridors lead off the hall, and that's a lot of shoe leather if you get lost.

Members of the public whose cases are scheduled for judgment later in the day in one of the 64 courts stand huddled in earnest conversation with solicitors. All the day's cases are listed in showcases, but that's as far as you can go. Though not legally restricted from entering, visitors are customarily not allowed to watch cases in progress. To witness a trial you have to make your way to the public gallery of the Old Bailey, the most famous criminal court in the world.

"Justice is not blind at the Old Bailey," declared the City of London Corporation 75 years ago when the **Old Bailey** (or the Central Criminal Court, to give it its proper name) was built. To emphasize the point, they made sure that their version of the Goddess of Justice, the statue that sits on the building's green dome high above the traffic jams holding the scales of justice and the sword of retribution, was one of the only ones in the world without a blindfold.

Criminal justice in England and Wales focuses on the Old Bailey, and within the walls of its 23 courts you can hear the verdicts of major trials, many of which are referred to the High Court judges as a last resort. The most famous and most important cases are heard in the surprisingly small Court Number One, a wood-paneled courtroom whose dock floorboards have creaked under some of the most notorious criminals in the history of 20th-century Britain. These include American-born Dr. Crippen, accused of murdering his wife, Belle Elmore, and cutting her up into pieces before eloping with his mistress. More recent trials have included that of M.P. Jeremy Thorpe, acquitted of conspiring to murder his ex-lover, and the "Yorkshire Ripper," the late-1970s rapist and murderer.

Covent Garden

London's newest village, at least on the visitors' map, is Covent Garden. Within the space of a few years the city's old fruit-and-vegetable market (just west of the Inns of Court) has been transformed into one of the liveliest and loveliest urban centers in Europe.

In underground cellars once used to store bananas, young sophisticates now pick cherries off the ends of tiny paper parasols resting on the edges of cocktail glasses. From stalls in the central Apple Market, where Granny Smiths and Cox's Orange Pippins were once stacked, shoppers now buy elaborately patterned sweaters and scores of other products handmade by the craftspeople who sell them. And in high-ceilinged warehouses that once stored crates of carrots, parsnips, potatoes, and other roots, Filofax clutchers now dine on nouvelle cuisine served by bow-tied waiters whose own social background would not permit them to take on such menial and deferential roles anywhere else in Britain.

In an earlier incarnation, Covent Garden was also a very fashionable part of town. Inigo Jones designed **St. Paul's Church**, popularly known as the actors' church, as well as the piazza on which it stands. The story has it that the earl of Bedford (the original landowner) told Jones that his budget would only stretch to cover a barn, so the architect promised the "most beautiful barn in the country." The church was completed in 1633 as part of London's first square, modeled after the Italian piazzas Jones had studied in his travels. It was later destroyed by fire but rebuilt to its initial specifications.

The original Theatre Royal, where Nell Gwynn sold oranges, opened in 1662, and soon afterward the **Royal Opera House** opened its doors. But the area's early elegance did not last long. The presence of the wealthy drew rogues—the poet Dryden was beaten up in an alleyway outside the Bucket of Blood pub, now the Lamb and Flag. It is no coincidence that London's first police force, the Bow Street Runners, was established just around the corner.

Attracted by the security of the strong arm of the law, a new wave of prosperity followed. The renaissance was marked by the construction of the Central Market buildings in 1830, when the duke of Bedford decided that something smarter was needed to replace the rows of shanty vegetable stalls that had stood their ground since the 17th century. Coffeehouses also flourished; Dr. Johnson first met Boswell in a small establishment, now fittingly called Boswell's, on Russell Street.

In 1974, after three centuries of trading, the market vendors moved out to modern premises across the River Thames at Nine Elms. They left behind a mass of grimy buildings, and an enormous debate began on just what to do with such a potentially prime site on the fringes of the West End. Restoration work on the old buildings was started, but the transition was not accomplished without opposition—mainly from neighborhood residents, who would have preferred to see the development of a simple residential community, not an upscale designer village.

One of the more welcome additions to the neighborhood is the collective **Courtauld Institute Galleries**, which recently moved from Bloomsbury, where only a third of the collection could be seen at any time, to Somerset House on Tavistock Street off the Strand. Painters who are represented in this rich collection include 19th-century masters—Bonnard, Degas, van Gogh, Seurat, Manet, Monet, Cézanne—as well as such other luminaries as Rubens, Michelangelo, Brueghel, Dürer, Tintoretto, Kokoschka, Rembrandt, Gainsborough, and Bellini.

The Covent Garden area offers some of the best of London's shopping, not for basics (there is only one butcher shop, and even that is mostly a purveyor of game) but for fashionable, boutique-type wares. Lots of old traders remain: Anello and Davide, the theatrical shoemakers; the Drury Tea and Coffee Co.; Stanfords, the map shop. Covent Garden itself and neighboring streets such as Long Acre contain scores of galleries and bookshops, clothing boutiques, epicurean and organic food stores, gift shops, and others whose products all bear a stamp of design that far exceeds the functional.

Many shop fronts are based on original designs, and in the north hall, site of the old Apple Market, a flavor of the old market days remains. Forty original wrought-iron stands, salvaged from the Flower Market, are now rented to traders and craftspeople who sell their goods beneath the magnificent glass roof. As for the Old Flower Market itself—on the eastern side of the piazza, completed in 1872 and staffed entirely by women—it now houses the **London Transport Museum**'s collection of early buses and trams. The entrance to Britain's first **Theatre Museum** is next door at Tavistock Street, within walking distance of the Royal Opera House and many other theaters.

Every lunchtime you will find performances by buskers, all carefully screened by the Covent Garden management, in front of the portico of St. Paul's Church, the very spot where George Bernard Shaw's Eliza Doolittle first met Professor Higgins, and under the 1830s roof of the Apple Market.

At night the activity takes on a different rhythm. When the stores close—mostly not until 8:00 P.M.—people drift to the pubs and wine-and-cocktail bars, then on to restaurants. You can eat African at the **Calabash**, Italian at **Orso**, American at **Joe Allen's**, Chinese at **Poon's**, classic English at the **Opera Terrace**, French at **Mon Plaisir**, Japanese at **Ajimura**, Mexican at **Café Pacifico**, and expensively at **Inigo Jones**.

Bloomsbury

Sinatra's "foggy day in London town" touches Bloomsbury in a surprisingly dramatic mood. The British Museum, he croons, has lost its charm, which is a curious attribute ever to apply to such a hefty, solid chunk of masonry, even on the sunniest of days. And, just to correct those misconceptions, London's traditional pea-soup fog, in which Sinatra's lyricist was no doubt once engulfed, is now only to be experienced in ancient horror movies.

The **British Museum** is at the heart of Bloomsbury, a fitting edifice for this, the most cerebral area of town. The great repository of treasures, many blatantly stolen from Egypt and other lands at a time when Britain's imperialist arrogance, not to mention its archaeological light-fingeredness, exercised no ethical restraints on other peoples' property, is invariably among the top half-dozen priorities of overseas visitors to London (although the last time most Londoners will have paid their respects is on a compulsory tour organized by a teacher who felt it would do his or her restless charges good).

Construction of the present building, with its ancient Greek influences (rather ironic, considering the recent tussle over the fate of the Elgin Marbles), was completed in the middle of the past century. It displayed the grime of all those years, too, until its recent cleaning. The building houses a vast collection, spread among some 75 rooms, galleries, and landings. Museum freaks will obviously need to tackle the lot, devoting their entire vacation to poking around. Others will prefer to edit their visits to some of the essential viewings. These must, of course, include the **Elgin Marbles**, if only to see the cause of the dispute between the authorities in Britain and Greece concerning their permanent home. You'll find them displayed in the Duveen Gallery. The Grenville Library contains the **Magna Carta**, one of the most important documents in the history of democracy, while the prize in the Egyptian Sculpture Gallery is the **Rosetta Stone**. All these are housed on the ground floor. In the Egyptian Gallery upstairs are the famous mummies, arguably the museum's most interesting exhibits. Save time, also, for a tour of the Reading Room (on the hour, 11:00 A.M. to 4:00 P.M.), a stunning library in which rows of desks radiate out from a central area beneath a 40-foot dome. The library is shortly to be rehoused, so see it while you can.

Other Bloomsbury museums include the **Percival David Foundation of Chinese Art**, on Gordon Square, which includes superb porcelains; the tiny one-room **Jewish Museum** in Upper Woburn Place, Tavistock Square; **Dick-**

ens's house at 48 Doughty Street; **Pollock's Toy Museum**, at 1 Scala Street, with the original "Penny Plain Tuppence Coloured" Toy Theatres as well as 19th- and 20th-century toys; and the **Wellcome Museum of Medical Science**, at 183 Euston Road, where entry is restricted to students in the field, although the entrance hall, with its mock-historical pharmacies, is well worth a peek.

If the British Museum represents Bloomsbury's seat of knowledge, the **University of London** is its seat of learning. American visitors, in particular, will be surprised at the relatively small acreage that such an important educational institution occupies. This is partly because there are no halls of residence as such, but also because several of the surrounding "ordinary"-looking buildings have been bought by the university for the use of individual faculties.

The university is a relative newcomer to Bloomsbury—the tall Senate House was begun only in 1932—but since so many of its parts are found in older buildings, its geographical roots seem much older. Among the most important of the larger buildings are University College and, on the opposite side of Gower Street, University College Hospital.

Sadly, the tallest building in Bloomsbury also happens to be one of the ugliest. The Post Office Tower, which dominates London's skyline (it's the second-tallest structure in London, after the NatWest Bank building in the City), is widely despised, though it has a good reason for being there, since its ungainly stature affords the necessary ground clearance for its communication functions. At least, that's the excuse.

There are, as in any section of any city, other monstrosities. But Bloomsbury is one of the most intact corners of Georgian London, its leafy squares little changed since their drawing rooms witnessed the frantic exchanges of artistic, literary, and philosophical banter by the early 20th-century Bloomsbury Group. Most members of this circle (Virginia Woolf and her sister, Vanessa Bell, Rupert Brooke, D. H. Lawrence, art critic Roger Fry, Lytton Strachey, Clive Bell, Maynard Keynes, and E. M. Forster) didn't have far to travel when visiting—they lived in either Bedford, Woburn, Russell, Gordon (Virginia Woolf lived at number 46 before she married), Tavistock, or Fitzroy squares. Bloomsbury Square has sadly lost all its original architecture; only **Bedford Square** and **Fitzroy Square** are still lined with their original tall, dark, and extremely handsome mid-18th-century terraced houses. The core of most squares is still a quiet patch of green, though when in the shape of lush gardens they are usually closed to the public (the residents have keys).

Brunswick Square is the black sheep of Bloomsbury—its dimensions have narrowed and its beauty has disappeared since the construction of an ugly housing block, and a small, modern cinema, the Renoir, has been plunked in the center, alongside a Safeway supermarket and other commercial outlets.

With all of its literary connotations, it's small wonder that Bloomsbury has sprouted a plethora of publishing houses. And when you want to see what they've produced, try some of the area's many bookshops—**Dillons** is the largest, built to serve the university, its distinctive navy blue and gold window display hogging the northern end of Malet Street. For browsing for secondhand or more specialized tomes, head south of Russell Square to the network of narrow streets around **Museum Street**.

Soho

Since the beginning of the century, Soho has enjoyed a dubious reputation. Mere mention of the word still conjures up images of sleazy clubs, brothels, gambling parlors, and Mafia plots (both the Italian and Chinese variety). It is a world where, by night at least, tourists either fear to tread or do so with adrenaline pumping through their veins.

Although a great deal has been done to rid the area of its women of the night—not so long ago one third of all its houses were brothels—it is only recently that the authorities have begun to stem the tide of sex shops and peep shows that blossomed in their place. Soho is not a no-go. It may not appeal to your taste, but, compared with most other sin centers of the world, it is relatively tame. In any case, irrespective of whether it has cleaned up its act, Soho cannot be ignored. To do so would be to turn your back on the highest density of good dining to be found in the whole of London.

The area runs diagonally across Leicester Square, bordered by **Charing Cross Road** (famous for its bookstores—Foyle's, Zwemmer's, Collet's, and others) and the shopping thoroughfares of Oxford and Regent streets. Stand in the middle of Leicester Square and you may or may not be in Soho. Depending on exactly where you are, you might even find you have one foot in Soho and the other in the West End. **Leicester Square** is a good place to begin a Soho saunter. It is difficult to imagine, despite the grass underfoot and the giddy heights of the plane trees, that in Henry VIII's time the area was at the heart of a royal hunting ground, surrounded by open country and rural villages, with the City of London still a few miles off to the east. The very name Soho is derived from an old hunting cry, the contemporary equivalent being "tallyho."

The actual square, known originally as Leicester Fields, was named after the earl of Leicester, who built its first town house on what is now the site of the Angus Steak House, on the northern side of the square. Soon other houses went up in what was one of the country's earliest spates of property speculation. Once commoners moved in to occupy them, however, the earl moved out. Today the square is a bright-lights mecca that mainly entices out-of-towners in search of a newly released movie (there's also a ticket booth selling seats for same-day theater performances at half price).

Soho's social history is colorfully cosmopolitan. The French Huguenots fleeing the consequences of the revocation of the Edict of Nantes, Greeks escaping the Turks, the Swiss, Italians, Germans, Jews, and other refugees have all immigrated to Soho in large numbers, most sharing backgrounds of persecution in their home countries. By 1914, for example, one third of the houses were occupied by Jews, a figure that will come as a surprise to people who think of the East End as the traditional Jewish district in London.

The cosmopolitan mix today is best seen in the enormous number of Continental restaurants. Stand, for example, on the corner of Leicester Street (just north of the square) and Lisle Street, and you'll see Poon's Chinese restaurant virtually next door to Manzi's Italian fish restaurant, which, just to add to the confusion, used to be a German hotel whose visitors' book recorded Karl Marx and his wife and children as onetime guests.

Among the many echoes of the French accent in Soho is **The French House** at 49 Dean Street, a regular pub but one as close as you're likely to come to a French bar in London (although its owner, Gaston, recently retired). It is complete with photos of French boxers lining the walls and with not-too-distant memories of Charles de Gaulle, who, during the war, patronized the bar along with other members of the Free French movement. There's also the

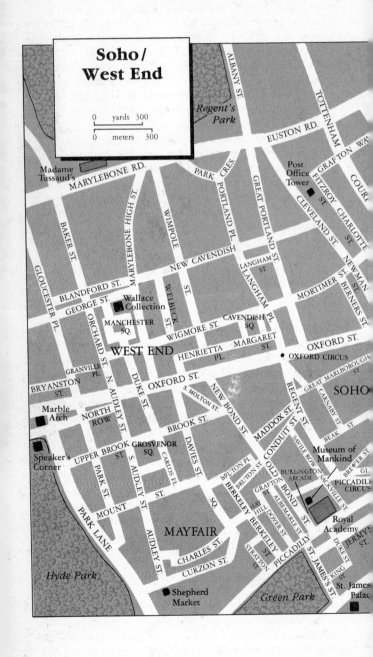

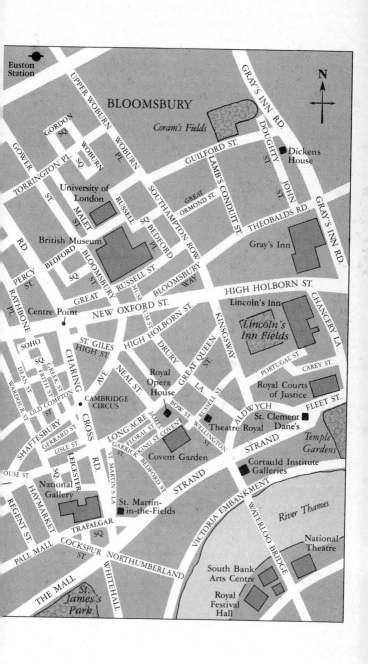

Euston
Station

BLOOMSBURY

N

GRAY'S INN RD.

UPPER WOBURN PL.

GORDON SQ.

WOBURN SQ.

WOBURN PL.

Coram's Fields

DOUGHTY ST.

Dickens House

GOWER ST.

TORRINGTON PL.

GUILFORD ST.

LAMB'S CONDUIT ST.

JOHN ST.

University of London

MALET ST.

RUSSELL SQ.

SOUTHAMPTON ROW

GREAT ORMOND ST.

THEOBALDS RD.

GRAY'S INN RD.

RD.

British Museum

BEDFORD SQ.

BLOOMSBURY ST.

BEDFORD PL.

Gray's Inn

PERCY ST.

GREAT RUSSELL ST.

MUSEUM ST.

BLOOMSBURY WAY

HIGH HOLBORN ST.

RATHBONE PL.

Centre Point

NEW OXFORD ST.

KINGSWAY

Lincoln's Inn

Lincoln's Inn Fields

CHANCERY LA.

SOHO SQ.

ST. GILES HIGH ST.

HIGH HOLBORN ST.

DRURY LA.

GREAT QUEEN ST.

PORTUGAL ST.

CAREY ST.

GREEK ST.

CHARING CROSS RD.

AVE.

NEAL ST.

DEAN ST.

FRITH ST.

Royal Opera House

Royal Courts of Justice

FLEET ST.

WARDOUR ST.

OLD COMPTON ST.

CAMBRIDGE CIRCUS

BOW ST.

RUSSELL ST.

ALDWYCH

St. Clement Dane's

LONG ACRE

JAMES ST.

FLORAL ST.

KING ST.

Theatre Royal

WELLINGTON ST.

Temple Gardens

SHAFTESBURY

GERRARD ST.

LISLE ST.

GARRICK ST.

Covent Garden

STRAND

STRAND

Cortauld Institute Galleries

ST. MARTIN'S LA.

BEDFORD ST.

OUSE ST.

National Gallery

LEICESTER SQ.

VICTORIA EMBANKMENT

River Thames

HAYMARKET

St. Martin-in-the-Fields

WATERLOO BRIDGE

National Theatre

REGENT ST.

TRAFALGAR SQ.

PALL MALL

COCKSPUR ST.

NORTHUMBERLAND

South Bank Arts Centre

WHITEHALL

THE MALL

St. James's Park

Royal Festival Hall

delightfully bohemian **Pâtisserie Valerie** in Old Compton Street and **Maison Bertaux** in Greek Street, perfect places to rest weary sightseeing feet over a coffee and croissant or *gâteau*.

If Londoners had to pick a single street that summed up the essence of Soho, the honors would go to **Old Compton Street**. No more than 200 to 300 yards long, it contains an Algerian coffee store, a French restaurant, a Spanish deli, an Italian pizzeria, a Malaysian restaurant, a Vietnamese restaurant, and, one of the most recent arrivals, an American diner called Ed's. The area's diversity is well summed up by the newsagent called A. Moroni & Son, who sells just about every newspaper in the world (though not, surprisingly, *The New York Times*).

The last ethnic group to move into Soho in significant numbers was the Chinese from Hong Kong. It wasn't until 1981 that the area in which they settled, centered on the now pedestrianized **Gerrard Street**, became officially recognized as **Chinatown**. The Chinese have totally revitalized the area, which used to be a run-down, typical inner-city slum. Although London's Chinatown is far smaller than its counterparts in, say, New York City or San Francisco, the area's shops, restaurants, and overall atmosphere are almost completely Chinese, and, yes, there are telephone boxes shaped like pagodas (though they are just as likely to be out of order as any other public telephone in London).

Soho has numerous blue plaques commemorating the famous and red lights announcing the presence of the infamous. No matter where you walk in Soho and no matter what ethnic stamp is currently on the street, evidences of its history abound. William Blake was born here, Hazlitt died here. Take a look at the Loon Fung supermarket on Gerrard Street, and you'll spot a plaque that describes the time that the writer John Dryden lived there. Just a few doors along the road, in the house now occupied by the Loon Fung restaurant, the writer and statesman Edmund Burke resided. On the opposite site of the street, you'll spot an original 18th-century building with a portico, now the Loon Moon supermarket, that is famous for a former occupant, the Turk's Head Tavern. The Turk, mentioned by Dickens and by Boswell in his biography of Johnson, was the great literati hangout of the day (interestingly, the current media hangout is Groucho's, just around the corner on Dean Street).

The parish of Soho was once far grander in scale than it is now and had the Church of St. Martin's-in-the-Fields as its parish church. As the area grew in popularity as a residential section of town, the scale became unmanageable, and the parish was split in two. St. Anne's was built as the new Soho's parish church—but, since the war, all that remains is a tower with a unique barrel-shaped clock, the only one in London. It is best seen from the spot where Romilly Street meets Dean Street, although at present it is surrounded by building construction that eventually will spawn a community center, representing the spirit of a newer, cleaner Soho, a phoenix rising from an image-poor past.

But back to the blue plaques. Casanova lived on Frith Street and also on nearby Meard Street, which still contains a row of mid-18th-century brick houses, among the oldest in the area. Chopin gave a recital in one. Jean-Paul Marat lived on Romilly Street in a house with a distinctive bay-window overhang, or "jetty." He came to London not as a revolutionary but as a doctor, working on a treatise on eye diseases.

Another unifying Soho theme, apart from history, sexual innuendo, and good eating, is music. In the 1950s it was famous for its coffeehouses, which spawned the U.K.'s first superstars of pop. Though all of the original venues are gone, Soho is still the place to hear music. **Ronnie Scott's** is the jazz epicenter, located, coincidentally, opposite a brick building where Mozart came to entertain at the age of eight. Just a few yards away, on the same side of the road, yet another blue plaque marks the spot where, at the embryonic stage in the development of another branch of entertainment, John Baird demonstrated the very first television set.

To most people, **Soho Square** is the heart of the area. It is certainly its greenest core, with a statue of King Charles II standing among the trees, holding what looks like a spout in one hand. It is a spout; the King used to be a fountain "powered" by a row of windmills along what is now Oxford Street. The square was once a garden for the exclusive use of residents, but they departed and the park became public, a popular summer retreat for lunchtime sandwich-eaters and more than a scattering of winos. A close inspection of the building that looks like a Tudor hunting lodge in the center of the square will reveal that it is mock Tudor, dating back to the 1930s but built as a replica of the type of lodges that used to be dotted around the royal hunting grounds in case of rain. It is now a tool shed.

The West End

Although visitors may find the nomenclature to be rather confusing geographically—it's in central, not western, London—Londoners never think twice about the West End's location. To them the West End means central shopping (and the theater). If you want to immerse yourself in the commercial heart of town, just mingle with the lunchtime office workers or weekend suburban pilgrims in the country's biggest stores.

Two miles of crowded pavement line **Oxford Street**, the West End's main artery, trampled daily from Marble Arch to the Centrepoint skyscraper at Tottenham Court Road. Its reputation has been carried to all corners of the globe, yet its days as London's premier shopping street seem numbered. There was a time when no self-respecting chain of stores would fail to open a branch on Oxford Street; without the address, a concern would hold little credibility in the retail hierarchy. But nowadays a disloyal shopping public, hungry for more fashionable styles and ever watchful of the avant-garde, has tended to give the street a wide berth and is taking its credit cards to more fashionable, polished rivals along Kensington High Street, in Covent Garden, and on Fulham Road in Chelsea.

Commercially, at least, it is still viable for a retail outlet to have at least one branch on Oxford Street—Saturday crowds justifying police megaphones to move them out of the way of oncoming buses cannot be bad for business. (There's even a regular shuttle-bus service that ferries shoplifters to the police station.) But the traditional Oxford Street names would probably be far happier if the tacky discount stores, furiously trying to unload cheap sweatshirts, plastic watches, tasteless imitations, and gimmicky paraphernalia, weren't their neighbors. Even offshoot Carnaby Street, a West End high spot during the swinging 1960s, is now surviving on its reputation alone; in reality, its veneer is more than a trifle jaded.

Largely it's the quality department stores (Selfridge's, John Lewis, Marks and Spencer, C&A, Debenhams, and British Home Stores) that keep the lunchtime, Saturday, and late-night Thursday shopping crowds flowing down

Oxford Street. They have survived as the great British shopping institutions, giant magnets without which Oxford Street would have died.

Marking the street's Park Lane (western) extremity, **Marble Arch** deserves a brief mention. Built by George IV to celebrate England's victory over Napoleon, it originally stood outside Buckingham Palace. But state coaches couldn't pass between its chubby, Portland stone piers, or "legs," and in 1851 it was moved to the West End. If Marble Arch figures high on the tourist's list of London sights, to native motorists it signifies little more than nonstop, bumper-to-bumper traffic jams.

St. Christopher's Place, an alley so narrow you could easily miss it, leads off the north side of Oxford Street almost opposite Bond Street and is lined with high-fashion, one-off boutiques, stores that sell just one example of a particular design. The Warehouse clothing store and the home-furnishing frippery store, The Reject Shop, are doing a roaring trade in the Plaza shopping mall. And running at a tangent to the mainstream traffic off the south side is super-chic South Molton Street.

Manchester Square, north of Oxford Street behind Selfridge's, contains the **Wallace Collection**. When the first marquis of Hertford started amassing 18th-century paintings and French furniture and artworks, the collection was housed in Paris, but by the time it was in the hands of Richard Wallace, five generations later, it was in England; it was opened to the public in 1900.

Take a sharp turn to the south at Oxford Circus, step down **Regent Street**, and you take a giant stride up the elegance scale. The street, modeled by John Nash in the early 19th century, was originally planned to run straight from the prince regent's home, Carlton House, to the new Regent's Park, but Nash interrupted the tedium of the endless avenue approach with his unmistakable, lavishly expensive curves. Immediately attractive to the rich and famous (Nash himself lived at number 14; Lady Hamilton, Admiral Nelson's renowned mistress, resided down the road at number 25), Regent Street soon became an attractive proposition for shopkeepers, too.

Although large chunks have been reconstructed over the years, Regent Street, now controlled by the Crown Estates Commissioners, is enjoying a revival. The mock-Tudor-style Liberty's and Dickins & Jones department stores, and the racks of trenchcoats at Burberry's on Lower Regent Street, for example, are still there, and the grim airline offices and fusty one-off stores are being gradually nudged out by a brigade of parquet-floored, marble-pillared designer newcomers like the U.S.–imported Gap, Next, and the popular Laura Ashley fabric outlets.

Window-shop, if nothing else, on **Bond Street**. A jewelers' lair for decades, the street has retained its sumptuous image with sky-high rents and retail prices to match. The same applies to **Jermyn Street** just south of Piccadilly, toward the Thames—where you must be rich *and* male because a large proportion of shops (Bates, Harvie & Hudson, and Astleys, for example) cater exclusively to men with a whim for a jar of mustache wax or a badger-hair shaving brush.

Two of the West End's biggest shopping attractions are on Piccadilly—**Burlington Arcade**, built in 1819 as Britain's first covered shopping mall, and the affluent **Fortnum & Mason** emporium. Even the royal family stocks up on groceries in its frogs'-legs-to-*fines-herbes* food hall. Weary shoppers who wander off in search of sustenance can choose from two of London's most palatial afternoon tea haunts—the Soda Fountain in Fortnum & Mason and, a scone's throw away, down Piccadilly to the west, the Palm Court Room in the Ritz hotel. If they're both full, cross the road and listen to the harpist in the lounge of the Hotel Meridien.

Follow such heavenly delights with a visit to the **Royal Academy** in Burlington House, a close Piccadilly neighbor. The grand courtyard, filled with snaking lines at peak visiting times (especially on Sunday mornings during the annual Summer Exhibition), fronts a Renaissance-style building. Inside is a grand, sweeping staircase and galleries of treasures, including Michelangelo's *Madonna and Child*.

At the back of Burlington House is the more modest, though equally Italianate looking, **Museum of Mankind** (6 Burlington Gardens), whose exhibitions always focus on non-Western cultures. Within the same building is the British Museum's ethnographic collection, including a skull carved from a single piece of Mexican crystal.

London is at her most gaudy and flirtatious with tourists in **Piccadilly Circus**. Walls of neon lights flicker day and night, captured by a million camera shutters. As part of the Circus's general face-lift, the aluminum statue of Eros (officially the Angel of Charity), once marooned in the tawdry center of the Circus, has been renovated and is now back in the limelight on the south side. Approval of his new good looks is welcome: When Eros was unveiled in 1893, *The Times* described him as the "ugliest monument in any European capital, more suited to the musical hall," while many simply frowned on his nakedness.

Piccadilly's newest brand of entertainment is the **Trocadero Centre** in Coventry Street, which has a Brass Rubbing Centre, a Guinness World of Records exhibit, and a multivisual show, *The London Experience*. The complex, with its shops and restaurants, is open seven days a week.

The back doors of the Trocadero open onto Shaftesbury Avenue, the West End's evening breadwinner. More than 100 years old (its centenary was in 1987), the heart of London's theater district has six theaters and two cinemas. Shaftesbury Avenue was named after the 19th-century philanthropist the earl of Shaftesbury, who carried out much of his alms-giving work in this area; its construction actually resulted in the demolition of several squalid Dickensian slums. The first theater to go up along the new avenue was the Lyric, in 1888. The Royal English Opera House on Cambridge Circus followed, but demand for fine singing was slack. The music hall was in fashion, and the theater was renamed the Palace. Musicals are still the staple diet of London's theater, particularly if they're written by Andrew Lloyd Webber and Tim Rice, the Rodgers and Hammerstein of the 1980s. The Palace, in fact, is now owned by Lloyd Webber and once housed *Jesus Christ Superstar,* the second-longest-running musical in the history of British theater.

The Apollo, the Globe, the Queen's, and the Shaftesbury complete the six. Originally the New Prince's theater, the Shaftesbury is most famous for its misfortune: A gas explosion interrupted Fred and Adele Astaire's dancing in Gershwin's *Funny Face,* while later the musical *Hair* literally brought the house down when part of the ceiling collapsed.

Mayfair

Between the West End and Hyde Park you'll find Mayfair. The small, appealing parts of Mayfair are the rows of elegant brownstones that were the original *Upstairs, Downstairs* houses of London's upper (and lower) echelons. Concentrated chiefly in Mayfair's two most famous squares, Grosvenor (home of the U.S. embassy) and Berkeley, these brownstones boast top-floor and basement servants' quarters that today command some of the highest rents in town, while the mews houses, once the stable yards for the coach and horses (with upper-floor living accommodations for the driver), sell for small fortunes.

The essence of Mayfair is its elegant shops and squares, though working Londoners are also aware that the city's most prestigious office buildings tower above it. Window shoppers and those with great amounts of money should head for Brook Street, South Molton Street (one of the city's most elite, pedestrianized precincts), Bond Street, and Savile Row. Smaller showrooms and galleries are to be found on Dover Street, also home to **Brown's Hotel** at number 22, London's renowned "gentleman's" hotel, founded by a former butler to Lord Byron and now owned by Trusthouse Forte. The hotel has worked hard to preserve a sense of quietude and privacy, and it still attracts some of the city's most gentrified visitors. It also serves an excellent traditional tea.

Curzon Street, part residential (number 19 marks the spot where Disraeli died in 1881) and part commercial, backs onto **Shepherd Market** (the name belies its wealth), a delightful "village" of narrow streets, period houses, and pubs like Ye Grapes, cafés geared for alfresco dining, and tiny courtyards—the whole linked by a series of archways. It is also noted for its prostitutes.

Thanks to the heavy traffic and plethora of motorcycle messengers in central London, a quiet stroll around Berkeley Square is possible only on a Sunday. Nevertheless, it's not difficult to appreciate the grandeur of its 200-year-old plane trees (all that remain of Berkeley Woods), which shelter some of the city's most beautiful architecture. Two buildings to look out for are number 45, the former home of Clive of India, and number 50, where **Maggs**, the antiquarian book specialists, is open to book lovers.

Westminster

Westminster is London wearing its most royal plumage and governmental robes. On the map, the area officially defined as the City of Westminster is vast, bordered by Camden on the north and the Thames on the south, but even Londoners rarely relate the name to its full territorial stake. The name really connotes Whitehall, the Houses of Parliament, Westminster Abbey, the Prime Minister's official residence at 10 Downing Street, and St. James's Park. Westminster is a residential borough, but its palaces and government offices, including the bulk of the ministry headquarters, overshadow the lives of its ordinary citizens.

Buckingham Palace is Westminster's prize showpiece. It was built for a duke in 1703 and bought by King George III in 1762. John Nash, to whom London's present-day aesthetics owe so much, played a significant part in the building's restructuring in 1825, although many of the trimmings that you see today were the result of a face-lift in 1913 by Sir Aston Webb. Today's palace is yesterday's Buckingham House, a beautiful pillared and porticoed mansion house carved in white Portland stone, overlooking a semicircular bow of manicured gardens. The grandeur continues inside, from the bedchambers to the state rooms; even the stable block is magnificent. Until the 19th century, the royal family would use Buckingham House as its personal residence, minutes down the road from its official home, St. James's Palace in Pall Mall at the foot of St. James's Street (south from Piccadilly). The red-jacketed and shakoed guards in front of the palace in St. James's are much photographed. (See below for the Changing of the Guard ceremony.)

It wasn't until 1837, when Queen Victoria spread her bustle on the throne, that the role of Buckingham Palace became official. **St. James's Palace**, Henry VIII's turreted gift to Anne Boleyn when they were first married, is now virtually redundant, though any announcement of a change of ruler is traditionally made from its Friary Court balcony.

If the gold Royal Standard flag is flying high above Buckingham Palace, the Queen is in residence. Occasionally, you may catch a glimpse of one or another of the royal family sitting rather anonymously in the back of a sleek black Daimler.

The palace is not open to run-of-the-mill sightseers. Two or three times a year, however, a few thousand members of a more esteemed public—aristocrats, sporting personalities, the higher echelons of local government, and the like—are invited within this inner sanctum to one of the Queen's summer garden parties. The even luckier, if that is the right word, are invited here to investitures, when knighthood and other honors are bestowed. But there are compromises. The **Queen's Gallery**, just around the corner in Buckingham Gate, is open every day except Mondays for exhibitions of paintings from the royal collection. In the **Royal Mews**, on Buckingham Palace Road, open on Wednesday and Thursday after-

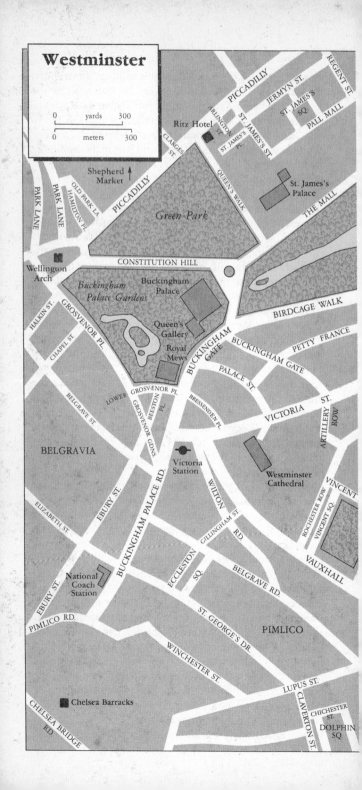

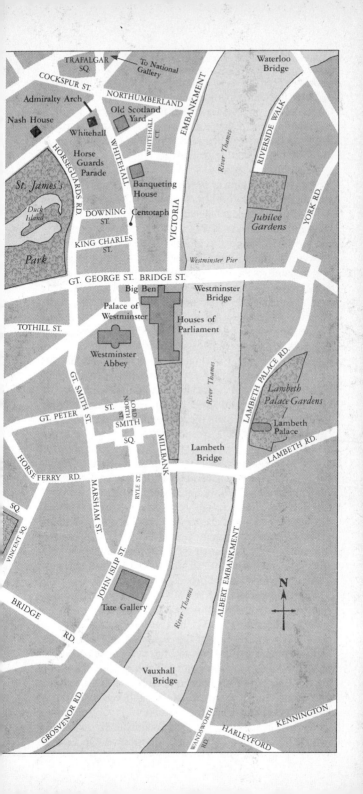

noons, are the family's Cinderella-like coaches, including the cherub-covered Gold State Coach, which carried the Queen from the palace to Westminster Abbey for her coronation. The Glass Coach, which transports royal brides, is on show, as are some vintage royal cars, such as the 1901 Daimler built for Edward VII.

Westminster is London's venue for pomp and circumstance. The **Changing of the Guard** at Buckingham Palace, a military pageant of horse guards and infantrymen dressed in black bearskins and red tunics, is the familiar image most often chosen to depict London on postcards and posters around the globe. At 11:00 every morning between April and July (alternate days, August to March), the St. James's Palace detachment of the Old Guard is inspected in Friary Court. Carrying the Colour (the regimental flag), it then marches off via the Mall, the wide formal boulevard designed by Charles II. At Buckingham Palace the palace detachment is lined up and inspected. The St. James's detachment enters by the South Gate and together with the Buckingham detachment awaits the arrival of the New Guard (at 11:30). Led by a regimental band, the New Guard marches into the palace forecourt via the North Centre Gate, having earlier assembled at Wellington Barracks in Birdcage Walk. By 12:05 it's all over for another day (except for the duties of the street cleaner).

Pall Mall, which runs from St. James's Palace to Trafalgar Square, was conceived by Charles I so that he could play *pallemaille,* a newfangled game he had discovered across the Channel, roughly equivalent to English bowls. He leased a house here to Nell Gwynn, who poutingly insisted that she should own the freehold of the house—after all, her "services" to the Crown were given freely. Charles agreed, and 79 Pall Mall is still the only privately owned property on the broad avenue.

The top (east end) of Pall Mall opens up into **Trafalgar Square**. Laid out by John Nash in 1820 as part of his grand design, it's rather a hodgepodge of architectural styles. The focal point of the square is its central area, with fountains by Lutyens and the granite Nelson's Column by William Railton (with a statue of Lord Nelson on top by Baily and four bronze lions by Landseer forming the base plinth). Trafalgar Square is home to flocks of pigeons and is always the terminus of political rallies and demonstrations, the anti-establishment shade of which Nelson would no doubt disapprove. On December 31 the political causes give way to a raucous crowd in an alcoholic haze cheering Big Ben's midnight chimes.

The **National Gallery**, by far the most beautiful building in Trafalgar Square, is backed by the National Portrait Gallery. Climb the steps up to the National Gallery, a grande dame built in Classical style, and look back a second for a sweeping view of Trafalgar Square. Now get on with the art on the inside. The gallery was opened in 1838 to house the national collection of masterpieces (at the time the gallery shared its premises with the Royal Academy, but for reasons of space the latter has since moved to Burlington House, Piccadilly). All the great periods of European painting are represented in the National—works by Botticelli and Bellini hang in the Italian rooms, alongside Leonardo da Vinci's *Virgin and Child with St. Anne and St. John the Baptist*. Constable's *Haywain* and Gainsborough's *Mr. and Mrs. Andrews* are also here, as well as a copious number of Dutch and Flemish paintings.

The original aim of the **National Portrait Gallery**, around the corner in St. Martin's Place, was to portray Britain's history through paintings, sculptures, miniatures, and photographs of the country's historical personalities. With so many famous people now represented here, it has become a visual *Who's Who*. Start at the top and work your way down in chronological order. The majority of people you'll see (apart from other visitors) are no longer alive, with the notable exception of the current royal family.

From the square, a stroll down Whitehall takes you past some of England's most prestigious civil service departments, including the Treasury, the gigantic headquarters of the Home Office and the Foreign Office, and the stark new Ministry of Defence building. On the left is the **Banqueting House**, a superb example of Palladian-style architecture built by Inigo Jones for James I in 1619 and still used for official receptions. Its ceilings are like miniature versions of those in the Sistine Chapel, decorated with nine remarkable paintings by Rubens (they brought £3,000 and a knighthood to the artist). Thirty years after the hall was built, Charles I stepped from one of its windows onto the waiting scaffold where he was executed.

Old Scotland Yard (the former office of the Metropolitan Police, as seen in a thousand B-movies) is also along Whitehall, though the headquarters have since shifted to

Victoria Street, also within the Westminster boundary. A military presence is maintained at **Horse Guards Parade**, in the form of two Household Cavalry sentries who sit motionless, immune to the persistent flash of cameras (though they do change shifts every so often), and a ceremonial guard is mounted daily at 11:00 A.M. (Sundays at 10:00 A.M.) A few yards farther down Whitehall is the Cenotaph, the stunted Lutyens monument to the soldiers who fell during the two world wars.

Winston Churchill's bunker, some 70 feet below Whitehall, the Cabinet's secret bombproof headquarters during World War II, opened its 16-foot-thick walls to visitors as a museum a few years ago. Nothing has changed in this six-acre maze of rooms and corridors since the Blitz: According to the map room and various notices around the place, the war is still going on. Sir Winston's bed and the telephone cabinet (disguised as a lavatory) from which he would phone President Roosevelt are just as they were.

Britain's prime ministers have never had to walk far to work. Behind the famous black door of **10 Downing Street**, with its lion-shaped brass knocker, is an eight-room top-floor apartment; state rooms used for official receptions and banquets on the middle level; and Cabinet room, anterooms, and offices on the ground floor, opening onto private gardens. Even when she attends sessions in Parliament, Margaret Thatcher has only to walk down Parliament Street, the name given to the lower portion of Whitehall, though she is invariably driven. Downing Street is currently closed to pedestrians, so no one much at all walks on it at present.

The **Palace of Westminster** is an extravagant example of Gothic style. Its lean clock tower has four clock faces, each measuring 23 feet across, and its 13.5-ton bell, Big Ben, chimes each quarter-hour. The palace is another one of London's most photographed sights. The familiar view is taken from across the river. Although visitors to Britain can always line up outside for tickets to the visitors' (or "Strangers' ") gallery, for a closer inspection of the Houses of Parliament you will have to take an organized tour. British residents can apply to their Member of Parliament; non-British residents must apply well in advance for tickets from their embassy or contact the Know Where Agency (P.O. Box 38, Sevenoaks, Kent TN13 3LN; Tel: 732-45-79-02), which will arrange a tour with an M.P. (or, more often, a retired employee of the House supplementing a pension).

The typical tour begins in Westminster Hall, the oldest and most historic part of the parliamentary complex and home to the original law courts before they moved farther north to their present site around Chancery Lane. These courts witnessed the kinds of state trials that have made history, including that of Guy Fawkes, the man who attempted to blow up the Houses of Parliament with kegs of gunpowder in 1605 and whose effigy now sits atop thousands of bonfires every November 5. From Westminster Hall the tour moves on to scrutinize the Royal Gallery, the Prince's Chamber, the Lords' Chamber (where every bill passed by the Commons or initiated in the Lords has to receive the Peers' assent before becoming law), the Members' Lobby, and the royal throne in the Peers' Chamber. Those stationary figures in the Central Lobby are prime ministers Churchill, Lloyd George, Arthur James Balfour, Herbert Asquith, and Clement Attlee.

The highlight of any tour is the **House of Commons**, the arguments and debates of which are broadcast and now televised into every British home. This world of green leather benches (in contrast to the red of the House of Lords) seats 437 M.P.s plus 15 Commons officials at any one time. (There are fewer seats than M.P.s entitled to them.)

In the Norman Porch, you can see a collection of some two million parliamentary records, including the original copies of all acts of Parliament, dating as far back as the Middle Ages.

Next door to Parliament stands **Westminster Abbey**, the second most famous church in England. It is the royal church, where monarchs are crowned on the ancient coronation chair, a piece of furniture that has been serving its regal purpose of succession since William the Conqueror became King on Christmas Day, 1066.

The abbey was originally owned by a Benedictine monastery, one of the few that managed to escape Henry VIII's dissolution, which destroyed much of ecclesiastical England. Now, some five million people visit the abbey each year, so if you come in search of spiritual peace and sanctuary, you'll be a shade disappointed. Even the burial space is overpopulated with kings and queens, from Edward the Confessor, who founded the abbey in 1065, to Elizabeth I, as well as such historic literati as Chaucer, Tennyson, Dickens, Kipling, Hardy, and Browning. The top seed are buried in the Poets' Corner; Ben Jonson was actually buried upright—by choice, as it happens, but it certainly made a contribution toward alleviating the space problem.

One can only praise the Classical-style **Tate Gallery**, built near Pimlico on a millbank, a section of the river's north shore upriver from Parliament between Lambeth and Vauxhall bridges. The gallery's origins date back to 1897, when the country was looking for a home for a national collection of British art. Sugar magnate Sir Henry Tate put forward the money, plus his personal collection of 64 paintings. Many a Londoner's Sunday afternoon is spent browsing its galleries—the original 64 paintings have been joined by continually changing exhibitions as well as a permanent collection of British works from the 16th to the early 20th century, vast collections of Impressionists, and, since 1916—when it was decided the Tate would not just be an extension of the National Gallery— many works of modern art from abroad. Matisse, Braque, Chagall, and Picasso share hanging space with Jackson Pollock, Henry Moore, Barbara Hepworth, and Alberto Giacometti. In its Clore Gallery, the Turner Bequest contains more than 300 oil paintings. The entire collection has recently been rehung and rearranged in simple chronological order, tracing the development of British art from 1950 to the present day. The results are impressive. The Tate has a good restaurant (lunches only, famed for its wine list) and a self-service cafeteria. A minor detour across to the south bank here will bring you to **Lambeth Palace**, a Medieval building and the London residence of the Archbishop of Canterbury for more than seven centuries. It's open to groups by prior arrangement (apply to the Palace Secretary; Tel: 928-8282) from 10:00 to 5:00, Mondays through Fridays. The **Institute of Contemporary Arts**, far more youthful and a shade more radical in spirit than the Tate, with often obscure and controversial items within its contemporary exhibitions, is in Nash House on the Mall. It features three galleries plus a cinema, a theater, and a restaurant.

For such a central city borough, Westminster has a surprising amount of greenery. With its fashionable promenades, lanes, and walkways, **St. James's Park**, the oldest royal park in London, has been compared with Versailles. James I, a passionate lover of wildlife, stocked it with deer; Birdcage Walk, which runs along its southern flank, was named after a string of aviaries established by Charles II Nowadays the fauna is limited to birds and lunchtime office workers enjoying an alfresco sandwich. Duck Island, in the middle of the curvaceous lake (another Nash creation), is a private sanctuary for several species of birds. There's even a lodge on the island, a whimsical gesture from Nash. Stand on the small bridge that hoops over the lake and you could be in a Hans Christian Andersen story, as you look across the water at the turrets and minarets of St. James's Palace surrounded by trees.

After a turn around St. James's Park, Charles II would habitually stroll up Constitution Hill, which cuts through neighboring **Green Park**. Although only the Queen Victoria Memorial comes between them and they both border on the Buckingham Palace grounds, Green Park has a completely different nature from St. James's. It's much smaller (53 acres in contrast to St. James's 93) and has rejected any attempts at floral trimmings, opting for just an ample rash of trees and grass. As its name suggests, it remains an expanse of simple, unadulterated green and the optimal place to walk off a breakfast or a grander feast at the neighboring Ritz hotel.

The quarter of St. James's is an almost exclusively male preserve, its domain defined by the presence of a number of gentlemen's clubs, the most famous being Brooks's, Boodle's, White's, and the stuffy like. Walk down Lord North Street late at night, for example, and you could be back in Georgian London. Step inside these inner sanctums of conservatism (subject to invitation, of course, and your sex), and the only event likely to disturb the status quo is the creak of a chubby leather-backed chair, the tinkle of ice against crystal, the rustle of the pink pages of the *Financial Times,* and the slow ticking of a grandfather clock. You can occasionally peek through the windows at such scenes, but only at that time of day when the inside lights have been fired and the curtains have yet to be drawn on the outside world.

Knightsbridge-Belgravia

Think of Knightsbridge, and you'll think of **Harrods**. The two words seem to reinforce each other in a fragrant blend of high income and refined taste. No matter where in the world you normally do your shopping, Harrods deserves a pilgrimage and at least a small spree.

They say a customer once went into the Harrods pet department and asked for an elephant. "Certainly, sir," replied the assistant. "African or Indian?" Your own needs might be rather more basic, but whether you go to

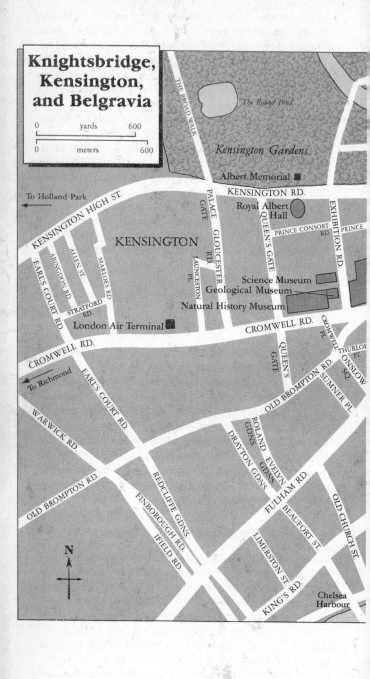

Knightsbridge, Kensington, and Belgravia

| 0 | yards | 600 |
| 0 | meters | 600 |

THE BROAD WALK

The Round Pond

Kensington Gardens

Albert Memorial

KENSINGTON RD.

To Holland Park

KENSINGTON HIGH ST.

PALACE GATE

GLOUCESTER RD.

Royal Albert Hall

QUEEN'S GATE

PRINCE CONSORT RD.

EXHIBITION RD.

PRINCE

KENSINGTON

ABINGDON RD.

ALLEN ST.

MARLOES RD.

EARL'S COURT RD.

STRATFORD RD.

LAUNCESTON PL.

Science Museum

Geological Museum

Natural History Museum

London Air Terminal

CROMWELL RD.

CROMWELL PL.

THURLOE ST.

ONSLOW SQ.

CROMWELL RD.

To Richmond

QUEEN'S GATE

OLD BROMPTON RD.

SUMNER PL.

EARL'S COURT RD.

WARWICK RD.

ROLAND GDNS.

EVELYN GDNS.

DRAYTON GDNS.

FULHAM RD.

OLD CHURCH ST.

OLD BROMPTON RD.

REDCLIFFE GDNS.

FINBOROUGH RD.

IFIELD RD.

BEAUFORT ST.

LIMERSTON ST.

N

KING'S RD.

Chelsea Harbour

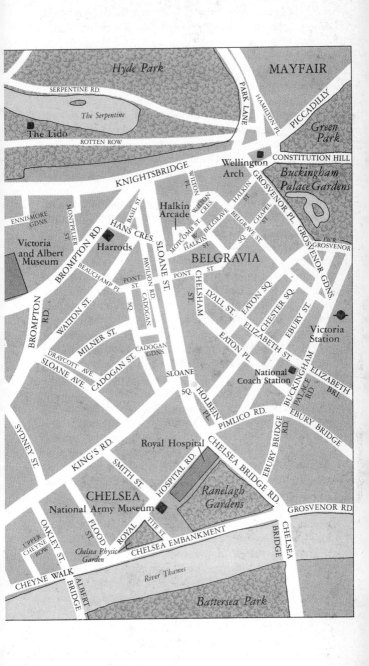

Harrods to buy or to browse, you can't fail to be bowled over by the sheer weight of style, let alone the store's contents.

Harrods is the largest store in Europe. It has its own bank, and, just to reel off a few of its stock statistics, it sells 150 types of pianos, 9,000 ties, 450 kinds of cheese, 130 kinds of bread, 85 different brands of malt whiskey, and more or less anything else that is made on the globe. If you want just a taste, head for the Food Hall, a palatial, beautifully tiled, magnificently stocked emporium. The store's own-brand items, often packed in distinctive green tins with the Harrods label, make easy and popular presents.

Harvey Nichols, nearby at Knightsbridge and Sloane Street, is London's "other" department store. Harrods may have its special Queen's entrance, but Harvey Nichols is the store where you're more likely to come across Princess Di casting an eye over the stock of designer labels. Apart from the main shopping arteries of Brompton Road and Knightsbridge proper, another shopping mecca that principally caters to the wealthy residents around and about is **Sloane Street**. The very name has spawned its own London social type whose style, in the words of *The Official Sloane Ranger Handbook* (by Ann Barr and Peter York), is all about "quality, conservatism, and classicism." And that's exactly what you can expect from the majority of stores on Sloane Street.

The tiny streets that lie in the elbow formed by Knightsbridge—the street as distinct from the environs—and Sloane Street constitute a neighborhood of expensive town houses and small, exclusive stores selling antiques, paintings, haute couture gowns, and pretty frippery. Cross Sloane Street, and Belgravia's Halkin Arcade, in particular, which spans Motcomb and West Halkin streets, has more priceless items in its windows than you'd come across in a sheikh's palace—which is, indeed, the ultimate destination of many of the pieces.

Those in search of **Belgravia** won't find a sign, but they've found it once they're in Wilton Crescent, Belgrave Square, Eaton Place, or Eaton Square. Belgravia, lying just east of Sloane Street, was a neat, early 19th-century development later rebuilt in Classical style.

Surprisingly, it is not the generously proportioned, 18th-century Grosvenor Square, home of the U.S. embassy, but Belgravia's Chester Square that has earned the nickname "American Square in Mayfair," on account of its high proportion of ex-pats in residence. In recent times they have included Henry Fonda, Tony Curtis, and Robert Wagner. Today's residents are as likely to be seen in the area's top Italian restaurant, **Mimmo d'Ischia** (on Elizabeth Street), presided over by the flamboyant Mimmo and his lively team of waiters, or on the opposite side of the street in the **Ebury Wine Bar**, which specializes in steaks grilled before your eyes (if you sit at the counter, that is).

Knightsbridge is home to **Beauchamp Place** (pronounced *Beecham*), off Brompton Road west of Harrods. Contrary to recent shopping trends, Beauchamp has remained a refreshingly anachronistic oasis of small, primarily independently owned boutiques and restaurants (some of the most interesting of which are in unprepossessing basements). Originally a row of Regency houses, this narrow, 400-yard-long road has more variety than many shopping streets ten times the length. Its name recalls the time when French nobles took up residence in Knightsbridge to escape the egalitarian consequences of the Revolution.

Knightsbridge is not only an elegant place to shop but an elegant place to live as well. Even the Queen lives just around the corner. The sweeping crescents, anonymous mews, and manicured squares—with their smart Rollers, Jags, Bentleys, and Daimlers patiently waiting like faithful retainers at the curbside—all lie within an easy stroll of both the quality shops and **Hyde Park**, that vast, pool-table expanse of greenery (at 360 acres, the largest in London) surrounding the mile-long Serpentine lake, and the setting of Kensington Palace, the home of Prince Charles and Lady Diana in neighboring Kensington Gardens.

Hyde Park is London's equivalent of New York's Central Park, a place to let off pent-up urban steam by jogging or hiring a rowboat, or even a horse from Lilo Blum's stables. If you opt for the latter, you can follow the hoofprints of the palace guards, who canter around a mile-long sandy track known as Rotten Row in the wee hours every morning. In addition to the before-work, after-work, and weekend activity, the park still lives up to its popular image—nannies wheeling perambulators along the Broad Walk, children throwing crusts of bread to the ducks, model boats making their way sedately across Round Pond, Sunday brass-band concerts, small-time politicos expounding on a soapbox at Speakers' Corner in the northeast corner (Britain's symbol of democracy, where anyone can express whatever opinion he or she may hold dear), and spartan swimmers plunging from the Lido into the Serpentine at 5:30 A.M., often breaking a layer of ice to do so.

Notting Hill

The broad Bayswater Road, which forms the northern boundary of Hyde Park, begins its journey at Marble Arch. Once past the park, it almost immediately becomes the southern boundary of Notting Hill, where a large part of the city's West Indian immigrants have settled. They've been increasingly joined by professionals who find the combination of ethnic color in cafés and shops and the gentility of five-story houses on tree-lined avenues like Elgin Crescent irresistible.

Sensationalized newspaper headlines of riots and robberies invariably follow Notting Hill's August Bank Holiday Caribbean Carnival, but don't let them put you off going, either to the Carnival itself—Westbourne Grove and Ladbroke Grove in particular are jam-packed with stalls, floats, and people dancing in the streets to reggae steel bands—or at any other time of the year, especially weekends.

Saturdays at the **Portobello Road Market**, where you will find antiques, Victoriana, and a variety of junk, are already on the tourist circuit. What you don't want to miss are the many small, specialized art and photographic galleries that have recently opened along Kensington Park Road, which is parallel to Portobello, and down various side streets.

If you'd like an American-style breakfast, start the day relaxing over your newspaper in the multilevel **Gate Diner**, also on Kensington Park Road. More serious eating takes place at **Monsieur Thompson's** nearby at number 29, or at **Leith's** at number 92. **Julie's Wine Bar and Restaurant** opposite David Black Oriental Carpets on Portland Road also attracts the smart set.

Chelsea

Like the Roman Empire, ancient Greece, and the Weimar Republic, Chelsea has already wallowed in its golden era. Its heyday in the annals of history is not rooted in its military supremacy or imperialistic acquisitiveness but in the ephemeral world of fashion. The Chelsea that attracted the attention of the world in the early 1960s was symbolized by the scantiest of all emblems: the miniskirt. Chelsea earned its place on the map by virtue of its highly talented designers, as well as the scores of artists, writers, and musicians who came to live within its geographical and emotional boundaries. It was the birthplace of "Swinging London," a notion born of an alchemy of coincidences— an enormously attractive environment, proximity to central London, and the then-low rents.

The decade of the 1960s was not a unique time of creativity for Chelsea. Scores of famous people, particularly in the arts and literature, have lived in the village, among them Charles Kingsley, Dante Gabriel Rossetti, Mark Twain, T. S. Eliot, Henry James, Oscar Wilde, and the so-called sage of Chelsea, Thomas Carlyle, whose Queen Anne house on Cheyne Row is open to view during the summer.

Chelsea, between Knightsbridge-Kensington and the Thames, still merits a visit today, and not just to mourn its passing glory. Chelsea is a delightful environment in which to live or, as a compromise, to visit. Its terraces and squares, studded with trees and lined by rows of pretty, pastel-painted town houses that look like overgrown dolls' houses, would seem more in keeping with a rural than an urban context. King's Road, supposedly named after the path that Charles II took to visit Nell Gwynn—who then lived in the neighboring borough of Fulham—is still one of the best shopping streets in London; in many ways the street is better than ever, since the retail action now stretches from Sloane Square in the east along the New King's Road continuation and on into Fulham Road, which is parallel to King's Road to the north.

There's no longer any need to groan at how the outlandish punks have added a stamp of mockery to the majesty of Chelsea's fashion pedigree. Although it's only a few years since this was their territory, today there's hardly a safety pin, bald scalp, or studded jacket to be seen; instead, the Saturday crowds are sporting checkered Paul Smith suits, tartan kilts, wedge haircuts, and sensible shoes. They spend small fortunes in interior-decor stores like Habitat and meet for lunch in the Habitat Café.

Clothing stores still predominate, but there are also plenty of antiques arcades and art galleries. If you happen to be partial to Victorian and Edwardian lighting, find your way to **Christopher Wray's** period light emporium at 600 King's Road. He stocks hundreds of models, mostly original, some quality reproductions. The street is also heavily endowed with lighting stores of the modern-design type. **Antiquarius** is a covered, 200-stall antiques market selling Art Deco and Art Nouveau designs, English porcelain, watercolors, and period jewelry and clothing.

In between is a generous sprinkling of pubs and restaurants, many occupying the same site for 20 years. The most famous pubs include **The Man in the Moon** and the **Markham Arms**; plant-filled and patioed, the latter witnesses an extensive pavement throng of lager drinkers in summer. The Pheasantry, a popular 1960s meeting place with an unusual arched entrance and guild plaques, now houses a complex of several Spanish restaurants. **Dominic's Bistro** is still attracting aficionados of candles in Chianti bottles.

Perhaps the busiest eatery of them all, on account of its minute proportions, is **The Chelsea Bun Diner**, tucked down a side road on Limerston Street. Arrive any time between 7:00 A.M. and 11:30 P.M. and you can be served a foaming cappuccino, a traditional English breakfast, a sandwich, or a burger. Everything's homemade, but the owners have no liquor license, so you must bring your own bottle.

Places of historical interest include the **Chelsea Physic Garden**, the second-oldest botanical garden in England. Its 5,000 plant species include—as the name suggests—the medicinal variety as well as Britain's biggest olive tree (there used to be cannabis, too, until 1982, when a dedicated home botanist jumped over the wall in the middle of the night and took the specimen for home cultivation). The **National Army Museum**, which records the history of the British military, is also in Chelsea, as is the **Royal Hospital**, home of the highly photographed Chelsea Pensioners, originally founded by Charles II "for the support and relief of maimed and superannuated soldiers." When Mary Quant designed the miniskirt, originally sold on King's Road in her store Bazaar, those uniformed pensioners, sharing the frame with pretty girls with dead-straight hair, heavy eyes, and lots of leg, were the photographic cliché of London.

South Kensington

You may feel that Chelsea falls short on serious culture, but neighboring South Kensington more than compensates for it. **Exhibition Road**, a 20-minute walk to the north, was Prince Albert's special project. As Queen Victoria's consort, he was able to wield the power to open the Great Exhibition in Hyde Park in 1851. It was such an immense success that in 1856 all profits were used to buy the Gore Estate, on which, he demanded, a collection of educational establishments should be built. Judging by the hordes of schoolchildren filing into the estate's grand collection of museums, which spill down Cromwell Road, his wishes have been well respected.

Queen of them all is the **Victoria and Albert Museum**, home to a vast collection of fine and applied art. It's the sort of museum best tackled by studying the plan, picking your favorite handful of "theme" rooms, and ignoring the rest. In fact, those who decide to "do" all the galleries would be wise to invest in a pair of hiking boots—they stretch a total of seven miles. At least the abundance keeps people coming back, discovering something new each visit. Don't miss the collection of Chippendale furniture, John Constable's English landscapes on the first floor, or the Jones Collection, a riveting display of French aristocratic interior decor, painting, furniture, ceramics, and other decorative arts, including examples of Marie Antoinette's lavish tastes. The costume court contains one of the greatest clothing collections in the world, popular with pencil-wielding fashion students. The rest of the museum's collections can only be listed: Japanese, Islamic, British art and music, Raphael cartoons. . . .

Just west on Cromwell Road is the **Natural History Museum** and its more specialized adjunct, the **Geological Museum**. From the outside the Natural History Museum resembles a grand sandstone church; the massive interior can be divided into five main departments—botany, entomology, mineralogy, paleontology, and zoology. It's one of the city's most popular museums; most Londoners, even if they haven't visited, have at least seen pictures of the skeletons of the *Brontosaurus rex, Tyrannosaurus rex,* and other dinosaurs in the magnificent central hall. After that, it's a question of which awe-inspiring sight to look for first. The ceiling of the Whale Hall in the west wing has to be seen to be believed: Skeletons and models of several species of mammals hang from it like spiders on webs. There are also fossil collections, galleries of birds, underwater creatures and coral, plants and minerals, plus a gallery devoted to simple ecology.

For fans of "hands-on" displays, the **Science Museum**, just north of the Geological Museum on Exhibition Road, is unbeatable, with knobs to twiddle, lights to flash, electric shocks to be administered, and plenty of bleeping sound effects. Children make up a generous proportion of the museum's devotees—there's even a Children's Gallery on the lower ground floor devoted to teaching simple scientific ideas using dioramas and working models. Older visitors, having mesmerized themselves with the Foucault pendulum that hangs near the entrance on the ground floor (its slow deviation proves that the earth does indeed rotate), usually head straight for the Apollo 10 space capsule and simulated moon base in the new Exploration of Space Gallery. But the museum also caters to steam engine buffs (Puffing Billy, the world's first locomotive, is in the road and rail transport wing) as well as lovers of astronomy, nuclear physics, modern technology (see The Challenge of the Chip display), photography, electricity, and navigation.

The **Royal Albert Hall** is also in this area, north of the Science Museum on Kensington Road, just across from Kensington Gardens. If it were in Spain you'd swear the hall was a bullring. A multipurpose venue, it hosts everything from Rolling Stones concerts to political conventions, graduation ceremonies of the University of London and boxing matches, but is perhaps best known as the site of the summer Promenade concerts, or "the Proms."

Richmond

Identifying Richmond on any map of London has never been difficult. At the region's heart lies a gigantic green expanse, seen at the map's bottom left-hand corner. If you fly into Heathrow from the east, the area will appear as a sea of green floating below the left-hand windows. Richmond is a prosperous borough that not only has more open spaces than any other in London but also has hundreds of listed buildings—and even the trees have preservation orders slapped on them. Should circumstances not allow you to live in Richmond, there's no excuse for omitting it from a London visit.

Richmond upon Thames, to give the borough its full name and pertinent location, spans the banks of the river upstream from central London between Hammersmith Bridge and Hampton Court. Despite its proximity to central London (30 minutes by tube), it's actually a borough of individual, small "villages": Barnes, Ham, Kew, Teddington, Twickenham, and Mortlake, all of which have managed to cling to significant shows of antiquity.

The name Richmond is inherited from a palace rebuilt by Henry VII, who in turn had borrowed the name from his Yorkshire earldom. Although all that remains today of the original building is the Gatehouse just off Richmond Green, during the 15th century Richmond Palace was a favorite Tudor retreat. Shakespeare staged performances of his plays here, while the wardrobe that Queen Elizabeth I stored in the palace—it contained well over 2,000 dresses—would put Joan Collins to shame. Both Henry VIII and Elizabeth I died here. The palace's importance gradually declined until it was finally demolished in 1660, after the Restoration.

The most scenic way to approach Richmond is aboard one of the boats that chug up from Westminster Pier during the summer. Once you step ashore you'll find yourself in the middle of a completely self-contained village. There's likely to be a cricket match in mellow swing on the Green, the locals (anyone from barristers and bankers to writers and actors) toing and froing, with liquid refreshments in hand, between their patch of spectator grass and the beery interior of the Cricketers pub.

Different styles of architecture jostle for position—Georgian, Palladian, Tudor, and Victorian—but the last definitely predominates. Minutes away are the Richmond Theatre and aging, narrow walkways and streets like Old Palace Lane, which runs from Trumpeters' Court to the river, and **Maids of Honour Row**. The latter is a famous row of four tall 18th-century houses, complete with wrought-iron gates and railings, on the Green, built in 1724 for the companions of Caroline, wife of the future King George II. But the name is now more synonymous with the **Maids of Honour Tearoom** on Kew Road. You can either line up for a table and wallow in the cottagey ambience, or take out a bag of scones, cakes, and Maids of Honour curd tarts (made from a secret recipe) and eat them at leisure down by the river.

Summer is the best time for a **riverside walk** (in spring and autumn, heavy tides have been known to flood the walkway). Low tide in hot, dry weather reveals the river's steep, sandy banks. Low-slung trees trail their leaves in the water, and ducks, swans, and moorhens rock along on the wash left by motorboats revving past. The most hectic time for the river (not to mention its wildlife) is March, when the **Oxford and Cambridge Boat Race** is held. Cutting through the waters from Putney to Mortlake, this is an amateur race for rowing "eights" and an important competition for the two universities, whose respective rowing teams practice for months beforehand. It lasts about an hour and a half; the best viewing points are on the Surrey bank above Chiswick Bridge, Mortlake close to the finishing line, or anywhere else along the towpath. Be sure to wear something of either light blue (Cambridge) or dark blue (Oxford) to show your allegiance.

Richmond's stretch of river is also active during **Swan Upping**, an ancient and rather curious pageant held every July. The Worshipful Companies of Vintners and Dyers, along with representatives of the Queen, spend one week rowing their half-dozen Thames skiffs upstream from Sunbury to Pangbourne, ceremoniously catching swans, counting them, and nicking the beaks of the year's new batch of cygnets. The tradition dates back to the Middle Ages; its original purpose was to establish the ownership of these then-profitable, prestigious, and tasty birds. The Crown can still lay claim to any unmarked swans, a right that is today administered by the Lord Chamberlain's office and implemented on the spot by Captain Turk, the Queen's official Swan Master. At present only some 200 swans are to be seen in the entire Lower Thames, and the Swan Upping ceremony has become a crucial census for ecological reasons.

The least urban of London's boroughs, Richmond contains three royal parks as well as the Royal Botanic Gardens at Kew. All four are popular weekend haunts. **Richmond Park**, the largest of the royal parks, covers 2,500 acres and was first enclosed by Charles I as a deer park. In fact, it's still worth your trouble to pack a pair of binoculars so you can examine at close range the large herds of fallow and red deer that roam freely.

The park's woodland gardens and Isabella Plantation are at their best from mid-April to the end of May, when the azaleas and the rhododendron dell are in full bloom. Historic buildings include the King's Observatory; the White Lodge, built in 1727 as a hunting lodge for King George II (open only in August); and Princess Alexandra's home, Thatched House Lodge. Stop for tea at **Pembroke Lodge**, a restaurant and café with its own garden and terrace. This place, ideal for pensive reflection, was the childhood home of the philosopher Bertrand Russell.

For years it cost only two pennies to enter the turn-stiles of Kew's **Royal Botanic Gardens**. The fee has now risen to one pound, but that's still an enormous bargain. The 300 acres of landscaped gardens, originally made up from the grounds of Richmond Lodge and Kew Palace, contain more than 25,000 species of plants from all over the world. A cry went up throughout the land at the havoc that the hurricane of October 16, 1987, wreaked on Kew, toppling 800 trees and destroying in one night 150 years' careful nurturing. Though the worst-hit areas are now open again, restoration work still continues, especially on river and lakeside areas. The magnificent Palm House reopened in spring 1990 after extensive renovation of the 19th-century conservatory.

Aircraft destined for Heathrow Airport fly overhead at the peak rate of one a minute, creating an incongruous din as visitors wander the paths through groves, wood-lands, and rock gardens, stopping to visit the Orangery, the four temples, the tall red Pagoda, or one of the plant houses. These fine Victorian conservatories, with such names as Alpine House, Water Lily House, Temperate House, Palm House, and the new Princess of Wales conser-vatory, are an architectural blend of cast iron and glass. The 17th-century Dutch House is one of the exceptions; this sturdy, red-brick and gabled building is all that re-mains of Kew Palace.

The Temperate House, one of the biggest hothouses, is dominated by a single giant palm whose towering leaves brush the ceiling. Visitors can walk along an upper bal-cony for aerial views of fountains and ponds full of orna-mental fish. When visiting the houses be prepared for abrupt climatic changes—within the space of a few paces, you can be transported from the tropical rain forests of South America to the arid desert of Arizona.

For the most delightful river walk to be had in these environs, head for the stylish Hammersmith Bridge and walk along the north bank toward Chiswick. The best time for such a walk is early on a summer's eve, when you can buy a glass of "bitter" ale in any (or each) of four charming pubs—the **Blue Anchor**, the **Rutland Arms**, the **Ship**, and the **Dove**—and sit and sup in the open with a friendly crowd, idly watching the scullers whose boat-houses line the banks below the bridge. **Hammersmith Terrace** is a delightful row of Georgian houses, several with their tiny gardens right above the river, separated from the houses by the towpath. William Morris used to live in Kelmscott House. Just before you reach Chiswick Square, step into the churchyard of St. Nicholas, where the painters James Whistler and William Hogarth are buried. Beyond lies **Syon House**—most famous for Robert Adam's Great Hall—the London residence of the duke of Northumberland. The house is open to the public, although Syon is most famous for its gardens—the 18th-century handiwork of Capability Brown, who included a lake, conservatory, aviary, and aquarium in his designs. He had nothing, however, to do with the Heritage Motor Museum, which is also on the grounds and houses a collection of British cars from 1895 to the present day, nor with the London Butterfly House, which displays numerous species fluttering madly in a tropical greenhouse. More energetic walkers can cross Hammersmith Bridge and follow the south bank as far south as the **Bull's Head** pub in Barnes, their faces held toward the setting sun.

Hampton Court

Richmond Palace was originally called Shene, but when Henry VIII made Richmond Park the place to hunt, outsiders built hunting lodges, and it became, at the same time, a popular stopping-off place for boats on their way up-river to Hampton Court Palace. Unlike other palaces, which have stood empty as museums, Hampton Court has been lived in continuously since it was built by Cardinal Wolsey, the Lord Chancellor of England, in 1515. George III was the last sovereign in residence; today, it is partly occupied by pensioners of the Crown, the "Grace and Favour" tenants. The palace is unique in that it represents the very best examples of English architecture of both the 16th and the early 18th centuries. And the location, hard on the Thames, is stunning.

In March, 1986, a fire caused severe damage to the palace. Amazingly, although many works of art were destroyed or damaged, most of the palace's valuable contents, including the outstanding collection of 500 Renaissance paintings, were saved. The building itself, however, suffered enormously. The fire gutted the King's Audience Chamber, the Cartoon Gallery (named for the Raphael cartoons bought by Charles I and moved to the Victoria and Albert Museum more than a century ago), and State Apartments designed by Sir Christopher Wren for King William and Queen Mary. Restoration work will almost certainly stretch into the next decade, but most of the palace was open to the public a week after the fire.

Although inhabited by a succession of kings and queens, Hampton Court is probably best known for its associations with Henry VIII. When he became owner, he extended the palace in earnest, including the building of Chapel Court as a nursery for Prince Edward, his son and heir. But by the time William and Mary came to the throne, the Tudor style was considered rather passé, and they commissioned Wren, the architect of St. Paul's Cathedral, to demolish the entire palace and build a new, more symmetrical, more spacious residence on a scale that would rival Versailles. Since the palace was so fully inhabited, Wren could only work on a little at a time, and, mercifully for architectural posterity, the money ran out before he could implement his grand designs. Hence the uniqueness of Hampton Court: One of the most complete examples of a Tudor palace coexists harmoniously alongside buildings by England's greatest architect.

The most popular element of Hampton's horticulture is its **maze**, first planted in 1714. It may not look too challenging from the outside, but it can take up to an hour or more to get out of the half-mile of yew-hedge labyrinth. So don't leave finding the way out till the main gates are about to close. Some visitors from abroad, it is said, have even seen their homebound aircraft pass overhead, having missed a Heathrow departure just down the road.

Camden Town

The charm of Camden Town, the lively, streetwise district bang in the center of north London and a ten-minute subway ride due north of Tottenham Court Road, lies mainly in its social and cultural mishmash. Along its core arteries (Camden High Street, Chalk Farm Road, and Parkway), plant-filled wine bars and bistros, antiques shops, and smart clothing boutiques rub shoulders with disheveled discount stores, secondhand music retailers, and the pulpy droppings from the fruit and vegetable market on Inverness Street. Harmless down-and-outs, occupants of the Arlington Road shelter for the homeless, are deep in inebriated conference on most street corners.

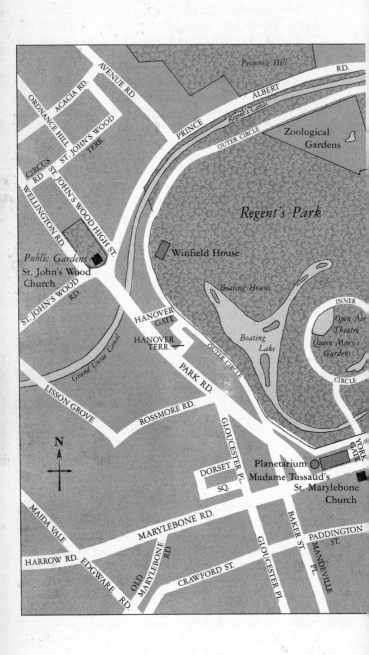

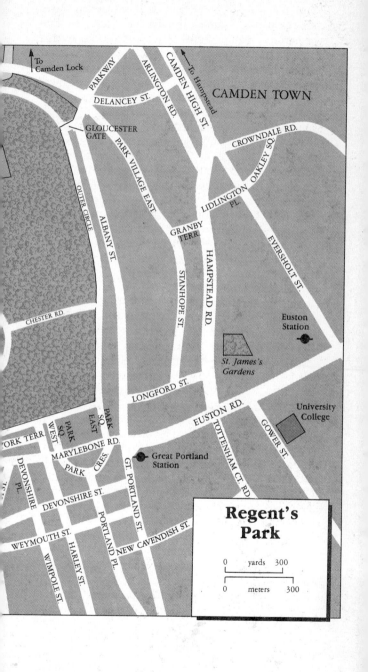

To Camden Lock

CAMDEN TOWN

PARKWAY

ARLINGTON RD.

CAMDEN HIGH ST.

To Hampstead

DELANCEY ST.

GLOUCESTER GATE

CROWNDALE RD.

PARK VILLAGE EAST

LIDLINGTON PL.

OAKLEY SQ.

OUTER CIRCLE

ALBANY ST.

GRANBY TERR.

HAMPSTEAD RD.

EVERSHOLT ST.

STANHOPE ST.

CHESTER RD.

Euston Station

St. James's Gardens

LONGFORD ST.

EUSTON RD.

University College

YORK TERR.

PARK SQ. WEST

PARK SQ. EAST

TOTTENHAM CT. RD.

GOWER ST.

MARYLEBONE RD.

PARK CRES.

Great Portland Station

DEVONSHIRE PL.

GT. PORTLAND ST.

DEVONSHIRE ST.

PORTLAND PL.

WEYMOUTH ST.

HARLEY ST.

NEW CAVENDISH ST.

WIMPOLE ST.

Regent's Park

| 0 | yards | 300 |
| 0 | meters | 300 |

The slightly jaded, hippie ambience of **Camden Lock's weekend market** is famous throughout London. Its scale is generous, spilling from the cobbled lockside area around the stagnant basin waters to Chalk Farm Road, almost as far as the former Roundhouse Theatre, located in an old brick-built railway locomotive shed. The blue-canopied stalls are surrounded by trendy shops and renovated haylofts and warehouses.

Anyone wishing to sell his or her wares to the battalions of yuppies and punks lines up at nine in the morning and, if lucky, is allocated a stall. The market has everything from potted palms to pine furniture, handmade jewelry to Hawaiian shirts, posters to pure-wool sweaters, antiques and bric-a-brac to high-tech gift items.

In the middle of this friendly chaos, two French-inspired restaurants are doing a roaring trade. Camden Brasserie and Le Bistroquet stare in quasi-hostility at each other across Camden High Street just south of the bridge over the Regent's Canal. **The Brasserie** is the cheaper of the two. Like the black-and-white photos of the market's punk fans that line the walls, the menu rarely changes, but that doesn't deter the arts and media clientele, many of whom saunter over from the futuristic-looking TV-AM building just around the corner. **Le Bistroquet** is more chic, more expensive, and more imaginative. Ceiling fans rotate, spiky-haired waiters and waitresses whiz between the tables, dishes such as fish *en papillote* are unveiled, reeking of capers and fresh fennel, and the smart talk flows.

The 50 acres of **Primrose Hill**, an offshoot of Regent's Park to Camden's south, are a voluptuous green hummock on an otherwise pancake-flat horizon. This area earned its name from its wildflowers, although, in the 18th century, the area blossomed with as many derelicts as blooms, and only the foolhardy would dare cross its boundaries once night had fallen. Today, Primrose Hill's Regency terraces rank among the most salubrious and expensive in north London. On Sunday afternoons the grassy mound is busy with kite-flyers and walkers who climb to its summit to enjoy one of the best panoramas of London.

The purpose of the closest, most prominent structure on the southern horizon would be impossible to guess. It is an aviary, designed by Lord Snowdon and standing within the **London Zoo** in Regent's Park, one of the city's biggest tourist attractions. Open seven days a week, it was founded by Sir Stamford Raffles (a name more immediately associated with the hotel in Singapore, the British trading colony he founded).

Apart from the aviary, other highlights of the menagerie, which is home to more than 5,000 animals, include a tropical house, where hummingbirds freely commute between thick foliage and your head; an "open-plan" lion house; an insect and arachnid house (not for the spider-phobic); and a tigers' den, where only a pane of glass separates you from the sharp canines of roaring beasts. There's also a rich-smelling elephant house, where the public can witness regular teeth-cleaning and toe-filing sessions; several high-octane monkey houses; and the Moonlight World, where nocturnal fauna are deceived into activity at hours to suit visitors.

Chalk Farm, the area tightly bordered by Primrose Hill, Regent's Park Road, and a main railway line, had been a fairly run-down precinct until gentrification occurred in the 1970s. The main thoroughfare is Regent's Park Road; its lower portion is now a neighborhood of shops that seem to sell a blend of everything—wine and kitchen equipment included—that a wealthy community could possibly need. There's also a smattering of restaurants, including the refined **Odettes** and **Lemonia**, a classy Greek eatery.

A large proportion of Camden is made up of parklands. During the British civil wars of the 17th century, the future of **Regent's Park**, arguably London's most urban park, looked gloomy, as most of its trees were razed to be used as firewood for the needy. It was John Nash who, at the end of the 18th century, backed by the prince regent, engineered today's pièce de résistance. Today, within the manicured hedges that line the Outer Circle road lie 500 acres of gardens, shrubbery, and bird life, all in a basic Victorian format, right down to an old-fashioned bandstand where tubas and trumpets entertain lunchtime and Sunday-afternoon picnickers. (It suffered catastrophically in a recent terrorist-bomb explosion, but is back in action.)

More modern trappings include a boating lake (formed by damming the River Tyburn), a children's boating pond, the zoo, and ornamental bridges. There's also an open-air theater, where the New Shakespeare Company performs a program of three or four plays throughout the summer. The glades and woods provide the perfect setting, and the audience, sitting on tiered seats exposed to the elements, can move around with the scenes when necessary, clutching plates of food and glasses of wine.

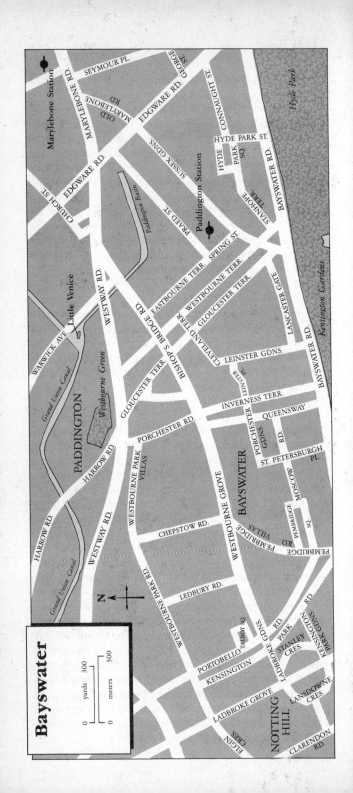

Once inside the Queen Mary's Gardens, within the Inner Circle road, the sounds of London are reduced to that of an occasional airplane. This fragrant enclave is a mass of 20,000 perfumed rose bushes grouped around a landscaped rock pool on the site where Nash originally planned to build a royal palace for the prince regent.

The Outer Circle road is lined with **Nash terraces**— smart, cream-colored, porticoed and pillared buildings that nowadays function as fashionable offices as well as private homes. The houses were originally built to raise money for the Crown and attracted the well-known and well-to-do—Hugh Walpole lived at 10 York Terrace, for example; King Edward VIII's lover, Mrs. Simpson, was ensconced at 7 Hanover Terrace; and the author H. G. Wells lived at 13 Hanover Terrace.

The only significant dwelling *within* the park is Winfield House, once the mansion home of Woolworth heiress Barbara Hutton. It's now the official London residence of the U.S. ambassador. You can view it only through the closely guarded gates at the bottom of the drive on the Outer Circle road. Almost opposite, straddling the south end of St. John's Wood High Street, is the Central Mosque, copper-domed and minareted, one of the most incongruous sights in the vicinity. At sunset it can be mistaken for a mutant sun lowering its obese body below the skyline trees.

The **Regent's Canal**, part of the Grand Union Canal network, flows around the northern perimeter of the park (you can see some of the zoo animals from the water) before taking a dogleg up to Camden Lock. Its total length runs to eight miles, from the pretty core of **Little Venice** west of the park near Paddington Station to Limehouse in the Docklands at the east. Several longboats operate regularly in summer between Camden and Little Venice, including the *Jenny Wren, Jasons Trip,* and the London Waterbus Company, which operates regular service on the Zoo Waterbus between Camden Lock and the zoo. *My Fair Lady* serves lunch and dinner; non-dining passage is not offered. You can catch these boats near the Warwick Avenue and the Camden Town Underground stations.

Little Venice is north of **Bayswater Road**, the northern boundary of Hyde Park; **Queensway**, a main neighborhood shopping and dining street, runs north off Bayswater. The boat ride takes you along the still waters, past rows of Georgian houses, to Little Venice, where you can break your journey with a jar of ale in the tiny, low-ceilinged **Warwick Castle** pub (especially vital if, as an alternative, you cover the one and a half miles by foot).

Marylebone Road

When Madame Tussaud, a French sculptress and one of King Louis XVI's tutors, arrived in London with a bizarre collection of wax facsimiles of heads that had rolled during the French Revolution, she could not have dreamed that **Madame Tussaud's**, the exhibition she established on the southern fringes of Regent's Park on the Marylebone Road in 1835, would eventually become London's most-visited attraction. Today, visitors line up far down the street to see lifelike figures of historical, political, royal, and show-business personalities. In the **Planetarium** next door, there are permanent constellation exhibitions plus, every evening from Wednesday through Sunday, laser shows accompanied by rock and classical music. Try to avoid the lines by going early and avoiding Saturdays, when the ranks of tourists are swelled by British out-of-towners.

Marylebone Road (originally St. Mary-le-bourne; *bourne* meant "river" in the 18th century) is long and busy. It is also the location of St. Marylebone Church, most famous for its tiered tower and cupola. The church is wedged into the opening of Regent's Park's York Gate, one of the main entrances to the park, built in 1817. Marylebone Road's offshoots, their northern reaches almost in Regent's Park, the southern almost in Oxford Street, include Harley Street, where the country's top physicians have clinics, and Wimpole Street, where Robert Browning courted Elizabeth Barrett. **Baker Street**, the biggest and longest, is most famous for the fictional address of detective Sherlock Holmes at number 221b. In his day, that part of Baker Street was known as York Place. Today, thanks to the renumbering of the street in 1930, the house at 221b is inhabited by the Abbey National Building Society, whose employees must every day reply politely to "Dear Sherlock Holmes" letters.

The more interesting and prettier Marylebone High Street is lined with shops and small cafés. **Maison Sagne**, at number 105, is one such refreshment house. This Swiss *pâtisserie* and bakery, established in 1921, is still baking pastries and cakes on the premises. Antiquities can be found in **Blunderbuss** on Thayer Street (the southern continuation of High Street). The eclectic shop is full of pistols, helmets, swords, and other military bric-a-brac.

Chiltern Street, parallel to and east of Baker Street, is interesting for its fashionable boutiques for men and women, its antiques stores, and its music and musical instrument shops stocking oboes, flutes, and early-music instruments.

Islington

One of the first of London's "villages" to be gentrified and have the prices of its rows of basic artisan dwellings inflated by an influx of middle-class residents, Islington suffers from a proliferation of real-estate agents whose windows advertise "bijoux" properties with quarter-of-a-million-pound price tags for the tiniest. Well connected by subway (Highbury & Islington stop on the Victoria line, the Angel on the Northern line, a 15-minute ride northwest of central London), Islington has come a long way since its days as one of London's seediest working-class boroughs.

The Domesday Book records Islington as a small settlement within the Great Forest of Middlesex, a largely rural, dairy-producing district supplying London. In the 17th century, when plague and fire caused a mass exodus from central London, Islington became a fashionable residence for the nobility and otherwise well-heeled (Charles and Mary Lamb lived here) who were attracted by its health-inducing spas. By the 19th century Islington was a curious mixture—the construction of better roads and the introduction of railways resulted in the development of fine terraces and squares, but the central core had declined and was crawling with grime, poverty, and working-class slums, although George Orwell, Walter Sickert, and Evelyn Waugh all made their homes here.

Today, Islington is the undisputed territory of the intelligent socialist. Ruled by a council of liberal tendency, it's a borough that survives on meager finances but doles out welcome bowls of sympathy. Such a reputation has made it a place of refuge for struggling minority groups and has spawned countless voluntary self-help associations, among them the Islington Voluntary Action Council, designed to help those who would doubtless suffer discrimination elsewhere.

However, as with all deprived areas (Islington is the eighth-poorest borough in London), its low property prices have attracted an influx of the upwardly mobile.

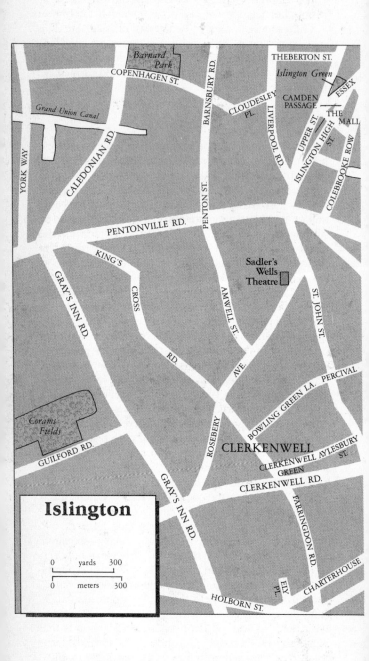

Barnard Park

THEBERTON ST.

COPENHAGEN ST.

Islington Green

BARNBURY RD.

CLOUDESLEY PL.

CAMDEN PASSAGE

ESSEX

Grand Union Canal

LIVERPOOL RD.

UPPER ST.

THE MALL

YORK WAY

CALEDONIAN RD.

ISLINGTON HIGH ST.

COLEBROOKE ROW

PENTON ST.

PENTONVILLE RD.

KING'S

Sadler's
Wells
Theatre

ST. JOHN ST.

GRAY'S INN RD.

CROSS

AMWELL ST.

RD.

AVE.

BOWLING GREEN LA.   PERCIVAL

Corams
Fields

ROSEBERY

CLERKENWELL

GUILFORD RD.

CLERKENWELL
GREEN

AYLESBURY
ST.

CLERKENWELL RD.

GRAY'S INN RD.

FARRINGDON RD.

Islington

ELY
PL.

CHARTERHOUSE

| 0 | yards | 300 |

| 0 | meters | 300 |

HOLBORN ST.

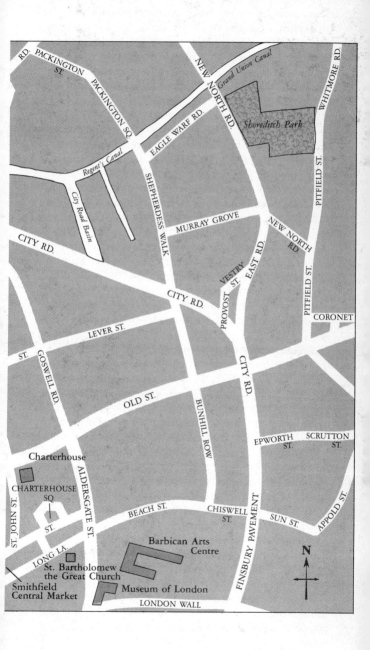

Rubbing shoulders with those relying on state support, the newcomers are buying the last of the borough's decaying properties and converting them into smart, terraced residences. And they buy all their fixtures and fittings in **Upper Street**. Aptly named, not only for its clientele but for its contents, Islington's main thoroughfare is adrift in wine bars, restaurants, designer kitchen accessories shops, and all the other late 20th-century paraphernalia.

Of course, there are antiques stores. Islingtonians frequent **Camden Passage**, a narrow, flagstoned, pedestrians-only street behind the miniature Islington Green. Wrought-iron shop signs advertise numerous antiques emporiums: Franco's, The Furniture Vault, Gordon Gridley, Ark Angel, and Laurence Mitchell, to name a few, plus **The Angel Arcade**, a Gothic precinct of 20 shops selling silver, porcelain, rare books, and objets d'art. Finbar Macdonnell has a caged mynah bird whose chirruping will distract your browsing through his old prints and engravings. And if you wind up in **The Mall**, on neighboring Islington High Street, you may never come out—it contains a bewildering 35 galleries of antiques and decorative arts. On Wednesday mornings and all day Saturdays there are also rows of antiques stalls in Camden Passage.

A large part of the borough of Islington is dominated by a district to the south called **Clerkenwell**, named after the Clerks' Well, which was discovered in 1924 in what is now the *New Statesman/Society* building. The well was christened after the Medieval parish clerks of the City of London, who performed miracle plays near here on the banks of the River Fleet. The **Charterhouse**, a beautiful, towered building near the Aldgate Underground stop and the Smithfield market (see below), owes its foundation to Sir Walter de Manney, who recognized its potential as a center of prayer and place of refuge for plague victims. Since then the Charterhouse has been home to Carthusian monks, a palace visited by Elizabeth I, and a famous boys' school. Large chunks of it were destroyed during the Blitz bombings; what remains is home to the Charterhouse Pensioners and is open on Wednesdays for guided tours.

The fertile meadowland on which Clerkenwell was founded is alive with spouting wells. Some are still quite productive, like the one under the **Sadler's Wells Theatre** (home to the Royal Ballet Company) on Rosebery Avenue. The purity of the local well water attracted beverage makers such as Gordon's, famous for its gin distillery, and Samuel Whitbread; both still occupy their original sites. In fact, the Whitbread Brewery Shire Horses still clop along their morning delivery rounds to pubs in the City and also turn out for the Lord Mayor's Show and other ceremonial occasions.

No wonder Islington's wine bars are so well stocked. **Serendipity**, in The Mall, is a cool, conservatory-like cocktail bar. **The Dome**, on Islington High Street, has a Parisian ambience, particularly when the windows are opened wide in summer and the smell of croissants drifts into the street. A glass of wine at these places is a good way to begin a night that may include theater: Many a West End box-office success has begun on the tiny stage at the back of the **King's Head** pub in Upper Street. Performances are held nearly every night. When the show ends, live music in the bar begins. The pub's old decor and gentrified spit-and-sawdust feeling is heightened by the staff's quaint habit of using a cash till that dates back to pre-decimalization days, so keep your currency converter handy or be prepared to trust the change.

After the theater, you can squeeze into **Minogues** on Theberton Street, one of London's few Irish pub/ restaurants, for flowers on the table and traditional dishes from the blackboard menu. **Young's Chinese** is a short distance away on Upper Street; the nearby **Upper Street Fish Shop** is bright, breezy, and a bit upscale, at least for a fish-and-chip shop.

You'll have to get up early to catch the market traders at **Smithfield**. This wholesale meat, poultry, and game market at the southern side of Clerkenwell near the Barbican Underground stop, though of little initial attraction to the visitor, has been a London tradition since the 12th century (in those days the cattle were live). Located on the site of Islington's old Caledonian livestock market, it extends over eight acres, has 15 miles of rails capable of hanging 60,000 sides of beef, and is active Monday to Friday. The Norman **St. Bartholomew the Great Church**, one of the oldest in London, lies a few minutes' walk to the east of the market. It contains the only pre-Reformation font in the city. There is also a restaurant here called **Café du Marché** that looks as if it belongs somewhere on Paris's Left Bank. It's hard to find, though: Stand on Charterhouse Square, look north, and you'll see it tucked down a tiny alleyway.

Hampstead

Hampstead is London at its most rural. Drop strangers in the heart of the 800 acres of leafy, luscious **Hampstead Heath** and they will swear on oath that they have been abandoned in some remote English shire, a verdant, bushy-tailed wilderness far from the madding crowds. Only when their ears turn away from birdsong to the distant hum of metropolitan traffic will they accept the urban coordinates. Stuff them into a taxi and they can be in central London in 20 minutes.

As a place to live, Hampstead's tree-lined lanes and twisting alleys have long been prominent addresses in the pages of *Who's Who*. Early residents included Robert Louis Stevenson, D. H. Lawrence, John Keats, John Galsworthy, George Orwell, William Blake, and John Constable. By the early 1900s Hampstead had become London's Montmartre, full of painters and their contemporary equivalent of wanna-bes. Wander around the streets today and you'll see many of the distinctive blue plaques that denote the fame of an earlier inhabitant.

Hampstead Heath is one of the "lungs of London." Tranquility and clean air (at least by city standards) are its stock in trade, and the lichen grows thick. Judging by the real-estate prices, which rank among the highest in the city, such virtues have much appeal today. Among the rich and famous residents are Jeremy Irons, John Le Carré, Frederick Forsyth, and Boy George. Hampstead being what it is, no one appears to spare a second glance when one of the media mortals is seen buying out-of-season asparagus at a local greengrocer, taking tea at Louis *pâtisserie,* or sipping a slow cappuccino at the Dome Café.

Despite the massive heath, the appeal of Hampstead is all too easy for the London visitor to miss. Emerge from the Hampstead subway station into a busy intersection lined with unexciting shops and you'll immediately wonder what the fuss is all about and turn around to check the station name. Turn left down Hampstead High Street, though, and left again into Flask Walk, and the pace takes a turn for the best.

The very name Flask puts things into immediate historical context. It is derived from the bottles of medicinal waters that once were filled from nearby chalybeate springs and sold here. The shops now go in for Perrier and other variations on the *eau* theme, but several are well worth a browse. One of Hampstead's many pleasant pubs, **The Flask**, is also on the Walk.

Hampstead is the one place in London where a map and compass are as useful to the tourist as a handful of currency. To get the best of the greenery, you need to walk in, around, and through the Heath, and, with luck, return to the point where you started. Take heart in the knowledge that even locals go astray.

Follow Flask Walk into Well Walk, another place with obvious watery associations, and pause at number 40, once the home of John Constable, England's finest landscape painter. From his house, after a couple more minutes, you should come face-to-face with the Heath. The point to head for, out of sight but likely to be known to the passing strollers, joggers, dog walkers, bird watchers, and the like, is **Kenwood**.

A very large and very white house across the Heath, northeast from where you are standing, Kenwood is a classic example of the 18th-century species of gentleman's country home. First owned by Lord Chief Justice William Murray, who employed Robert Adam to enlarge and embellish the property, Kenwood is now a bequest to the nation. It contains a fine collection of paintings by Rembrandt, Vermeer, Rubens, and others. During the summer there is a series of open-air concerts on the grounds.

From Kenwood, walk through the rhododendron gardens, littered with the occasional piece of weathered sculpture, along the linden-shaded gravel path, and ask to be pointed to the Spaniards Inn, reputedly an old haunt of Dick Turpin, the highwayman. From there, through the still narrow gap between the inn and the tollhouse, both 18th-century, head south along Spaniards Road (or, better still, follow a more rural course parallel to the busy thoroughfare) toward Whitestone Pond, whose dark waters mark the highest place in London (437 feet). Just before you reach the road, you will catch a glimpse of the distant city skyline growing out of the Thames valley, a spectacular sight when the afternoon sun is low on the horizon, striking gold against the city structures.

Since this is the high point of the walking tour, you might like to take time out at **Jack Straw's Castle**, a white wooden eyesore of a pub. Or you can follow North End Way to the popular **Bull and Bush Tavern**, built on the site of a 17th-century farmhouse that was briefly home to Hogarth.

Hampstead has a few other important landmarks, well worth a detour before you scurry back to more central parts of town. One is **Keats House** on Keats Grove (open to the public), set in the delightful garden where the poet composed *Ode to a Nightingale*. Another is the 17th-century **Fenton House** at Hampstead Grove, with an interesting collection of paintings, furniture, and ceramics and a highly regarded collection of early keyboard instruments. A third landmark is the remarkable 18th-century terrace of "brownstones" along Church Row. With the Church of St. John's at the end of the row, which is planted with trees along its center, the scene is quintessentially English. Imagine it with a dusting of snow and you have the makings of a classic Christmas card.

If the day is fine, head for Highgate. Close to another Flask pub (this one, with its large courtyard and outside summer tables, looks extremely rural) lies **Highgate Cemetery**. It is divided into two sections: The one to the east of Swains Lane is the newer half, containing the grave and bold bronze bust of Karl Marx; the one to the west is a tangled, overgrown, rather bizarre yet beautiful world of vaults and other monumental masonry.

East End

London's East End is not an obvious goal for visitors. It is far from refined, short on interesting shops, relatively light on historic buildings, and lacking in greenery. But for anyone interested in London as a sociological phenomenon, the East End—located at the eastern end of the city and hugging the northern bank of the Thames—is an essential detour.

Although London has nowhere near the same melting-pot alchemy that, say, New York does, it has certainly welcomed its fair share of huddled masses. The first to stake a claim were the Huguenots in the 16th century. Close on their heels came Sephardic Jews, Irish Catholics who excavated the city's docks, Polish and Russian Jews escaping the pogroms, and later, though less concentrated as a group in this particular section of town, thousands of Central European Jews fleeing Nazi persecution.

In 1887 a sociological study described Whitechapel as simply the "dwelling place of the Jews," a place where they practiced tailoring and other traditional skills. Today, the East End is still steeped in Jewish history. For example, Bevis Marks, near Aldgate Underground station, is

Britain's oldest surviving synagogue, built for the Sephardic community in 1701. Jewry Street is nearby, and there is even a Jewish soup kitchen on Brune Street. Cable Street is famous for the "battle" in which Jewish resistance to a march by Oswald Mosley and his Black Shirts stemmed the rising tide of Fascism in Britain.

In recent years there has been a shift in the ethnic makeup of the East End. Many Jews have moved out, upgrading their properties and buying in more desirable parts of town (particularly in the northwest London suburbs of Golders Green and Hendon; most of the Orthodox have moved to Stamford Hill). Even the Great Synagogue of Duke's Place closed in 1978, and so have ten others in the neighborhood, as the Jewish population has declined from 125,000 in 1900 to around 12,000 today.

Their places have been filled by a fresh wave of immigrants from the Indian subcontinent, notably Bengal and Bangladesh, who have taken over the lower-priced real estate as well as the traditional sweatshops. There are now as many *halal* butchers in the main shopping streets as there are kosher. On one street corner, where Fournier Street meets Brick Lane, there is a structure that was built as a Huguenot chapel, later became a synagogue, and is now a mosque.

The East End has always been on the "other" side of the tracks, a tough, working-class district of terraced houses, outside lavatories, and communal baths. At the end of the past century its slums were notorious. They inspired, among others, the American philanthropist George Peabody to finance the building of apartment blocks in an effort to alleviate the worst areas of overcrowding. Crime and prostitution flourished here, and this was the setting of the macabre deeds of Jack the Ripper.

Before you venture east, try to catch at least one episode of Britain's most successful soap, "Eastenders." Like all soaps, it pays only lip service to the truth, but it will introduce you to the mood and at least familiarize you with the Cockney dialect. Anyone born within the sound of Bow Bells, it is said, is a true Cockney, and most of the East End's places of interest lie within their decibel radius.

If you can choose the day for your visit, save the East End for a Sunday morning. Do this not so much for any religious resonances—though many beautiful churches designed by Christopher Wren and Nicholas Hawksmoor (including Christ Church, Hawksmoor's masterpiece, which overshadows Spitalfields fruit and vegetable mar-

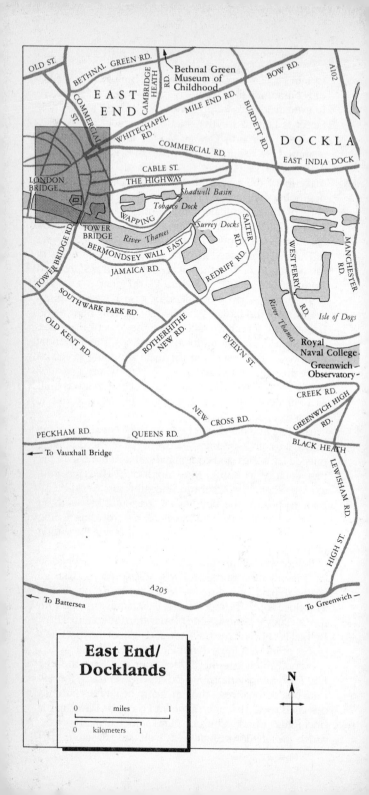

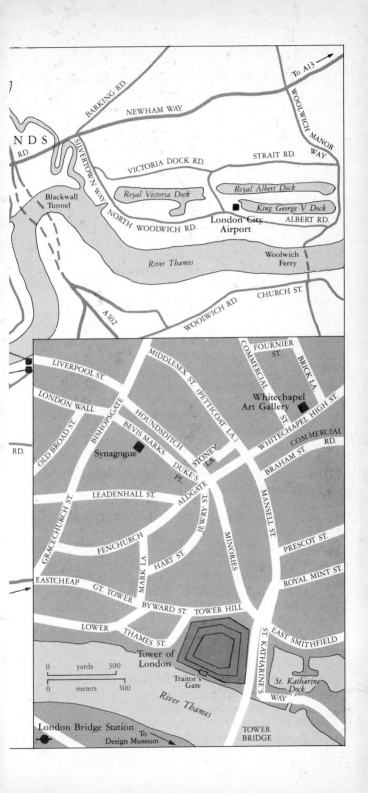

ket) lie within the area—but for its **Petticoat Lane market**. You won't find that name on a map, though; just take the tube to Aldgate and follow the crowds. If you prefer to trust a map, look for Middlesex Street and you'll find yourself in the heart of the action.

There are a few antiques and bric-a-brac stalls but nothing to compare with, say, Portobello Road or Camden Lock. In fact, the market's name hails from the days when it was predominantly a clothes market, but today's wares are as much the celebration of plastic and fly-by-night manufacturing as anything remotely tied to nostalgia. The pleasure of Petticoat Lane is just listening to the patter of the stall holders, barrow boys, costermongers, and fly-boys, the unlicensed traders who are always ready to flee at the first sign of a bobby. You should simply drift along with the crowd, soaking up the sheer vitality of the occasion. This is an extremely popular market, almost an institution among local residents, so you'll mingle with just about all of the Cockneys in London.

Petticoat Lane is one of those classic markets where they say you can find whatever was stolen from you the week before. Don't trust the irresistible prices, explained away by an unfortunate accident whereby the merchandise just happened to fall off the back of a lorry, a popular Cockney euphemism for hot goods. Be equally wary, despite the temptations, of Club Row, where they sell pleading dogs of dubious pedigree and caged birds whose vocabulary usually turns out to be as extensive as that of their canine neighbors, again contrary to the vendors' promises.

There are other interesting sights in the East End worthy of higher cultural esteem. The **Whitechapel Art Gallery** is one of the best in London (the Tate recently recruited a new chief curator from its portals), while opposite the Whitechapel Underground is the London Hospital, most famously the home of Joseph Merrick, better known as the Elephant Man. Cinema devotees will want to check out the Coronet on Mile End Road, not for its current screen presentations but to pay respects to the site of the music hall where Charlie Chaplin made his debut. And a great favorite for a family outing is the **Bethnal Green Museum of Childhood** on Cambridge Heath Road, with collections not only of children's toys but also of costumes and furniture.

With all its ethnic origins, you won't go hungry in the East End, but you may have to leave your food prejudices behind. **Tubby Isaacs' seafood stall** on Greatorex Street is just one institution, a place to buy a small plate of jellied eels, whelks, cockles, and winkles. You might like to risk your palate on the hot to very hot dishes at the Indian restaurants on Brick Lane, basic in price but with burning consequences. **Bloom's**, on Whitechapel Road, the East End's main artery, is London's best kosher restaurant. Takeout sandwiches and borscht followed by salt beef are the order of the day here.

Docklands

Visitors to London beware. The capital is changing faster than any other city in the world except perhaps Paris, Hong Kong, or Tokyo. But stick to the familiar haunts of the City and the West End, visit such popular landmarks as Westminster Abbey, the Houses of Parliament, St. Paul's Cathedral, and Buckingham Palace, and you won't notice a thing. Even many Londoners are none the wiser—their typical reaction, when shown what's happening on their very doorstep, is amazement at just how much has already been altered.

Venture just five minutes or so east from the Tower of London, and you'll come across the fringes of a London that is undergoing massive redevelopment on a scale seen only on two previous occasions—after the Great Fire and during the 1950s, when London repaired the ravages of war. Although work began only in the early 1980s, the Docklands has already become the most important and exciting inner-city development in Europe.

The area that is destined to become the new London is the old docks, a vast acreage of basins, locks, and canals where, during the peak of the country's imperial power, raw materials were unloaded from the colonies and manufactured goods were exported to the rest of the world. But with the gradual loss of empire and the undermining of England's commercial supremacy, coupled with the growth of containerized traffic, the docks gradually dwindled in importance. Decline led to decay and the vast landscape became a giant urban wasteland.

In a location as big as central London itself (a land area equivalent to that stretching from Marble Arch to the Tower of London and from Waterloo to Euston), old warehouses—some still smelling of the spices they once stored—are now being renovated and slowly transformed into chic stores, wine bars, restaurants, exhibition centers, craft workshops, art galleries, museums, and hotels. One of the first to open its doors is **Tobacco Dock**, with dozens of shops, restaurants, and other establishments based in the restored shell of the old tobacco warehouses. There are two replica 18th-century ships permanently moored at the nearby quay that you are welcome to board.

Within a five-minute walk of Tower Bridge is **St. Katharine Dock**. This restored Docklands area houses England's historic ships collection, full of old Thames sailing barges. Modern yachts anchor in a basin surrounded by arcaded warehouses constructed by Scottish engineer Thomas Telford and the Dickens Inn, a wooden warehouse now converted into a pub with a sawdust floor and two restaurants. On the other side of the river, a short but breezy walk across the Tower Bridge, is the new **Design Museum**, housed in Butlers Wharf (see below). Established by the Conran Foundation, it is a museum of everyday objects and an exploration of why they look the way they do.

Ecology has not been ignored in the grandiose schemes. Mudchute is a 32-acre working farm that even raises sheep for slaughter, and the Stave Hill Ecological Park, right in the heart of the Surrey Docks, contains 400 species of flora. Canals that were filled in during the 1960s, having ceased to function as commercial arteries, are now being dug out for purely aesthetic considerations. With its eight miles of River Thames and 460 acres of retained water, the Docklands has already been compared with Amsterdam and Venice—which is where several architects have looked for inspiration.

Top names in architecture, both British and foreign, have been recruited to renovate warehouses, some of which survive from the 1790s (although most are from the 19th century), and design new residential and commercial buildings. Sir Terence Conran, fresh from revitalizing the high streets of Britain, has done a similar job on **Butlers Wharf**, an outstanding remnant of original 19th-century riverside warehouses, turning it into shops, homes, restaurants, offices, and the above-mentioned Design Museum.

A transformation is planned for the pumping station on **Shadwell Basin** in Wapping, built by the London Hydraulic Power Company in 1890 as one of five stations of its kind, providing power not only to the surrounding docks but also throughout central London (for everything from raising the curtains at Drury Lane to lighting Joseph Kennedy's house when he was the U.S. Ambassador to Britain). Plans are not settled at this writing.

The Light Railway serves the new breed of residents, workers, and visitors some 20 feet above street level, using many of the original Victorian viaducts and running from the Tower of London through a series of stations to the Isle of Dogs (see below). In October 1987 the London City Airport was opened. A mile-long runway, sandwiched between the Royal Albert and George V docks, accommodates 50-seater DeHavilland Dash-7 aircraft that link the Docklands with Jersey, as well as cities on the Continent within a 400-mile radius of London. Just 15 to 20 minutes after collecting their baggage, less than half the time it takes to journey out to Heathrow, arriving travellers can be in the heart of the City, making the airport an ideal gateway for financiers and other business people. The Docklands has, in other words, turned full circle: It was here, because of the commercial importance of the Thames and the dock system, that London was able to become the financial capital of the world, and it is here that its success may once again be ensured.

From the visitor's point of view the most exciting aspect of the Docklands is not what's new but what's old. Historic watering holes such as the **Prospect of Whitby**, the **Town of Ramsgate**, the **Three Suns**, the **Angel**, the **Grapes**, and the aptly named **House They Left Behind** are all part of the Docklands fabric. Several of these places back onto the Thames; on a fine summer evening you won't find a more absorbing sight than, say, from the tiny balcony at the back of the Grapes, the view across the drift of the tide to the Surrey Docks.

There are more than 100 listed buildings in the area, including half a dozen Hawksmoor churches, which are being spruced up and their courtyards cleared of their years of matted vegetation, and Edward III's moated manor house, which was discovered by workers digging a foundation in the vicinity of the Rotherhithe docks. A large chunk of Britain's maritime history was spawned by London's docks. Most 18th-century Royal Navy vessels, for a start, were built here, as was the *Great Eastern,* the largest ship built in the past century. Some are now permanently berthed in the docks as tourist attractions; the *John W. Mackay,* probably the oldest steam-driven cable ship in the world, is among them, berthed in the West India docks.

The Docklands is also Charles Dickens country. The

Quilp residence in *The Old Curiosity Shop* was at Tower Hill, and Quilp's Wharf was across the river at Shad Thames. Just behind Hawksmoor's St. George's-in-the-East in Wapping was the site thought to be the opium den Dickens visited shortly before he died. Lizzie Hexam lived in Limehouse, and so did Miss Abbey Potterson, the proprietress of the Six Jolly Fellowship Porters (alias the Grapes) in *Our Mutual Friend.* Jacob's Island (which Dickens called Folly Ditch) was the home of Bill Sikes, and where he was hanged in *Oliver Twist.* The **George Inn**— still a pub—in Southwark's High Street appeared in *Pickwick Papers* and *Little Dorrit.* The George has been preserved and is now owned by the National Trust.

What's best about the Docklands is that this is a living environment, not an artificial stage set manicured for tourists. When the Docklands really was docks, high walls kept Londoners from seeing, let alone enjoying, their backyard acres of water. Today, with the building of scores of walks along the Thames and canals, an entire waterscape is opening up before their eyes.

Greenwich

Greenwich, the historic maritime heart of London, lies some five miles east of the center of town, on the southern shore of the Thames. Since its maritime traditions still shape its present-day appeal, it is especially fitting to arrive in Greenwich by boat at Westminster Pier or Charing Cross Pier. Step off the pier and, within a few paces, you can be mounting the gangplank of the *Cutty Sark,* a magnificent clipper that plied 19th-century trade routes carrying cargoes of tea, the brew that oiled the cogs of an empire.

Within a few yards, dwarfed by the soaring masts of the *Cutty Sark,* is the comparatively tiny *Gipsy Moth IV,* the yacht that carried Sir Francis Chichester on the first solo circumnavigation of the globe in 1966–67. Nearby is the Royal Naval College, inspired by Wren, Hawksmoor, and Sir John Vanbrugh, and, just across the main road, the **National Maritime Museum**, which brings Britain's rich seafaring heritage vividly alive. Housed in a grouping of some of the country's finest 17th-century buildings, the museum displays paintings, models, and real-life boats, as well as exhibits that evoke some of the country's great naval battles and the voyages of discovery by Captain Cook and other adventurers. Nearby is Inigo Jones's

Queen's House, restored by the National Maritime Museum and opened by the Queen in May 1990. It was once home to Queen Henrietta Maria, the wife of Charles I.

After exploring these sights, take a climb through Greenwich Park to the top of the hill where, from the ankles of the statue of General Wolfe, you'll enjoy a grand view of the river. Try to time your climb so you are at the summit at 1:00 P.M., when the famous ball drops from the top of the **Old Royal Observatory**. The moment marks the correct Greenwich Mean Time. The observatory, part of the Maritime Museum, houses the largest refracting telescope in the U.K. as well as an extensive collection of historical timepieces and astronomical instruments. A plaque marks the Greenwich Meridian, the spot that defines the zero line of longitude—stand astride it and you'll have one foot in the Orient, the other in the Occident. Farther downstream, and included on many riverboat trips, is the new Thames Barrier, a curious, menacing structure designed to regulate the flow of water and prevent high tides from encroaching on much of the city's terra firma.

An interesting alternative return route to central London is to follow the foot tunnel beneath the Thames from Greenwich to the **Isle of Dogs**, so called because Charles II used to exercise his spaniels in the then-rural parts. After admiring the view of Greenwich as painted by Canaletto, you can catch the Light Railway back to Tower Bridge.

GETTING AROUND

The telephone area code for inner London (roughly anywhere within a four-mile radius of Trafalgar Square) is, with one or two exceptions, (071). The area code for outer London is (081). Throughout this chapter we have given the area code only if it is (081); if it does not appear, you can assume that the area code is (071).

Airports

Heathrow (Tel: 081-759-4321; British Airways, 081-897-4000) is 15 miles west of the city and can be reached in 45 minutes on the Piccadilly Underground line from Central London (one stop before the last for Terminal 4, last stop for Terminals 1, 2, and 3); trains run every five minutes, 20 hours a day. Airbuses pick up at several points throughout the main hotel areas of central London. **Gatwick** (Tel: 081-668-4211) is 30 minutes from Victoria Station by British Rail Gatwick Express (every 15 minutes from 5:30 A.M. to

11:00 P.M., hourly service throughout the night). Combined Gatwick Express/Underground tickets are available from any Underground station.

British Rail

London is served by several railway stations whose lines fan out like spokes on a wheel to various destinations of day-trip interest to the visitor. The best single source of information is the **British Travel Centre** at 12 Regent Street; open Mondays through Fridays, 9:00 to 6:30, Saturdays, 9:00 to 5:00, and Sundays, 10:00 to 4:00; Tel: 730-3400 Mondays to Saturdays. Inquiries about specific services can be directed to the various stations: Charing Cross (Tel: 928-5100); Euston (Tel: 387-7070); Holborn Viaduct (Tel: 928-5100); King's Cross (Tel: 278-2477); Liverpool Street (Tel: 283-7171); London Bridge (Tel: 928-5100); Marylebone (Tel: 262-6767); Paddington (Tel: 262-6767); Victoria (Tel: 928-5100); Waterloo (Tel: 928-5100). (For all of these numbers, a central stacking system ensures that phone calls are answered in strict rotation, so be patient and wait for a reply.) For information on the area of England each station serves, see Useful Facts at the front of this book.

Visitor Information

The most detailed sources of information for visitors to London are the weeklies *Time Out* and *City Limits,* which come out on Wednesdays and are sold at all newsstands. *The Standard,* London's weekday evening newspaper, is also a useful source of information, particularly on entertainment. Major tourist-information centers include:

London Tourist Board and Convention Bureau, 26 Grosvenor Gardens, London SW1W ODU, open Mondays through Fridays, 9:00 to 6:00 (Tel: 730-3488); **London Tourist Information Centre** at the following locations: Victoria Station Forecourt, open daily, 9:00 to 7:00, later in July and August; Selfridges department store (basement), Oxford Street, open 9:30 to 6:00, Mondays through Fridays, except Thursdays, 9:30 to 8:00; Harrods department store (fourth floor), Knightsbridge, open Mondays through Saturdays, 9:00 to 6:00, Wednesdays, 9:30 to 7:00, Saturdays, 9:00 to 6:00; Heathrow Terminals 1, 2, and 3 Underground Station, open daily, 8:00 to 6:30; Tower of London (west gate), open Mondays through Saturdays, 9:30 to 6:00, Sundays, 10:00 to 6:00; **British Travel Centre**, 12 Regent Street, near Piccadilly Circus, open Mondays through Fridays, 9:00 to 6:30,

Saturdays, 9:00 to 5:00, Sundays, 10:00 to 4:00 (Tel: 730-3400). There are also Tourist Information Centres in Clerkenwell, Croydon, Greenwich, Harrow, Hillingdon, Kingston-upon-Thames, Lewisham, Richmond, Tower Hamlets, and Twickenham.

Guided Tours
London Transport (Tel: 222-1234) operates half- and full-day tours from Victoria Coach Station, Buckingham Palace Road. For information, maps, and brochures contact the British Travel Centre, 12 Regent Street, Piccadilly Circus (Tel: 730-3400). Other tours are operated by **Cityrama** (Tel: 720-6663) and **Harrods** (Tel: 581-3603). Both *Time Out* and *City Limits* give details of the numerous independent lecturers and walking-tours available. There are also taxi guide services; details are available from Tourist Information Centres.

Underground (Tube) and Buses
London Transport has a 24-hour travel-information telephone service (Tel: 222-1234; English only) and also operates **Travel Information Centres** at the following stations: Charing Cross, Euston, King's Cross, Oxford Circus, Piccadilly Circus, St. James's Park, and Victoria.

The first trains run from 6:00 or 6:30 A.M. (later on Sundays) and the last at approximately midnight. Children under five ride for free, and those under 14 ride at reduced fares, as do 14- and 15-year-olds with a Child Rate Photocard (available from post offices in the London area; be sure the child has a passport-size photo and proof of age). Free maps of tube and bus services and a huge number of ever-changing leaflets describing various fares and special passes are available at Underground and bus stations. The map of the city bus network is posted on tube station platforms, bus shelters, and main bus stations. Individual bus routes are detailed at bus shelters.

Fares on both tube and bus are computed according to stages and zones; therefore, a relatively short bus ride crossing three fare zones will cost the same or more than a much longer ride in a single zone.

Tourist Passes
The **London Explorer** pass allows unlimited travel on all London red buses (except structured sightseeing tours) and almost all Underground routes (including Heathrow by Airbus or tube) for one, three, four, or seven days.

Children under 16 receive reduced rates. The **Capitalcard** offers unlimited off-peak travel (after 9:30 A.M. Monday through Friday) throughout London by train, Underground, or bus for one day; both passes are available at British Rail and Underground stations.

Taxis

London's black cabs are rated the best in the world. Any cab with its yellow "For Hire" sign lit should stop if you flag it, and provided your journey is under six miles and within the borders of London, the cab must take you where you want to go. (A taxi-share scheme has also been recently introduced.) You may telephone the following companies to arrange for a taxi: **Radio Taxis** (Tel: 272-0272, 272-3030, or 253-5000; 24 hours); **Addison Lee** (Tel: 720-2161); **Abbey Car Hire** (Tel: 727-2637).

Driving in London

Do not use your car in London unless it is absolutely necessary: Traffic is extremely dense, traffic jams are the rule of thumb, and parking places—if you can find one—are expensive. **National Car Parks** has several locations throughout London; two of the more central ones are on Cavendish Square (Tel: 629-6968) and on Brewer Street near Piccadilly Circus (Tel: 734-9497). The NCP at the National Theatre, Southbank (Tel: 928-3940), is less expensive. A free list of locations is available from NCP, 21 Bryanston Street (Tel: 499-7050). The North and South Circular ringroads of London are easily accessible from the city center and link up to all major motorways around London.

Rental Cars

Budget: Central reservations (Tel: 0800-181-181; toll free); King's Cross Station (Tel: 837-9877); NCP car park, Semley Place, near Victoria Station SW1 (Tel: 730-5233). **Avis:** 68 North Row, near Marble Arch W1 (Tel: 629-7811); Gatwick Airport (Tel: 0293-297-21); Heathrow Airport, Hounslow, Middlesex (Tel: 081-897-9321). **Godfrey Davis Europ car:** Central Reservations (Tel: 081-950-5050); King's Cross (Tel: 387-2276); Heathrow Airport (Tel: 081-897-0811). **Hertz:** Central Reservations (Tel: 081-679-1799); near Victoria Coach Station (Tel: 730-8323). It is best to pick up a car at one of the London airports, which has the added advantage of getting you familiar with driving on the left before you hit the traffic in central London.

Boat Excursions

Boats leave from Westminster Pier and travel up the Thames to Kew every 30 minutes from 10:30 to 3:30. Trips upstream to Hampton Court leave at 10:00, 10:30, 11:30, and noon (Tel: 730-4812). **Zoo Waterbus** departs from Little Venice, near the Warwick Avenue/Camden Town tubes, for trips on the Regent's Canal (Tel: 482-2550); **Jasons Trip** also offers cruises along the canal from Camden Town tube (Tel: 286-3428). Riverboat Information Service, a recorded message giving the times and routes of river trips, can be reached at 730-4812.

There is a new **Riverbus** service operating high-speed catamarans every 20 minutes from Chelsea harbor to Greenwich via Charing Cross Festival pier, Swan Lane pier, London Bridge pier, and West India Dock pier. Boats operate from 7:00 A.M. to 8:00 P.M. weekdays only (weekend service is planned). Fares depend on the length of your journey; Tel: 512-0555.

Excursions

Green Line/London Country buses leave from Marble Arch, Hyde Park Corner, Oxford Circus, and Victoria Coach Station for various towns of interest in the surrounding area. For information on routes and fares (including the Diamond Rover tickets, valid for one to three day's unlimited travel on the network) call 081-668-7261. Several companies also offer one-day tours, including **Harrods** (Tel: 581-3603), **Frames Rickards** (Tel: 837-3111), and **Evan Evans** (Tel: 930-2377).

—David Wickers

ACCOMMODATIONS

Part of the pleasure of visiting London is staying in a hotel that is typically and eccentrically British. London is rich in just such places. Many London hotels occupy converted town houses full of hidden corners and great charm. Others are refurbished Victorian and Edwardian hostelries in which no two rooms are alike. Even new hotels in London often try to make each room different from the next.

The following list is far from comprehensive, but it includes some of the best ones in different price ranges. As prices are always subject to change, we indicate only the general range you can expect to pay. An inexpensive double among *our* recommendations would be around £40; moderate, roughly £60 to £110. Expensive will be around £160 and, of course, on up. Keep in mind that as London is crowded with visitors year round, it is always best to book well in advance. Also, as London is such a huge city, you should decide upon the area in which you wish to stay before you make your booking; there is no point in saving money on a hotel only to spend it on travelling to and from the places you wish to visit.

The telephone area code for inner London, including all accommodations listed here, is (071).

Tower/City

The Tower Thistle Hotel. Despite its ugly modern exterior and out-of-the-way location on the edge of the City, just east of the Tower of London, this moderately priced hotel does have its pluses: a most wonderful position on St. Katharine's Dock, unmatched views, and attractive rooms.

St. Katharine's Way, E1 9LD. Tel: 481-2575; Telex: 885934; Fax: 488-4106; in U.S., (212) 689-9284 or (800) 882-4777; Telex: 6718291; Fax: (212) 779-0732; in Canada, (416) 441-1048 or, in Ontario and Quebec, (800) 268-7866; in Australia, (008)22-1023 or (02) 261-4399.

Whitehall/Strand

Royal Horseguards Thistle Hotel. Large but cozy, this pleasant and moderately priced hotel has much to offer at a reasonable price, primarily location. It is within walking distance of most of Westminster's historical sights as well as the theaters, and it occupies the elegant quarters of the old National Liberal Club, between the War Office and Victoria Embankment. (The club still occupies the end building in this terrace.) There is a good restaurant and bar in house.

2 Whitehall Court, SW1A 2EJ. Tel: 839-3400; Telex: 917096; Fax: 925-2263; in U.S., (212) 689-9284 or (800) 882-4777; Telex: 6718291; Fax: (212) 779-0732; in Canada, (416) 441-1048 or, in Ontario and Quebec, (800) 268-7866; in Australia, (008) 22-1023 or (02) 261-4399.

The Savoy Hotel. Built on the site of the Medieval palace of Savoy, this is probably London's best-known luxury hotel and is doubtless the one with the most fascinating history. It was built by the brilliant impresario Richard D'Oyly Carte out of the profits he made on his productions of the operettas of Gilbert and Sullivan, which were performed at his Savoy Theatre next door. When he took his productions of Gilbert and Sullivan to America, he was so impressed by the standards of the luxury hotels there that he decided to build a comparable one in London. He certainly succeeded: The Savoy was the first hotel in the world to be lit by electricity and the first hotel in London to have elevators. Another first, but nothing to do with Mr. D'Oyly Carte, was the invention of the martini in the **American Bar**. Next to this popular gathering spot is the **Savoy Grill**, a favorite place for after-theater suppers.

The Strand, WC2R 0EU. Tel: 836-4343; Telex: 24234; Fax: 872-8901; in U.S. and Canada, (800) 223-6800; in New York State, (212) 838-3110; in Sydney, (02) 233-8422; in the rest of Australia, (008) 222-033.

Bloomsbury

Hotel Crichton. This 19th-century house across from the British Museum in Bloomsbury is a well-run and inexpensive hotel and is understandably popular. The large breakfast (included in the price) is a good start to a day of sightseeing.

36 Bedford Place, WC1B 5JR. Tel: 637-3955; Telex: 22353; in U.S., (800) MIN-OTEL.

The Kenilworth Hotel. This recently refurbished hotel on the edge of Bloomsbury and close to the British Museum caters to business meetings and small conferences. Even so, it's well equipped for tourists, too, and is a good value.

97 Great Russell Street, WC1B 3LB. Tel: 637-3477; Telex: 25842; Fax: 631-3133; in U.S., (212) 473-8377, (203) 454-1957, or (800) 44-UTELL; in Ontario/Quebec, (800) 268-7041; in Toronto, (800) 387-1338; in Vancouver, (800) 663-9582; in Australia, (008) 22-11-76.

North of Oxford Street

Dorset Square Hotel. This small, attractive hotel occupies several 19th-century town houses on the corner of two-and-a-half-acre Dorset Square, just to the southwest of Regent's Park (the site of the original Lord's Cricket Ground, created by Thomas Lord in 1787 and a mecca for cricketing fans from all over the world). Despite the discreet town-house atmosphere and its very moderate price, the Dorset Square offers all the most up-to-date facilities: state-of-the-art security systems, 24-hour room service, and secretarial services.

39-40 Dorset Square, NW1 6QN. Tel: 723-7874; Telex: 263964; Fax: 724-3328; in U.S., (800) 543-4138.

Mandeville Hotel. Tucked away in Marylebone north of Oxford Street near Wigmore Street, Wigmore Hall, and the Wallace Collection, this attractive and reasonably priced hotel is a favorite of busy executives who make use of its restaurant, coffee house, two bars, and comprehensive business services.

Mandeville Place, W1M 6BE. Tel: 935-5599; Telex: 269487; Fax: 935-9588; in U.S., (402) 493-4747 or (800) 44-UTELL; in Canada, (416) 967-3442; in Australia, (02) 235-1111.

Mostyn Hotel. Relaxing comfort is what the Mostyn is all about, a welcome relief from the bustle of Marble Arch and Oxford Street. In 1740, Lady Black of George II's court commissioned John Adam to build her a grand house. Her home, which is now listed by the Historic Buildings and Monuments Commission as being of national importance, has been skillfully incorporated into the rest of the present building, but you can see part of the original structure as you enter the restaurant and cocktail bar. The grand staircase, superbly molded ceilings, wall paneling, and handsome fireplaces all show the airy spaciousness of the 18th century. Moderate.

Bryanston Street, W1H 0DE. Tel: 935-2361; Telex: 27656; Fax: 487-2759.

Ramada Hotel. This large and highly decorated Victorian hotel, once Berners Hotel and recently upgraded as part of the moderately priced Ramada chain, is situated in the heart of rag-trade land, just north off Oxford Street and close to Soho. Its splendid marble entrance hall is a popular meeting place for Londoners.

10 Berners Street, W1A 3BE. Tel: 636-1629; Telex: 25759; Fax: 580-3972; in U.S., (800) 228-9898 or (800) 228-2828; in Toronto, (416) 485-2610; elsewhere in Canada, (800) 268-8998; in Australia, (008) 22-24-31 or (02) 251-8888.

The Savoy Court Hotel. In a quiet mews just moments from the noise and bustle of Oxford Street sits this small, reasonably priced, and unpretentious hotel. Maybe its greatest asset is that it is almost next door to one of the biggest Marks and Spencer stores in Europe, as well as being one minute from Selfridges. So for those intent on shopping this is a wonderful site, with a cocktail bar and restaurant to revive you when you return exhausted with your purchases.

19–25 Granville Place, W1 0EH. Tel: 408-0130; Telex: 8955515; Fax: 493-2070.

Mayfair

Brown's Hotel. In 1830, James Brown, a gentleman's gentleman who was married to Sarah, the lady's maid to Lady Byron, bought the first of the large Mayfair houses that make up this most understated but elegant hotel. Over the next 150 years another 11 houses in Dover Street and Albemarle Street were acquired, making the hotel a veritable rabbit warren but in no way detracting from the impeccable service that makes this one of the most civilized places to stay in London. The cozy, paneled public rooms are crammed every afternoon as people enjoy the delicious afternoon tea for which Brown's is famous. It was in this hotel, in 1876, that the first successful telephone call was made in Britain—between the youthful inventor Alexander Graham Bell and the young son of the landlord, Henry Ford. It was also from this hotel that Theodore Roosevelt walked to his wedding at St. George's Church in Hanover Square, and just a few years later Franklin and Eleanor Roosevelt spent several days of their honeymoon in the same suite. Expensive.

Albemarle and Dover streets, W1A 4SW. Tel: 493-6020; Telex: 28686; Fax: 493-9381; in U.S. and Canada, (800) 225-5843; Telex: 6852554; in Australia, (02) 267-2144 or (008) 222-446.

The Chesterfield. Created from a gracious town house in the heart of Mayfair, close to Berkeley Square and Curzon Street, the Chesterfield is a gracious hotel. Named after the fourth earl of Chesterfield, who was a local landowner, this hotel has an affiliation with the English Speaking Union, whose headquarters, Dartmouth House, are next door. The interior is warm and inviting, and the staff is very friendly and helpful. The rates are moderate and members of the English Speaking Union receive a 20 percent discount.

35 Charles Street, W1X 8LX. Tel: 491-2622; Telex: 269394; Fax: 491-4793; in U.S., (800) 223-9868; in Toronto, (800) 268-7041; in Vancouver, (800) 663-9582; in Australia, (008) 22-11-76.

Claridge's. This wonderful hotel in the heart of Mayfair, near New Bond Street, may remind you of the great transatlantic liners, and the service is comparable, too. Quite simply, Claridge's is the ultimate in London luxury and discreet service, which is probably why guests of the royal family are frequently put up here. The rooms are among the most comfortable and best equipped anywhere, yet they still retain the grace and style of another era. During World War II, Claridge's became a haven for exiled royalty and heads of state. An amusing story is told of a diplomat who telephoned Claridge's and, asking to speak to the King, received the reply, "Which king?"

Brook Street, W1A 2JQ. Tel: 629-8860; Telex: 21872; Fax: 499-2210; in U.S., (212) 838-3110 or (800) 223-6800; in Canada, (800) 223-6800; in Australia, (008) 22-20-33 or (02) 233-8422.

The Connaught. This establishment is more like a very select club than a hotel; most of the guests have been staying—and eating at the renowned **Connaught Grill**—for years. The high standards this hotel, near the U.S. embassy, maintains are all the more valuable these days, when they are so rare. Most of the staff has been here for years, providing impeccable service. Both the hotel and the grill are hard to get into.

16 Carlos Place, W1Y 6AL. Tel: 499-7070; Fax: 495-3262; in U.S., (212) 838-3110 or (800) 223-6800; in Canada, (800) 223-6800; in Australia, (008) 22-20-33 or (02) 233-8422.

The Delmere Hotel. Close to Paddington Station and Bayswater, this is the best choice on a street of small hotels. With 40 rooms, which were attractively converted from a large town house, it caters not only to the vacationer but also to the business traveller, offering all the usual support services, including fax machines. Moderate.

130 Sussex Gardens, W2 1UB. Tel: 706-3344; Telex: 8953857; Fax: 262-1863.

The London–London Hotel. This newly opened hotel is inexpensive but has high standards, with all the usual facilities. Converted from several large houses in a quiet London square, it is close to Paddington Station, which serves the west of England as well as some of the nearer tourist destinations such as Windsor. The hotel is also close to the Bayswater district north of Hyde Park, and, for those who like to shop, Oxford Street is a reasonable walk away. Thatchers, the hotel restaurant, specializes in meat-free food.

2–14 Talbot Square, W2 1TS. Tel: 262-6699; Fax: 723-3233.

St. James's

Dukes Hotel. This small and attractive hotel is hidden discreetly in a courtyard brimming with flowers. With service that matches its comfort, no wonder it is recommended by regulars who wouldn't stay anywhere else. Expensive.

35 St. James's Place, SW1A 1NY. Tel: 491-4840; Telex: 28283; Fax: 493-1264; in U.S., (212) 779-1888 or (800) 544-7570; in Australia, (02) 360-1666.

The Ritz. This is where the word "ritzy" originated, and everything about it is just that—from the service to the decor, from the opulent public rooms, the most beautiful in London, to the elegant guest rooms and suites. The **Palm Court** is the best place in London for afternoon tea; the magnificent, gilded dining room looks out onto Green Park. The Marie Antoinette Suite, next to the dining room, is where Winston Churchill, General Eisenhower, and General de Gaulle planned the invasion of Normandy.

Piccadilly, W1V 9DG. Tel: 493-8181; Telex: 267200; Fax: 493-2687; in U.S., (800) 222-0939; in Canada, (416) 924-1711; in Australia, (02) 264-9966.

The Stafford Hotel. Reached from St. James's Street through a cobbled mews (although there is a more conventional entrance in the front of the hotel), this is one of London's treasures. The smallish and expensive hotel occupies two converted 19th-century town houses just to the east of Green Park. Public rooms are formal but welcoming, and attention to detail is in evidence everywhere—comfort even extends to a tunnel leading from the hotel beneath nearby buildings into the park. The restaurant is expensive but excellent. In the cellars, hidden away among the bottles of wine, is a small, private, and fascinating museum of wartime memorabilia, complete with sandbags and posters of the period. During World War II this was a bomb shelter for the American and Canadian officers who used the hotel as a club.

16-18 St. James's Place, SW1A 1NJ. Tel: 493-0111; Telex: 28602; Fax: 493-7121; in U.S., (800) 544-7570; in Canada, (800) 468-7745; in Australia, (02) 360-1666, (02) 264-9966, or (008) 25-1664.

Sloane Square/Victoria Station

Eccleston Hotel. Within easy walking distance of Victoria Station and its trains to Continental Europe and Gatwick

Airport, and Victoria Coach Station and the Underground, both with their links to Heathrow, this large and efficiently run hotel is an ideal location for the business traveller or the vacationer. Although inexpensive, the Eccleston offers most of the facilities you would expect to find in a more expensive hotel. Office facilities can be organized.

82-83 Eccleston Square, SW1V 1PS. Tel: 834-8042; Telex: 8955775; Fax: 630-8942; in U.S., (617) 581-0844 or (800) 223-6764.

The Elizabeth Hotel. Situated in one of the many garden squares of London, only a few doors away from one of the former residences of Sir Winston Churchill, this small and inexpensive hotel has a loyal following among travellers. Full English breakfast is included in the price. An unexpected bonus is that residents may use the tennis court in the communal gardens.

37 Eccleston Square, SW1V 1PB. Tel: 828-6812.

Goring Hotel. This, perhaps London's best small hotel, is still owned by the same family that built it in 1910. (The Goring was the first hotel in the world to have central heating and private bathrooms in every room.) Much loved by regulars, it occupies a quiet position by the Royal Mews of Buckingham Palace and is close to Victoria Station. Many of the rooms, as well as the comfortable and pleasantly seedy lounge and bar, overlook a garden. The motto of this hotel is "There is no longer a Mr. Claridge at Claridge's, there is no longer a Mr. Brown at Brown's, but there will always be a Mr. Goring at Goring's!" Moderate.

15 Beeston Place, Grosvenor Gardens, SW1W 0JW. Tel: 834-8211; Telex: 919166; Fax: 834-4393; in U.S., (312) 251-4110 or (800) 323-5463.

Royal Court Hotel. Location is this hotel's appeal—on Sloane Square in the heart of Chelsea, between Peter Jones, one of London's very best department stores, and the Royal Court Theatre, renowned for producing avant garde plays, and near all the shopping on the King's Road. Moderate.

Sloane Square, SW1W 8EG. Tel: 730-9191; Telex: 296818; Fax: 824-8381; in U.S., (800) 44-UTELL.

The Rubens Hotel. Built at the turn of the century to serve Victoria Station, this moderately priced hotel, situated opposite the Royal Mews, has recently been refurbished. It is attractively decorated, with large public rooms. Included in its many facilities are five meeting rooms that can be rented for conferences or social occasions. Located close to excellent underground and bus services, as well as the major trains of Victoria Station, The Rubens is particularly convenient.

Buckingham Palace Road, SW1W 0PS. Tel: 834-6600; Telex: 916577; Fax: 828-5401.

St. James's Court. Originally built at the turn of the century as grand apartments, by London standards this hotel is huge, with 390 bedrooms—but this does not mean it is without character; far from it. Recently upgraded, the St. James's is built around a landscaped central courtyard with a magnificent fountain. The building boasts the world's largest brick frieze, which depicts scenes from Shakespeare, but for more modern taste the facilities also include three very good restaurants, a health and leisure center, and a large business center. Considering its position, south of Buckingham Palace and close to St. James's Park, the St. James's Court is very reasonable.

Buckingham Gate, Westminster, SW1E 6AF. Tel: 834-6655; Telex: 928225; Fax: 630-7587; in U.S., (212) 972-6830, (402) 498-4300, or (800) 44-UTELL.

The Willett. In a small street of large red-brick houses is the inexpensive Willett. It is close to Sloane Square in the heart of Chelsea and so very close to many of the good shopping areas. A sumptuous English breakfast buffet is included in the price.

32 Sloane Gardens, SW1W 8DJ. Tel. and Fax: 824-8415; Telex: 926678.

Knightsbridge/Kensington

The Abbey Court. Newly and very elegantly converted from a large town house, this small hotel offers very personal and friendly service and moderate rates. Snacks and drinks are available around the clock and a full English breakfast can be served in your room every morning. This area of London (Notting Hill; just west of Bayswater and north of Kensington Gardens) abounds with restaurants of every kind for other meals.

20 Pembridge Gardens, W2 4DU. Tel: 221-7518; Telex: 262167; Fax: 792-0858.

Basil Street Hotel. This moderate and wonderfully old-fashioned and eccentric hotel has a large clientele who wouldn't stay anywhere else. In an excellent position in Knightsbridge off Sloane Street, it is perfect for shoppers—which is probably why the large room to the left of the entrance is set aside for women from the country who come to London to shop. In fact, the whole hotel has a very clubby atmosphere and is furnished throughout with comfortable chairs and writing desks. The staff-client ratio is higher than it is anywhere else in London, and the staff tends to stay.

8 Basil Street, SW3 1AH. Tel: 581-3311; Telex: 28379; Fax: 581-3693; in U.S., (402) 493-4747 or (800) 44-UTELL.

The Beaufort. On a cul-de-sac of very large, terraced houses near Harrods, this small hotel is privately owned and attractively decorated in country-house style. Guests are given their own key to the front door when they arrive so they come and go as though the hotel were their own home in London. Continental breakfast is served in your room or in the small sitting room and there is a complimentary 24-hour bar. Expensive.

33 Beaufort Gardens, SW3 1PP. Tel: 584-5252; Telex: 929200; Fax: 589-2834; in U.S., (800) 548-7764.

The Berkeley. This modern luxury establishment, close to Hyde Park and the shops of Knightsbridge, has all of the old-fashioned values you expect from a great London hotel. Unusual for London, though, are its penthouse swimming pool, beauty and health center, and a basement garage (a great plus in a city where parking is such a problem). Secretarial and valet service; 24-hour room service.

Wilton Place, SW1X 7RL. Tel: 235-6000; Telex: 919252; Fax: 235-4330; in U.S., (212) 838-3110 or (800) 223-6800.

Capital Hotel. Small, quiet, and beautifully decorated, and just around the corner from Harrods and the bustle of Knightsbridge, this hotel is a gem, though expensive. The restaurant (one of the best in London) is a favorite of gourmets, but if you want to cook for yourself there are some private luxury apartments available in the house next door (see below).

22-24 Basil Street, SW3 1AT. Tel: 589-5171; Telex: 919042; Fax: 225-0011; in U.S., (212) 725-5880 or (800) 223-5695; in Canada, (416) 447-2335.

11 Cadogan Gardens. There is no sign on the door of this small, moderate hotel off Sloane Street south of Harrods to suggest that it is anything other than a private house. Nor is there a reception desk or a restaurant; just a visitor's book and room service. Ring the bell next to the front door, and a manservant will let you in. Created from several Victorian houses, this hotel is much favored by diplomats and art dealers. Room service provides light meals, but for anything more substantial just venture down the road, where you'll find plenty of excellent restaurants.

11 Cadogan Gardens, SW3 2RJ. Tel: 730-3426; Telex: 8813318; Fax: 730-5217.

Gore Hotel. This pleasant and moderately priced small hotel across from Kensington Gardens, west of Royal Albert Hall, is very quiet yet close to all the activity of South Kensington. It has a pleasant lounge and a restaurant that serves light meals.

189 Queen's Gate, SW7 5EX. Tel: 584-6601; Telex: 296244; Fax: 589-8127; in U.S. and Canada, (800) 528-1234; in Australia, (02) 212-6444.

The Halcyon Hotel. Newly converted from two large houses on the corner of Holland Park (west of Hyde Park/Kensington Gardens), the Halcyon, although expensive, is already popular with theater people. No doubt they are drawn here by the greenery beyond the front door and the tastefully decorated rooms, designed to make you feel like a guest in a country house. The restaurant is highly regarded.

81 Holland Park, W11 3RZ. Tel: 727-7288; Telex: 266721; Fax: 229-8516; in U.S., (212) 490-2244 or (800) 323-7500.

L'Hotel. This delightful small hotel on the street behind Harrods has an air of the country about it, so it is no surprise that it is frequented by people who come up from the country to shop or attend meetings and who neither want nor need all the services of a larger hotel. The guest rooms are simple, as befits L'Hotel's moderate rates, but they are most attractive, with pine and brass fittings. There are no public rooms, but the bistro in the basement, **Le Metro**, is very popular with hotel guests and neighborhood residents alike. L'Hotel is a sister hotel of the Capital Hotel next door.

28 Basil Street, SW3 1AT. Tel: 589-6286; Telex: 919042; Fax: 225-0011; in U.S., (212) 725-5880 or (800) 223-5695; in Canada, (416) 447-2335.

Hyde Park Hotel. At 10:30 every morning, you can see the Horse Guards riding past this stately hotel, one of London's oldest, on their way from the Horse Guards Barracks next door to the changing of the guard at Whitehall. Many debutantes' parties are held here, maybe because the young Guards officers are close at hand to act as escorts. With a lovely dining room overlooking Hyde Park, and several bars and lounges, this member of the Trusthouse Forte Group is a favorite meeting place for

Londoners and visitors alike. All rooms have recently been redecorated and are partially furnished with antiques.

66 Knightsbridge, SW1Y 7LA. Tel: 235-2000; Telex: 262057; Fax: 235-4552; in U.S. and Canada, (800) 225-5843; Telex: 6852554; in Australia, (02) 267-2144 or (008) 22-2446.

The Knightsbridge. This is a small, cozy, unpretentious place, and one of the least expensive of several small hotels on this quiet cul-de-sac just west of Harrods, off Brompton Road. Don't expect much more than a bed, Continental breakfast, and a front-door key. Spend your money instead in the delightful restaurants in nearby Beauchamp Place.

10 Beaufort Gardens, SW3 1PT. Tel: 589-9271; Fax: 823-9692.

The Pelham Hotel. This recently opened hotel is a hidden treasure situated in South Kensington, a very popular corner of London that is close to many important museums, as well as to the shops and restaurants of Knightsbridge. Like numerous other London hotels, The Pelham comprises two very large converted houses, but the standard to which they have been converted is extra-ordinary. It is owned by Kit and Tim Kemp, who also own the Dorset Square Hotel, and their attention to detail is exceptional. Luxury exists here, but happily not at luxury-hotel prices.

15 Cromwell Place, SW7 2LA. Tel: 589-8288; Telex: 8814714; Fax: 584-8444; in U.S., (800) 553-6671.

Portobello Hotel. Media people tend to frequent this moderately priced hotel in a hard-to-find corner of Holland Park, within a stone's throw of Portobello Road market and all the fun shops and restaurants of this corner of town, west of Hyde Park/Kensington Gardens. The bar/restaurant is open to guests 24 hours a day and the whole place has a very easygoing atmosphere. Rooms range in size from a ship's cabin to very large, but they all have the necessary amenities. The hotel is equipped with a special clean-air system pioneered in Scandinavia.

22 Stanley Gardens, W11 2NG. Tel: 727-2777; Telex: 268349; Fax: 792-9641.

Whites Hotel. Looking like a beautiful white wedding cake, this recently restored, large, and expensive hotel is in a wonderful position, with views over Kensington Gardens and Bayswater. On weekends, the railings of the park become an open-air picture gallery where artists hang their paintings in the hopes of making a sale. The public rooms are most attractive, and the bedrooms have been decorated in an unusual and luxurious style, with all comforts included. Office facilities can be arranged.

90-92 Lancaster Gate, W2 3NR. Tel: 262-2711; Telex: 24771; Fax: 262-2147.

16 Sumner Place. Built in 1848, these four interconnecting and charming town houses create an agreeable ambience for those who like pleasant surroundings but don't want to break the bank. And it's very well placed in South Kensington, too. The hotel has two drawing rooms, one of which provides tea and coffee throughout the day, the other a delightful conservatory drawing room overlooking the very attractive walled garden.

16 Sumner Place, SW7 3EG. Tel: 589-5232; Telex: 266638; Fax: 584-8615.

Apartments

For those who want to look after themselves when they come to London, the answer is to rent a serviced apartment, of which there are many. Although they are not necessarily cheaper than hotels, you do get more space for your money. Here are some of the best.

Capital Apartments. These serviced luxury apartments are just next door to the Capital Hotel with all its facilities, including its marvelous restaurant, just in case cooking for yourself doesn't fascinate.

26 Basil Street, SW3 1AT. Tel: 589-5171; Telex: 919042; Fax: 225-0011.

Dolphin Square. Not far from the Tate Gallery, this is the largest apartment complex in Europe and offers the biggest range of apartments. They are perfectly adequate but definitely not in the luxury class, although the in-house facilities make up for this. There is a shopping arcade with baker, butcher, grocer, ticket agency, two licensed bars, squash and tennis courts, and a very good restaurant of the brasserie type that overlooks the large swimming pool. There is also a large central garden.

Chichester Street, Pimlico, SW1V 3LX. Tel: 834-9134; Telex: 913333; Fax: 798-8735.

Draycott House. Just off Sloane Square, these exceedingly well designed apartments—always very popular despite the high prices—are temptingly close to the shops and restaurants of Knightsbridge and the King's Road in Chelsea.

10 Draycott Avenue, SW3 3AA. Tel: 584-4659; Telex: 916266; Fax: 225-3694.

Durley House. These excellently placed apartments, on Sloane Street between Chelsea and Knightsbridge, were taken over in 1989 by the ubiquitous Kemps of Dorset Square and Pelham Hotel fame, who are fast becoming the leading entrepreneurs in the small-hotel world of London. Refurbished to their usual high standard with exquisite taste, the formerly ramshackle Durley House is no longer recognizable. The only drawback to this sort of makeover is that such excellent service and comfort don't come cheap, and the price has more than doubled in the past year. (But included in these rates is the use of the tennis courts in Cadogan Square Gardens.)

115 Sloane Street, SW1X 9PG. Tel: 235-5537; Telex: 919235; Fax: 259-6977; in U.S., (800) 553-6674.

47 Park Street. This is the place for those looking for unashamed luxury and privacy. Although Mayfair is synonymous with elegance, these sumptuous serviced apartments are the top of the tree. The entrance hall is commanded by a concierge who will look after you down to the smallest detail, and the in-house restaurant is none other than the Michelin-starred **Le Gavroche.** Even breakfast, served in your suite, is a gastronomic delight.

47 Park Street, Mayfair, W1Y 4EB. Tel: 491-7282; Telex: 22116; Fax: 491-7281.

In the English Manner. This firm offers over 50 luxurious apartments in various areas and price ranges, in and around London. All are attractively furnished and on arrival fresh flowers and breakfast provisions await you.

Lancych, Boncath, Pembrokeshire SA37 0LJ. Tel: (02) 397-7444; Fax: (02) 397-7686; in U.S., P.O. Box 936, Alamo, CA 94507; Tel: (415) 935-7065 or (800) 422-0799 outside California; Fax: (415) 934-9260.

—Katie Lucas

DINING

There is no gourmet area in London, although Soho, shedding its red-light image, is becoming increasingly well endowed with decent eateries. Covent Garden, on the other hand, has more than its share of mediocre establishments that have a fast turnover of tired shoppers and hungry theatergoers.

Some of Britain's best chefs are firmly ensconced in the top hotels; others move around, taking with them a steady band of dedicated followers to unlikely backwaters of

London. And while London's ethnic restaurants have always been its most inexpensive eateries, a number of Indian, Japanese, Chinese, Thai, and Lebanese establishments now offer some of the best food in the capital in fashionable designer settings.

The following selection takes in London restaurants in all price ranges, serving all types of ethnic food, in all of London's diverse neighborhoods.

English

Restaurants that look and feel like dining rooms of private homes are very much in vogue in London these days. **Launceston Place** (sister of Kensington Place; see below), in a quiet street of the same name behind Kensington High Street, achieves a candlelit intimacy in a crowded couple of rooms full of fine oil paintings and mirrors. The moderately priced menu here is decidedly British—roast beef and Yorkshire pudding on Sundays, and a groaning cheese board—as is most of the clientele. Tel: 937-6912.

At 21 Romilly Street in Soho, **The Lindsay House** attempts to make you feel as if you are a guest in a private town house: You ring the bell to enter, drink an aperitif in front of an open fire in the downstairs sitting room, and eat upstairs among drapes, flounces, and flowers from an elaborate and moderately priced 18th-century English menu that includes traditional English puddings. Even so, the place hasn't quite managed to exorcise the ghost of the Chinese restaurant that occupied these quarters before it. Prix-fixe lunch from 12:30 to 2:30 P.M. and dinner from 6:00 P.M. until midnight, 7:00 to 10:00 P.M. on Sundays. Tel: 439-0450. The **English House** (in Milner Street, off Cadogan Square) and the **English Garden** (in Lincoln Street, off the King's Road) are similar.

Leith's occupies three Victorian houses knocked into one at 92 Kensington Park Road. Prue Leith, the talented principal of Leith's School of Food and Wine, owns this establishment, refurbished with French silver, English bone china, and Dartington glass. Swivel chairs make for relaxing dining, spotlights ensure that you can see how good the food is, and the Wagons Leith, trolleys for hors d'oeuvres and desserts, are outstanding. Dishes include charcoal-grilled rib of beef, ox tongue, and their unfussy like. There are also English cheeses, and herbs and vegetables from Prue's own farm in Gloucestershire. The prix-fixe menus (including VAT and service) are a good value (the price depends on the number of courses you have), and the interesting and long vegetarian menu is made up entirely of home-grown produce. Dinner only. Tel: 229-4481.

The grill and the main restaurant in the **Connaught Hotel** (on Carlos Place in Mayfair) continue to serve excellent traditionally British food in an Edwardian setting that never seems to change. Tel: 499-7070.

Brasseries and Cafés

Brasseries and cafés are usually cheaper than more formal restaurants, and many serve meals—which tend to lean toward French—all day from breakfast onward.

Currently popular with Londoners is **Kensington Place** at 205 Kensington Church Street, the noisy Continental sister of the more formal Launceston Place. Revolving doors lead to a high-tech glass-fronted brasserie that concentrates on exciting and unfussy European dishes with the freshest of ingredients. It is reasonably priced and always crowded. Open every day from 9:00 A.M. to midnight. Tel: 727-3184.

The Continental-style **Soho Brasserie** at 23 Old Compton Street serves typically French dishes such as fish soup, as well as snacks at the long bar (which is a popular drinking venue). On summer evenings when the restaurant gets crowded, the full-length doors are opened and patrons spill out onto the sidewalk. Open noon until 11:30 P.M.; closed Sundays. Tel: 439-9301.

At 48 Greek Street in Soho, the street-level brasserie **L'Escargot** is the "in" lunch place for members of the media who don't belong to the Groucho Club around the corner in Dean Street and who prefer not to pay the higher prices upstairs (a restaurant for more than 100 years). The brasserie menu offers modern English dishes and the wines are celebrated. You can only make reservations for the evening. Lunch is served Mondays through Fridays from noon on, and dinner Mondays through Saturdays from 6:30 to 11:15 P.M. and Sunday evenings from 6:00 to 11:15 P.M. Tel: 437-2679.

Off Piccadilly, **Langan's Brasserie** on Stratton Street is always crowded (but it's big so you can usually get in). The two floors (upstairs is more quiet but they don't serve the famous spinach soufflé) are jammed with splendid paintings, lots of large round tables, and a regular influx of conversation stoppers, including the occasional entertainers (Michael Caine is one of the owners). The long menu offers dishes, including daily specials, of variable quality, and the tab can be relatively low if you watch what you order. Service may be interminably slow, but you can't come to London without eating here. Open Mondays through Fridays 12:30 P.M. to 2:45 P.M. and 7:00 P.M. to 11:45 P.M., Saturdays 8:00 P.M. to 12:45 A.M. Live band in the bar after 9:00 P.M. Tel: 491-8822.

Le Caprice on Arlington Street in Mayfair is chic, stylish, and frequented by stars. Reserve well ahead, unless your name will get you in. The decor is black, white, and chrome, with photos on the walls. Simple snacks and diet-conscious meals are served from noon to 3:00 P.M. and 6:00 P.M. until midnight; brunch on Sundays until 3:00 P.M. Tel: 629-2239.

Joe's Café, in Draycott Avenue at Brompton Cross, opposite the Conran Shop, is frequented by well-dressed people from the fashion and pop worlds and is about as far removed from a café as you can get. Waiters sport black waistcoats and white shirts that match the black-and-white decor and black-and-white tagliatelle. The lunch menu includes salads, bagels, and a few hot dishes, while evening meals are more formal, though still quite inexpensive. The bar is open weekdays from 6:00 P.M. to 9:00 P.M.; otherwise, you have to eat. They also serve Saturday breakfast and brunch on Sundays. Tel: 225-2217.

If you're shopping in Knightsbridge, the Emporio Armani Express at 191 Brompton Road (Tel: 823-8818), one of the smartest cafés in town, is convenient. It looks a bit like a railway carriage and serves modern Italian dishes as well as cakes and espresso during store hours: Mondays through Saturdays 10:00 A.M. to 6:00 P.M.; 7:00 P.M. on Wednesdays. Tall Orders at 676 Fulham Road (at the far end) is a gimmick that works. Modern European food is served warm (not hot) in Chinese-style wicker dim sum baskets stacked high. Dishes here include grilled swordfish with white beans in virgin olive oil, and salmon carpaccio with guacamole. Prices are very reasonable and there is an animated, lively atmosphere, as well as music (although the din often drowns it out). Open seven days a week from noon to midnight. Tel: 371-9673.

Overlooking the river, the Serpentine Restaurant offers reasonably-priced dinner party-style food in a conservatory setting. Tel: 402-1142.

French

A few of London's French restaurants regularly receive the highest accolades from food critics. Three are particularly outstanding (note that they are all very expensive in the evening and closed on weekends): **Le Gavroche**, at 43 Upper Brook Street (Tel: 408-0881), is owned by one of London's best-known chefs, Albert Roux, and offers an affordable lunchtime menu and dishes that range from the simple to the sophisticated; **La Tante Claire**, 68 Royal Hospital Road in Kensington (Tel: 352-6045), boasts chef Pierre Koffmann, who is renowned for his pig's trotters dish, and an outstanding-value set lunch menu; and **Chez Nico**, 35 Great Portland Street in the heart of the garment district, but a stone's throw from Oxford Street, where owner Nico Ladenis's largely classical French menu has been satisfying his discerning followers for years. The food is simply outstanding and presented immaculately. There is an absence of salt cellars on the tables, on account of Nico's knowledge of how food *should* taste. (He claims many of his customers need educating; if you want to get as far as the stunning chocolate desserts, don't ask for the salt.) A meal here is almost a theatrical experience. The prix-fixe lunch menu is good value. Tel: 436-8846.

Nico's old premises at 48a Rochester Row are now called **Very Simply Nico** and offer an informal brasserie-style experience with a reasonably priced set menu. Open every day except Sundays with lunch from noon to 2:00 P.M. and evening meals from 7:00 P.M. (no lunch on Saturdays). Tel: 630-8061.

Le Mazarin consists of a series of alcoves leading off a main dining area in an elegant pink basement at 30 Winchester Street, just beyond Victoria Coach Station. With exquisite sauces and quality ingredients, chef-proprietor René Bajard delights gastronomes who don't want to spend a week's wages on a meal. The set lunch and dinner menu, an excellent value, may include foie gras, game, and shellfish; the gastronomic menu is only a little more expensive. Closed Sundays and Mondays. Tel: 828-3366.

The French food at the **Auberge de Provence** brings the cooking of the south of France into a somewhat drab restaurant in the St. James's Court Hotel. As at the Oustaù de Baumanière in France, on which it is modeled, cloches are lifted to reveal colorful Provençal ingredients skillfully combined. Vegetarians are well catered to, and the wine list is carefully chosen. The excellent prix-fixe lunch menu attracts local business people. South of Buckingham Palace at Buckingham Gate. Tel: 821-1899.

The south of France atmosphere also prevails in Pierre

Martin's fish restaurants. Popular among celebrities who don't mind rolling up their sleeves and tucking in to the vast *plateau des fruits de mer* is the simple, crowded **Le Suquet** at 104 Draycott Avenue at Brompton Cross. Tel: 581-1785.

La Croisette, 168 Ifield Road (north of the Fulham Road but nearer the Old Brompton Road—look for the awning), was the first of Martin's chain to open, in 1975. Ring and you will be ushered into a crowded basement where London's French come for the fixed menu and to socialize over the enormous cork platters loaded with crab, langoustines, winkles, oysters, and mussels. La Croisette is 100 percent French, down to the youthful staff in Cannes tee-shirts, the paintings of the Mediterranean, and the unsalted butter; a trio strums guitars on some nights. Closed Mondays. Tel: 373-3694.

At Martin's **Le Quai St. Pierre**, 7 Stratford Road just off the Earl's Court Road, you can sit at the counter under a huge umbrella or at a table in the only slightly more formal dining room up the spiral staircase. What this place lacks in finesse it makes up for in atmosphere. Closed Sundays. Tel: 937-6388. Nearby, at 116 Finborough Road, the **Bouillabaisse** specializes in the famous soup; Tel: 370-4183, dinner only.

La Croisette is best for an intimate evening, Le Quai St. Pierre more fun if you're in a party, Le Suquet if you like star-spotting. All are excellent value for the money.

In Knightsbridge are the two St. Quentin restaurants, which are owned in part by the Savoy Group. The **St. Quentin**, a bustling, elegant French establishment on two floors (opposite the Brompton Oratory) at 243 Brompton Road, serves a reasonable prix-fixe lunch. Tel: 589-8005. The **Grill St. Quentin** occupies a huge, bright, and warmly lit basement reminiscent of La Coupole in Paris at 2 Yeoman's Row. Closed Sundays. Tel: 581-8377.

Bernard Gaume at the Hyatt Carlton Tower at 2 Cadogan Place in Knightsbridge is well respected for his French (but not nouvelle) cuisine in the **Chelsea Room**. The restaurant has a sunny conservatory from which you can see the gardens of Cadogan Place; there are deep settees on which to relax over a drink in the adjoining bar; and the moderate, prix-fixe lunch menu includes half a bottle of wine—unusual for London. The likes of Lords Lichfield and Snowdon are drawn here for the breakfasts. Tel: 235-5411.

Other excellent hotel restaurants include the intimate

Le Soufflé on the ground floor of the Inter-Continental in Hamilton Place (on Hyde Park) and the opulent **Oak Room** on the ground floor of the Meridien in Piccadilly. At Le Soufflé, Peter Kromberg is at the helm and offers imaginative soufflés and a consistently high standard of French cuisine. There is a short set menu at lunch, five courses in the evening, and Sunday brunch (closed Saturday lunch). Tel: 409-3131. The decor couldn't be more different in the grand gilt and mirrored Oak Room, though the food is similarly acclaimed. Tel: 734-8000. Closed Saturday lunch and Sundays. Both are expensive.

The **Four Seasons**, at the Inn on the Park hotel on Park Lane, is a palm-filled room in which the esteemed young Bruno Loubet offers *cuisine du terroir* (classical bourgeois cooking) as well as dishes that are low in cholesterol. Although the dinner menu is expensive, there is a reasonable *menu du jour* at lunch. Tel: 499-0888.

You can eat inexpensive French food in London's numerous brasseries (see Brasseries and Cafés).

Indian

Some of London's best Indian restaurants are unpretentious places, but those of the new school have turned up the lights, spruced up the decor, and begun to offer cocktails as well as beer with their curries. Leading the band of these upscale Indian restaurants are **The Last Days of the Raj** at 22 Drury Lane and the **Red Fort** at 77 Dean Street, both in Soho, **Jamdani** at 34 Charlotte Street, specializing in unusual dishes, and **Lal Qila**, at 117 Tottenham Court Road. All are moderately priced and offer North Indian cuisine. At the **Bombay Brasserie** adjoining Bailey's Hotel in Courtfield Close (140 Gloucester Road in South Kensington), the decor is impressively colonial in style—chandeliers, ferns, a conservatory, paddle fans, and a white piano. You can sample food from all over India; here, as at many Indian restaurants, the buffet lunches are the best buy.

Far Eastern

London's Chinatown is in Soho. Most of London's best Chinese restaurants are here, south of Shaftesbury Avenue in and around Gerrard Street. **Fung Shing** in nearby Lisle Street, **Good Food** in Little Newport Street, and **Wong Kei** at Wardour Street are authentic old-school Cantonese establishments where you can eat cheaply and well.

You can get some of London's best wind-dried food (a Chinese process of hanging out food to dry naturally) at the ever-popular **Poon's** at 4 Leicester Street, as well as at the vast **Chuen Cheng Ku**, 17 Wardour Street (it's been there 20 years or so), and **New World**, in Gerrard Place. **Yung's** in Wardour Street appeals to insomniacs, because it is open from 4:00 P.M. until 4:00 A.M.

London's first formal Chinese restaurant was Ken Lo's **Memories of China** in Ebury Street, Victoria (Tel: 730-7734). A second branch, **Memories of China Chelsea**, overlooks the boats in Chelsea Harbour and, unlike most other Chinese restaurants, offers a menu that roams the regions, an inexpensive dim sum brasserie, and Sunday brunch. Celebrities, businesspeople, and royalty drop in by yacht, with and without bodyguards. You can arrive by river boat (from the Embankment) or approach by land via Lots Road. Two floors, "Ming dynasty" gold and blue decor, and a pianist. Tel: 352-4953.

For beautifully presented Chinese food and a backdrop of water cascading down the walls, try **Zen** in Chelsea Cloisters on Sloane Avenue (Tel: 589-1781) or **Zen Central** at 20 Queen Street off Curzon Street in Mayfair (Tel: 629-8089). Both attract a fashionable clientele, including Chinese.

It's well worth the journey out to the Fulham Broadway for a meal at the **Blue Elephant** restaurant, almost opposite the Underground station at 4–5 Fulham Broadway. Here, in an exotic jungle of ferns and bamboo, an ever-smiling staff exquisitely presents moderately priced Thai dishes and beautifully sculpted fruit (Tel: 385-6595). Popular Thai restaurants in Soho are **Chiang Mai** at 48 Frith Street (Tel: 437-7444), **Bahn Thai** almost opposite on the same road, where there is a choice of hundreds of dishes (Tel: 437-8504), and **Sri Siam** at 14 Old Compton Street (Tel: 434-3544).

Some of London's most expensive Japanese restaurants are in the City near St. Paul's. **Miyama** in Godliman Street (Tel: 489-1937) caters to businesspeople on expense accounts and is closed on weekends; **Ginnan** in Cathedral Place serves up fast lunches for quite a bit less but is closed on Saturdays at lunch; both places close at 10:00 P.M. Elsewhere in London, the expensive **Suntory** at 72–73 St. James's Street (south of Piccadilly) is popular among discerning Japanese (Tel: 409-0201); the **Miyama** at 38 Clarges Street (Tel: 499-2443; closed Sundays and Saturday lunch) off Piccadilly near Green Park is much less expensive, especially at lunchtime; the prix-fixe meals at **One Two Three**, 27 Davies Street in Mayfair (Tel: 409-0750), are also a good value. It is closed on weekends. The basement **Ikkyu**, 67 Tottenham Court Road near Goodge Street Station, is handy for shoppers. Closed Saturdays and Sunday lunch; Tel: 636-9280.

Middle Eastern

The Lebanese **Al Hamra**, almost opposite the Curzon Cinema in Mayfair's Shepherd Market, is much more sophisticated than you might expect a restaurant specializing in Middle Eastern cooking would be. The tables are close together, so if you're not sure what to eat, follow the example of a neighboring diner. You are sure to be safe if you stick with the hot and cold starters (wiped up with pita bread) and the salads, which come in huge baskets and include plenty of chunky raw vegetables. Open until midnight every day. Tel: 493-1954. Insomniacs can find Middle Eastern solace at **Maroush II**, 38 Beauchamp Place, until 4:30 A.M. (Tel: 581-5434), and at the slightly cheaper **Maroush**, 21 Edgware Road near Marble Arch, until 1:00 A.M. Tel: 723-0773. **Maroush III**, nearby at 62 Seymour Street, is open until 12:30 A.M. Tel: 724-5024.

Greek

Greek restaurants aren't currently in vogue in London, but the old standbys do a brisk business, among them the **White Tower**, 1 Percy Street, Tel: 636-8141 (closed weekends). The less expensive **Beotys**, 79 St. Martin's Lane (near the theaters) has been around for more than 40 years; it starts serving pre-theater dinners at 5:30 P.M. (closed Sundays; Tel: 836-8768.) For a livelier atmosphere you can watch plates being thrown around and dance on the tables in **Anemos**, 32 Charlotte Street. Still lively but a bit less raucous is the crowded and candlelit **Kalamaras** in Inverness Mews, an alley behind Queensway, the area just north of Hyde Park. Authentic Greek food, not Cypriot, as in most of the city's "Greek" restaurants; open until midnight. Closed Sundays and at lunch; Tel: 727-9122.

Eastern European

For years, socialist M.P.s and intellectuals have enjoyed Eastern European food of the sauerkraut and black-cherry soup variety at the **Gay Hussar**, 2 Greek Street (near Soho Square). The management has changed but you can still sit in old-fashioned comfort and eat smoked goose with a bottle of Champagne. Tel: 437-0973. Closed Sundays; dinner from 5:30 P.M. Waiters at **Bloom's**, 90 Whitechapel High Street in the East End, dispense Middle-European Jewish chicken soup and gefilte fish to customers with minimal grace, as they have for years. Tel: 247-6001.

American

If you're in the mood for a hamburger, the place to go is the **Hard Rock Café**, at the Hyde Park corner end of Old Park Lane—that is, if you can stand loud music and don't mind sharing a table or lining up to get in. In Soho, **Ed's Easy Diner**, a small, neon-lit café wedged into the corner of Old Compton Street and Moor Street, serves quick, sit-at-the-chrome-counter, 100 percent additive-free burgers and soda. In the jukeboxes on the counter, 5p buys 1950s rock and roll. There is also a branch on King's Road at number 362. **Joe Allen's**, in a brick basement at 13 Exeter Street just behind Covent Garden, livens up with a theatrical crowd late at night. The **Rock Island Diner** on the top floor of the London Pavilion at Piccadilly Circus is a huge 1950s-style eatery with a Chevy suspended over the bar. The DJ plays 1950s music, there's sometimes a roller-skating maître d', and food is of the meatloaf and steak sandwich variety, plus milkshakes and cocktails. Open seven days a week, 11:00 A.M. to 11:30 P.M. No need to reserve ahead, but you may have to stand in line.

Italian

Orso at 27 Wellington Street in Covent Garden is currently trendy. Decorated in 1930s style and sister to Joe Allen's, its regularly changing menu includes pizzas and pasta. Open noon to midnight. Tel: 240-5269. Rivalling it in popularity is **Cibo** at 3 Russell Gardens, with authentic peasant food served against a backdrop of modern art. Tel: 371-6271; closed Sunday dinner.

It's well worth the journey to the **River Café**, Thames Wharf, Rainville Road, between Putney and Hammersmith bridges. Converted from an old water warehouse, it has splendid Thames views, simple, white decor, and authentic regional Italian food with the emphasis on Tuscany. The proprietors even grow their own herbs. The menu changes twice daily, and you can dine outside in summer. Open weekdays for lunch and dinner, for lunch only on weekends, with last orders at 9:30 P.M. Tel: 381-8824 or 385-3344.

At **Kettners**, a reasonably priced eatery in Soho at 29 Romilly Street, you may feel like lingering longer. Despite the refined Edwardian atmosphere, though, Kettners is actually a branch of Pizza Express, and it serves hamburgers, too. The Champagne bar is a fashionable Soho meeting place and is open until midnight. There is a cocktail pianist every evening and on Thursdays and Fridays at lunch.

Going up in price: **San Lorenzo**, just past Harrods at 22 Beauchamp Place, attracts a steady band of devotees (including the rich, the royal, and the famous) who eat pasta among the potted plants (Tel: 584-1074). **Santini**, at 29 Ebury Street near Victoria Station, attracts businesspeople at lunch. It is quiet and airy, and the menu hovers around specialties of the Veneto. Tel: 730-4094. The owners' newest restaurant, the fashionable **L'Incontro** at 87 Pimlico Road, also specializes in dishes of the Veneto. There is a pianist every evening except Sundays. Tel: 730-3663.

Scandinavian
You can get an authentic lunchtime Scandinavian smorgasbord in the comfortable **Causerie** at Claridge's, where you may find yourself in the company of royalty. Closed Saturdays; lunch from noon to 3:00 P.M., dinner from 5:30 to 11:00 P.M. Also has pre- and post-theater menus. Tel: 629-8860.

Eclectic
Several London restaurants include English dishes on an eclectic menu. One of London's most accomplished yet modest young chefs is Alastair Little, who runs a stylized, simple, monochrome café to which he's given his name in Soho's Frith Street. With its black lacquered tables, bright lighting, and unpretentious decor, at first glance **Alastair Little's** looks like a Japanese restaurant. Actually, you might get something vaguely Chinese from the menu . . . or French, or Danish, or British: whatever takes the chef's fancy. Little changes his menu twice daily, and his imaginative and moderately priced dishes are recognized as being some of the most exciting in London. Lunch from 12:30 to 2:30 P.M.; dinner from 7:30 to 11:30 P.M. Closed Sundays and Saturdays lunch. There's also a small downstairs bar (no reservations accepted for dinner) for fish, including sushi, and cold dishes. No credit cards. Tel: 734-5183.

Sutherlands, on neighboring Lexington Street, is more

formal than Little's: a tiny, serious, stylish restaurant on street level, serving some of the best food in London. Tel: 434-3401. Closed Saturday lunch and Sundays.

Clarke's at 124 Kensington Church Street also takes its name from its enterprising owner. You don't get a choice on the evening menu (you do at lunchtime), but don't let that put you off. Whatever comes out of the basement kitchen (which you can view from the dining room) is good. The menu roams through Italy, France, and California, although Sally Clarke also regularly offers English cottage-made cheeses and home-grown vegetables and fruits. The menu changes nightly; closed weekends. Tel: 221-9225.

Renowned chef Simon Hopkinson, who has no patience with nouvelle cuisine, is at the helm of the spacious, bright dining room of **Bibendum**, on the first floor of the Michelin Building on Fulham Road. Elegant and fashionable, Bibendum attracts serious food lovers and celebrities. The menu is mostly expensive (though lunch is more of a bargain—try the fish and chips) and spans France, Italy, and Britain. Tel: 581-5817.

South of the Thames and a bit off the beaten track, **Harvey's** at 2 Bellevue Road, overlooking Wandsworth Common, is an outstanding restaurant owned by the talented chef Marco Pierre White, who offers inspired food at fairly reasonable prices, especially at lunchtime. Worth travelling out of your way for. Closed Sundays and Mondays. Tel: 081-672-0114.

Early and Late

Apart from brasseries, which serve meals all day, most London restaurants don't start serving until 7:30 P.M. and stop at 11:00 P.M., so you have to make plans if you want to eat before or after the theater, unless you fancy Chinese or other ethnic (many are open after midnight).

Some theaters and concert halls have their own restaurants (including the South Bank complex, the Mermaid, the Barbican, and the Palace Theatre). Many theaters have sandwiches and coffee available in the bar.

In Covent Garden, the French **Café du Jardin** at 28 Wellington Street serves a pre- and post-theater supper from 5:30 to 11:30 P.M. Royal Opera House patrons, rather more formally attired than the rest of the clientele, wander in clutching their programs, and waiters wend their way between tables balancing trays of Cognac. Sit at ground level to be seen, downstairs to get on with it. The food, though inexpensive, is as erratic as the service. Tel: 836-8769.

Magno's, around the corner in Long Acre, is rather more formal but also relatively inexpensive, and its pre-theater menu of simple, quick dishes that change weekly is an especially good buy. Tel: 836-6077.

Rules, at 35 Maiden Lane, serves traditional English food in a decor to match and is open from noon to midnight.

The **Savoy Grill**, in the famous luxury hotel off the Strand, is within walking distance to the theaters and offers a pre-theater menu. After the show, you can go back for dessert and coffee in the Thames Foyer. Jackets and ties are required in both places. Tel: 836-4343. If you don't meet the dress code, **Upstairs at the Savoy** will serve you relatively inexpensive snacks, oysters, Champagne, and vintage wines by the glass noon to midnight weekdays and 5:00 P.M. to midnight Saturdays (closed Sundays). You can sit at the marble counter or at one of the tables along a narrow corridor, from which you have a fascinating view of arrivals at the front entrance. They also offer a breakfast buffet on weekdays (8:00 to 10:00 A.M.).

One of London's best-loved oyster and Champagne bars, **Green's**, at 36 Duke Street in St. James's (near Jermyn Street), starts serving at 5:30 P.M. The atmosphere is formal (regulars include royalty) but some of the traditional English dishes, including kedgeree and bangers and mash, most certainly aren't. Tel: 930-4566.

Le Caprice, on Arlington Street in Mayfair, is open from 6:00 P.M. to midnight daily, as is Kensington Place (see Brasseries, above). **The Causerie** at Claridge's has an early buffet supper from 5:30 P.M. You can get reasonably priced snacks at **Fields**, a huge restaurant/coffee bar in the crypt of St. Martin-in-the-Fields Church (near Charing Cross Station) until 8:30 P.M.

The **Terrace Garden** at the Meridien, Piccadilly, is open every day from 7:00 A.M. to 11:30 P.M. for an inexpensive breakfast, lunch, dinner, a light French snack, or tea. In this spectacular conservatory overlooking Piccadilly a pianist plays most evenings.

Across the river on the South Bank, **RSJ**, behind the National Theatre at 13a Coin Street, is a restaurant in a converted hayloft offering imaginative French dishes. Fixed price menu or à la carte. Open for lunch and from

6:00 P.M. with last orders at 11:00 P.M.; closed Sundays. Tel: 928-4554.

—*Susan Grossman*

PUBS AND BARS

PUBS

Publicans know a lot about beer, rather less about spirits, and hardly anything about wine, which probably reflects the proportions they sell of each. The majority of pubs are owned by breweries, giving them an overwhelming influence on the pub's stock, appearance, and staff. "Tied houses," as they are known, principally sell the beers from the brewery that owns them. The rest, offering a fine miscellany, are known as "free houses."

A recent change in the law allows pubs to set their own open hours, between 11:00 A.M. and 11:00 P.M. After a period of experimentation with this new freedom, the practical effect, born of competition, is that most pubs feel obliged to stay open all that time, and the round-the-clock drinker can seem as much of a fixture as the sign warning minors off alcohol.

There are between 5,000 and 6,000 pubs to serve London. Their durability is graphically demonstrated in the colossal development of the old dockland area, where, in a great wasteland of demolition, only pubs—dozens of them—were left as coping stones waiting for a new community to grow up around them.

The visitor should be aware that some popular pub names are adopted many times over. In London there were at last count 25 pubs called The King's Head and 12 The Queen's Head; there are 22 Railway Taverns; the emblem of spring, The Green Man, is used 19 times, likewise The George, The Coach and Horses, The Crown, The Rising Sun, The Red Lion, and The Blue Posts are each to be found in all sorts of incarnations. So, in asking directions or instructing a taxi, it is wise to give not only the name of the pub but also to specify the street.

Beer drinkers keen to extend their knowledge can do so in **The Sun**, opposite the Children's Hospital in Great Ormond Street in Holborn, which has the largest selection of cask-conditioned ales in the world—187 at the last count, with oddities such as Oy Vay, weissbier (a grain),

Merrie Monk, and Old Scrap Cyder. (An early evening tour of the 1688 cellar to see how beers are prepared can be arranged by calling the landlord; Tel: 405-8278.)

Pubs change, if slowly. Two very fine summers have prompted the pubs to set out tables and chairs on the sidewalks in Continental style. The big difference in London, though, is the gradual blurring of distinctions between the plush saloon bar and the more basic and lower-priced public bar.

Central London

Just as time begins for the British at Greenwich, so distances are measured from Trafalgar Square. Appropriately, one of the pubs against which others could measure themselves can be found at one of its corners, where St. Martin's Lane leaves it, a dart's throw from the statue of poor Edith Cavell. This is **The Chandos**—spacious, good beer, quick service, and a slightly more dashing menu than most that includes such items as beef olives, steak-and-pepper pie, and smoked mackerel. The pub is very much a meeting point, with six ground-floor cubicles, like little chapels with their stained-glass windows looking onto the square, and the Opera Lounge upstairs (the English National Opera is housed a few doors up the road), with deep leather armchairs and blessed freedom from Muzak.

Farther up the lane, past an eclectic shopping alley called Cecil Court, which travellers should note as the collectors' hub for original Baedeker guides, are two curious places. **The Green Man & French Horn** is very long and thin, like a cul-de-sac with a ceiling, the result of joining two pubs together. Victorian prints on the walls here illustrate the gloomy story of the decline of a drunkard and his family. Opposite, **The Salisbury** is much more ample, an island bar set in an ocean of rococo decoration and kitsch.

Among the plethora of pubs around Piccadilly Circus and the great shopping arteries (the electronics of the Tottenham Court Road, the rag trade and shoe leather of Oxford Street, and the travel, fashion, ceramics, and silver of Regent Street) it is hard to finger many of real distinction. But there are a few shining exceptions. On Beak Street, on the Soho (east) side of Regent Street, **The Old Coffee House**, with its burnished brass and copper fittings, comfortable furniture, and crimson carpet, has a relaxed ethos and an amiable staff serving a wide range of bottled and hand-pumped beers.

Carnaby Street, that magnesium flare of the Swinging Sixties, offers **The Shakespeare's Head** at the corner of Great Marlborough Street, with wooden floors, good hot food, and an upstairs restaurant, but otherwise nothing to write home about. In Soho, choose **The Dog & Duck** on Bateman Street (a small street between Dean and Greek streets). Go not for food but for the company of the flotsam and jetsam of bohemian society, a contrast with the monogrammed gear of the staff. Small and rowdy, it has an upstairs snug (a small private room) with saucy cartoons and postcards and cozy casement tables from which to look down on the street action. **The French House** on Dean Street, with a somewhat raffish clientele and a staff that knows more about wine than most, has a reputation that dates from World War II, when it was the off-duty rendezvous of the Free French Forces in Britain.

If you penetrate the hinterland north of Oxford Street into Marylebone, you will see an odd and exclusively summer phenomenon of recent times in the complex of streets beyond Selfridge's—great swarms of yuppies drinking on the sidewalks, men and women alike in uniform charcoal-gray suiting, gathered like colonies of seals outside such places as **The Lamb & Flag** on the corner of James and Barrett streets.

But the year-round special in Marylebone is **The Prince Regent** on Marylebone High Street. The portrait of the prince himself is a complete fantasy, not the corpulent Prinny we think of but a handsome Young Lochinvar. The pub has a strong miscellany of local regulars, drinking under cartoons and prints and enjoying its celebrated collection of cheese dishes.

And, in cobbled Weymouth Mews, parallel to Portland Place, is one of the oldest pubs in London, **The Dover Castle**, a coaching inn where horses were changed on the first stage from the City en route to Oxford. The lounge and pleasant back room of this free house are very busy at lunch and early evening with a crowd of media, design, and advertising people.

Go east from Tottenham Court Road and cross Gower Street to find **The Museum Tavern**, standing opposite the British Museum in Great Russell Street. With so many scholars and literati restoring their parched gray cells here, plus the pub's eccentric practice of serving afternoon tea, it is not surprising that a neighboring publisher has produced an account of its history, which dates from 1723.

Heading south and east across Kingsway, stop for a quick one at **The Queen's Larder** in the alley leading into Queen Square (there are hospitals of all sorts in this area and therefore doctors and nurses too) on the way to the always fashionable **The Lamb** in Lamb's Conduit Street, where you'll find hospital people at midday, theater people at night. Brass rails around the tables stop the drinks from falling off; strange old pivoting panels at the bar were apparently devised to prevent the staff from hearing private conversations. A rare feature is a nonsmokers' cubbyhole. On the walls are rows of faded sepia pictures of theatrical divinities, with Hogarth prints and *Vanity Fair* cartoons.

The City

A jungle by day, a desert by night, the City has always had different hours and rules for its pubs—and its own police force to see them observed. The tendency is to close by 8:00 P.M., and to not open at all on weekends. In the shorter time frame, however, the old, heavy-beamed pubs like **Olde Wine Shades** on St. Martin Lane and **Ye Olde Mitre** in Ely Place off Holborn Circus do brisk enough business with the stockbrokers, financiers, and conveyancers to compensate. The beer fancier curious to know what happens when a pub brews its own stuff can try **The Market Porter** on Stoney Street south of the Thames across London Bridge and off Borough High Street.

This last pub's name suggests the great wholesale food markets that once pulsed within the City precincts and enjoyed special indulgences for thirsty early-morning traders. The last significant example of these, still on its original site, is the Central Meat Market, which has stood at Smithfield since the tenth century. The license to operate from 5:30 A.M. is still exercised by some pubs here; two in particular are recommended for the opportunity for lively, humorous trader talk and a hearty breakfast with ale. **The Cock Tavern** is in a basement down steps from the second archway; **The Fox & Anchor** is adjacent to the entry to serene Charterhouse Square. Market porters critical of the beef served in cafés on Smithfield have sometimes taken their own steak in to fry, but that is not necessary in The Fox & Anchor.

The southern neighbors of Smithfield are St. Bartholomew, London's busiest hospital, and The Old Bailey, the central criminal court. Opposite St. Bart's is **The White Hart**, a serviceable and friendly establishment; opposite The Bailey formerly stood **The Magpie & Stump**, a ferment of gossip and good low-life stories spun by a clientele composed largely of lawyers and journalists. Dissolved in redevelopment for three years, an embryonic new version is now in place for opening in 1991.

A find north of Smithfield is **The Crown**, a 17th-century inn on an attractive small square called Clerkenwell Close. The square's great feature is the Marx Memorial Library, a mass of socialist literature from seething tracts and compassionate novels to stolid economic analysis assembled to honor the author of *Das Kapital,* who labored at the British Library nearby on his seminal work. Apparently apolitical, the pub nevertheless still separates the plusher saloon area from the public bar; it also has a backroom restaurant and an upstairs room where one-act plays today carry on the tradition of evening entertainment that once took the form of music-hall performances.

Chelsea

The King's Road, and those that lead off it, are very well provided with pubs. On the main drag itself is **The Markham Arms**, a famous socialite center from the 1960s. It still has a name, but some of its feel is gone, and the section of old photos labeled "Memory Lane" has the pathos of a lost estate. **The Chelsea Potter**, another great source for the gossip columnists, holds up better. Its very young clientele chatters like starlings, though the pub is so dark it looks closed from the outside.

The Six Bells by the Town Hall (between Sloane Square and the King's Road) has been renamed **Henry J. Bean's** ("But his friends all call him Hank") and transformed into a cocktail zoo with heavy-metal sounds, fast food, and fancy drinks. The hundreds of customers in this grand old barn average age 19, but the big garden in the rear remains a great romantic asset. At **The Cadogan Arms** on the corner of Old Church Street you'll find another young and lively but less frantic crowd, a jeans-and-sweaters bunch swarming on split levels. From here on east the pubs have lately taken to offering breakfast from 9:00 A.M. and sometimes earlier—the full-scale bacon, eggs, sausage, tomato, toast, and marmalade meal. At the end is

The Man in the Moon, a free house with heavy maroon drapes, caramel-colored lighting, throbbing music, and its own theater club upstairs (see Fringe Theater, below).

WINE BARS

The closer association of Britain with Continental Europe has not yet, from the wine drinker's point of view, had any very noticeable effect on prices, but the reductions must surely come when the Common Market drops trade barriers at New Year's 1993. Knowledge and appreciation of wines and places dedicated to their drinking have already improved, resulting in an increase in the number of wine bars, which have been taking some of the custom from the pubs.

The expansion has had two styles: the masculine and the contemporary. The older is the masculine manner, leaning heavily on tradition and characterized by oak beams and counters like ramparts, clumsy, comfortable furniture—big casks often standing in for tables—a sprinkling of sawdust on the stone floors, typically, a full-dress battalion of high-quality Champagnes such as Veuve Clicquot, and a cumulus cloud of cigar smoke. Many of the best examples of this are to be found among the 40 owned by Davys, as well as among the chain run by Balls Brothers. There is naturally a strong concentration in the City, among which **The Bottlescrue** in Bath House on High Holborn, **The Pulpit** in Worship Street (north of the Liverpool Street Station), and **The Boot and Flogger** in Redcross Way (in Southwark south of the Thames) will educate while slaking a violent thirst, in a dark and dignified ethos suitable to conversation about the bottom line.

The ancestor of them all is **Olde Wine Shades**, St. Martin Lane at Cannon Street, opened in 1663 and the only such establishment to survive the Great Fire three years later. Its owners run another, even more celebrated, place, **El Vino's** on Fleet Street, which proffers a similar choice of fine wines, Port, and Sherries drawn from a great parade of casks. Although the national newspapers are now scattered away from Fleet Street, something of the former mood persists, with old fire-brigade journalists reminiscing about their best stories. The rule here barring women has been abrogated, but it is still preferred that women sit at a table rather than stand at the bar, and wear skirts rather than trousers. The dress rule for men is particularly strict: In the absence of jacket or tie you will be asked to leave. (A few doors down, opposite the ancient and also vinous **Olde Cheshire Cheese** pub, is a Tie Rack shop.)

An entrepreneurial New Zealander, Don Hewitson, is now making a mark with a slightly lighter version of this style, putting French art posters on the walls, white cloths on the tables, and offering tasty meals at around £10. His little empire comprises **Shampers** in Soho's Kingly Street (parallel to Carnaby Street), **The Cork and Bottle**, in a cramped basement on Cranbourn Street (the continuation of Long Acre near Covent Garden), and the much ampler flagship, the award-winning **Methuselah's** on Victoria Street, which is much liked by younger people (and not merely the trendies).

The contemporary style in wine bars has had a variable pattern, shifting to adapt to designer-fashion currents, merging at the one end with restaurants, like the Soho Brasserie, at the other with cocktail bars like The Long Island Iced Tea Bar in Cranbourn Street, or with tourist-oriented places that have exotic themes, such as the Spanish *tapas* bar whirl of **Brahms and Liszt** in Covent Garden. Generally they do not serve beer, but offer a wide range of wines, among them French, Alsatian, German, Italian, Spanish, and occasionally Australian vintages, with prices starting at £6 a bottle and commonplace Champagnes at £17 to £20.

There is no such phenomenon in London as the American singles' bar scene, but it is fair to say that some, like **Le Cochonnet** in outlying Maida Vale (northwest of Paddington), which has a wine list as long as a telephone directory, are chummier than others. Among a relaxed miscellany that stand out for amiability are **Morgan's** in Soho's Ganton Street, for its reasonably priced meals and a barman with both a genuine delight in wine lore and a wish to lead his patrons in the right direction; **Volkers**, handily sited in the Haymarket, for its excellent stock and the unique opportunity to drink pink Champagne from a bottle clamped in a pewter cuirass while sitting at the bar on a copper milk churn filled with Champagne corks; and **The Metro** by Clapham Common Underground Station, a great meeting point with a glass roof like a conservatory's that the neighborhood cats frequent. The Metro sells no beer, but if one of your party is a beer-drinker and fetches in a crate of the stuff, nobody minds.

COCKTAIL BARS

American bars and cocktail bars are as close to being synonymous in the British mind as Coke and Pepsi. An excellent choice with discretion and style, where a woman on her own may pause without discomfort, is the bar in **Brown's Hotel** on Albemarle Street. On the same wavelength, with senior barmen who know what goes into a daiquiri or a Tom Collins, a whiskey sour or a planter's punch, the nookeries of **Durrant's** on George Street in Marylebone, **The Connaught** on Carlos Place in Mayfair, and, through a door on an inner courtyard off St. James's Street, **The Stafford** on St. James's Place—all have the pukka tone (meaning they're first-class).

The dazzling white counter and Art Deco of the **Savoy Bar** conjures up the spirit of 60 years ago, when the creative barman Harry Craddock developed and expanded the cocktail range way beyond the confines of its original definition—a concoction of any spirit with water, sugar, and bitters. The period design persists, though the menu lacks imaginative spring. Nevertheless, with its Champagne cocktails, sharp old-fashioneds, Moscow mules, and some knockouts like the brandy Alexander and the black Russian for nightcaps, the Savoy keeps the faith. Expect to find similar standards in the Ritz and Claridges.

The luxurious old favorites just mentioned have their counterparts in new branches of several chain hotels—the Hilton, by the BBC on Portland Place (which has a fine opportunity in taking over the old Langham Hotel), the Mayfair, and St. George's Hotel, opposite the new Hilton, with a bar on the 15th floor high above the spire of All Souls Church—but the character of the bars in these latter-day establishments fluctuates with the changing tides of customers.

Vogue curiosities include the basement art gallery effect of **Freud's** at the High Holborn end of Shaftesbury Avenue and—a common phenomenon—the bar that suddenly changes its style on the whim of the owner, one example being **Efes II**, formerly The Manhattan, in Great Portland Street. The bar now looks down on a kebab restaurant. It still serves the cocktail that has lately been mandatory, and after which another busy house on Cranbourn Street, with live music, has renamed itself: **The Long Island Iced Tea Bar.**

—*Alex Hamilton*

ENTERTAINMENT AND NIGHTLIFE

THEATER

Periodic crises threaten to darken one theater or another as developers encroach or the art houses find their subsidy inadequate even when they are booked solid, and the old Savoy was recently burned out. Nonetheless, just over 50 commercial playhouses soldier on. **The National Theatre** in the South Bank complex comprises three separate stages; **The Royal Shakespeare Company** performs in the Barbican complex in the City; and that other stalwart of the classical repertory, **The Old Vic**, lies just south of Waterloo Bridge. The vehicle of much serious modern work, **The Royal Court**, dominates Sloane Square in Chelsea. In the summer, defying the vagaries of the weather, the **Open-Air Theatre** in Regent's Park mounts a Shakespeare repertory season every year. The citadels of entertainment are **Drury Lane Theatre** (musicals) and **The London Palladium** in Soho (celebrity shows).

Newspaper listings are rarely comprehensive enough to satisfy either cinema or theater goers. The best service is provided by three weekly guide magazines: *Time Out* (published every Wednesday), *What's On* (Wednesday), and *City Limits* (Thursday); these publications also include information on productions at outlying theaters.

The largest ticket-selling organization in Britain, for live events and sporting occasions as well as theater, is the **Keith Prowse** agency, which has many shops and also booths in large hotels. For half-price tickets (plus booking fee) to same-day performances in West End theaters with seats to spare, apply to the **ticket booth in Leicester Square** between 2:30 P.M. and 6:30 P.M. Turning this idea on its head, a new charity venture with impeccable theatrical sponsorship, **West End Cares**, opened in 1990 to sell tickets at twice their face value for the best seats in the house at sold-out smash hits (Tel: 976-6751).

Fringe Theater

Innumerable elements make up the lively phenomenon of the London fringe theater: one-act plays, satirical revues, stand-up comedy, bravura solo acts, dramas that passionately argue political causes, expressionistic shows with no discernible argument, a local playwright working the parish pump, and a foreign import in translation for the first time. The fringe is a sprawling network that includes the by-products of established theaters near the middle of town, like **The Theatre Upstairs**, part of The Royal Court Theatre in Chelsea's Sloane Square, as well as very successful venues that, properly speaking, are not in London at all, like **The Warehouse** at Croydon, which has a strong attraction for London audiences.

Among the many, some of which have a transient, fitful career, half a dozen are worth distinguishing. In Islington they are **The King's Head** and **The Old Red Lion**; in Hammersmith **The Lyric Studio**; in Chelsea at the far end of the King's Road from the Royal Court, **The Man in the Moon**; at Shepherd's Bush Green **The Bush**; and in Notting Hill **The Gate**.

This last is particularly loved by the critics for its habit of introducing unknown foreign plays, but as a rule fringe managements do not have settled polices of commitment and prefer a varied diet. The fact that many are advertised as clubs is not often a bar to entry. Election to membership can generally be achieved almost spontaneously, and the fee—as low as 40 pence in the case of The Man in the Moon—is rarely a serious deterrent. Comfortable seating is not the strong point of such theaters; people like them for more important reasons that include an interest in discovering new talent and in enjoying the camaraderie that can form in their casual atmosphere. One of the longest established fringe theaters, with a consistently high standard, is **The New End** in Hampstead.

Children's Theater

Aside from the pre-Christmas season, when the playhouses break out in a rash of pantomimes, not a great deal is done on the London stage for children. However, there are a few specialists who fill their schedules with a range that runs from classics to mixed-media entertainments involving slides, film, modern rap, and music hall. The principal pillars are **The Unicorn Theatre** at Great Newport Street and **The Polka** on the Broadway, Wimbledon. **The Royal Britain Children's Theatre** is in Aldersgate Street in the City. **The Little Angel Marionette Theatre**, in Dagmar Passage off Cross Street in Islington, puts on performances for the very young as well as older kids, and in the same line there is the **Puppet Theatre Barge**, moored in Little Venice. Some public libraries have also taken to putting on children's shows, notably

Willesden Green Library. Children's cinema, incidentally, can be found at the Barbican and at the ICA on Pall Mall.

CLASSICAL MUSIC, BALLET, AND OPERA

From cinema to theater to concert hall to opera house the prices rise in geometric progression, and at the top end patrons could feel themselves under pressure to make a commensurately heavy investment in their personal wardrobes. However, neither tickets nor clothes need be too extravagant in the "gods," or highest seats, of the showcase of opera, **The Royal Opera House**, Covent Garden (but demand heavily exceeds supply). The classic repertory is sung in translation at The London Coliseum in St. Martin's Lane, home of the **English National Opera**. Both of these regularly include ballet in their schedules, but the heart of the balletomane lies in **Sadler's Wells**, a cultural enclave as remote as a desert fort at the northern end of Rosebery Avenue north of Farringdon Road (it can be reached on the number 38 bus from Piccadilly; the nearest Underground stop is the Angel).

The principal concert halls are those in the **South Bank complex**: Purcell Room, Queen Elizabeth Hall, and Royal Festival Hall, overlooking the River Thames. There is also **The Royal Albert Hall** in Kensington (where the annual Promenade Concerts are held) and **The Barbican Arts Centre** in the City. At the same level of intimacy as the Purcell, **The Wigmore Hall** in Wigmore Street in Marylebone schedules recitals and chamber music.

In summer, open-air concerts, some with fireworks, are held by the lake on the grounds of **Kenwood House** on Hampstead Heath. Take a blanket, a thick sweater, and picnic (proper plates and glasses, please). No other prescriptions on dress are needed for audiences of serious music; the majority of listeners at the great concert halls tend to dress formally but not competitively.

JAZZ

London is not Copenhagen or Chicago for jazz. **Ronnie Scott** seems to have propped it up in his club in Soho's Frith Street since almost before the big band became obsolete, distributing the foreign strains through an unrivaled sequence of eminent player-guests (Tel: 439-0747). More recently arrived, but thoroughly established among addicts for its nightly variety as well as quality, are **The Bass Clef** on Coronet Street, Islington, and the **100 Club** at 100 Oxford Street. After the **Pizza Express** on Dean Street and the **Dover Street Wine Bar**, the dilettante is clutching at straws of the Sunday Jazz Brunch at the Hotel Russell kind, which must be a contradiction in terms, but farther out there are a couple of good jazz pubs, **The Bull's Head** at Barnes and **The Prince of Orange** on the Mile End Road. Some 25 years ago Philip Larkin suggested that as jazz increasingly became a composer's art, it would move from the club to the concert hall, but that transition has not yet been realized in London.

DISCOS AND LIVE MUSIC

Believe no disco recommendation until you're in. Being admitted to a disco is generally a matter of matching its style and paying its admission price, but in the case of a few, whose attraction for an older set is their exclusivity, introduction by a member is needed and a hefty entrance fee is exacted. When a place makes it into print, one part of the crowd is ready to say it's history. **Annabel's**, on Berkeley Square, has lasted a few years and is entitled to be called semi-permanent. It is notorious for its undisco-like patrons, entry fee of £25, and annual membership of £500. **Stringfellow's** in Upper St. Martin's Lane is another place for the affluent, with a £300–1,000 annual membership, and non-members introduced at £8–15 per session.

Coming off this high plateau, the **Café de Paris** in Coventry Street (off Piccadilly Circus) and **The Hippodrome** on Charing Cross Road seem to get the most repeat business, and kind words for their music and pace. **The Hammersmith Palais** has been here forever, opening at least 20 years before Granddad came here to jive during World War II; now restyled, it is a good, modern disco near the Hammersmith Broadway tube station. **The Wag Club** on Soho's Wardour Street has a truly young crowd at the leading edge of streetwise.

But, while **Gossips** on Dean Street in Soho, **Limelight** on Shaftesbury Avenue, and the cheerfully extroverted biggie on Leicester Square, the **Empire Ballroom**, all have their regulars and deserve them, some of the best disco action is a moveable feast, like the crap games immortalized by Damon Runyon. Look for the strangely dressed sidewalk line, buzzing with anxiety as they hope to impress the men at the door with their street smarts and rightness for this evening's session.

Country-and-western music has its own special havens, most often arts centers or pubs like the **King's Head** out at Crouch End (in north London beyond Islington), the **White Horse** at Hampstead, and **The Swan** at Stockwell (south of the river and east of Clapham). Its Art Deco temple is the old **Astoria Theatre** on Charing Cross Road, where people can also dance on the two floors that once were the stalls and the dress circle.

CLUBS, CABARET, AND CASINOS

The term "clubs" covers a multitude of sins and, no doubt, as many virtues. There are three main types, in addition to the residential kind that are run by the social, political, sporting, and artistic networks of the country and are joined only through introductions, and then generally for life, such as The Oxford & Cambridge, The Travellers, White's (Tory politics), The Garrick (publishers and literary intellectuals), and The Caledonian (Scottish regiments).

The first kind of club are those of the same caliber as those mentioned above but are open to all, or have reciprocal arrangements with certain clubs overseas, such as **The American Club** in Piccadilly or **The Royal Overseas League** in St. James's Street. **The Sloane Club** in Sloane Street, Knightsbridge, was founded as a ladies-only club but now accepts men as well. Peter de Savary's **St. James's Club** is also unrestricted in its membership, but a night there can be as expensive as a life subscription to many other clubs.

The second kind of club is the nonresidential members' club, often with a restaurant and spacious bar, such as **The Groucho Club**, a media enclave on Dean Street, and the ad world's rendezvous, **The Moscow Club** on Frith Street. (If you want to join either of these you must be nominated by a member.)

The third kind usually switches on after nightfall. It may be quite demure, like **The Spanish Garden Club** off Maddox Street, or somewhat raunchy like **The Pinstripe** on Beak Street, where drinks are served by topless French maids. Women accompanying men into cellar drinking clubs with topless entertainers such as are found in **The Gaslight Club** on Duke of York Street must be prepared for basilisk stares from the regulars.

Two clubs that depend on old-fashioned "glamour," with cabaret, sophisticated trappings for food and drink, and hostesses (but with an easy welcome for couples), are **Churchill's** by the Royal Academy in Piccadilly, and **The Director's Lodge** in Mason's Yard off St. James's. Both have erotic cabaret as a staple, but licensed striptease clubs with pretentions at a Continental level are few—girls with bodies that seem to have been turned on a lathe show them off on the stage of Raymond's durable **Revuebar** on Brewer Street in the 30-years-and-counting Festival of Erotica. The same Raymond also runs the adjoining **Madame Jo Jo's**, a campier and more louche venue.

The Clubman's Club in Albemarle Street (Tel: 493-4292) offers membership to selected clubs all over Britain for an annual subscription.

Casinos

The style of London gaming houses is quite unlike that to be found anywhere else. You must apply for membership 48 hours in advance, so don't leave a flutter until your eve of departure, and the dress code of suit and tie for men is strictly enforced. There is no cabaret and no drinks or tips at tables. The settings, however, are generally grand, the meals good, and the level of play interesting to international gamblers. The picture cards, so to speak, are **Crockford's** (Tel: 493-7771) and **Aspinall's** (Tel: 629-4400), both on Curzon Street. Less exalted but still useful cards are **The London Park Tower Casino** (Tel: 235-6161) and the hotel casinos of the Ritz and the Hilton.

There are some 20 casinos in London, and the **British Casino Association** (Tel: 437-0678) in Leicester House on Leicester Street will provide callers with venues, rules, and regulations.

DINNER AND DANCING

Ballroom dancing has become more of a sport or a hobby these days than a social accomplishment, but the traditional dance rhythms are still to be heard accompanying diners in the great hotels, particularly at the Savoy, the Ritz, and the Park Lane Hilton. However, there are a number of ethnic restaurants—Greek, Italian, Spanish, Portuguese—with small dance floors and live music where couples who are a little rusty on the steps and use a pump handle action with their arms will not feel shamed by their performance. Among these are **Barbarella 2** (Italian) on Thurloe Street in South Kensington, **Costa Dorada** (Spanish) on Hanway Street in the West End, the **Grecian Taverna & Grill**, also in the West End, on Percy Street, and **Os Aquanos** (Portuguese) on Porchester Road in Bayswater.

THE RIVER

When the legendary stacks of gold coins of the working city are transformed by night into reflections on the river of the lights of the buildings, the Thames takes on a different character. Many people like to take a dinner cruise or hitch up to one of the many pubs that give on to the water. The stretch involved is essentially between Greenwich to the east and Kew Gardens to the west, and the cruise departure point is most often Westminster Pier. Which direction the boat travels varies and is generally the decision of the captain on the day. **Catamaran Cruises** sails into (or away from) the sunset every evening except Saturdays (Tel: 839-3572). **Romance of London** operates three-hour cruises only on Sundays (Tel: 620-0474). **Tidal Cruises** offers a disco with supper (Tel: 839-2164).

Because there is no company as yet that sets passengers down at any of the river pubs, you will have to reach them by road. Those that are particularly worth the effort are **The Doves** in West London's Chiswick, **The Samuel Pepys** on Brooks Wharf, Upper Thames Road near Blackfriars Bridge, where it occupies an old tea warehouse, **The Anchor**, a creaking warren on the south bank of the Thames near Southwark Bridge, (resonant with the echoes of Dr. Johnson), and the Medieval **The George**, off Borough High Street near London Bridge, whose cobbled yard is the set for Morris dancing and Shakespeare plays. (Take the Underground to the London Bridge Station for Brooks Wharf and Bankside.) **The Dickens Inn** at St. Katharine's Dock is a lively and popular place in this blossoming area.

GOING HOME

The last Underground trains run out of central London on weekdays at varying times between 11:30 P.M. and 1:00 A.M. (the Piccadilly line) but midnight is the safer average, and 11:30 P.M. on Sundays. Night buses have Trafalgar Square as their hub—look for the prefix N on the number and on the bus stop. About a third of London's 16,000 taxis are in action on the night shift, which is considered anything from 8:00 P.M. onward. The worst times for finding cabs are at around 7:00 P.M. (when the day shift is going home and the night shift is not yet on the scene, and they are wanted by workers leaving the office and others going out to dinner and the theater) and at 11:00 P.M., when there is a general exodus from theaters, pubs, and restaurants. But at 1:00 A.M. there is often quite a fair supply, particularly near bridges where cabs are coming back into the center (such as Parliament Square or the Aldwych). Oddly enough, although there is a small supplement after 8:00 P.M., the fare at night tends to be lower because of the relatively traffic-free movement.

—*Alex Hamilton*

SHOPS AND SHOPPING

It is probably true to say that you can buy anything in London, from a stuffed elephant to a Victorian coatrack. From the ultimate in fashion and furnishings to a prehistoric tool or a 19th-century walking stick, you can find whatever you want, plus much that you didn't even know existed, for this is a city that prides itself on the idiosyncrasy of its shops. Randomly scattered throughout the capital, many of the most interesting ones are in quite unexpected places. While London's main shopping streets may seem much like those in Paris or New York, slip away down a side street or a cobbled alley and you enter the shopping capital of the ancient world. London is just about up among the front-runners in fashion and design, but it is indisputably top of the league for antiques and eccentricity. There is simply no other capital city in the world that offers such a diversity of things to buy.

The best bargains are to be had at the twice-yearly sales, from June until August and from mid-December through January. Most shops close at 5:30; late-night shopping, until 8:00, is on Thursdays in the Oxford Street area and on Wednesdays in Knightsbridge. Marks and Spencer and Harvey Nichols both stay open late on other nights, too. Many of the shops in Covent Garden and Tobacco Dock are open until 8:00 most evenings.

If you're taking the goods you buy out of England, you can claim back the VAT from a shop or store if it operates an export scheme (check first). Take your passport with you. You fill in a form, get it stamped at customs (for EC countries, upon your return), and mail it back to the shop, which should then send you a refund. There may be a small administrative charge, and you may have to spend a minimum to qualify.

Eccentric Shops

If you want to browse for old prints and books, there are several shops—with drawers stuffed full of originals—alongside one another in the narrow Museum Street opposite the British Museum (see below). **Arthur Middleton** in New Row (which runs into St. Martin's Lane) sells scientific instruments from the 18th and 19th centuries, as does **Arthur Davidson** in Jermyn Street, who also specializes in curiosities and German furniture. For silver the **London Silver Vaults** in Chancery House in Chancery Lane (closed Saturday afternoons) consist of underground corridors full of individual, mostly pricey stalls. For formal and classical furniture displayed in almost museum-like showrooms, head for **Mallett and Son** in New Bond Street. If you're interested in antique clocks and watches dating from the 17th to 19th century, again splendidly displayed, try **Camerer Cuss & Co.** in Ryder Street, near Green Park tube station (closed Saturdays). **Jean Sewell Antiques** in Campden Street near Portobello Road and Notting Hill Gate specializes in exquisite 18th- and 19th-century English porcelain, both complete sets and individual items.

Covent Garden

Covent Garden is an attractive place to shop for many reasons. For one, the shops are located near one another, either in the covered market itself or in the streets leading off the central piazza. For another, many of London's best-known shops (especially high-fashion) have branches in Covent Garden, and this is also the place for affordable attire, the unusual, and British crafts.

At delightfully old-fashioned **Crabtree and Evelyn** in James Street, beautifully packaged soaps, herbs, and preserves are displayed on old wooden counters. Just north, Neal Street has many of the area's most interesting shops: **Neal Street East** is crammed with Eastern goodies; the Tea House sells leaves and bags of every conceivable flavor; and the Hat Shop provides that final touch in fashion. **Neal's Yard**, just off Neal Street, caters to health-oriented shoppers. Old-fashioned remedies are made up to suit individual ailments in **Neal's Yard Apothecary** (they also offer various therapies). There's also a whole-food warehouse, a farm shop, and a bakery in the Yard.

If you're into astral travel, **Mysteries** in Monmouth Street, London's largest psychic shop, sells everything from tarot cards to astrological charts. For conventional routings, try **Stanfords** map shop in Long Acre.

For British-made goods—especially Fair Isle sweaters—there is the **Scottish Merchant** in New Row. **Naturally British,** also in New Row, has a good range of gifts, clothes, and toys. The **Museum Store** has collectibles from galleries and museums around the world. If you're shopping for children or have them in tow, head for the tiny **Doll's House Toys Ltd.** on the ground floor of the Market. It is crammed with miniature British structures, from Elizabethan cottages to Victorian shops. **Pollock's Toy Theatres** and the **Puffin** bookshop, both upstairs, are also worth a visit. On the corner of King and Bedford streets is **Hackett,** the gentleman's outfitters.

St. James's/Piccadilly

St. James's is a small, exclusive area south of Piccadilly that has yet to be molested by developers and where a number of Victorian-fronted shops still hold the exclusive Royal Warrant (shops or manufacturers that officially supply the Queen and her family). It is one of the few areas of London where parts of your anatomy, whatever its dimensions, can be fitted out with tailor-made British goods and where, unusual for London, the customer is always right. Should you wish to purchase a British bowler hat, **James Lock & Co.** (established 1676) in St. James's Street will oblige.

In **Jermyn Street,** which runs into it, you can get pin-striped shirts, dressing gowns, ties, and other accessories from **Turnbull & Asser,** visit several exclusive designer boutiques for men, including the shirtmakers **Hilditch & Key,** and buy fragrances in **Floris,** a family firm that has been making English products for five generations.

For a Burberry, that most popular of all London purchases, keep walking along Jermyn Street east to the Haymarket, where you'll find **Burberry's** (there are other branches in Regent Street and in Knightsbridge next to the Scotch House). The Haymarket leads north to busy Piccadilly, which is home to such old established stores as **Simpson's** (off-the-rack suits and "country" clothing), **Lilly-whites** (sports clothes and equipment), **Hatchards** book shop, and **Fortnum & Mason**, where the Food Hall will dispatch hampers of exotic goodies all over the world.

Fortnum & Mason, like Harrods, is worth visiting just for the ambience. They supply groceries to royalty, make majestic picnic hampers for Christmas or occasions like Ascot, have an elegant restaurant and **The Fountain** (which is excellent for snacks), and pride themselves on a standard of service that has largely disappeared in stores elsewhere. They package their own products, from bath oils to marmalade, and sell rare Port, a variety of teas in pretty tins, fashion on the upper floors, and 18th-century antiques.

Burlington Arcade (parallel to Old Bond Street) has elegant, exclusive, small—though expensive—boutiques mostly selling jewelry and woollens. You can buy Irish linen from the **Irish Linen Company**'s tiny shop, jewelry from the **Goldsmiths & Silversmiths Association**, fine porcelain from **Zelli**, or animal bronzes from **Christie**.

In Piccadilly there are several covered shopping malls, including the Trocadero, the center of tourist London, with tacky souvenir shops and cheap restaurants and boutiques, as well as entertainment. The London Pavilion around the corner at the bottom of Shaftesbury Avenue is another covered shopping venue worth visiting.

Bond Street

Old Bond Street leads north toward Oxford Street. You'll pass the Italian shoemaker **Ferragamo**, the English "By Royal Appointment" shoemaker **Rayne**, and numerous art and antiques galleries, including **Agnew's** for old masters and **Thomas Gibson Fine Art**. Farther up the street you'll find the **Fine Art Society**. Then come **Chanel** and **Gucci**, **Tiffany** and **Cartier**, with **Piaget** and **Georg Jensen Silver** across the road. **Asprey** is one of the most famous names and sells divine gifts and antique and modern jewelry. Once over the small pedestrianized section, Old Bond Street becomes New Bond Street. You'll find **Tessiers**, the silversmiths, **Polo Ralph Lauren** across the road, and then **Sotheby's**.

Sotheby's, the biggest London auction house, conducts various specialized sales that attract international dealers (they have an export scheme). Almost all the auction houses are open to the public, with viewing days preceding the days of sale. Although some of the sales are well publicized, with items going for millions of pounds, some are modest affairs. Sales may be of anything from old masters to household items, with special days allocated to different items. Sotheby's, along with **Christie's** in King Street near Green Park tube, is perhaps the most famous. Also worth visiting are **Phillips** (in Blenheim Street near Bond Street, in Lisson Grove near the Marylebone Road, and in Salem Road in Bayswater), and **Bonhams** in Montpelier Street in Knightsbridge.

North of Sotheby's going toward Oxford Street, the **White House** sells exclusive linens and exquisite clothes for children; the **Bond Street Antique Centre** is opposite, and beyond that **Kurt Geiger** shoes and the narrow entrance to the **Bond Street Silver Galleries**.

Oxford Street Area

Oxford Street has everything except exclusivity. To the Anglo-Saxons it was the "Broad Military Way," the route for armies marching westward. Today, the armies are shoppers, but Oxford Street is still a battleground. Shops and stores offer the cheapest prices in London (and some of the shoddiest goods); there are more than 30 shoe shops alone. The **John Lewis** department store has excellent quality and is "never knowingly undersold"; their own brand is Jonelle. There are two branches of **Mothercare** (for maternity wear and children's clothing) and two of Marks and Spencer, with the flagship at Marble Arch, opposite Selfridges. On four floors (with food in the basement) **Marks and Spencer** is almost overwhelmingly enormous. Quality and design are of the highest order, though—notice especially the superb cashmere sweaters and London's best buys in sexy silk lingerie. Keep your receipt in case you need a refund.

HMV, at 363 Oxford Street near the Bond Street tube station, claims to be the largest record store in the world, and the **Virgin Megastore**, near the Tottenham Court Road Underground station, retaliates by claiming to be the best. **Selfridges** department store has an excellent linens department and a mouth-watering food hall. Behind it to the north, St. Christopher's Place is easy to miss but worth finding for its affordable boutiques—**Whistles**, especially, for women's fashion—and simply to escape the crowds at lunch, when restaurants let tables spill out onto the pavement in summer. On the other side of Oxford Street, behind the Bond Street tube, pedestrian-only South Molton Street has expensive designer boutiques such as **Browns** (men and women) and **Joseph**

(which carries women's clothing); **Butler & Wilson** for affordable fashion jewelry; and top hairdressers and shoe shops. For a selection of antiques, the covered emporium **Gray's Antique Market**, on the corner of Davies Street, offers a vast choice of items (jewelry and small items) from individual collectors (closed weekends).

Walking east from Oxford Circus you'll come across another branch of **Marks and Spencer**, and a little farther on, on the opposite corner of Berners Street, is a new £100 million shopping mall, the **Plaza on Oxford Street**, the largest to open in the West End. It has a total of 70 shops and is open on weekdays from 10:00 A.M. to 8:00 P.M. (7:00 P.M. on Saturdays).

An unlikely survivor of the old-school-type shop is **James Smith and Sons** in New Oxford Street (just west of the intersection on Oxford Street known as Centre Point), specializing in umbrellas. Tottenham Court Road, which runs north from Centre Point, is where to go for stereo equipment and other electronics, as well as for furniture in shops like **Heals** and **Habitat**, which both sell contemporary designs at reasonable prices—otherwise the street is of little interest to shoppers.

The Charing Cross Road, running south from Centre Point, is lined with both new and secondhand bookshops. **Foyles**, near Centre Point on the west side of the street, is enormous but chaotic; doubtless they will have what you're after, but chances are no one will be able to find it. There are drawers stuffed with sheet music on an upper floor. A central branch of **Waterstone's**, one of a chain of bookstores now owned by W. H. Smith, is in the Charing Cross Road. All the assistants are university graduates and know how to help. The shops stay open until very late, and some branches also are open on Sundays. Background music is classical, often opera.

Regent Street

Two of the best reasons for shopping in Regent Street, the elegant, curving avenue laid out by John Nash to connect Piccadilly Circus with Oxford Street, are **Hamleys** enormous toy shop and Liberty's, both of which offer relative calm after the packed stores in Oxford Street. **Liberty's**, in a mock Tudor-style building, is gloriously old-fashioned, with exquisitely carved wood paneling in the elevators and galleries lining the main shopping floor. The store has an excellent selection of gifts, fabrics, lace, and quality china. Other Regent Street stores include a large branch of **Laura Ashley** and, for conventional classic fashion, **Jaeger**, **Austin Reed**, and **Aquascutum**. There is also a branch of **Moss Bros**, for gentlemen who need to rent a dinner jacket in a hurry. **Wedgwood**, which sells glass, ovenware, vases, jewelry, and crystal as well as its own famous china, is on the corner of Oxford Street; and farther along Regent Street is **Gered Wedgwood**, **Spode** and **Garrard**, the Queen's jewelers, which sells everything from china animals to antique silver. Good bargains are to be found in June and in the mid-December sale. Between Regent Street and Bond Street you'll find **Hardy Amies** and **Gieves & Hawkes**, among several tailors in the famous Savile Row. They will supply you with a tailor-made suit—but as this isn't Hong Kong you'll have to pay for this privilege in both time and money.

Soho

Gone are the porn shops and peep shows, replaced by stylish bars and brasseries, art galleries, and trendy shops. Some of the old, established family firms selling everything from fabrics to Italian salami are still here, fortunately, and the whole area, determined not to go the way of Covent Garden, has become synonymous with quality and style, with prices that even Londoners can afford. There is no single shopping street in Soho. In Beak Street, **Anything Left Handed** sells just that, from pens to cooking utensils. There are two long-established family firms here: **John Wilkes**, the gunsmith, and **H. J. Spiller**, which sells 17th-century picture frames. In Golden Square, **Bennetts Cashmere House** has been in business for more than 30 years.

Bloomsbury

This is not a great shopping area, with one exception: Museum Street, opposite the British Museum, the place to go for shops specializing in old prints and second-hand books. Visit **Bloomsbury Rare Books** at number 29 and **The Print Room** at number 37 next to the Museum Tavern. The quality Scottish woollens at **Westaway and Westaway** in Great Russell Street are an especially good buy. Within walking distance in Gower Street (to the south) is the enormous, efficiently run bookshop of the University of London, **Dillons**. The British Museum itself has a small shop that sells reproductions of Roman and Greek jewelry as well as prints and books.

Knightsbridge/Fulham/South Kensington

The designer shops, jewelers, and boutiques in the Brompton Road are overshadowed by **Harrods**, which offers a wide range of goods from around the world and is famed for its sales, Food Hall, and perfumery. Many of these other shops, though, are well worth a stop. For example, the **Scotch House**, across the street from Harrods, is excellent for woolens. **Harvey Nichols**, the area's other department store at the Knightsbridge end of Sloane Street, is usually less crowded than Harrods, but it is no less chic. This is an especially good place for classic and designer clothes. There is a menswear department and a good self-service restaurant in the basement. Another plus: Their fashion shows are fun. Sloane Street runs south all the way to Chelsea and the beginning of the King's Road, and has lots of excellent shops—many of them expensive clothing boutiques. Walking south, on the right you'll pass **Kenzo** (with the black and chrome L'Express café on the lower floor); **Katharine Hamnett**'s shop, with an aquarium in the window; **Joseph Tricot**; and **Yves Saint Laurent**. Across the street you'll see **Nicole Farhi**, **Giorgio Armani**, and **Jaeger**, which is just north of the Hyatt Carlton Tower. If you're gasping from the exercise—and at the prices—relax over the Hyatt's splendid cream tea (with a harpist) in the ground floor **Chinoiserie**.

Walking west along Brompton Road from Harrods you'll soon come to Giorgio Armani's **Emporio Armani**, which has an Italian café, and then to Beauchamp Place, a small shopping street where **Bruce Oldfield**, **Whistles**, and several expensive fashion jewelers have their shops. A few blocks past Beauchamp Place, Brompton Road bends to the south and becomes Fulham Road. Here, at the intersection known as Brompton Cross, you'll find **Jasper Conran** and the huge Michelin building, which houses **The Conran Shop**, with affordable designer furnishings and fabrics, Italian cookware, books, gifts, even English teas and preserves. Should you need a revitalizing snack at this point, there is a Champagne and oyster bar in the building, as well as the Bibendum restaurant. Almost opposite is **Joseph**, displaying all of his collections, including one for men, under one roof. Back on Fulham Road, you'll come to a branch of **Butler & Wilson** (costume and semi-precious jewelry) at number 189, then **Oggetti's** for flashy designer gifts, and the

Sleeping Company, stuffed full of lacy cushions and silk sheets.

Chelsea and King's Road

King's Road begins at the south end of Sloane Street, in Sloane Square. On the northwest corner of the square is **Peter Jones**, an upscale branch of the John Lewis partnership. Walking west on King's Road from here, you'll pass an almost continuous string of shops selling clothes by British and overseas designers, shoes, and wild extremes of fashion, from the 1950s biker's look to Japanese cocktail wear. A new shopping center, **King's Walk Shopping Mall** at 122 King's Road, has a piazza-style forecourt. Its striking design, with wall-hugging elevators and bridges, is more New York than London. **Antiquarius**, opposite the small Chelsea Cinema and near Chelsea Old Town Hall, consists of stalls from which you can buy secondhand goods, from fine art to 1920s flapper dresses. Past the Chelsea Old Town Hall (nearly opposite the fire station) is **Givan's**, stocked with fine Irish linen.

The shops peter out a bit and then pick up again just before World's End, where there is a row of good antiques shops and **Chelsea Rare Books** at number 313. A bit farther on, the rambling **Furniture Cave** on the corner of Lots Road sells quality secondhand furniture. There are several auction rooms on Lots Road and, at the bottom, the entrance to the Chelsea Wharf (home of the Memories of China Chelsea restaurant and a river boat stop). The King's Road continues for a while past a few more expensive antiques shops and **Christopher Wray's** vast lighting emporium at number 600, and then becomes the New King's Road with five outlets of the gentlemen's outfitters **Hackett**, where you can fit yourself out with anything from riding gear to formal evening wear. Just before Parson's Green is the **Antique Print Gallery**, which specializes in rare and original horse-racing prints and carries often humorous ones dating back to 1880.

Kensington

Like Oxford Street, Kensington High Street is lined with similar department stores and chain outlets. The nearby **Kensington Market** has seen better days, but the leather is cheap. Next to the Royal Garden Hotel is the **Hyper Hyper** fashion emporium (the huge white statues outside make it hard to miss), where trendy Londoners snap up clothes from new young designers. Next door is **Next**'s glass showcase, with affordable fashion for all the family.

Kensington Church Street runs into Kensington High Street across from the House of Fraser. Walking up it to the north you'll come to a branch of **Crabtree & Evelyn**, with its beautifully packaged toiletries. Almost opposite is **Amazon**, specializing in designer samples. Continuing north around the bend you'll come to several quality art galleries and antiques shops, such as **Kensington Fine Arts**, as well as two excellent restaurants, Clarke's and Kensington Place.

If you're shopping for children it's worth continuing west along Kensington High Street toward the Commonwealth Institute, past another branch of **Mothercare** and **Waterstone**'s bookshop (on the corner of Allen Street) to **The Early Learning Centre** (on the corner of Abingdon Road) and **The Children's Book Centre** for books and toys (just before Earls Court Road). At the bottom of Queensway, off the Bayswater Road north of Hyde Park, is the new **Whiteleys** development, an old department store now stylishly revamped with numerous restaurants, boutiques, and a large multiscreen movie theater under one roof. If you're an after-midnight person, Queensway, which attracts a cosmopolitan crowd, is always lively until the early hours, with many shops and snack bars along it staying open late.

East End/Tobacco Dock

Three times the size of Covent Garden, Tobacco Dock, to the east of the city, behind Wapping High Street, is a new development that hasn't really taken off yet. The shops (open daily until 8:00 P.M. and until 10:00 P.M. on Fridays) and restaurants are converted Victorian warehouses and restored Georgian vaults. Entertainers and themed attractions, including two sailing ship replicas, give the whole area a village atmosphere. Take the Docklands Light Railway or Docklands Minibus from Tower Gateway next to the Tower Hill tube to Shadwell or Wapping, from which it is a five-minute signposted walk. Parking is available.

ANTIQUES MARKETS

The antiques traders in **Portobello Road** just off to the northwest of the Notting Hill Gate tube may well spot you coming and inflate their prices accordingly, but you can still pick up some interesting jewelry, prints, and artifacts here, either from the stalls on Saturdays (8:00 A.M. to 5:00 P.M.) or from the shops on either side of the street.

Islington's **Camden Passage Market** on Wednesdays and Saturdays (8:30 A.M. to 3:00 P.M.) is smaller than the one on Portobello Road but still interesting, and the shops in the area are well worth checking out for larger items. **Camden Lock** near Camden Town is being redeveloped and attracts large crowds at weekends. You can buy crafts, handmade jewelry, old postcards, and the like, though you're unlikely to find anything of much value and the area is often quite littered.

The market stalls in the center of **Covent Garden** sell antiques on Mondays, general goods Tuesdays through Fridays, and handmade British crafts on weekends. Dealers and the public buy from the outdoor **New Caledonian Market** (also known as Bermondsay Market) on Fridays from 5:00 A.M. to noon on the corner of Long Lane and Bermondsey Street south of the river off Tower Bridge Road. There are a few antiques stalls in the East End's Brick Lane, Whitechapel, on Sundays (9:00 A.M. to 2:00 P.M.).

—*Susan Grossman*

DAY TRIPS FROM LONDON

OXFORD, CAMBRIDGE, WINDSOR, BRIGHTON

By Anthony Burton and Frank Dawes

OXFORD

Visitors to Oxford tend to arrive with a ready-made image in mind: Matthew Arnold's description of "that sweet City with her dreaming spires." That is not always what they find, particularly if they arrive by public transportation. Emerging from the railway station, passengers are confronted by a brewery and an old jam factory. The latter, once the source of Oxford's famous marmalade, now houses an antiques market where the atmosphere is friendly and there are bargains to collect. Bus travellers are dropped in one of the city's more nondescript quarters.

The best way to get an instant feel for Oxford is to find a vantage point with an overall view, and a literally central spot is where the main streets converge, at Carfax. The 14th-century **Carfax Tower** (all that remains of St. Martin's Church, which was demolished in 1896) is open to visitors who, when they have wound their way up the spiral stairs, will find all Oxford laid out before them. This is where you should begin your tour of Oxford.

MAJOR INTEREST

Carfax Tower
The University colleges
Radcliffe Square
Bodleian Library
Bookstores on Broad Street
Sheldonian Theatre
Science Museum
Ashmolean Museum

To the east, High Street—always known as "the High"—curves away to the distant hills. To the north is Cornmarket Street. Between these two streets is an enticing array of domes, pinnacles, and towers. St. Aldate's, to the south, is dominated by the ornate Tom Tower, marking the entrance to Christ Church College. Beyond it is the Thames, or (as it is more popularly known in its passage through Oxford) the Isis. To the west are sadder sights. Queen Street leads to a mishmash of modern shopping areas and parking lots. The old castle lies this way, but the romantic battlements are now the site of the local jail, and all that remains of the Norman fortress is a grassy mound.

From the Carfax Tower, the areas of rewarding exploration are apparent. The rich golden stones of the old, which on a sunny day seem to glow with their own inner light, offer a far greater lure than the neon and plastic of the new. Thus, visitors to Oxford are drawn to the city's main claim to fame, its ancient university.

Travellers here frequently ask to be directed to the university, only to be told that it is all around them—as you can clearly see from the top of Carfax Tower. The university is made up of 35 separate colleges, each with its individual history and traditions, yet all growing from a single root. To understand the system you must step back some 700 years. Medieval learning drew its strength from the church, which was the major center of study and which controlled virtually all forms of education. By the 13th century Oxford was home to a guild of teachers, the Universitas, whose students were housed in communal halls. From these grew the colleges, each with its chapel for prayers and its quadrangles, around which were grouped rooms for students and teachers. Common facilities, such as libraries, soon developed to serve all the colleges. But the heart of the teaching system remained

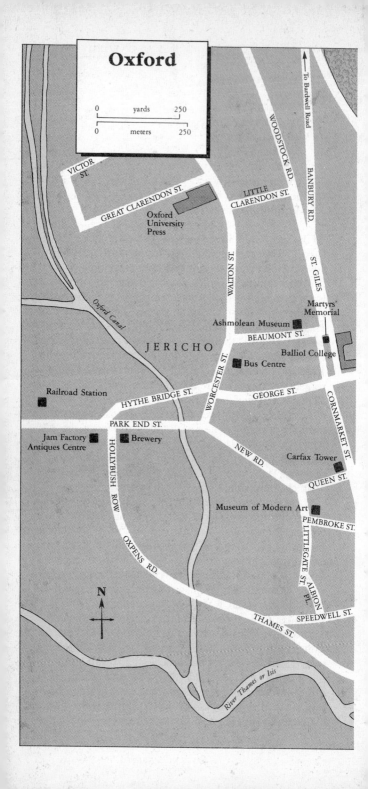

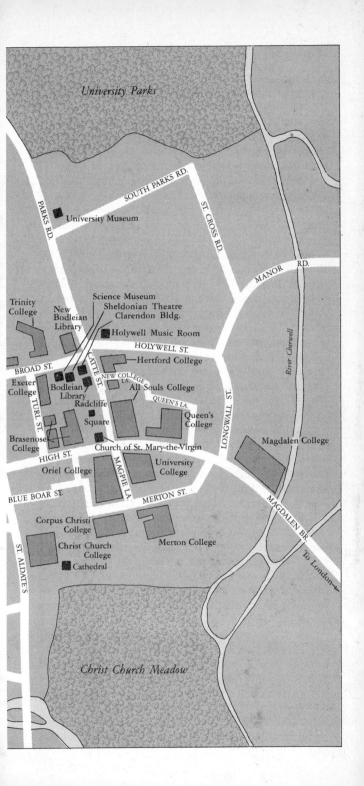

the tutorial, the meeting of teacher and student in the comfortable, informal surroundings of a college room.

Great variety exists among the colleges, certainly in appearance. There are grand colleges, with architecture so classically formal it approaches pomposity, and others where you might feel you had strayed into the garden of some old country mansion. To understand the colleges, it may help to take a little time at the beginning of the tour and look at one in detail.

Christ Church College

As you descend Carfax Tower and walk south on St. Aldate's, the first college you come to is Christ Church. The site originally held an Anglo-Saxon nunnery, but the church was rebuilt several times before the Norman church of St. Frideswide was begun there in the 12th century. In 1525 Cardinal Wolsey arrived with typical bravado and plans to demolish all that was old and raise a new college with a new chapel. The cardinal's fall brought a change of plans and patrons. Henry VIII took over, and Cardinal College became Christ Church. In the process, St. Frideswide's was saved, first as the college chapel, later as **Oxford Cathedral**.

Given its powerful patronage, the college was inevitably built on a grand scale and improved and developed over the centuries, with much of its present formal beauty due to the influence of the architect Sir Christopher Wren. The formal entrance, topped by the tall **Tom Tower**, is intended to impress the visitor, and it does. Each evening during term time the great bell in the tower tolls 101 times, once for each member of the original foundation of the college. Once inside the quad you are in an enclosed space, the self-contained world of the college. All around are the buildings that house students and dons, but the sheer size of the open grounds prevents any sense of claustrophobia. Meanwhile, the eye is drawn to the tower and spire of the cathedral. Thus, the architecture expresses the college's religious and scholarly heritage. Christ Church has an air of spaciousness, fronting a wide street with the open green of Christ Church Meadow alongside. Beyond the main quad are subsidiary quads and such important buildings as the college kitchens.

Famous alumni of Christ Church include the mathematics tutor C. L. Dodgson, better known as Lewis Carroll. He might have been amused by some of the antics of the 20th-century undergraduates: A swan was once discovered languishing in Tom Quad, formally attired in black bow tie; on another occasion, when Dean Lowe of Christ Church landed in Christ Church Meadow in a helicopter, he was greeted by a choir of undergraduates singing "Lo, he comes in clouds descending."

Christ Church creates its own unmistakable atmosphere, just as every other college at Oxford does, and if it can boast of former members as diverse as Lewis Carroll, William Penn, and W. H. Auden, so can they.

Other Colleges and Landmarks

If you go back up St. Aldate's and then take a stroll down Blue Boar Street, a quite different sense of space and time develops. The noise of traffic recedes, and the narrow lane briefly opens out into Oriel Square, bounded by the **Peckwater Quad** of Christ Church and Oriel and Corpus Christi colleges. What is at once so striking is that Oxford really is a mixture of quite disparate styles: **Oriel** is grandly Jacobean, with its strong rhythms of shaped gables, while **Corpus Christi**, altered and enriched though it has been over the years, has a feel of almost domestic intimacy. It is typical of Oxford that there should be curiosities to look out for, such as Corpus Christi's pelican sundial with its strange perpetual calendar.

Beyond the square, the way continues its ever more secretive path up cobbled Merton Street, past **Merton College**, which received its first statute in 1263 and is generally regarded as the oldest of the colleges—though the claim is strongly contested by two others, Balliol and University. Merton can at least claim to have some of Oxford's oldest buildings, and nowhere can you feel closer to the Medieval heart of the university than in **Merton Chapel**, with its beautiful stained glass.

Merton Street bends through a right angle, and the mood changes again, quite dramatically, for there at the end is the High, dominated by colleges and two churches set among many old houses of character (virtually all now converted to shops). To the west are crowded city streets, to the east openness and light—no accident but a reflection of the fact that the former lay within the old city walls, the latter outside them. To the east the view is dominated by **Magdalen College** (pronounced *maudlin*), its elaborate stonework gleaming from a recent cleaning. It is the focal point for one of Oxford's most popular traditions. Each May Day morning at 6:00, a hymn is sung from the tower, signaling the start of a pre-breakfast round of roistering that fills the surrounding streets, not to mention the surrounding pubs, which are opened early specially for this one day of the year. From here you can hire punts to explore the River Cherwell. A favorite excursion is to punt down to the **Victoria Arms**—universally known as the Vicky Arms—for a well-earned pint of beer on the lawn. It takes approximately two hours from Magdalen Bridge. A shorter, one-hour trip is possible by hiring a punt upstream at Bardwell Road.

West toward the city center down the High, the scene is one of rather formal grandeur, with the classicism of **Queen's College** setting the dominant note. But to reach the core of the university complex you must turn off the High onto Catte Street to **Radcliffe Square**. An urban space that captures the imagination, the square owes its impact to the genius of the architect Nicholas Hawksmoor, who suggested that the library, the **Radcliffe Camera**, be built as a rotunda. His own design was not used, however, and the work was given to James Gibbs, though both men received fees. So there it sits like the hub of a wheel, positively inviting you to look outward to the splendors on every side.

To the south is the **Church of St. Mary-the-Virgin**, with its tall tower. The main body of All Souls College comes into view to the east, and Brasenose College is to the west, while to the north is the Bodleian Library. But it is not just the magnificence of the buildings that gives the square its special character. The Camera is the principal undergraduate library, so it is constantly surrounded by a clutter of bicycles and a whirl of students who are there to work, not merely to gaze.

The **Bodleian Library** is rather more solemn, a research library used by scholars from all over the world. Statistics, for once, do give some notion of scale: five million volumes, spread along 81 miles of shelving, with seating for 2,078 readers. What statistics cannot do is convey the air of antiquity of a library whose heart is now four centuries old. Modernization has been slow. Heating was introduced only in 1821, which is why the oath all new readers must take includes a vow "not to bring into the Library or kindle therein any fire or flame." Visitors who want to see the oldest part of the library must make arrangements in advance, but it is well worth the effort.

Visitors should call the Bodleian (Tel: 27-71-65) and book a tour; there are four a day, starting at 10:30 A.M., from mid-March to the end of October, with limited visits in winter. No children under 14 permitted.

Broad Street

Opposite the Bodleian is New College Lane, spanned by Oxford's version of the Bridge of Sighs, which unites the two parts of Hertford College.

Those tempted to explore will find ever more secluded alleyways that end surprisingly at a country-pub-come-to-town in the shape of the thatched **Turf Tavern**. Just around the corner at the end of Broad Street is one of the undergraduates' favorite pubs, the **Kings Arms**, where you can choose between the big open bar at the front and the cozy paneled back bar, which until very recently was exclusively a male preserve. Still reserved for men is the famous bathing spot on the Cherwell, Parson's Pleasure, where gentlemen can bathe in the nude. Those who prefer wider vistas will certainly find just that in Broad Street. Close at hand is the **covered market**. Stalls originally cluttered and blocked the surrounding streets before they were moved into this specially built market hall. Here the colleges buy their provisions; many of the stalls sell very traditional English food—from the specialists in game, whose stalls, in season, are festooned with pheasant and partridge, to the sellers of English cheeses. But Broad Street caters to a quite different need: For book lovers, it is as close to heaven as they are ever likely to get. Here virtually anything can be found, from the most esoteric textbook to the latest paperback. There are shops specializing in art books, children's books, and even antiquarian books. Trinity, Balliol, and Exeter colleges manage to squeeze in among the booksellers and still leave space for a small group of historic buildings.

The **Sheldonian Theatre** was not designed as a theater in the modern sense but as a site for ceremonials. The first work of Sir Christopher Wren ("the first" in the sense that it was the first to be begun; Pembroke Chapel at Cambridge, though completed earlier, was started later) soon found other uses. Home for a time to the University Press, it later became a concert hall and remains one today. The Sheldonian and the delightful little **Holywell Music Room** up Holywell Street are part of Britain's musical history—Haydn performed here and so did Handel. In July there is the Handel in Oxford Festival; hearing the composer's works in the ornate setting of the Sheldonian is not unlike hearing Mozart in Salzburg.

Broad Street is a cheerful place, but it has had its moments of horror. An iron cross outside Balliol marks the spot where the Protestant martyr Thomas Cranmer, Archbishop of Canterbury, was burned at the stake in 1556, and an old gate in Balliol Quad is still said to show the scorching of the flames. Bishops Hugh Latimer and Nicholas Ridley were also burned nearby, and all three are commemorated in the Martyrs' Memorial in St. Giles.

Opposite the memorial on Beaumont Street is Oxford's best-known hotel, the stately and very traditional **Randolph**. Those looking for somewhere less overwhelmingly grand to stay need only walk up St. Giles to the ivy-covered **Old Parsonage** at the end of Banbury Road. Along here, too, are two of Oxford's favorite, if contrasting, restaurants. **Brown's** has good food at reasonable prices and is invariably bustling, noisy, and crowded but full of atmosphere. **Gee's Restaurant**, at 61a Banbury Road, is very different: Housed in an elegant Victorian conservatory, it boasts one of the best and most sophisticated French menus in the country (to reserve, Tel: 535-40 or 583-46). Another popular restaurant in this area is **Munchy Munchy** at 6 Park End Street. Its plain appearance gives no hint of the exotic flavors of Ethel Ow's authentic Indonesian cooking.

Broad Street has one more building of note, not perhaps the grandest but one that has a fascinating history. The tiny **Science Museum**, which holds an array of beautiful old scientific instruments, began life in the 17th century as home to Elias Ashmole's Cabinet of Curiosities, the world's first public museum. The Ashmolean collection outgrew its old quarters and found a new, classically styled home in Beaumont Street—it is not unlike a British Museum in miniature. The **Ashmolean Museum** today covers a wide range of exhibits from Egyptian mummies to 19th-century paintings. The ceramics are particularly fine, and among the gems of the art collection are a number of beautiful, haunting paintings by Samuel Palmer.

During the mid-19th century, Oxford decided it needed a natural history museum, and again a new style was pioneered, an almost riotously elaborate Gothic, using the new building materials of iron and glass. This, the **University Museum**, is on Parks Road. As well as housing the natural history collection, it is home to the Pitt-Rivers Collection of ethnography, an extraordinary assemblage of objects from around the world, including such bizarre items as shrunken human heads. The 20th century abandoned elaboration, and the **Museum of Modern Art** on Pembroke Street is housed in a converted warehouse—very bare, very austere, but a perfect setting for its constantly changing exhibitions. The restaurant in the basement is a popular place for a lunchtime snack, when the diners are often as colorful as the pictures on the walls.

A new addition to the Oxford scene, opened in spring 1988, combines something of the museum world with a good deal of show business and high-tech wizardry. At **The Oxford Story** on Broad Street, visitors follow the evolution of the university and meet some of the great thinkers and personalities who have been "up at Oxford."

University Oxford is what most visitors rightly wish to see. There is another city, too, however—the city where William Morris began making motorcars, the city of little terraces that run down to the canal in the area known as **Jericho**. This maze of narrow streets was once home to the working-class families of Oxford but now has become fashionable. The past is still preserved, however, in simple pubs such as the **The Bookbinders Arms** on Victor Street—a reminder that the Oxford University Press is not very far away. Oxford is still a city where town and gown both have an important part to play.

—*Anthony Burton*

CAMBRIDGE

In the perpetual pairing of Cambridge with Oxford, Cambridge always comes second. It is Oxford and Cambridge, or even Oxbridge, but never the other way around, except perhaps in the specialized world of the scientist. This is perhaps a reflection of history, for the university at Cambridge began with an exodus of scholars from Oxford after a quarrel between town and gown at the beginning of the 13th century. Yet, paradoxically, Cambridge contrives to appear the older city, more closely tied to its Medieval past. Here, the influence of the university is overwhelming; it is an inescapable presence in a way that is never quite the case at Oxford. But if it is the university that has made Cambridge the fascinating and beautiful place it is today, it is the River Cam that first brought the

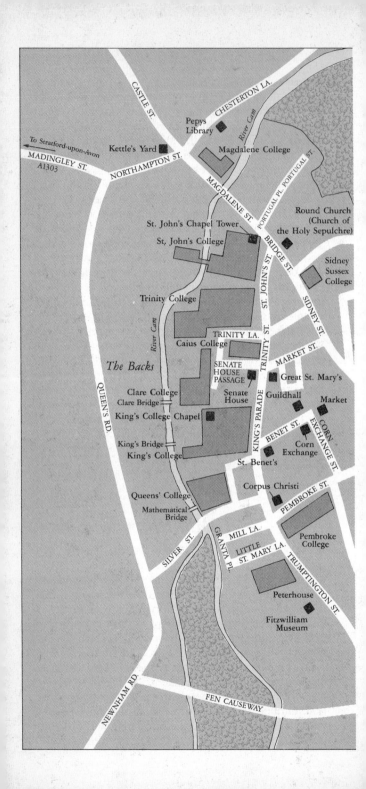

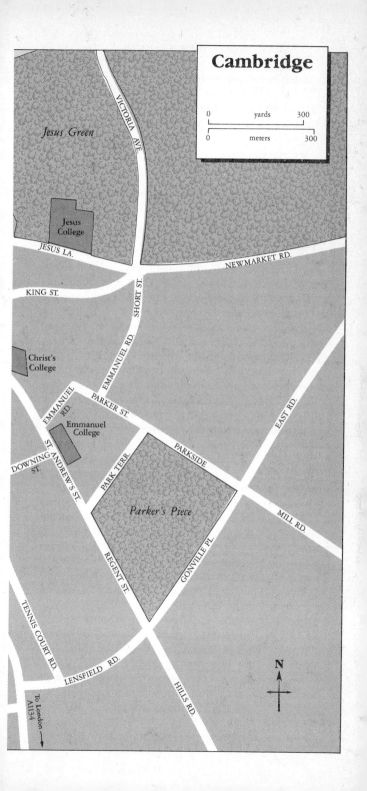

city into being. It was at the crossing of the river that the settlement of Cam-bridge grew, and it is the river that today threads together the different parts of the city's past to make a coherent whole.

MAJOR INTEREST

The Backs
University colleges
King's College Chapel
Kettle's Yard
Round Church
Fitzwilliam Museum

From the river, the visitor passes **the Backs**, which are exactly what the name suggests—the green space in back of the colleges, along the river's edge. But the unimaginative name gives no notion of the enchantment here, where the stone towers and turrets of colleges and chapels are reflected in the quiet waters of the Cam. By far the best way to take in this view is from a punt, the traditional narrow, flat-bottomed boat propelled by pole. These can be hired either by the bridge at Magdalene Street or by Mill Lane. It is possible to take "chauffeured punts" and let someone else do the poling. Those who choose to be punted rather than punt may fancy themselves in some English Venice, a feeling reinforced as you pass under Cambridge's bridges, particularly the local version of the **Bridge of Sighs** at St. John's College. The oldest bridge, at Clare College, was built in the 1630s, and the oddest is the Mathematical Bridge at Queens' College. A shapely wooden arch, it was constructed entirely without nails, from straight timbers that notch together like a Chinese puzzle. It was certainly a puzzle that proved too complex for generations of drunken undergraduates. They were capable of dismantling it, but putting it together again was quite beyond them. Eventually, authority had to step in, and the bridge sections are now bolted together.

The views of the colleges from the Cam include what is perhaps the city's most famous—**King's College** and its **Chapel**. The latter is on every tourist itinerary and deservedly so, for it is one of the great buildings not just of Cambridge but of the world. Its majesty is apparent from the outside, but its true glory is its interior.

Cambridge University is, like Oxford, the sum of its colleges, and while there are many similarities in organization, there are subtle differences as well. Colleges in both universities are usually built around squares, but what is a quad at Oxford is a court at Cambridge, and undergraduates here never have tutorials—they go for "supervisions" instead. For visitors, however, the most obvious difference lies in building materials: Whereas in Oxford stone rules, here warm red brick dominates. Most of the colleges are open to visitors except during the examination period, which runs from early May to mid-June. But even when they are closed, much of the colleges' magnificence is on display. Indeed, it is the cumulative effect of college architecture that gives Cambridge its unique atmosphere, and that visitors tend to remember far more clearly than any nice points or fine details.

The geography of Cambridge is comparatively simple. Starting in the north, below the river crossing of Bridge Street, the main road divides. One branch becomes Sidney Street, changing to St. Andrew's Street and continuing as Regent Street. The second branch, starting as St. John's Street, continues on as Trinity Street, King's Parade, and Trumpington Street. Both these routes are lined with colleges, and the space between is given over to town affairs, to the Guildhall, the Corn Exchange, and the still-flourishing market—a proper market with stalls selling everything from fresh meat to fine books.

Exploring the Colleges

Beginning a tour of Cambridge on the far side of the Cam, at Magdalene Bridge (originally Great Bridge), the spot where the Roman road crossed the river, you come first to **Magdalene College** (pronounced *maudlin*), founded in 1542. Although it is not one of the grander colleges, the splendor of its Renaissance gateway can be admired, while the extremely Gothicized church can be left to those with enthusiasm for heavy-handed Victorian restoration. The college has much of interest besides its architecture. The **Pepys Library** contains Samuel Pepys's bequest, which includes the famous diaries written in the author's unique shorthand and the more easily deciphered pocket book of Sir Francis Drake. In the 17th century there was a strong Puritan element in the college, and one member who left for the New World, Henry Dunster, went on to become the first president of Harvard College.

Magdalene and its immediate surroundings show how rich and diverse the charms of Cambridge can be. You could spend a contented day without straying more than a few hundred yards from here. Magdalene Street itself has a wealth of ancient buildings. Look, for example, at number 25, now a shoe shop but basically a timber-framed Medieval building with an upper story jutting outward and embellished with lovely, ornate carving. Just north of the crossroads, in the corner between Northampton Street and Castle Street, is one of the city's most surprising finds, known somewhat prosaically as **Kettle's Yard**. Here is the house of the art collector Jim Ede, who died in 1990. Nothing on the outside prepares you for the interior. This really is a home, not a museum, so arranged that the visitor feels the owner might turn up at any moment to resume residence. Ede bought the then unfashionable and unwanted work of his contemporaries—from Gaudier-Brzeska to Ben Nicholson—and he had special affection for the paintings of the Cornish primitive Alfred Wallis.

Across the bridge, visitors who enjoy exploring back streets will find an area that once housed college servants but now comprises what the local real-estate agents would call "desirable residences." It also has its oddities and surprises. On the corner of Portugal Street, an aged police notice announces that hand carts and trolleys are not allowed in, while nearby Portugal Place has a genteel terrace that ends with the High Victorian Gothic of St. John's chapel tower. Back on Bridge Street is the popular student pub the **Baron of Beef**, and just a little closer to the city center is another of Cambridge's more pleasing oddities. The church of the Holy Sepulchre is usually known simply as the **Round Church**, for the very good reason that it is indeed round. Originally built in the 12th century, it contains a ring of stone heads—from fiercely mustachioed warriors to even fiercer demons—that stare down at the visitor.

The Round Church stands by the point where Bridge Street and St. John's Street diverge, at **St. John's College**, which boasts one of the most attractive and ornate gatehouses of all the colleges. Typical of many, it was built of both red brick and stone. In addition to a statue of the saint, the gatehouse bears a variety of heraldic emblems, from Lancastrian roses to mythical creatures with horns and tusks known as yales. They are the emblems of Lady Margaret Beaufort, under whose will the college was founded in the 16th century. These you might expect, but the builders had a sense of humor. A field of marguerites makes a visual pun on the founder's name, and among the daisies is a rabbit hole with a fox disappearing down one end and a rather smug rabbit popping out the other.

St. John's Street leads to Trinity Street and **Trinity College**, where you might notice that the heraldic ornaments on the great gate are the same as those at St. John's—not surprising, since Henry VIII was Lady Margaret's grandson. The statue of Henry clutches an orb in one hand and—thanks to generations of undergraduates—a chair leg in the other. Trinity's **Great Court** is the largest in Cambridge, and college athletes test their prowess by attempting to run a circuit while the clock is striking 12:00. The apple tree on the lawn is descended from one that stood in the garden of a former member of Trinity, Sir Isaac Newton.

Trinity Lane is one of those curved, narrow ways that promise fresh delights just around the corner. Here it leads on to **Gonville and Caius College**, begun by Mr. Gonville and enlarged by Dr. Caius and usually known simply as Caius (pronounced *keys*). It has three gates: The undergraduate enters in Humility to Tree Court, passes through Virtue to Caius Court, and leaves the college via Honour. The lane leads on past Senate House Passage and the 18th-century classical formality of Senate House itself, where university degrees are conferred in a ceremony that, because of the numbers involved, takes two days. After that comes Clare College, closely followed by King's.

King's is a delight, but the **King's College Chapel** is the inevitable focus of attention. Seen across from the Backs it is majestic; up close the detail is revealed; and inside the full splendor appears. It might never have been so splendid but for the turbulence of Medieval life. The chapel was begun in the reign of its founder, Henry VI, but the long and bloody Wars of the Roses caused numerous interruptions, and it was completed by Henry VIII. His devices—the Royal Arms, portcullis, Tudor rose, dragon, and greyhound—can be seen everywhere in the building. More important, English architecture had reached a period of great elaboration; hence we have what is literally the chapel's crowning glory, the intricate tracery of the beautiful fan-vaulted roof. The chapel's proportions are noble and the vast areas of stained glass send a warm light washing over the intricate details of carving and tracery. If you left Cambridge having seen nothing else, you would go away content.

King's has an appropriate companion in nearby **Queens' College**, named after its two founders, Margaret of Anjou and Elizabeth Woodville. Where the former college is all grandeur, the latter has a feeling of pleasant domesticity, with buildings of mellow brick that could be part of a country house.

Back on Trinity Street, now become King's Parade, the clock on **Great St. Mary's Church** rings the hours with a familiar chime, for it is the same as Big Ben's at Westminster—although first struck at St. Mary's. Church bells are also cause to visit St. Benet's Church, where modern bell-ringing, or change-ringing, was begun. There are two ways of ringing bells. The simplest is one in which the bells play a melody. In change-ringing, however, the bells ring peals, each one differentiated from the next by the order in which the bells are rung. It is a system of great, almost mathematical complexity whose nearest musical equivalent might be a Bach fugue. Change-ringing, still widely practiced in English churches, was invented by a parish clerk at St. Benet's named Fabian Stedman. Another reason to visit the church: It boasts a Saxon tower, the city's oldest building.

Where King's Parade becomes Trumpington Street, water courses run down deep gulleys on either side. These once brought drinking water to the city's center, and the man largely responsible was Thomas Hobson, who owned extensive livery stables. His customers were forced to take whichever horse was nearest the door, a practice that gave rise to the expression "Hobson's choice."

Off Trumpington Street is Pembroke College, with a **chapel** by Sir Christopher Wren, the first of his architectural works to be completed—giving Cambridge a Wren "first" to set beside Oxford's Sheldonian Theatre. Nearby **Peterhouse**, the oldest of the colleges, dating to 1281, has a famous curiosity. Looking up at the top of the building near the church, you can see an iron bar across a window. The poet Thomas Gray had it placed there to anchor a fire-escape rope. This proved too tempting for his fellow undergraduates, who put a tub of water at the bottom and yelled "Fire!" He was so upset by the experience that he packed his bags and moved to Pembroke College.

Trumpington Street leads on to the **Fitzwilliam Museum**, which has the solemn appearance associated with much Victorian architecture, having been built in 1848. Once past the somewhat dourly tiled entrance, rather reminiscent of a grandiose public lavatory, you will find a fine collection of art and antiquities, with the work of French and English Impressionists doing a great deal to lighten the overall sense of darkness that seems to pervade the university museum. There are temporary exhibitions mounted throughout the year and special exhibitions and concerts during the Cambridge Festival. If, by now, you are tempted by the thought of afternoon tea, then the thing to do is to leave the Fitzwilliam for **Fitzbillies**, Cambridge's most famous tea shop, at 52 Trumpington Street, or, if the riverside still exerts its appeal, then the **Garden House Hotel** in Granta Place for cream tea on the lawn stretching down to the water. The Garden House is also recommended for an overnight stay. The **University Arms** on Regent Street is another excellent accommodation. Those on the lookout for something equally traditional but a little stronger than tea might care to sample the beer at the 17th-century coaching inn **The Eagle** on Benet Street. And if a full-scale meal is in order, there is no shortage of restaurants, from the excellent Chinese fare of **Tai Cheun** on St. John's Street to the Swiss fondues at **Flames** on Castle Street. Fine though international restaurants are, visitors to Cambridge are more likely to be wanting something as English as a punt on the Cam, and what could be more English than a cricket pavilion? **Hobbs Pavilion** restaurant on Parker's Piece is just that, though the proprietors cannot guarantee you will have any cricket to watch.

—*Anthony Burton*

WINDSOR

From a plane approaching London's Heathrow Airport, or across the fields from a car on the M 4, the crenelated walls of Windsor Castle and its one big, round, hollow tower look like a child's dream of a heavenly sand castle.

Closer, from the three-mile-long avenue of trees called Long Walk, it seems to belong in Camelot rather than in this world of airports and freeways. Yet Windsor Castle, just 21 miles west of London, is uniquely a part of both: the home and fortress of nine centuries of English monarchy and of the present helicopter-hopping, polo-playing royal family.

MAJOR INTEREST

Windsor
The Guildhall (Wren, royal portraits)
Madame Tussaud's Royalty and Empire Exhibition

The Castle
St. George's Chapel (Chapel of the Order of the
    Garter)
The State Apartments
Queen Mary's dolls' house

Windsor Great Park
The Royal Mausoleum at Frogmore House
Windsor Safari Park

Around Windsor
Eton College
Runnymede

When Queen Elizabeth I commanded William Shake-speare to write a play for her court, this town of red-roofed houses became the setting for *The Merry Wives of Windsor*. The **Garter Inn** pub stands on the site of the Harte and Garter, where Sir John Falstaff and his cronies roistered.

At the Victorian (1849) Central Railway Station, **Madame Tussaud's** 130 life-size models evoke a later period: the precise moment on June 19, 1897, when Queen Victoria stepped off the train with her entourage in readiness for the celebration of her Diamond Jubilee the following day.

The Guildhall is a handsome colonnaded building erected in the 17th century by Sir Christopher Wren. It houses a small museum of local history, but its main attraction is its collection of royal portraits.

A good place to dine in Windsor is **The Castle**, a Georgian coach inn opposite its namesake that offers a plain à la carte menu. However, to escape the crowds it is worth taking a half-mile walk across the pedestrians-only bridge to the town of Eton. **Christopher**, on Eton's High Street (closed Saturday lunchtimes and at Christmas), is fashionable and not terribly expensive. (If you want to splurge and sample some of the finest food in Britain, go six miles upriver to Bray for a meal at the **Waterside Inn**. The restaurant, run by the celebrated Roux brothers of France, has views of smooth lawns and summerhouses, weeping willows, boats, and swans on the river. Book in advance; Tel: 0628-206-91.)

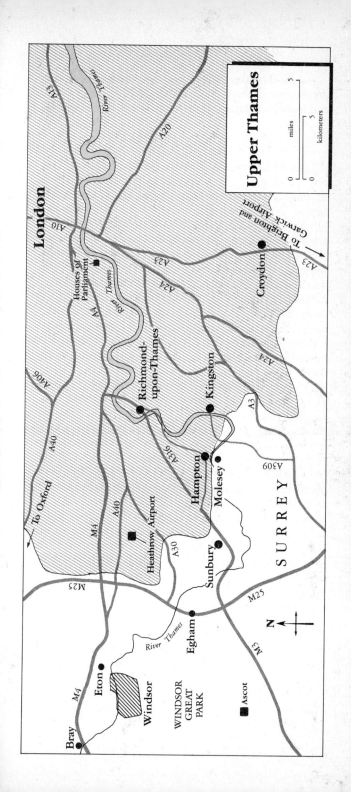

The royal borough is overshadowed by the huge castle perched on its chalk ridge above the River Thames and dominating the approaches from London.

The Castle

It is not difficult to picture Henry VIII, bloated with excess and age, dragging his ulcerated leg through the cloisters of Windsor, where courtiers plotted and whispered of heresy and treachery. It's said that his halting steps can still be heard there. It was to Windsor that Henry fled in August 1517, when the "sweating sickness" struck the capital. But the epidemic followed the King, carrying off some of the royal pages who slept in His Majesty's chamber. The arms of Henry, along with the Tudor rose and the pomegranate of his first wife, Catherine of Aragon, are engraved in stone above the entrance gate named after the King. But Henry is only one of 41 monarchs who have added to and altered the castle that William of Normandy began just four years after he defeated Harold at the Battle of Hastings. The original Norman round tower, which surveys the Thames as it winds through its green valley, is surrounded by other towers, walls, courts, lodges, and chapels built by successive royal dynasties. Plantagenets, Tudors, Stuarts, and Hanovers have added to the castle over the years. (The only interruption in the near millennium of royal residence at Windsor was the bitter decade of the Civil War in the 1640s.) The most recent occupants, the Windsors, so renamed their House of Saxe-Coburg and Gotha in 1917, when anti-German feeling was high. A new addition to the grounds is the Tudor-style mansion that the Duke and Duchess of York designed for themselves.

Tradition rules here at Windsor, the heart of the system that from an island of warring barons created a nation and an empire upon which, it was said, "the sun never set." British tradition is glorified every morning from Mondays through Saturdays at 11:00 with the elaborate rituals of the changing of the guard. Soldiers in their red tunics and black bearskin helmets stamp their boots and make the ancient walls ring. The same troops, in flak jackets rather than scarlet, embarked for the Falklands War in the summer of 1982. At Combermere Barracks on St. Leonard's Road, just a few blocks from the castle, is the **Museum of the Household Cavalry**. The Household Cavalry can also be seen mounting the guard daily at the

Horse Guards opposite Whitehall in London. The museum tells the story of the Blues (who, confusingly, wear red plumes in their helmets) and the Life Guards (white plumes) from 1685 to the present.

The **Chapel of the Order of the Garter**—St. George's Chapel—is the first building you see when you pass through the Henry VIII Gate. Carved choir stalls in the chapel include those of the Knights of the Garter, an order that, according to romantic legend, Edward III founded in 1348 after he picked up a garter the Countess of Salisbury dropped while they were dancing. He rebuked the tittering courtiers with the words *"Honi soit qui mal y pense"* ("Evil be to him who evil of it thinks"), and this is the motto inscribed in gold letters on the dark blue velvet garter that to this day members wear beneath the left knee.

Edward IV began building the present chapel where the processions and ceremonies of the Knights of the Garter are enacted. Their banners are hung in the choir. The chapel was completed by Henry VIII, who shares a tomb there with Jane Seymour, his favorite among his many wives. The body of Charles I, beheaded in the Civil War and brought secretly to Windsor, was found nearby in the chapel vault when it was opened by George IV in the early part of the 19th century. Apart from Henry and Charles, eight other kings of England, including three from the present century, rest in peace beneath the chapel's fan-vaulted ceiling.

When George IV came to the throne late in life (he was prince regent for years during his father's madness), he transferred the family apartments from the dank north wing to the southern and eastern sides of the castle. He built the Grand Corridor to connect them with the **State Apartments**. The richly furnished State Apartments are used for royal ceremonies and receptions but are otherwise open to the public. The Queen's Presence Room is still as Charles II decorated it, commissioning the Neapolitan artist Antonio Verrio to paint the ceiling. The walls are adorned with late 18th-century Gobelins, other tapestries, and royal portraits. In the sequence of rooms with majestic titles there are carvings by Grinling Gibbons, etchings by great masters, priceless porcelain and furniture, and paintings by Rubens, Rembrandt, Van Dyck, Canaletto, Dürer, Holbein, Reynolds, and others. The aptly named Grand Staircase is dominated by a vast, gleaming suit of armor made to measure in 1540 for gouty Henry VIII. The

Waterloo Chamber, created by George IV as a memorial to those who brought down Napoleon, has a carpet 80 feet long and 40 feet wide without a seam in it. It was made in India for Queen Victoria and is probably the largest example of its kind in the world.

Everything in Windsor Castle is on a regal scale—everything, that is, except the **dolls' house** presented to Queen Mary in 1923 by the architect Sir Edwin Lutyens. It is on a scale of 12:1, and so is everything in it, including works of writers such as Chesterton and Kipling and paintings of Orpen and Munnings, down to electrical and plumbing fixtures of Lilliputian proportions. Like the State Apartments nearby, it is open to inspection.

Windsor Great Park

The 4,800-acre park, lying on the far side of the castle in a wide loop of the River Thames, was a hunting ground for William the Conqueror. Herds of deer roam here still. At the farthest end of Long Walk from the castle is an equestrian statue of George III dressed as a Roman emperor—a suitably sardonic memorial to the king who lost the American colonies.

On the grounds of Frogmore House, a royal residence dating from 1697 in a quiet corner of the park, is the **mausoleum**. A masterpiece of mosaic and monumental masonry, it is a reminder of the Victorian way of death. Victoria, the Widow of Windsor, had it built for her beloved consort, Albert, whom she mourned for 40 years before she joined him. In the burial ground outside lie the remains of the king of the briefest reign, Edward VIII, and the woman for whom he gave up the throne of England, Wallis Simpson.

A one-mile motor route takes visitors around **Windsor Safari Park**, two miles southwest of Windsor on B 3022, through an unexpected reserve of lions and tigers, elephants and camels, zebras, bears, wolves, and baboons living wild in the green English countryside. The white turrets and battlements of the mansion overlooking the park, built half a century ago by an American automobile tycoon, are a pastiche of the real thing just down the road.

Eton and Runnymede

Eton College, that oldest of old schools that molded no fewer than 20 British prime ministers, stands modestly beside the High Street of the little town from which it takes its name, just across the river from Windsor. Some of the buildings, including the exquisitely painted Chapel, date from the school's founding by Henry VI in 1440. A tower completed by Roger Lupton in 1520 looks down on the cobbled schoolyard and the playing fields beyond, on which the Battle of Waterloo was supposedly won. There is a wall against which a game peculiar to Eton is played annually. The younger boys still wear the inimitable Eton jacket and stiff collar, and the "Eton Boating Song" is still sung.

One fine summer's morning in 1215 King John and his entourage rode out from Windsor Castle to meet the King's disaffected barons, assembled on Runney Mede, and to sign the Magna Carta. All English-speaking peoples, including those who went to America, have benefited from this charter of liberty. The water-meadows of **Runnymede** beside the Thames, two miles northwest of Egham on A 308, remain virtually untouched by the passing centuries. A small Classical-style temple was erected in 1957 by the American Bar Association, and nearby a memorial to President John F. Kennedy stands at the foot of Cooper's Hill. At the summit is another memorial, commemorating the 20,456 Allied airmen who died in World War II and have no known graves. Their names are recorded in the cloister.

Royal Windsor Horse Show

The Royal Windsor Horse Show is held in Home Park in mid-May. Members of the royal family play an active part, whether it be show jumping or driving. The best way to see the show, which is done while drinking Champagne and eating smoked-salmon sandwiches, is to become a member. Write to The Secretary, Mews, Windsor Castle, Berkshire. For those who would rather listen to Baroque music than compare the finer points of horseflesh, the Windsor Festival runs from late September through October.

—*Frank Dawes*

BRIGHTON

Queen Victoria was not amused by Brighton; George IV, as Prince of Wales ("Prinny" to fashionable Regency society), adored the place, which he first visited one Sunday in September 1783 when it was just a small fishing town called Brighthelmston.

Brighton is a town built on misbehavior. Prinny installed his morganatic wife, Mrs. Maria Fitzherbert, here in a house he built for her in Old Steine, a triangular garden at the center of Brighton. Today the house is a YMCA hostel. In less permissive times it was an open secret that unmarried couples, or at least couples who were not married to each other, slipped down to Brighton for an illicit weekend of pleasure. Titled men kept their actresses here. Brighton was known as early as the mid-18th century, when a local doctor published a pamphlet recommending the "oceanic fluid" as a curative, to be taken both by bathing and by drinking.

Fifty years ago Graham Greene used the resort as the backdrop for *Brighton Rock,* a novel about sleazy crime amidst the seaside trippers and at the racecourse in the hills above the town. The "rock" of the title is not a geographical feature but a stick of rainbow-hued candy, very hard on the teeth, with "Brighton" spelled out in red sugar all the way through its white core. Greene's boy-gangster, Pinkie, would have no difficulty in recognizing Brighton—and its rock—today.

Less than an hour from London by train, and easily within commuting distance, Brighton is nonetheless a smart place to live, much favored by creative people such as the late Lord Olivier. Apart from Greene, Terence Rattigan and Noël Coward found inspiration here. Not so long ago, kippers could be had for breakfast on the Pullman service to town, but alas, the *Brighton Belle* is no more. Frankly, the steeply shelved beach of large round pebbles is nothing to write home about, except that a section of it just west of the marina is reserved for nudists. But Brighton still *revels* in naughtiness and is always fun to visit, even for a day—though it has enough to keep you entertained and occupied for much longer.

MAJOR INTEREST

The Lanes (antiques shopping)
Royal Pavilion and The Dome
Palace Pier views of the coast
The Aquarium
Volk's beachside railway

Trim suburbs climbing inland up the grassy slopes of the Downs, manicured public lawns, and bright ribbons of flowers give no hint of the centerpiece that, when revealed, hits the visitor smack in the eye. It is a palace from the hills of northern India, complete with minarets and onion domes, magically transported and set down in the midst of an English garden. The **Royal Pavilion** was built not by a Mogul emperor but by the extravagant, debauched, lecherous, eccentric George IV. About the time of his father's terminal bout with madness, George hit upon the idea of transforming the mansion he had built in Brighton into an Eastern fantasy palace. His architect was John Nash, who laid out London's Regent's Park and Regent Street and redesigned Buckingham Palace. No expense was spared. The result, the Royal Pavilion, convinced some people that the family insanity was hereditary. Among some of the more polite remarks were these: "This pot-bellied palace, this minaret mushroom, this gilded dirt pie, this congeries of bulbous excrescences . . ."

The interior was no less exotic than the exterior, satisfying the prince's taste for chinoiserie, which can still be viewed today, together with marvelous Regency furniture, porcelain, glass, silver, and gold plate. Many of the pieces are on loan from Queen Elizabeth II. The Music Room is a Nash masterpiece, in which a 70-strong royal orchestra would play while Prinny sang to his guests. Gutted by a fire in 1975, the room was expensively restored, then wrecked again when a three-ton minaret crashed through the roof during the great windstorm of 1987, which also devastated the lovely central parks of Brighton. Once again, Brighton has restored the Music Room to its original splendor.

By the time the pavilion was completed, the prince regent had become king and lost interest in it. But the fashion he had started rolled on. **Regency Square**, just across the promenade from West Pier and planned as the Royal Pavilion neared completion, provides the grandest example of the genre of bay windows, balconies, and wrought-iron tracery in the houses that line it.

Before he built the Pavilion, George commissioned William Porden to build stables and a riding school in the style of a Muslim mosque. Today **The Dome** is the home of the Brighton Philharmonic Orchestra and is also used for events as varied as rock concerts, trade-union conferences, and the degree-conferring ceremonies of Sussex University, whose campus, designed by Sir Basil Spence in the 1960s, is high on the Downs out of town. The adjoining stables fronting Church Street serve as Brighton's public library, art gallery, and museum.

The Lanes

Nowhere is the atmosphere of Brighton, a heady mixture of colorful history and present glamour, more in evidence than it is in what remains of Brighthelmston, a square mile of small weatherboarded houses and twisting alleyways called The Lanes. Book and antiques shops, jewelers and junk dealers, pubs and restaurants are crammed into these pedestrians-only byways, the entrances to which are clearly marked in the wider streets surrounding them.

At the center of this Medieval enclave is **Brighton Square**, a 20th-century traffic-free shopping precinct; open-air cafés give it a Continental feel. Certainly you will hear a variety of European tongues here, and not only from tourists—Brighton is a busy center for English-language schools.

There is no need to confine your shopping to The Lanes, of course—Brighton has more than its share of stylish emporia, which have helped it earn its reputation as "London by the sea." Among the many fine stores in North Street, the department store **Hannington's**, the oldest (1808), prides itself on its knowledgeable and courteous staff. **Wyn Gillett**, at 34 Upper North Street, sells antique linen and lace in pristine condition. **Graham and Jo Webb**, at 59 Ship Street, specialize in antique music boxes, some of which play whole operatic overtures. Even farther off the well-beaten tourist track, in a narrow lane off Gloucester Road near the railway station, is **Pyramid**, which has a wide range of Art Deco pieces, from tea services and lampshades to telephones and mahogany-cased radios. The address is 9a Kensington Gardens.

The best-known seafood restaurants in Brighton are **English's** and **Wheeler's**. Lesser known, and less expensive, is **D'Arcy's** in Market Street, where the plaice and other fish are fresh from the Channel. The **Eaton Garden Restaurant** in Eaton Gardens, Hove (which adjoins Brighton on the west), also serves excellent fish and good old-fashioned English fare such as steak, kidney, and mushroom pie. For those seeking a traditional English tea, the **Mock Turtle Restaurant** at 4 Pool Valley serves a good pot of tea with lashings of homemade cakes and jams on Wood's willow blue-and-white china. Brighton has numerous first-rate French restaurants, too, among them **La Marinade** in Kemp Town and **Le Grandgousier** in Western Street, where rich sauces, garlic, and *l'escargot* provide a whiff of the land just across the Channel. New restaurants open as others fade away.

Between The Lanes and the sea is the newly built **Hospitality Inn Brighton**, boasting a four-story plant-filled atrium, two restaurants, and a fully equipped health club and swimming pool. It sits in stark contrast to its neighbor, the **Old Ship Hotel**, which is more than four centuries old. Thackeray stayed at the Old Ship while writing *Vanity Fair*, Charles Dickens gave public readings of his works in the ballroom, and Paganini gave a recital here in 1831. More recently the late poet laureate Sir John Betjeman was an habitué. Locally caught seafood is a specialty, and the cellars are extensive.

Just a short walk westward along King's Road, facing the sea, are Brighton's finest hotels: the **Brighton Metropole** and the **Grand**. Stately neighbors, they have been extensively renovated and both feature indoor swimming pools. Accommodation in either one includes well-appointed suites as well as rooms with all modern facilities.

The Esplanade and Piers

It would be unthinkable to visit Brighton without taking a sniff of sea air and a stroll along "the front," which is as gaudy as the promenade at any other popular seaside resort. Between Brighton's two piers are fast-food joints, fish-and-chip cafés, cockles-and-whelks stalls, amusement arcades, bumper cars, paddling pools, putting greens, and sleazy shops selling a range of awful kitsch. Among the crowds taking the air are the inevitable dropouts, eccentrics, and punks, whose purple hair and safety-pin adornments have become as much a part of the tourist scene as the Beefeaters at the Tower of London.

The view from the end of **Palace Pier**, stretching a third of a mile into the sea from Grand Junction Road and Marine Parade, takes in a wide section of English Channel coast, including the beginning of the white cliffs to the east. This is the younger of the two Victorian piers. The **West Pier**, recently saved from demolition by local enthusiasts, once again offers to visitors the slot machines that were shown in Richard Attenborough's satiric film *Oh, What a Lovely War*. Brighton and adjoining Hove, incidentally, were a center for movie-making before Hollywood set eyes on its first hand-cranked camera.

Brighton's **Aquarium**, next to Palace Pier, is well past its centennial and still displays sea lions, seals, and turtles, as well as thousands of fish. Dolphins perform daily in the 1,000-seat Dolphinarium. Also at hand is Britain's first public **electric railway**, Volk's. Opened in 1883 and travelling for a mile along the edge of the beaches (including the one for nudists), it carries passengers in little yellow wooden cars with open sides. The service runs from Easter to October and is inexpensive. At the farthest end of Brighton is one of the town's newer attractions, the largest yachting marina in Europe, opened by the Queen in 1979.

The Brighton Festival

In 1967, Lord Olivier brought the festival to his home town. Held every year in May, it is now one of Europe's liveliest, rivaling the more famous one in Edinburgh. It encompasses theater, jazz, classical music, big bands, opera, rock, cabaret, poetry, fireworks, and such eccentric experiments as a conducted tour of the sewers and the world's smallest theater—an actor on a motorbike with an audience of one in the sidecar. On the first Sunday in November, fans turn out for the London-to-Brighton Veteran Car Run.

A pleasant 20-mile drive west of Brighton, **Arundel** has both a fine castle, the ancestral home of the Dukes of Norfolk, and a Roman Catholic cathedral (see the Literary Southeast chapter).

—*Frank Dawes*

GETTING AROUND

Oxford
Oxford, 57 miles northwest of London, is reached by rail from Paddington Station, by bus from Victoria Coach Station, and by road via A 40 and M 40.

Cambridge
Cambridge, 55 miles north of London, is reached by rail from Liverpool Street Station, by coach from Victoria Coach Station, and by car via M 11.

Windsor

By car, leave London through Hammersmith and follow the M 4 to Junction 6. Windsor is 39 minutes by train from London's Paddington Station to Windsor and Eton Central; the trip takes 55 minutes from London's Waterloo to Windsor and Eton Riverside. You can also reach Windsor by Green Line bus from Victoria Coach Station.

Brighton

By car, Brighton is just 53 miles south of London on A 23. From London's Victoria Station, Brighton is reached in a mere 51 minutes by express trains, which run hourly. National Express buses make the trip from Victoria Station in two hours. Gatwick Airport lies midway between London and Brighton.

ACCOMMODATIONS REFERENCE

Oxford

▶ **The Old Parsonage Hotel.** 3 Banbury Road, **Oxford** OX2 6NN. Tel: (0865) 31-02-10.

▶ **The Randolph Hotel.** Beaumont Street, **Oxford** OX1 2LN. Tel: (0865) 24-74-81; Fax: (0865) 79-16-78.

Cambridge

▶ **Garden House Hotel.** Granta Place, Mill Lane, **Cambridge** CB2 1RT. Tel: (0223) 634-21; Telex: 81463; Fax: (0223) 31-66-05.

▶ **University Arms.** Regent Street, **Cambridge** CB2 1AD. Tel: (0223) 35-12-41; Telex: 817311; Fax (0223) 31-52-56.

Brighton

▶ **Brighton Metropole.** King's Road, **Brighton** BN1 2FU. Tel: (0273) 77-54-32; Telex: 877245; Fax: (0273) 20-77-64; in U.S., (402) 493-4747 or (800) 44-UTELL.

▶ **Grand Hotel.** King's Road, **Brighton** BN1 2FW. Tel: (0273) 211-88; Telex: 877410; Fax: (0273) 20-26-94.

▶ **Hospitality Inn Brighton.** King's Road, **Brighton** BN1 2GS. Tel: (0273) 20-67-00; Telex: 878555; Fax: (0273) 82-06-92; in U.S., (213) 937-2530, (201) 587-1555, or (800) 228-9898.

▶ **Old Ship Hotel.** King's Road, **Brighton** BN1 1 NR. Tel: (0273) 290-01; Telex: 877101; Fax: (0273) 82-07-18.

THE LITERARY SOUTHEAST
KENT, SUSSEX, SURREY

By Frank Dawes

Within a chalk oval formed by the hill ranges of the North and South Downs between London and the English Channel, many of England's great writers took root. Inside that oval lies the Weald (pronounced *wheeled*), the old Saxon word for wood. Across the North Downs to Canterbury in the east winds the Pilgrims Way trod by Chaucer. The chalk oval meets the Channel in a series of cliffs, a bastion against would-be invaders of the island, and folds itself away inland into the open plains that stretch, prairie-like, westward toward the mysterious circle of Stonehenge, older than the Pyramids, marking the calendar of the seasons since prehistoric times (covered in our Cotswolds to Winchester chapter).

This is Dickens and Kipling country and the favorite retreat of the Bloomsbury writers Virginia Woolf and E. M. Forster. Others identified with the area—from Kent through Sussex to Surrey—include 17th- and 18th-century poets, diarists, travellers, and thinkers such as William Cobbett, Jonathan Swift, John Evelyn, Thomas Paine, and Daniel Defoe, as well as more contemporary literary figures such as A. A. Milne, Henry James, H. G. Wells, and Winston Churchill (who, though primarily thought of as a statesman, was awarded the Nobel Prize for Literature in 1953).

Our perceptions of the landscape, towns, and villages of this small corner of England encompassing the counties of Surrey, East and West Sussex, and Kent—all of them only an hour or two's drive south of London—have been shaped by the words of this celebrated company. Who can drive the byroads of the Southeast, winding through green meadows and woods and over gentle hills, without remembering Chesterton's lines: "Before the Roman came to Rye or out to Severn strode, the rolling English drunkard made the rolling English road"?

The rivers of the Southeast, once navigated far inland, ripple down to the sea, providing sport for anglers and canoeists: the Ouse, Arun, and Adur in Sussex and Kent's Medway, dallying through orchards and hop fields to its confluence at the sea with the greatest British waterway of all, the Thames. Norman churches, castles, ruined abbeys, stately homes, and country houses, Tudor beams and thatch, clapboard inns and oasthouses, bluebell woods and gardens laid out centuries ago can be discovered along these riverbanks and in the narrow country lanes.

Most of this part of England was covered in forest when the Normans invaded in the 11th century, and a few places still are, even though 15 million trees, mostly beech and oak, were knocked down by 100-mile-per-hour winds in October 1987. (Six of the seven oaks planted at Sevenoaks in Kent to mark the coronation of King Edward VII in 1902 were blown down.)

There had been nothing like it in the Southeast since the Great Storm of 1703, when Daniel Defoe noted 17,000 uprooted trees in Kent alone before he gave up counting. The climate here may be notoriously unpredictable, but it is not usually given to such extremes. Like the English people, the gentleness of the landscape can be deceptive; history has shown that both are tough enough to survive almost anything.

MAJOR INTEREST

Westerham and the Weald
Chartwell (Churchill)
Great houses of Kent
Long Barn (The Nicolsons)

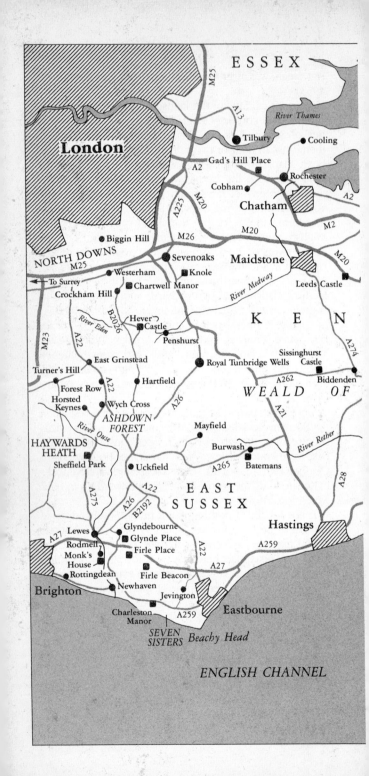

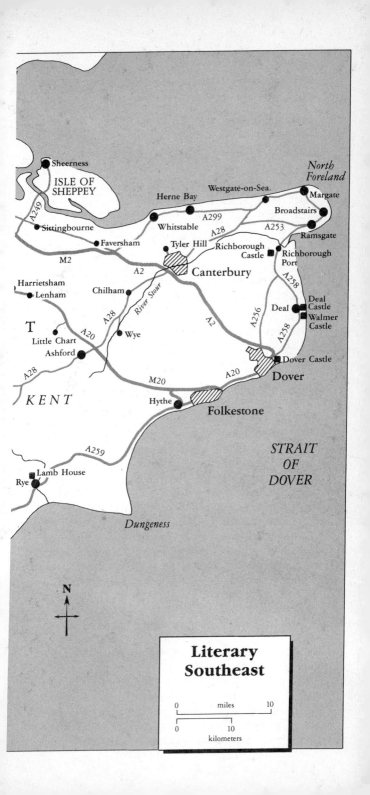

Literary Southeast

| 0 | miles | 10 |

| 0 | 10 | |
kilometers

N

STRAIT
OF
DOVER

*North
Foreland*

Margate
Broadstairs
Ramsgate

Westgate-on-Sea
A253

Herne Bay
Whitstable
A299
A28

Richborough
Castle
Richborough
Port

Sheerness
ISLE OF
SHEPPEY

A249

Sittingbourne
Faversham
M2

Tyler Hill
Canterbury
A2

Harrietsham
Lenham
Chilham
A28
River Stour
A2

A256

Deal
Castle
Walmer
Castle

A258

T
Little Chart
Ashford
A20
Wye

KENT

A28

M20
Hythe
A20
Folkestone

Dover Castle
Dover

A259

Lamb House
Rye

Dungeness

Pilgrims Way
Canterbury

Dickens Country
Medway towns and Broadstairs
The Channel coast

Sussex by the Sea
Batemans (Kipling)
Rye (Henry James, E. F. Benson)
Charleston and Monk's House (Virginia Woolf,
    et al.)
Arundel and Amberley

Surrey
Abinger Hammer (E. M. Forster)
Hog's Back and Devil's Punch Bowl

Hampshire Borders
Chawton (Jane Austen)
Selborne (Reverend Gilbert White)

WESTERHAM AND THE WEALD

A few miles east of Gatwick Airport on M 25, the motor-way that orbits London, signs indicate the turning-off point for Chartwell and Hever Castle, a convenient gate-way to the Weald of Kent, which Winston Churchill loved so much. Chartwell, where Churchill lived for more than 40 years, lies among the wooded hills two miles to the south of **Westerham**, a country town to which peace has returned now that much of the heavy traffic bypasses it on the motorway. William Pitt the Younger used a timbered cottage on the outskirts of Westerham as a summer home. General James Wolfe, who died at age 32 on the Plains of Abraham at Quebec in 1759 while wresting control of Canada from the French, spent part of his childhood in the town, in a gabled 17th-century house that is now a museum of this epic expedition. Mementos of his life can be seen among the fine paintings, furniture, tapestries, and china. General Wolfe's statue shares the town square with another, of Winston Churchill.

Three miles north of the town on A 233, which scales the steep bank of the North Downs, is Biggin Hill, one of the airfields from which Churchill's Few took off in their Spitfires and Hurricanes to do battle with the Luftwaffe in the skies over Kent in the summer of 1940. Biggin Hill was also the control center for Sector "C" of the Royal Air Force Fighter Command during the Battle of Britain and, as such, came under heavy air attack. A chapel stands on the site of one of the bombed hangars, in commemoration of pilots and ground crew who lost their lives.

Chartwell Manor

Churchill bought this old manor house, riddled with dry rot, in 1922 for the marvelous views from its hill down to the wooded valley. The Churchills moved in two years later, after it had been reconstructed with a new wing (which the young statesman called "my promontory") and many French doors, making house and garden one. It was now a fine mansion with five reception rooms, 19 bedrooms and dressing rooms, eight bathrooms, and three cottages on 80 acres. "Winnie" dug out ornamental ponds, lakes, and a heated, floodlit swimming pool. He created waterfalls and erected a brick wall around the kitchen garden with his own hands—for which he was invited to become an "adult apprentice" in the builders' trade union; he accepted.

Between the ages of 55 and 65, Churchill produced a stream of books, including *My Early Life: A Roving Commission,* with its nostalgia for a glorious past when Britannia ruled the waves; *World Crisis,* a history in several volumes of World War I and a vindication of his own part in it; *Thoughts and Adventures,* a collection of his best newspaper articles; *Great Contemporaries,* biographical essays; and, most ambitiously, a multivolume life of his ancestor, the Duke of Marlborough. His *History of the English-speaking Peoples,* begun in 1938, was interrupted by World War II and was completed and published in four volumes after it, together with his entirely subjective account, *The Second World War.*

Most of this work was done at Chartwell, hardly the lonely writer's garret. Churchill commanded large fees, and he employed a researcher and a whole team of secretaries whom he worked at a ferocious pace, starting when he sat up in bed early in the day and finishing at three or four the following morning as he paced up and down, still dictating (the track worn across the carpet in his study is visible). The rooms still seem to echo with Churchill's voice and the laughter and conversation that animated the dinners attended by a continual flood of visitors, from government officers and academics to foreign statesmen, newspaper owners, and celebrities such as Charlie Chaplin.

House and garden were a source of delight to Churchill through all the years he lived there, until his death at the age of 90.

Hever Castle

From the summit of Crockham Hill near Chartwell, the Weald spreads out in green and brown patchwork south and southeast to the horizon. There are so many fine historic houses within the area that it would take a week to visit them all. Hever Castle, 5 miles south of Chartwell and up a small lane off B 2026, or an hour by train from London to the tiny local Hever station, should not be missed. In Tudor times it was the home of the Bullen (or Boleyn) family, and it was here that Henry VIII wooed Anne Boleyn. The original moated manor, dating from the 13th century, was bought by William Waldorf Astor in 1903, restored, and surrounded by a newly built village in mock Tudor style. Astor created an Italian garden with classical statues and sculptures, including a carved marble relief that was part of the triumphal arch erected by Rome's Emperor Claudius in A.D. 51 at Richborough on the Kent coast to mark his conquest of Britain. This treasure, one of only two surviving remnants of the arch (the other is in the Louvre in Paris), is now displayed inside Hever Castle. Its American owner took British citizenship and became the first Viscount Astor of Hever. The Astors still live at Hever Castle.

Penshurst Place

An old stone bridge crosses the River Eden at Hever. A few miles downriver, where the Eden flows into the River Medway, is Penshurst Place, which can be reached either on B 2176 or, if you can read an Ordnance Survey map, through a variety of delightful but unclassified lanes that play hide-and-seek with the river among the woods and meadows. The stately edifice where the Elizabethan soldier, poet, and statesman Sir Philip Sidney was born is entered through Leicester Square, named after the Earl of Leicester. The Great Hall, with its minstrels' gallery and armor, goes back to the 14th century. Penshurst is the ancestral home of the Sidney family, and Viscount de

L'Isle continues the family tradition as a soldier (he won the Victoria Cross at Anzio), a diplomat, and a landowner.

The **Spotted Dog** at Smarts Hill, half a mile from Penshurst, is a charming old Kentish clapboard pub with a terrace looking over the Weald. A traditional Sunday lunch is served in the low-beamed bar, and a variety of tasty pub food, including Speldhurst sausage, is available at all times. The pub is very popular with locals, so it is advisable to book in advance for sit-down meals in the restaurant (Tel: 0892-87-02-53).

Knole

Another ancestral home, begun in the middle of the 15th century by the then Archbishop of Canterbury and given by Queen Elizabeth I to courtier-poet Thomas Sackville in 1603, is Knole, on the outskirts of the country town of **Sevenoaks** on A 225, 12 miles north of Penshurst. The Sackville-Wests still live there, although the mansion and its furnishings, tapestries, silverware, and paintings, including portraits by Reynolds and Gainsborough, have been given to the National Trust. Knole, which stands in a great park where deer roam freely, was described by Virginia Woolf in her novel *Orlando* as "a town rather than a house," a fitting description of a building that covers three acres and has seven courtyards, one for each day of the week; 52 staircases, one for each week of the year; and 365 rooms, one for every day of the year. Virginia Woolf's friend Vita Sackville-West, also a writer, grew up here.

Sissinghurst Castle
and Long Barn

Vita and her husband, the diarist, biographer, diplomat, and politician Harold Nicolson, created two other notable houses and gardens in the Weald. Two years after their marriage in 1913 they bought 15th-century Long Barn, where William Caxton is said to have been born. They extended and developed it, and laid out a garden with the help of Edwin Lutyens. It is 2 miles south of Sevenoaks, off A 21, but it is not open to visitors.

In the 1930s the Nicolsons bought and restored Sissinghurst Castle. Visitors can see the first-floor room in which Vita Sackville-West wrote her poetry, with a view of the garden, and also her library. Sissinghurst is richly furnished with polished oak and Persian carpets and its gardens are still acclaimed as some of Britain's finest. (Sissinghurst is just off A 262 near the village of Biddenden.)

THE PILGRIMS WAY

"He knew the tavernes wel in every toun," wrote Geoffrey Chaucer in the prologue of his *Canterbury Tales,* and 600 years after the words were written, there are as many old villages and pubs along the Pilgrims Way. To follow the route taken by the Medieval pilgrims across the shoulder of the North Downs from Winchester, the ancient Saxon capital, to Canterbury still calls for good boots and a stout heart, but the way is marked. For much of its length, the Pilgrims Way crosses open country, over fields and through woods that have never known tarmacadam or concrete. The nearest modern roads heading in more or less the same direction are the M 20 motorway and the M 25 London Orbital, which passes just north of Sevenoaks at Junction 5.

Beyond Maidstone, the Pilgrims Way passes near **Leeds Castle**, built in the 12th century from the original ninth-century fortress in the middle of a lake, and still in use for high-security summit meetings. Lord Culpepper, who was the governor of Virginia from 1680 to 1683, used Leeds Castle as his English country seat after Henry VIII had converted it into one of his many royal palaces. It contains superb Medieval accoutrements, French and English furniture, tapestries, and Impressionist paintings, and has a newly planted maze of 3,000 yew trees.

Ringlestone, one of those marvelous inns that Chaucer would recognize, with its blackened beams, brick floors, and a fireplace with an inglenook, is a mile or so farther along A 20 at **Harrietsham**. If you are looking for a simple place to stay the night, as well as good food and wine, the **Harrow Inn** at Warren Street, just off A 20 and close to the M 2, was once a forge and a resting place for pilgrims going to Canterbury. Nowadays the fare it serves is far from simple—venison in cherry and wine sauce or beef and pheasant casserole, for instance—and it uses local produce. There are just seven bedrooms, four of which have private baths.

Eastwell Manor, on the other hand, offers elegance in its oak-paneled bar and baronial dining room. A period mansion on 3,000 acres of private parkland just outside Ashford, it was completely rebuilt in the 1920s. The bedrooms are huge and the bathrooms sumptuous. It is, of course, expensive, as is the **Ashford Post House** on the Canterbury Road at Ashford, which incorporates a 15th-century manor house with a 17th-century barn converted into a restaurant. **Ashford**, a cattle-market town and railway center, is due to become the passenger terminus of the Eurotunnel, with parking for 6,000 vehicles, but until the tunnel's completion in 1993 the countryside around it slumbers on.

Timeless villages with broad greens where cricket is played on weekends, oasthouses with white cowls where hops are dried for the breweries, and apple orchards that burst into oceans of pink and white in May are the stuff of H. E. Bates novels. Bates made his home at **Little Chart**, a few miles west of Ashford, the site of a large green (known in these parts as a *forstal*) where cattle were penned or forestalled before going to market in Ashford.

At **Chilham** (a few miles north of Ashford), a village dating from Medieval times, a "pilgrims' fayre" is held on Spring Bank Holiday, with local people in costume setting up market stalls. The main street leads past a carved-timber Wealden house to the **Woolpack Inn**, where the oak-beamed bar is hung with hop vines and ancient pews are arranged around the inglenook fireplace. Roast beef and steak, Guinness, and oyster pie are served. There are 14 bedrooms, three in converted stables, eight in a separate building across the courtyard, and the remainder in the original inn.

Canterbury

From Chilham, it's 6 miles north on A 28 to Canterbury, whose splendid cathedral tower, "Bell Harry," can be seen from afar across the Garden of England, whether you approach from inland or from the white cliffs that guard the coast. The cathedral has been the mother church of English Christianity since Pope Gregory sent Saint Augustine here in A.D. 597. Saint Augustine (not the Augustine of the *City of God*) founded the abbey that bears his name outside the city walls and started another church on what is believed to be an earlier Roman site beneath the nave of the present Norman cathedral. Six hundred years later an event occurred that was to make Canterbury a center of pilgrimage and inspire great writers: murder in the cathedral. On December 29, 1170, Archbishop Thomas à Becket was waylaid and assassinated by four knights who had overheard King Henry III cry out in frustration, "Who will deliver me from this turbulent priest?"

The response of Rome was to make Becket a martyr-saint and start the procession of pilgrims, which continued over the next 400 years until Henry VIII, breaking with Rome, denounced Becket for "treason, contumacy, and rebellion." The pilgrims came to pray at two hallowed places—the spot in the northwest transept where the knights cut Becket down, and his tomb in the crypt. Vials containing watered-down drops of Becket's blood were sought as relics and charms because it was believed he had died in the name of Jesus and in defense of the Church.

Soon after Becket's murder, a fire destroyed the Norman choir and the chapel beneath which his tomb lay. Stone was shipped from Caen up the River Stour to William of Sens, who created an early Gothic cathedral and shrine of St. Thomas the Martyr on the site. When William was crippled after falling from scaffolding, William the Englishman took over and completed Trinity Chapel. The feet and knees of pilgrims wore grooves in the mosaic tiles in this holy place; not even Henry VIII could erase these marks of devotion. Nor did Henry destroy the chapel's 12 inspiring stained-glass windows showing the miracles of Christ and some of the cures attributed to the murdered archbishop. These windows represented to unlettered pilgrims a "Poor Man's Bible."

A new exhibition in the Medieval **Church of St. Margaret**, a short walk from the cathedral gatehouse, employs the latest visual, aural, and olfactory technology to give 20th-century visitors a taste of what it was like to be a pilgrim in Chaucer's time and travel on foot from the Tabard Inn at Southwark in London to the martyr's tomb. The work of Heritage Projects, which created the Jorvik Viking Center (see the York chapter), it re-creates Chaucer's band of travellers: the Reeve, the "verray parfit gentil Knight," the beery, blowsy Wife of Bath, and others—warts and all—including a drunken reveler with pockmarked face recalling "So was hir joly whistle wel y-wet." Whether or not you approve of Chaucer's masterpiece being turned into a "pop-up book," the project should help spread appreciation of Chaucer's work and the story of Becket.

Holograms and computers play a part in the City Council's Canterbury Heritage Exhibition in the 13th-century **Poor Priests' Hospital**, on the banks of the Stour just off the High Street. The visitor is conducted on a walk through time, viewing silver spoons left by the Romans, *mazers* (drinking bowls) from Medieval hospitals, a fully threaded loom of the Huguenots, who made Canterbury famous as a weaving town, and a re-creation of the fire-bomb Blitz of 1942, which destroyed a quarter of the city.

Parts of the city are still enclosed within Medieval walls, and the keep of the ancient castle survives, together with the ancient buildings lining the narrow streets that defied the ravages of the Luftwaffe. The King's School, clustered around Green Court behind the cathedral, numbers among its former pupils the Elizabethan dramatist Christopher Marlowe (who was born, the son of a shoemaker, in Canterbury) and Somerset Maugham. The University of Kent, founded in 1961, surveys the panorama of history from a hill named after Wat Tyler, who led the Peasants' Revolt 600 years ago.

There are numerous old Canterbury inns that the pilgrims knew, but none is more welcoming than the **Falstaff Hotel**, in St. Dunstan's Street beside West Gate. It was built in the 15th century and, despite modernization of its 24 bedrooms, has preserved its oak beams and paneling. The inn serves hearty, old-fashioned English food such as steak-and-kidney pudding. The **County Hotel** in High Street is the most central choice, and its restaurant, **Sullys**, is recommended. But for the region's finest English and French cooking (duck roasted with apples and served with a brandy sauce, perhaps) and a wine list of impressive variety, drive 10 miles out to the **Wife of Bath Restaurant** in Wye, off A 28 in the direction of Ashford.

DICKENS COUNTRY

North of Maidstone back near Sevenoaks, Pilgrims Way loops across the River Medway by the same bridge that carries the modern M 2 motorway toward the Channel ports. The Romans came this way after invading the Kent coast at Richborough and put up a bridge downriver from the modern motorway. The town the Romans established here, Durobrivae, now **Rochester**, grew as a staging post on Watling Street, the great highway across England. When the Normans invaded, they too grasped the strategic situation of Rochester and built a castle, the keep of which survives. In due course they replaced the adjacent Saxon church, the second-oldest bishopric in Britain (after Canterbury), with a building that forms the core of the existing modest cathedral. In the south transept there is a brass memorial to the writer who spent the impressionable years of his childhood and the later part of his life in or near this city, and used it in several of his novels.

When Charles Dickens lived here, between the ages of 5 and 10, Rochester had already merged with its bustling neighbor, Chatham, a dockyard with a long history of building warships, from those that defeated the Spanish Armada to H.M.S. *Victory,* the flagship at Trafalgar. Indeed, a young midshipman named Horatio Nelson joined his first ship, H.M.S. *Raisonnable,* here. Today the fleet has gone, and **Chatham Historic Dockyard**, with its 18th-century ropewalk and the mid-Victorian steam sloop H.M.S. *Gannet,* is open to visitors.

Charles Dickens was born at Portsmouth in a little terraced house in Old Commercial Road, now a museum. His father, who moved the family to Rochester when Charles was five, was a navy pay clerk who sometimes took his son with him as he went about his official business. Charles watched the ropemakers and smelled the tar, stood under the wooden walls on the slips amid oak chips and wood shavings, and sailed down the river to Sheerness and the Thames, passing the black hulks where convicts awaited transportation to Botany Bay. Red-coated soldiers paraded in Chatham Lines on the hill above the town, and in the High Street was Simpson's coach office, operating the Blue-Eyed Maid along the old Roman road to London. The massive square **keep of Rochester Castle** offered then, as now, captivating views of the Medway estuary, the North Downs, and the cathedral to anyone willing to climb the 150 steps to the top.

The Bull Inn, where Mr. Pickwick stayed, and the Blue Boar of *Great Expectations* were, and are, none other than the **Royal Victoria and Bull**, a 400-year-old coaching inn that is still open as a hotel and that serves you good plain English food, in the High Street. Miss Havisham's haunting, cobwebbed Satis House is in reality the 16th-century Restoration House in Maidstone Road, but it is not open to visitors.

On rural outings, with father orating all the way, the Dickenses went as far as **Cobham** on the Dover–London road (A 2) and visited the church of **St. Mary Magdalene** (boasting the finest collection of Medieval brass memorials to knights in armor and their ladies in England) and the half-timbered **Leather Bottle Inn**, still open for drink and food, which later became a setting in *Pickwick Papers*. **Cobham Hall**, an Elizabethan red-brick manor with a broad colonnaded front, is today a girls' school, but it is open to visitors at certain times during school breaks. Its octagonal corner towers and array of chimneys remain as they were when Dickens senior and junior admired them on their walks, before entering the shadowy glades of Cobham Wood to come out, two miles farther on, by Gad's Hill, where Falstaff waylaid travellers. Here the boy feasted his eyes on the white portico of an ivy-fronted rose-brick mansion overlooking the valley of the Medway—**Gad's Hill Place**—where John Dickens told his son that he might one day live if he worked very, very hard. Indeed, after using many of the images planted in his head as a child in his brilliantly successful novels, Dickens bought Gad's Hill and lived there for 14 years until his death.

Gad's Hill Place is not open to the public, but the Swiss chalet that Dickens installed on the grounds has been moved to the **Dickens Centre** in Eastgate House on High Street in Rochester. Eastgate House figures in his last, unfinished work, *The Mystery of Edwin Drood,* as the Nun's House, Cloisterham. Dickens, who loved dramatics and reading his own works on stage, would surely approve of the theatrical display of some of his unforgettable characters at the center, which uses a sound and light show to bring them vividly to life.

The Lonely Shore

To the north of Rochester and Chatham, between the estuaries of the Medway and the Thames, is a mysterious area of creeks and marshes, ditches and mud flats, where herons fly over the ancient Hundred of Hoo and there are no major roads (the "Hundred" is the name formerly given to a subdivision of a county in England). Tankers, container ships, and the occasional passenger liner pass by on their way to and from Tilbury. Oil refineries glow on the Essex shore across the Thames estuary, and the long pier of Southend-on-Sea can be seen in the distance on a clear day, but it is hard to believe that this desolate place is a mere 40 miles from central London.

In the churchyard at **Cooling**, 13 stones mark the graves of the children of the Comport family from Decoy Farm who died from marsh fever. Dickens, venturing out from Gad's Hill Place in search of atmosphere, found it here and described it in the opening chapter of *Great Expectations,* when young Pip startles Magwitch, an escaped convict hiding among the gravestones. The place has lost none of its atmosphere of brooding isolation, especially when the wind is sighing through the reeds. Cooling was the setting of Joe Gargery's forge. As you go eastward from Rochester and Chatham, along the northern edge of Kent, the scene is altogether more hospitable, more as Mr. Jingle described in *Pickwick Papers:* "Kent, sir—everybody knows Kent— apples, cherries, hops, and women." The M 2 dashes on, but several delightful places may be reached via the old Roman road to Dover. These include **Sittingbourne**, where ocher-sailed, tarred Thames barges can be admired at the Dolphin Yard, and **Faversham**, where Shepherd Neame has been brewing ale from local hops since the 16th century.

A branch (A 299) off the old Dover Road brings you to the seaside town of **Whitstable**. Sample the "Whitstable Natives" (oysters) at **Wheeler's Oyster Bar**, with views across the bay to the Isle of Sheppey. Next are Herne Bay, Westgate-on-Sea, and Margate. As you follow A 299 around the headland of North Foreland, where for nearly five centuries a light has warned ships of the treacherous Goodwin Sands just offshore, you come to Broadstairs. This is the resort where Dickens spent many of his summers, writing feverishly and enjoying the "rare good sands," as he called them, and the brisk and bracing air.

Broadstairs

According to Dickens, Broadstairs at the North Foreland "beat all other watering places." When Dickens first took his wife and infant son here for a long summer holiday in 1837, it was little more than a fishing village at the edge of the chalk cliffs. "I have walked upon the sands at low-water, from this place to Ramsgate," Dickens wrote in a letter at the time, "and sat upon the same at high-ditto till I have been flayed with cold. I have seen ladies and gentlemen walking upon the earth in slippers of buff, and pickling themselves in the sea in complete suits of the same. I have seen stout gentlemen looking at nothing through powerful telescopes for hours."

Dickens was 25 and already famous for *Pickwick,* which was into its final installments. *Oliver Twist* was pouring out of him, and in the following year he would undertake his investigation of the notorious Yorkshire schools that led to *Nicholas Nickleby.* He wrote the last lines at two o'clock on the afternoon of September 20, 1839, in a rented house overlooking the sea, and immediately dashed off to Ramsgate to send the copy to the printers in London.

Among the places he rented here were 37 Albion Street and Lawn House, and while the family members were getting "as brown as berries" and Broadstairs filled with his friends, *The Old Curiosity Shop* and *Barnaby Rudge* flowed from his writing table. He wrote most of *David Copperfield,* his "favorite child," in a house built like a fort on the cliff overlooking Viking Bay. It is now known as **Bleak House**, and, like the **Dickens House Museum** nearby, it contains fascinating memorabilia of the author. Indeed, there are reminders of Dickens at every corner of this charming town, with its little harbor and sandy beach protected by a small pier.

The Channel Coast

It is possible to walk, as Dickens did, from Broadstairs south to the busy harbor of **Ramsgate** along the sands at low tide. From here all the way south along the Channel to Hythe the coast is at once a fortress and a gateway to the Continent, which can be seen in clear weather across the narrow **Strait of Dover**. The **North Downs Way**, a trail 141 miles in length across Surrey and Kent from Farnham to Dover, crosses rivers and highways. The middle part of it follows the Pilgrims Way, but it continues beyond Canterbury just south of Dover Harbor to the sea at Shakespeare Cliff, a massive chalk headland 300 feet high with a dizzying view over the Channel that is described in *King Lear* and is now the scene of Channel tunnel work.

This natural ditch has been England's bastion against invasion since the Normans came, and it was reinforced by formidable castles at Dover, Walmer, and Deal. The ruined castle at **Richborough** (just south of Ramsgate and Pegwell Bay), the main landing place for the invading forces of Emperor Claudius in A.D. 43, was last used for coastal defenses in World War II—when soldiers on guard duty reported seeing whole cohorts of ghostly Roman legions marching into the sea. There are traces of the foundations of the enormous triumphal arch that would have been visible for miles out to sea (a fragment of it is kept at Hever Castle), and ancient coins, ornaments, and weapons are displayed in the museum on the site.

Large vehicle-carrying ferries and Hovercraft shuttle back and forth across the Channel from **Dover** and **Folkestone**, the twin gateways in the wall of chalk. Between these and Ramsgate there is a long stretch of sand dunes that forms a 700-acre wild bird reserve, the Sandwich Bay Nature Reserve, and provides the setting for three championship golf courses: the Royal Cinque Ports, Royal St. George's, and Prince's. Ian Fleming, the creator of James Bond, liked to relax here, and he used the background for 007's game in *Goldfinger*.

SUSSEX BY THE SEA

Around on the English southern coast west of the promontory of Dungeness, where two nuclear power stations rear up from misty marshes, is the town of Rye (see below), guarded by a Medieval gateway. West from Rye, the outer edge of the chalk oval shows itself again in white cliffs flanking the seaside towns of Hastings and Eastbourne, with their piers, promenades, and bandstands, and reaches a magnificent crescendo in the Seven Sisters beyond Beachy Head, where the **South Downs Way** begins its long haul west to Hampshire. The cliffs stand between the open sea and the wide expanse of what Kipling called "our blunt, bow-headed, whale-backed Downs."

Six miles inland from Eastbourne by A 259 and B 2105, signposted to Jevington, is the **Hungry Monk**, a secluded restaurant in extended Elizabethan cottages serving sublime food and wines at very reasonable prices. It is open for dinner only and Sunday lunch, and advance booking is essential; Tel: (03212) 2178.

Kipling Country

Rudyard Kipling brilliantly fused the present and the past of Sussex in *Puck of Pook's Hill,* when two children act out their version of *A Midsummer Night's Dream* as Puck conjures a Roman centurion, Viking raiders, a Norman knight, a Renaissance craftsman, and smugglers. Kipling loved Sussex so much—"Yea, Sussex by the sea!"—that he spent the second half of his life here, between world travels.

The Elms, where Kipling lived with his wife and three young children at the turn of the century, is perched on the cliff top at **Rottingdean** just east of Brighton, with the Downs behind it. It faces the village green and duck pond near the Plough Inn. **The Grange**, next door, is a museum of Kipling letters, manuscripts, and books. Kipling scoured East Sussex with his wife in one of the early automobiles (which often broke down) looking for a country seat. They found what they were looking for, among the "trees and green fields and mud and the gentry," just outside the village of **Burwash**, about half-way between Eastbourne on the coast and Royal Tunbridge Wells to the north.

Batemans, the solid Jacobean mansion built by a 17th-century ironmaster, lies at the end of a lane that Kipling described as "an enlarged rabbit hole." He bought Batemans in 1902 and lived there for the next 34 years. It is half a mile off A 265, the way clearly marked by signs. The hedgerows are trimmed back, but otherwise it is as Kipling left it. His 1928 Phantom I Rolls-Royce stands in the garage. A short walk through the garden and over a stream brings you to the ancient water mill mentioned by Kipling in *Puck of Pook's Hill* and restored by him to provide electricity for his country estate. Beside it, one of the oldest water-driven turbines in the world now stands idle, but once a week the great spur wheel and hurstings still grind whole-wheat flour for sale to visitors.

Kipling and his wife laid out the formal garden, beyond which—over a hedge clipped into the shape of battlements—are the meadows, streams, and woods he so lovingly described. The views are framed in the mullioned windows of the gabled stone house, in which a timber staircase leads to a book-lined study and the French walnut table "ten feet long from north to south and badly congested" at which Kipling wrote *If* and *Puck*.

The exit road from Batemans emerges at the end of the tile-hung and weather-boarded High Street of Burwash. Among the inscriptions on the village war memorial is "Lieut. John Kipling, 2nd Irish Guards, killed 29 September 1915, aged 18." Kipling never wholly recovered from the loss of his only son on the field of Flanders. Opposite the memorial and the Norman Church of St. Bartholomew is the 17th-century **Bell Inn**, where apple logs burn in the grate, pints of Harveys and King & Barnes are drawn by hand pump, and the accents around the dart board are distinctively Sussex. There are five simple yet comfortable guest bedrooms, one of them so old that the floor slopes beneath the low oak beams. Even older, and boasting oak carvings by Grinling Gibbons, is the **Middle House Hotel** in the nearby village of Mayfield on what used to be the London-to-coast road (A 267). Good food is served in comfortable surroundings.

Rye

Kipling often drove down the road that winds along the border between East Sussex and Kent and along the River Rother to Rye at the coast southeast of Burwash to visit Henry James at **Lamb House**. Stephen Crane, who settled nearby at Hastings, and H. G. Wells would drop by, too, and talk away sunny afternoons in the walled garden of the unpretentious two-story red-brick house that stands on a bend of West Street leading out of Church Square. E. F. Benson, whose Mapp and Lucia novels are set in Rye, lived in the house later, under the name of Tilling. The Garden Room, where James wrote *The Ambassadors, The Wings of the Dove,* and *The Golden Bowl,* was wrecked during a World War II air raid, and there is little physical evidence of his tenure from 1898 to 1914. But out of season, when what he called the "various summer super-numeraries" have gone, it is still easy to see why, having been to the far end of Florida, the writer preferred this far end of Sussex.

The **Mermaid Inn** here in quaint Mermaid Street (re-built in 1420) contains priest holes and a secret staircase dating from the days when it was a notorious haunt for smugglers. Queen Elizabeth really did sleep here—in 1573.

In High Street, opposite the old grammar school that figures in Thackeray's *Denis Duval,* the **George Hotel** keeps up the coaching-inn tradition of comfortable rooms and good food, especially with fish delivered fresh from nearby Hastings. The banquet hall has a minstrels' gallery, and logs blaze in cavernous fireplaces. The George con-tains timber from one of Drake's "wooden walls," or wood-built ships, broken up at Rye after the defeat of the Spanish Armada. The sea is now two miles away, but Rye has managed to stay active.

Ashdown Forest

The pretty road from London toward Lewes (A 22) runs through East Grinstead, near which are several notable hotels in substantial grounds. Two, **Alexander House** and **Gravetye Manor**, are historic houses with lovely gardens (those of the latter were created by the horticulturist William Robinson when he owned the estate). Expect to pay for *haute cuisine* served in a gracious style. **Effingham Park** is on 40 peaceful acres only five minutes from Gatwick Airport. Its amenities include a leisure club, a nine-hole golf course designed by Francisco Escario, and a collection of vintage and classic cars.

From East Grinstead the A 22 road continues through Forest Row, a country town, and Ashdown Forest, a remnant of the Roman forest of Anderida, once a center of the Wealden iron industry. This is A. A. Milne and **Winnie the Pooh country**. Just outside the village of Hartfield, a couple of miles to the east of Forest Row, is a 100-acre wood, Piglet's Quarry, and, hidden up a trail, Pooh Bridge, from which you can drop sticks in the rushing stream and then race them. The "enchanted place" of *The House at Pooh Corner* is Gills Lap, at the very top of the forest, from where you can see "the whole world spread out until it reached the sky."

At Wych Cross, the right fork (A 275) goes via Sheffield Park and its magnificent gardens with five lakes laid out by Capability Brown. This is one end of the Bluebell Railway (which makes a five-mile run through lovely countryside to Horsted Keynes). The A 275 continues to Lewes.

Lewes

The steep, narrow streets of this town, which can be reached by rail from London via Haywards Heath in one minute over the hour, are paved with literary and historical associations. **Southover Grange** in Keere Street, part of Anne of Cleves's divorce settlement with Henry VIII, was once the home of the diarist John Evelyn, "a studious decliner of honours and titles," and the **White Hart Hotel** on High Street was where Thomas Paine held the debating club that he was later to call the cradle of American independence. The White Hart offers present-day debaters 19 bedrooms and Harveys real ale, but **Shelleys Hotel** nearby, in a 17th-century manor with private gardens, is

the best hotel in town, if rather more expensive. Lewes is
a lively, sturdy place set in a hollow of the Downs and a
convenient base for exploring the countryside that some
of the most influential figures in post-Victorian arts made
their own: Virginia Woolf and her husband, Leonard, the
critic Clive Bell, and the biographer Lytton Strachey; painters such as Duncan Grant, Vanessa Bell, and Roger Fry
(who was also an art critic); and the economist John Maynard Keynes. Most of them had known one another at
Cambridge before they lived and loved together in
Bloomsbury and here in East Sussex.

Charleston

Virginia Woolf discovered this 18th-century farmhouse in
the shadow of Firle Beacon, the highest point on the
Downs east of Lewes, before the period between the wars
when she wrote her seminal novels. Several fine houses lie
in the shelter of the steep north-facing slope, including
Firle Place, the home of the Gages, one of whose ancestors,
General Thomas Gage, was commander-in-chief of the
British forces at the outset of the American Revolution; the
16th-century Glynde Place; and nearby **Glyndebourne
Manor**, famed for its summer opera season. (Just north of
here toward Uckfield on the A 26 is **Horsted Place**, an
outstanding Victorian mansion now run as a top-class ho-
tel. It was sold in 1983 following the death of Lord Rupert
Nevill, whose wife has been closely associated with the
Glyndebourne Festival.)

Virginia Woolf was much taken with Charleston and
told her sister Vanessa and her sister's husband, Clive Bell:
"If you lived there you could make it absolutely divine."
The Bells took her advice and moved in, together with
Duncan Grant, painting every surface—fireplaces, bed-
steads, bookcases, tables—with loose swirls and messy
colors in divine inspiration. The walled garden is filled
with sculpture and mosaics as much as with flowers and
shrubs. A restored Charleston is now open to the public,
echoing with the voices of T. S. Eliot, Lytton Strachey, the
Bells, and the Woolfs.

Monk's House

Leonard Woolf bought this modest house near the church
in the village of Rodmell, four miles southeast of Lewes,
for £700 just after World War I ended. It is now owned by

the National Trust but can admit no more than 15 people at a time. Although this was a retreat from the Woolfs' Georgian townhouse in Tavistock Square, London, in a sense Bloomsbury came with them—so many of their friends had houses or cottages in the area. Virginia spent the summer of 1924, as she did many summers, writing at Monk's House: "a very animated summer." She was on the threshold of confirming her own "queer individuality" as a novelist with the experimental *Mrs. Dalloway,* and women, as she remarked later in *A Room of One's Own,* were not supposed to compete with Shakespeare or to write novels. Seventeen years later, depressed by the bombing of her beloved London, she drowned herself, not far from Monk's House, in the Ouse, which flows through Lewes and down to the sea at Newhaven; her ashes were scattered in the garden of the house. Her husband stayed on at Monk's House until his death in 1969.

SURREY-HAMPSHIRE BORDER

The two halves of the chalk oval discussed earlier converge inside the Hampshire border in the direction of Salisbury Plain, which E. M. Forster considered to be the "heart of our island," and which we cover below in the chapter The Cotswolds to Winchester. He wrote in *The Longest Journey:* "The Chilterns, the North Downs, the South Downs radiate hence. The fibres of England unite in Wiltshire, and did we condescend to worship her, here we should erect our national shrine." His home, West Hackhurst, is at **Abinger Hammer** in Surrey, near the North Downs Way.

The curious name of this hamlet derives from an iron-forging hammer of the 16th century, which was powered by the fast-flowing stream that now feeds watercress beds. A clock overhanging the Dorking–Guildford road (easily reached from M 25) marks the site of the old forge, and the figure of a smith strikes the hours on the bell with a hammer. Abinger Hammer was one of the last places where the Surrey iron industry survived, but its origins go back to the Stone Age settlement excavated on the grounds of the Manor House in the 1950s.

Six miles to the north in Stoke d'Abernon (near the junction of A 3 and M 25) is an opulent 19th-century mansion that formerly belonged to the Bryants, a family

that made its fortune in the match industry. The house has now been expensively restored as the **Woodlands Park Hotel**. Edward VII and Lillie Langtry were often house-guests here when it was a private residence.

Beyond the old posting town of Guildford (another ornate clock overhangs its Georgian High Street), the road to Winchester (A 31) runs along a ridge known as the **Hog's Back**. Frensham Great Pond, one of the largest lakes in southern England, and the **Devil's Punch Bowl**, a depression scoured out of the landscape by running water, lie to the south, flanked by the Portsmouth road (A 3). **Frensham Pond Hotel** at the water's edge has an air of quiet exclusivity. Its amenities include an indoor swimming pool and squash courts. The country here is a mixture of woodland and wide expanses of heather that you can roam at will while admiring the distant views.

The **William Cobbett Inn**, a pub at **Farnham**, a Georgian red-brick country town of unsullied charm off A 31 west of Guildford, was formerly The Jolly Farmer. It was renamed in honor of the celebrated author of *Rural Rides,* who was born here in 1763. Cobbett, the son of a farmer, served in the army in Canada and worked as a teacher in the United States before coming home to start a weekly paper, the *Political Register.* An out-and-out radical, he championed the cause of farm laborers.

Cobbett is not the only literary figure connected with Farnham. Jonathan Swift wrote *Tale of a Tub* when he was secretary to Sir William Temple at Moor Park, which stands on the outskirts of the town. "Good God! What a genius I had when I wrote that book," he said later. At Moor Park he began his friendship with Hester Johnson, the subject of his *Journal to Stella,* published long before *Gulliver's Travels.*

Jane Austen Territory

The North Downs Way trail begins (or ends, depending in which direction you are walking it) at Farnham. Just out of town, A 31 leaves Surrey and crosses the rolling plain to the Hampshire town of Alton. A mile beyond is the village of **Chawton**, where Jane Austen spent the last eight years of her life. The two-story red-brick building here, originally an inn, was where she put the finishing touches to *Pride and Prejudice* and wrote in quick succession *Emma, Mansfield Park,* and *Persuasion.* The building is now a museum, furnished in early 19th-century style and

containing personal effects such as a patchwork quilt that Jane made with her mother and her desk, bureau, and music books. In the bakery is the cart that the family hitched to a donkey for the short trip into Alton. Just outside the garden wall, beside the Winchester road, are two oak trees planted by Jane in 1809 when the family moved in. She wrote at the time that the cottage "when complete, would all other houses beat." Although her brother Edward inherited a fine manor house in a wooded park outside the village, Jane lived happily in the brick cottage and anonymously published her acutely observant novels of middle-class provincial society. She is buried in the cathedral at Winchester, near Saint Swithun, who, according to local legend, governs the summer rainfall.

A mile or two south of Chawton on B 3006 is the village of **Selborne**, whose natural history was chronicled by the Reverend Gilbert White in his classic work, *Natural History and Antiquities of Selborne,* published in 1789. His house, **The Wakes**, which stands near the church and village green, is now a museum and library dedicated to White and to Captain Lawrence Oates, who died with Robert Falcon Scott on an expedition to the South Pole. White was born and died in this village, which remains virtually as it was. From the village, the Zig-Zag Path climbs to the top of a beech-covered hill called the Hanger, where White made many of the notes for his book. From this vantage point, he could see the slopes of the South Downs rolling away toward the southeast into West Sussex. The South Downs Way, which is accessible to horseback riders and cyclists as well as hikers, begins just a few miles away at Harting. It is just 80 miles east by this trail, along the crest of the hill range that forms the bottom half of the chalk oval, to meet the sea at the white cliffs of Beachy Head on the south coast.

Arundel Castle

A splendidly impressive Norman castle in a wooded park towers above the Medieval town of Arundel on the River Arun 20 miles west of Brighton on A 27. Arundel is the seat of the dukes of Norfolk, England's foremost Roman Catholic family, and the castle has a notable collection of paintings, including works by Van Dyck, Gainsborough, and Reynolds. The collection, along with apartments in the castle, may be toured by visitors.

The dukes also built the Gothic-style Roman Catholic cathedral of St. Philip Neri, the second most imposing feature of this small country town. **Pogey's** on Tarrant Street offers a complete contrast to the Medieval and Gothic surroundings with its Art Deco interior and inventive menu, which ranges from moderate to expensive.

Another historic castle (in the village of Amberley in the lee of the South Downs outside Arundel) became a hotel and restaurant in 1988. Its great walls, battlements, and oak portcullis are intact, yet every room (each named after a different Sussex castle) has its own Jacuzzi. **Amberley Castle** was attacked by Cromwell and twice visited by King Charles II. The barrel-vaulted dining room contains a fine Restoration mural of him and Catherine of Braganza. Some 36 acres of former chalk pits in the pretty thatched village have been turned into an open-air museum with its own narrow-gauge railway and a collection of industrial steam and diesel engines dating from 1880. The water meadows of the River Arun, habitat for a great variety of flora and fauna, including Bewick swans that fly in from Siberia every winter, are a nature reserve. There are seven hides, all of them suitable for disabled visitors, and wheelchairs can be borrowed without charge. Arundel and Amberley can be reached easily by rail from London's Victoria Station, or on A 29.

GETTING AROUND

All the places mentioned in this chapter are within an hour or so of central London by rail or road. The two major international airports of the region, Heathrow and Gatwick, are linked by the London Orbital Motorway (M 25) and provide convenient gateways for exploring the Southeast without becoming entangled in London traffic. The channel ports of Dover, Folkestone, and Newhaven are the entry points for those arriving from Europe, while Southampton (see the following chapter) handles the few long-distance passengers arriving by sea aboard the *QE2* and other liners. Most major car-rental companies have facilities at these ports and airports.

ACCOMMODATIONS REFERENCE

▶ **Alexander House.** Fen Place, **Turners Hill** RH10 4QD. Tel: (0342) 71-49-14; Telex: 95611; Fax: (0342) 71-73-28.

▶ **Amberley Castle. Amberley,** near Arundel BN18 9ND. Tel: (0798) 83-19-92; Fax: (0798) 83-19-98.

▶ **Ashford Post House.** Canterbury Road, **Ashford** TN24

8QQ. Tel: (0233) 62-57-90; Telex: 966685; Fax: (0233) 64-31-76; in U.S., (212) 541-4400 or (800) 223-5672.

▶ **Bell Inn.** High Street, **Burwash** TN19 7EH. Tel: (0435) 88-23-04.

▶ **County Hotel.** High Street, **Canterbury** CT1 2RX. Tel: (0227) 76-62-66; Telex: 965076; Fax: (0227) 45-15-12.

▶ **Eastwell Manor.** Eastwell Park, **Ashford** TN25 4HR. Tel: (0233) 63-57-51; Telex: 966281; Fax: (0233) 63-55-30; in U.S., (212) 535-9530 or (800) 223-5581.

▶ **Effingham Park Hotel.** Copthorne RH10 3EU. Tel: (0342) 71-49-94; Telex: 95649; Fax: (0342) 71-60-39.

▶ **Falstaff Hotel.** 8–12 St. Dunstan's Street, **Canterbury** CT2 8AF. Tel: (0227) 46-21-38; Telex: 96394; Fax: (0227) 46-35-25.

▶ **Frensham Pond Hotel.** Churt, near Farnham GU10 2QB. Tel: (0251) 25-31-75; Fax: (0251) 25-26-31.

▶ **George Hotel.** High Street, **Rye** TN31 7JP. Tel: (0797) 22-21-14; in U.S., (212) 541-4400 or (800) 223-5672; Fax: (0797) 22-40-65.

▶ **Gravetye Manor.** Vowels Lane, near **East Grinstead** RH19 4LJ. Tel: (0342) 81-05-67; Telex: 957239; Fax: (0342) 81-00-80.

▶ **Harrow Inn.** Warren Street, near **Lenham,** Maidstone ME17 2ED. Tel: (0622) 85-87-27.

▶ **Horsted Place.** Little Horsted, **Uckfield** TN22 5TS. Tel: (0825) 755-81. Telex: 95548; Fax: (0825) 754-59; in U.S., (312) 954-2944 or (800) 323-7308.

▶ **Mermaid Inn.** Mermaid Street, **Rye** TN31 7EU. Tel: (0797) 22-30-65; Telex: 957141.

▶ **Middle House Hotel.** High Street, **Mayfield** TN20 6AB. Tel: (0435) 87-21-46; Fax: (0435) 87-34-23.

▶ **Royal Victoria and Bull Hotel.** 16–18 High Street, **Rochester** ME1 1PT. Tel: (0634) 462-66; Fax: (0634) 83-23-12.

▶ **Shelleys Hotel.** High Street, **Lewes** BN7 1XS. Tel: (0273) 47-23-61; in U.S., (402) 493-4747 or (800) 44-UTELL; Fax: (0273) 48-31-52.

▶ **White Hart Hotel.** 55 High Street, **Lewes** BN7 1XE. Tel: (0273) 47-46-76; Telex: 878468; in U.S., (602) 954-7600 or (800) 528-1234; Fax: (0273) 47-66-95.

▶ **Woodlands Park Hotel.** Woodlands Lane, Stoke D'Abernon, **Cobham** KT11 3QB. Tel: (0372) 84-39-33; Telex: 919246; Fax: (0372) 84-27-04.

▶ **Woolpack Inn.** High Street, **Chilham** CT4 8DL. Tel: (0227) 73-02-08; Fax: (0227) 73-10-53.

THE WESSEX SHORE

WEST SUSSEX, HAMPSHIRE, DORSET

By Frank Dawes

Y ou will search in vain for the name Wessex on any modern map, but when the Normans crossed the Channel to invade England in 1066, this Saxon kingdom—extending inland from the south coast and the Isle of Wight and with its capital at Winchester (see The Cotswolds to Winchester)—was at the height of its power. Nine centuries later the same coast, stretching west from Sussex across Hampshire to Dorset and on to Devon, was the scene of preparations for a massive movement of Allied troops in the opposite direction to liberate Nazi-occupied France. Operation Overlord, the code name for the landings in Normandy on June 6, 1944, is commemorated by the Overlord Embroidery in the D-Day Museum at Portsmouth, an even more monumental piece of needlework than the Medieval Bayeux Tapestry that records William the Conqueror's triumphant expedition.

The Dorset coast is one of magnificent views from cliffs of chalk, sandstone, and limestone along crescent beaches ranging from golden sand to shingle to giant's pebbles. Other broad vistas open up inland, the folds of a cataclysmic convulsion millions of years ago, golden with gorse in spring and purple with the heather of late summer when rare species such as the brown and black Lulworth Skipper butterfly can be spotted. This is Thomas Hardy country. On Bulbarrow Hill, he wrote,

There are some heights in Wessex,
Shaped as if by a kindly hand,
For thinking, dreaming, dying on . . .

And this is as true today. Visitors come from every part of the globe to see for themselves the places that Hardy describes in his novels under fictitious names. "Sandbourne" is parvenu Bournemouth, still the queen of south-coast resorts as it was in Victorian times. East along the coast the great natural harbors of Southampton, Portsmouth, and Chichester, from which Britannia ruled the waves, are now given over to leisure and tourism, like that offshore chunk of England across the tidal Solent, the Isle of Wight. New industries have sprung up around these conurbations, whose housing estates spread farther and farther afield, but the 90,000 acres of the New Forest, so called by the early Norman kings who used it as a hunting ground, remain inviolate.

MAJOR INTEREST

Chichester
Cathedral
Roman palace

Portsmouth
Historic ships
D-Day Museum

Southampton
Queen Elizabeth II home port
Broadlands stately home

Isle of Wight
Cowes Regatta (birthplace of America's Cup)

New Forest
Wildlife, walks

Bournemouth
British seaside at its best

Dorset coast
Unspoiled scenery, wildlife, Coast Path

Dorchester
Thomas Hardy country

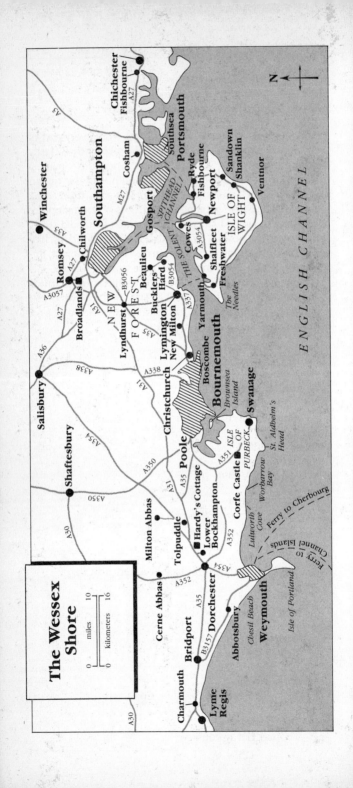

THE HARBOR CITIES
Chichester

A 16th-century Market Cross neatly marks the intersection of two straight Roman roads at the heart of this ancient city, ten miles west of Arundel (see Literary Southeast). Chichester was originally surrounded by a wall, parts of which, both Roman and Medieval, survive. The largest **Roman palace** uncovered in Britain (excavated in the 1960s) is at Fishbourne a mile to the west; it boasts 12 recently uncovered mosaic floors and a museum. The **cathedral** in the city center is Norman, with a 15th-century detached bell tower, the only one of its kind in England, and a Victorian-era spire (replacing the original one, which was blown down in a storm in 1861) that can be seen from afar. Among the cathedral's other notable features are an altar cloth by John Piper and windows by Marc Chagall. The buildings on the largely pedestrian-only streets around it are well-preserved Georgian and include the **Ship**, where General Dwight Eisenhower dined on the eve of D-Day. Originally built as a house for one of Nelson's admirals, it has 36 rooms for guests who like its casual Georgian style. Somewhat larger and up-dated with all the late 20th-century amenities is the **Dolphin & Anchor**, which faces the cathedral yet has parking. Chichester is famed today for the annual summer drama season in its Festival Theater, sited in a 40-acre park on the outskirts of town. The theater offers four plays a year from May to September that run the gamut from classical to modern and star such luminaries as Glenda Jackson and Vanessa Redgrave.

Chichester Harbour, reached from the town center by winding roads or canal, is a wide, landlocked lagoon divided by peninsulas with tidal creeks running off in all directions. It's a mecca for sailors, water-sports enthusiasts, anglers, and bird-watchers. One of the prettiest of the villages on its shores is **Bosham** (pronounced Bozzam), where King Canute is reputed to have ordered the tide to reverse to prove to his courtiers that he wasn't as powerful as they thought. The tide is as invincible as ever and is apt to submerge the cars of visitors who ignore warning notices.

Portsmouth

The A 27 road, skirting Chichester Harbour inland, crosses the Hampshire border west to Portsmouth, whose harbor has been the home base and fortress of British sea power since the 15th century. It has been known to generations of sailors as "Pompey," but today there are fewer warships to be seen than ever before and interest is focused on relics. It was Henry V who built the Round Tower at The Point, guarding the narrow entrance to the harbor from the Spithead channel. In 1545 Henry VIII, watching his fleet engage the French from the battlements of his newly built castle at nearby Southsea (now a seaside resort area), recoiled as his pride, the *Mary Rose*, suddenly keeled over for no apparent reason and went down with all hands. Four centuries later Prince Charles, having served at sea in the Royal Navy, led a remarkable salvage operation to raise *Mary Rose* from the seabed, and today its Tudor timbers are preserved for all to see under a fine spray of water inside a special hall that is the centerpiece of **Her Majesty's Dockyard** (entered through Victory Gate). Alongside the *Mary Rose* are Admiral Nelson's flagship, *Victory*, and *Warrior*, the world's first ironclad warship, dating from 1860 and restored to its former glory as the showpiece of Queen Victoria's navy. The First Fleet to the convict colony of Australia sailed from Portsmouth in 1788; today's voyages from the ferry terminal are to the nearer destinations of Le Havre and Cherbourg, Caen and St. Malo, and Guernsey and Jersey.

Portsmouth is rich in naval and military museums—the **Royal Naval Museum**, in a Georgian warehouse in the dockyard; the World War II submarine *Alliance* at Gosport, on the opposite side of the harbor mouth (crossed by ferry at The Hard, a boarding point near the Portsmouth railway station); at Southsea Castle, mentioned above; and at the Royal Marines' Eastney Barracks in Southsea, where the splendidly ornate Victorian officers' mess is on view. The seaside promenade here has a newer attraction in the **D-Day Museum**, which includes reconstructions and films of the invasion in which a million and a half Americans, British, and Canadians were transported across the Channel, as well as numerous exhibits and a gallery containing the **Overlord Embroidery**. It took 20 needlewomen five years to reconstruct this saga of our times in 34 panels (41 feet longer than the famous tapestry at Bayeux). Even the museum in the house at 393 Commercial Road, where

Charles Dickens was born in 1812, has a military connection, because his father was a navy pay clerk, although it now contains Dickens memorabilia.

Old Portsmouth is best explored on foot, as its streets are quite narrow and twisting. Three pubs you might stop in at for drinks or a bar lunch are **The Lively Lady**, **The Seagull**, and **The George Tavern**. This last, on Queen Street near the dockyard gates, dates to 1781 and specializes in dessert puddings.

The **Holiday Inn**, a newish hotel of 170 rooms with full facilities, stands alongside North Harbour at Cosham, nearly four miles from Old Portsmouth. The **Crest**, just as large and well equipped (including an indoor swimming pool), with rooms reserved for nonsmokers, is only a mile away overlooking the promenade at Southsea.

Southampton

Three gentle Hampshire rivers—the Test, Itchen, and Hamble—flow into the tidal Southampton Water, which is next door to Portsmouth Harbour and, until the advent of mass air travel, was the major gateway to Britain for those crossing the Atlantic. The *Queen Elizabeth II* and other ocean liners can still be seen arriving and departing on a double tide that first flows in from the Solent, the channel separating the mainland from the Isle of Wight (see below), and then two hours later from Spithead. Southampton Docks isn't what it was in its heyday, and the city fathers have been looking to their history to boost tourism revenue. The *Mayflower* set sail for the New World from Southampton in 1620, a fact that is emphasized by the Pilgrim Fathers Memorial near Royal Pier. Another memorial (in East Park) commemorates a much later and less propitious maiden voyage from Southampton—that of the *Titanic*. Unfortunately, much of old Southampton was flattened by bombing during World War II, but substantial sections of the Medieval walls and the old northern gate to the city (the Bargate) survived and are incorporated in the Town Walk Walkway, a signposted tour (brochures are available at the Visitors Centre). Imaginative use has been made of the few surviving buildings of antiquity; some are museums, while others have been developed as new marinas and shopping centers such as Ocean Village and Town Quay. They make an ideal setting for the television soap opera "Howard's Way," which has restored some of the glamour lost when Greta Garbo last

walked down the gangway of the *Queen Mary*. The Southampton International Boat Show in September is said to
be the biggest of its kind in Europe. This is only one of
many annual events here, which also include a Film
Festival, a Balloon and Flower Festival (July), and a Jazz
Festival (November), as well as the Sailing Regatta (August) and the Powerboat Grand Prix (end of September).

Southampton has a surprising variety of cuisines from
which to choose. **Pearl Harbor,** at 17 Above Bar, does
Chinese quite well. Three choices in the Ocean Village
complex are **Dolphin's** (American food and cocktails),
Los Marinos (Spanish), and the **Village Pâtisserie** (cakes
and tea).

No fewer than three large new hotels were opened
here in 1990: the **Hilton National** at Chilworth, and the
Novotel and **Hotel Ibis** near each other on the waterfront; the favorite remains **The Dolphin**, which has been a
landmark in the High Street for years with its bow windows, archway, and wrought-iron traceries.

Broadlands, "one of the finest houses in all England,"
according to Lord Palmerston, who once lived there, lies
just 8 miles north of Southampton on the A 3057 outside
the country town of Romsey. In more recent times Queen
Elizabeth and Prince Philip began their honeymoon there,
an example followed in due course by their son Prince
Charles when he married Lady Diana, now the Princess of
Wales. It would be hard to think of a more romantic place
than this mid-Georgian mansion set in gardens landscaped
by Capability Brown beside the River Test. Both garden
and house, packed with paintings by Van Dyck and others,
fine china, and furniture and mementos of Lord and Lady
Mountbatten (whose last home it was), are open to summer visitors.

THE ISLE OF WIGHT

A network of ferries, Hovercraft, catamarans, and hydrofoils carries passengers and cars the four miles across the
water from Southampton to this island that in prehistory
was joined to the mainland. From Southampton you can
catch the ferry at the terminal near the Royal Pier; there
are also ferries from Portsmouth and Lymington.

The Isle of Wight was already an island when Vespasian
conquered it for Rome in A.D. 43 and called it Vectis,
meaning "separate division." Despite modern transport,

the Isle of Wight is still a land apart, indefinably different from the county of Hampshire "over the water." It isn't large (23 miles from end to end), and its safe, sandy beaches, often reached by gentle wooded ravines known as "chines"—Shanklin Chine, Brook Chine, Whale Chine, and Blackgang Chine (the last named after notorious smugglers)—have made it a longtime favorite for family holidays. There's a coastal footpath around the whole island, and walking is rewarded by marvelous views of sea and landscape and a rich variety of flora and fauna.

Behind the seaside towns of Sandown, Ventnor, Ryde, and Shanklin on the east coast the green downs, where sheep graze, rise to a height of 787 feet, meeting the English Channel on the south shore in a series of chalk cliffs that culminate at the western point in **The Needles**. These three gleaming white 100-foot-high escarpments reach out to the lighthouse that warns shipping to keep clear. Alum Bay here is noted for the varying colors of its sands. Near Freshwater Bay, just east of The Needles, is **Farringford**, where the poet Alfred Lord Tennyson lived for nearly 40 years. It's now a hotel with 20 bedrooms and self-catering cottages. Facilities include an outdoor swimming pool, croquet lawn, and a nine-hole golf course. Tennyson Down is named after the poet, who said the air was "worth sixpence a pint," and a monument to him crowns the summit. The **Albion Hotel** at the water's edge shares the views and offers comfortable accommodation and good food at very reasonable prices.

A nice place to stop for lunch is the **New Inn** in Shalfleet on the road between Yarmouth and Newport. This pub specializes in fresh fish, conger eels, and mussels in garlic; try any of these with Pompey Royal Ale (made in Portsmouth) in the pub's garden.

Historic buildings on the island open to visitors include **Carisbrooke Castle**, parts of which date from the 12th century and where Charles I was a prisoner, and **Osborne House**, the Italianate villa built by Queen Victoria as an escape from the cares of ruling an empire and where she died in 1901. Both are within easy reach of **Newport**, the sleepy capital, which lies inland on the River Medina on the north half of the island, and **Cowes**, which spans both banks of the same river where it enters the Solent on the northern shore. It was the Royal Yacht Squadron at Cowes that in 1851 offered a 100-guinea trophy for a race around the island; won by the schooner *America* for the New York City Yacht Club, the award has ever since been known around the world as the America's Cup. Cowes is to yachting what Wimbledon is to tennis or Ascot is to racing; each August, boats of every description, from dinghies to the Royal Yacht *Britannia,* descend on the little town for the regatta known simply as Cowes Week. The atmosphere is as bubbly as the Champagne that flows freely.

Cowes, Ryde, and Fishbourne are the gateways for visitors crossing by ferry from Portsmouth and Southampton, but the shortest route is at the western end of the island between Yarmouth, another yachting center on the estuary of the River Yar, and Lymington, on the mainland between Bournemouth and Southampton.

THE NEW FOREST

Lymington, at the southern approaches to the New Forest, southwest of Southampton, is an attractive sailing and fishing resort with chandlery stores and tackle shops lining the busy jetties. You can rent a boat to fish for bass in the Solent or buy a day ticket to cast for trout on the River Lymington. And if you are looking for somewhere to stay, you will have a hard time choosing from among the many pleasant hotels in and around the New Forest. West of Lymington on the A 337 toward Christchurch is **Chewton Glen**, one of the finest country-house hotels in England, standing in 30 acres of private parkland. Facilities include a heated outdoor pool, tennis, golf, croquet, and, indoors, billiards and snooker. Captain Frederick Marryat (1792–1848), the author of *Mr. Midshipman Easy* and *Children of the New Forest,* stayed here in the early 19th century, and the period suites are named after characters from the latter book. The food is excellent—haute French cuisine in an elegant atmosphere—and, of course, the prices reflect this. More moderately priced, but still very comfortable, is the **Montagu Arms**, part of which dates from the 18th century. Sited among wooded hills on the Beaulieu River, it offers excellent food and wine and traditional individual rooms with full facilities, including log fires in winter. Nearby are the ruins of **Beaulieu Abbey**, founded in 1204, and the adjoining **Palace House**, the ancestral home of the Montagus of Beaulieu and open to visitors. The present Lord Beaulieu is the chairman of English Heritage and runs the **National Motor Museum**, located on his grounds. It tells the story of motoring from

1899 onward with a comprehensive display of historic vehicles and Disney World–style "time journeys." Transport around the park is by monorail, miniature train, or veteran open-topped London bus.

Just over two miles downriver (there is a marked trail along the bank) where the Beaulieu widens to meet the Solent, the village of **Bucklers Hard** recalls the days when the great oaks of the forest were carted or rolled here to be hewn and shaped into men-of-war for the British fleet. A substantial number of the ships that defeated the French at Trafalgar came from these slipways. There's a maritime museum and the historic **Master Builder's House**, a quiet, 23-room hotel with beguiling views of the estuary. In the opposite direction from Beaulieu village on the B 3056, Beaulieu Road Station, a stop on the railway line from Southampton to Bournemouth, is the annual scene on five widely separated days of the **New Forest Pony Sales**. The ponies can be seen roaming freely together with deer and other wildlife in the 90,000 acres of unspoiled heath, bog, and woodland glades, through which the B 3056 continues northwest to Lyndhurst, the capital of the New Forest and crossroads of most of the routes through it.

There are several car parks in the beech and oak forest around **Lyndhurst**, which is at the heart of the forest. You'll find leaflets describing various nature walks here or at the Forestry Commission Office in town. As you explore the forest along these trails, watch for fallow and roe deer, buzzards and other birds of prey, and a great variety of more bird life attacted by the bogs and marshes.

Lyndhurst is the seat of the Verderers' Court, which meets six times a year at Queen's House for the business of protecting and maintaining the forest entrusted to it 600 years ago (and that's the estimated age of the Knightwood Oak, which grows to the west of town and measures more than 21 feet in girth). The Court's orders are carried out by mounted rangers. The residents retain the rights granted them in the Middle Ages to cut turf, gather firewood, and feed their pigs on forest acorns. These days, however, citizens concentrate on catering to visitors with hotels and guesthouses, pubs and tearooms, and antiques and souvenir shops. If you can brave the traffic in the High Street, the **Crown** is an inviting, Old-World establishment that offers the charm of a timbered, ivy-clad façade, a wood-paneled bar, cozy lounges, and 43 well-kept rooms. The 300-year-old **Waterloo Arms Pub** on Pike's hill offers reasonably priced meals in a building crammed with souvenirs and artifacts from around the world, ranging from a boomerang to a stuffed crocodile. **The Castle Inn** is a thatched 17th-century pub with a terraced garden. As you appreciate the nooks and crannies indoors and out, you can sip from a wide range of beers, from Devenish Dark Mild to Great British Heavy.

THE DORSET COAST
Christchurch, Bournemouth, Poole

These three Dorset towns have merged in recent years into a coastal conurbation separated from Southampton by the wild spaces of the New Forest. **Christchurch** takes its name from its parish church, the largest in England with the two oldest bells, which were cast in 1370. The town's origins go back to Saxon times when it was one of King Alfred's fortresses against the marauding Angles and Danes. It appears later in the Norman Domesday Book as Twynham, or "town between two waters," because it stands at the confluence of the Rivers Stour and Avon (not to be confused with other Avons to the north). These waterways are a peaceful retreat for anglers, and the harbor is often full of yachts.

Bournemouth begins as you head west out of Christchurch on A 35, although the city center is six miles down the sandy beach. In 1989 its long-held reputation as the Queen of the South Coast was reinforced when it was named "Resort of the Year" by the English Tourist Board. It was a certain Dr. Granville in the mid-19th century who first recommended Bournemouth's mild and bracing air for those "in delicate health." Villas sprouted among the heathland and pinewoods through which the "chines," or valleys, descended to the shore on either side of the Bourne valley. In *Tess of the D'Urbervilles,* Thomas Hardy calls the town "Sandbourne" and describes its two new railway stations, gaslit piers, and promenades as "a glittering novelty." Robert Louis Stevenson wrote *Kidnapped* and *The Strange Case of Dr. Jekyll and Mr. Hyde* during the 1880s in a house on the avenue now named after him. Surprisingly, the graveyard of St. Peter's Church contains the heart of Percy Bysshe Shelley, which was brought back from Italy in 1822 by a companion; the rest of Shelley's ashes stayed in Rome. The only museum devoted to the poet's life and work is at **Shelley Park** on

Beechwood Avenue in suburban Boscombe, which was formerly the home of his son, Sir Percy Shelley.

Prime Minister Benjamin Disraeli stayed at the **Royal Bath Hotel** for the sake of his health, and he might haved benefited still more from the pool, sauna, and gymnasium provided there today. He might not, however, have approved of the Bournemouth Casino, which operates separately but on the same premises as the hotel. Competing with the town's oldest hotel, the new **Norfolk Royale** offers comparable health and fitness facilities and reserves a percentage of its rooms for nonsmokers and women guests only. **Langtry Manor** capitalizes on the fact that it was built by the future King Edward VII as a love nest where he could be with his mistress Lillie Langtry; it offers four-poster beds and six-course Edwardian dinners. Medium-priced hotels such as **Durley Hall** or **Marsham Court** have no such claims to fame but do have outdoor swimming pools and snooker indoors and are convenient for shops and the beach.

Crust, on the town square, is unquestionably Bournemouth's finest restaurant. Cane furniture and potted palms are the setting for excellent fresh fish and vegetables, attentive service, and a good wine list.

Bournemouth has one of the country's widest range of hotels outside London and some of the best shopping, with antiques, Victoriana, and Art Deco specialties in its Boscombe and Pokesdown suburbs. The main shopping area, with all the major stores represented as well as the local, family-run department store **Beales**, is around the square in the city center. The beach has a European Community "Blue Flag" for cleanliness, and the parks and gardens are kept in immaculate condition by a regiment of 230 municipal gardeners.

The city has six entertainment centers attracting top talent in summer, and its own symphony orchestra. Sporting activities range from ten-pin bowling and ice skating to cricket, golf, tennis, fishing, sailing, and powerboat racing.

With a population of 150,000 and still growing, blooming Bournemouth has all but engulfed **Poole**, its neighbor to the west. But this ancient port, which once traded with Newfoundland and the other colonies of the New World, jealously preserves its Georgian Custom House, Guildhall, and various harbor buildings. **Purbeck Pottery** on the Quay is a good place to buy examples of this local craft at reasonable prices. Poole Harbour, from which cross-Channel ferries operate to Cherbourg, is an enormous area of water crammed with all kinds of leisure craft and protected by a narrow spit called Sandbanks, whose beaches live up to its name.

Inside the harbor is the island where the Boy Scout movement was founded with a summer camp held in 1907 by Lord Baden-Powell. **Brownsea Island**, a 500-acre tract of wild heath and woodland, is now the property of the National Trust, which runs a shop here selling books about the Scout movement. The island can be reached by ferry from Sandbanks or Poole Quay from April to September.

Overlooking the harbor from Canford Cliffs is **Compton Acres**, seven gardens landscaped in various styles from around the world, including Japanese, Italian, and Roman schemes, with a subtropical woodland glen.

In Poole, **Fishnets** serves up a fixed-price Scandinavian smorgasbord in an old mill on the quay.

Swanage to Weymouth

Swanage is a quiet little seaside town on the Isle of Purbeck (an island in name only) to the south of Poole Harbour. Its most notable features—the Wellington Clock Tower and the carved stone façade of the town hall—both came from London, but there is also a 13th-century parish church next to the Millpond and a local museum in the Old Tithe Barn. Nearby is the village of **Worth Matravers**, famous for centuries for the quarrying of the dark gray Purbeck marble that went into the building of churches and cathedrals, including Salisbury, up and down the country. The ruins of **Corfe Castle** dominate the *corfe* (Anglo-Saxon for pass or cutting) through the Purbeck Hills. Both the castle and the village that grew up around its domed green hill are entirely of gray Purbeck stone.

From here westward is the least touched stretch of the South Coast, in marked contrast to that running eastward from Bournemouth. The southern shore of Poole Harbour is almost entirely given over to nature reserves, where adders and lizards may be encountered as well as wildfowl. A mile from the village of Studland is the **Agglestone**, a huge triangular chunk of ironstone that, it's claimed, the Devil planned to drop on Salisbury Cathedral—but its weight proved too much for him. There are other interesting natural formations at the sea's edge: Old Harry and Old Harry's Wife, off the Foreland, are pillars of chalk named for the Devil. The Great Globe in Durlston Country Park near Durlston Head is man-made, however, from Portland stone.

The **Dorset Coast Path** follows the clifftops along the coast around St. Aldhelm's Head, where no main roads run and where guillemots and razorbills wheel round a Norman chapel perched on the headland as a marker for vessels in the Channel.

Since World War I, a great slice of the coast inland from oyster-shaped Lulworth Cove and Worbarrow Bay has been reserved for military use as a tank-training course and firing range. Ironically, this has preserved it from the worse depredation of "development" that has turned so much of Britain's coast into a ribbon of highways and housing, marinas, trailer parks, power stations, pylons, container ports, and drilling rigs. Wildlife, undisturbed by the gunfire, flourishes in the 7,000 acres of the range, and access on the Coast Path is allowed to visitors at most weekends and during public holidays. Barn owls nest in the rafters of the village of Tyneham, abandoned to the military in 1943. An exhibition in the church relates the long history of the valley in which it stands. Another piece of nature's sculpture to be seen from the Coast Path as it continues west toward Weymouth is Durdle Door, an arch of limestone jutting out into the sea from a sandy beach.

Weymouth, at the western end of this stretch of coast, is an elegant resort of porticoed Georgian buildings that owes its legacy to George III himself, the first monarch to use a bathing machine, during a visit to the town in 1789. (A bathing machine is a changing room on wheels invented for modesty's sake; a bather entered it, wheeled down to the water, changed into swimming clothes, and slipped into the ocean without anyone seeing.) The **Gloucester Hotel** was formerly the King's summer home. His statue overlooking the promenade and the sands, put up in 1810 for his golden jubilee, is now one of the sights of the town. Another is the brightly painted clock tower erected on the promenade for Queen Victoria's similar anniversary in 1887. As Weymouth is a port, the harbor at the mouth of the River Wey is busy with small boats and ferries and hydrofoils on their way to and from Cherbourg and the Channel Islands. (The hydrofoil to the Channel Islands runs only in summer.) To the south, the Isle of Portland reaches out toward Portland Bill with is attendant lighthouse and the Victorian Trinity House Tower.

The 66-room **Portland Heights Hotel** combines fine views over the "island" (it is, in fact, joined to the mainland by a causeway next to the final stretch of Chesil Beach) with squash and swimming in a heated pool. Portland is the "Isle of Slingers" in Hardy's novels, and prisoners used to break rock in its quarries. Portland stone went into many buildings, not the least of which is Buckingham Palace.

Chesil Beach, stretching in a ten-mile crescent from Portland west to Abbotsbury, is one of Britain's most unusual natural phenomena. This barrier of shingle, up to 40 feet high, encloses a lagoon called the Fleet. The pebbles on the beach are graded larger and larger toward Portland, but no one has been able to explain why. The stories of Chesil are of sailing ships driven by gales into the shingle and of hundreds of lives lost. **Moonfleet Manor**, overlooking Chesil Beach and the sea five miles west of Weymouth, features in John Meade Faulkner's Victorian smuggling saga *Moonfleet*. It is now a 38-room hotel with lawn bowling, three squash courts, tennis, snooker, and an indoor swimming pool.

Abbotsbury has one of the largest tithe barns in the land, a thatched 15th-century structure, and a Swannery started in the 11th century by Benedictine monks who reared the birds for meat. Today the abbey is no more, but the only nesting colony of mute swans in Britain survives, ranging from 500 in summer to a thousand in winter. They feed on the rare eelgrass that grows around the Fleet. The **Ilchester Arms** is a comfortable and inexpensive place to stay in this delightful village of thatch and orange-colored stone, but there are just ten rooms, so advance booking is advised.

HARDY COUNTRY
Dorchester

The Hardy Monument that stands on gorse-covered Black Down just inland from Abbotsbury is not in memory of the famous novelist, as might be supposed, but of Thomas Masterson Hardy, the captain of the *Victory* at Trafalgar, to whom Nelson addressed his dying words, "Kiss me Hardy." The gallant captain, who went on to a vice-admiralship and a knighthood, lived in Portesham at the bottom of the hill. By coincidence, the 1840 birthplace of the other Thomas Hardy is just a few miles away on the other side of the county market town of Dorchester, which is directly north of Weymouth. The small thatched cottage in the woods at Higher Bockhampton ("Mellstock" in his novels), just ten minutes from a parking lot, is in the care of the National Trust and open to visitors. **Yalbury Cottage** at Lower Bockhampton serves an excellent dinner and has just ten rooms for those who wish to linger overnight to soak up Hardy atmosphere.

The A 35 leads on to Dorchester through Tolpuddle, the village of the trade-union movement martyrs, and Puddletown ("Weatherbury"). If Hardy visited Dorchester today he would instantly recognize the town that he describes in *The Mayor of Casterbridge*. He would also recognize the accents of the farmers bargaining over cattle and crops in the market and drinking locally brewed ale in the pubs.

Dorchester's handsome main street is lined with solid buildings of Portland stone; the Antelope Hotel, where Judge Jeffreys sentenced 74 men to be hanged and quartered for joining the duke of Monmouth's rebellion of 1685, and the Shire Hall, where the Tolpuddle Martyrs were sentenced to transportation to Australia in 1834, are unaltered. So, too, are the 15th-century St. Peter's Church, which Hardy as a young architect helped to restore, and Max Gate (just outside the town), the house he designed and in which he spent his last years as a rich and famous author. It is, alas, undistinguished and not open to visitors. Thomas Hardy's tomb in the churchyard at Stinsford is midway between Max Gate and Higher Bockhampton. "Thrown aside as dead" as a baby, Hardy nonetheless lived to be 87 and "a miserable old fellow," as far as Dorchester folk were concerned. Certainly his monument wears a melancholy air.

The **King's Arms**, with 31 rooms, a restaurant, and parking facilities, or the much smaller **Casterbridge**, which has no restaurant but is very cozy, make convenient bases for exploring winding Wessex lanes inland "far from the madding crowd" and for visiting thatched villages such as the model Georgian Milton Abbas and Cerne Abbas, which are among the most idyllic in England.

The county isn't large; it is only 27 miles northeast to Shaftesbury, the hilltop town to which Hardy gave its old name of Shaston in the Wessex novels. You can see the window from which Sue in *Jude the Obscure* jumps on her wedding night, and if you need a cream tea after that excitement, you will find it under the gnarled beams and old cider flagons in **King Alfred's Kitchen** here. The views from the 700-foot-high plateau over the Blackmoor Vale of "little dairies" (as Hardy described the area in *Tess of the D'Urbervilles*) are worth a detour, as are the abbey ruins and a fascinating local museum at the top of cobbled Gold Hill.

Abbotsford to Lyme Regis

The coast is as lovely and untouched to the west of Weymouth and Dorchester as it is to the east. The extremely wide streets of **Bridport** ("Port Bredy" in several Hardy novels) are evidence of its long history of ropemaking, for this is where workers twisted the hemp. Indeed, it's claimed that the cultivation of hemp and flax was first introduced here by the Romans. Certainly, in the days of sail, to say that someone has been "stabbed by a Bridport dagger" meant he had been hanged. Today the old ropewalks have been abandoned, but nets are still made for fishing. There is a museum and art gallery and an open-air market on Wednesdays and Saturdays.

Great golden cliffs stretch west around the bay to **Lyme Regis**, which owes the second word of its name to a charter from King Edward I, who used its harbor to send ships out to fight the French in the latter part of the 13th century. Three centuries later ships sailed from here against the Spanish Armada, and in 1685 the duke of Monmouth raised his standard on the beach west of the harbor where he had landed to launch his ill-fated rebellion against his uncle, James II.

The 18th-century **Alexandra Hotel**, set in spacious gardens overlooking Lyme Bay, with 27 rooms and a sun lounge, or **Mariners** in Silver Street, with 15 rooms and a garden, serving set meals with wines at moderate prices, are pleasant places to stay in this colorful small resort. The stone breakwater called The Cobb that protects the harbor achieved unexpected international fame in the early 1980s when the actress Meryl Streep, mysteriously cowled, posed on it during the filming of the novel *The French Lieutenant's Woman*. Its author, John Fowles, lives locally and is something of an authority on the fossils from the cliffs that are displayed in the museum, some of which date from 200 million years ago. The first major discovery—of the complete 21-foot-long skeleton of an ichthyosaur in the cliffs of Black Ven near where the River Char enters the sea—was by Mary Anning, the 12-year-old daughter of a carpenter, in 1811. The area is now a nature reserve.

The cliffs of sandstone topped with bright yellow gorse climb from Charmouth to 618 feet at Golden Cap, the highest point on England's south coast. This 2,000-acre estate embracing farmland, woods, cliffs, and glorious beach is regarded as the crowning achievement of the National Trust's Enterprise Neptune, which, since 1965, has fought to protect coastline not already spoiled. There are 15 miles of footpath (including the Dorset Coast Path) for exploring places with intriguing names like Cain's Folly, Doghouse Hill, and The Saddle. The fields have not been turned over to prairie, and in the hedgerows yellowhammer and wren can be seen and heard and wildflowers such as agrimony, spear, and stemless thistle grow vigorously.

GETTING AROUND

As in the Literary Southeast, most of the places in this chapter are easily reached from central London by road and rail within a couple of hours. Gateways to the main routes are provided by the London Orbital Motorway (M 25), which also links the major international airports of Heathrow and Gatwick. The Wessex Shore is especially convenient for those arriving by sea at Southampton aboard the *Queen Elizabeth II* and other ships. Local ferries make the crossing to the Isle of Wight in 30 minutes to an hour from Portsmouth, Southampton, or Lymington, the Hovercraft in ten minutes from Southsea, and the hydrofoil almost as speedily from Southampton.

ACCOMMODATIONS REFERENCE

▶ **Albion.** Gate Lane, Freshwater Bay, **Isle of Wight** PO40 9RA. Tel: (0983) 75-36-31; Fax: (0983) 75-52-95.

▶ **Alexandra Hotel.** Pound Street, **Lyme Regis** DT7 3HZ. Tel: (0294) 720-10.

▶ **Casterbridge.** 49 High East Street, **Dorchester** DT1 1HU. Tel: (0305) 640-43.

▶ **Chewton Glen.** Christchurch Road, **New Milton** BH25 6QS. Tel: (0425) 27-53-41; Telex 41456; Fax: (0425) 27-23-10.

▶ **Crest.** Pembroke Road, **Portsmouth** PO1 2TA. Tel: (0705) 82-76-51; Telex: 86397; Fax: (0705) 75-67-15.

▶ **Crown.** High Street, **Lyndhurst** SO43 7NF. Tel: (0703) 28-29-22; Fax: (0703) 28-27-51.

▶ **Dolphin.** 35 High Street, **Southampton** SO9 2DS. Tel: (0703) 33-99-55; Telex: 477735; Fax: (0703) 33-36-50.

▶ **Dolphin & Anchor.** West Street, **Chichester** PO19 1QE. Tel: (0243) 78-51-21; Fax: (0243) 53-34-08.

▶ **Durley Hall.** 7 Durley Chine Road, West Cliff, **Bournemouth** BH2 5JS. Tel: (0202) 76-68-86; Fax: (0202) 76-22-36.

▶ **Farringford.** Freshwater Bay, **Isle of Wight** PO40 9PE. Tel: (0983) 75-25-00.

▶ **Hilton National.** Bracken Place, Chilworth, **Southampton** SO2 3UB. Tel: (0703) 70-27-00; Telex 47594; Fax: (0703) 76-72-33.

▶ **Holiday Inn.** North Harbour, Cosham, **Portsmouth** PO6 4SH. Tel: (0705) 38-31-51; Telex: 86611; Fax: (0705) 38-87-01.

▶ **Hotel Ibis.** West Quay Road, **Southampton** SO1 0RA. Tel: (0703) 63-44-63; Telex: 477698; Fax: (0703) 22-32-73.

▶ **Ilchester Arms.** 9 Market Street, **Abbotsbury** DT3 4JR. Tel: (0305) 87-12-43.

▶ **King's Arms.** 30 High East Street, **Dorchester** DT1 1HF. Tel: (0305) 65-353; Fax: (0305) 60-269.

▶ **Langtry Manor.** 26 Derby Road, East Cliff, **Bournemouth** BH1 3QB. Tel: (0202) 23-887; Fax: (0202) 29-01-15.

▶ **Mariners.** Silver Street, **Lyme Regis** DT7 3HS. Tel: (0297) 42-753; Fax: (0297) 42-431.

▶ **Marsham Court.** Russell Cotes Road, East Cliff, **Bournemouth** BH1 3AB. Tel: (0202) 22-111; Telex: 41420; Fax: (0202) 29-47-44.

▶ **Master Builder's House. Bucklers Hard** SO42 7XB. Tel: (0590) 61-62-53; Fax: (0590) 61-26-24.

▶ **Montagu Arms.** Palace Lane, **Beaulieu** SO42 7ZL. Tel: (0590) 61-23-24; Fax: (0590) 61-26-24.

▶ **Moonfleet Manor.** near **Weymouth** DT3 4ED. Tel: (0305) 78-69-48; Fax: (0305) 77-43-95.

▶ **Norfolk Royale.** Richmond Hill, **Bournemouth** BH2 6EN. Tel: (0202) 21-521; Telex: 418474; Fax: (0202) 29-97-29.

▶ **Novotel.** 1 West Quay Road, **Southampton** SO1 0RA. Tel: (0703) 33-05-50; Fax: (0703) 22-21-58.

▶ **Portland Heights.** Yeates Corner, **Portland** DT5 2EN. Tel: (0305) 82-13-61; Fax: (0305) 86-00-81.

▶ **Royal Bath.** Bath Road, **Bournemouth** BH1 2EW. Tel: (0202) 25-555; Telex: 41375; Fax: (0202) 54-158.

▶ **Ship.** North Street, **Chichester** PO19 1NH. Tel: (0243) 78-20-28; Fax: (0243) 77-42-54.

▶ **Yalbury Cottage. Lower Bockhampton** DT2 8PZ. Tel: (0305) 26-23-82.

THE COTSWOLDS TO WINCHESTER

By Bryn Frank

Bryn Frank is the author of several books about Britain, including Discover Scotland, Everyman's England, *and, most recently,* Short Walks in English Towns. *He has also contributed to* National Geographic, *among many other publications and guidebooks. A native of rural Northumberland, he writes widely about travel.*

Oxford makes such a convenient day trip from London that it is all too easy for visitors to look no farther. Bath, of course, is very much on the tourist beat, but what lies between that and Oxford is one of southern England's best-kept secrets: lonely rolling uplands bordered by prosperous arable farms, ancient forests, and the still-tangible remains of prehistoric settlements, which indicate that what we now know as Wiltshire (around the Salisbury Plain) was once highly populated. The M 3 motorway is one of England's best landscaped: On it you reach Winchester and, beyond that, across a swath of little-known, deeply rural countryside, Salisbury and its cathedral, which boasts the tallest spire in England. Cathedral aside, Salisbury has remained intact and charming despite the vicissitudes of the late 20th century.

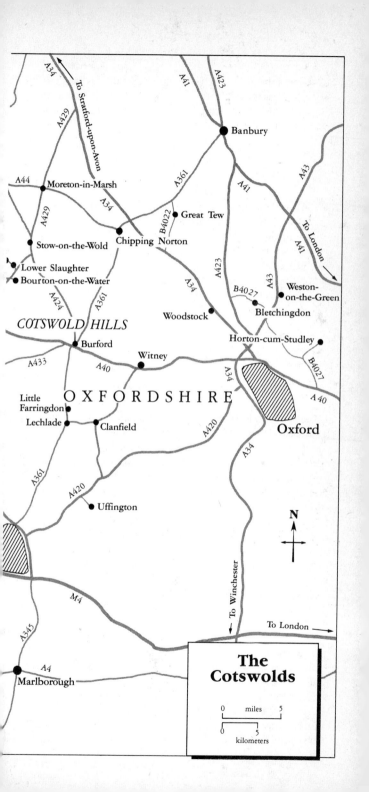

North of the M 4, which runs due west out of London to Bristol across the top of the Salisbury Plain, lie the famous Cotswold hills, with Bath at their southwestern end and Oxford to their east.

MAJOR INTEREST

The Cotswolds: charming country towns and inns
Bath: Roman Baths, Royal Crescent, Pulteney
 Bridge
Salisbury Cathedral
Stonehenge
Stourhead House and gardens
Winchester Cathedral
Avebury Stone Circle and Silbury Hill

THE COTSWOLDS

Largely unspoiled, the Cotswold hills are rural England at its best. They are almost too good to be true. Even the name, which confuses foreigners and even the English who claim to know this exquisite corner of the country, is a charmer. It comes from an amalgam of two Anglo-Saxon words meaning "sheepfold" and "open, unculti-vated uplands."

Hard to define geographically, the Cotswolds stretch very roughly from Cheltenham in the west to Oxford in the east, from near Evesham (southwest of Stratford-upon-Avon) in the north to Cirencester in the south. You can choose Bath at their far southwest as a base for a Cotswold exploration, though Cirencester, Cheltenham, and Oxford, which all offer a good choice of hotels, would also serve.

Whatever town you use as a base, a good road map— some of the larger gasoline stations have a wide selec-tion—is essential in the Cotswolds. With the exception of half a dozen picturesque villages and small towns, the best of the region is hidden from view. Even so, country buses are adequate and rural taxis are accustomed to transporting people fairly long distances; no part of the Cotswolds is dramatically remote.

Cotswold Villages and Towns

Some of the villages and hamlets on the extreme edges of the Cotswolds are the ones that keep most to themselves. Try **Uley**, south of Stroud, in the heart of the country where Laurie Lee set his perennial best-seller *Cider with Rosie*. He describes the region as "a mystery land of difficult hills and deeply wooded valleys." Nearby **Owlpen** is dominated by a fine, sprawling Tudor manor house with a church and a steep hillside behind. Accommodations are available in the cottages on the estate (Tel: 0453-86-02-61). Another self-catering accommodation is **Langford House Cottages**, owned by Lady de Mauley, on A 361 in Little Faringdon near Lechlade (Tel: 0367-522-10).

At roughly the opposite edge of the Cotswolds, near Chipping Norton, north of Oxford, is **Great Tew**, until recently so run-down and neglected that it seemed ready to crumble into dust. But this slice of English village life has been reprieved and is now undergoing renovation without detriment to its original charm.

Just south of the busy A 40 road that links Cheltenham and Oxford lies **Withington**, one of those villages that even people who claim to know the Cotswolds may not be able to place. The best reason to go to Withington is to see the nearby **Chedworth Roman Villa**.

Visiting the villa, built around A.D. 150, you will need only a little imagination to translate the mosaics and the painted walls into a warm and habitable dwelling. It was probably built not by Romans at all but by locals (most likely the ancient Dubonnic tribe) in the Roman style. A highly recommended detour, it is in a fine, peaceful, partly wooded setting.

For those who prefer a less rural base, **Cheltenham** can be recommended. It has some fine Regency architecture, dating from its days as a spa town, and was the 1989 winner of the "Beautiful Britain in Bloom" competition. There is excellent shopping, especially for clothing and antiques, and in early July, the Cheltenham International Festival of Music takes place. Also, there's the Cheltenham Literature Festival in October and, for horse racing fans, the Cheltenham Gold Cup meeting in March. For accommodations, see below in this section. Among other Cotswolds towns, **Stow-on-the-Wold** (east of Cheltenham) is exceptional and will probably be your favorite. It is high lying, surrounded by windswept countryside. "Stow-on-the-Wold, where the wind blows cold," runs an old adage. Its marketplace, as if to protect itself against the winter weather, is enclosed almost completely by inns and shops, including a hardware store and newsagent's, of the old-fashioned kind: Courtesies of "Good morning" and "Good evening" still prevail here. There is a cozy tea shop, **Edward's Café**, on the marketplace. The church is probably most famous as the site where Cromwell, during the Civil War, incarcerated several hundred Royalist troops, shooting two "*pour encourager les autres*." On the outskirts of the little town, on the A 424 road, is the pleasant, low-ceilinged **Unicorn Hotel**, featuring especially a few charming attic rooms. Another good hotel is the **Wyck Hill House**, with spacious bedrooms and a cedar-paneled library, and a comfortable bar with leather armchairs downstairs.

Bourton-on-the-Water, just southwest of Stow-on-the-Wold, is smaller and different: Unashamed commercialization meets the "olde world" here. The village is an essential stop on day trips by bus that aim to capture some of the Cotswolds' flavor and also offer the chance to spend money on knickknacks. Don't miss the model village; of course, you can also purchase a model of the model village. Here and elsewhere in the Cotswolds, portable antiques are a good buy. They are not particularly cheap, but the quality is good, and browsing for them is a pleasure.

Two other essential stops are **Burford** and Chipping Campden. The former, set on a steep hill, is a fairly short, easy side trip west on A 40 from Oxford. It is a busy place, well served by coaching inns, a couple of them of great character. The **Bull Hotel** is outstanding for a drink or a snack and offers accommodations. **Chipping Campden**, north of Stow-on-the-Wold, is more low-lying and a little quieter, though equally popular with tourists. Its covered market building, built in 1627 "for the sale of cheese, butter and poultry," is a picture-postcard classic. (*Chipping* means "market," and the town was the center of the region's Medieval wool trade.) There is a small rural museum here and, on the outskirts, an impressive "wool church," whose construction was financed by money made from the Cotswolds' famous sheep. Chipping Campden also has two fine inns. The modest **Noel Arms Hotel** dates from the 14th century; the cozy **Cotswold House Hotel and Restaurant** is known for its food and the care and attention given to its guest rooms: Each one has its own theme. A few minutes' drive from Chipping Campden is **Charingworth Manor**, a quiet inn full of antiques.

The Cotswolds are not rich in castles and houses, but

there are a few fine and much-photographed exceptions. Among these is **Sudeley Castle**, once the home of Henry VIII's last wife, Catherine Parr. Set in superb gardens, it is conveniently and attractively located on the edge of the underrated (and less touristy) town of Winchcombe northeast of Cheltenham. You should go there near the end of the day and hang back so you can appreciate the atmosphere without being jostled by too many tourists. The **Sudeley Castle Cottages** are effectively within the castle grounds.

About 4 miles to the north is **Hailes Abbey**, the substantial excavated remains of a Cistercian abbey founded in 1246. **Snowshill Manor**, a small, unassuming manor house 3 miles due south of Broadway and northeast of Cheltenham, contains eclectic artifacts collected by a previous owner, of which Japanese armor and penny-farthing bicycles are just two examples. **Arlington Row** in Bibury, east of Cirencester, is a classic: a line of gray-stone woolworkers' houses dating from the early 17th century and now owned by the National Trust. Gardeners will appreciate **Hidcote Manor Garden** (4 miles northeast of Chipping Campden), considered by many to be the most influential example of English landscape architecture of this century. Created by American Major Lawrence Johnston in 1913, it actually took 30 years to complete. It features some remarkable topiary and many irresistible alleyways.

This is some of the finest walking country in England, but until you get out and walk, you won't realize just how high some of the terrain is. **Broadway Hill** (1,025 feet), immediately southeast of Broadway, and **Cleeve Hill** (1,083 feet), near Cheltenham, are the two highest points in the Cotswolds. Both are accessible to reasonably energetic walkers, who will be rewarded on clear days with spectacular views. Broadway Hill offers views as far west as the Black Mountains of mid-Wales and as far north as the Wrekin, another distinctive outcrop, in mid-Shropshire.

Even if you're not a walker, the area is well worth an overnight stop: The **Lygon Arms**, in the town of **Broadway** itself, is one of the best-known country hotels in Britain. Many a hunting scene has been painted or photographed outside its mellow exterior. If you take a suite, you can have your own log fire. For energetic guests there are archery ranges and an all-weather tennis court on the grounds, and golf (with lessons if desired) at an excellent nearby club. And up Fish Hill, on the outskirts of the village, is the very welcoming **Dormy House Hotel**, with especially pleasant dining rooms. **Buckland Manor**, just out of town, is a fine, partly 12th-century manor house that has been impeccably converted; its restaurant is also highly regarded. Broadway has several antiques shops, art galleries, and print and antiquarian bookshops.

Good hotels are among the many attractions elsewhere in the Cotswolds, too. If you are looking for a metropolitan base, the **Queen's Hotel** in Cheltenham is smart and central. It is used mainly by businesspeople on weekdays but travellers appreciate its weekend package deals. The **Golden Valley Thistle Hotel** on the outskirts of town is also smart, modern, and very well appointed. Both have good and comfortable restaurants. South of Cheltenham at Birdlip, **Kingshead House** offers food and lodging. It is run by a hardworking, dedicated couple, Warren and Judy Knock, who serve imaginative, not-too-expensive meals. The **Plough at Clanfield,** on the Cotswolds' southernmost edge near Lechlade, is a well-maintained Elizabethan manor house with a stylish restaurant and whirlpool baths. The **King's Head Hotel** at Cirencester is a coaching inn of great antiquity, a major attraction in this golden-stone market town near the southwestern corner of the region. The **Lords of the Manor,** at Upper Slaughter near Bourton-on-the-Water just southwest of Stow-on-the-Wold, is yet another of the region's fine, high-ceilinged country houses that will transport you miles away from everyday cares—except perhaps when it comes time to pay the bill. It has a formal restaurant with elaborate classic dishes as well as innovative ones. **Lower Slaughter Manor,** a fine renovation of an imposing family house, is in the lovely village of Lower Slaughter. The stroll uphill through the woodlands to Upper Slaughter is delightful. **Studley Priory Hotel**, at Horton-cum-Studley, is another rambling, historic stone building. Those who have seen the film *A Man for All Seasons* might recognize the view from the back garden, as a crucial scene in the film was shot here. In Woodstock the **Feathers Hotel** and **The Bear Hotel** are accommodations of great character, the latter a coaching inn with paneled bars, low ceilings, and lots of atmosphere. None of these hotels is cheap, but special weekend deals can bring prices down substantially.

The Cotswolds are also superb picnic country, or you can wash down your bread and cheese or your game pie and salad with a pint or two of ale from a low-ceilinged pub that still sells beer from one of the local breweries.

BATH

Bath is not a Cotswold town, but it is nicely situated on the outermost southern fringes of the area. If you are travelling by road from the Cotswolds proper, there is a good chance that you will slip down into Bath via A 46. The ancient city is also just an hour and a half by train from London's Paddington Station. It is said that around 875 B.C. Bladud, the father of King Lear, allowed a herd of sickly pigs in search of acorns to wallow in mud that seemed to cure them of all known ills. Thus were Bath's spa waters discovered. (If you visit the Circus, note the acorn motifs on top of the terrace of houses.)

The Romans rediscovered the health-giving waters after their invasion of Britain in A.D. 43, and in this comparatively balmy and prosperous part of the country, they found reasonably acquiescent local tribes and relaxation from the more strenuous and warlike northern border of the empire straddled by Hadrian's Wall. They built a series of baths and a temple to Sulis Minerva: Sul was an ancient Celtic deity, and Minerva, the Roman goddess of healing. The settlement was, however, known as Aquae Sulis (waters of Sul). They also built a swimming pool, a feature not usually included in a Roman spa (in England, apart from Bath, only Wroxeter, near Shrewsbury, is known to have had one). The baths were similar to today's Turkish baths and were as much a place to gossip and relax as to get clean. Bathers had to wash without soap, which had yet to be invented. Instead, dirt was literally scraped off, and bath oil was much in evidence.

After the Roman occupation, Bath continued as an important center. In the tenth century the foundations of the many-windowed abbey (one reason the abbey became known as the "lantern of the west") were laid. In 973 the coronation of Edgar, the first English king, took place here. The abbey is the focal point of **Abbey Church Yard**, a spacious, traffic-free open area abutting the Pump Room and the entrance to the baths. Buskers and other street entertainers perform in the open air in summer; it is a delightful place to watch the world go by.

James I's Queen Anne put Bath's supposedly health-giving waters back on the map in 1707. Taking the waters became *de rigueur,* but not in the Roman bath; that was not rediscovered until 1878. The 18th-century architects who re-created Bath, rendering it among the finest cities in all

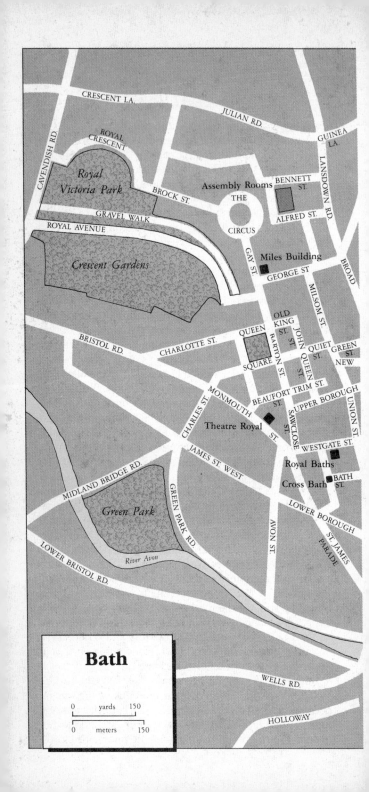

Bath

```
0        yards       150
|------------------------|
0        meters      150
```

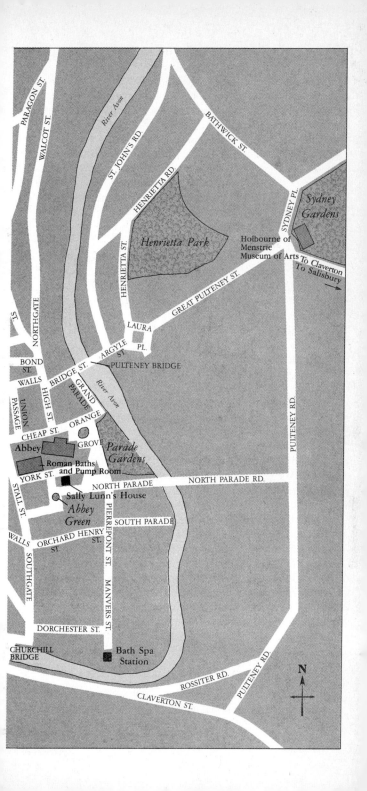

of Europe, showed little interest in the Romans' achievements. Supreme among the architects were Yorkshire-born John Wood and his son, also named John. The former's greatest lifetime project was the **Circus** (he would probably not have appreciated the five great plane trees the Victorians planted); that of the younger Wood was the **Royal Crescent**. Seldom do the outskirts of a city have such a focal point. The Scottish architect Robert Adam built the **Pulteney Bridge**, a classic piece of neo-Palladian design. Do not miss this. It is the second-oldest surviving bridge in England to have houses and shops built on it (only Lincoln's High Bridge is older).

Jane Austen—who actually disliked the city for its stuffiness and the garishness of its newly quarried stone (now beautifully mellowed)—described it in her novels. The early- and mid-18th-century entrepreneur and fashion arbiter Beau Nash turned Bath into a city of elegance and charm. To get a little closer to this remarkable man, you can have a meal at **Popjoy's** on Sawclose, in the last house in Bath to be occupied by Nash.

The Victorians almost ruined the city center—one of their worst excesses involved introducing trees in squares and precincts never intended to have them.

Over the centuries, as now, the springs have gushed forth about a million gallons of water a day, at a constant 120 degrees F. But you will not be able to bathe at all, as the baths of the 17th and 18th centuries are undergoing extensive renovation. You *will* be able to drink the water in the **Pump Room**, water that Sam Weller in Charles Dickens's *Pickwick Papers* described as "having a wery strong flavor o' warm flatirons". When you visit the baths, take advantage of the brief guided tour; some of the guides are exceptionally witty and informative. At the end of the tour you may opt for morning coffee or afternoon tea in the Pump Room, accompanied by the strains of a resident string trio. To see the rest of the city center, walk to the tourist information center at The Colonnades, Bath Street, for information on joining one of the excellent guided tours.

Bath Museums

Bath has such a rare and impressive link with the past that its handful of exceptional museums constitutes almost an embarrassment of riches. One of the best in the entire west of England is **Number 1 Royal Crescent**. Few of the houses in the Royal Crescent are still complete private homes, but Number 1 comes surprisingly close to capturing the atmosphere of a family house of the late 18th century (Bath's heyday), with exquisite antique furniture, a fine staircase, even a sedan chair parked in the hall. The dining room is laid out exactly as it would have been for a dinner party of 200 years ago, with real food. The book and gift shop is excellent.

The 18th-century Assembly Rooms—a charming and spacious setting—house the **Museum of Costume**, which is closed for renovation until late spring 1991. The **Holburne of Menstrie Museum of Art** is worth the picturesque half-mile walk over the Pulteney Bridge and along Great Pulteney Street. It is both a fine house and a repository of old masters, rare books, gold, and silverware. The museum is becoming increasingly well known for its Crafts Study Centre's concerts, lectures, exhibitions, and classes; these activities are especially popular with single travellers.

If the walk to the museum is too long, a highly recommended open-top bus (pick it up at any of a dozen or more convenient points) stops at the museum's entrance. This open-top tour is a happy marriage of rural and urban sightseeing. Looking down on the city as the bus makes its way across the surrounding hills is a treat. On the route, two miles from the city center, is the early 19th-century **Claverton Manor**. This American Museum is unique in Britain, having been created in 1961 by two antiques collectors, one an American, to help improve understanding between two increasingly distinct cultures. Among the exhibits is a collection of traditional quilts and a special reconstruction of aspects of the opening of the American West. Winston Churchill gave his first political speech at Claverton at a fête on July 26, 1897.

Until recently there was a dearth of good hotels in Bath; now there are several. The modern **Hilton National**, on the banks of the River Avon close to Pulteney Bridge, was once considered an architectural blot on the horizon. It seems now to have been accepted and is much used by groups on the better bus tours, as well as business people. More recent still is the **Bath Spa Hotel**, ten minutes' walk from the city center in a restored 19th-century mansion.

The **Royal Crescent**'s location is exceptional: right in the center of the Royal Crescent, overlooking Royal Victoria Park. (A memorable anecdote is told about the future Queen Victoria visiting this part of Bath as a young girl. A gust of wind blew up her skirts, after which she was known locally as "bandy legs." Deeply offended, she never came here again.)

A short stroll away along Gravel Walk and then across Queen Square is the comfortable **Francis Hotel**. Part of the extensive Trusthouse Forte chain but with more character than many in the group, it is popular with overseas visitors. The softly lit, very large restaurant of the hotel overlooks the square, another open space designed by the elder John Wood. The hotel was one of the buildings destroyed in this part of the city during a raid by the Luftwaffe in 1942. As rebuilt it fits attractively into its surroundings. The **Priory Hotel** has a feeling of the country, though it's just a mile from the city center. It dates from 1835 and has a fine restaurant that emphasizes imaginative game dishes in season. This is a connoisseur's establishment, very discreet and comfortable. The **Paradise House**, in a Georgian building across Churchill Bridge, has Laura Ashley decor and is quiet. A mile or so from the city center on Newbridge Hill lies the highly regarded **Apsley House Hotel**, a William IV mansion. There are only seven large bedrooms, and a much-admired restaurant.

Good bar lunches are to be had in the **Crystal Palace Tavern** in Abbey Green and at **Sally Lunn's**, known for its traditional teas and "Sally Lunn" buns, but also a fine example of late 17th-century architecture in its own right. A popular, sometimes crowded, wine bar with a proper restaurant as well is **The Moon & Sixpence**, 6A Broad Street.

Recently moved from the center of Bath to the village of Box, a few minutes' drive east on A 4, is the well-respected **Clos du Roy**—a restaurant in an elegant 18th-century house serving expensive, rich, imaginative dishes. Clos du Roy's original premises are now occupied by **Garlands** (7 Edgar Buildings, George Street), proferring ambitious dishes and good sweets. **Tarts** (8 Pierrepont Place) is an inexpensive, lively, bistro-style establishment.

Those people who like their travels to have a focal point should visit the Bath Festival (first half of June) or the Bath Antiques Fair (in May). The former is probably best known for its national theme: In 1990 it was Spanish, in 1989 German.

Salisbury Plain

From Bath it is a quick trip east on A 4 to Avebury (of the Stone Circle), which we cover after Winchester and Marlborough below; or it is only 15 miles south on A 36 to Warminster, on the westernmost edge of mysterious Salisbury Plain. If you tell someone in any of the local pubs around the plain that you've seen a flying saucer, you will not be laughed at. More UFOs have been sighted here than anywhere else in Britain—especially in the 1960s, when hardly a month went by without news of something extraterrestrial being spotted on a hillside. Doubters attribute the sightings to the presence of nearby military installations, and the romantic associations of Salisbury Plain help get the imagination working, too.

You can also make the trip from Bath to Salisbury by train; the route is comparatively roundabout but scenically very pretty. Best of all, the line passes through **Bradford-on-Avon**, an exquisite town that is known for its antiques shops, including a porcelain specialist and an art gallery that welcomes browsers. Something of a poor man's Bath, Bradford-on-Avon has, among other attractions, a Saxon church and a 14th-century tithe barn. The town's prosperity came, not untypically, from wool production, but the last mill closed in 1905. A "day-return" ticket between Bath and Salisbury costs just over £6, and you can stop to shop in Bradford-on-Avon without extra charge. A few minutes' walk away in the village of Avoncliff you will find the charming 17th-century inn called **The Cross Guns**—all low ceilings, horse-brasses, and oak beams. If you want somewhere even more special to stay, there is **Woolley Grange Hotel** standing on the edge of Bradford-on-Avon in 14 acres of grounds. It's elegant and spacious, and small children are welcome.

Salisbury Plain is just one part of the chalky upland that dominates much of rural Wiltshire. It has been described as a rumpled plateau surrounded by steep slopes, and though it is on average just 500 feet above sea level, it seems higher. It appears soft and pleasant enough on a summer afternoon, but when the wind moans across the grassy, uninhabited hills it is a different proposition. For many centuries this has been a military testing ground. The Romans crisscrossed it, and army maneuvers first took place here during the Napoleonic Wars. Most notable are the region's remnants of never-quite-forgotten

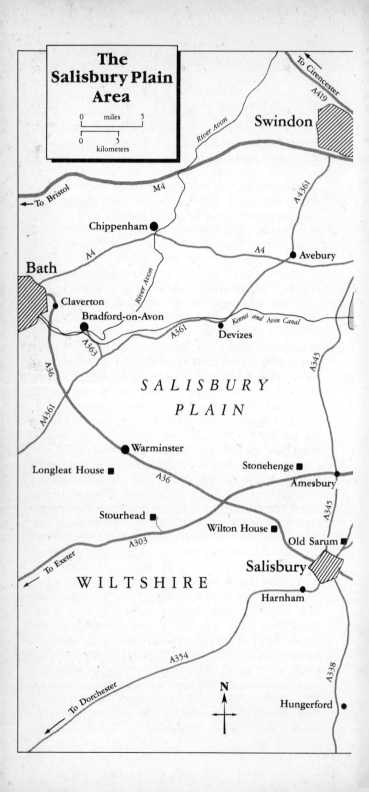

The Salisbury Plain Area

| 0 | miles | 5 |
| 0 | kilometers | 5 |

To Cirencester

Swindon

River Avon

A419

M4

To Bristol

A4361

Chippenham

A4

Avebury

Bath

A4

River Avon

Claverton

Bradford-on-Avon

Kennel and Avon Canal

A361

Devizes

A363

A345

A36

A4361

SALISBURY
PLAIN

Warminster

Stonehenge

Longleat House

A36

Amesbury

A345

Stourhead

Wilton House

A303

Old Sarum

To Exeter

Salisbury

WILTSHIRE

Harnham

A354

A338

To Dorchester

N

Hungerford

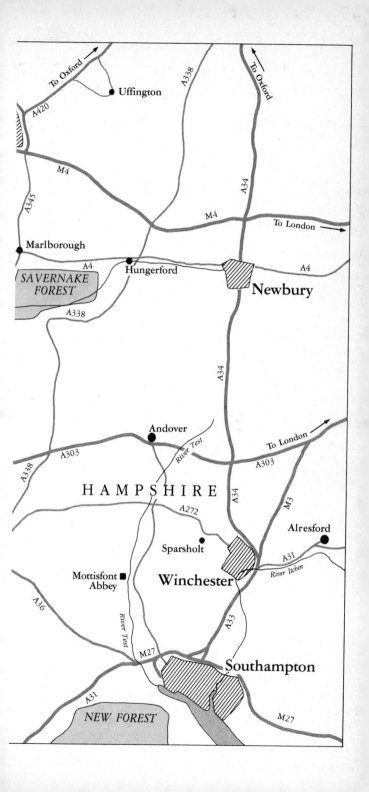

3,000- to 4,000-year-old tribes: Stonehenge (which we cover below, after the town of Salisbury) and the even more mysterious and romantic Avebury Stone Circle, which actually encompasses an ancient village.

Stourhead—in contrast to the exposed Salisbury Plain and other Wiltshire uplands—is 2,500 acres of some of the National Trust's finest garden property. Located southwest of Warminster, it is due south of the equally famous Longleat House—the family home of the marquesses of Bath, built in 1580. Longleat was the first country house in Britain to open to the public and, in 1966, was the first of many to create a safari park containing wild animals on its grounds.

Stourhead is a fantasy world of ornamental lakes and gardens, set off by bizarre bridges, a classical temple, and even a market cross. The gardens were laid out in the 1740s, and as you stroll through them you may feel you have stepped into a classical Italian landscape painting. This is the perfect place for a picnic: Try a local pork pie (a Wiltshire specialty) or pastries from one of Marlborough's fine pâtisseries. (See Around Winchester, below, for Marlborough.) A Hampshire wine such as Hambledon might complete the feast. Stourhead House, the focal point here, tends to take second place to the gardens, yet it has some fine Chippendale furniture, landscape paintings, works by old masters, and Grinling Gibbons carvings (those distinctive limewood representations of fruit, leaves, and birds).

SALISBURY

Part of the appeal of England's cathedrals, whether identifiable by spires or towers, is that so many of them are visible from a great distance. Salisbury's distinctive single spire—at 404 feet the tallest in Britain, beating Norwich by 89 feet—dominates the city. Many a first-time visitor who has had trouble negotiating the approach to Salisbury and the city ring road has been frustrated by the sight of the spire cropping up tantalizingly in apparently different places.

The history of Salisbury, which is due south of the great mass of Salisbury Plain, is closely interwoven with that of the cathedral. Neatly extending beyond the boundaries of the cathedral's close—perhaps the most harmonious and beautiful in the country—the town has retained its original Medieval layout. It is graced by a huge marketplace, a 13th-century poultry cross, an exceptional parish church that was a "chapel of ease" to the cathedral, and a handful of highly evocative and historic coaching inns that seem to have stepped straight out of the pages of Dickens's *Pickwick Papers.*

The **water meadows**, from which John Constable painted several pictures of the cathedral, have been jealously guarded, with no building allowed. The walk across them to Harnham Mill—now incorporating a small hotel, a restaurant, and a café on the edge of the small village of Harnham, onto which Salisbury proper has never encroached—is recommended. The river that tumbles beside Salisbury's town mill and meanders toward Harnham in the shadow of the cathedral is a tributary of the Salisbury Avon, not to be confused with the Avon that flows through Shakespeare's Stratford. The name *Avon,* by the way, is derived from the Celtic word for "water." It is entirely characteristic of Salisbury that the **Salisbury Arts Festival** is low-key and little known beyond a certain radius (and so less crowded as well). It takes place each September. Not far away in **Wilton House** near Salisbury and **Longleat House** (see above) musical events are regularly held.

Salisbury Cathedral

Salisbury Cathedral, and thus most of the city we see today, was built on virgin land, following a move in 1219 from Old Sarum, on high ground two miles north of Salisbury. **Old Sarum,** a very worthwhile detour for visitors who want to explore Salisbury's origins, was probably occupied during the Iron Age. The Romans had a defensive fort here called Sorbiodunum. In the Domesday Book, the settlement appears as Sarisberie. Due to a lack of fresh water, Bishop Poore, incumbent at the original cathedral, requested papal permission to build a new cathedral. Legend has it that Poore fired an arrow into the air, vowing to build wherever it landed. A good way to see Old Sarum is to attend the open-air plays (often Shakespeare) performed here in summer.

The new cathedral was consecrated a remarkably brief 38 years after the first foundation stone was laid. This first half of the 13th century saw a magnificent surge of Gothic architecture (Amiens and Lincoln cathedrals were created at roughly the same time). Even so, Salisbury is memorable, with a long nave—second only to Winchester's—that can be taken in at one glance. The cathedral is full of unique architectural detail: rare 13th-century stone friezes in the octagonal Chapter House and a clock mechanism of 1386—the oldest piece of machinery still working in the country, perhaps even in the world. Also contained in the cathedral is the best preserved of the four extant copies of the Magna Carta. This has been safely contained within the building since 1225, except between 1940 and 1945, when it was hidden in a nearby quarry to protect it from German bombing. The famous spire—so often pictured on chocolate boxes and calendars—was not part of the original cathedral plan but was begun in about 1330.

The earliest houses in the cathedral close were built partly from stones brought from Old Sarum, and these early remains can be detected alongside state-of-the-art Georgian red brick and later stucco that make the close a paragon of domestic architectural harmony. The close is, literally, an enclosure, as the four gates through which most visitors pass are actually closed at night, continuing a centuries-old curfew.

The easterly **St. Ann's Gate**, perhaps the most exciting approach to an English cathedral precinct, closes off St. Ann's Street. The gate, attractive and intriguing in itself, effectively divides the workaday streets of the town from the rarefied setting of the cathedral. In a room above, it is said, the young George Frederick Handel gave his first public recital in England. Beyond the close, the simple arrangement of houses and streets that followed immediately in the wake of the construction of the cathedral comprised neighborhoods that were known as "chequers," usually taking their name from inns. So there were precincts known as the White Hart Chequer, the Black Horse Chequer, and the **Cross Keys Chequer**, the last of which survives in the heart of the city, a few yards from the Guildhall, where a small shopping precinct still carries the name.

No transport is needed within this compact city, which has no hills to discourage the stroller. **St. Ann's Street** might appear on the map as an unlikely detour, but it is worth the short walk. This street is a microcosm of the best of several centuries of English domestic architecture. Walk up the street—it is a dead end—and then retrace your steps; it makes a fine approach to the cathedral, whose spire is visible as you walk along. Joiners' Hall, now owned by the National Trust, was once the guildhall of the Joiners' Company, which was created in 1617.

Salisbury Museums

The most popular of the city's museums is the **Salisbury and South Wiltshire Museum**—with good reason. It is especially strong on archaeological finds tracing the prehistory of Wessex, which was one of Britain's most advanced and populous regions long before the Roman invasion. Better still, artifacts from Stonehenge are included, so this makes an excellent appetizer if you are en route to that monument.

Mompesson House, in Choristers' Green, on the northern side of the close, is one of the finest of the National Trust's urban properties. It is a recently lived-in house overlooking the northern flank of the cathedral with a warm and harmonious interior of about 1740. Also worth seeing from the outside, although its interior is closed to the public, is the **College of Matrons**—dating from 1682 and originally founded as a home for widows and unmarried daughters of clergymen—near High Street Gate and Malmesbury House, one of the finest houses in the close.

Exploring Salisbury

St. Thomas's Church holds its own even against the cathedral, and parts of it are older. Just 100 yards from Market Square, it commands the commercial quarter. The church houses a famous painting known colloquially as *Doom,* an impressive Medieval work depicting both highborn and common men and women emerging from a graveyard on their way to either heaven or hell.

You can finish off your visit to St. Thomas's by stopping at nearby **Snell's**, a stylish coffee room/delicatessen that is renowned for its handmade chocolates and other confectioneries.

Markets are held in Salisbury on Tuesdays and Saturdays. The Tuesday charter was granted in 1227, but the practice gradually became daily until neighboring towns objected. Thus the twice-weekly compromise. Above the library at one side of the marketplace is a clock celebrating the Queen's 1977 Silver Jubilee. Another royal event recalled here is the coronation of Edward VII, in celebration of which 4,000 people sat down to roast beef and a choice of dessert. At the southeastern corner of Market Square is the mainly 18th-century Guildhall, and just across Queen Street, which runs past it, is the Cross Keys Chequer shopping precinct.

A few yards beyond the Cross Keys Chequer precinct is the house of John A'Port, a wool merchant and six-time mayor of Salisbury. The house is now a china and glass emporium called **Watson's** in which visitors are encouraged not just to browse among the crystal and Wedgwood but also to look at a cutaway section of the first floor's original structure, as well as a series of before-and-after photographs of the restoration. Another remarkable city-center building is the Hall of John Halle, now the lobby of the Odeon movie theater. The hall dates back to about 1479.

Salisbury has an exceptional inn—the **Red Lion**, the original coaching yard on Milford Street, with a bright red stone lion on which children like to sit and have their photographs taken. In the heyday of the coaching era this was the starting point for the "Salisbury Flying Machine," which departed for London every night at 10:00. The public rooms of the Red Lion have resisted late 20th-century tarting up and remain oak-paneled, labyrinthine, and full of nostalgia, but bedrooms are modern and generally comfortable. If you pop in here for a drink you half expect an ostler to emerge touching his forelock or a serving maid to come to your table bearing a jug of ale made on the premises. Walking south from the Red Lion along Fish Row and Butcher Row—clues to the nature of commercial life in Salisbury 400 or 500 years ago—you'll come to Poultry Cross, a small stone shelter that has stood here for about 600 years. It is one of only four of its kind in the country. Directly opposite is the ancient **Haunch of Venison** pub, a beautifully preserved, traditional chophouse. Good, inexpensive bar meals, as well as traditional roasts, are served in this low-ceilinged, bustling place, and a bizarre tale is still told of a mummified hand found in the dark recesses of the pub in 1905.

For unusual souvenirs try **Beach's Bookshop** on High Street, a large secondhand emporium in which the assistants actually wear uniforms. It is very good for books on local topography and history. Directly across the road from Beach's is **Mitre House**, now a tea room and shop selling teas (run by the fine-tea specialists Betjeman and Barton). Bishops were traditionally robed here before their enthronement. The National Trust shop on High

Street sells things like needlepoint kits, luxury soaps, embroidered and printed tea towels, coffee-table books, commemorative plaques, and a traditional run of portable souvenirs—all displayed in a genteel environment. From Beach's it is just a few hundred yards to the Old George shopping mall and, beyond that, to Bridge Street and another good source of books, **The Everyman Bookshop**. There is also a fine antiques shop on St. Ann's Street: **Ian Hastie**. At 37 Catherine Street is **The Antique and General Trading Centre**, a three-story antiques and bric-a-brac emporium.

Salisbury has no restaurants of national renown, and its ethnic restaurants (Indian and Chinese) tend to be of the friendly neighborhood variety, with no pretensions—just filling meals at good value. Salisbury seems best for solid pub fare: game in season, locally made meat pies, fish and chips. There is a large and popular fish-and-chips shop, **Stoby's**, between Fish Row and Market Square. The **White Hart** on St. John Street—also a hotel—serves good hot bar lunches, and you will rub shoulders with comfortable solicitors in Harris tweed and ladies in Pringle sweaters. In the hotel foyer residents will be waiting for friends behind their *Daily Telegraph*s. The 13th-century **Rose & Crown Hotel** also serves traditional English food and has lots of atmosphere. For something different, at a very reasonable price, try **Mainly Salads** on Fisherton Street or **Mo's** on Milford Street; both are suitable for vegetarians. An alternative on a pleasant summer day would be to buy some fruit and cheese from the market and eat it in the shade of the Poultry Cross.

STONEHENGE

Just to the north of the city is Salisbury Plain, where thousands of the sheep that made Salisbury so prosperous once grazed. Of all the tangible reminders that in prehistoric times this was a popular and comparatively sophisticated patch of England, none is better known than Stonehenge.

Stonehenge, at the southern edge of the plain just eight miles north of Salisbury, is probably bigger in your imagination than in its actual physical presence. As has often been pointed out, its 162 stone blocks—unadorned, undressed, and only about 35 steps from one side to the other—would fit into the Library of Congress rotunda or within the dome of St. Paul's Cathedral. Nonetheless, each year it inspires approximately three quarters of a million people to go on a pilgrimage. These numbers are swollen by modern-day Druids, pop fans, and latter-day hippies who crowd onto Salisbury Plain for the summer solstice and for officially illegal rock festivals held to coincide with it. It is mainly on account of these celebrants that access to Stonehenge is much more restricted than it has ever been. Barbed-wire barricades have turned this into a look-but-don't-touch monument—no more KILROY WAS HERE engraved into the stone with penknives.

This most famous of all Britain's stone circles is one of Europe's greatest enigmas. A thousand years before the Egyptians built the pyramids, Neolithic farmers lived on the windswept chalk plateau. There was little wood and less stone, but they built burial chambers around which Stonehenge eventually grew—first as a cemetery, then as a temple. Over the years it was put to many uses, which is one of the reasons Stonehenge has so puzzled later generations.

As trade routes became busier and the population increased, Stonehenge and similar burial grounds took on the role of meeting places, not only for traders but also for participants in seasonal fertility rituals. Stonehenge was almost certainly not constructed because of any astronomical significance.

Among the earliest visitors to Stonehenge were the Druids, Celtic priests who came over from the Continent about 300 B.C., when Stonehenge had lain abandoned and unused for more than 1,000 years. They took it over for ceremonial purposes (though not, as used to be fancifully supposed, for ritual slaughter).

In 1130 Henry of Huntingdon, a dean at Lincoln Cathedral, was commissioned to write a history of England, and he included Stonehenge. He borrowed from an even earlier chronicle—largely fictitious—that claimed Merlin, seer and prophet to King Arthur, had the stones removed from Ireland and reconstructed on Salisbury Plain.

Charles II was among the "great and good" to be fascinated by Stonehenge, and he commissioned Inigo Jones, the superb architect of St. Paul's, Covent Garden, and the Banqueting Hall in London, to solve the mystery. Jones concluded that as "those ancient times had no knowledge of public works, either sacred or secular, for their own use or honour of their deities, they could not be responsible for such an impressive structure." It must, ergo, have been Roman in origin.

Samuel Pepys took a day trip from Salisbury but found the cost of his party's saddle horses rather high. Of the site he was characteristically blunt: "Worth going to see. God knows what their use was." James I was utterly intrigued and commissioned John Aubrey, best known for his *Brief Lives,* to produce a thorough survey. But Aubrey was much more impressed with nearby Avebury Stone Circle, and his work at Stonehenge was skimpy. Among all the dross was the correct suggestion that this was a residential site of early British tribes.

People seem to have great difficulty counting the stones. There was even a legend from Elizabethan times that no ordinary mortal could count the stones twice and arrive at the same figure. Jonathan Swift, the author of *Gulliver's Travels,* and Celia Fiennes, the late 17th-century traveller and diarist, were among those who made a stab at it. Each came up with a different number, and Swift hedged his bets—"either 92 or 93."

The Layout of Stonehenge

As you approach Stonehenge, you first come upon a ditch and a bank about 100 feet from the first stones. Inside this are the 56 Aubrey holes, found to contain remains of cremated human beings, and what is effectively a gateway to the site known as the slaughter stone, now fallen. The Heel Stone, a so-called sarsen stone, stands outside the entrance. (The word *sarsen* probably comes from *saracen,* or, simply, strange or alien; the term "Heel Stone" is derived from a mark on the surface that resembles a man's heel.) The Heel Stone is the only one to have survived from the first circle of stones that appeared here around 1800 B.C. It was erected exactly in line, with other stones, with the point at which the sun rises above the horizon during the summer solstice.

Between 1700 and 1600 B.C. the construction of the second stage of Stonehenge began. Blue stones were transported from Wales and erected in two concentric circles. This was the work of the Beaker Folk, farmers from the Continent. The construction of Stonehenge III began after 1600 B.C., when the blue stones were moved and 80 huge sarsen stones were transported here from the Marlborough Downs. These were formed either into a ring of upright stones, connected by carved lintels, or an inner horseshoe shape.

Later (also part of Stonehenge III) an oval arrangement of blue stones was erected within the sarsen horseshoe, and a block of sandstone, also from Wales, was erected in the center. It became known as the Altar Stone. Finally, in about 1300 B.C., the residents rearranged 19 blue stones into their current configuration.

Traditionally, the time to visit Stonehenge is at the summer solstice, usually the nights of June 21 and June 22. You'll need a ticket from English Heritage (Tel: 071-973-3580). A word of advice: Try to visit Stonehenge when the rest of the world has decided to miss it. Dull, even rainy, days are good; misty or foggy ones are better still. It all helps to get the imagination working. But even when the site is closed, it is possible during daylight hours to see a certain amount of Stonehenge from the road.

Mottisfont Abbey

A visit to Salisbury and Winchester cathedrals has been called the best day's outing in southern England. And Mottisfont Abbey, set in a gentle valley by the River Test (famous for its trout fishing), is almost exactly midway between the two, making for an added bonus. The abbey takes its name from the Saxon "moot" (council) once held on the site, and from a nearby spring, or font. In the 18th century the abbey became a country house, and it is now owned by the National Trust. The house is open only at limited times, but the lovely gardens are usually accessible and are delightful for picnicking. Mottisfont is a rural interlude between the two inevitably bustling and well-trodden tourist hot spots. Highly recommended for a light lunch or afternoon tea are the Post Office tea rooms in the village center.

WINCHESTER

When the Romans reached this part of the south of England, Winchester was well established as the most important city in the land. The Normans adopted it as their capital after the 1066 invasion, and Winchester almost became the English capital for all time. But London's geographical advantages, particularly its position on the Thames, were too strong to ignore.

Winchester's spectacular cathedral, which has the longest nave of any in England, was begun in 1079 and not completed until 300 years later. The presence of this mighty church—certainly more than the effective status as capital—made Winchester the most important market town in Wessex.

The town is comparatively small and intimate, though you might not think so on a hot day as you try to escape into the air-conditioned comfort of the larger-than-average branch of Marks and Spencer. On such a day be sure to stroll along the bank of the River Itchen, close to the spacious grounds of Winchester College on your right. To experience the Medieval aspect of town, walk along the back lanes leading to and around the school.

Much Medieval prosperity derived from wool, and Winchester enjoyed its share of this wealth. The bishops of Winchester held the charter for a great annual wool fair, and funds from this enabled Bishop William of Wykeham in 1382 to found **Winchester College**, possibly the oldest of the country's "public" schools (although this claim is disputed by King's School in Canterbury). The school offers occasional organized tours to the public, and its buildings are just several among many that make Winchester worth visiting on its own account and not just for the cathedral. The grounds and buildings are lovely, reminiscent of some of the larger Oxford and Cambridge colleges. Other essential sights include the **Castle Hall**, which is all that remains of the Norman castle that was largely destroyed by Cromwellian troops in 1651. Here you'll find "King Arthur's Round Table," but do not assume Arthur or Merlin (elusive figures at the best of times) ever sat at it: It has been scientifically dated at around 1400. It is interesting to compare the Purbeck marble pillars in Castle Hall with those in Salisbury Cathedral. Nearby, there is a small museum in the Westgate, one of two surviving gateways from about 1200.

The truth about King Arthur, who he was and where he held court, is unclear, but there is no doubt that King Alfred, much ahead of his time, created a powerhouse of culture in fertile Wessex. He died in 899, after fortifying 20 or more towns and translating Latin texts into the vernacular Saxon. He also wrote the very first English history. His statue, erected in 1901 to mark the 1,000th anniversary of his death—actually two years too late—stands in Winchester's main street, Broadway.

If you are really adventurous, you may apply for the

wayfarer's dole of bread and ale at the **Hospital of St. Cross**, founded in 1137 by a grandson of William the Conqueror. Note the ruffed gowns of the pensioners who reside at the hospital. Only a tiny token of bread and ale is now available, but at least you become part of an 800-year-old tradition. You can also make a literary pilgrimage of sorts in Winchester. Jane Austen and Izaak Walton both died here—Austen in 1817 in a house on College Street, Walton in 1683 in a house on Dome Alley (a cul-de-sac at the end of St. Swithun's Street) in the cathedral precinct, although neither house is open to the public. Finally, in your wanderings around Winchester, do not miss **Kingsgate**. It is almost in the same league as Salisbury's St. Ann's Street, a rare example of harmonious domestic architecture.

The Cathedral

This is the longest Medieval church not only in England but in the whole of Europe. Part of the foundations, discovered during excavations in the 1960s, date from about 645, though the earliest material is from the 11th century. The cathedral close, while not in the same class as Salisbury's, has some special buildings, including some dating from the 13th century.

For all the cathedral's rare and beautiful tombs and its outstanding collection of antechapels and chantries, the tomb of the ninth-century bishop Saint Swithun is the most popular attraction. Swithun was a man of such great humility that he refused to allow his own burial in the church proper. It is said that when his bones were brought into the cathedral to be reinterred on July 15, 971, it rained heavily for 40 days. Legend now holds that if it rains on July 15, it will do so at least in part for each of the next 40 days.

Among the details some visitors miss is the Winchester Bible, an illuminated 12th-century volume housed in the oldest book room in Europe, dating from about 1150. And in one transept are two wooden benches thought to be Norman—they are certainly the oldest pieces of oak furniture in the country. There are also several chests said to contain the bones of Saxon kings, including Canute and Ethelwulf. Jane Austen is commemorated by a stone in the floor of the nave, but no direct reference is made to her novels in the inscription. Most recent among things to see is the cathedral's Triforium Museum—sculpture, wood, and metalwork reflecting 1,000 years of the building's history.

Like Salisbury, Winchester has an abundance of secondhand bookshops. The long-established **Wells** is small but charming and sells prints too, at the cathedral end of Kingsgate Street. It has a new-books branch in College Street. A bigger secondhand bookshop is **Gilberts** in The Square—excellent browsing. For a variety of interesting antiques, try **Blanchards** on Jewry Street. This street is filled with antiques and bric-a-brac shops.

There are fewer well-known restaurants in Winchester than pubs, which offer a wide range of hot and cold bar lunches. The **Royal Oak**, off Royal Oak Passage, is one of several contenders for the title of the oldest drinking spot in Britain; it is part Saxon. Another small pub near the cathedral, the **Eclipse**, was originally the rectory for the little church of St. Lawrence, and it predates the cathedral itself. It offers traditional English food such as toad-in-the-hole (sausage cooked in batter) and kedgeree (fish, rice, eggs, and condiments). For Itchen trout or pork in cream and cider sauce, with a better-than-average glass of (pub) wine, look for the **Wykeham Arms** pub on the corner of Kingsgate and Canon streets. **Mr. So**, a Chinese restaurant on Jewry Street, compares well with most Chinese restaurants in London.

You may be lucky enough to find local venison—from New Forest deer—in some of the restaurants in and around Winchester; the spacious and well-run restaurant of the **Wessex Hotel**, considered Winchester's best hotel, is one such source. If you decide to stay at the Wessex, be sure to request a room with a cathedral view. When the Trusthouse Forte chain put up the hotel in the 1960s, it was considered an eyesore, but now it seems to have settled into its city-center background. Another nice place to stay is the **Lainston House**, just west of town in the village of Sparsholt (a short taxi ride from Winchester). This luxurious retreat, popular with a well-heeled clientele, occupies a 17th-century country house surrounded by many acres of grounds. It offers an inexpensive and elegantly served table d'hôte lunch.

Around Winchester

From Winchester, Newbury and the A 4 lie about 25 miles due north. Close to workaday Newbury, and westward along A 4 (which is dotted with old coaching inns) are the historic towns of **Hungerford** (famous for its antiques shops) and **Marlborough,** where another famous public school (former poet laureate John Betjeman was one of its pupils) offers residential summer courses for outsiders. Try to visit Marlborough on a Saturday, when the open-air market is held under multicolored awnings. It has just enough of the atmosphere of bygone centuries to add spice to your trip. Good old-fashioned pubs and tea shops are a bonus. In warm weather a stroll from the elegant, mainly red-brick High Street down to the cool and shady riverside is pleasant. **Alresford,** sometimes called New Alresford, is a comparatively unspoiled market town of 18th-century coaching inns and wide, tree-lined streets just 6 miles to the east of Winchester on A 31.

Known mainly to local people but highly recommended for a change of pace are the cool and dappled glades of **Savernake Forest,** a short drive to the east of Marlborough. Its Grand Avenue of beeches is four miles long.

A few miles to the west of Marlborough are partly intact prehistoric settlements that some feel surpass the magic of Stonehenge. The **Avebury Stone Circle** is impressive: Its massive boulders actually surround a substantial village. The circumference of the earthwork encloses 30 acres, ten times the space occupied by Stonehenge. But even less is known about Avebury than Stonehenge. It has been called "all things to all men": Military experts have tended to label it a military camp; sociologists think it was a gigantic market and meeting place; astronomers assume it was devised to predict a cosmic event.

Silbury Hill, within walking distance of the Avebury Stone Circle, is even more intriguing. This unlikely, entirely man-made conical mound, which stands by a Roman road, may have been a burial chamber. Silbury Hill is railed off, but **White Horse Hill,** near the village of Uffington—birthplace of Thomas Hughes, the author of *Tom Brown's School Days*—is not. It lies northeast of Swindon. A not-too-difficult climb from the village, it offers superb, panoramic views and a close-up look at what some people say is a Neolithic cutting of a horse, from which the hill gets its name. (Recent research indicates that it was cut between the first century B.C. and A.D. 871.)

GETTING AROUND

The best way to see rural England is by rental car, and this is especially true in the Cotswolds. In summer you can also rent a bicycle. There are cycle shops in the larger towns, such as Noah's Ark in Cirencester, Thames and Cotswold Bikes in Tetbury, and Jeffrey's Toy Shop in Moreton-in-Marsh.

This region of the south of England is mercifully free of traffic congestion, which makes car travel a pleasure. Even cities such as Oxford, Bath, Salisbury, and Winchester are not too bad for drivers, though Salisbury's ring road can leave you looking for a way into the very center. Perhaps by way of compensation, Salisbury's car parks are better than most.

A good way to see the Cotswolds by car is to leave A 40 near Burford and drive northwest through Burford to Broadway and then southwest on B 4632 through Winchcombe toward Cheltenham and Cirencester. Oxford lies just off the M 40 motorway from London, currently being extended northward. Bath is just a few miles off M 4; Winchester is easily reached from London via M 3.

Country buses fan out from the larger towns to the rural villages, but sometimes they run only on market days or on market days and Saturdays. Sunday travel by public transportation can be well-nigh impossible. Train service survives in the Cotswolds, even in the face of government equivocation, but really only on the idyllically pretty line from Oxford to Worcester and between Swindon and Gloucester. Salisbury, Winchester, and Bath are all easily accessible by train from London—Bath from Paddington Station and Salisbury and Winchester from Waterloo.

ACCOMMODATIONS REFERENCE

▶ **Apsley House Hotel.** 141 Newbridge Hill, **Bath** BA1 3PT. Tel: (0225) 33-69-66; in U.S., (708) 251-4110 or (800) 323-5463; Telex: 449212; Fax: (0225) 46-98-45.

▶ **Bath Spa Hotel.** Sydney Road, **Bath** BA2 6JF. Tel: (0225) 44-44-24-; Fax: (0225) 44-40-06.

▶ **The Bear Hotel.** Park Street, **Woodstock** OX7 1SZ. Tel: (0993) 81-15-11; Telex: 837921; Fax: (0993) 81-33-80.

▶ **Buckland Manor. Buckland,** near Broadway WR12 7LY. Tel: (0386) 85-26-26.

▶ **Bull Hotel.** High Street, **Burford** OX8 4RH. Tel: (0993) 82-22-20.

▶ **Charingworth Manor. Charingworth,** near Chipping

Campden GL55 6NS. Tel: (0386) 78-555; Fax: (0386) 783-53.

▶ **Cotswold House Hotel and Restaurant.** The Square, **Chipping Campden** GL55 6AN. Tel: (0386) 84-03-30; Fax: (0386) 84-03-10.

▶ **Dormy House Hotel.** Willersey Hill, **Broadway** WR12 7LF. Tel: (0386) 85-27-11; Telex: 338275; in U.S., (312) 251-4110 or (800) 323-5463; Fax: (0386) 85-86-36.

▶ **Feathers Hotel.** Market Street, **Woodstock** OX7 1SX. Tel: (0993) 81-22-91; in U.S., (312) 251-4110 or (800) 323-5463; Fax: (0993) 81-31-58.

▶ **Francis Hotel.** Queen Square, **Bath** BA1 2HH. Tel: (0225) 42-42-57; Telex: 449162; in U.S., (212) 541-4400 or (800) 223-5672; Fax: (0225) 31-97-15.

▶ **Golden Valley Thistle Hotel.** Gloucester Road, **Cheltenham** GL51 0TS. Tel: (0242) 23-26-91; Fax: (0242) 22-18-46.

▶ **Hilton National.** Walcot Street, **Bath** BA1 5BJ. Tel: (0225) 46-34-11; Telex: 449519; Fax: (0225) 46-43-93.

▶ **King's Head Hotel.** Market Place, **Cirencester** GL7 2NR. Tel: (0285) 65-33-22; Telex: 43470; in U.S., (602) 954-7600 or (800) 528-1234; Fax: (0285) 65-51-03.

▶ **Kingshead House. Birdlip** GL4 8JH. Tel: (0452) 86-22-99.

▶ **Lainston House Hotel. Sparsholt** SO21 2LT. Tel: (0962) 635-88; Telex: 477375; Fax: (0962) 726-72.

▶ **Langford House Cottages.** Little Faringdon, **Lechlade** GL7 3QN. Tel: (0367) 522-10; Fax: (0993) 84-28-79.

▶ **Lords of the Manor. Upper Slaughter**, near Bourton-on-the-Water GL54 2JD. Tel: (0451) 202-43; in U.S., (212) 714-2323, (800) 522-5568, or (800) 223-6764; Fax: (0451) 206-96.

▶ **Lower Slaughter Manor. Lower Slaughter**, near Bourton-on-the-Water GL54 2HP. Tel: (0451) 204-56; Telex: 437287; Fax: (0451) 221-50.

▶ **Lygon Arms.** High Street, **Broadway** WR12 7DU. Tel: (0386) 85-22-55; Telex: 338260; in U.S., (800) 243-9420; Fax: (0386) 85-86-11.

▶ **Noel Arms.** High Street, **Chipping Campden** GL55 6AT. Tel: (0386) 84-03-17; Fax: (0386) 84-11-36.

▶ **Owlpen Manor.** Owlpen, near Dursley GL11 5BZ. Tel: (0453) 86-02-61; Fax: (0453) 86-08-19.

▶ **Paradise House.** 86-88 Holloway, **Bath** BA2 4PX. Tel: (0225) 31-77-23.

▶ **Plough at Clanfield.** Bourton Road, **Clanfield** OX8 2RB. Tel: (0367) 812-22; Fax: (0367) 815-96.

▶ **Priory Hotel.** Weston Road, **Bath** BA1 2XT. Tel: (0225) 33-19-22; Telex: 44612; in U.S., (212) 696-1323; Fax: (0225) 44-82-76.

▶ **Queen's Hotel.** The Promenade, **Cheltenham** GL50 1NN. Tel: (0242) 51-47-24; Fax: (0242) 22-41-45.

▶ **Red Lion Hotel.** Milford Street, **Salisbury** SP1 2AN. Tel: (0722) 233-34; Telex: 477674; Fax: (0722) 257-56.

▶ **Rose & Crown Hotel.** Harnham Road, **Salisbury** SP2 8JQ. Tel: (0722) 279-08; Telex: 47224; Fax: (0722) 33-98-16.

▶ **Royal Crescent.** 16 Royal Crescent, **Bath** BA1 2LS. Tel: (0225) 31-90-90; Telex: 444251; in U.S., (212) 535-9530 or (800) 223-5581; Fax: (0225) 33-94-01.

▶ **Studley Priory Hotel. Horton-cum-Studley** OX9 1AZ. Tel: (0867) 352-03; in U.S., (212) 714-2323, (800) 552-5567, or (800) 223-6764; Fax: (0867) 356-13.

▶ **Sudeley Castle Cottages.** Sudeley Castle, **Winchcombe** GL54 5JD. Tel: (0242) 60-41-03; Fax: (0242) 60-29-59.

▶ **Unicorn Hotel.** Sheep Street, **Stow-on-the-Wold** GL54 1HQ. Tel: (0451) 302-57; in U.S., (402) 493-4747 or (800) 44-UTELL; Fax: (0451) 310-90.

▶ **Wessex Hotel.** Paternoster Row, **Winchester** SO23 9LQ. Tel: (0962) 616-11; Telex: 47419; in U.S., (212) 541-4400 or (800) 223-5672; Fax: (0962) 84-15-03.

▶ **White Hart Hotel.** 1 St. John Street, **Salisbury** SP1 2SD. Tel: (0722) 274-76; in U.S., (212) 541-4400 or (800) 223-5672; Fax: (0722) 41-27-61.

▶ **Woolley Grange.** Woolley Green, **Bradford-on-Avon** BA15 1TX. Tel: (0221) 647-05; in U.S., (800) 848-7721; Fax: (0221) 640-59.

▶ **Wyck Hill House.** Stow-on-the-Wold GL54 1HY. Tel: (0451) 319-36; Telex: 43611; Fax: (0451) 322-43.

DEVON AND CORNWALL

AND THE
ISLES OF SCILLY

By Ken Thompson

Ken Thompson is a newspaper and broadcast journalist who has lived in Cornwall for nearly 30 years. His holiday guide, Discover Cornwall, *has won national design awards.*

Devon and Cornwall have a certain magical quality. Perhaps it is the magnificence of 650 miles of coastal scenery, which is unsurpassed in either England or Wales. Or maybe it is the unhurried pace of life in the relaxing and mild climate of this far southwesterly corner of Britain. Perhaps it is the delight in discovering why the Isles of Scilly will forever be known as the Fortunate Isles. Whatever it is, Devon and Cornwall offer an attractive combination of scenic beauty and historical and cultural interest.

MAJOR INTEREST

Seaside villages, art colonies
Mild climate
Celtic culture

Devon
Dartmoor and Exmoor parks
Exeter Cathedral

English Riviera resort area
Plymouth Hoe
Barbican and Mayflower Steps
Buckland Abbey
Buckfast Abbey
Clovelly
Dart Valley Steam Railway

Cornwall
Land's End
Truro Cathedral
Tintagel Castle
St. Michael's Mount
Cotehele House
Trerice Manor
Polperro

Isles of Scilly
Uncrowded beaches
Sea life
Tresco Abbey and Gardens

DEVON

Whether you enter the county from Somerset to its north or from Dorset to its east, it scarcely requires a frontier post to proclaim that you have reached the geographical gateway to southwest England: Devon. Gone are the familiar English villages with their houses and shops grouped around a proud, Gothic country church. Instead, whitewashed, cob-walled farm cottages with reed-thatched roofs punctuate the landscape alongside fields of rich red soil, lush green hillsides, and combes (or coombs), the short valleys climbing inland from Devon's famed seacoast.

This ancient Celtic kingdom, once called Dumnonia, boasts 2,000 square miles of some of the finest and most varied scenery in Britain. At its heart is the hauntingly beautiful Dartmoor National Park, the last largely unspoiled wilderness left in England. Here you will find granite tors and sweeping moorland, sparkling streams and wooded valleys, ancient stone circles and clapper (or

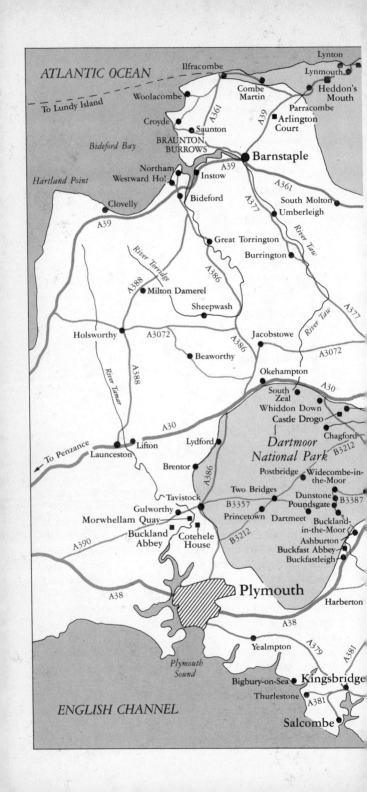

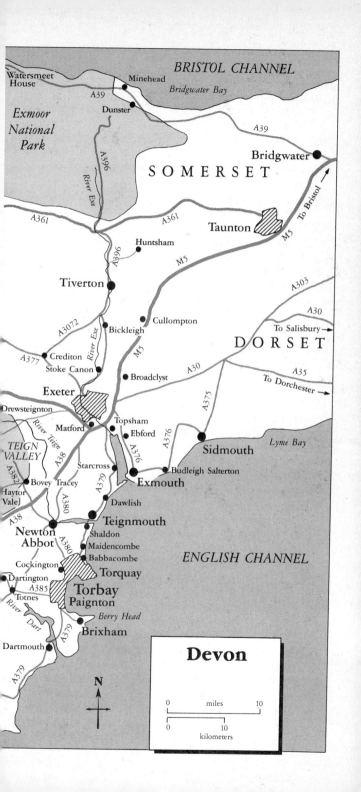

packhorse) bridges, historic towns and charming villages around which wild ponies graze placidly.

Devon has two fine cities: Exeter, with its 14th-century cathedral and historic Guildhall, and Plymouth, the great naval port from which Sir Francis Drake sailed to defeat the Spanish Armada 400 years ago and that will forever be associated with the Pilgrims. Fleeing religious persecution, they sailed from here in 1620 and subsequently founded the township of Dorchester in Massachusetts.

Like Cornwall, Devon has two contrasting coastlines. Overlooking the Atlantic to the north are the rugged cliffs and great expanses of sand called the "golden coast." In the south are towering red sandstone cliffs that slip down into river estuaries and palm-fringed bays, a surprising touch of the tropics.

When driving down to Devon from points north, it is best to leave the M 5 at Bridgwater and take A 39 toward the coast road and Minehead. This route will give you the option of exploring Exmoor, a park that Devon shares with neighboring Somerset.

It would be uncharitable not to mention an architectural gem you will encounter while crossing Exmoor en route for North Devon: the historic market town of **Dunster**, although geographically speaking it belongs to neighboring North Somerset. Dunster Castle, built on the site of a Saxon fortress, dominates the main street. The town also features an octagonal 17th-century Tudor yarn market, once used for the sale of locally woven cloth. The main street is perhaps the best surviving example of life in Medieval England and should not be missed. Dunster lies just south of the A 39 road inland from the coastal resort of Minehead.

NORTH DEVON

Exmoor National Park is softer and more undulating than Dartmoor and has been described by English poets as "The Little Switzerland of England" for its springtime carpets of primroses. It is not difficult to understand why, in 1869, Richard Doddridge Blackmore chose the wild beauty of Exmoor as the setting for his romantic novel *Lorna Doone*. You may recall that Lorna, rescued from the clutches of a band of outlaws by John Ridd, was shot during their wedding in **Oare Church**, which still stands on the northern edge of Exmoor and is worth visiting.

Your first encounter with North Devon after Exmoor is likely to be at the twin towns of **Lynton** and **Lynmouth**. Since 1890, Lynton, with its magnificent hilltop views, and Lynmouth, with its delightful harbor, have been linked by a water-operated cliff railway that descends 500 feet down a steeply wooded valley and remains to this day one of the most remarkable railways in the world.

There's a great deal to see in this part of Devon, quite enough to justify an overnight stop, and a good place to stay is the **Rising Sun**, a 14th-century thatched smugglers' inn alongside Lynmouth's tiny harbor and the East Lyn salmon river. Full of character, it is only a few miles from the Brendon (Doone) valley, which features in *Lorna Doone;* Blackmore wrote part of the book during his stay at the Rising Sun. Next door is the cottage in which the poet Percy Bysshe Shelley and his bride, Harriet, spent their honeymoon in 1812.

An alternative base from which to explore this area is the **Woodlands Hotel**, a country guesthouse at Lynbridge in Lynton. It stands in an acre of grounds running down to the West Lyn River and has private fishing rights that guests are encouraged to use. It is one mile from Lynmouth.

While you are here, be sure to visit Watersmeet, which lies in a very picturesque valley adjoining the Lynmouth–Barnstaple Road (A 39) about 1½ miles from Lynmouth. This is superb walking country. Here, at the confluence of the East Lyn River and Hoar Oak Water, the National Trust maintains an information center.

Before leaving Exmoor, visit the **Brass Rubbing Center** in Lynton on Queen Street. You might then head for the **Exmoor Bird Gardens** at Parracombe on your way west to Combe Martin and Ilfracombe. Incidentally, there's an interesting inn at Combe Martin—**The Pack o' Cards**, built in the shape of a deck of playing cards. It's a good place for a coffee break.

West of Exmoor, in steep wooded country northeast of Barnstaple on A 39, is **Arlington Court**, an early 19th-century house with a fascinating assemblage of objets d'art, model ships, pewter, costumes, and furniture of the past century. The stables contain a collection of horse-drawn vehicles, and Shetland ponies and Jacob sheep graze in the surrounding parkland. The late Sir Francis Chichester, that remarkable seafarer who single-handedly circumnavigated the globe, once lived here; now both house and gardens are in the care of the National Trust.

The town of **Ilfracombe**, North Devon's premier resort, grew up around its old harbor; it nestles in a valley surrounded by spectacular cliffs and rolling countryside. From a small fishing village, Ilfracombe emerged to be an extremely select resort in the Victorian era, when the advent of the railways first made seaside vacations practical.

Devon is one of those places where you can step back in time, a reverie helped along by the four-poster beds that many hotels provide. One such establishment is the **Heddon's Gate Hotel** at Heddon's Mouth near Parracombe, which lies between Lynton and Ilfracombe. Here you can enjoy the atmosphere of an original Victorian morning room and an Edwardian sitting room and sleep in a four-poster with interior lighting and wrap-around drapes.

Make a point of visiting **Chambercombe Manor**, a 16th-century house 2 miles southeast of Ilfracombe. Built in 1500, it contains an interesting collection of Tudor and Jacobean furniture and Cromwellian armor. And, time permitting, take a boat trip from Ilfracombe (or Barnstaple) to **Lundy Island**, 25 miles out into the Bristol Channel where it meets the Atlantic Ocean. The Landmark Trust administers it, and you'll find the journey well worthwhile, if only to see the colony of puffins that breeds there.

The North Devon coast is incomparable where Exmoor meets the sea, and nowhere is this more apparent than at Woolacombe, Croyde, and Westward Ho!, three resorts with fine beaches much sought after by surfers. **Croyde** is a particularly attractive village of thatched and color-washed cottages at the foot of steep, grassy downs, just north of Saunton Sands and Braunton Burrows.

You will have no difficulty finding a hotel in this area. There is a wide choice, ranging from the sumptuous **Saunton Sands Hotel** to the Old World **Kittiwell House Hotel**, at the eastern end of Croyde, with its Elizabethan restaurant. Kittiwell may offer 20th-century comforts, but you can still ask for a room with a four-poster bed.

Inland from here you will enter a different world: "Tarka Country," the countryside of the two rivers, the Taw and the Torridge, which Henry Williamson immortalized in his nature classic, *Tarka the Otter*.

Close to the mouth of the River Taw stands the ancient market town of **Barnstaple**, reputedly the oldest borough in England, having been granted its royal charter by Queen Elizabeth I in the 1580s. Barnstaple has been a

major seaport and commercial center since the Middle
Ages; five ships sailed from here in 1588 to help Sir
Francis Drake defeat Spain's Armada.

Be sure to visit the Pannier (basket) Market on Tuesdays,
Fridays, and Saturdays (the market dates to 1714); St. Peter's Church, with its twisted spire; and the Old Quay. You
should also cross the Long Bridge, with its 16 arches
spanning the River Taw. The bridge is one of the oldest
structures in the town and easily the most impressive.

One of the most exciting ideas of recent times here is
the development of the **Tarka Trail**, a long-distance footpath that follows in the footprints of Tarka the Otter, as
described in Williamson's book. The route also incorporates one of the loveliest train journeys in England—the
Tarka Line—which runs from Barnstaple along the banks
of the River Taw and on to Exeter.

If you have a day or two to spare, you can explore the
Taw, Torridge, and other Tarka Country landmarks with
Trevor Beer, a writer and wildlife artist (Tel: 0271-73520).

There is an excellent choice of hotels in this area,
including the highly rated **Park Hotel** overlooking the
river in Taw Vale (formerly the North Devon Motel, it was
totally refurbished in 1990), and the **Royal & Fortescue
Hotel**, a charming old coaching inn that was patronized
by Edward VII, Prince of Wales, and still retains its character and charm. In neighboring Bideford, the **Royal
Hotel** successfully combines 400 years of history with
every modern comfort. The Kingsley Room retains the
plaster ceiling designs originally imported from Venice.
Also on the banks of the River Torridge you will find the
equally inviting **Yeoldon House Hotel**.

The ancient port and market town of **Bideford** is rich in
history. Two fine ships were sent from here to help Sir
Francis Drake defeat the Spanish Armada, and the J. Hinks
and Son boatyard on the Torridge still builds replicas of
these historic vessels. The most notable was a copy of the
Golden Hind, which recently sailed to London's Tower
Bridge before crossing to America.

The **Torridge** is a spate river; the chance of catching a
salmon here depends on the height and color of the
water. The river is also known for the large sea trout that
travel it as early as April and May; the main run, however,
begins in June, and July and August are the best months
for the angler. Brown trout are also plentiful. If you want
to fish the river, you could do worse than stay at the **Half
Moon Inn** at Sheepwash near Beaworthy, where Water

Authority licenses are issued and they know all about the sport.

Before reaching Hartland Point, and Devon's northern boundary with Cornwall, you should stop at **Clovelly**, a colorful fishing village clinging dramatically to a steep hillside over the sea, with quaint cobbled streets that can be negotiated only on foot. Animal lovers will be glad to know that a Land Rover has replaced the donkeys that were formerly the only other means of transportation back up the hill.

If you intend to go on to Cornwall from here (or even if you don't), an overnight stop at the **Woodford Bridge Hotel** at Milton Damerel, on A 388 between Bideford and Holsworthy, would be a wise choice. It is a superb thatched and whitewashed 15th-century coaching inn (its roof is the longest thatched one in England) set in 20 acres of attractive gardens; its indoor heated pool is the envy of many much larger establishments. You may feel that this is Devon at its most glorious.

South from the Coast

Heading south down A 386 from Bideford toward Oke-hampton you will encounter **Great Torrington**, the home of Dartington Glass, where you can watch skilled workers dressed in period costumes demonstrating the art of glassblowing.

In Torrington there's an interesting place to eat, **Rebecca's** in Potacre Street. Unfortunately, it is closed on Sundays, but on the other six days of the week they will cook to order any English dish you choose from the menu. Rebecca's comes highly recommended—HRH Prince Edward was among recent satisfied customers.

If you find this part of Devon to your liking and wish to explore further, spend the night at the 250-year-old **Northcote Manor Hotel**, a 12-room country-house hotel at Burrington, near Umberleigh.

Before heading south toward Exeter, it would be worth making a slight detour to visit **Quince Honey Farm** on A 361 at South Molton. The farm is hailed as the world's most important honeybee exhibition; in the 25,000-square-foot apiary you can actually open the hives at the press of a button and see the colonies at work.

En route southeast to Exeter along A 396 there are a number of attractions worth visiting. At Tiverton you can take a trip on the Grand Western Canal in a horse-drawn barge. In the valley of the River Exe, at Bickleigh Mill, is Devonshire's Craft Center, where local crafts are made and sold.

For mild eccentricity **Huntsham Court Country House**, an impressive Gothic mansion near Tiverton, is hard to beat. The hotel is as relaxed as the land around it and prides itself on a country house-party atmosphere. It is stuck in a Victorian time warp, with its 15 guest bedrooms all named after composers, so you may find yourself keeping company with Mr. Beethoven or Mr. Brahms. There's also a great place to eat in Tiverton—**Hendersons** in Newport Street, highly regarded for its organic cuisine.

This area abounds in country house–type hotels. One worthy of special mention is the **Bickleigh Cottage Country Hotel**, at Bickleigh Bridge near Tiverton, which also incorporates The Trout Inn. Bickleigh, a thatched and whitewashed establishment, is 4 miles south of Tiverton on A 396 and 10 miles north of Exeter.

EXETER

Exeter was originally settled by the Celtic people of Devon and Cornwall, the Dumnonii. The city, standing at what was then the head of the navigable waters of the River Exe, was later used as an administrative center by the Romans.

In the third century A.D. Exeter was fortified by a massive stone wall, and parts of this defense system can still be traced in town at Rougemont Gardens, Southernhay, and below South Street. An early Norman tower can also be seen at Rougemont, as can the remains of a Norman keep.

For over 600 years **Exeter Cathedral** has been standing much as it appears today, but its history goes back more than 1,000 years. It had three predecessors on the same site: a Saxon church rebuilt in 1050 to become the first cathedral, a Norman cathedral with north and south towers built to the east of it in 1160, and a larger cathedral incorporating the best of its predecessors into a Gothic-style structure in 1270. The nave was completed in 1370 and the West Front, with its wealth of sculpture and 300-foot-long stone vaulting—considered among the finest of its kind in Europe—a few years later. The Chapter House, built originally in 1224 but reconstructed in the early 15th century, should also be visited if only to view sculptures of the stages of the Creation as told in both the Old and New Testaments. They were installed in 1974 and are the work of local sculptor Kenneth Carter.

Exeter has a great deal from its historic past to show the visitor. In the busy High Street is the 14th-century Guildhall, from which Exeter has been governed since Saxon times. It is one of the oldest municipal buildings in the country and is still in use. Not far from it is the entrance to the Underground Passages, Exeter's Medieval aqueducts, which can be toured between 2:00 and 5:00 P.M. Tuesdays through Saturdays.

St. Nicholas Priory, a Medieval building containing period furniture, is in fact the restored guest wing of a Benedictine priory founded in 1070 by monks from Battle Abbey in Sussex, which itself was founded by William the Conqueror. The surviving features include a Norman undercroft, a 15th-century guest hall, and the kitchen.

The **Royal Albert Memorial Museum**, named in 1868 in memory of Queen Victoria's consort, houses a collection of paintings by well-known British artists, including many who lived and worked in Devon. Also on display is Exeter silver, pottery, porcelain, and glass. The important **Rougemont House Museum of Costume and Lace** on Castle Street displays fashions through the ages in a series of period rooms in an attractive Regency house overlooking the castle and Rougemont Gardens.

Since 1981 the Exeter Ship Canal and Quay Development Trust has been revitalizing the quay, which is becoming an important center for leisure activities. High on the city's list of tourist attractions is the **Exeter Maritime Museum**, down by the River Exe. There are boats from Arabia and China, Africa, the Americas, Britain, and the Mediterranean on display; nowhere else in the world can you inspect such an amazing collection of canoes, punts, coracles, rowboats, and steamers—afloat, indoors, and ashore.

As you might expect, the quay has always played an important role in the lives of Exeter's citizens, but never more so than in the days of the prosperous wool trade. Cloth exported from here brought wealth to Exeter during Tudor and Stuart times. Today, in the Quay House Interpretation Center, you can see displays relating to the use of the river and riverside areas throughout history.

Exeter has a wide choice of accommodations. The exquisitely restored Georgian **Royal Clarence**, just a few yards from the cathedral, is steeped in history and furnished with genuine antiques. Also centrally located in the heart of Exeter are the **Rougemont Hotel** in Queen Street; the **St. Olaves Court Hotel** in Mary Arches Street; and the **White Hart** in South Street. A Crest hotel, **Buckerell Lodge**, can be found out along Topsham Road.

Restaurants abound, but we suggest you try **The Tudor House**, in Tudor Street, which dates from the 15th century. One of the oldest buildings in Exeter, it has elegantly beamed parlors and bars, and recently received the coveted European Heritage Award. You'll find it at the bottom of Fore Street, just minutes away from the House That Moved (a house that was lifted intact and wheeled to a new location during recent city center development). Also highly recommended are the **Cloisters** restaurant in Broadgate, just off Cathedral Yard and located in yet another historic building; **Mad Meg's**, a Medieval-style restaurant in Fore Street; and **The Ship Inn** in Martins Lane, which specializes in pub food and bar meals.

Around Exeter

Killerton, an 18th-century house at Broadclyst on the road out of Exeter to Cullompton, is the administrative headquarters of the National Trust in Devon. Dating back to the Civil War, Killerton was substantially rebuilt in 1778. It houses the **Paulise de Bush Costume Collection**, which traces 200 years of fashion in a series of period rooms, and stands in 15 acres of gardens containing many rare trees and shrubs.

A convenient base from which to visit Exeter is the **Devon Motel** at Matford, close to Junction 31 of the M 5 motorway, which provides a unique blend of Georgian elegance and modern motel amenities for the travelling motorist. The smaller **Ebford House Hotel**, near Topsham and also convenient to the city, is a lovely Georgian country-house hotel that has managed to retain a homey atmosphere. To reach it, leave M 5 at Junction 30 and follow the signs for Exmouth (A 376).

There's an interesting restaurant at the **Chimneys Hotel** in Starcross, 15 minutes from Exeter on A 379; this Victorian residence enjoys a reputation for its menu of fresh local seafood including lobster, crab, mussels, and oysters. And, 4 miles from Exeter, at Stoke Canon, the **Barton Cross Hotel** has successfully combined 17th-century charm with 20th-century international standards of comfort and service under its thatched roof. Among Devonians it is noted for its exceptional food and wine.

WEST OF EXETER

Head out of Exeter along A 30 toward West Devon and the historic market towns of Tavistock and Okehampton. About halfway between the two towns you will come to **Lydford**, with its famous gorge. The gorge is a deep ravine scooped out by the River Lyd, which plunges into a succession of whirlpools, among them the awesome Devil's Cauldron, and culminates in the 90-foot-high White Lady waterfall.

Just a few miles along A 30 outside of Exeter is **Castle Drogo**, standing 900 feet above a wooded gorge and commanding views over the eastern slopes of Dartmoor National Park. This 20th-century masterpiece, completed shortly before World War II, is the work of architect Sir Edwin Lutyens, and despite its Medieval appearance it has such modern amenities as its own hydroelectric system.

It follows that in an area of such outstanding beauty there must be a range of hotels to match. The two-star **Lydford House Hotel**, near the famous gorge, has four-poster beds and its own riding stables to boot. In the delightful village of South Zeal (on the south side of A 30 and 14 miles from Exeter) you will come across an ancient country inn, the **Oxenham Arms**, and a thatched cottage, **Poltimore**. Both accommodations serve good food and are ideal stopping points if you are overnighting on your way to Dartmoor. A hotel of exceptional character and charm is the **Arundell Arms Hotel** at Lifton, on A 30 from Okehampton toward Launceston. It is England's best-known fishing hotel and controls 20 miles of salmon, trout, and sea-trout fishing on the River Tamar and four tributaries.

Dartmoor National Park

Dartmoor National Park, which occupies some 365 square miles, is an area of exquisite beauty, peace, and tranquility where Bronze Age people made their home thousands of years ago. It consists chiefly of two high plateaus that rise in places to 2,000 feet. There are also areas of moorland, enclosed farmland and wooded valleys, sparkling streams and rivers, and great granite tors, weathered into curious shapes by exposure to the elements.

Whether you join one of the many organized walks or venture out onto Dartmoor alone, make sure you are well equipped to withstand sudden changes in the weather. The villages on and around the moor are a delight; watch for the wild ponies that are allowed to wander at will across the open land and through village streets.

Take time to visit **Tavistock**, the market town on the western edge of Dartmoor where Sir Francis Drake was born. Largely Victorian in character, it reflects the copper bonanza of the late 19th century. Or go over to **Okehampton**, widely regarded as the "capital" of the Northern Moor, and see what remains of its Norman castle, built as a stronghold from which to subdue the rebellion that broke out in the southwest following the Battle of Hastings.

Dartmoor's loveliest villages include **Widecombe-in-the-Moor**, the much-photographed cottages that cluster around **Buckland-in-the-Moor**, and **Postbridge**, where you can see the best clapper (wooden) bridge on Dartmoor. Down from the heights, on the western and northern fringes of the national park, respectively, are the legendary hilltop church at **Brentor** and the cob-and-thatched village of **Drewsteignton** in the Teign valley. And be sure to sample a Devonshire cream tea at the **Badgers Holt Café** in Dartmeet.

When **Dartmoor Prison** was built at Princetown in 1803 to accommodate the growing number of French prisoners taken during the Napoleonic Wars, it's doubtful anyone guessed that nearly 200 years later it would become an object of curiosity for tourists, who often pose for photographs in front of its forbidding gates.

On the eastern edge of Dartmoor stands **Buckfast Abbey**, a Benedictine monastery in the valley of the River Dart, off the Exeter–Plymouth road (A 38). Here monks have restored a Medieval monastery to its former splendor. The abbey restoration, completed in 1938, took four monks 31 years to accomplish. It contains many art treasures, including stained-glass windows made in the abbey workshops, and is open to visitors.

There are many places to stay on Dartmoor, and the challenge is to select the most interesting one. Take, as an example, **Teignworthy**, a country-house hotel in the tiny hamlet of Frenchbeer, in the north of the park near Chagford, where the style of cooking is a blend of simple French provincial cuisine and nouvelle cuisine. Eating here is an experience not to be missed. The same might be said of the **Horn of Plenty** restaurant at Tamar View House, Gulworthy, near Tavistock, where the international cuisine of Sonia Stevenson is exceptional. Besides the classical menu, there are regional menus that change monthly, and in 22 years the proprietors of the Horn of Plenty have concocted 130 menus without ever once repeating themselves.

The **Cherrybrook Hotel** at Two Bridges in the center of the Dartmoor National Park is another ideal touring base. To reach this small hotel, exit the Exeter–Plymouth road (A 38) at Ashburton. You will find it cozy and moderately priced, with a low-beamed lounge/bar and good home cooking. You can arrange for dinner and breakfast or for lodging alone. Another hotel of distinction is the **Holne Chase Hotel and Restaurant**, between Ashburton and Two Bridges on the southeastern fringe of Dartmoor. It looks over the valley of the River Dart and owns the rights to a mile of salmon fishing.

TOWARD THE ENGLISH RIVIERA

When you leave the hilly uplands of Dartmoor, you have a choice. You can either set off to the southeast to Torquay, Devon's premier south coast resort and self-styled "Queen of the English Riviera," or set course for Plymouth, to the southwest of the moor.

Torbay—the coastal metropolis created by Torquay, Paignton, and the fishing port of Brixham—is a good choice, and for a change it is possible to leave the strain of driving and join the **Dart Valley Steam Railway** at Buckfastleigh southeast of Buckfast Abbey. The seven-mile journey follows the River Dart to **Totnes** (just west of Torbay), a royal borough in Saxon times that still contains many historic and interesting features.

In Totnes's narrow streets and alleyways you can see a thousand years of history. Especially worth visiting are the 16th- and 17th-century houses in High Street and Fore Street. From early May to the end of September, try to be in town on a Tuesday morning, when the townsfolk dress in period costume and hold an Elizabethan market day. Also visit the 14th-century castle and its circular keep.

Before you visit palm-fringed Torbay, spend a day farther along the coast toward Exeter at **Exmouth**, a traditional resort with a two-mile-long esplanade. Unspoiled **Budleigh Salterton** nearby is the site of Bicton Park's 50 acres of enchanting gardens—Italian, American, Oriental, and Hermitage styles—and a host of additional attractions, including falconry displays. Farther east of Exmouth, elegant **Sidmouth**, with its Georgian and Regency architecture, annually plays host to the International Folk Dance Festival, which attracts colorfully costumed performers from all over the world. It's usually held in August.

There's a wide selection of accommodations in this part of South Devon, but little to surpass the four-star **Victoria Hotel**, which welcomed its first guests during the last year of Queen Victoria's reign. The hotel is adjacent to the property that was once Queen Victoria's official Sidmouth residence. If you are looking for a simple bed-and-breakfast establishment, try **Willmead Farm** in Bovey Tracey, near Newton Abbot (north of Torbay), a thatched house built around 1450.

Although reference is made in the section on West Cornwall to the fact that the famous potter Bernard Leach established his studio at St. Ives, which can be seen to this day, it is worth noting on your travels through Devon that his son, **David Leach**, is now practicing the skills that Japanese potters taught his father. David Leach's studio is in Bovey Tracey at the extreme eastern slopes of Dartmoor. You can visit his studio and see him at work while travelling down from Dartmoor to Torbay.

THE ENGLISH RIVIERA

Although it may seem unlikely, there is such a place as the English Riviera. It consists of 22 miles of unspoiled coastline around Torbay in South Devon. There are three major resort areas and 18 beaches and secluded coves, all in a unique environment of exotic plants and palm trees, beautiful gardens, and salty harbors.

Fashionable **Torquay**, with its large, modern hotels, has been compared to Cannes; Paignton's long, safe bathing beaches are perfect for family holidays; and Brixham is a thriving little fishing port steeped in history. It was 300 years ago that William of Orange landed at Brixham to claim the throne and become King William III of England. Paignton, too, is not without its history. **Oldway Mansion**, built in 1871 for sewing-machine millionaire Isaac Singer, is well worth a visit; his son, Paris, extensively altered the mansion in the style of the great palace at Versailles.

Torbay

Torquay's palm trees, exotic flowers, and shrubs give the resort a Mediterranean atmosphere. While there, make sure to visit the completely thatched village of Cockington, with its famous forge, and include Kent's Cavern and the Model Village at Babbacombe in your tour of the town, as well as the Aircraft Museum on the road (A 385) to Totnes. Agatha Christie was born in Torquay in 1890. The Agatha Christie room at the Torre Abbey mansion displays some memorabilia relating to her.

For accommodations in Torquay try the **Livermead House** and the **Livermead Cliff**, two independently owned and related hotels on the seafront. If you are willing to go a few miles inland, there is the enchanting **Cott Inn** (circa 1320) at Dartington, one of the five oldest inns in England. The roofing thatch is 187 feet long. While in Torquay visit the elegant **Boulevard Restaurant** on the waterfront overlooking the international yacht marina, and the recently opened Fleet Walk restaurant and shopping complex.

In the village of Harberton, near Totnes, is the 17th-century **Ford Farm House**, where you can be assured of a warm welcome from Mike and Sheila Edwards.

Just 3 miles from Torquay is the **Orestone Manor House**, a country-house hotel at Maidencombe that was once the home of John C. Horsley, an artist and the brother-in-law of the engineer Isambard Kingdom Brunel (see Plymouth, below), who lived close by. Rudyard Kipling lived next door.

Adjoining Torbay are the popular holiday resorts of **Teignmouth** and **Shaldon**, set on the estuary of the River Teign and linked by bridge and passenger ferry. Close by, northeast of Teignmouth, is the equally attractive resort of **Dawlish**, where a stream and colorful gardens dominate the town center.

Toward Plymouth

Tucked in between Torbay and Plymouth is yet another attractive part of Devon known simply as the **South Hams**. Here, beyond Berry Head, you will find the historic port of

Dartmouth, with its strong maritime associations, including the Britannia Royal Naval College; the sailing center of Salcombe; and the busy little market town of Kingsbridge. It would be difficult to imagine a more idyllic setting for a restaurant than the promenade at Dartmouth overlooking the picturesque River Dart. There on the South Embankment at the sign of the **Carved Angel**, you will find Joyce Molyneux serving freshly caught salmon—from the Dart, naturally—in a Champagne sauce, or grilled lobster with tarragon butter. Don't be surprised to find Mediterranean overtones and liberal use of the finest olive oils. Lunch comes out around £25 and dinner about £33.

There are some remarkably interesting hotels in the South Hams district: at Salcombe, the **Soar Mill Cove Hotel**, overlooking one of the most beautiful coves in England; and the **Tides Reach Hotel** on the South Sands at Salcombe. In the same category are the highly regarded **Thurlestone Hotel** near Kingsbridge and **Piper's Bench** at Thurlestone, a small, colonial-style hotel that arranges golf, sailing, and fishing holidays. The elegant **Buckland-Tout-Saints Hotel**, at Goveton near Kingsbridge, is one of the finest Queen Anne–style manor houses in southwest England. In their **Queen Anne Restaurant** at the Buckland-Tout-Saints Hotel the Shephard family holds court, serving excellent sirloin steaks fanned out on the plate with intensely reduced red wine sauce. The ceviche of lemon sole is to be recommended and, for something sweet, try the pear frangipane with clotted cream.

If you would like to turn back the clock 70 years and spend your vacation in the manner of the 1920s, you can do just that at the **Burgh Island Hotel**. This "great white palace" of a hotel on Burgh Island, just off the coast at Bigbury-on-Sea, has been lovingly restored and reopened in true Art Deco style by London fashion consultants Beatrice and Tony Porter. For a fairly modest outlay you can occupy a suite used by Agatha Christie during one of her working holidays here (one of 14 distinctive suites); dine in the restaurant once patronized by Edward VIII, who brought Wallis Simpson to Burgh Island to escape the attention of the press just prior to his abdication; and dance the night away under the Peacock Dome as Noël Coward did on many occasions. The remarkable thing—and this is what makes the Burgh Island Hotel so special—is that nothing has changed; it remains exactly as it was in the "jet-setting" 1920s.

PLYMOUTH

You could spend a week in and around the city of Plymouth and still not see everything, but wherever you look, the sea has created history. Sir Francis Drake, greatest of all Elizabethan seafarers, sailed from here aboard the *Golden Hind* in 1577 to circumnavigate the globe. When he returned three years later, he became Plymouth's mayor. Drake bought **Buckland Abbey** from Sir Richard Grenville, and here, north of Plymouth near Yelverton, you can inspect "Drake's Drum," which he carried with him on all his voyages. According to legend, the drum was beaten by unseen hands at times of national emergency to recall Sir Francis to England's aid.

On **Plymouth Hoe**, a promontory where he calmly finished a game of bowls before setting out to do battle with the Spanish Armada in 1588, Drake's immense contribution to England's maritime history is marked by an imposing statue. While on Plymouth Hoe be sure to see the latest addition to the city's attractions—**Plymouth Dome**, an award-winning exhibition center overlooking the world-famous Plymouth Sound. In 14 separate viewing areas you can see unfold the fascinating history of Plymouth.

Sir Walter Raleigh, born at Hayes Barton near Budleigh Salterton, also sailed from Plymouth to North Carolina in 1584, where he "discovered" the tobacco leaf and brought it back to England with him.

Today, Plymouth Sound is still busy with ships. Be sure to visit the **Barbican**, the old Elizabethan quarter, with its lively fish quay surrounded by restaurants, antiques shops, and inns with names that have a salty tang. Across the road from the fish market is the **Island House**, where the Pilgrim Fathers, their names listed on an outside wall, spent the night before they left from the **Mayflower Steps** in 1620 on their perilous voyage to America.

Other plaques commemorate the return of the Tolpuddle Martyrs (six agricultural workers who dared to form Britain's first trade union) from Australia in 1838 and the first seaplane flight across the Atlantic in 1919. Up a narrow cobbled street (inappropriately named New Street) an Elizabethan house (circa 1584) is one of many old buildings preserved around the Barbican.

Visit the **Royal Citadel**, a 17th-century fortress alongside the Hoe, to look far across Plymouth Sound; while there, climb **Smeaton's Tower**, the first true lighthouse, which John Smeaton built on the Eddystone Rock, 11 miles off Plymouth. It was replaced in 1884 and now stands on the Hoe.

Three miles east of the city center toward Kingsbridge is **Saltram**, a remarkable George II mansion with its original contents, situated in a landscaped park and administered by the National Trust.

Find time while you are in Plymouth to inspect the **Tamar Road Bridge**, which links the city with Cornwall to the west. When it opened in 1962 it replaced a steam-driven chain ferry. Take an even closer look at the railway bridge alongside it and marvel at the engineering skill of Isambard Kingdom Brunel, who built it in 1859 to carry the Great Western Railway from Plymouth into Cornwall.

Plymouth offers a range of fine hotels, including the **Mayflower Post House Hotel**, the **Plymouth Moat House**, and the quiet Victorian elegance of **The Grand Hotel** on Plymouth Hoe, together with a Holiday Inn and a **Novotel** on the outskirts of the city. New to Plymouth is the 135-room **Copthorne Hotel**, which became one of the area's top hotels on the day it opened in 1987. On a central site and with two restaurants, **The Burlington** and **Bentleys**, which have quickly achieved recognition, the Copthorne has brought international standards of excellence to Plymouth. It offers a taste of Elizabethan England at moderate rates that include breakfast.

CORNWALL

Cornwall, whose mild climate and great natural beauty are perhaps its main attractions, is virtually an island. It is distanced from the neighboring county of Devon on the south coast by the River Tamar, which for all but a few miles forms a natural border "with England," or so native Cornish men and women will have you believe. Throughout history Cornwall's sons and daughters have behaved as if theirs is a land apart, and in certain respects you will find yourself agreeing with them.

Kernow is the name the Cornish proudly attribute to their Celtic homeland. Once across the fine modern road bridge that carries you into Cornwall by the southern

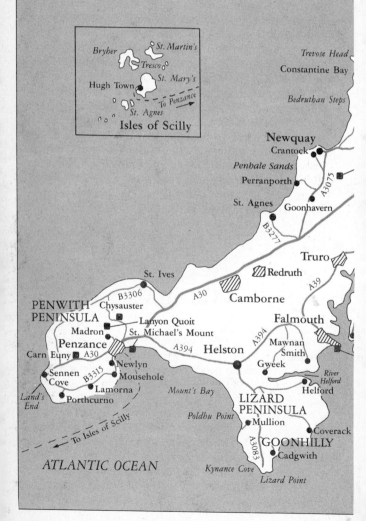

Cornwall

0 miles 10

0 10 kilometers

ATLANTIC OCEAN

Bryher
St. Martin's
Tresco
Hugh Town
St. Mary's
St. Agnes
To Penzance
Isles of Scilly

Trevose Head
Constantine Bay
Bedruthan Steps

Newquay
Crantock
Penhale Sands
Perranporth
St. Agnes
Goonhavern
B3277

Truro

St. Ives
B3306
A30
Redruth

PENWITH
PENINSULA
Chysauster
Camborne
Falmouth

Lanyon Quoit
Madron
St. Michael's Mount
A394
A39

Penzance
Carn Euny
A30
Helston
Mawnan
Smith
Newlyn
Gweek
Sennen
Cove
B3315
Mousehole
*River
Helford*
Lamorna
Porthcurno
Mount's Bay
Helford

*Land's
End*

LIZARD
PENINSULA

To Isles of Scilly
Poldhu Point
Mullion
GOONHILLY
Coverack
Cadgwith

ATLANTIC OCEAN

Kynance Cove
Lizard Point

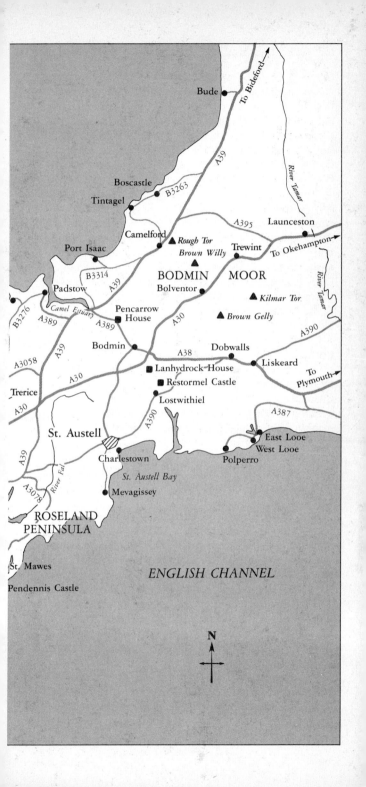

route—A 38—you will notice the many Celtic place names, similar to those found in Scotland, Wales, Ireland, Brittany, and the Isle of Man. You can recognize them by the prefixes Tre (farm or village), Pol (anchorage), Pen (head or end), Ros (heath or spur), Res (ford), Kelly (grove), and Car (camp or fort). These prefixes extend to Cornish surnames as well. As the saying goes: "By Tre, Pol, and Pen, you may know the Cornish men."

Cornwall also has its own language, though it is seldom spoken today except by students encouraged to keep it alive by the Cornish Language Society. Similar to the Welsh language, it remained Cornwall's mother tongue until the 18th century, when it was superseded by English, save in a few fishing villages around Penzance. Dolly Pentreath, who died in 1777 at Mousehole, in West Cornwall, is reputed to have been the last native speaker of the Cornish language. (You can still see her house in Mousehole.)

Counting all the inlets, creeks, and river estuaries, Cornwall is gifted with England's longest and most glorious coastline, 326 miles, bounded on the north and west by the Atlantic Ocean and on the south by the English Channel.

Along its northern shoreline, from Bude to Land's End, majestic cliffs brace themselves against the sea, interspersed by steep-sided valleys formed by fast-flowing rivers and streams. This coast contains some of Europe's finest surfing and bathing beaches—magnets that attract three million visitors to Cornwall annually, mostly in July and August.

By contrast, along its southern English Channel shore from Plymouth Sound to Land's End, Cornwall presents a softer picture, one of less rugged cliffs; instead, headlands reach out to sea to form magnificent bays, estuaries, and creeks that draw an admiring yacht set.

Inland, Cornwall exchanges the grandeur of its coastal scenery for rugged moors, the best example being **Bodmin Moor,** in the county's craggy uplands, where the landscape resembles Dartmoor. The highest points on Bodmin Moor are Brown Willy (1,375 feet) and Rough Tor (1,311 feet), near Camelford.

Not every visitor falls under the spell of Cornwall's beautiful and varied scenery. Many are drawn to the county instead by its wealth of archaeological and historic sites—dolmens and stone circles from the Stone Age, Bronze Age burial chambers, Iron Age hill forts, castles, keeps, and coastal fortifications.

In addition to numerous hill forts and cliff castles, the Iron Age Celts left behind fascinating villages like **Chysauster**—already in existence for two centuries before the Romans arrived—and **Carn Euny**, both near Penzance. Both are now in the care of English Heritage and are open to the public.

Celtic saints, who came to Cornwall mainly from Wales and Ireland in the sixth and seventh centuries, are venerated in the names of many Cornish villages, such as St. Ives, St. Ewe, St. Issey, St. Tudy, St. Breward, and St. Madron. The father of Cornish saints was Saint Petroc, who established monasteries at Padstow and Bodmin. Then there was Saint Piran, patron saint of tin miners, whose ancient oratory lies buried beneath the sand dunes near Perranporth. Saint Piran's cross (a white cross on a black background, symbolizing white metal being extracted from the black tin ore) has been adopted as Cornwall's emblem.

The Romans came here seeking tin; so too did the Phoenicians. Disused winding-engine houses punctuate the landscape in parts of the county, reminders of the fact that tin was once the lifeblood of the Cornish economy. The industry was revived in the early 1970s, when tin again became profitable to mine. The market subsequently collapsed, enjoyed a brief recovery from 1988 to 1989, but early in 1990 received another setback when falling tin prices forced the £6 million Wheal Jane mine near Truro to close, causing the loss of 150 jobs. China-clay extraction, almost unique to Cornwall and parts of Devon, is an industry that, like agriculture, fishing, and tourism, is still of prime importance to the region.

NORTH CORNWALL

Many overseas visitors take the northern route (A 39) into Cornwall, following the coast road down from North Devon after stopping at Lynton, Lynmouth, and Clovelly, and enter the county at the aptly named Welcome Cross, not far north of the holiday resort of Bude.

"King Arthur's country" is the romantic label tied to this part of North Cornwall, which incorporates the charming coastal villages of Boscastle and Tintagel. From **Boscas-**

tle's tiny quay there is a view of 14th-century cottages clinging to the steep wooded hillsides above a fast-flowing river. The harbor is one of Cornwall's most picturesque spots.

Tintagel is famed for its 12th-century cliff-top castle ruin, in which the legendary folk hero King Arthur, who fought the Saxons, is said to have been born. Whether or not this is true, the gaunt shell of the castle, perched precariously on a rocky ledge overlooking the Atlantic, is an evocative sight (but you need to be fairly agile to get there).

While visiting Tintagel it would be a pity to miss the Old Post Office, a 14th-century building in the main street; it is a photogenic monument to the past.

Inland from Tintagel and Boscastle, and well worth seeing, are Launceston's ruined Norman castle with its imposing keep; Methodist John Wesley's cottage at Trewint, astride the A 30 trunk road; and the **Jamaica Inn**, at Bolventor on Bodmin Moor. (The slate-hung pub is immortalized in Daphne du Maurier's novel of the same name, with its tale of wrecking and smuggling.) Dozmary Pool on Bodmin Moor is the legendary resting place of King Arthur's sword, Excalibur.

An ideal base from which to explore this part of North Cornwall is the lovingly restored **Port Gaverne Hotel**, a 17th-century inn nestled in a fishing cove near Port Isaac. The fact that for many years the 18-room hotel, which has an international clientele, has been owned by genial Americans Fred and Midge Ross is an added attraction for the many U.S. visitors who stay there. The hotel is recognized for its good dining; the restaurant specializes in freshly caught local seafood.

Just a short distance from Port Gaverne is **St. Enodoc Churchyard**, wherein former Poet Laureate Sir John Betjeman is buried. He spent childhood holidays in this area and was greatly influenced by Cornwall in his writing. If you've time for a round of golf, the excellent course at Trevose Head is only just across the Camel estuary.

Continuing westward from here, find time to stroll around the busy little harbor at **Padstow**, where the quayside architecture owes much to the Flemish influence and where every May Day morning the residents take part in the oldest dance festival in Europe, the 'Obby 'Oss (Hobby Horse).

Two hotels in this area commanding attention are the **Old Custom House Inn** on the South Quay at Padstow and the **Treglos Hotel** at Constantine Bay near Padstow, where they still clean your shoes, carry your luggage, and serve you personally with early morning tea.

Inland again from here is **Lanhydrock**, an imposing mansion near Bodmin, set in acres of parkland and colorful gardens. Originally built in the 17th century, it was largely rebuilt in the grand Victorian manner following a fire in 1881. This great house, cared for by the National Trust, awaits your arrival as if time had stood still. Close by, and still family-owned and -occupied, is **Pencarrow**, a stately home that contains a collection of fine paintings by Sir Joshua Reynolds and period furniture.

MID-CORNWALL

Cornwall's premier resort, **Newquay**, which grew from a tiny fishing port, has seven miles of the finest coastline and beaches in Europe. The incredibly beautiful **Bedruthan Steps**, just to the northwest, are large black rocks in the sand that are said to have been used as stepping stones by Bedruthan, a legendary local giant. Drop in at the **Old Albion Inn**, a pub that was once a smugglers' haunt at Crantock, and at **Trerice**, an Elizabethan manor house built in 1571 and now preserved by the National Trust.

An overnight stop at Newquay's **Headland Hotel**, which occupies a ten-acre natural headland and is surrounded on three sides by the sea, could prove one of the high points of your visit to Cornwall, especially if you are here during one of their hot-air balloon festivals.

St. Agnes, a former tin-mining village southwest of Newquay, has recently risen to prominence with the television serialization of Winston Graham's best-selling *Poldark* novels. Many of the scenes were shot in the Trevellas valley on the outskirts of the village. There are at least two other reasons for going there: "Cornwall in Miniature," and "The World in Miniature," at nearby Goonhavern, remarkable theme parks featuring authentic models of favorite landmarks in Cornwall and the rest of the world.

As you continue west along the north coast toward St. Ives you will pass through the town of Redruth. Worth a stop here is **The Chart Room**, a restaurant housed in the Inn for All Seasons on the inner bypass road. It boasts an imaginative menu that changes weekly, and map charts adorning the walls that create elegant and warm surroundings.

WEST CORNWALL
St. Ives

This once-small fishing port, with its maze of cobbled streets and stone cottages clustered around the picturesque harbor, has changed little through the centuries. Here among the narrow streets, alleyways, and courtyards—bearing such improbable names as Teetotal Street and Upalong and Downalong—fish cellars and shops jostle with craft workshops, art galleries, and sail lofts turned into studios. There has been an artists' colony in St. Ives for close to 100 years, and as a center for the arts the resort enjoys an international reputation, so much so that London's famed Tate Gallery is now building a "Tate of the West" on a site overlooking Porthmeor Beach to display paintings from the St. Ives and Newlyn schools.

Of foremost interest is the **Barbara Hepworth Museum and Sculpture Garden**, another outpost of the Tate Gallery that has on permanent display sculptures by the late Dame Barbara Hepworth, whose home this was. She did some of her best work here between 1949 and 1975, when she died tragically in a fire. It was also in St. Ives that Bernard Leach revived the potter's art during the 1920s, and his work can be purchased in the pottery shop in The Stennack. (His son is also a potter; see the Toward the English Riviera section, above.)

The **Sloop Inn** on the harbor wall is a favorite pub with fishermen and artists, but if you have in mind to stay a while, the 50-bedroom **Porthminster Hotel**, which looks down over the harbor, will give you an excellent base from which to explore Land's End peninsula. From most of the rooms you can look out across St. Ives Bay as far as Godrevy Lighthouse.

Land's End

Land's End is to Cornwall what Jerusalem is to the Holy Land, the saying goes, and indeed it remains today one of the most important and best-loved landmarks in Britain, with a million visitors making the annual pilgrimage to this most westerly location in England.

Land's End point is privately owned. Since 1987 it has been the property of the entrepreneur and yachtsman Peter de Savary, who offers sightseers to Land's End an exciting experience. He has created a visitors' center called The Last Labyrinth and built a cable suspension bridge across a deep, rocky gorge to provide an unparalleled glimpse of the grandeur of the Cornish coastline.

Under de Savary, the formerly unpretentious Land's End Hotel has been redesigned and upgraded and has now emerged as **The State House**, which bills itself as the First and Last Hotel in England. Here, for a moderate outlay, you can occupy one of its 34 luxuriously appointed rooms with four-poster beds and en suite facilities. From its cliff-top position the hotel commands unrivaled views of the Longships Lighthouse and the Isles of Scilly beyond. You can dine in the hotel's **Observatory Restaurant** and enjoy its romantic backdrop of ocean and sky.

An interesting stopover at Cornwall's western extremity would be the 17th-century fishing inn **Old Success**, nestling down in Sennen Cove. Old Success offers excellent accommodations, including three suites, two of them with four-poster beds. The inn retains the robust seafaring flavor of a maritime village. Fresh fish dishes are available throughout the day, as are "proper" Cornish pasties—a taste of the true Cornwall.

Leaving Land's End by the B 3315, travelling northeast toward Penzance, you'll come across many more of Cornwall's treasures. At Porthcurno, for instance, you can visit the unique open-air Minack Theatre, on a craggy cliff high above the sea. Here, in the summer months, touring theater companies stage a variety of live entertainment, ranging from Greek tragedy to drawing-room comedy, with the English Channel as a backdrop.

Make stops at Lamorna, a tiny cove approached through a narrow valley blooming with wild flowers, and at **Mousehole**, with its diminutive harbor and wild-bird hospital. Take refreshment here at **The Ship Inn**, where Dylan Thomas enjoyed a drink while in Cornwall. During December, taste the specialty of the house, "starry gazy pie"—a pie containing seven different species of fish, with pilchards' heads and tails poking up through the pastry . . . if you dare.

Penzance

From Mousehole it is just a short drive along the south coast road to Penzance. You will pass Newlyn, home port of Cornwall's largest fishing fleet.

West Cornwall is packed with ancient sites and monuments and is, in fact, a living museum. You can meet girls turned to stone for dancing on a Sunday (The Merry Maidens, a Bronze Age stone circle near Lamorna) or climb through a holed stone reputed to cure your backache and other ailments (Men-an-Tol, on the moors between Madron and Morvah near Penzance).

Among the most ancient objects are the great quoits and chambered cairns (ancient burial chambers), built between 4,000 and 6,000 years ago. The biggest of the quoits, Chun, is at Zennor, but **Lanyon Quoit**, between Madron and Morvah near Penzance, is the most famous and more easily reached.

Penzance, boasting the only promenade in Cornwall, is the major town on the Land's End peninsula. It is the administrative center for West Cornwall, the district describing itself as Penwith, a Cornish word meaning "extreme end." The town is full of historical and archaeological interest.

It lies on the sheltered curve of Mount's Bay, which takes its name from the island castle of **St. Michael's Mount**, rising 238 feet above the sea a mile offshore. At low tide the castle is linked to the mainland at Marazion (which in the Middle Ages was a Jewish settlement) by a granite causeway over which it is possible to walk to the mount, but at high tide the only way to get there is by boat. It was originally the site of a Benedictine monastery established by Edward the Confessor.

From the highest point on the romantic island castle (which has a "twin" in Mont-St-Michel on France's northwest coast near Avranches) there are on a clear day uninterrupted views that take in The Lizard, as this part of the Cornish peninsula is called, to Land's End. Although it is still the home of Lord and Lady St. Levan, St. Michael's Mount is today one of the most visited properties administered by the National Trust.

If you are interested in antiques, you will love the **Queen's Hotel**, an elegant Victorian property on Penzance's promenade. Every room is different, and many of them are furnished with genuine antiques. The hotel has long been renowned for its collection of fine art, prints, and originals from the Newlyn School of Art—and the finest of freshly caught fish from nearby Newlyn Harbour. For good measure, the Queen's Hotel has recently opened **Strollers**, a brasserie and bar with a super-informal atmosphere and decor that includes traditional Cornish granite warmed by pine gazebos, rich fabrics, brass, and polished wood surfaces. The excellent, imaginative menu features fresh Newlyn fish and the very best local produce. Strollers's cocktails are also proving very popular.

Before leaving Penzance, stroll up Chapel Street behind the parish church. There you will discover, tucked away amid the Regency and Georgian town houses, the **Dolphin Tavern**, in which Judge Jeffries, nicknamed "The Hanging Judge," held court; the ornate Egyptian house, the ground floor of which is now a National Trust shop; the **Turk's Head**, an inn dating from 1233, when Turks visited Penzance during the Crusades; and the **Admiral Benbow Coffee Tavern**, decked out like an old sailing ship.

Following the road out of Penzance to Madron, stop at Trengwainton to see the magnificent subtropical gardens filled with fuchsias, exotic magnolias, rhododendrons from Nepal and Assam, and rare maples from China and Japan.

The Lizard Peninsula

We're fortunate that there is one district of Cornwall that, even today, remains largely undiscovered—the Lizard Peninsula, the most southerly point in England. You really do need a car to see it properly.

This region contains some of the finest coastal scenery in Cornwall, including Lizard Point, Church Cove, Kilcobben Cove, Kynance Cove, and Mullion Cove, in addition to the much-admired villages of Coverack and Cadgwith.

At its head is the quaint old town of **Helston**, where every year, on or about May 8, elegantly dressed couples dance in and out of the houses and shops in the ancient Furry (or Floral) Dance—a delightful spectacle. Should you happen to be near Helston at the time, and not mind crowds, you might join the 10,000 people who attend every year.

You can see tomorrow's world today at **Goonhilly Earth Station**, which provides a fascinating glimpse into the science of satellite communications. Here, at the heart of one of England's oldest nature-conservation areas, is one of the most complex pieces of high technology in the world, its vast, saucer-shaped aerials looming against the skyline, a familiar landmark. In its control center you can see pictures beaming in from all corners of the world. Through Goonhilly, millions of telephone conversations, facsimile calls, and television transmissions pass each year. It is a far cry from the day when Marconi, from this same spot, bridged the Atlantic by sending out the first radio signals from Poldhu Cove. The Earth Station is 7 miles from Helston on B 3293.

There are other tourist attractions on the Lizard Peninsula. Flambards, Cornwall's leading theme park, features an authentically reconstructed, life-size Victorian village complete with shops, carriages, and costumes, and there is a seal sanctuary at Gweek.

For accommodations in the area: The **Polurrian Hotel** in Mullion, which has commanding views from the cliff top above Mullion Cove, claims to be Cornwall's most elegant hotel, with its own leisure complex, including tennis courts and a heated pool. Freshly caught lobster is a specialty of the house. The Polurrian has been tastefully restored after losing its roof in the January 1990 storms.

THE FALMOUTH SOUTH COAST AREA

From here it is but a short ride to **Falmouth**, gem of the Cornish Riviera, which has the third-largest natural harbor in the world and, it follows, a great maritime history, dating back to the era of the post office sailing packets, the tea clippers, and windjammers—great square-riggers from sailing's glory days. If you want to be pampered during your stay in Cornwall, then make for the **Budock Vean Golf and Country House Hotel**. It's set in 65 acres of subtropical gardens at Mawnan Smith, between the River Helford and Falmouth, and provides its own private golf course, a spectacular indoor swimming pool (with poolside log fire in winter), and championship-standard allweather tennis courts. The hotel's **Duchy Restaurant** has a growing reputation for its cuisine, which includes the famous Helford oysters.

Today, Falmouth is a very fashionable holiday resort, yet it is largely unspoiled. As you might expect with such a large harbor, Falmouth offers an exciting range of water sports and activities. Sea and river trips are popular. Inquire at the Prince of Wales Pier in Falmouth about a boat trip up the River Fal, landing at Truro, if tidal conditions permit. It is a beautiful ride. Subtropical gardens and coast walks around Falmouth itself also hold great appeal. A unique annual festival held every April and May

opens to visitors some 70 gardens, many of world renown. Be sure to visit **Pendennis Castle** and its twin (one
mile across the estuary at St. Mawes), built on the instruc-
tions of Henry VIII to guard the entrance to the harbor
against marauding pirates. Both castles contain exhibitions of arms and armor.

On the seafront a short, level walk from the town and
harbor of Falmouth stands the **Royal Duchy Hotel**, only
100 yards from the beach. This first-class hotel enjoys a
reputation for comfort and the quality of its cuisine.

Another good choice for dinner is the recently opened
Livingstons, which commands superb unobstructed views
across Falmouth Bay from its position above the Seahorse
Inn overlooking Maenporth Beach on the outskirts of
Falmouth. Livingstons has already established itself as an
excellent restaurant, offering a sophisticated and airy decor and a very warm, relaxed atmosphere for diners. The
chef was formerly at the famous London nightclub
Annabel's. You may need to reserve; Tel: (0326) 25-02-51.

Roseland Peninsula

It is only 20 minutes' drive from the Royal Duchy north
to **Truro**, the commercial and administrative center of
Cornwall. A fine Gothic-style cathedral dominates the
city center. The latest and most up-market addition to
Cornwall's wide range of hotels is the **Alverton Manor
Hotel,** standing in six acres of parkland in the center of
Truro and providing gracious country-house living at its
best. The 150-year-old building is interesting both historically and architecturally and has been restored to
incorporate every modern comfort. The suites have
been individually designed. The food, too, is of a high
standard, prepared under the supervision of a chef direct from London's famous Dorchester Hotel.

On your way back south to **St. Mawes**, at the tip of the
Roseland Peninsula and facing Falmouth across the estuary (where the average winter temperature is only five
degrees cooler than in the south of France), be sure to
visit the 13th-century church at **St. Just-in-Roseland,** a
village that stands at the head of a lovely creek.

THE SOUTH COAST TOWARD PLYMOUTH

Your next port of call must be **Mevagissey**, another picturesque village, with its enclosed harbor, a safe haven for
the fishing fleet, for which Cornwall is renowned.

From Mevagissey, proceed to the typically Cornish
coastal village of Charlestown, with its **Shipwreck Centre**
and **Heritage Museum**, in St. Austell Bay. The **Carlyon
Bay**, near St. Austell, is the most prestigious hotel on the
Cornish Riviera. Standing in 250 acres, much of which is
given over to subtropical gardens, it has its own championship 18-hole golf course and a large leisure complex
with both indoor and outdoor heated swimming pools.

Rejoining the main road (A 390) near Lostwithiel,
which has 800 years of history, pause to visit **Restormel
Castle**, former home of the first duke of Cornwall, the
Black Prince. It is a perfect stone circle surrounded by a
moat.

Still to be enjoyed (especially for railroad buffs) is the
Dobwalls Family Adventure Park in the eastern half of
Cornwall, at Dobwalls, near Liskeard, adjoining the main
road (A 38). There is a host of attractions here, including
replicas of the Rio Grande Western Railroad and the
Union Pacific Railroad of America. Nowhere else will you
find superb working, passenger-hauling models of both
of the world's largest steam and diesel locomotives—Big
Boy William Jeffers and Centennial. You can also enjoy an
Edwardian experience by strolling down a lantern-lit London street, faithfully reproduced, or through the High-
lands, taking in the largest and most important collection
of paintings by Britain's greatest natural-history artist,
Archibald Thorburn. This is a truly outstanding theme
park.

Your next stop should be the showpiece harbor at
Polperro, one of the prettiest villages anywhere. The
famous author Sir Arthur Quiller-Couch (or "Q" to his
friends and readers) lived in Polperro. The main attraction here is the "House on the Props," a house supported
above the ground in the manner its name suggests.

Before retracing your steps east back into Devon across
the Tamar Bridge, take a stroll around **Looe**. In reality, it is
East Looe and West Looe, two ancient boroughs separated
by a narrow tidal river and united by a seven-arched

stone bridge. Together they form a popular resort of a quaintness and charm found only in communities whose sea-directed history goes back hundreds of years.

ISLES OF SCILLY

From the bridge of the steamship *Scillonian III* the view is breathtaking: nearly 100 heather-clad islands and islets rising from the Atlantic depths as if pushed above the surface by an unseen force from the legendary, submerged land of Lyonesse. No matter in which direction you look as you approach the Isles of Scilly, the sea dominates the landscape, and it is the relationship between the sea and the land that makes the archipelago so attractive. Yet only five of the islands are inhabited: St. Mary's and the "off-islands" of Tresco, St. Martin's, St. Agnes, and Bryher. Ferries make one trip daily each way between Penzance and St. Mary's.

St. Mary's, the commercial and social center of Scilly, is home to most of the 2,000 Scillonians. The capital, Hugh Town, is little more than a village by mainland standards. Even so, there is a good selection of hotels, guesthouses, restaurants, and inns, and there are two banks and a post office.

Tresco contains the famous **Abbey Gardens**, created in 1834 by Augustus Smith, in which exotic plants and shrubs from all over the world flourish. Also worth visiting is the **Valhalla Maritime Museum**, containing a collection of figureheads salvaged from ships wrecked on the rocky shores of Scilly.

St. Martin's, noted for its flowers and white sandy beaches, has a population of 83 and a school with just a handful of pupils. **St. Agnes**, the most southwesterly community in the British Isles (population: 65), is surrounded by deep, clear water. It is joined to the still smaller island of **Gugh** by a sandbar that is covered at high tide. From here you can gaze upon the infamous Western Rocks, the graveyard of many fine ships.

Bryher, a favorite with many tourists, has the smallest population (56) of the inhabited islands. It is wild and rugged in the north but to the south has a sheltered bay around which are grouped guesthouses and a few shops and cafés. The islanders are hospitable and their island beautiful.

During the main season local boatmen arrange trips from the quay at St. Mary's and other islands to Samson, Nornour, St. Helen's, and Tean, all of which are uninhabited; visitors go there to view seal colonies, seabirds, and lighthouses.

Scilly, low in the sea, fails to trap weather fronts, which explains why these "fortunate" islands enjoy more hours of summer sunshine than mainland Britain and are a good deal warmer. Frosts seldom occur here in winter, and this has enabled the islanders to become Britain's leading producers of naturally grown narcissus and daffodils, including the well-known Soleil d'Or variety. Growers start picking them as early as November, but generally they are exported to the mainland in bud from December onward.

The same favorable climate ensures that early (new) potatoes grown on Scilly reach market that much sooner than supplies from either the Channel Islands or mainland Cornwall. However, to balance its economy, Scilly has come to rely increasingly on the influx of summer visitors, and tourism is today the chief preoccupation of many islanders. During the peak months of June, July, and August upward of 2,000 tourists descend on Scilly every week, a number equal to the islands' entire resident population (hence the need to book well in advance if you are planning to stay here in high season).

Exploring the Islands

Ask any visitor what he likes most about Scilly and he will probably list peace, quiet, tranquility; the absence of traffic, urban stress, pollution, and commercialization; the seclusion, the uncrowded beaches, the natural beauty, the wildlife, the Old World charm and hospitality. In short, the islands are a paradise from which to escape the pressures of modern living and find a sense of timelessness and the open-handed friendliness of the Scillonians.

The mile-long walk around Garrison Hill on St. Mary's is an unforgettable experience, providing superb views of the "off-islands" and a chance to inspect an Elizabethan fort, **Star Castle**, built in 1593 to guard the island against pirates and the threat from Spain. The inner building is now a hotel, the dungeons a bar. The 26-room Star Castle, which still forms part of the Royal Garrison property on St. Mary's and as such is part of the Duchy of Cornwall, boasts that every subsequent heir to the English throne has stayed here, from Charles I to the present Prince of Wales and Princess Di. The sharp-eyed might get a glimpse of Tamarisk, the royal bungalow owned by Prince Charles, Duke of Cornwall.

When the feet begin to tire, you can board a bus outside the Town Hall (and Tourist Information Center) in Hugh Town for **Vic's Tour** of the island. It takes just over an hour, covers seven miles, and is accompanied by a not only informative but also highly entertaining commentary by the driver. The trip was devised in 1947 by local wit Vic Trenwith. Today his nephew Ron Perry carries on the family tradition of a side-splitting tour of St. Mary's.

You can visit what are known to Scillonians as the "off-islands." Dolphins, porpoises, and whales are regularly sighted here; giant turtles are occasionally seen. Chief interest, however, lies in the colonies of the Atlantic grey seal, which breeds within the outer reefs. Bird watchers will be fascinated by the sight of puffins, shearwaters, petrels, and roseate terns.

The pollution-free atmosphere and frost-free climate of Scilly combine to create conditions that support a range of very rare plants, including more than 250 varieties of lichen. Plants introduced from the Mediterranean and other subtropical regions to the famous **Tresco Abbey Gardens** have spilled over to bring further color to the natural flora of all the islands.

Generations of Scillonians have kept watch for ships in distress in the rock-infested seas around the islands, and there are museums on St. Mary's that tell the maritime story of Scilly. **Hugh Town Museum** has on permanent display artifacts salvaged from wrecks together with a collection of coins brought up from the ocean floor. The **Longstone Heritage Center**, about a mile from Hugh Town, houses a collection of coins and priceless porcelain salvaged from a Dutch East Indiaman, together with ancient cargoes and brass bells from ships that centuries ago found a watery grave off these islands. More recently, in March 1967, the 61,000-ton super-tanker *Torrey Canyon* struck the Seven Stones reef, northwest of Scilly. Her crew was saved, but 119,000 tons of crude oil polluted the sea on both sides of the English Channel, killing thousands of seabirds and devastating marine life (the area has since recovered).

Outstanding among places to stay on Scilly is the **Island Hotel** at Tresco, which is the first choice of an international clientele. Typical of the guesthouses on St. Mary's is **Westford House** in Church Street. Like so many Scillonians, proprietors Tim and Barbara Simpson are extraordinarily accommodating. They walk down to the cobblestoned quay to meet guests disembarking from the *Scillonian* and arrange for luggage to be delivered to the door. Hotelkeeping on this level is a very personal business.

The island of St. Martin's now has its own exclusive hotel, opened in the spring of 1989. The **St. Martin's Hotel** seems a world apart from mainland England, and because of its inaccessibility it is the ultimate escape for some. Its owner, Robert Francis of the luxury Polurrian Hotel at Mullion (see The Lizard Peninsula, above), offers a free helicopter shuttle between the two hotels for guests who wish to spend time at each location.

GETTING AROUND

The introduction and completion of the motorways network and major road improvements in the southwest have made the journey to Devon and Cornwall by road from London, the Midlands, and the North of England simplicity itself. Bus travel is growing in popularity, and the fares are relatively inexpensive.

A long-distance service operates from London's Victoria Coach Station by way of the M 4 motorway to Bristol and the M 5 from Bristol to Exeter. (Or, if you are driving a rented car, an alternative route from London is by way of the M 3 motorway and subsequently the A 303 or A 30 to Exeter.)

National Express operates a Rapide service from London, offering hostess-served refreshments, reclining seats, and toilet facilities. The bus reaches Truro in the center of Cornwall in under six hours.

For the motorist it is important to know that traffic does build up at the approaches to Devon and Cornwall on the peak Saturdays of the holiday season—generally the last two Saturdays in July and the first two Saturdays in August. Try to avoid these snarls by travelling at times other than weekends. During the summer, Holiday Routes, clearly marked "HR," are introduced. They use a network of minor roads, taking a less busy and more leisurely route to your destination. Maps showing the Holiday Routes can be obtained from tourist boards, information centers, and motoring organizations.

Devon and Cornwall are served by fast, direct, and frequent rail service from London, the Midlands, and the North. Intercity expresses operate from London's Paddington Station to Exeter in two hours, Plymouth in three hours, Truro in four and a half hours, and Penzance in five hours. They include the famous Cornish Riviera express, which now has a full Pullman car service.

If you are planning to arrive at Heathrow or Gatwick, buses of Railair Links now operate to Reading, where you can connect with British Railways' high-speed Intercity express trains and reach Exeter in just under two hours, and arrive in Penzance at the end of the line in under five hours.

However, if you are in a hurry to reach Devon and Cornwall, you can fly on Brymon Airways (the West Country's own airline) to Devon's principal cities: Exeter from Gatwick and Plymouth from Heathrow. Brymon can also fly you direct into Cornwall from Heathrow to Newquay's Civil Airport, using a 50-seater turboprop De Havilland Dash 7.

Exeter Airport is becoming recognized as a gateway to Devon, handling traffic from Gatwick, Belfast, Dublin, the Channel Islands, and the Isles of Scilly. It connects to Dinard (France) and Paris, and a service is being introduced linking Plymouth, through the new London City (Docklands) Airport, to Paris, Brussels, and Amsterdam.

From Plymouth's City Airport at Roborough, Brymon operates direct services to Heathrow, London City, Gatwick, Newquay, the Isles of Scilly, Jersey, Guernsey, Cork, and Aberdeen.

The Isles of Scilly

The Isles of Scilly Steamship Company provides ferry service between Penzance and St. Mary's. Boats leave from Penzance daily at about 9:15 A.M. and return from St. Mary's at about 4:15 P.M.; the crossing takes about two-and-a-half hours each way; Tel: (0736) 620-09. The company also operates a Skybus between Land's End airport and St. Mary's, making about 12 flights each way daily during July and August, fewer at other times of the year. British International Helicopters has approximately hourly service from Penzance to St. Mary's and Tresco during the summer season; Tel: (0736) 638-71. You can reach the Isles of Scilly from either Penzance Heliport or Land's End Airport in 20 minutes. Local companies provide frequent boat service between the isles.

ACCOMMODATIONS REFERENCE

▶ **Alverton Manor Hotel.** Tregolls Road, **Truro** TR1 1XQ. Tel: (0872) 766-33; Fax: (0872) 22-29-89.

▶ **Arundell Arms Hotel.** Fore Street, **Lifton** PL16 0AA. Tel: (0566) 846-66; Fax: (0566) 844-94.

▶ **Barton Cross Hotel. Stoke Canon,** near Exeter EX5 4EJ. Tel: (0392) 84-12-45; Fax: (0392) 504-02.

▶ **Bickleigh Cottage Country Hotel. Bickleigh Bridge,** near Tiverton EX16 8RJ. Tel: (0884) 52-30.

▶ **Buckerell Lodge Crest Hotel.** Topsham Road, **Exeter** EX2 4SQ. Tel: (0392) 524-51; Telex: 42410; Fax: (0392) 41-21-14.

▶ **Buckland-Tout-Saints Hotel. Kingsbridge** TQ7 2DS. Tel: (0548) 85-30-55; Fax: (0548) 85-62-61; in U.S., (212) 779-1888 or (800) 544-7570.

▶ **Budock Vean Golf and Country House Hotel. Mawnan Smith,** near Falmouth TR11 5LG. Tel: (0326) 25-02-88; Fax: (0326) 25-08-92.

▶ **Burgh Island Hotel. Bigbury-on-Sea,** South Devon TQ7 4AU. Tel: (0548) 81-05-14.

▶ **Carlyon Bay Hotel.** Near St. Austell, **Cornwall** PL25 3RD. Tel: (0726) 81-23-04; Fax: (0726) 81-49-38.

▶ **Cherrybrook Hotel. Two Bridges,** Yelverton PL20 6SP. Tel: (0822) 882-60.

▶ **Copthorne Hotel.** Armada Center, Armada Way, **Plymouth** PL1 1AR. Tel: (0752) 22-41-61; Telex: 45756; Fax: (0752) 67-06-88; in U.S., (402) 493-4747 or (800) 44-UTELL.

▶ **Cott Inn. Dartington,** near Totnes TQ9 6HE. Tel: (0803) 86-37-77; Fax: (0803) 86-66-29.

▶ **The Devon Motel.** Matford, **Exeter** EX2 8XU. Tel: (0392) 592-68; Fax: (0392) 41-31-42.

▶ **Ebford House Hotel.** Exmouth Road, Ebford, **Exeter** EX3 0QH. Tel: (0392) 87-76-58; Fax: (0392) 87-44-24.

▶ **Ford Farm House.** Harberton, **Totnes** TQ9 7SJ. Tel: (0803) 86-35-39.

▶ **The Grand Hotel.** The Hoe, **Plymouth** PL1 2PT. Tel: (0752) 66-11-95; Telex: 45359; Fax: (0752) 60-06-53.

▶ **Half Moon Inn.** The Square, **Sheepwash** EX21 5NE. Tel: (0409) 233-76.

▶ **Headland Hotel.** Headland Road, **Newquay** TR7 1EW. Tel: (0637) 87-22-11; Fax: (0637) 87-22-12.

▶ **Heddon's Gate Hotel. Heddon's Mouth,** Parracombe EX31 4PZ. Tel: (0598) 33-13.

▶ **Holne Chase Hotel and Restaurant.** Tavistock Road, **Poundsgate,** near Ashburton TQ13 7NS. Tel: (0364) 34-71; in U.S., (800) 323-6855; Fax: (0364) 34-53.

▶ **Huntsham Court Country House. Huntsham** EX16 7NA. Tel: (0398) 62-10 or 63-65; Fax: (0398) 64-56.

▶ **Island Hotel. Tresco,** Isles of Scilly TR24 0PU. Tel: (0720) 228-83.

▶ **Kittiwell House Hotel and Restaurant.** St. Mary's Road, **Croyde** EX33 1PG. Tel. and Fax: (0271) 89-02-47.

▶ **Livermead Cliff Hotel.** Seafront, **Torquay** TQ2 6RQ. Tel: (0803) 29-28-81; in U.S., (602) 954-7600 or (800) 528-1234; Fax: (0803) 29-44-96.

▶ **Livermead House Hotel.** Seafront, **Torquay** TQ2 6QJ. Tel: (0803) 29-43-61; Telex: 42918; in U.S., (602) 954-7600 or (800) 528-1234; Fax: (0803) 20-07-58.

▶ **Lydford House Hotel. Lydford,** Okehampton EX20 4AU. Tel: (0822) 823-47; in U.S., (800) MIN-OTEL; Fax: (0822) 442.

▶ **Mayflower Post House Hotel.** Cliff Road, The Hoe, **Plymouth** PL1 3DL. Tel: (0752) 66-28-28; Telex: 45442; in U.S., (212) 541-4400 or (800) 223-5672; Fax: (0752) 66-09-74.

▶ **Northcote Manor Hotel. Burrington** EX37 9LZ. Tel: (0769) 605-01; in U.S., (602) 954-7600 or (800) 528-1234.

▶ **Novotel.** 270 Plymouth Road, Marsh Mills Roundabout, **Plymouth** PL6 8NH. Tel. and Fax: (0752) 22-14-22; Telex: 45711; in U.S., (800) 221-4542.

▶ **Old Custom House Inn.** South Quay, **Padstow** PL28 8ED. Tel: (0841) 53-23-59.

▶ **Old Success Inn. Sennen Cove,** Land's End TR19 7DG. Tel: (0736) 87-12-32.

▶ **Orestone Manor House.** Rockhouse Lane, Maidencombe, **Torquay** TQ1 4SX. Tel: (0803) 32-80-98; Fax: (0803) 32-83-36.

▶ **Oxenham Arms. South Zeal,** Okehampton EX20 2JT. Tel: (0837) 84-02-44.

▶ **Park Hotel.** Taw Vale, **Barnstaple** EX32 9AD. Tel: (0271) 721-66; Fax: (0271) 785-58.

▶ **Piper's Bench. Thurlestone** TQ7 3NG. Tel: (0548) 56-01-57.

▶ **Plymouth Moat House.** Armada Way, **Plymouth** PL1

2HJ. Tel: (0752) 66-28-66; Telex: 45637; Fax: (0752) 67-38-16.

▶ **Poltimore. South Zeal** EX20 2PD. Tel: (0837) 84-02-09.

▶ **Polurrian Hotel.** Polurrian Cove, **Mullion** TR12 7EN. Tel: (0326) 24-04-21; Telex: 94015906; Fax: (0326) 24-00-83.

▶ **Port Gaverne Hotel. Port Gaverne,** Port Isaac PL29 3SQ. Tel: (0208) 88-02-44; Fax: (0208) 88-01-51.

▶ **Porthminster Hotel. St. Ives** TR26 2BN. Tel: (0736) 79-52-21; in U.S., (602) 954-7600 or (800) 528-1234; Fax: (0736) 79-70-43.

▶ **Queen's Hotel.** The Promenade, **Penzance** TR18 4HG. Tel: (0736) 623-71; Fax: (0736) 500-33.

▶ **Rising Sun Hotel.** Harbourside, **Lynmouth** EX35 6EQ. Tel: (0598) 532-23.

▶ **Rougemont Hotel.** Queen Street, **Exeter** EX4 3SP. Tel: (0392) 549-82; Fax: (0392) 42-09-28.

▶ **Royal Clarence Hotel.** Cathedral Yard, **Exeter** EX1 1HD. Tel: (0392) 584-64; Fax: (0392) 43-94-23.

▶ **Royal Duchy Hotel.** Cliff Road, **Falmouth** TR11 4NX. Tel: (0326) 31-30-42; Fax: (0326) 31-94-20.

▶ **Royal & Fortescue Hotel.** Boutport Street, **Barnstaple** EX31 1HG. Tel: (0271) 422-89.

▶ **Royal Hotel.** Barnstaple Street, **Bideford** EX39 4AE. Tel: (0237) 47-20-05; Fax: (0271) 785-58.

▶ **St. Martin's Hotel. St. Martin's,** Isles of Scilly TR25 0QW Tel: (0720) 220-92; Fax: (0720) 222-98.

▶ **St. Olaves Court Hotel.** Mary Arches Street, **Exeter** EX4 3AZ. Tel: (0392) 21-77-36; Fax: (0392) 41-30-54.

▶ **Saunton Sands Hotel. Saunton,** near Braunton EX33 1LQ. Tel: (0271) 89-02-12; Fax: (0271) 89-01-45.

▶ **Soar Mill Cove Hotel. Malborough,** Salcombe TQ7 3DS. Tel: (0548) 56-15-66; Fax: (0548) 56-12-23.

▶ **Star Castle. St. Mary's,** Isles of Scilly TR21 0JA. Tel: (0720) 223-17.

▶ **The State House. Land's End,** Penzance TR19 7AA. Tel: (0736) 87-18-44; Fax: (0736) 87-18-12.

▶ **Teignworthy.** Frenchbeer, **Chagford** TQ13 8EX. Tel. and Fax: (0647) 333-55.

▶ **Thurlestone Hotel. Thurlestone,** near Kingsbridge TQ7 3NN. Tel. and Fax: (0548) 56-03-82; in U.S., (602) 954-7600 or (800) 528-1234.

▶ **Tides Reach Hotel.** South Sands, **Salcombe** TQ8 8LJ. Tel: (0548) 84-34-66; Fax: (0548) 84-39-54.

▶ **Treglos Hotel. Constantine Bay**, near Padstow PL28 8JH. Tel: (0841) 52-07-27; Fax: (0841) 52-11-63.

▶ **Victoria Hotel.** The Esplanade, **Sidmouth** EX10 8RY. Tel: (0395) 51-26-51; Fax: (0395) 57-91-54.

▶ **Westford House.** Church Street, **St. Mary's**, Isles of Scilly TR21 0JT. Tel: (0720) 225-10.

▶ **White Hart Hotel.** South Street, **Exeter** EX1 1EF. Tel: (0392) 798-97; Fax: (0392) 501-59.

▶ **Willmead Farm. Bovey Tracey** TQ13 9NP. Tel: (0647) 72-14.

▶ **Woodford Bridge Hotel. Milton Damerel**, near Holsworthy EX22 7LL. Tel: (0409) 264-81; Fax: (0409) 265-85.

▶ **Woodlands Hotel.** Lynbridge, **Lynton** EX35 6AX. Tel: (0598) 523-24.

▶ **Yeoldon House Hotel.** Durrant Lane, **Northam**, near Bideford EX39 2RL. Tel: (0237) 47-44-00; in U.S., (602) 954-7600 or (800) 528-1234.

EAST ANGLIA
SUFFOLK AND NORFOLK

By Katie Lucas

Katie Lucas, a well-known travel writer who specializes in Britain, has lived in Suffolk for 26 years. Her London-based company, Grosvenor Guide Service, organizes tours of Britain for individuals and small groups.

Although it is barely 60 miles from the noise, bustle, and bright lights of London, the county of Suffolk, the center of East Anglia, could be in another world. (The other counties of East Anglia are Essex—from London up to Colchester—and, north of Suffolk, Norfolk, of which only Norwich is covered in this chapter.) Perhaps because it is situated on the easternmost point of Britain, it has, until very recently, stayed aloof from the vagaries of fashion and modernization. The people of East Anglia seemed content with a bad road system from London because they felt it kept intruders out; only the hardy, that is, got through. Natives of Suffolk and Norfolk turned their faces toward the sea, rather than to the rest of Britain.

But everything changes. With the advent of the Common Market and the demise of the London docks, the East Coast ports have come to prominence because they are numerous (Suffolk is a maritime county with 40 miles of coastline) and efficient, with excellent labor relations. Therefore the roads to London are improving fast, which, in turn, has brought light industry and electronics concerns to the area. Until very recently, laborers in these parts could expect to work on the land for their entire lives. But as farm mechanization increased and production dropped to fit in with the new Common Market agricultural quotas, the pool of the unemployed grew. This unexpected spurt into the 21st century by this most agricultural of counties could not have come at a better time: Today Suffolk has one of the lowest unemployment rates in the country. And because intervening stages have been bypassed, the development in Suffolk could well serve as a model for the rest of Britain. Most of the horrors perpetrated in the 1960s and 1970s by planners with grandiose ideas have passed it by, and modernization seems to have been carried out more sympathetically here than elsewhere in Britain.

MAJOR INTEREST

Tranquil, unspoiled Medieval villages with small inns and magnificent churches
Haunting seacoast marshlands

Suffolk
Churches at Blythburgh, Lavenham, and Framlingham
Abbey at Bury St. Edmunds
Orford Castle ruins
Medieval village of Kersey
Ickworth art collection
Framlingham Castle ruins
Otley Hall

Norfolk
Norfolk Broads
Norwich: Cathedral, Norman Castle, Bridewell Museum

SUFFOLK

East Anglians as a race, and Suffolk people in particular, are very hardy, having fought with, and learned to live with, the wild North Sea over the centuries. They are independent and private people, and they have an honesty that is very appealing. It is no accident that most of the great dissenters in British history have come from East Anglia. They also have one of the most attractive

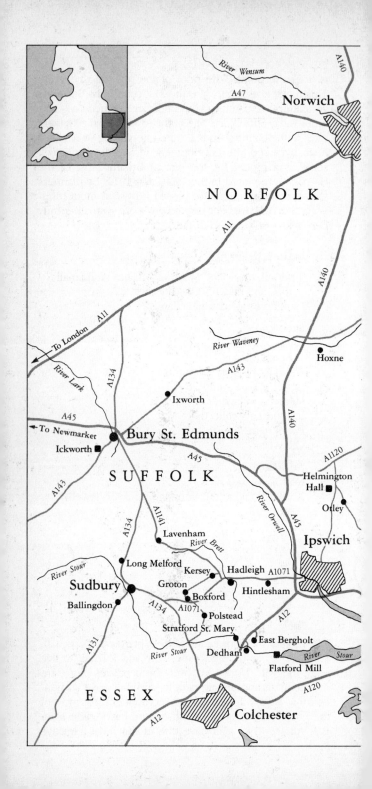

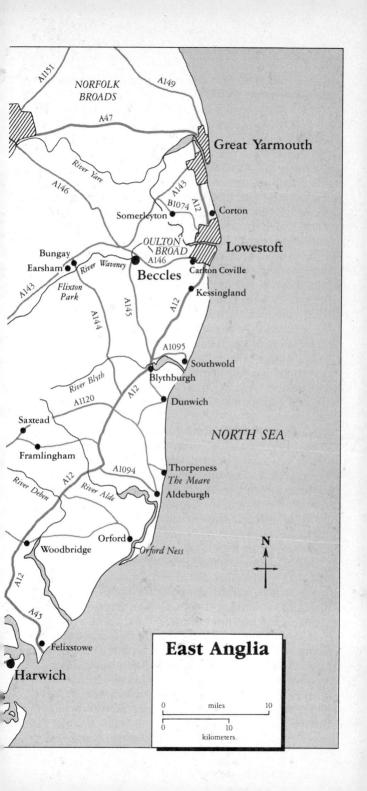

East Anglia

dialects in Britain, with almost every sentence ending in the interrogative. In the midst of Suffolk, you still meet people whose accent is so strong that it is almost impossible to understand them.

Suffolk has a rich racial heritage. In A.D. 43 the Romans came and made Colchester in Essex their capital city. From this base, which they called Camulodunum, they dominated the local Celtic tribes—the Iceni and the Trinobantes—establishing camps all over East Anglia. But by the fifth century their lines of communication to Rome had been stretched too far, so they departed, leaving the native Celts prey to the next invaders, the Anglo-Saxons. Like their successors, the Anglo-Saxons came over the North Sea; their intention was not to pillage and plunder, however, but to make their home here. They were basically village people who lived in small communities but who liked independence and self-sufficiency—characteristics they have passed on to their Suffolk descendants of today.

The Vikings, who crossed the North Sea in their longboats, were the next to land on these shores. They mixed with the local population, and their descendants are very visible today. Many Suffolk place names also show a Nordic influence.

After the Vikings came the Normans, in the Conquest of 1066. They themselves were Vikings who had settled earlier in Normandy and adapted themselves to the French culture and language. The Normans were great castle and church builders, and most of the castles you see today in Suffolk are Norman. Although many are in ruins, enough still stand to show how impressive these magnificent structures must have looked to the downtrodden Anglo-Saxon population.

The Flemish were another major influence in Suffolk. They left Flanders in the 1330s because of restrictive guild practices and brought their technology, which was weaving, to Britain at the invitation of Edward III. They created great wealth in the area. Until the 18th century Suffolk was famous for its wool trade; it produced almost all the worsted used in England and nearly a third of the woolen cloth. The result of all this money and energy can be seen in the area's magnificent churches, built by rich men in gratitude to a munificent God. It can also be seen in the wool towns, many of which are gems of Medieval architecture, with their half-timbered buildings a riot of color, ranging from a gentle shade of cream through pink and orange to a rather violent reddish-dung hue. These colors are actually all variations on a theme: The daub covering the wattle between the timber frames is a mixture of horsehair or cow dung, plaster, lime, and varying amounts of oxblood. Although the paint is now manufactured in a factory, an attempt is still made to emulate the color; in fact, you'll find Suffolk Pink listed in any paint catalog.

Of course, the traffic has not been entirely one-way. Early in the 17th century a group of Puritans set forth from the Suffolk coast for the New World. The best known of all the ships that sailed to America, the *Mayflower,* started her journey in East Anglia. The Puritans were the first of many dissenters to sail to America and found colonies. They named their new towns and villages after the ones they left behind, and the surnames of many of the eminent citizens on the East Coast of America were originally surnames from the East Coast of England.

Suffolk is a large and currently underpopulated county, although at the time of the Domesday Book in 1086 it had the densest population in Britain. But since the mid-1960s the population has grown by a third. Fortunately, the landscape has remained unspoiled and the pace of life gentle. Suffolk is expansive and beautiful in a quiet, understated way. High Suffolk, which runs from Cambridgeshire in the west to about ten miles inland from the coast, is rolling and fertile: a domestic landscape of fields and hedgerows, isolated and often moated farmhouses, and remote and beautiful flint church towers—far too many, it would seem, for the sparse population. There is a timeless and ancient feeling to this land.

Nearer the sea, where many estuaries punctuate the coastline, Suffolk feels untamed and wild. As you look across reed-fringed marshes, with the curlews wheeling overhead through the huge East Anglian skies, you will sense the mysterious quality of this area.

Over the centuries this conjunction of space and light has given rise to the greatest concentration of English artists in the country. Constable came from Dedham, Gainsborough from Sudbury, and Turner painted Orford. This still holds true, although now other kinds of artists—composers, musicians, novelists, and craftspeople—are represented as well. One of the best-known music festivals in Britain is the Aldeburgh Festival. Founded just after World War II by the composer Benjamin Britten, it is held for two weeks every June in churches, village halls, and maltings near the coast at Aldeburgh. (Maltings are large buildings where barley was malted for brewers. Now they frequently serve as concert halls.)

June is a wonderful time to be in Suffolk, particularly with the festival to enjoy. But Suffolk is beautiful throughout the year, and there is always plenty to see and do whatever the season. In fact, it is difficult to write about Suffolk without constantly using superlatives. It generates them.

THE IPSWICH AREA
Stratford St. Mary

The entry to Suffolk could scarcely be more dramatic. A few miles northeast of Colchester on the London road, A 12, you descend Gun Hill into Dedham Vale, and there, on the far side of the River Stour, lies gently rolling Suffolk. It is unmistakable because it has hardly changed since John Constable immortalized it in his paintings.

The first group of villages you come to are all connected with Constable. The first of these is Stratford St. Mary, which was a Roman settlement called Ad Ansam. It has an attractive winding main street, bordered by a lovely stream and lined with interesting timbered houses and inns. The biggest is **The Swan**, a former coaching inn with stabling for 100 horses that was a main staging post on the road to Ipswich. Most of the pubs in Stratford St. Mary serve food at lunchtime, and The Swan has a garden beside the stream where you can eat and drink on sunny days. Like those in most towns and villages in Suffolk, many of the pubs here offer bed-and-breakfast accommodations, although The Swan does not.

The A 12, which used to be a meandering street, now runs between the village and its impressive flint church, which can be reached via an underpass at the end of the street. You often see this church in the paintings of Constable, and inside you will see reproductions of some of his works.

The church, **St. Mary's**, was built mostly in the 15th and 16th centuries by prosperous cloth merchants, although it was added to and restored by the Victorians. On its exterior there are some interesting flushwork inscriptions (flint and freestone decorations are called flushwork). These include the letters of the alphabet, which were probably used by passersby as an aid to prayer.

The interior of the church is lofty, with a finely carved 16th-century angel roof. The church is used quite a bit, despite its position on the edge of the village. Among its most interesting modern possessions are the hassocks, which were embroidered by the women of the village and which fall into three design groups: depicting the life of the village, the life of the church, and nature.

If you wish to go no farther on your first night in Suffolk, you will find the **Maison Talbooth** on the banks of the River Stour at Gun Hill in nearby Dedham to be one of the best hotels and restaurants in the area. If, instead, you would rather carry on into the depths of Suffolk, but would first like a civilized meal, this is definitely the place for you. Having a drink on the terrace by the river while watching the swans drift past will introduce you to the joys of Suffolk at the outset of your adventure.

East Bergholt

East Bergholt (just east of Stratford St. Mary), whose name in Old English means "wooded hill," stands on a south-facing slope on the Suffolk side of Dedham Vale. It is an unusual village: long and rather straggly, with six distinct settlements. Several contain modern housing built to cope with the rise in population that this area's easy access to London, Ipswich, and Colchester has prompted over the past 20 years. The heart of the village is the church, the post office, and several pubs.

From the 13th to the 16th century East Bergholt was an important cloth-making center. As a result, there are many imposing timber-framed houses that were built by wealthy cloth merchants (although several of these homes now have brick façades that were added in the 18th and 19th centuries). The **Hare and Hounds** pub on Heath Row is a good example of this, and it also serves a delicious and inexpensive lunch. While ordering in the bar, be sure to look up at the elaborate ornamentation on the Tudor plaster ceiling. If you wish a more leisurely meal, the **Fountain House**, right in the heart of the village, serves good English food.

East Bergholt must be one of the most often painted villages in the world. Constable, who was born here in

1776, depicted it many times; 21 of these paintings hang in the Victoria and Albert Museum in London. Constable was the son of a prosperous mill owner who wanted him to enter the family business. He actually did work at Flatford Mill for a short time, but fortunately he was allowed to follow his own desires. Although his birthplace no longer survives, there is a plaque on the original railings by the church to commemorate the site. His first studio, a small cottage in the center of the village, has survived and is also marked by a plaque. It is now part of the local gas station, and if you poke your head around the door, you will see plastic bottles of oil and antifreeze incongruously placed on old dressers.

In the church of **St. Mary the Virgin** there is a monument to Constable's wife, Maria Bicknell, who was the granddaughter of the rector, Dr. Rhudde, and in the churchyard are the graves of the artist's parents. (He was not buried in Suffolk but instead in Hampstead parish church in London.) The church is imposing, even though the west tower was never completed. There is a legend that at the end of each day the devil undid the work the builders had just done. Eventually they gave up and built a wooden cage in the churchyard in which the five bells are hung upside down. These are rung by hand, and it is fascinating to watch the bell ringers at work on Sundays.

Down on the banks of the Stour at Flatford stands one of East Bergholt's best-known houses—**Willy Lott's cottage**, which is instantly recognizable to anyone familiar with Constable's painting. Willy Lott worked as a millhand for Constable's father at **Flatford Mill**, and he lived in the cottage for 88 years. Constable also painted the mill several times. Built in 1733, it is now a field study center owned by the National Trust; for information on forthcoming courses, Tel: (0206) 29-82-83. Other buildings on the old mill site house two museums, one with displays on the life of Constable and the other showing agricultural artifacts. There are also a tea shop and a National Trust shop that sells preserves, china, potpourri, herbs, and gardening implements.

If, after all the walking you have done, you feel like sitting down, you will find your opportunity here, for beside the little wooden bridge over the Stour is a mooring where you can rent rowing boats by the hour. Drifting along the water will give you another view of this beautiful river that has inspired so many great paintings.

Sudbury

Sudbury (northwest of East Bergholt, at the intersection of A 131 and A 134) is very ancient and the largest of the wool towns. It is a center for the surrounding villages and hamlets, and on market days, which are Thursdays and Saturdays, the hill in front of St. Peter's church is covered with stalls and thronged with people. People come not only to buy the fresh produce, clothing, kitchen utensils, and even car seats that are on sale but also to meet family and friends from the other villages in the pubs and tea shops. An added attraction on Thursday mornings is the livestock market in Burkitts Lane, and in the afternoon there is a secondhand goods and antiques auction. This market has been in existence since Saxon times and is noted in the Domesday Book of 1086.

Sudbury is an attractive town situated in a loop of the Stour. It has beautiful **water meadows** on three sides, which are traversed by well-signposted walks. These water meadows are unique in an ancient borough like this—in most prosperous towns any land with navigable water running through it is swallowed up for building. But the Freemen of Sudbury were given the ancient hereditary grazing rights to the common lands in the 13th century, and therefore they still afford grazing to the freemen of the borough—and wonderful walks for everyone else to enjoy.

Where there is a river, there is often a mill with its millpond; Sudbury is no exception. But when the mill here ceased to be used for milling, it was imaginatively converted into a hotel, the **Mill Hotel**. The old mill wheel is a room divider between the bar and the restaurant, which is itself the 300-year-old miller's house.

The river saved Sudbury from the decline of the wool trade that hit the other towns in the area at the end of the 16th century. At the beginning of the 18th century improvements in river transport made the North Sea just 15 hours away by barge. Although the land distance involved is only 20 miles, the roads at the time were so appalling and unsafe that the river trip was infinitely preferable. At the same time Sudbury's quay and warehouse were built in Quay Lane. With the coming of the railways in 1850, however, these buildings gradually fell into disrepair, and it is only recently that restoration has begun. **The Sudbury Quay** has been imaginatively restored by the Sudbury Dramatic Society, who reopened it in 1981 as an arts center, with a cinema, a theater, and a restaurant and bar with tables on the riverbank. While this conversion was taking place, the River Stour Trust dredged the channel and rescued a Stour lighter, one of the barges that plied its trade on the waterway, and it can be seen at the quay at any time.

Ironically, the railways that replaced the river have in turn gone into decline, and there is now infrequent train service to the south and none at all to the north. The track that went to Bury St. Edmunds has been lifted altogether, and the two-and-a-half-mile **Valley Walk** to Long Melford now runs along it. The station buildings have been turned into the town's museum.

The Market Hill, St. Peter's church (now redundant, that is, no longer needed by the parishioners and under the care of the Redundant Churches Fund), and a statue of Thomas Gainsborough are at the center of town. Roads radiate from here; on the roads to the west, particularly, there are several very fine timbered houses, notably the Chantry and the Salter's Hall on Stour Street and the 15th-century Priory Gate (all that remains of the 13th-century Dominican priory) on Friars Street. Beside the gate is the oldest inn in Sudbury, the 400-year-old **Ship and Star**. This was probably the priory's guesthouse for pilgrims, but it is now an interesting pub and a good spot for lunch. If you wish to have something more substantial, **Friars Restaurant**, just a few yards away, serves British food in its 15th-century establishment.

The wealth of Sudbury came not only from the wool trade but also from silk weaving. The town still has rows of three-storied silk weavers' cottages, with large first-floor windows where the loom stood. Even today fine silk is woven here, including that used to make the wedding dress of the present Princess of Wales.

Thomas Gainsborough was born in Sudbury in 1727 on what is now called Gainsborough Street. **Gainsborough's House** is actually two 15th-century cottages, but two years before Thomas was born his father connected them with the red-brick façade we see today. The house has been turned into a museum, with a permanent display of some of Gainsborough's work, including a marvelous and recently discovered painting of Hadleigh Church that he did when he was only 15 years old.

Past Gainsborough's House, the road turns right to **St.**

Gregory's Church, the mother church of Sudbury. Part of this handsome structure may date back to the eighth century, although Simon of Sudbury, named Archbishop of Canterbury in 1375, was responsible for much of the building we see today. This remarkable local man, who studied at the universities of Cambridge and Paris, became chaplain to Pope Innocent VI in Rome, then papal nuncio to Edward III, before becoming chancellor of England in 1380. One of his acts was to impose a poll tax of three groats per head. The downtrodden and poverty-stricken peasants responded with the Peasants' Revolt. They marched on London, extracted Simon from the Tower of London, where he had taken refuge, and beheaded him on Tower Hill. Then they displayed his head on London Bridge. His body was buried in Canterbury Cathedral, but his head is contained in the vestry of this church and can be seen upon request.

The prize possession of the church is the magnificent font cover. During World War II this was protected with sandbags, but, sadly, it did suffer some damage; recently it has been restored. In the chancel, which is as long as the nave, the original misericord seats can be seen. When the seats were upturned, the clergy could perch themselves on the finely carved ledge during the interminable services.

Near the entrance to the churchyard is a small green. There is a touching memorial here to the 486th Bombardment Group of the U.S. Air Force, which flew 191 combat missions over Nazi-occupied Europe from May 1944 to July 1945. During World War II many U.S. forces were stationed in Suffolk because it was flat enough for airfields and near the Continent. Several USAF bases remain here.

On the far side of the church is the Croft. Some time ago workers were digging here when they came upon a mass of headless skeletons. It is thought that these are the remains of the rebels who supported Wat Tyler in the Peasants' Revolt and who were beheaded in Market Square in 1381. Simon of Sudbury, it seems, was not the only person to lose his head.

Next, stroll across the bridge at the Croft, along the water meadows, past the water mill, which is now the hotel, and on to Ballingdon Bridge and **All Saints Church**. Although there was a church here as early as the 11th century, the present structure is mainly 15th century, and the very fine pulpit is of the same date. Close by, under the vicar's lawn, is the mass grave of 18th-century smallpox victims.

Just around the corner is Ballingdon Bridge, which has always been an important entry gate from the county of Essex into Suffolk. To the right (where a pub now stands and where rowing boats can be rented) was a Templar hospital, which was founded in the reign of King John and endowed by tolls from the bridge.

Long Melford

Long Melford (north of Sudbury on A 134) is aptly named. The beautiful tree-lined main street is more than a mile long, and it is one of the widest in Suffolk. It has an attractive mixture of shops and houses, mostly timber framed, though many were refronted in the 18th and 19th centuries. Many of the shops sell antiques; Long Melford is in fact one of Britain's most important antiques centers. Under the west side of the High Street is one of the largest Roman settlements discovered in Britain.

After the road crosses the bridge, at the mill ford, the village opens up into a huge village green; it is triangular in shape and one of the largest in Suffolk. On the edge of the green stands **Melford Hall**. This imposing, turreted, red-brick house, set behind a high wall and an interesting gatehouse, was built in the 16th century and is where Queen Elizabeth I began her Suffolk perambulations in 1578. It is now administered by the National Trust and is open to the public.

The other large house in the village is a moated Elizabethan house, **Kentwell Hall**, which is approached down a long avenue of lime trees planted in 1678. This house had become derelict, but in 1970 the new (and present) owners began a careful restoration of it. It is open to the public. On several weekends a historical re-creation of the Tudor period takes place here, with the staff dressing, talking, and behaving as they would have in Tudor times.

Long Melford Church has been called the jewel in the crown of Suffolk; it can certainly lay claim to being the most beautiful of the county's 500 churches. It stands on the highest point of the green, behind the Holy Trinity Hospital almshouses, and in appearance is more like a cathedral than a church. As with so many other churches, the previous church on this site has been incorporated into the present 15th-century structure. The names of the donors are inscribed in the elaborate flushwork of the exterior. Inside the church the overwhelming impression is of incredible light, particularly on a fine day, when the sunlight pours through the clerestory windows. In all, there are 100 large windows.

Like many churches in Suffolk, this one suffered both during the Reformation and at the hands of General Dowsing, the parliamentary commissioner for Oliver Cromwell, who was put in charge of removing, by whatever means he had at hand, any popish imagery he could find. This included stained glass, font covers, bench ends, and, of course, commemorative brass. His soldiers shot at the decorative glass and angel bosses in the roofs; with their swords they would slash bench ends; and it was not unknown for them to stable their horses in the naves of churches.

Fortunately, though, a great deal of the Medieval glass was spared here and can be seen in the windows commemorating the Clopton family, who were great benefactors. In the Clopton Chapel, through the door on the left at the east end of the church, is one of the most important pieces. It is a tiny lily window that represents the Holy Trinity. The corresponding chapel on the other side of the high altar is the Lady Chapel; its entrance is outside the church, through the door near the porch. It was used as a schoolroom in the past, and there is still a multiplication table on the wall.

There are so many pubs, hotels, and restaurants in Long Melford that it is difficult to choose where to eat. The picturesque coaching inn, **The Bull Hotel**, serves all types of food and has rooms available. For a more personal stay as well as very good food, the **Black Lion Hotel and Countrymen Restaurant** on the green is the place to go. For a cozy and simple lunchtime pub, the **Crown Inn**, opposite the Bull, fits the bill nicely.

Lavenham

Lavenham (northeast of Long Melford on A 1141) is one of the finest Medieval towns in England, and it is the most famous of the wool towns. So picturesque is it that the local inhabitants have to suffer not only tourists but regular invasions by film and television companies as well. It is not uncommon to arrive in Lavenham and find the whole of the wonderful market square filled with actors

in historical costumes, horses, carriages, and all the paraphernalia of filmmaking.

The town is built on a hill, with its triangular market
square at the top. In the center is the **Guildhall**. This
magnificent building was erected by the Guild of Corpus
Christi—the guild of the cloth workers—in 1520, and it is
now a museum showing the rise and fall of the wool
trade. For at least 500 years wool was Lavenham's main
source of wealth; indeed, during the reign of King Henry
VIII, this was the 14th-wealthiest town in England.

From the market square, streets run higgledy-piggledy
down the contours of the hill, and each is lined with
superb half-timbered houses and cottages. At the corner of
Lady Street is the 14th-century **Swan Hotel**. During World
War II, the bandleader Glenn Miller had his last drink here
before flying from the local U.S. Air Force base, and on the
walls of the Old Bar there are many signatures and squadron badges left by U.S. airmen of the 487th Bombardment
Group, which was based here. There is a memorial to
them in the town.

Opposite the Swan is the **Priory**, which was the home
of Benedictine monks until Henry VIII dissolved the monasteries in 1536. It then became the home of a clothier,
and the original Lavenham wool mark remains on the
outside wall. This is a magnificent building that, after
years of neglect, has recently been restored and is now
open to the public. Buffet lunches, as well as coffee and
tea, are served in the priory refectory. Another good place
to have lunch is the **Greyhound Inn**, a small and cozy pub
close to the Swan.

A rich wool town would be expected to have a magnificent church, and Lavenham does: The **Church of SS. Peter
and Paul** is among the finest in Suffolk. It sits, dominated
by its massive tower, on another hill to the south of the
town. It has very elaborate flushwork, and the heraldic
devices of the de Veres, earls of Oxford, and the Spryngs,
a rich clothing family, appear many times. Both were
responsible for much of the work we see today. The
heraldic device of the Tudors, the Tudor rose, is also
much in evidence. John de Vere, who was the 13th earl of
Oxford, was Captain-General to Henry Tudor. He was
with Henry on the battlefield of Bosworth when Henry
picked the crown of England from a thornbush where it
had fallen after Richard III died, placed it on his own
head, and became the first Tudor king, Henry VII.

To the earl, the wealthy town of Lavenham was the

obvious place to build a grand new church upon the accession of the Tudors to the throne. He approached the townspeople, who were enthusiastic about the idea, and over the next 40 years most of the old church, apart from the chancel, was pulled down and the present glorious church built.

The tower is 141 feet high, and it contains eight bells. One, cast in 1625, has been described as the finest-toned bell in England and probably in the world. From the interior the tower arch is very beautiful, as is the west window beyond it. Yet until 100 years ago it was obscured by the organ and the choir loft; then the organ was moved to the Branch Chapel. The bellows of the organ had to be pumped by hand, and, indeed, the handle is still there in case of emergencies. During World War II, however, the 487th Bombardment Group of the U.S. Air Force generously paid for an electric blower, which still happily puffs away.

In the chancel, which predates most of the church by at least 100 years, there are some fine misericords. One of the finest, under the rector's stall, depicts a man holding a pig under his arm; he makes the pig squeal by pressing it with his elbow. On the chancel floor you will see a square of carpet. Under it is the only remaining floor brass in the church. It dates from 1631 and shows a tiny baby. This was Clopton d'Ewes, the son and heir of the lord of the manor, Sir Symonds d'Ewes. The baby died when he was only ten days old, but, commemorated in this way, he will never be forgotten.

Kersey

If Lavenham is a most perfect Medieval town, then Kersey, 8 miles to the southeast, must claim to be a most perfect Medieval village. Kersey is set on two steep hills; its main street starts at the top of one, by the church of St. Mary, and runs down to a water splash, where ducks have the right of way. The street then climbs the next hill. For most of its length it is lined with a picturesque jumble of weaver's cottages, pubs, and merchants' houses, outside one of which hangs the sign of a horse's tail, the symbol of a veterinarian.

Because of its commanding position the tower of the church is visible for miles around, and it is well worth climbing to the top to see its spare, simple interior. The oldest part dates back to the 12th century.

Groton

There is no village of Groton as such, just a series of small hamlets 3 miles southeast of Kersey, a church, and, of course, a pub. Were it not for the Winthrop connection, one would drive through Groton without noticing it.

Adam Winthrop, a rich clothier from Lavenham and the grandfather of John Winthrop, was granted Groton manor in 1544 by Henry VIII. John Winthrop, who was born in 1588, inherited the lordship of the manor and was made patron of the church when he was 30. Twelve years later, in 1630, he led the Great Puritan Emigration to New England, setting sail with 15 ships and nearly 1,000 emigrants. He subsequently became the first governor of Massachusetts.

The old manor house where he lived no longer exists, but the mulberry tree under which he played as a boy can still be seen, as can the imposing church, with its many Winthrop memorials and tombs, including those of John Winthrop's father and grandfather and his first two wives.

Boxford

The charming village of Boxford lies between Sudbury and Kersey, just south of Groton, in the valley beside the River Box. It was here that travellers forded the river on their way south to Essex or on to Sudbury; hence the name. This village has a sleepy quality; there is a feeling here that little has changed in hundreds of years. Although this was an important wool town from the 15th to the 18th century, it was also important as a brewing town, and there was a sizable brewery behind the White Hart Inn, along with a large malting. All that is left now of this industry and activity is the pub. (Milling was the other big local industry.)

As you cross the bridge to the lovely 14th-century church of **St. Mary**, you'll pass the spot where, in 1620, the horses of John Winthrop of Groton bolted, and his "coach was broken into pieces on the logges and high stumpes of the Causeye." Among the many delights in this church is a memorial to a woman who was "four times widowed, and hastened to her death by a fall in her 113th year 1738."

Hadleigh

Hadleigh, set east of Boxford in some of the finest countryside in Suffolk, is a beautiful, bustling market town. For centuries it was one of the richest of the cloth towns; now it is a thriving center of both commerce and small industry. It is also one of the 51 English towns listed as having special historical and architectural importance.

As is true of most Suffolk towns, its most noticeable feature as you approach is the church. But this church, **St. Mary's**, is different from others in the region because it has a large, lead-covered spire. The church and churchyard are part of a magnificent complex of Medieval buildings, including the enchanting 15th-century **Guildhall**, which has, oddly, two overhanging upper stories, and the 15th-century Deanery Tower. The Guildhall was the home of the five Hadleigh guilds, which were social and religious organizations. The relatively large number of guilds reflects the importance of this town. The Deanery Tower served as the gatehouse to the now demolished rectory. In Gainsborough's House in Sudbury there is a painting of this group of buildings as they looked in 1748.

St. Mary's is the fourth-largest church in Suffolk. Over the centuries, as the town became richer, the church was enlarged. But the tower is actually part of the earliest structure and is therefore narrower than the rest of the church. The spire was added in the 13th century, along with the Angelus bell, one of the oldest bells in the country. When the bell was cast, the founder forgot to invert the inscription in the mold, so the words on the bell have to be read backward. As you enter St. Mary's, you will be exhilarated by its loftiness, light, and immense feeling of space. Although General Dowsing and his gang of gun-happy Puritans did their work here, there are still plenty of treasures to see. The stone octagonal font has been in continuous use since the 14th century; the wooden font cover was erected in 1925 as a memorial to a Hadleigh man, John Overall, who played a major part in translating the Authorized Version of the Bible in 1611. Another memorial of interest here is one to Dean Hugh Rose. In 1833, in the Deanery Tower, Rose organized one of the first meetings of the Oxford Movement, a group concerned about the effect of the Industrial Revolution on the spiritual values of the Anglican Church. This church has a lived-in feel about it because it is very much part of the community it serves.

The town, like the church, is full of treasures, one being 49 High Street. This shop has a fine, original 15th-century oak door with carved spandrels, and over the shop windows is a row of stout pegs, used in the past for the display of saddlery. Richardson and Preece, also on High Street, next door to the White Lion Hotel, has an excellent example of 17th-century pargeting, a form of ornamental plasterwork in which the pattern or design is applied to the building. Inside this shop is a well-preserved 17th-century biblical wall painting.

On Market Street there are many more delights. The tiny 19th-century Corn (grain) Exchange, built in Neoclassical style, stands next to the flamboyant 19th-century Town Hall, which bears a fine coat of arms depicting sheep and wool sacks—the source of the town's wealth in the past. In front of the Town Hall is a most attractive cast-iron pump, which is also decorated with the town coat of arms. The final building at the bottom of Market Street is 17th-century Toppesfield Hall. Although it is not particularly interesting in its own right, you should stop here a while because this is the headquarters of the East Anglian Tourist Board. Although the parish churches are normally the best places to find the most comprehensive guides to towns and villages, it is also worthwhile to browse through the leaflets and pamphlets available here.

From Toppesfield Hall a lane leads south to the lovely River Brett. Spanning the river at this point is ancient **Toppesfield Bridge**, which was built in the 14th century. In 1591 it was judged "decayed and ready to fall down"—but it still stands.

Among several pubs in the town to be recommended for both lunch and dinner is the **Eight Bells Inn** on Angel Street. It has a very clubby atmosphere; although everyone seems to know everybody else, you will be made to feel welcome. For high days and holidays, **Hintlesham Hall**, in nearby Hintlesham on the Ipswich road, is one of the best restaurants in East Anglia. Not only is the food a delight but the hall itself is spectacular and offers accommodations.

Ipswich

Although most streets in Ipswich (east of Hadleigh, and the largest town in Suffolk) have evocative names from the past, the past they evoke is getting harder to recognize as more and more of this country town is swept away in the name of progress.

By the seventh century, Ipswich, situated on the River Orwell, was one of the largest ports in Britain. It remained so until the 18th century, when it went into a period of decline. It was rescued by the Industrial Revolution and more recently by the Common Market, which has thrust it (and its coastal neighbors Felixstowe and Harwich) into the forefront of trade with the rest of Europe. Ipswich is also notable because it is the town in which Mrs. Simpson obtained her divorce from Mr. Simpson, which left her free to marry the Prince of Wales.

In the center of town are a civic center (which houses the local information office), a theater, several cinemas, and the town's current pride and joy—a leisure pool, with waterfall, fountains, and wave machines. Like most ports, Ipswich has many pubs; one of the better ones for an inexpensive lunchtime meal is the **Swan** on King Street. Alternatively, for a more ambitious meal of fresh fish, go to **Mortimer's Fish Restaurant**, hidden away on an interesting corner of the docks on Wherry Quay. Nearby is the Old Custom House, a distinguished building of 1845. It was constructed at the same time as the 26-acre Wet Dock, which was once the largest in Europe.

For a port as large as Ipswich, there are surprisingly few hotels. So if you wish to stay, follow in the footsteps of Charles Dickens and Admiral Lord Nelson and go to the **Great White Horse** on Tavern Street. As coaching inn to the town, it has been looking after wayfarers for hundreds of years. Although the building was refronted in 1815, the 16th-century structure remains behind it.

The town has a red-brick Victorian museum (on Museum Street), which shows mainly archaeological and geological artifacts. Close to it, in lovely Christchurch Park, is **Christchurch Mansion**. This E-shaped Elizabethan house, where Elizabeth I stayed in 1561, is now open to the public, having been given to the people of Ipswich by the Cobbold brewing family. It is furnished like an English country house, and the pictures on show are predominantly by East Anglian artists such as Constable and Gainsborough. Another interesting building is the 15th-century Ancient House in Butter Market. Now a bookshop, it is worth going to see for the magnificent pargeting and plasterwork.

Although Ipswich was a walled town, nothing now

remains of the walls but the names of some of the streets in which the gates were situated, such as Northgate and Westgate streets. But the Medieval street pattern survives in the center of the town, as do some Medieval houses and shops. Some of the most distinguished of these are near the docks.

In East Anglia it is never easy to get away from Henry VIII, and Ipswich is no exception: This is the childhood home of his lord chancellor, Cardinal Wolsey, who was the son of a local butcher. On Silent Street there is a plaque on one of the houses noting this. On College Street, a crumbling red-brick gateway surmounted by the Royal Cypher is all that remains of one of Wolsey's more grandiose plans—a college of cardinals, which was still unfinished when he fell from grace in 1530.

In Wolsey's day the spiritual life of the town was well served by its many Medieval churches. These still stand, along with one of the country's first Nonconformist chapels, opened here in 1700 following the Toleration Act of 1689. This lovely and very peaceful building, the **Unitarian Chapel** on Friars Street, is full of delights: The original box pews and gallery and an elaborate carved pulpit, which is probably the work of the master wood-carver Grinling Gibbons, are among them. It is situated next to one of the most improbable buildings in Suffolk, a reflective black glass structure that has won many architectural awards but does rather lack charm, particularly when compared with its next-door neighbor.

CENTRAL SUFFOLK
Bury St. Edmunds

Just a country market town in size, **Bury St. Edmunds** (30 miles northwest of Ipswich on A 45) is nonetheless the second-largest town of Suffolk and very important in England's history. It has all the dignity and elegance of the Georgian age, but that is just a façade, because it is really a great deal older. The Normans laid out the town in a grid pattern that still exists, an unusual scheme in England, where roads tend to meander all over. Although the town's buildings are largely Medieval and even Norman, many were refronted in the 18th century, giving Bury St. Edmunds an intangible aura of Georgian balls and assemblies.

At the heart of the town are the ruins of the great **abbey**.

This was founded in 633 when King Sebert (or Sigebert) built a church on this spot in what was then the Anglo-Saxon settlement of Bedericksworth. It was burned down by the Danes but rebuilt in 903 to hold the body of the martyr, King Edmund. Young Edmund had been crowned King of East Anglia on Christmas Day, 856, but he was cruelly murdered by the Danes just 14 years later, on November 20, 870, because he refused to renounce his Christian faith. The Danes tied him to a tree at nearby Hoxne and used his body for target practice with their arrows, then beheaded him and left his body in a thicket. A wolf led the English to his remains, and this is why the town's coat of arms shows a wolf holding a human head.

In 1095 a stone church replaced the chapel. It was huge—more than 500 feet long—because the saint's body had become an object of pilgrimage. Many miracles are said to have occurred at the church until it was closed by King Henry VIII at the dissolution of the monasteries.

But even more important than the miracles was the meeting in this abbey church, in front of Saint Edmund's tomb, of the barons of England on November 20, 1214. At this meeting they swore to obtain the ratification of the Magna Carta from King John; just a few months later—on June 15, 1215, at Runnymede near Windsor—they did. The motto of Bury St. Edmunds is "Shrine of the King, Cradle of the Law." Among the ruins at the site of the high altar are two plaques commemorating this important historic event; one lists the barons who were present.

The monastery here was one of the most important and powerful in the land. Judging by the remains, the abbey must have been enormous. Among many other privileges, it had the right to mint money, which was granted by Edward the Confessor in 1065 and continued until 1325. At least once, in 1327, the townspeople rebelled against its tyranny and destroyed the great abbey gate. The present gate was completed in 1347 and is a fortress as well as a gate. The area inside is a pleasant place in which to stroll, with gardens planted among the gray stone remains and a bowling green and a tennis court on the greensward that leads down to the River Lark. Spanning the river is the attractive 12th-century Abbot's Bridge; nearer the gate is the Old English Rose Garden. This was given to the people of Bury by John T. Appleby of the United States, who was stationed here during World War II. It is a memorial honoring the men of the U.S. Air Force who died from these shores.

The **Cathedral Church of St. James** dates mainly from the 16th century, although some parts are much older. It became the cathedral church of St. Edmundsbury and Ipswich in 1914, making Bury St. Edmunds the cathedral town of Suffolk. The west front is imposing; it is richly carved with the emblems of Saint James and Saint John. The interior is lofty and painted white.

Close to St. James is the **Norman tower**. This impressive building dates from 1148 and is one of the most perfect examples of Norman architecture in Britain. It is now used as the belfry for the cathedral, with a peal of ten bells. It was originally designed to be the gateway to the massive abbey church, whose west front is across the churchyard. The west front is 250 feet wide, which gives some indication of the size of the church. This is the oldest surviving part of the abbey; three arches, into which houses have been built, are still visible.

Nearby is the 14th-century **Chapel of the Charnel**. The entrance to the crypt of this chapel was undiscovered until 1844; when opened it was found to be filled with bones to a depth of two feet.

On the far side of the churchyard stands **St. Mary's Church**. This lovely church is one of the largest in England. It was built in 1433 and is the fifth on this site. The nave has a magnificent angel roof; of particular note is the chantry chapel of John Baret, a wealthy clothier who died in 1467. Its decorations include 100 stars, all of which have looking-glass centers to reflect the light.

In this church is the grave of Mary Tudor, onetime queen of France, and sister to the King of England, Henry VIII. When her first husband, Louis XII, died, she returned to England and married her first love, Charles Brandon, Duke of Suffolk. The granddaughter of this union was Lady Jane Grey, the nine-day queen. One of the windows in the church was given by Queen Victoria as a tribute to Mary Tudor.

Stephen Gardiner, Bishop of Winchester and Lord High Chancellor of England, was the son of a cloth worker from Bury St. Edmunds. He became secretary to Cardinal Wolsey (who also came from Suffolk) and succeeded him upon Wolsey's fall from power in 1527. Gardiner served Henry VIII well, although he was not a Protestant. But during the reign of Henry's son, Edward VI, he was imprisoned in the Tower of London because he was a Catholic. When Mary I came to the throne she made him Lord High Chancellor, and together they attempted to restore the Roman Catholic faith in the most horrific way. The religious persecution they started sent 300 martyrs to be burned at the stake. Even Gardiner's hometown was not spared this horror: In the churchyard stands an obelisk to the 17 Protestant martyrs who suffered death by burning in Bury St. Edmunds under the edict of Stephen Gardiner.

On the west side of the abbey gates is Angel Hill, a large open space that was very attractive before it was converted to a parking lot. Every Georgian town has an assembly room, and Bury St. Edmunds is no exception: On Angel Hill stands the Athenaeum, which was the social hub of the town. Not only were balls and masques held here, but famous actors and authors of the day gave readings of their works. Among their number was Charles Dickens, who stayed next door in the **Angel Hotel**. This attractive hotel, with its Georgian frontage, is still the best place to stay here; its cellars, which date from the 13th century, have been converted into an atmospheric restaurant. A poet of note who lodged here was Edward Fitzgerald. In his youth he attended King Edward VI's School in Bury St. Edmunds, and he stayed at the hotel the night before he died, after revisiting the school.

Another attractive Regency building is the **Theatre Royal**, one of only three remaining Regency theaters in the country. It was designed by William Wilkins, the designer of the National Gallery in London, in 1819. Subsequently it fell into disrepair and became a brewery warehouse for the local concern, Greene King. It was restored in the 1960s and is now very much used by the town.

Suffolk brewers generally make very good beer, and Greene King is no exception. You should sample their wares while in town, possibly at **The Nutshell**, the smallest pub in England. It is situated at the junction of Abbeygate Street and the Traverse. While it's definitely worth one glass just to say you've been there, only 100 yards away, on Whiting Street, is **The Mason's Arms**, an excellent and cozy pub. The landlord looks after his guests, and the food is good.

After you leave The Mason's Arms, continue down Whiting Street until you reach Churchgate Street. This was designed by the abbots to be a kind of triumphal avenue to the abbey church and was laid out so that one could look straight down, through the Norman arch and the west doors, right to the high altar. Unfortunately, the townspeople foiled this plan by slanting the street slightly away from the gate. If you look at the town map, you will see that the same thing has happened to Abbeygate Street.

To the left, on Churchgate Street, is the red-brick **Unitarian Chapel** of 1711, which is one of the oldest in existence. Its interior is particularly fine and has an interesting double-decker pulpit.

Turn right on Churchgate Street and you'll come to Guildhall Street. The oldest part of the **Guildhall** here dates from 1250, but it was refronted in 1809, and the entrance porch is early Tudor—quite a hodgepodge. Continue up to Butter Market and to possibly the oldest example of domestic Norman building in East Anglia—**Moyses Hall**. This fascinating building may have been a Jewish merchant's house, but he certainly couldn't have stayed there long, because the Jews were expelled from Bury St. Edmunds in 1190. After many vicissitudes, including a term as the house of correction, Moyses Hall became the town museum in 1898. As such, it is interesting, well laid out, and has good temporary exhibitions from time to time. Among the fascinating relics on display are the remains of William Corder, who murdered Maria Marten in the Red Barn at Polstead in 1827. A book recounting his crime has been bound with his skin and is on view, as are his scalp and death mask. His skeleton is preserved in the West Suffolk Hospital. All very macabre.

Ickworth

Just 3 miles southwest of Bury St. Edmunds stands Ickworth, the home of the marquess of Bristol. This extraordinary house is more than 600 feet long, has a 100-foot-high central dome, and stands in a magnificent deer park. Although the land has been in the family since 1485, the present house was built in 1800 to house the art collection of the fourth earl of Bristol. It is open to the public and certainly worth seeing.

Newmarket

The approach to Newmarket (west of Bury St. Edmunds on A 45) is unmistakable. On each side of the road are more than 50 stud farms and racing stables, in which trainers keep and work with up to 100 horses at a time. Beyond the stables lie the heaths, where horses can be seen exercising from very early in the morning, a magical sight.

Newmarket has been the capital of English horse racing since King Charles II established it as the headquarters of the sport during his reign (1660–1685). He loved the town and was a regular visitor. In the 1750s the Jockey Club in High Street was founded for gentlemen interested in the sport, but it soon developed into the racing world's administrative authority, and any raffish connotations it may have had in the past certainly don't apply today. It is very grand and very respectable.

Horse racing is the main industry of Newmarket. Each year there are about 30 racing days on two lovely courses, The Rowley and The July, and on these occasions this sleepy little town bursts at the seams with people pouring in for the great contests such as the Two Thousand Guineas in the spring, and for the less august but equally enjoyable events at which winning and losing money adds to an afternoon's excitement. The Newmarket Sales are run by Tattersalls auctioneers several times a year and usually coincide with the race meetings. These sales are world renowned, drawing buyers from around the globe to purchase horses of their choice.

The town itself is basically one straggly main street, in the center of which is the **Rutland Arms Hotel**. An attractive Georgian building, the hotel really comes to life during the race meetings. It is possible to eat at the bar or the restaurant, or stay the night. Close to the hotel is the National Horseracing Museum, definitely worth a visit. It tells the history of racing from Roman times to the present day.

UP THE COAST
Woodbridge

Woodbridge (northeast of Ipswich on A 12) is an old market town of great character set in the valley of the River Deben. This is a short, very beautiful river that offers excellent sailing, as it is only a few miles from the North Sea, as well as pleasant riverside walks for the landlubber. In the Middle Ages Woodbridge was a thriving commercial port, and a maritime atmosphere lingers still. It continues to thrive, partly because of its geographical position, which makes it both a sailing and a holiday center, and also because it is a shopping and administrative center for the surrounding villages.

The railway line divides the town from the river. To arrive here by rail (take the East Suffolk line from Ipswich) is a great joy because the last mile of the journey runs along the water to the ramshackle station. On the far side of the river is the site of the **Sutton Hoo burial**, one of the greatest Anglo-Saxon treasures ever found in Britain. In 1939 archaeologists discovered the magnificent regalia of a seventh-century East Anglian king in one of the 11 boat graves that lie on the high land beside the Deben. That treasure can now be seen in the British Museum in London.

Beside the station is the newly restored Riverside Theatre/Cinema, which has a very good bar and restaurant. Behind this, on the quay, is the 18th-century **tide mill**. This stands on the millpond, which, when the mill was in operation, would fill up at high tide. The gates would then be closed, and the water would flow back to the river through a channel cut beside the tide mill, turning the mill wheel as it did. This is an unusual system, and there were very few such in the country. The first tide mill here was built in 1170; the present one, built in 1793, was in use until 1956 and was the last working tide mill in the country. The machinery has now been restored, and the mill is open to the public. The millpond has been given new life as a marina for yachts.

From the quay several charming roads and lanes lead up into the town. They are all lined with a wealth of interesting buildings, many of which date back to the 15th century. The main shopping street in Woodbridge is the Thoroughfare, and from it runs Church Street, which leads up to Market Hill. This street and Market Hill are lined with antiques shops (Woodbridge is an important antiques center) and picture galleries. In the center of the market square stands the **Shire Hall**. This elegant building, with its Dutch gables, is basically Elizabethan and serves as the magistrates' court every second Thursday, when bewigged barristers can be seen climbing the external double staircase to plead the cases of their clients inside.

In a Georgian house on the south side of the square is the **Woodbridge Museum**. Quite apart from providing a great deal of information about Woodbridge, this small, well-laid-out museum tells the story of the Sutton Hoo burial in an interesting way.

Behind the museum is St. Mary's Church. Its massive 15th-century flint tower stands 108 feet high and provides a useful guide for yachters as they return to harbor. At the entrance to the square is the **Bull Hotel**. Edward Fitz-Gerald, the poet who translated the *Rubáiyát of Omar Khayyám*, used to meet his friends in this 18th-century coaching inn. Tennyson and Thomas Carlyle, both of whom made the journey to Woodbridge to see FitzGerald, stayed in the Bull while they were here.

On the other side of the Bull is New Street, a total misnomer, as can be seen by the great age of many of its buildings, including the timbered pub, **Ye Olde Bell and Steelyard**. The Steelyard was a lever machine for weighing carts and their loads. Last used in 1880, it can still be seen on the exterior of this fascinating building, which is a good stopping place for lunch, unless you wish to follow in the footsteps of the literary giants of the past and lunch at the Bull Hotel. If you prefer grander surroundings, the **Seckford Hall Hotel**, in the country outside Woodbridge just 1 mile from Market Hill, is the place. Thomas Seckford was the local landowner, after whom one of the streets leading out of Market Hill was named. He built the lovely red-brick almshouses in that street in 1587, as well as much of the chancel in St. Mary's Church. Seckford Hall was his family home and is now an attractive hotel.

Orford

The small and enchanting red-brick village of Orford (east of Woodbridge) is remote. It is bordered by the remnants of an ancient oak forest, and some of the trees that line the road are 1,000 years old. The present village is all that remains of a very much larger Medieval port, evident from the ruins of the castle and the church. Over the centuries the river silted up, and the great shingle bank formed by the tides opposite the harbor mouth, Orford Ness, cut off direct access to the sea. It is now a sailing center, offering safe mooring and quick access to the North Sea, which is just four and a half miles along the spit.

Although fishing and farming are its main industries, Orford is also a favorite vacation village. Possibly because of this, it has one of the best and simplest fish restaurants in Britain—the **Butley Orford Oysterage**. It specializes in smoked fish (which the proprietors smoke themselves) and oysters from its own beds in the adjoining Butley Creek. All three pubs in the village serve food of varying types; the most simple and most fun pub is the **Jolly Sailor**, down near the quay. It also offers bed-and-breakfast accommodation. These pubs date from the days when the port was flourishing, as do the lovely fishermen's cottages on Quay Street.

All that is left of **Orford Castle** is the keep, the final stronghold in times of siege. It is well worth the climb to the top of this imposing 90-foot building because the views out to sea and of the surrounding countryside are spectacular. The castle was built in 1165 by Henry II to keep the rebellious Baron Bigod at bay. It was the only royal stronghold in East Anglia at the time, and it is the oldest castle in England for which pipe rolls (the building and financial records from the King's Exchequer) exist, as well as lists of the provisions needed to supply the castle's garrison. The castle must have been huge, judging by the remains of its fortifications, which can be seen in the form of small hills around the keep. This is a perfect place for a picnic: Children and dogs can safely run up and down the hills. And, of course, they must tour the castle and be told about the Green Man of Orford. This poor fellow was a merman who was caught by local fishermen. He was taken to the castle and imprisoned in the dungeon. Although he was tortured, he never spoke to his captors, and eventually he managed to escape to sea again.

St. Bartholomew's Church, on the far side of the market square from the castle, is a massive structure whose tower echoes the castle keep. In the churchyard, at the eastern end of the church, are the remains of what must have been a superb Norman edifice. The early 14th-century tower of the present church collapsed in 1830 (it was partially rebuilt in 1971). As you enter the church, you will see three of the bells to the left, as well as the old village stocks, which, when in use, would have stood in the market square to detain offenders. Although General Dowsing visited this church and removed many of the memorial brasses, 11 remain. After a visit to the vicarage, and payment of a small fee, brass rubbings may be taken. In June of every year operatic concerts and performances of the Aldeburgh Festival are held at St. Bartholomew's. The composer Benjamin Britten performed his church parables here, including the first performances of "Noye's Fludde" and "Curlew River."

The **King's Head**, which is next to the church, was the coaching inn of the village; now it is a restaurant serving good food. The attached coach house is now a well-stocked craft shop. The inn was also the distribution center for smugglers and pirates who plagued this coast from the 17th to the 19th century. Next to the Oysterage in the Market Square is a small and reasonably priced antiques shop; it's fun to prowl around it after lunch.

Apart from Havergate Island, a reserve owned by the Royal Society for Protection of Birds where it is possible to bird-watch with a permit, most of Orford Ness (the promontory opposite Orford) has been taken over by the Ministry of Defence. Although a ferry temptingly runs from the quay to the ness, the public is not permitted (but see Dunwich, below, for information on obtaining a bird-watching permit.). In World War I a squadron of aircraft was based on the spit, and there was a camp for prisoners of war. Between the wars the first experiments with radar took place here, and until recently a huge early-warning radar station was sited on the ness.

A fascinating way to see some of this, and to learn more about the history of the area, is to take a trip on the **Lady Florence**, a 35-ton vessel that cruises from Orford Quay several days a week. An interesting commentary is delivered by the skipper, Geoffrey Ingram-Smith; if you wish, you can partake of a delicious homemade meal served on board while you listen. (Tel: 0394-45-02-10).

Otley

Just a few miles northwest from Woodbridge lies the straggling village of Otley. Although it is not scenically interesting, it has great historical importance. In 1602 Bartholomew Gosnold set off from Otley Hall for the New World in a 56-foot-long vessel called *The Concord*. After 49 days at sea he reached Massachusetts, landing at Cape Cod, which he named Gosnold's Hope. However, because his sailors caught many cod when they were fishing, he renamed it. Gosnold named Martha's Vineyard after his two-year-old daughter Martha, who had died just prior to his departure. When Gosnold and his crew returned home they were in better health than when they had left, so Gosnold decided, with Captain John Smith (of future Pocahontas fame) and several other East Anglian entrepreneurs, to return and found a permanent settlement in the New World. On December 20, 1606, a flotilla of three boats—the *Susan Constant,* the *Discovery,* and the *Godspeed,* which was under the command of Gosnold—left England. After a far more difficult voyage than expected, they sailed up a majestic river, which they named the James River, after the king. Here they settled on May 23, 1607, and built a township called James Towne. Sadly, on August 22, Gosnold died of swamp fever.

It well shows the adventurous spirit of the Elizabethan age that Gosnold left home at all, because his house, **Otley Hall**, nestled in the countryside near Woodbridge, is so beautiful that it is hard to imagine anyone forsaking it. The Gosnolds had acquired the property in 1450 but, because of their failing fortunes, were forced to sell the estate in 1674. For the next 250 years it was leased by absentee owners to local families, who retained its important historical features.

Today Otley Hall is owned by John Mosesson, who has restored the house and garden most charmingly and in keeping with the period. As Mr. Mosesson is very aware of its historical importance, he opens the house to the public on selected days. North Americans, as you might expect, are particularly welcome (Tel: 0473-392-64). The house has marvelous woodwork, oak beams, linenfold paneling, and a moat. It is altogether delightful.

The nearby **Otley House** offers comfortable bed-and-breakfast accommodations, with a charming hostess and delicious food.

Helmingham

Helmingham is just 1 mile northwest of Otley. Most of the village is owned by one family, the Tollemaches, and it is their house, **Helmingham Hall**, that sits in an ancient deer park amid large herds of both red and fallow deer. The family have owned the house since it was built in 1480. It is surrounded by a wide moat, over which is a drawbridge that is raised every night. The house is not open to the public, but the park and gardens are open on Sunday afternoons for enjoyable strolls along herbaceous borders and through immaculate kitchen gardens.

Framlingham

As you approach Framlingham (about 7 miles northeast of Otley) you will see three buildings that dominate this little market town. At the top of the slope on which the town is built stand Baron Bigod's castle and the large and beautiful church of St. Michael the Archangel. In the flat meadowland below is the huge red-brick Victorian school. Stroll up the hill and you will pass many more buildings of great character. Among them is the **Crown Hotel**, the old coaching inn where the mail coach would have called with travellers and the mail. The interior is cozy and beamed, and bar meals are served, as well as meals in the restaurant. The atmosphere is leisurely except on Saturdays, which are market days, when the whole town bustles and the triangular marketplace outside is full of stalls. The Crown has 14 bedrooms, one of which has an enormous four-poster bed.

Roger Bigod's Castle, which was started in 1100 by Roger Bigod, has an interesting history. The Howards, who became the dukes of Norfolk and the premier Roman Catholic family in England, lived at Framlingham until 1555. During the reign of Henry VIII the family suffered greatly. Although the third duke successfully promoted the interests of his two nieces with the king, the results were disastrous: Both Anne Boleyn and Catherine Howard became queens, but Henry sent them to the block. Then the duke's son and heir, the poet earl of Surrey, was taken off to the Tower of London and beheaded. The third duke himself almost suffered the same fate, but Henry died the night before the duke was due to go to the block. The fourth duke was beheaded by Henry's second daughter, Elizabeth I. It is strange indeed that the family endured such hardship, because Henry's illegitimate son Henry Fitzroy, duke of Richmond, was betrothed to the daughter of the third duke.

Edward VI, the only legitimate son of Henry VIII, died when he was sixteen. During his brief reign, however, he gave Framlingham to his half-sister, Mary, daughter of Catherine of Aragon. When he died in 1553, Mary sought refuge at Framlingham while she prepared to do battle with her cousin, Lady Jane Grey, who had usurped her throne. Nine days later she was proclaimed Queen Mary I here. In 1555 the Howards moved to Arundel Castle in Sussex. Eventually, the estate was bought by Sir Thomas Hitcham, who willed it to Pembroke College, Cambridge, still the lords of the manor today.

Apart from one dwelling house, no other building remains within the curtain wall. It is still possible, however, to climb the staircase in one of the 13 towers in the wall and enjoy the magnificent views of the surrounding countryside from the top of the castle.

The **Church of St. Michael the Archangel** is a short

stroll from the castle; indeed, it once had a private entrance for nobility from the castle. As you can imagine, the magnificence of the Howards is reflected in the church, and the Howard tombs are particularly outstanding. The third duke ordered the old chancel to be pulled down and a new one built as a mausoleum for the family. Even Henry Fitzroy lies here.

Most of the church was built between 1350 and 1555, although the chancel arch certainly dates from the 12th century. The chancel is unusually large compared with the small nave, but it is balanced by the majestic 96-foot-high square tower. In the nave, at the entrance to the tower, is an organ built by Thamar of Peterborough in 1674. It is the only complete one left (both the case and pipes remain), all the rest having been destroyed during the Commonwealth. As a result, it is much in demand by organists from around the world. The final treasure here is *The Glory,* the mystical painting at the center of the church's reredos, which dates from 1720. *The Glory* is depicted as a flame-colored circle surrounded by clouds and symbolizes looking through the veil into eternity. It is truly magnificent.

Just a mile to the west of Framlingham, on Saxtead Green, stands a fine example of a Suffolk **post mill** still in working order. This windmill dates from 1796, although records of mills on this site date back to 1309. It is open to the public.

Aldeburgh

The fame of Aldeburgh (east of Framlingham on A 1094) is disproportionate to its size. Composer Benjamin Britten and singer Peter Pears came to live here in 1946; in 1948 they founded the **Aldeburgh Festival**, one of the most famous music festivals in Britain. Moreover, in 1745, the poet George Crabbe was born here while his father was the local customs and excise officer—probably a fairly thankless task because of all the smuggling along the coast at that time. Crabbe wrote about his hometown in a poem called "The Borough," and one of the characters in it was the fisherman Peter Grimes; Benjamin Britten turned this tragic story into his first great opera.

Aldeburgh is also famous for having a lazy wind—one that blows through, not around, you. But on a sunny summer day, this is the most enchanting of English seaside towns, and even on a bleak winter day it has a unique fascination.

Although Aldeburgh is the home of many writers, musicians, and artists, it is also very much a fishermen's town, from the fishing boats pulled up on the shingle beach to the huts where the catch is sold. And when the festivalgoers leave the **Cross Keys pub** on Crag Path, it reverts to the locals, many of whom are fishermen. This atmospheric pub serves a very good lunch. On a sunny day you can sit outside, watch the seaside activity, and admire the lifeboat that stands on the shingle at the station of the Royal National Lifeboat Institution, just behind the pub.

From the 15th to the 17th century this town was a prosperous port. But as with many towns on this part of the East Coast, much of Aldeburgh has disappeared under the sea over the centuries. In the past 400 years alone at least half the town has vanished. In the old council chamber of the town, the Tudor **Moot Hall**, which stands on the edge of the sea, there is a small museum of local history; among the interesting artifacts on display are two maps, one showing the Moot Hall in its present position on the edge of the sea and the other showing it as it was in the past, standing in the center of town. Just south of the town, the former village of Slaughden disappeared within the last century. All that remains is the Martello Tower, standing in splendid isolation on its spit of land between the River Alde and the sea. This is the most northerly of the great impenetrable fortresses built during the Napoleonic Wars. In this century, buildings put up for similar reasons (though not, of course, against the French) are the concrete pillboxes that can be seen in fields on the side of the road as you approach Aldeburgh.

The **Parish Church of St. Peter and St. Paul** stands on the high ground at the entrance to the old town, and it is a noted landmark to sailors. The original church was Norman, but in 1525 it was altered and enlarged. It has been the setting for many illustrious concerts of the Aldeburgh Festival over the years, and it is fitting that the graveyard is the final resting place for festival founders Britten and Pears. The parents of the poet George Crabbe, who was also the curate of this church in 1781, are buried here too. There is a bust of Crabbe in the Chapel of St. Clement and St. Catherine. Close by is the Benjamin Britten Memorial Window. It is the work of artist John Piper, a close friend of Britten's, and it depicts the composer's three church parables: "Curlew River," "The Burning Fiery Furnace," and "The Prodigal Son." Just to remind visitors of the ever-present danger of the sea, a touching copper memorial inside the west door was erected to the seven members of the Aldeburgh lifeboat who lost their lives when the boat capsized in a storm on December 7, 1899. On the south wall are some interesting plans of the church and a key to who is buried where.

Opposite the church is a large Georgian house, now the **Uplands Hotel**. This comfortable, privately run inn was the childhood home of the remarkable Elizabeth Garrett Anderson, the first woman in Britain to qualify as a physician and a surgeon, who in 1908 also became the first woman mayor of Aldeburgh.

Down the hill from the church, on the right of High Street, is the cinema. Aldeburgh is one of the few towns in the area with a cinema, and on rainy days and when the north wind is blowing off the sea it is a haven for evacuees from the seafront. Among the more popular places to go on fine days are the yacht club at Slaughden on the River Alde and the beach at Thorpeness. In the opposite direction from the cinema, on the left at the bottom of the hill, is the **Wentworth Hotel**, a pleasant place both to eat at and to stay. It has been in the hands of one family since 1920, and present owner Michael Pritt, who took it over ten years ago, has carried out extensive and attractive renovations.

Along the sea wall as you head south is Aldeburgh's largest hotel, the **Brudenell**. Named for a distinguished local family, it is owned by the Trusthouse Forte chain and has a slightly more individual flavor than many of its partners in the group.

Thorpeness

Just a mile north along the beach from Aldeburgh is the village of **Thorpeness**, the brainchild of one man, Stuart Ogilvie, who designed it as a holiday village in 1910. He created the Meare, a delightful and shallow lake where children can rent boats and go off adventuring to the Pirates' Lair, Peter Pan's Island, and Wendy's House. It's all slightly shabby now but still enormous fun for children, and it also has good picnicking sites (if the ducks don't get the food first). From the Meare you can see the **House in the Clouds**, an eccentric building that looks like a dollhouse on a column but is actually a water tower set on top of living accommodations. Adjacent to it is a windmill, which is now the information center for the Suffolk Heritage Coast.

The beach at Thorpeness is one of the best in Suffolk. If you are brave enough to venture into the cold North Sea you will find that the water is marginally warmed by the outfall from Sizewell Nuclear Power Station, which is a mile to the north along the coast—perhaps a dubious benefit. A more positive aspect of the coast is that there are two fine golf courses here, at Thorpeness and Aldeburgh.

Dunwich

Another few miles along the coast north of Aldeburgh is the minute clifftop village of Dunwich. Like Aldeburgh, this village has suffered from the rampaging sea, but to a much greater extent. In the seventh century Dunwich was such a large and prosperous city that Saint Felix, the first bishop of East Anglia, set up the first Cathedral See of East Anglia here, effectively making this the regional capital. In the early Middle Ages the sea, on which the fortunes of this great port depended, started to invade, and since then almost everything that existed here has been washed away, including nine Medieval churches and two monasteries. The last of these, All Saints, disappeared at the beginning of this century, leaving one solitary tombstone on the cliff as a memorial. There is a local legend that when a gale is blowing at sea, the bells of the churches can be heard ringing beneath the waves. The little local museum is a good way to learn about this lost city. There is a good pub here, the **Ship Inn**, which serves food and where, if you engage a local in conversation, you may be told many more legends of this extraordinary part of the coast.

Adjacent to the village is Dunwich Heath and Minsmere Reserve. Here there are hides, run by the Royal Society for the Protection of Birds, from which you can watch the ever-fascinating bird life of the Suffolk coast. (For permission to use the hides write to: Royal Society for the Protection of Birds, The Lodge, Sandy, Bedfordshire SG19 2DL; Tel: 0767-68-05-51.)

Blythburgh

Blythburgh, northwest of Dunwich, is another small village that was once a large and thriving port. Now all that is left is a huddle of cottages; the White Hart pub, which was the old courthouse; and the magnificent **Church of the Holy Trinity**, also called, with justification, the Cathedral of the Marshes. As you approach from any direction, its 14th-century tower dominates the skyline with breathtaking grace and beauty. Although the church is huge, the combination of its intricate flushwork and enormous clerestory windows give it an effect of almost floating above the landscape. The vast interior, painted white, is very bare and wonderfully simple; its light and spaciousness will make your spirits soar. During the Aldeburgh Festival the church is the site of many concerts, and as you sit there listening to the music, it is a joy to look upward at the angel roof. General Dowsing did his best to destroy this architectural feature by urging his Puritan soldiers to fire their muskets at it; in fact, during recent restoration work, musket balls were found in some of the woodwork.

Southwold

On May 28, 1672, the English and Dutch fleets engaged each other in the Battle of Sole Bay. It was a fight with no real victor but plenty of carnage. The previous day was Whit Monday, a public holiday, which for the English meant a day devoted to drinking. Thus was the fleet caught totally unprepared; hundreds of sailors were too drunk to move, and it took four hours to round up the few capable of getting on board.

The lovely town of Southwold (northeast of Blythburgh) is so demure and delightful that it is hard to imagine anything so horrific happening near its coast—so close, in fact, that the citizens lined the cliff to watch the spectacle. Yet on these same cliffs is another reminder of a particularly bloody battle: six 18-pound Elizabethan cannons, which were last used at the Battle of Culloden in Scotland, when the Scots were decisively beaten by the English. The cannons were presented to the town in 1746 by the victor, the Duke of Cumberland. During World War I they were temporarily buried when the Germans, claiming that the cannons were fortifications, bombed the town.

One of the best-known landmarks of Southwold is the white-painted lighthouse on the cliffs. Also on the cliffs is the **Sailors' Reading Room**, which is open to anyone who wishes to look at its collection of artifacts, old photographs, and almost anything else connected with the sea.

Close by is Adnams Brewery. Some of the best beer in England is brewed here, and you can sample it at the pub opposite, **The Sole Bay Inn**. The beer is still delivered locally by magnificent gray dray horses, a wonderful sight as they pull carts loaded with barrels through the lanes.

Special features of this delightful watering place are the greens, seven open spaces that were actually created by the Great Fire of 1659, when much of the town was destroyed. After the fire these spaces were left open as firebreaks. Much of the quaint town you see today was built immediately after the fire, and since this is the closest point in Britain to Holland, there is a strong Dutch influence in many of the houses. This style mixes well with the Georgian and Victorian buildings that went up later. In Victorian times Southwold was a popular bathing resort, and as a result a small, and very unpredictable, rail line ran here until 1929.

From the greens, the great common leads down to the town marshes on the River Blyth and to the now silted-up Southwold Harbour. At the beginning of the 16th century the harbor was the source of much prosperity for the town. But as the century drew to a close the North Sea—which seems to draw mercurial delight in eating away the cliffs of some towns and depositing them at others in the form of sand and shingle—did its worst by blocking off Southwold's harbor. Despite an attempt by most able-bodied inhabitants of the town on April 12, 1590, to cut through the shingle and clear the entrance to the harbor, only shallow-drafted vessels can use the waterway.

From the sea four landmarks mark the entrance to the channel: Walberswick and Blythburgh churches on the south, and the lighthouse and Southwold Church on the north. **Southwold Church** is huge, evidence of a once-large congregation. It is dedicated to Saint Edmund, King and Martyr, the last king of East Anglia, who was martyred by the Danes at Bury St. Edmunds. Built in the 15th century, it is full of treasures such as the glorious painted rood screen, which dates from 1500 and is one of the most beautiful in England, and the pre-Reformation pulpit, which is unique in that it stands on one slender pillar. In 1930 the people of Southold, Long Island, USA, provided funds for the pulpit's restoration in memory of John Youngs, who in the 17th century set off with the Puritans from Southwold, where his father was the vicar, for the New World. He founded the settlement of Southold and died there in 1672. Another famous son of Southwold is George Orwell.

In the Lady Chapel are two interesting signs of Henry VIII's presence in East Anglia. On the roof are two carved bosses: One represents Mary Tudor, his sister, who is buried in Bury St. Edmunds; the other is of Charles Brandon, Duke of Suffolk, who was Mary's second husband. Together they looked after Henry's affairs in Suffolk. Other aspects of the church include the 15th-century Jack o' the Clock, or Southwold Jack, as he is known locally. He stands in the north arch of the tower, and when the service is about to start, he strikes the bell with the battle-ax he holds in his right hand.

Southwold has many tea shops, but for either a simple or an elaborate meal the **Crown Hotel** is the place to go. It is almost next door to the **Swan Hotel**, the old coaching inn of the town; rooms can be had in both establishments. It should be mentioned here that the wine buyer at Adnams Brewery, Simon Loftus, is renowned throughout Britain for the choice and quality of the wine he sells. The Crown Hotel is a showplace for the brewery, and the wine bar at the Crown recently won the national Wine Bar of the Year award.

AT THE NORFOLK BORDER
Bungay

The River Waveney divides the counties of Suffolk and Norfolk, and the prosperous and attractive towns of Beccles and Bungay are built on it. (Bungay is at the intersection of A 143 and A 144, northwest of Southwold and west of Beccles.) Lovely as the Waveney looks today, as it skirts commons, golf courses, and children's playgrounds, it has been the cause of much death and destruction. From 802 to 1000 the Danes sailed up it in their longboats and sacked and pillaged the area. Part of the inheritance they left can be seen in many of the local place names.

In the center of Bungay, behind the Swan Hotel, are the remains of **Hugh Bigod's Castle**. From this huge Norman keep, which stood 90 feet high when it was built in 1165, Hugh terrorized the local countryside as had the Danes before him. It was not until King Henry II built Orford Castle and established a stronghold in East Anglia that Hugh Bigod was finally tamed. All that remains of Hugh's fortress are some ruins and fragments of stone incorporated in buildings throughout the town.

In 1160 Gundreda, Roger Bigod's wife, founded a Benedictine priory near the castle. As were other monasteries, this one was dissolved in 1536 by Henry VIII, although some ruins remain in the churchyard at the east end of **St. Mary's Priory Church**. In 1577 the church was full for morning service when a terrible storm suddenly shook the town. Lightning hit the tower, twisting the wheels of the clock and hurling down stones. In the midst of this tumult the devil himself, in the shape of a black dog, ran through the church, leaving two dead men behind. A black dog running on a bolt of lightning can now be seen on the town's coat of arms. Renowned for its fine tower, this handsome church sadly became unable to sustain a congregation large enough for its enormous size. However, the Redundant Churches Fund has since restored it, and the building is now used for flower festivals, concerts, and exhibitions.

The very much smaller **Church of the Holy Trinity** shares the churchyard with St. Mary's. Its round tower is the oldest building in Bungay (predating the castle by about 100 years) and is possibly the oldest round tower in the country. One noteworthy feature of the church is its finely carved Elizabethan pulpit. The church paid five shillings for it in 1558, and the church wardens retain a record of that transaction.

Bungay is the only community in Britain that still has a town reeve. The holder of this ancient Saxon office, which was replaced in most towns by the Norman title of mayor, was responsible to the county shire reeve, known to us as sheriff, who in turn was responsible to the King.

Market day in Bungay is Thursday. In the past, farmers and market women displayed their wares at the **Butter Cross**, which stands at the middle of the marketplace. This attractive centerpiece to the town was created in 1689 to replace a much older cross that was destroyed in a terrible fire in 1688. The Butter Cross was also where offenders were detained and displayed. The stocks were kept there, as was a cage for the detention of prisoners. For culprits guilty of more serious offenses, there was a small dungeon beneath the floor, and if you look hard you will see a pair of wrist irons fixed to a pillar. No doubt all this explains why the figure of Justice surmounts the cross, although, interestingly, unlike most of her counterparts, this Justice does not wear a blindfold.

The **Bungay Museum**, which is situated in the Council Offices on Broad Street, gives a good view of the town. Its contents include a model of the castle as it was in the 13th century that illustrates what it would have been like to live there in those days.

One of the largest employers in the town is the printer Richard Clay and Company. Founded as John and R. Childs in 1795, it has grown over the years to become one of the most renowned printing firms in Britain. This is not the end of Bungay's literary associations: The famous writer Sir Henry Rider Haggard lived just a mile from the printing works, and the Aldeburgh poet George Crabbe spent several years studying at the grammar school in Bungay.

Bungay is also known to cricketers as the source of the best cricket bats. The willows are grown on the marshes and then made into bats in a factory in town.

The town has several good inns that serve lunch; highly recommended are **The Three Tuns** for good pub fare or **Brownes Restaurant** for a more leisurely meal.

Three miles from Bungay is the village of Flixton. During World War II a U.S. Air Force airfield was located here; the village is now the home of the **Norfolk and Suffolk Aviation Museum**, which has a varied collection of aircraft from all periods. Also just outside the town, at the village of Earsham, is the Otter Trust. The world's largest group of otters is kept here in seminatural surroundings by the River Waveney.

Beccles

Beccles (east of Bungay on A 143) is an enchanting town with many Georgian buildings; it suffered a terrible fire in 1586 that destroyed most of the earlier structures. Even the 14th-century church of **St. Michael**, which was built of stone, was severely damaged when all of its woodwork, including the roof, went up in flames. Today, the church stands in the center of the town, between the Old Market Place and the New Market Place; both, needless to say, are very old. One unusual feature of the church is the 97-foot-high campanile, with its peal of ten bells, which stands apart from the main structure. During the construction of the church the builders felt that the cliff overlooking the River Waveney (on which the tower would have stood if it had been built in the normal place) was not strong enough to bear the enormous weight. The peal of ten bells is one of the finest in East Anglia, and the church is a center for bell ringers from all over the country.

Although there are several porches by which to enter the church, the most impressive is the 15th-century South Porch, the Pride of St. Michael. It is two stories—34 feet—high and has elaborately carved stonework that was once highly colored. The priest's chamber above the porch has a squinch window that looks into the church; through it the priest could watch the altar unobserved. This chamber is now used for Sunday school. Close to the staircase that leads to the chamber is the font. Its bowl was carved in the 12th century and is the church's most ancient possession.

In this church in 1749 the curate Edmund Nelson married Catherine Suckling, who was the daughter of the rector of the nearby village of Barsham. They subsequently moved to the Rectory at Burnham Thorpe in Norfolk, where their son Horatio was born. He grew up to become the greatest of Britain's naval heroes, Admiral Lord Nelson. The other East Anglian curate who married in this church was the poet George Crabbe.

Close to the church, in Old Market Place, stands **St. Peters House**. Originally a chapel dedicated to Saint Peter, in 1536 it was seized by Henry VIII and subsequently became a residence that, with some alterations, has remained ever since. It is now a small hotel and serves meals. As can be imagined, it has an interesting interior.

Another old building in the town is the 16th-century **Roos Hall**. This handsome Elizabethan structure, with its battlemented gables (gables designed to look like the top of a castle wall) was once the home of an ancestor of Lord Nelson. The **Beccles and District Museum** is in Newgate; here you can see a printing press dating to 1842, as Beccles, like Bungay, is the home of an old, established printing firm. William Clowes started printing in London at the end of the 18th century. The company moved to Beccles in 1873 and printed, among many other books, the works of Beatrix Potter. The town's Baptist Chapel is called the Martyrs Memorial after three victims of religious persecution who were burned to death in the marketplace in 1556. It is hard to imagine such horrors occurring in this peaceful town, but when Mary I came to the throne such things happened all over England.

From many points around town glimpses can be caught of the delightful River Waveney and the bustling activity upon it. You can get a particularly attractive view by leaning over the old wall on the top of the cliff behind the church. If you descend the steps here and walk beside the red-brick walls to your right, you will eventually come to the town yacht station. This is another good vantage point from which to observe the river life, and it is situated next to some attractive old maltings. One of these has been converted into a restaurant, **The Loaves and Fishes**, an interesting place to stop for lunch (Tel: 71-38-44).

The little fishing village of Kessingland, on the coast between Southwold and Lowestoft east of Beccles, is the site of the popular **Wild Life and Rare Breeds Park**. The park has a collection of exotic wild birds and animals and, of all things, a large Wurlitzer organ, which is a great attraction.

Lowestoft

Lowestoft (east of Beccles on A 146) is the most easterly point in Britain, and the golden weathercock atop St. Margaret's Church is the first object in the country to catch the light of the morning sun. Since the 14th century, when the little fishing village started to grow, it has become both one of the largest fishing ports in the country and a popular vacation resort. Over the last 20 years it has grown even more as a supply town for the North Sea oil rigs and as a food-processing and shipbuilding center. Many of the huge trawlers that put to sea for 12 days at a time were built at the local yards, as was Richard Branson's *Virgin Atlantic Challenger II*. And, of course, when the fish is brought back to Lowestoft it is sold at the town's fish market, either to be processed locally or sent inland to be sold fresh.

The coming of the railway in 1847 provided a big boost to the town. It carried fish out to the great urban centers and vacationers into the town, where they could take advantage of the newly built pier and hotels and, of course, the fresh but rather fishy air.

The docks are in the center of the town, and a swing bridge over the main road allows vessels to sail in and out of the inner harbor. The two-hour guided tours of the 63-acre fish markets and the docks are interesting and sometimes include a tour of a trawler. Tours can be booked at the Tourist Information Centre, which is situated on the Esplanade by the South Beach. It is also possible to buy a box of smoked fish from one of the local shops to be sent as a gift to a friend.

Lowestoft is renowned for its miles of firm, golden-sand beaches. On the **South Beach** there are all the usual pleasures of a large English seaside resort: Punch and Judy shows, trampolines, yacht ponds, a pier, and a lifeguard on duty. Naturists (nudists) are permitted at the northern end of the **North Beach**, at Corton, where the beach merges into the dunes and marram hills. Still farther north is Pleasurewood Hills, an American-style theme park, offering a day's entertainment for one entrance fee. Lowestoft is also the birthplace of the composer Benjamin Britten, who later moved south along the coast to Aldeburgh, where he founded the Aldeburgh Festival.

There are many more recreational facilities in the area, as well as several attractive parks. At **Sparrow's Nest Park**, site of the local theater, is the most easterly public bar in Britain, **The Bar of the Sparrow's Nest Theatre**. The Maritime Museum at Bowling Green Cottage is also in Sparrow's Nest. On the cliff above is beautiful Belle Vue Park, the site of a memorial to the men of the Royal Naval Patrol Service who have no grave but the sea. In front of the memorial stand three ancient cannons.

On Oulton Broad, one of the finest stretches of inland water in the country and the site of speedboat racing on Thursday evenings in the summer, is **Nicholas Everitt Park**. In the park's Broad House is the Lowestoft Museum, which has a collection of local archaeological finds and a fine assortment of Lowestoft's famous porcelain.

Just 4 miles northwest of Lowestoft is the picturesque village of **Somerleyton**. Sir Samuel Morton Peto, the railway builder and founder of modern Lowestoft, bought the estate here in 1844 and restored it. Today it is the home of Lord and Lady Somerleyton and is open to the public; there are many attractions for children as well as adults here, including a miniature railway and a maze.

NORFOLK

Norfolk, north of Suffolk, is a large county of huge skies, flat landscape, water, and windmills. With the Wash to the northwest and the North Sea to the north and east, Norfolk is half surrounded by water and, in fact, for centuries was inundated by it. In the 17th century Charles II invited engineers from Holland to solve the problem, which they did by digging drainage canals, or fens, at the west of the county, creating that mysterious area called Fenland. Having been reclaimed from the sea, the soil is very fertile—rich, black, and peaty—and the terrain is very flat, making for perfect agricultural conditions. Approaching Norfolk from the west you will be struck by mile after mile of neatly laid out rows of vegetables and small farmsteads. Because many of the roads are causeways, you have a perfect view down into the fields.

In the east of the county are the **Norfolk Broads**, another unique feature of the East Anglian landscape. A network of lakes and canals, the Broads cover a large area of Norfolk bordering Suffolk. Three major rivers flow into this system, creating more than 120 miles of navigable water. The Broads are one of the most popular holiday destinations in northern Europe.

Boats of all sizes, from a small Norfolk sailing boat to a large ten-berth cruiser, can be rented for anything from a weekend to a month (for booking information see Getting Around section). For the enthusiast, the sailing boat is hard to beat, and it is a magical sight to see the sails of these small craft appearing to float through the fields. The waterways twist and turn and go back on themselves so much that the Broads often remain hidden until you are actually on them.

In the center of this fascinating county is the regional capital of East Anglia, Norwich.

NORWICH

George Borrow said, "A fine old city, Norwich," and so it is. It is also a civilized one, with the Theatre Royal (one of the best provincial theaters in England), many excellent museums and art galleries, and much in the way of contemporary arts and crafts, both to view and to buy. Norfolk attracts many artists and artisans, writers, poets, and composers, who find the remote location and atmosphere conducive to their work, the locals tolerant, and the rents lower than in many other parts of England. This is naturally reflected in the social and artistic life of the county.

Probably the best view of Norwich is from Mousehold

Heath on the northeast of the city. Although Norfolk is mostly flat, Norwich is in a valley, and from the Heath you have a marvelous view down into the old walled city. In the foreground is the cathedral with its tall spire, which at 315 feet is the second highest in England (after Salisbury), and like Salisbury Cathedral it sits on a winding and photogenic river, in this case the Wensum. Another ancient building in view is the dominating Norman castle on its mound in the center of the town. Everywhere church towers rise above the fine Medieval buildings; legend has it that among the streets and alleys of this ancient city there are 52 churches, one for every week of the year.

The Market Place

Although very little is left of the city walls, the area within them was for many centuries the second-largest city in England, after London. Today Norwich gives the impression of an attractive and bustling country town rather than a city, with the **Market Place** at its heart. The center of this large and colorful open space is filled with the gaily roofed stalls of the market traders, and it is surrounded by buildings from many periods. The largest of these, and one of the most modern, is the City Hall, which is at the top of the square on the west. (Behind it on Upper St. Giles Street is Greens, one of the best fish restaurants in the area). City Hall's predecessor, the **Guildhall**, is on the north of the square. The latter, a churchlike flint building, was started in 1407, and from then until 1938, 529 mayors presided over the impressive Council Chamber, with its 15th-century glass and Tudor carved ceiling. Displayed within is the sword captured from the Spanish Admiral of the Fleet at the Battle of St. Vincent by Admiral Lord Nelson, who presented it to the town. Nelson was a local boy, having been born the son of the parson of Burnham Thorpe and educated at Norwich School before going off to sea. Although built as the Council Chamber, the Guildhall has also been a cloth market and a prison. Today there is a magistrates' court on the second floor and, on the ground floor, the Tourist Information Centre, worth a stop not only to look at the architectural detailing but also to find out what is on in town.

On the south side of the Market Place is the magnificent **Church of St. Peter Mancroft**. It is a great joy to be in the vicinity of this church on Sundays, because it houses

13 bells, making it one of the finest and most historic set of bells in the world. The church is the center of campanology in East Anglia. Sixty feet tall from the floor to the great hammer-beam roof and 212 feet in length, with huge windows on the north and south, the interior of the church gives the impression of vastness and light. Contributing to this effect is the glorious East Window, a treasure that boasts some of the finest Norwich glass of the 15th century, the same era as the church.

All major cities in the 18th century had a place of assembly where the gentry, notables, and dandies would meet during the season, and Norwich is no exception. Behind St. Peter Mancroft on North Theatre Road is the elegant **Assembly House**, built in 1754 by Thomas Ivory. People would gather there for tea or to play cards in the smaller rooms, and balls and assemblies would take place in the lovely Music Room. One of the greatest of these events was the victory ball to celebrate the Battle of Trafalgar—the battle in which Lord Nelson lost his life. The Assembly House is a good place to meet before attending the Theatre Royal next door, as the Music Room is now a restaurant, with an art gallery in one of the other rooms. The Theatre Royal is thriving today, with all the national touring companies making a stop at Norwich.

Running along the bottom (east side) of the Market Place is Gentleman's Walk, a higgledy-piggledy collection of shops, restaurants, and pubs. On the right at the end of the walk is London Street, one of the main shopping streets of Norwich and very enjoyable to stroll down, as this was one of the first pedestrian malls in England.

The Castle

Standing on its man-made mound overlooking all of this a few blocks east of the Market Place is the Norman castle. Built originally of wood in 1067 in the first flurry of Norman defensive construction, it was rebuilt in stone about 60 years later. Its present appearance dates from 1834, when it was refaced with Bath stone. Until 1220, a Norman nobleman was appointed constable of the castle as the King's representative in Norwich, but from that date until 1887 the castle served as the county jail and, indeed, was the site of public executions. It is now a museum and well worth visiting. The galleries show the historical and cultural growth of Norfolk, as well as geological and archaeological finds in the area. But perhaps the most popular galleries are the Art Galleries, which have an unrivaled collection of the Norwich school of painting. The group of artists who formed the Norwich Society were all local men who painted their beloved East Anglian landscape. The two most prominent among them were John Crome, who founded it in 1803, and John Sell Cotman; all told, there were about 30 members, most of whom are well represented here.

The views from the castle's ramparts are spectacular, with the spires and towers of the city's 32 surviving churches much in evidence (several of these have been converted to other uses).

Around the Castle

To the north of the castle can be seen a network of little streets and alleys, of which the enchantingly Medieval Elm Hill is the heart. From here it is a short stroll past the **Briton's Arms**, once a pub, now a café/restaurant and a good place for lunch. This 15th-century house, which, unusually for Norwich, is thatched, is the oldest in the street. Be sure to visit the **Bridewell Museum**, a display of local industries and crafts, in Bedford Street. It is fascinating, as Norwich has always had a wide variety of industries, mustard making, shoemaking, and printing being just three. It is housed in a 14th-century merchant's home, which became a prison in the 16th century and a factory in the 19th century before being turned into a museum.

A few blocks west is another merchant's house that has been turned into a museum: the **Strangers Hall** in Charing Cross. This large Medieval house, the oldest part dating from 1320, is now a museum of English domestic life. The merchants who lived here were wealthy, leaving the house much enlarged and the many rooms filled with lovely furnishings. Just to the west on St. Benedicts Street is **Pinocchio's**, which serves very good Italian food.

Enchanting cobbled streets of Medieval shops and houses, most of which are color-washed, lead down from the castle area to Tombland and the cathedral. At the top stands the old church of **St. Peter Hungate**, which is now a museum of church art. This little building is beautifully kept, with highly polished tiled floors and a display of Medieval illuminated manuscripts and Russian icons, as well as fascinating ironwork signs of the mayors of Norwich.

From Medieval times Norwich had a very strong, if sometimes turbulent, ecclesiastical life. Most of the great preaching orders had priories within the city walls, which were demolished at the Reformation, when Henry VIII dissolved the monasteries. One of the very few in England to survive was the nave and chancel of the Dominican Friars' church. The nave is now **St. Andrew's Hall**, and the chancel **Blackfriars' Hall**. The splendid Perpendicular building, across the street from St. Peter Hungate, was acquired by the Norwich Corporation in the 16th century and has been used since that time for civic occasions. Many members of the royal family have been entertained here, as have other distinguished visitors over the centuries. It has a good collection of portraits of local worthies, as well as the last portrait painted of Lord Nelson. The halls are also used for art exhibitions, flower shows, concerts, and the like. There is a coffee bar/café in the ancient crypt, which is another good place for lunch.

The name **Tombland** is macabre but apt, because it was here in Tombland Alley that many victims of the Great Plague were buried. On a happier note, the annual Saxon fair took place in this large open space facing the cathedral close until it was transferred to the Market Place. Note should be made of the marvelously lopsided Augustine Steward house, built in 1549. (Steward negotiated with the Crown over the acquisition of St. Andrew's Hall for the citizens of Norwich in the 16th century.)

The Maid's Head Hotel in Tombland is a great deal older and more fascinating than it looks from the outside. Queen Elizabeth slept here on her perambulations through East Anglia in 1578. Her mother's family, the Boleyns, came from Norfolk, and her grandfather, Sir William Boleyn, is buried in the cathedral. Pleasant rooms are available.

Norwich Cathedral

From Tombland there are two gates into the **cathedral close**, one of the largest and most attractive in England. On the green is the 14th-century flushwork St. Ethelbert's Gate, which was built by the townspeople after they fought with the Benedictine monks and set fire to the cathedral. Not too much damage was done, but as penance they were set the task of building this gate. Opposite the west end of the cathedral is the 15th-century Erpingham Gate. This is built in the Perpendicular style, of which it is a fine example, and a bust of Sir Thomas Erpingham, who was the commander of the English archers at Agincourt, can be seen in a niche over the arch. On the left through the Erpingham Gate is Norwich School, founded in 1316 as Carnary College and refounded by Edward VI in his name in 1553. As can be imagined of an institution of such age, it has had many famous pupils, but probably the most illustrious is Admiral Lord Nelson, whose statue stands nearby. In its ancient undercroft, the school chapel once housed the charnel house for the city churches.

The great **Cathedral Church of the Most Holy and Undivided Trinity** is one of the glories of England. The Norman Bishop Herbert de Losinga began building it in 1096, and much of that structure is still evident today in the nave and transepts. Great Norman columns march down the church to the apsidal east end, with ambulatory and side chapels. The side stalls are among the best there are, with carved misericords showing scenes from everyday life in Medieval times. Behind the high altar sits the Saxon bishop's throne, the only one of its kind in northern Europe. The soaring clerestory and lierne vaulting date from 300 years later and are glorious, as are the carved stone bosses, which were recently repainted and relit. The best way to examine the intricate detailing of these beautiful examples of Medieval workmanship so that you don't get a crick in your neck is to look into the mirrors provided around the nave.

Although the original Norman **cloisters** were destroyed by the citizens' riot in 1272, they were subsequently rebuilt, and therefore they are a mixture of periods. They are the largest of any cathedral in England, with a vast greensward in the center. The cathedral **library** is housed above the cloister and contains many rare books and manuscripts.

The simple grave of Nurse Edith Cavell is outside the east end of the cathedral in a plot of land called Life's Green. She, like Horatio Nelson, who is also commemorated in the cathedral close, was the child of a Norfolk parson. She worked in Belgium as a nurse, remaining there even when the Germans overran it in 1914. In 1915 Cavell was arrested and shot for aiding Allied soldiers to escape. After the war, her remains were brought back to England and given a funeral service in Westminster Abbey before being buried in Norwich. There is a statue of her in Tombland and another in Charing Cross Road in London. She is remembered each year on the Sunday morning nearest to October 12, the date of her death.

A walk east past some of the buildings that made up the Medieval complex of the priory, including the granary, brewery, infirmary, and refectory, leads into a lane that goes down to the River Wensum and **Pull's Ferry**. This is one of the city's most beautiful spots, a 15th-century water gate. When the Normans built the cathedral, they brought the stone from Caen in Normandy. The lane to the ferry was once a canal created to transport building materials to the site of the massive cathedral.

From Pull's Ferry there is a pleasant riverside walk through playing fields to the 13th-century Bishop Bridge. On the far side of the bridge was Lollard's Pit, the horrifying place where many martyrs were burned at the stake.

Bishopgate, the road leading west from the bridge back toward the cathedral, is believed to be the Roman road that crossed Norwich; on the right as you walk along it is the **Great Hospital**, built in 1249. Originally designed to house poor priests and laymen, it survived the Reformation by being taken over by the corporation. Today it is a retirement home, but much of it is open to the public and definitely worth a visit. The refectory can be seen, as can the cloister leading to the transept of St. Helen's Church, which acts as both the chapel and the local parish church. In the 16th century the nave and chancel were divided into wards for single men and women, and they are not open to the public.

If you are looking for a pub lunch this is the place to stop, because the ancient **Adam and Eve** is very close by. This attractive pub serves good, inexpensive food down near the waterfront, just off Bishopgate.

Other Sights in Norwich

There has always been a strong Nonconformist element in Norfolk, and this has resulted in several very attractive buildings being built over the centuries. Just west of the cathedral, cross the Fye Bridge to Colegate, once the home of the prosperous cloth merchants of Norwich. Two of the earliest Nonconformist chapels in England can be found here. The attractive **Old Meeting House**, which was built by the Congregationalists in 1693, is situated up an alley so that it could be defended against rioters, if need be. The Congregationalists were subject to persecution and had been forced to flee to Holland and America (where they founded Norwich, Connecticut) before they returned home after the Act of Toleration. The elegant **Octagon Chapel**, built by the Presbyterians in 1756 and later taken over by the Unitarians, was the work of the local architect Thomas Ivory.

The Quaker influence in Norwich has also been particularly strong. The Gurney family, of whom prison reformer Elizabeth Fry was the best known, attended the meetings at the Quaker Meeting House in Lower Goat Lane, which is just off the Market Place. The building dates from 1679.

One of the most fascinating houses in Norwich, indeed in England, is the **Music House** in King Street, several blocks southeast of the castle. Originally called the Jew's House, it was the home of two of the wealthiest Jews in 12th-century England, who were rich enough to live in whichever area of the city they chose rather than being restricted to the Gildencroft, the Jewish quarter. Possibly the oldest dwelling house in England, although much added to over the centuries, the basic structure is Norman. The house has been lived in by most of the illustrious families of Norwich. Each family made it grander and more suitable for their style of living. Although the house is now part of the Wensum Lodge Adult Education Centre, a bar is sited in the oldest part of the building and can be viewed in licensing hours.

Opposite the Music House was the cell of the 14th-century mystic Mother Julian, a Benedictine nun who wrote *Revelations of Divine Love,* possibly the first book ever written by a European woman. A chapel has been built on the site of the cell, incorporating stone from the original building. Close by is **Dragon Hall**, a really marvelous Medieval hall house that was once owned by a rich merchant. It is in the process of being restored, but even at this halfway stage, there is a great deal to see.

The River Wensum runs through Norwich, and there are many riverside walks to stroll along. There are also cruises that can be taken for an hour, half a day, or a day. This is a lovely way to see a lovely town. If you wish to stay beside the river, book a room at the **Nelson Hotel** on Prince of Wales Road.

GETTING AROUND
To reach Suffolk from London by road, take A 12 through the East End. An alternative route, approaching Suffolk from the west, is to take the M 11 toward Cambridge,

again through east London, then transfer to A 45 into Suffolk.

To reach Suffolk by train from London, go to Liverpool Street Station in the City area. The trains run hourly and reach Ipswich in 70 minutes. To go on up the East Coast, you will transfer to the East Suffolk Line, which runs every two hours. Suffolk can also be approached from across the Channel, as it has several major ports. The main passenger terminals are at Felixstowe and Harwich.

Norwich is about 50 miles north of Ipswich on A 140. The drive up the Suffolk coast on A 12 is longer (about 70 miles) but more scenic. Once in Norwich, cruises on the Norfolk Broads are an excellent way to see the county. Two firms headquartered in Norfolk are: **G. Smith and Sons**, Riverside Road NR12 8UD, Tel: (0603) 782-527; and **C. J. Lovewell Southern River Steamers**, 43 Ebbisham Drive NR4 6HQ, Tel: (0603) 501-220.

ACCOMMODATIONS REFERENCE

▶ **Angel Hotel.** 3 Angel Hill, **Bury St. Edmunds** IP33 1LT. Tel: (0284) 75-39-26; Telex: 81630; Fax: (0284) 75-00-92.

▶ **Black Lion Hotel and Countrymen Restaurant.** The Green, **Long Melford** CO10 9DN. Tel: (0787) 31-23-56; Fax: (0787) 745-57.

▶ **Brudenell Hotel.** The Parade, **Aldeburgh** IP15 5BU. Tel: (0728) 45-20-71.

▶ **The Bull Hotel.** Hall Street, **Long Melford** CO10 9JG. Tel: (0787) 784-94; Fax: (0787) 88-03-07; in U.S., (212) 541-4400 or (800) 223-5672.

▶ **The Bull Hotel.** Market Hill, **Woodbridge** IP12 4LR. Tel: (0394) 38-56-88.

▶ **Crown Hotel.** Market Hill, **Framlingham** IP13 9AN. Tel: (0728) 72-35-21; in U.S., (212) 541-4400 or (800) 223-5672.

▶ **Crown Hotel.** High Street, **Southwold** IP18 6DP. Tel: (0502) 72-22-75; Telex: 97223; Fax: (0502) 72-48-05.

▶ **Great White Horse Hotel.** Tavern Street, **Ipswich** IP1 3AH. Tel: (0473) 25-65-58; Fax: (0473) 25-33-96.

▶ **Hintlesham Hall. Hintlesham,** near Ipswich IP8 3NS. Tel: (0473) 872-68; Telex: 98340; Fax: (0473) 874-63.

▶ **Jolly Sailor.** Quay Street, **Orford** IP1 2NU. Tel: (0394) 45-02-43.

▶ **The Maid's Head Hotel.** Tombland, **Norwich** NR3 1LB. Tel: (0603) 76-11-11; Fax: (0603) 61-36-88.

▶ **Maison Talbooth**. Stratford Road, **Dedham**, Colchester CO7 6HN. Tel: (0206) 32-23-67; Fax: (0206) 32-27-52.

▶ **The Mill Hotel**. Walnut Tree Lane, **Sudbury** CO10 6BD. Tel: (0787) 755-44; in U.S., (212) 714-2323, (800) 522-5568, or (800) 223-6764; Fax: (0787) 31-00-33.

▶ **Nelson Hotel**. Prince of Wales Road, **Norwich** NR1 1DX. Tel: (0603) 76-02-60.

▶ **Otley House**. Otley, **Woodbridge** IP6 9NR. Tel: (0473) 89-02-53.

▶ **Rutland Arms Hotel**. High Street, **Newmarket** CB8 8NB. Tel: (0638) 66-42-51; in U.S., (402) 493-4747 or (800) 44-UTELL; Fax: (0638) 66-62-98.

▶ **St. Peters House**. Old Market, **Beccles** NR34 9AP. Tel: (0502) 71-32-03.

▶ **Seckford Hall Hotel**. **Woodbridge** IP13 6NU. Tel: (0394) 38-56-78; Telex: 987446; Fax: (0394) 38-06-10.

▶ **Swan Hotel**. High Street, **Lavenham** CO10 9QA. Tel: (0787) 24-74-77; Fax: (0787) 24-82-86.

▶ **Swan Hotel**. Market Place, **Southwold** IP18 6EG. Tel: (0502) 72-21-86; Fax: (0502) 72-48-00.

▶ **Uplands Hotel**. Victoria Road, **Aldeburgh** IP15 5DX. Tel: (0728) 45-24-20.

▶ **Wentworth Hotel**. Wentworth Road, **Aldeburgh** IP15 5BD. Tel: (0728) 45-23-12; in U.S., (212) 714-2233, (800) 522-5568, or (800) 223-6764.

THE HEART OF ENGLAND

STRATFORD AND WARWICK TO THE WELSH BORDER

By Angela Murphy

Angela Murphy, a British free-lance writer and photographer, has contributed to a number of guidebooks, including the Shell Weekend Guide Book *and* The Hachette Guide to Great Britain. *The Heart of England is her favorite part of Britain.*

Just a few hours from London is the region loosely known as the "Heart of England." This area, stretching from the ancient towns of Stratford-upon-Avon and Warwick west to the Welsh border, encompasses some of the finest and most historic countryside in England. Shakespeare country, centered around his birthplace, Stratford, and the mighty castle at Warwick, attracts many thousands of visitors every year. But if you explore the areas to the west you'll discover sleepy villages and bustling market towns that have remained largely unspoiled. A network of canals crisscrosses the land. Once essential in transporting goods across the country, they now provide a superb touring resource, and you should not fail to take at least one river or canal trip during your stay. (See Getting Around, at the end of this chapter, for specific booking information.)

MAJOR INTEREST

Shakespearean sites in Stratford
Warwick Castle
Kenilworth Castle
Worcester Cathedral
Malvern Hills
Chained Library in Hereford Cathedral
Forest of Dean
Tintern Abbey
Shrewsbury's historic buildings
Ironbridge Gorge industrial museum
Ludlow and the Shropshire Hills

STRATFORD-UPON-AVON

A visit to England would be incomplete without at least a brief stop at Shakespeare's birthplace, Stratford. Although it draws crowds of visitors from all over the world, Stratford is still a delightful town, with many less-frequented side roads where ancient houses and unusual crafts and antiques shops are to be found. Regular guided tours of Stratford and some of the nearby sites are available, and Guide Friday runs open-top double-decker buses connecting the Shakespeare properties every 15 minutes in summer and hourly in winter. Tickets can be bought on the bus or from the Guide Friday Stratford Centre of Tourism at 14 Rother Street.

To start your visit, see the lavish and spectacular audio-visual production called "The World of Shakespeare," just north of the Royal Shakespeare Theatre on Waterside. Superbly designed to present the everyday life of the Elizabethans, it can be a great help to visitors touring the general sites. Although the building is being sold, it is hoped that the production will continue. From here you can walk to the other side of Bridge Foot to catch the open-top Guide Friday bus in front of the Pen & Parchment Inn.

Stratford drew few Shakespearean pilgrims before the early 18th century, when interest in Shakespeare's writings revived. From then on there was a steady stream of literary visitors, encouraged by the first Shakespeare Festival, organized in 1769 by the celebrated actor and impresario David Garrick. Modern-day tourists visit the same places those first tourists did. There are a number of

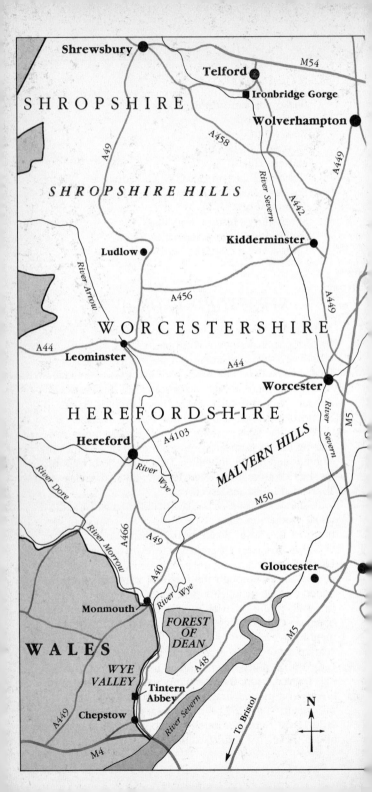

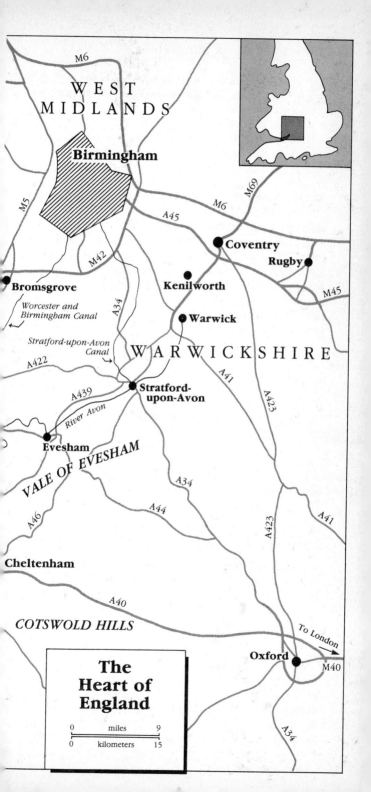

Tudor houses associated with Shakespeare, many of them run by the Shakespeare Birthplace Trust, which issues a combined admission ticket to all its buildings. The ticket is available at any of their properties.

Shakespeare's Birthplace, on Henley Street, has always been a popular venue, although it is in better condition than in past times and tourists are no longer offered chunks from the Bard's chair as expensive souvenirs. Walking from Henley Street to the site of Shakespeare's last home, **New Place**, visitors pass the late 16th-century **Harvard House** on the High Street. Now owned by Harvard University, the house was built by the grandfather of John Harvard, founder of the college. It contains a fascinating collection of books, pictures, and period furniture. Equally ancient is the building next door, which houses a pub, the **Garrick Inn**.

New Place was demolished in 1759 by its crotchety owner, the Reverend Francis Gastrell. He had already cut down Shakespeare's mulberry tree as a protest against the growing number of visitors who came to look at the poet's former home. Only the foundations of this house in Chapel Street remain (opposite the fine old Guild Chapel), and these are now in the center of some delightful gardens. They include a fine replica of a formal Elizabethan knot garden, comprising four "knotts," or beds filled with mixed herbs and flowers and divided by stone paths.

The gardens are entered through **Nash's House** next door, which was once owned by Shakespeare's granddaughter, Elizabeth Hall, and her husband, Thomas Nash. It is now the local history museum and is furnished in Elizabethan style. Also nearby, and well worth a visit, are the old **Grammar School**, which Shakespeare probably attended, and **Hall's Croft**. This lovely old house was the home of Shakespeare's daughter, Susanna, and her husband, Dr. John Hall. Beautifully furnished and maintained, it also contains an Elizabethan dispensary, complete with surgical equipment, herbs, and potions. The large walled garden behind the house is a delightful spot to sit and have tea.

Holy Trinity Church is just a short walk away. At this beautiful Medieval parish church on the banks of the River Avon, Shakespeare was both baptized and buried. Every year on the Saturday closest to Shakespeare's birthday (April 23) local and foreign dignitaries, figures from the theatrical world, and Shakespearean actors from the

Royal Shakespeare Company walk in procession to the church to lay flowers on **Shakespeare's Tomb** in celebration of the Bard's birthday. If your visit to Stratford coincides with this or with the traditional Mop Fair, usually held on or about October 12 (originally an annual hiring fair for servants, it is now an amusement fair), you will miss the summer crush of tourists and see some of the town's true life.

Following the river from Holy Trinity back toward the Clopton Bridge, you arrive at the **Royal Shakespeare Theatre**, which contains a small exhibition of paintings, costumes, and mementos. Shakespearean plays are performed here from the end of March to the end of January. A small number of medium-priced tickets are sold on the day of the performance, but advance booking is always highly advisable. The Royal Shakespeare Company will arrange tickets along with food and accommodations. Another fine theater, the Swan, has been built in the shell of the original Victorian Memorial Theatre (destroyed by fire in 1926) and is designed to resemble a Jacobean playhouse. The **Swan Theatre** stages the works of Shakespeare's contemporaries and followers, and a third theater nearby, **The Other Place**, stages modern productions (The Other Place has just been rebuilt; call ahead to be sure it is open; Tel: 0789-29-56-23 for bookings or 0789-691-91 for 24-hour recorded information, or write to the Box Office, Royal Shakespeare Theatre, Stratford-upon-Avon CV37 6BB). Visitors can also tour backstage at the Royal Shakespeare Theatre and view the costume exhibition most afternoons.

If you want a really good dinner try **Shepherd's Garden Restaurant** at the Stratford House Hotel or **Sir Toby's** in Church Street. Theatergoers and others can also dine at the Royal Shakespeare Theatre, either at the elegant **Box Tree Restaurant** overlooking the river (not always good value) or at the more informal **River Terrace Restaurant**. Just across the road is the popular actors' pub, the **Black Swan** (known to regulars as the "Dirty Duck"). In the center of town, the **Slug and Lettuce** pub-cum-bistro on Guild Street offers a lively alternative with an excellent range of dishes, in spite of its unappealing name. For more exotic but inexpensive fare, try the Italian **Sorrento** on Meer Street or, for first-class Indian food, **Hussain's** on Chapel Street. Also fun to eat at is **Fatty Arbuckle's**, opposite New Place on Chapel Street.

Other unusual attractions in town include the marve-

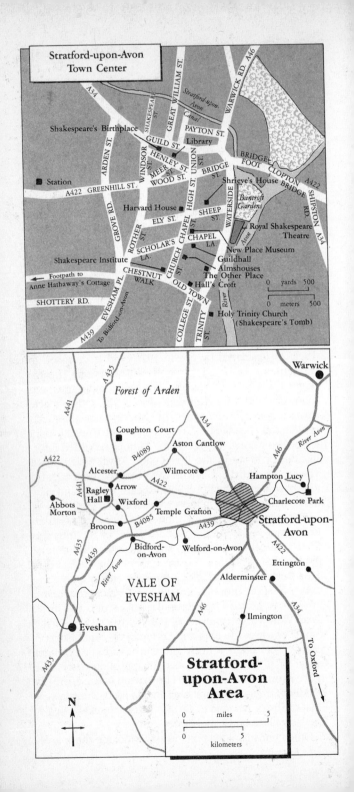

lous **Teddy Bear Museum** in Greenhill Street and the Brass Rubbing Centre in **Avon Bank Park** (between the Swan Theatre and Holy Trinity Church), where visitors can make their own brass rubbings. In Bancroft Gardens and just across the footbridge in Swan's Nest Lane you can take a cruise or rent boats for short excursions on the river or the Stratford-upon-Avon Canal, which branches off the Avon here. **The Water Rat** brasserie in Swan's Nest Lane has a lovely view of the river.

Visitors looking for reasonably priced accommodations are advised to book early and select with care from the many available choices. Several hotels offer reduced prices for weekend bookings. Two popular, upmarket, and very central hotels with strong historic connections are **The Shakespeare Hotel** on Chapel Street and the refurbished **White Swan Hotel** on Rother Street. Part of The Shakespeare inn was the 15th-century home of Sir Hugh Clopton, a former lord mayor of London who built the town's attractive bridge. The fine 16th-century wall paintings in the White Swan, uncovered in the 1920s, illustrate the story of Tobias and the angel and owe their remarkable state of preservation to Jacobean paneling.

Those on a more modest budget might try the small but exclusive **Stratford House Hotel**, just 100 yards from the theater on Sheep Street, which has a good restaurant— **Shepherd's Garden**—and will book theater tickets for you. Another pleasant hotel in a peaceful canal-side setting is **Duke's Hotel** on Payton Street. An excellent and inexpensive bed-and-breakfast accommodation out of town is **Folly Farm Cottage** at Ilmington, a beautiful village on the northern edge of the Cotswolds. Take a magical walk through this village's back alleys and finish off with a superb dinner at the restaurant of the **Howard Arms.**

There are also a number of fine hotels around Stratford. Three luxury establishments, housed in large, historic mansions, each with its own first-class restaurant, are the **Ettington Park Hotel** on the A 34 near Alderminster, the **Welcombe Hotel** on Warwick Road, and the **Billesley Manor Hotel** on the A 422 near Alcester. All three stand in superb parklands and offer a wide range of amenities. At a more moderate price, and with an excellent restaurant, there is the **Chase Hotel** in Ettington.

Attractions near Stratford

A pleasant stroll along the footpaths leading west from the town center will take you to the place where Shakespeare did much of his courting. **Anne Hathaway's Cottage** at Shottery is a classic thatched farmhouse containing original furniture and surrounded by an old-fashioned English garden. Visitors can get lunchtime snacks or excellent cream teas at the **Cottage Tea Garden** opposite.

To the north and west, little remains of the ancient Forest of Arden, which once covered most of the area. However, much of its timber can be seen in use as the frames and gables of houses in the local villages. Notable among these villages are lovely **Abbots Morton**, with its 14th-century stone church and thatched-roof letter box; **Aston Cantlow**, where Shakespeare's parents married; and charming **Wilmcote**, where his mother was raised.

Shakespeare's parents were a comparatively wealthy couple. His father was a glover and tanner, and his mother, Mary Arden, was the daughter of a prosperous farmer. Their attractive farm in Wilmcote is now a museum of farming and rural life, containing some interesting rooms, a dairy, and a cider mill. An exhibition (with demonstrations) and shop at the farm display the wares of many local craftspeople. The area has a pair of fine traditional English pubs with excellent home-cooked bar food: the **King's Head Inn** at Aston Cantlow (where Shakespeare's parents are reputed to have held their wedding breakfast in 1557), and the **Mason's Arms** in Wilmcote.

Legend has it that the young William Shakespeare poached deer in the grounds of **Charlecote Park** near Stratford to the east, and deer can still be seen grazing there. Whatever the truth of the tale, this magnificent Tudor mansion in its great landscaped park makes for a satisfying visit. Still the home of the Lucy family, the house is now the property of the National Trust, and the ground-floor rooms are open to the public from Easter to October. It has some impressive Victorian rooms, a vast kitchen and brewhouse, and a museum of local and family relics. While there, drive or walk to the village of **Hampton Lucy** to see the family church of St. Peter and a restored 18th-century water mill where traditional stone-ground flour is still made.

The countryside immediately south of Stratford is fairly flat meadow and farmland sustained by the River Avon. To the west, however, a number of pleasant villages with

Shakespearean associations lie on either side of A 439—notably Temple Grafton, Wixford, Broom, Bidford-on-Avon, and Welford-on-Avon. **Temple Grafton** was once the center of large-scale limestone quarrying, and nearby Hillborough Manor was the home of Anne Whateley, to whom Shakespeare may have been betrothed before he married Anne Hathaway. (The known facts are that 26-year-old Anne Hathaway, who had been working in the Whateley household, was pregnant when she married the 18-year-old Shakespeare. In the previous year, on November 27, 1582, a license had been issued for Shakespeare's marriage to 21-year-old Anne Whateley. On November 28, 1582, the records show that a license had been issued for his marriage to Anne Hathaway. Some scholars believe that the first entry was a clerical error, but the truth of the matter will probably never be known. We do know, however, that Anne Whateley left for an extended stay in Italy and that, shortly after her return to London, Shakespeare himself left for the capital.)

Wixford is named after its ancient ford, now replaced by a bridge. In Shakespeare's day the village belonged to the Throckmortons, a powerful Catholic family that lived at nearby **Coughton Court**. The ugly frontage here conceals a superb brick courtyard, and the house contains some interesting Gunpowder Plot relics.

The outstanding Palladian mansion **Ragley Hall** is set in a 400-acre park landscaped by Capability Brown a few miles west of Wixford. In addition to a remarkable collection of paintings and furniture, its great hall contains some of the most splendidly ornate plasterwork in Britain. A more recent treasure is *The Temptation* by Graham Rust, a magnificent mural painted (1969–1983) for the present Marquess of Hertford. Opposite the entrance to the hall, a mill has been converted into a delightful small hotel, the **Arrow Mill**, and makes an excellent base for touring the area. The village of Arrow, for which it was named, is nearby.

The little village of **Broom** contains a 19th-century mill and the 17th-century timber-framed **Broom Tavern**, an attractive pub with good bar food and a garden.

Just off A 439 is **Bidford-on-Avon**, quieter now that a bypass carries the traffic that once thundered through the ancient town center. There is a pleasant picnic spot by the Medieval stone bridge. Much of **Welford-on-Avon** has been built up, but the red, white, and blue maypole still stands, and village children dance round it every May Day.

The **Shakespeare Inn** here serves excellent homemade food in a cozy bar and doubles as the village library.

THE VALE OF EVESHAM

Southwest of Stratford, the River Avon flows through the Vale of Evesham, edged to the south by the Cotswold Hills. This fertile vale gained its fame for the fruit and vegetables grown there when the great abbeys dominated the region, and it is still well known as a major producer of vegetables and for its massed orchards of plums, cherries, and apples. In spring the orchards form part of a signposted "Blossom Trail" from Evesham; Tel: (0386) 44-69-44 for up-to-the-minute news of the blossoms.

The two great abbey towns of the region, Pershore and **Evesham,** both fell victim to the ravages of the Reformation. Evesham's Benedictine abbey, one of the finest ever built, was completely destroyed, leaving only its magnificent bell tower (1539) and the 14th-century half-timbered gateway in the marketplace. Among other fascinating displays of local history, a model of the abbey is on view in the **Almonry Museum** on Vine Street near Abbey Park. (It also houses the Tourist Information Centre.) Two fine Medieval churches in Evesham also survive from this era side by side—the townspeople's church of **All Saints** and the **Church of St. Lawrence,** built for the many pilgrims who flocked to pay homage to Simon de Montfort, a popular hero because of his role in founding the House of Commons. De Montfort was killed by Prince Edward (later Edward I) at the Battle of Evesham in 1265 and is buried beneath the abbey's high altar.

An attractive market town, Evesham has many interesting old buildings, including the beautifully restored Round House, which today contains the National Westminster Bank. At the town hall, the broad High Street splits into two roads leading down to the river. Between them lie the abbey ruins, surrounded by parkland that slopes gently down to the riverbank.

Just upstream from Workman Bridge, the modern **lockkeeper's house** deserves a look. It was built by the Lower Avon Navigation Trust, which, since the 1940s, has restored the Avon to navigation through voluntary labor contributions. In 1974, for the first time in more than a century, Stratford was linked with the Severn (which

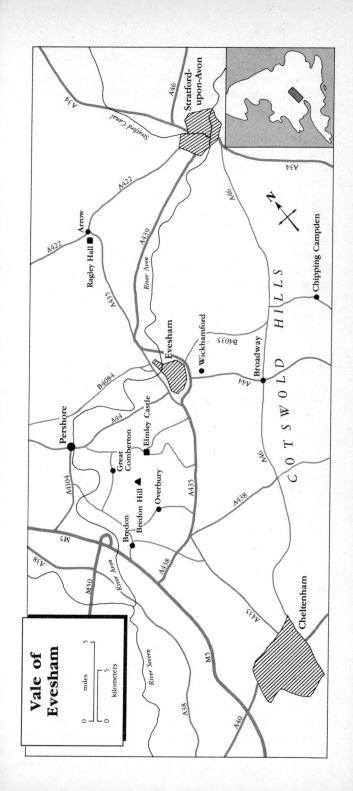

Vale of Evesham

Stratford-upon-Avon

Arrow
Ragley Hall
A422
A422
Stratford Canal
A34
A46
A439
River Avon
A435
A46

Evesham
Wickhamford
Pershore
B4084
A44
Great Comberton
Elmley Castle
Overbury
Bredon Hill
Bredon
A435
B4035
Broadway
A44
A46
Chipping Campden
A435
A438

COTSWOLD HILLS

M5
A4104
A38
M50
River Avon
A438
A38
River Severn
M5
A435
A40

Cheltenham

N

miles   5
0
kilometers 5
0

flows southwest down past Bristol), and a cruising route through the Avon, the Stratford Canal, the Worcester and Birmingham Canal, and the Severn was made available to pleasure craft. Fully equipped cruisers and barges can be hired in Stratford and Evesham (the **Original Boat Company** at Evesham Marina on Kings Road; Tel: 0386-489-06 or 478-13), or you can take cruiser trips on the river. Hourly river trips operate from Easter to September from the site of the Hampton Ferry (the oldest rope-pulled ferry in England) to the west of town. Evesham is a popular boating center, and a number of regattas are held here throughout the summer. The comfortable **Evesham Hotel** is a family-run, well-equipped Tudor manor house with attractive gardens on Cooper's Lane, off Waterside. It is sophisticated—yet has a friendly and slightly eccentric atmosphere. Just outside Evesham, in a major asparagus-growing area, **The Round of Gras** pub at Badsey serves famous asparagus suppers from May to mid-June. Also worth a detour, at any time of year, is **The Fleece Inn** at Bretforton, a 19th-century tavern, part of which dates from the 14th century.

At **Pershore**, to the west, the important tenth-century Benedictine abbey was largely destroyed during the dissolution of the monasteries. The townspeople paid to save the lovely 13th-century choir and transept; these now serve as **Holy Cross**, the town's parish church. Most spectacular is the impressive 14th-century lantern tower, standing on four great Norman arches, and two richly decorated 17th-century monuments to the Hazelwood family are also worth seeking out. Bridge Street and the High Street are lined with attractive Georgian houses, many with bow fronts and ornamental iron balconies. Several now house restaurants or tearooms. On the eastern side of the town, many of the hotels and inns back onto gardens by the river, including the friendly 16th-century **Angel Inn and Posting House**, which serves excellent homemade food. An important gardening center, Pershore has a large market on Wednesdays, Fridays, and Saturdays.

South of Pershore, across the Medieval bridge built by the Benedictine monks over the River Avon, the land rises slowly toward the summit of **Bredon Hill**. From here there is a fine view of Pershore across the broad, sheep-scattered plain by the river. At the summit of the hill are the remains of a large Iron Age fort, and the 18th-century tower **Parson's Folly**.

Surrounding the base of Bredon Hill are some charming examples of English country villages, with clusters of stone-built or half-timbered houses that are well worth a detour. The village of **Bredon** lies on the Avon and has a gigantic 14th-century tithe barn, while **Great Comberton** has one of the largest dovecotes in England, with more than 1,400 nesting holes. All the villages are easily visited by car or on foot, and the hill itself can be climbed from **Elmley Castle** to the north (fine 17th-century monuments are in St. Mary's church here) or from **Overbury** to the south (it has an attractive mansion). Journeying from Elmley Castle, you pass **Bell's Castle**, another 18th-century folly. On a fine day the beautiful Avon valley and as many as nine counties can be seen from the summit.

The country church at **Wickhamford**, 2 miles southeast of Evesham, contains the 17th-century tomb of one of George Washington's ancestors, Penelope Washington. Here you can see the Washington family coat of arms—three stars and one stripe—which served as a model for the U.S. flag.

WARWICKSHIRE OUTSIDE THE STRATFORD AREA

Stratford attracts hordes of visitors, as does Warwick, but the countryside of surrounding Warwickshire offers delightful exploration too. This has long been a prosperous place: The River Avon provided an early trade route to Bristol, and later the Stratford-upon-Avon Canal linked the area with the industrial center of Birmingham. Mighty castles also gave Warwickshire immense political importance in the Middle Ages. Today, the center of this region is Warwick.

Warwick

The historic town of Warwick, just 8 miles north of Stratford on A 46, merits at least a daylong visit, not only for its justly famed, monumental Warwick Castle but also for the town itself. Although it is the administrative capital of the county, Warwick is quite small, with a network of higgledy-piggledy streets, many fine old houses, and a special charm and intimacy. It is situated on top of a low hill overlooking the Avon, and its center is largely contained within a triangle of ancient streets grouped around St. Mary's Church in Old Square.

The base of this triangle is the High Street (leading onto Jury Street), which separates the town from the castle and connects the east and west gates of the town's original Medieval walls. Although the layout of Medieval Warwick has survived, fire destroyed much of the town in 1694, and most of the houses remaining date from the late 17th and 18th centuries. The fire also destroyed the main body of **St. Mary's Church**. (The nave and the superb tower were rebuilt in the early 18th century.) However, the jewel of the church survived: the 15th-century **Beauchamp Chapel**, with its famous tomb of Richard Beauchamp. Other remarkable tombs commemorate the various earls of Warwick, including the Dudleys and Grevilles.

Some ancient buildings still stand on the perimeter of the town, notably **Oken's House**, now a world-famous doll museum, and **Lord Leycester's Hospital** by West Gate. Home to retired military veterans since 1571, the hospital was founded by Elizabeth I's favorite, Robert Dudley, earl of Leicester. The half-timbered, overhanging façade of the group of buildings has an impressive and much-photographed lean, and if you walk through the tiny passage between the houses you will find a charming inner courtyard. The buildings, which include an unusual candle-lit chapel, date from the 12th to the 16th century; there is a small museum in the former guildhall. The **Brethren's Kitchen** tearoom here provides excellent light snacks and teas (open Easter to September).

The city's main local history museum is housed in the **Market Hall** on Market Place. As in other English towns, market stalls used to stand in the open arcades between the pillars supporting the hall. Although the arcades are now filled in, the hall still marks the site of the present-day marketplace and of the annual Mop Fair in October. A branch of the local museum specializing in folk life and the history of the Royal Warwickshire Regiment is housed in the Jacobean **St. John's House** at Coten End next to St. Nicholas' Park.

The town's star attraction is of course the magnificent **Warwick Castle**, which, with its battlements, towers, and beautiful gardens and the enormous mansion at its heart, covers the hillside between town and river. Warwick Castle was begun by William the Conqueror in 1068 on the site of an earlier fortification built by the great Saxon monarch Queen Ethelfleda. For several hundred years afterward, the castle, standing at a strategic crossing place on the river, was a vital link in the defense of the kingdom. As a result, it was regularly modernized and added to and was an important gift to loyal subjects from various kings and queens.

The castle became a subject of controversy in the 1970s when the present earl of Warwick sold a number of the family heirlooms and, finally, the castle itself along with its magnificent contents. Luckily, the buyers were the owners of Madame Tussaud's, the famous waxwork museum, and they have restored the castle beautifully. They have also added to the collection by buying items associated with the castle's history.

The castle is filled to the brim with visitors in high summer (to be avoided, if possible), and lines to see the state apartments have been known to stretch beyond the castle walls. However, in summer the grounds are at their best; so if you go and want to avoid the worst of the crush, visit in the early morning. Thursdays and Saturdays are the least crowded days. A winter's afternoon, when visitors are few, can be one of the most rewarding times to visit the castle.

The tour of the private apartments is thrilling. They have been arranged to replicate a weekend house party that occurred in June, 1898, complete with lifelike models of the distinguished guests and appropriate sound effects. It is one of the best-presented exhibits of its kind, and you may feel like an invisible eavesdropper who has travelled back in time. Other fascinating exhibits at the castle include the dungeon, fine armory, and the Medieval Great Hall. The main entrance and gift shop are in the stables (through the Castle Lane car park) on a hill above the castle and close to the town center.

A fine view of the castle can be had from the "new" **Banbury Bridge**, built in the 1780s to replace the old bridge at the foot of the castle walls. The delightful ribbon of ancient houses along Bridgend owes its survival to the decision made by George Greville, second earl of Warwick, to move the bridge upstream. Beautiful private gardens at 55 Mill Street are occasionally open for charity, and they too provide a magnificent view of the castle and the remains of the old bridge. However, the finest views of the castle are from the river itself. Boats can be rented riverside at St. Nicholas's Park, which also has recreational facilities and picnic areas.

The best food in town is to be found at **Randolph's**

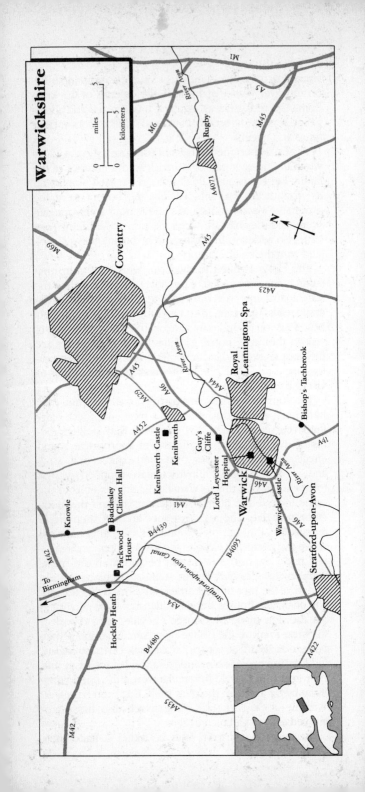

Warwickshire

miles
kilometers

N

Coventry

Rugby

Royal
Leamington Spa

Kenilworth Castle
Kenilworth

Guy's Cliffe

Lord Leycester Hospital

Warwick

Warwick Castle

Bishop's Tachbrook

Stratford-upon-Avon

Knowle

Baddesley
Clinton Hall

Packwood House

Hockley Heath

To
Birmingham

Stratford-upon-Avon Canal

River Avon

River Avon

M1
A5
M45
M6
M69
A46
A429
A45
A452
A41
A423
A444
A41
A46
A422
A46
A34
B4439
B4095
B4480
A435
M42
A4071

restaurant at 19–20 Coten End (reservations are advised; Tel: 0926-49-12-92). For less expensive fare in Warwick, try **Pizza Piazza** on Jury Street, which serves good home-made pizzas in a 15th-century house near East Gate. Light meals and afternoon tea can also be had at the **Number 5 Tearoom** at 5 New Street; and **Nicolini's Bistro** on Jury Street. You can even take part in a Medieval banquet at the castle if you reserve ahead; Tel: (0926) 49-54-21; Fax: (0926) 40-16-92.

If you want to stay in town, try the former country home of the earl of Leicester, the **Lord Leycester Hotel**, on Jury Street, or the **Westgate Arms** on Bowling Green Street, which has an elaborate formal restaurant and a good brasserie. Both hotels are comfortable and centrally located. For less expensive but very comfortable bed-and-breakfast accommodation try **Ashleigh House** in Henley-on-Arden, or **Northleigh House** at Hatton.

Just a mile north of Warwick on the road to Coventry is **Guy's Cliffe**, named after Guy of Warwick, the legendary hero of the Dark Ages who ended his days as a hermit in the caves above the river. Above the cliff are the ruins of an 18th-century house where the great actress Sarah Siddons once worked. Below, on the river, is a pleasant inn and steak house, **Saxon Mill Harvester**, where you can watch the mill wheel turning and water rushing under-foot. It is worth visiting for the magnificent setting.

Kenilworth

A great castle is also the main attraction at nearby Kenilworth, 5 miles north of Warwick on A 46. All that remains of this once formidable royal stronghold are some dramatic ruins left after Cromwell's troops disman-tled the castle at the end of the Civil War. The 12th-century keep of **Kenilworth Castle** and its outer curtain wall were once surrounded by a vast man-made lake that was a defensive system in the early Middle Ages. Later the lake became a place of entertainment and leisure, so much so that Elizabeth I and her 400-member retinue made four visits to the castle when it belonged to Robert Dudley. The best documented of these occurred in July 1575 and formed the background for the novel *Kenilworth* by Sir Walter Scott.

Today, the lake has been drained and the buildings are decayed and roofless. Their sheer scale, however, is very impressive, especially the walls of John of Gaunt's Great

Hall, the massive gatehouse, and the stables erected by the earl of Leicester. Your visit will be enhanced if you first tour the "World of Shakespeare" exhibit in Stratford, part of which illustrates Queen Elizabeth's triumphal procession to Kenilworth in 1575. Make sure, too, that you have a close look at the postcard sold at the castle—it shows a drawing of Kenilworth as it was during Elizabeth's visit.

Between the castle and Kenilworth's center is a large open space named **Abbey Fields**, in which stand the remains of the town's abbey. The main part of the town is modern, but the area near the castle (particularly Castle Green, Little Virginia on Castle Hill, and the High Street) has retained its original buildings, including many of the charming bow-fronted cottages characteristic of this region.

Just up Castle Hill is a pleasant, inexpensive restaurant called **George Rafters**, which serves lunch and dinner. For something a little more special, seek out **Restaurant Bosquet** on Warwick Road, which serves superb food and wine at reasonable prices (reservations are essential; Tel: 0926-524-63).

Royal Leamington Spa

A couple of miles east of Warwick on A 444 is Royal Leamington Spa, an elegant, early 19th-century Regency town with gracious houses and broad streets. Leamington and other important British spa towns such as Bath and Cheltenham (see The Cotswolds to Winchester chapter) came to prominence in the late 18th century on a wave of enthusiasm for "taking the waters" at mineral springs. By 1814 several baths had been built in Leamington, together with the large, distinguished buildings housing the Pump Room, the **Assembly Rooms**, and the **Public Baths**. The town continued to prosper in the early 19th century, a fact attested to by its spacious avenues and crescents lined with houses that are handsomely embellished with porticoes and ornate iron balconies.

Although the spa's popularity began to decline in the mid-19th century, the **Pump Room** still offers hydrotherapy and physiotherapy medical treatments (by prescription only); the facilities may be open to the public after restoration is completed. Just opposite the Pump Room, by the River Leam, are the delightful **Jephson Gardens**. Also worth a visit is the **Leamington Spa Art**

Gallery and Museum on Avenue Road, which has a fine collection of Dutch and Flemish masterpieces.

The shopping in Royal Leamington Spa is excellent; the High Street has a full range of shops, from Next to Marks and Spencer. There is also a wide variety of hotels, guesthouses, and restaurants to choose from here. For a pleasant, medium-priced hotel try the **Lansdowne Hotel** on Clarendon Street or the **Coverdale Private Hotel** on Portland Street. If you prefer more luxurious surroundings, head for **Mallory Court**, an outstanding country-house hotel with a superb restaurant, at Bishop's Tachbrook just south of Leamington.

Two stately homes are nearby: Baddesley Clinton Hall, 6 miles north of Warwick off A 41 at Knowle, and Packwood House, near A 34 at Hockley Heath. Both are owned by the National Trust. **Baddesley Clinton Hall** is a superb moated manor house, much of which dates from the 14th and 15th centuries. It has several priest holes (for concealing Catholic priests during the Reformation) and Elizabethan fireplaces; fine tapestries and some notable paintings hang in paneled rooms. A 17th-century yew topiary garden representing the Sermon on the Mount is probably the most famous feature of **Packwood House**, but the building itself is an outstanding example of domestic Tudor architecture, with some fine tapestries, needlework, and furniture on display.

WORCESTERSHIRE

Worcester

Thirty miles west from Stratford on A 422 is the ancient cathedral city of Worcester (pronounced W'sster). The city lies on the River Severn, just where the valley broadens into a wide, fertile plain. To the east, gently rolling farmland stretches to the valley of the River Avon and the Vale of Evesham, while to the west are the fertile, hopproducing slopes of the lovely Teme Valley and the sharply defined ridge of the Malvern Hills.

An important settlement as early as Roman times, Worcester later flourished as the marketplace for surrounding agricultural areas and as a staging post between the North and Gloucester and between Wales and London. Worcester has also played a vital role in British history: In 1651, at the Battle of Worcester, the city was the last in England to surrender to Oliver Cromwell. Today much of the old city has disappeared under successive layers of development, but enough fascinating reminders of its varied history remain to make a visit here rewarding. Its many attractions include some well-designed exhibitions, such as the Commandery and Tudor House, that bring these events to life.

If you are a first-time visitor, you should make the magnificent **Worcester Cathedral** your first stop. Originally the cathedral church of a Benedictine monastery that thrived here until 1540, it is built on a low hill overlooking the Severn, just upstream of the town's impressive arched bridge. Its majestic bulk dominates the city skyline and provides a spectacular backdrop to the well-known Worcestershire County Cricket Ground. (You can buy tickets for any of the matches at the grounds.) Parts of the present structure, notably the fine crypt, date back to Norman times, but most of the cathedral was constructed under royal favor during the 13th and 14th centuries, when a constant stream of pilgrims visited its tombs and surrounding monastic buildings.

Many of the monastery buildings have survived, including the magnificent round Chapter House and the monks' refectory (now the hall of the King's School). Viewed from across the college green, to the south of the cathedral, these buildings are testaments to the binding link between church and monastery that existed before the dissolution of the monasteries by Henry VIII. From this side it's possible to walk around the **cloisters**, where side doors lead to a tearoom and a shop; you can enter the cathedral itself through the "Prior's Door."

After the intimacy of the cloisters, the magnificent nave is a breathtaking sight. Take special note of the elaborately carved pulpits and tombs, especially that of King John, who was buried here at his own request in 1216. Other items of interest include some cunningly carved misericords under the choir seats, a carved marble reredos, and Prince Arthur's Chantry, with its delicate tracery. The cathedral's upkeep is expensive, and funded solely by donations, so you may wish to contribute as you leave.

The **Commandery**, an important 15th-century building, is southeast of the cathedral, next to the Worcester and Birmingham Canal at the foot of the hill. Erected on the site of a Medieval hospital, or commandery, this was the Royalist headquarters during the Civil War and the site of some of Charles II's war councils. The restored building, with its superb Great Hall, now houses a mixture of permanent displays and some very imaginative changing exhibitions illustrating the history of the Civil War and Charles II's flight from England. If you have limited time you should view the latter first, along with the dramatic audiovisual show that is also offered. Both will bring the history of the town and the Commandery to life. There is a very pleasant canal-side tearoom here, if you have the time.

Some of the best-preserved reminders of the city's past are the ancient half-timbered houses on nearby Friar Street, particulary the 15th-century **Greyfriars** and **Tudor House**, now a folk museum with a well-organized display of the social and domestic life of the town over the past two centuries. **King Charles's House** in New Street, now a restaurant of the same name, is where Charles II hid after he lost the disastrous Battle of Worcester in 1651.

Of the three things for which Worcester is most famous—gloves, sauce, and porcelain—glove making is the only industry to have declined significantly. The curious spire off Deansway, once part of a church, was renamed the Glover's Needle by the townspeople in honor of the trade. Worcestershire sauce is still made in quantity here at the Lea & Perrins factory. Its founder, C. W. Dyson Perrins, established the unique **Dyson Perrins Museum** of historic Worcester porcelain at the Royal Worcester Porcelain Company. On display is the first piece ever made here, the Wigornia cream boat.

The **Royal Worcester Porcelain Company**, founded in 1751, conducts fascinating tours of the factory continually every weekday, during which you can watch at close hand the processes used in making porcelain. You can buy the results in the retail showroom and seconds shop. Reservations are essential in the summer and advisable at other times; however, a phone call before 10:00 A.M. will sometimes produce a reservation for the same day (Tel: 0905-232-21; no children under eight). Longer (two hours) and more detailed connoisseur's tours are also available. A restaurant serves afternoon teas and light lunches. If you come to Worcester by car, you can park at the Royal Worcester factory for a small fee and walk up to the cathedral along the cobbled College Precinct. From there, it is a pleasant walk around the center of the town and then back down to the Commandery and the factory.

Other attractions in Worcester include the narrow-boats, or barges, in the Diglis Basin and on Lowesmoor

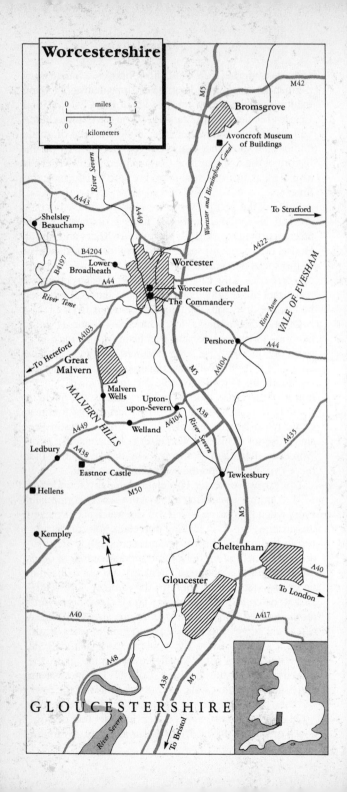

Wharf on the canal; **St. Helen's County Record Office**, housed in a former church at the corner of High Street and Fish Street, which holds the marriage document of William Shakespeare and Anne Hathaway; the **City Museum and Art Gallery**, near Foregate Street Railway Station; and the picturesque Pitchcroft Racecourse, by the Severn. Riverboats, rowing boats, and canoes can be rented at North and South Quay; you can also rent bicycles and accessories at the **Cadence Café and Cycle Hire**, at the Foregate Street Railway Station.

You can get light snacks at the Cadence Café; for more substantial fare try **Hodsons Coffee House**, at the top of the High Street near the cathedral (closed Sundays), or one of the little restaurants on Friar Street. For a more stylish meal, dine overlooking the river at **Brown's Restaurant**, a converted granary on Quay Street (lunch and dinner). Out of town, you can get excellent home-cooked meals and accommodations at **The Birche** (just 7 miles northeast of Worcester in Shelsley Beauchamp off B 4204). The newly restored **Fownes Hotel** on City Walls Road is an elegant modern hotel on the side of the canal.

The Malvern Hills

The famous English composer Sir Edward Elgar was born in the nearby village of Lower Broadheath and lived in Worcester. (A statue of him stands in Worcester at the top of the High Street, across from the cathedral.) His beloved Malvern Hills can be seen from the riverside garden in front of Worcester Cathedral, and the local tourist board has devised a 45-mile-long signposted **Elgar Trail** for motorists, which leads to the houses where he lived— including the soon-to-be-expanded **Elgar Birthplace Museum** in Lower Broadheath—and the places that inspired his music. An accompanying booklet and cassette are available.

These hills that inspired Elgar also provide some lovely walks. From their highest point, the **Worcestershire Beacon** (1,395 feet), just west of Great Malvern, you can walk the entire nine-mile range south to the Herefordshire Beacon. On a clear day you will be able to see into Wales. Nestled below the hills is the old spa town of **Great Malvern**, southwest of Worcester on A 449, built around a splendid priory church containing some stunning Medieval stained glass and tiles. This pleasant town holds an annual festival of music at the end of May called the

Malvern Festival. A comfortable, inexpensive guesthouse nearby is **One Eight Four**, at 184 West Malvern Road; **Holdfast Cottage** in nearby Welland is a rambling, reasonably priced guesthouse with views of the Malvern Hills. To the south, in Malvern Wells, is the small **Croque-en-Bouche**, one of the best restaurants in England. In high season you may have to book a month ahead (Tel: 0684-56-56-12).

Two other attractive towns just to the south of the Malvern Hills are **Ledbury** (on A 449) and Upton-upon-Severn (on A 4104, just off A 38). In Ledbury's Heritage Centre, in the **Old Grammar School** on cobbled Church Lane, offers exhibits such as one tracing the development of this thriving market town from its beginnings as an Anglo-Saxon village; the Medieval **Church of St. Michael's** has an interesting collection of tombs. There are many fine half-timbered houses in Ledbury; two of the town's most handsome old buildings are the oak-pillared **Market House** (1617) in Market Place and, beyond it, the 16th-century **Feathers Hotel**, which has a good restaurant and plenty of character. On the edge of town, the **Hope End Hotel** provides superb English cooking and comfortable lodgings in a delightful setting.

Eastnor Castle, 1 mile to the east of Ledbury, is a 19th-century building housing an important collection of tapestries, furniture, and ancient armor. Farther south, the historic **Hellens** mansion at Much Marcle is definitely worth a detour. This charming house has changed little since some major alterations made just before the Civil War. Two-hour guided tours leave hourly. The Norman church at nearby **Kempley** is famous for a remarkable series of 12th-century frescoes.

The beautiful old country town of **Upton-upon-Severn**, southeast of Great Malvern, is a perfect center for boating trips on the river. Information about boating and town and riverside walks can be obtained at the local Heritage Centre, a curious eight-sided cupola crowning an old church tower by the river; it is the town's oldest surviving building.

Just south of Upton is the lovely town of **Tewkesbury**, on the edge of the Cotswolds, which lie to the south in Gloucestershire (see The Cotswolds to Winchester chapter). It commands a historic and strategic position at the confluence of the Rivers Severn and Avon. The massive **Abbey**, which dominates the town, sits foursquare, seemingly rooted to the earth. Inside, the nave is striking in its simplicity. Its decorative elements are mainly confined to the east end, where there is a magnificent stained-glass window and a series of elaborate chantries. A tour of the town is worthwhile: It is full of interesting old buildings and attractive alleyways. Church Street contains two fascinating local history museums and some fine buildings. Stop for a delicious light dinner at **Oscar's** on the High Street (closed Sundays and Mondays) or for cream teas at **Wintor House** on Church Street (closed Mondays). Tewkesbury also has two important literary associations. Mrs. Craik wrote the 1856 novel *John Halifax, Gentleman* while staying at the charming **Bell Hotel** on Church Street, and there is a museum near the abbey commemorating the 20th-century novelist and short-story writer John Moore.

The **Tewkesbury Park Hotel**, on Lincoln Green Lane, is a large, tourist-oriented hotel. There is also a good small hotel in the area; the **Corse Lawn House Hotel**, to the southwest, is a spacious, peaceful country hotel with an excellent restaurant.

The town of Bromsgrove, 14 miles north of Worcester off M 5, is well worth a visit, chiefly for its fascinating **Avoncroft Museum of Buildings** just outside the town at Stoke Prior. The buildings range from a working windmill, which sells its own stone-ground flour, to a cockpit and a fully equipped nail- and chain-making workshop. They have been collected from all over Britain and re-erected in a large 15-acre park.

HEREFORDSHIRE AND THE WYE VALLEY AREA

From its source in the mountains of Wales, the River Wye runs down to rural Herefordshire and flows, twisting and turning, south from the cathedral city of Hereford, through Ross-on-Wye and Monmouth, and on to Chepstow at the mouth of the Severn. The Wye Valley and the ancient Forest of Dean, to the east, form one of the loveliest areas in Britain. Although not readily accessible by public transport, this is great touring country for motorists and provides many lovely walks, particularly along the river valley itself. From Stratford the best way to reach this region is on A 422 to Worcester, and from there A 4103 to Hereford.

Hereford

Hereford, just 26 miles from Worcester and 22 miles from the Welsh border, was once a Saxon capital and took its name from the ford here, the only way of crossing the river before bridges were built. For many centuries the city was battered by border conflicts, and its castle was destroyed and rebuilt several times. Finally, it was dismantled after the Civil War, and today all that remains is part of the moat around **Castle Green**. Hereford also became known as a thriving marketplace for the products of the rich agricultural land around it, especially the beef cattle. Indeed, it still has a thriving cattle and sheep market.

If you are travelling by car, one of the most attractive ways to approach Hereford is to park in the lot south of the old Wye Bridge (near the new bridge into the city from the south), and then walk across Bishop's Meadow to the **Victoria Footbridge**. There is a stunning view of the city's fine cathedral from here, and the footbridge leads to a pleasant walk through Castle Green and Redcliffe Gardens to the cathedral. It is possible to park closer to the city center, but there are more restrictions there.

Hereford Cathedral is the jewel of the city today. Although founded in about A.D. 700, the present building dates mainly from the 12th century and later. Inside, the massive bulk of its pillars and the imposing semicircular arches in the nave display its Norman origins, while the great sandstone tower is a 14th-century structure. Also notable are the lovely early English Lady Chapel and some fine sculpted tombs.

The cathedral's two greatest treasures are the famous **Chained Library** and the 13th-century **Mappa Mundi**—a unique five-foot-wide map of a flat world with Jerusalem at its center. This is now in the treasury and will soon be the centerpiece of a small, specially built museum. More than 1,400 books are chained to rods attached to the four 17th-century bookcases in the historic library. Its extraordinary collection of books includes a copy of the eighth-century Anglo-Saxon Gospels. Also worth visiting is the 15th-century **College of Vicars' Choral**, a quadrangle surrounded by cottages where the 27 priests who chanted the services lived.

The profile of the cathedral dominates the skyline, and the cathedral is surrounded by a Medieval network of ancient streets. The houses in this part of the city are of many different ages and include some fine Georgian buildings on **St. Owen's Street**, one of which is the **Green Dragon Hotel**, a well-restored coaching inn open to overnight guests. From the cathedral, Church Street, lined with attractive old buildings, leads up to the ancient Saxon marketplace of High Town, now a modern pedestrian precinct lined with stores. Only the 17th-century **Old House** in the marketplace is a reminder of an earlier age. This fine black-and-white timbered building houses a museum of 17th-century life and a brass-rubbing center and is well worth a visit.

Another fascinating building just outside the center of Hereford is Coningsby Hospital on Widemarsh Street. This delightful edifice contains the 13th-century **St. John Medieval Museum**, which has armor and relics from the crusaders' order of Saint John. The city's main museum and art gallery, with its fine collection of 19th-century watercolors, is near the cathedral and next to the library on Broad Street. If you'd like a more detailed look at the city and its surroundings, you should go on one of the guided city walks organized by the local tourist office (in St. Owen's Street).

Many visitors come to Hereford to visit H. P. Bulmer's world-famous cider factory, on Grimmer Road off Whitecross Road (book your tour in advance; Tel: 0432-35-20-00) and the **Museum of Cider** next door, open daily in summer. Cider making is closely linked with the history of this region, and the story of this industry is outlined in the museum. Many traditional cider makers still work in the villages around Hereford. Bulmer's also owns the **Railway Centre**, where its own train and the King George V, and Princess Elizabeth, and Clan Line steam locomotives are kept, with many other examples of steam-railway memorabilia. Both sites can be reached by a walk down Eign Street. Note that the Railway Centre is only open on weekends and on bank holidays from Easter to September.

One of the best months to visit Hereford is May, when the May Fair, Regatta, and a raft race down the river are held. In August, 1991, Hereford Cathedral is host to the annual Three Choirs Festival. (The location is alternately Worcester, Gloucester, and Hereford.) This is the oldest choral festival in Europe, and it features first-class orchestral, choral, and chamber music concerts. To book in advance, write to the Three Choirs Festival Office at the cathedral.

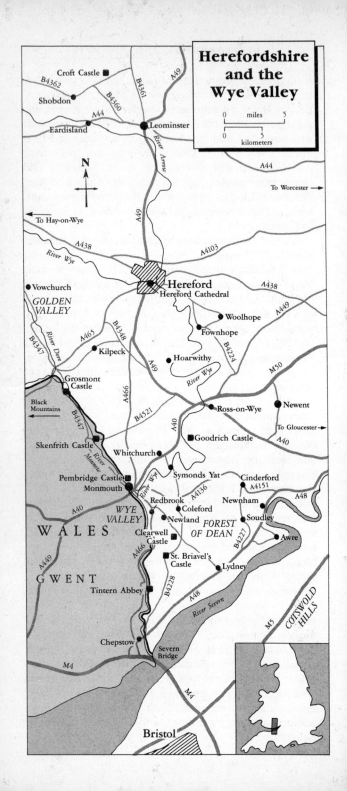

Herefordshire and the Wye Valley

miles 0 — 5
kilometers 0 — 5

N

Croft Castle
Shobdon
Eardisland
Leominster
B4362
B4360
B4361
A49
B4363
A44
River Arrow
To Worcester →
A44
To Hay-on-Wye
A438
River Wye
A4103
Vowchurch
GOLDEN VALLEY
Hereford
Hereford Cathedral
A438
A449
Woolhope
Fownhope
A465
B4348
Kilpeck
Hoarwithy
River Wye
B4224
River Dore
B4347
Grosmont Castle
A466
B4521
A49
Ross-on-Wye
Newent
M50
Black Mountains
To Gloucester →
Skenfrith Castle
River Monnow
Whitchurch
Goodrich Castle
A40
Pembridge Castle
Monmouth
River Wye
Symonds Yat
A4136
Cinderford
A4151
Newnham
A48
WALES
A40
WYE VALLEY
Redbrook
Coleford
Newland
FOREST OF DEAN
Soudley
GWENT
A449
Clearwell Castle
A466
St. Briavel's Castle
B4227
Awre
Lydney
Tintern Abbey
B4228
A48
River Severn
M5
COTSWOLD HILLS
Chepstow
Severn Bridge
M4
M5
M4
Bristol

Around Hereford

All year round Hereford is a popular center for exploring the immediate area as well as Wales and the Welsh Black Mountains. There is a string of fine Norman castles along the Welsh border, testaments to the long and troubled history of the border region. The finest are Croft, to the north near Leominster, and Grosmont, Skenfrith, Goodrich, and Pembridge, near Ross-on-Wye to the south. All have superb settings and are open to the public. There is a particularly fine walk from **Croft Castle** up to the Iron-Age hill fort of **Croft Ambrey**, with its magnificent views of the Welsh mountains.

It is an easy trip from Hereford north to the sleepy little town of **Leominster**. In addition to the nearby castle, this delightful old wool town boasts some gorgeous architecture, including a fine 12th-century **priory church**. On display in the church is a ducking stool last used as a punishment for troublesome women in 1809. About 6 miles west of Leominster is the church at Shobdon, a 1755 Rococo Gothic structure that looks like an elaborate piece of confectionery and, on the River Arrow, the delightful village of Eardisland (4 miles west on A 44).

Another popular regional base is the charming town of **Ross-on-Wye**, south of Hereford on A 49. (In summer this normally quiet little market town can get very busy, especially as the M 50/M 5 link here makes it very accessible from the Midlands.) Ross-on-Wye stands on a hill overlooking both a bend in the Wye and the Welsh hills beyond and has a fine 17th-century market house. The town owes much of its charm to the work of the town's most famous citizen, John Kyrle, the so-called Man of Ross, whose good deeds were immortalized in Alexander Pope's *Moral Essays* in the early 18th century. Just outside the town are the impressive **Hill Court Gardens and Garden Centre**.

The lovely town of **Newent**, a few miles east of Ross, is well worth visiting for the fascinating complex of Victorian shops called **The Shambles**, and for the world-famous **Falconry Centre** nearby, where visitors can see flying demonstrations and see every variety of birds of prey at close quarters. Between here and the Forest of Dean at Drybrook is **The Cider Press**, an excellent little restaurant. Many of the dishes served here are based on locally made cider. Teas are served in the mansion's attractive walled garden; reservations are recommended (Tel: 0594-544-472).

If you want to cycle around this region or canoe on the river, you can rent transport from **Pedalaway** in Llangarron. They will deliver anywhere in the area (Tel: 098-984-357). Charming lodgings can be found nearby at **The Butcher's Arms** in Woolhope, a traditional 14th-century half-timbered inn and restaurant. Here, you'll be close to the Wye and the villages of Fownhope and Hoarwithy, and the latter's lovely Italianate church.

Northwest of Ross and just south of A 465 is the little church at Kilpeck, with magnificent stone carvings. It is a fine example of Norman architecture and worth a detour. If you'd prefer to stay in a rural area, the **Croft Country Guest House** is a delightful but relatively inexpensive small country guesthouse at Vowchurch, at the heart of the so-called Golden Valley west of Hereford. The valley, which runs north to Dorstone, is named after the River Dore, which, in turn, may have taken its name from *d'or,* the French phrase for "of gold".

Hay-on-Wye

A trip that combines some wonderful natural sights with a cultural attraction leads west of Hereford to the town of Hay-on-Wye on the Welsh border. This small, sleepy Welsh market town, reached via A 438, has over the last ten years become a mecca for book lovers and is said to contain the largest number of secondhand books in the world. West from Hereford, the A 438 runs along the River Wye on the river's way down from the Black Mountains, which glower in the distance. If you take the first turn signposted to Hay, you will pass through the tiny hamlet of Bredwardine—famous as the parish of the late 19th-century Anglican curate and diarist Francis Kilvert. A booklet about Kilvert and a map of a walk around the village can be bought in the parish church.

Hay is dominated by its 12th-century castle, whose ruins now enclose the remains of a fine Jacobean mansion that is being restored after a recent fire. Its present owner, Richard Booth, was the first to open a secondhand bookshop in the town, and the growth of this and his own flair for publicity led to Hay's present renown. Hay now has over 20 major bookshops—some general and some specializing in subjects as diverse as the American Indian, poetry, cookery, children's books, and Dickensiana. Prices are extremely reasonable, especially when compared to those in London, and most shops are open every day. Call at the new tourist and crafts center near the car park at the top of the town for more information. Market day is on Thursday.

The Granary restaurant near the clock tower is a delightful health-food restaurant, or you can buy excellent picnic provisions at the **Hay Wholefoods and Delicatessen** on Lion Street. Hay also has a lively Festival of Literature at the end of May. For information and tickets write to the Festival Office, Hay-on-Wye HR3 5AD. For medium-priced accommodations, try the very central **Old Black Lion Inn**, a small pub with some nice rooms and a small restaurant, or **Bredwardine Hall Guest House** for a more rural and spacious setting.

The Wye Valley

South of Ross-on-Wye are the undulating hills and lovely woods of the Forest of Dean, which is bounded to the west by the magnificent Wye Valley. The River Wye flows in great loops through its beautiful wooded valley and provides some of the finest river views in Britain—and, incidentally, some of the best fishing. One of the most desirable ways to see and enjoy this spectacular piece of countryside is to walk alongside the river on part of the 34-mile **Lower Wye Valley Walk**. Guidebooks and cards describing the walk are available in local bookshops, and the walk, which runs from near Monmouth to Chepstow, is very well signposted. You can start anywhere. An alternative is to join one of the many guided walks organized by the Wye Valley Countryside Service year round. Details can be obtained from local Tourist Information Bureaux.

Particularly interesting on the first stretch of this walk are the view from Kerne Bridge, the formidable ruins of **Goodrich Castle**, and **Symonds Yat**, where there is a famous outcrop of rock 1,500 feet high. Hardy walkers can climb 400 feet up the hillside from the river for a marvelous view; the less energetic can drive to the forest parking lot at the top.

The east and west halves of the village of Symonds Yat are on either side of the river and are linked by two hand-operated ferries. Half-hour river tours can be taken from points on either side of the river. Symonds Yat East is the more attractive of the two little hamlets. It has a number of small guesthouses and a congenial pub, **The Saracen's**

Head. However, parking in the village is limited, so arrive early during the summer. The Wyedean Canoe and Adventure Centre here organizes canoeing, caving, and climbing trips and rents equipment (Tel: 0600-89-01-29).

Far less attractive but with lots of space for parking, Symonds Yat West and its garish entertainment complexes lie on the flat plain near the river. The first of these complexes contains a tropical butterfly garden and the rather more interesting **Jubilee Maze**—a traditional hedge labyrinth containing a museum of mazes. Nearer the river there are amusement arcades and, next to one of the river-trip pick-up points, a tropical bird garden. Farther downstream, where the river goes into a little gorge, **Ye Olde Ferrie Inn** has some large terraces facing across the river to Symonds Yat East and makes a pleasant stop for a meal or a drink.

If you take the exit off A 40 toward Symonds Yat East but make a right turn before reaching the town, you can follow the signs up Great Doward Hill to the **Rural Heritage Museum**. This collection of domestic and agricultural bygones in the midst of woodland must be one of the largest in England and is the remarkable result of one family's endeavors. Although not very well labeled, the collection is a fascinating mixture of everything from steam threshing machines and domestic mangles to a fully equipped blacksmith's shop.

Downstream from here is ancient **Monmouth**, just over the Welsh border. Situated where the River Monnow joins the Wye, the town was a strategic site from the time of the Romans and figured in the defeat of the Welsh princes in the 13th century. The bridge over the Monnow has a fine fortified gatehouse. **Great Castle House** (now a regimental headquarters and museum) stands on the site of the castle, which was destroyed during the Civil War.

The heart of the town is pretty **Agincourt Square**, with its attractive buildings and Saturday market. Here you can see statues of two of Monmouth's most famous sons—Henry V and Charles Rolls, co-founder of Rolls Royce and an early aviator. The **King's Head Hotel** here is the only coaching inn that survives. Nearby is a museum in the Victorian Market Hall largely devoted to a collection of memorabilia related to Lord Nelson (who visited here in 1802—see below—but otherwise has no connection to the town), donated by Rolls's mother. You can rent canoes, with or without instruction, at Monmouth Canoe Hire (Tel: 0600-34-61).

To the east of Monmouth, **Kymin Hill** is topped by the Round House, or Pavilion, built by a local dining club in 1793 so that they could enjoy the magnificent panorama at their weekly dinners. The same dining club (long since disbanded) built the nearby Naval Temple in 1800 in honor of Nelson, "the hero of the Nile." Admiral Nelson made a triumphant visit to the temple on August 19, 1802. You can reach Kymin Hill via an access road off B 4136 or by following part of the **Offa's Dyke Long-Distance Footpath** up the hill from Monmouth. This footpath runs the entire length of the English-Welsh border. Part of it follows the rampart built by the Saxon king Offa in the eighth century to defend England from the Welsh tribes. If you follow the footpath across the disused railroad bridge at Redbrook (on A 466 south of Monmouth), you can get a good meal at the **Boat Inn**, which has a lovely setting overlooking the River Wye.

The Forest of Dean

To the east of the Wye Valley in Gloucestershire is the Forest of Dean. Many of its 22,000 acres (about 20 miles long by 10 miles wide) are covered in mixed woodland—mostly oak and beech—and crisscrossed by hundreds of paths where wildlife of all kinds can be seen in abundance. The tourist board and some individuals have published maps of forest trails, and there is the signposted Forest of Dean Scenic Drive around the area.

Industry once flourished in the forest, chiefly charcoal burning and coal mining. Over a million tons of coal a year were being mined at the beginning of the 20th century. Today some small mines are still worked by the so-called Free Miners, who have a traditional right to dig coal. They are among the many Foresters who have retained inherited rights to graze their animals, mine for coal, and cut stone in the quarries. Fine monuments, including one of a 15th-century Forester showing his traditional dress and tools, can be found in the 13th-century **All Saints' Church**—the so-called Cathedral of the Forest—in Newland, west of Coleford. Even more unusual is the curious little brass there depicting a local miner. Just opposite the ancient lych-gate the **Ostrich** pub serves excellent bar food. The rights of the Foresters were maintained through meetings at the **Speech House**, which stands on the B 4226 halfway between Coleford and Cinderford. It is now an attractive hotel and an ideal center for exploring the forest.

Nearby, visitors can follow the remarkable **Sculpture Trail**, a three- to four-hour walk through the forest past more than 15 modern sculptures. **Piggies Parlour**, to the south in Parkend, serves appetizing meals in rooms hung with hundreds of old domestic artifacts, many of them for sale. Open Wednesdays through Sundays, noon to 9:00 P.M.

The **Clearwell Caves** (just south of Coleford off B 4228) are ancient iron mines that were worked for more than 2,500 years—until 1945. Guides from local mining families make a visit to this small mine and museum particularly interesting (open March to October). Guided walks through the forest also start from here four times a week, led by Timewalk (Tel: 0594-335-44). Nearby **Clearwell Castle** (1727) is the earliest neo-Gothic building in Britain and is now a charming country hotel and restaurant. You can also get snacks or full meals in the **Wyndham Arms**, a large Clearwell pub with an attractive garden and several rooms; children are welcome.

Some of the best views of the forest can be had from **St. Briavels Castle**, just south of Clearwell to the west of the forest. Royal visitors once stayed in this Medieval castle when they came to hunt wild boar and deer; it is now a youth hostel. A congenial and lively place for a home-made snack and a pint is the **George Pub** at the foot of the castle walls.

The **Dean Heritage Centre** at Camp Mill in Soudley, south of Cinderford, is on the other side of the forest. It is a fascinating collection of buildings situated in a beautiful wooded valley by a mill pond. The many exhibitions illustrating the life of the area include displays on "The Living Forest," as well as others on charcoal burning, woodcraft, and the region's industrial history; there is also a Museum of Forest Life. You can get information on nature trails and guided tours of the forest (open daily all year) here too. It is well worth a visit and serves as an excellent introduction to the whole area. For accommodations, the sheer beauty of its setting and some excellent home cooking make **The Old Vicarage** at Awre, east of Soudley and the Forest of Dean, hard to beat. Book ahead, as there are only a few rooms.

The widespread improvement of England's road system in the mid-18th century led to a rapid increase in travel for its own sake, and the beauty of the Wye Valley soon attracted many visitors. One of the most famous was William Gilpin, who wrote *Observations on the River Wye* in 1782. The Wye Tourists, as they came to be known, would usually take a boat trip south from Ross or Monmouth to Chepstow, and most stopped at the beautiful ruins of Tintern Abbey, just north of Chepstow.

Tintern Abbey

Tintern is known to many people through Wordsworth's poem "Lines Composed a Few Miles Above Tintern Abbey." Its majestic bulk, situated next to the river, is an impressive sight, even though the stone ruins are no longer romantically covered in ivy and moss, which were removed around the turn of the century.

An abbey was first built on this site for Cistercian monks in the early 12th century; however, the present building dates mostly from the 13th century, when it was rebuilt by Roger, earl of Norfolk. For several hundred years it was an important trading center, but it gradually declined and was stripped of its treasures at the dissolution of the monasteries. The roof was dismantled and much of the stone removed, but the mighty shell of the abbey remains, and it's still possible to trace the position of the domestic buildings attached to the church. A little museum and tourist information center stand nearby.

It is hard to believe that sleepy Tintern was also an industrial center for more than 300 years, and that works producing brass, iron, and wire lined the little Angidy valley. Nowadays just a few millponds and ruins remain to commemorate their passage. A mile above the abbey, the old Tintern railway station has been preserved. It has a picnic site and a car park, which makes this a convenient base for walks around the area.

Tintern contains quite a number of hotels. The **Royal George Hotel**, a long-established coaching inn, and the recently refurbished **Parva Farmhouse** both provide comfortable accommodations.

Chepstow

South of Tintern, the River Wye goes around in two giant loops before widening out on its way down to join the mighty Severn. Here, west of the river, is the Welsh town of Chepstow; at its northern edge is the famous Chepstow Racecourse at Piercefield Park, the site of both flat racing and steeplechasing events. The town, to the south, has been a trading settlement since Saxon times, and the first stage of **Chepstow Castle** was built here in 1067, just a year after the Norman Conquest.

The magnificent ruins of this once-mighty castle give a very clear picture of how it must have functioned. It stretches along the giant cliffs overlooking the River Wye on the north side of the town (there is a fine view of the castle from A 48) and is open to the public daily. There is a large car park at the foot of the hill and near the entrance to the castle. Across the road the **Castle View Hotel** serves good bar food. A small local history museum is located here as well. Walking up toward the town, you will see the **Stuart Crystal Craft Centre**, where you can watch artisans engrave lead crystal and then, if you wish, buy the end product.

An ancient town wall encloses the maze of steep, narrow streets that cluster above the castle, and the city's fine west gate still stands. The tourist information center is contained in its gatehouse. Close by, the church of St. Mary contains the tomb of Henry Marten. An unrepentant signatory of Charles I's death warrant, Marten spent 20 years under house arrest in the castle until his death in 1680. Book lovers will enjoy a visit to **Glance Back Books** in Upper Church Street. Its rabbit warren of rooms contains over 60,000 antiquarian and secondhand books as well as rare coins, postcards, medals, stamps, and prints.

The extremely luxurious **St. Pierre Hotel** in St. Pierre Park, a couple of miles west of Chepstow, provides an impressive array of facilities for its guests, including tennis and an internationally famous golf course.

South of Chepstow is the western end of the mighty Severn Bridge. This is where the M 4 motorway crosses from England to Wales, and it is also a convenient link straight into London or to the southwest of England.

THE UPPER SEVERN VALLEY AND THE SHROPSHIRE HILLS

Between the industrial city of Birmingham and the high, harsh mountains of the Welsh border country is the beautiful winding valley of the River Severn and the rich farming land and bare escarpments of the Shropshire Hills. The **Shropshire Hills** occupy a great triangle of land north of Herefordshire and Worcestershire, bounded by the Severn Valley to the north and east, the Teme Valley to the south, and the Long Mynd escarpment and Clun Forest to the west; they are bisected by A 49. Vivid reminders of the past fill this superb landscape, from fortified manor houses to later remnants of the Industrial Revolution. It is well worth making the effort of travelling off the beaten tourist track to get here.

The area has been settled from the earliest times. Traces of Bronze and Iron Age settlements and hill forts have been found at Caer Caradoc, near Church Stretton, and Croft Ambrey, near Leominster. One of the largest cities of the Roman era, Viroconium, stood near Wroxeter southeast of Shrewsbury, and later the area was heavily fortified by the Normans against the unruly Welsh princes. At the same time, land was cleared and small permanent communities began to develop in the valleys and on the lower slopes of the hills. Timber from the cleared forests provided frames for the area's characteristic black-and-white, half-timbered houses. Local oak was first blackened with pitch, then the frame was erected on a sandstone base, filled in with brick or wattle and daub, plastered, lime-washed, and finally roofed in Welsh slate. Dairy and sheep farming were the dominant industries, and, as local conflicts died out, the area rapidly grew in prosperity, which prompted the growth of several important market towns.

Shrewsbury

The most important market town in this area was Shrewsbury (pronounced Shrosebury), which is situated in a superb defensive position on gently rising ground enclosed by a tight loop of the Severn. This attractive, sleepy old town, in the center of Shropshire, about 25 miles west of Birmingham via the M 54 and A 5, retains much of its historic character.

At the time of the Norman Conquest, Shrewsbury already had five churches and a substantial castle, which was rebuilt by Roger de Montgomery, earl of Shrewsbury, in 1067. He also founded a Benedictine monastery just to the east of the town a few years later. Shrewsbury became an important strategic stronghold for England's rulers, and in 1283 it was Edward I's military base during his final defeat of the Welsh princes. During the period of

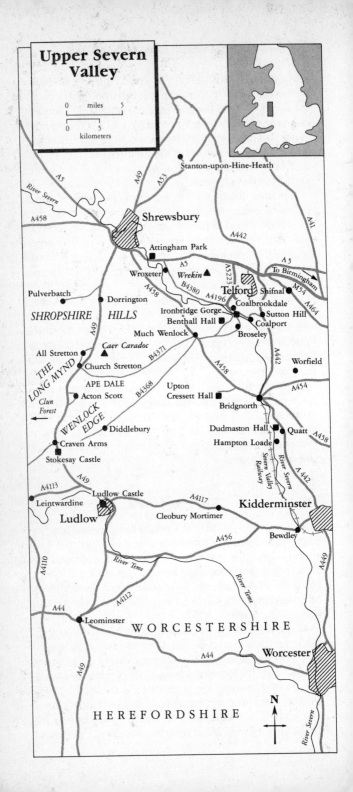

peace that followed, the town was a major center for trade between the Welsh and the English, and its two main bridges became known as the "Welsh" (to the west) and the "English" (to the east). Even today, a rich mixture of accents can be heard throughout the town on market days (Wednesdays and Fridays).

Shrewsbury's prosperity reached its height in Tudor times, but it remained a busy market center throughout the 18th and 19th centuries. However, the subsequent rise of the great industrial cities turned the town into a relative backwater. Today the happy result of Shrewsbury's decline is that many of a beautiful old buildings have been preserved, and some of its steep, winding streets with their curious names remain very much as they once were. A notable exception to this is the Market Hall in Bellstone, built in the 1960s. However, the market within this ugly building is worth a visit for a glimpse of local color and Midlands life (open Tuesdays, Wednesdays, Fridays, and Saturdays).

This is a lovely town to walk around; especially beautiful are **the gardens** by the river overlooking Shrewsbury School—particularly the Dingle Dell for its elaborate displays. These were once under the charge of one of Britain's most famous gardeners, Percy Thrower, who started the town's magnificent midsummer flower show.

Shrewsbury came to be called the "town of flowers," and in recent years the townspeople (with plenty of encouragement from the tourist board) have been living up to its reputation by filling every garden, tub, and window box in summer with a vast variety of blossoms.

Shrewsbury's once-great castle was largely dismantled after the town's stand against Cromwell in the Civil War. However, in 1787 the keep was transformed into a private house by Thomas Telford, the great civil engineer, for his patron William Pulteney, the local M.P. The castle now houses the Shropshire regimental museum. All that remains of the great Benedictine monastery of SS. Peter and Paul is the **Abbey church**, just over the English Bridge. It contains several interesting tombs.

One of the best ways to get to know Shrewsbury is to take an organized town walk. These are offered from May to October daily at 2:30 P.M.; lasting about two hours, they leave from the Tourist Information Centre in the Square. Failing this, follow one of the walking routes outlined in the information center's leaflets. You can arrange a tour in the off season through Tourist Information (Tel: 0743-507-61).

Some of the town's finest buildings were erected by the great cloth merchants of the 16th and 17th centuries. **Rowley's House**, on Barker Street, is one; Rowley's son built the neighboring Rowley's Mansion, one of the first brick houses in town. Together the two house a fine local history museum, which has a sizable display of important Roman remains from nearby Viroconium (see below). The oldest part of Shrewsbury is at the highest point of the town between the Square, Dogpole, and the pedestrian shopping area of Pride Hill. Many of Shrewsbury's fine old buildings are here, including the Old Market Hall, Ireland's Mansion on the High Street, the Abbott's House in Butcher Row, and the group of Medieval buildings in St. Alkmund's Place known as **Bear Steps**, part of which houses a pleasant tearoom. Just across St. Alkmund's Place from here, **St. Julian's Craft Centre** is well worth a visit for local crafts shopping (open daily except Thursdays and Sundays).

Architectural splendors from the Georgian Age are also in abundance in Shrewsbury, especially between St. John's Hill and Belmont. One of these, in College Hill, is now the **Clive House Museum**, with a beautiful garden. The period rooms provide an elegant setting for a specialized collection of Shropshire pottery and porcelain. Another attractive Georgian building is now the Parade Shopping Centre in St. Mary's Square.

Most of Shrewsbury's inns and restaurants are in the center of town around Butcher Row, St. Alkmund's Place, and Wyle Cop (cop means "hilltop" in Welsh). The **Lion Hotel**, an old coaching inn with leaded windows on Wyle Cop, is large and comfortable and has an elegant Adamstyle ballroom. However, the best hotel is the **Prince Rupert**, part of which is housed in a 17th-century mansion. Centrally located in Butcher Row, the hotel has recently been refurbished to a very high standard.

For an excellent but not too expensive meal, try the **Cornhouse Restaurant and Wine Bar**, at the bottom of Wyle Cop. Simpler fare is available at the **Old Vestry** restaurant, a vegetarian eatery at St. Julian's Craft Centre in St. Alkmund's Place (closed on Sundays and bank holidays). The **Good Life** is another good-value vegetarian restaurant, in a delightful 14th-century building in Barrack's Passage, off Wyle Cop (closed Sundays). An excellent out-of-town restaurant, **Country Friends**, in

Dorrington south of town on the A 49, serves seasonal food in an attractive old building.

The Upper Severn Valley and Ironbridge Gorge

From Shrewsbury, the Severn continues to wind eastward across a broad, fertile plain broken occasionally by hilly outcrops. The most spectacular of these is the abrupt, conical shape of the **Wrekin** east of Wroxeter, which, at 1,334 feet, affords some fine views to those hardy enough to climb it. One of Shropshire's greatest houses is nearby at Atcham: **Attingham Park** (4 miles southeast of Shrewsbury on A 5), a magnificent Georgian mansion built for the first Lord Berwick. Its impressive state rooms are lined with paintings and fine furniture, and it has a superb collection of Regency silverware acquired by the third Lord Berwick in Italy. The great park was elaborately landscaped by the legendary gardener Sir Humphry Repton.

Just south on B 4380 at Wroxeter is another historic site, but from a much earlier period. The Roman city of **Viroconium**, built between A.D. 50 and 125, was the fourth-largest Roman city in Britain. Although little of the original town remains standing, the Roman baths there show how much still lies under neighboring fields and are well worth a visit.

The real gem of this part of the Upper Severn Valley is **Ironbridge Gorge**, an area that is celebrated throughout Britain as the birthplace of the Industrial Revolution. Today nearly 6 square miles of the gorge, from the town of Coalbrookdale in the north to Coalport in the south, is a museum where the remains of Britain's Industrial Revolution have been restored and rebuilt into a fascinating exhibit.

This area's unique combination of natural assets—coal, timber, ironstone, clay, limestone, and water transport—created ideal conditions for the development of the region's fledgling iron-smelting industry. It expanded even more rapidly after 1708, when Abraham Darby arrived and began to use coke rather than charcoal to fuel his furnaces. Rapid advances in the mass production of iron followed, and in 1779 Abraham Darby III built the massive **Iron Bridge**—the first cast-iron bridge in the world. Today it takes a leap of imagination to understand what a masterpiece of invention and engineering skill it was at the time. At the other end of the gorge, a thriving ceramics industry developed around the Coalport China Works.

After the decline of its industries, the area remained relatively untouched for more than 90 years, until some of its industrial buildings were restored in the 1960s. It is now the country's largest museum, and to do it full justice you'll need two days. There are six museum sites: the **Severn Warehouse Visitor Centre**, which offers an exhibition introducing the area and an audiovisual show on its history; the **Coalbrookdale Museum of Iron and the Old Furnace**; the Iron Bridge; the **Coalport China Works Museum**, which has a fascinating display of some of the finest china produced in Britain; the **Jackfield Works and Tile Museum**; and the **Blists Hill Open Air Museum**, a recreation of a Victorian township where the everyday life of local tradespeople is reenacted around the visitor.

If your time is limited, start your tour at the visitors' center in the Severn Warehouse, then visit the Coalbrookdale Museum of Iron and the Old Furnace, Blists Hill, and the Hay inclined plane, which moved boats between the two levels of the Shropshire Canal. The bridge and Ironbridge town are nearby; you can get a light meal and other refreshments in the town, which also contains some fascinating antiques shops, or at various tearooms throughout the museum complex. (For more on the subject of the early industry in this area, see the chapter The Industrial Heritage.)

Other attractions in the region include the 12th-century **Buildwas Abbey** (off B 4380, 2 miles east of Ironbridge), which, with its fine vaulted chapter house, stands in a picturesque setting by the river. South of Ironbridge are the Elizabethan Benthall Hall, with its delightful church; the charming little village of Broseley; and **Much Wenlock**, a small market town with many old timbered buildings and the extensive ruins of a 12th-century priory (worth a visit for its famous topiary). **Scott's Coffee and Wholefood Shop** on the High Street here serves an excellent and inexpensive light lunch (except Wednesdays).

Just to the northeast is **Boscobel House**, where the future King Charles II hid in the "royal oak" while fleeing Cromwell, and **Weston Park**, a beautiful house designed by Lady Wilbraham in the 17th century. Weston has an assortment of Georgian furniture and a particularly fine collection of paintings, including some by Holbein, Gainsborough, and Van Dyck. The Capability Brown–designed park has architectural and nature trails, an aquarium, and the Weston Park miniature railway. The park is crowded in summer with families from the neighboring industrial cities and is also host to various fairs.

The best accommodations in the immediate vicinity of Ironbridge are at the **Telford Hotel, Golf and Country Club** at Great Hay in Sutton Hill, just north of Coalport. This comfortable, welcoming hotel is contained in a series of modernized farm buildings and houses. It has an indoor swimming pool and squash courts. Nearby at Shifnal is **Park House Hotel**, in two adjoining Georgian houses. Park House is a luxurious hotel with a grill room and an excellent, though formal, restaurant.

The Shropshire Hills

To the south of Shrewsbury lies the vast area known as the Shropshire Hills. These 300 square miles of land, where the wild Welsh mountains gradually give way to the gentler vales and uplands of the Midlands, have been designated an "Area of Outstanding Natural Beauty." It's best to explore the hills by car at first, but whenever possible, get out and walk. From Shrewsbury, A 49 goes directly south to the town of Craven Arms along the path of an ancient Roman road between the two massive escarpments—the Long Mynd (west) and Wenlock Edge (east)—that run northeast to southwest. The **Long Mynd** dominates the landscape, rising abruptly from the valley to a high (1,700 feet) plateau of heather-covered moorland 10 miles long. A series of valleys cuts into its eastern edge, and these provide fine walks for both the serious walker and those who prefer a gentle stroll.

One popular short walk begins in the parking lot at the National Trust Information Centre (which has a shop and café) in Carding Mill Valley and climbs up to New Pool Hollow. (Carding Mill Valley is about 12 miles south of Shrewsbury off A 49 near All Stretton.) You can also drive up the Long Mynd on minor roads, and on a fine day you may get some good views of hang-glider enthusiasts from the southern end of the ridge. To the west is a strange outcrop of rocks known as the **Stiperstones**. Legend has it that devils gather here to select a leader on midwinter nights.

There is a small, comfortable hotel—the **Stretton Hall Hotel**—near the little market town of Church Stretton on the A 49, at the foot of Long Mynd. One of Shropshire's most famous literary figures, the novelist Mary Webb, spent her honeymoon here and named it Shepwardine in her novels. The **Acton Scott Historic Working Farm** nearby provides a fascinating glimpse of life as it was on a 19th-century farm before the advent of mechanization, and it is well worth a detour (open daily, April to October).

Wenlock Edge is a narrow, wooded limestone escarpment stretching southwest from Much Wenlock near Ironbridge for 15 miles. A footpath along its crest is part of the unofficial long-distance footpath, the **Shropshire Way**. B 4371 runs along the top of Wenlock Edge, and if you drive, it's possible to leave your car at any of the small parking areas along the road and explore the area on foot. (Be careful of the unfenced "edge" itself.) There are excellent views across Ape Dale to the Stretton Hills. Southward, past the town of Craven Arms on A 49, is the massive 13th-century fortified manor house of **Stokesay Castle** (open daily except Tuesdays, April to October; in November, open on weekends). This unusual building is being renovated by English Heritage and, although empty of furnishings, is well worth a visit.

Ludlow

The major town in this region is the ancient market center of **Ludlow**, south of Craven Arms on A 49. It is famous for its attractive black-and-white half-timbered houses and the great Norman **Ludlow Castle**. The town's wealth was built on the wool trade, which is celebrated in the local museum at Butter Cross. The **Church of St. Laurence** is one of the largest and finest Medieval churches in the country; it contains several fine monuments, some notable wood carvings, and lovely stained glass. **Broad Street**, which runs southeast from the church, has claims to being Britain's prettiest street.

Ludlow is an excellent center for exploring the beautiful rolling landscape to the north and west, the "blue remembered hills" that the poet A. E. Housman described in *A Shropshire Lad* (his ashes are scattered in the St. Laurence churchyard). The composer Ralph Vaughan Williams was also inspired by this landscape when he wrote his celebrated and haunting vocal piece, "On Wenlock Edge."

It is well worth visiting Ludlow during the Ludlow Festival, during the last week of June and the first week of

July. The castle makes a spectacular backdrop for the Shakespeare play performed on the castle grounds. Reserve ahead, as there are rarely tickets available on the night of performance; also, dress warmly and bring blankets, cushions, rainwear, a picnic basket, and a warming drink to the play (Tel: 0584-872-150 for information, May through July).

In Ludlow, **Aragons** restaurant on Church Street serves delicious food in pleasant surroundings. There are also two delightful and inexpensive vegetarian restaurants in town—**Hardwicks**, in Quality Square, and the **Olive Branch** on Old Street (both open 10:00 A.M. to 5:00 P.M.).

Ludlow has two excellent hotels. **The Feathers Hotel** is an attractive Jacobean half-timbered building in the town center; **Dinham Hall Hotel** near the castle is a superb new hotel in a large Georgian house with an exceptional restaurant. Less expensive is the charming **Redfern Hotel**, east of Ludlow in Cleobury Mortimer, which has a good restaurant.

Directly south of Ludlow on A 49 is Leominster and, beyond that, Hereford, discussed earlier.

Bridgnorth

Bridgnorth (northeast of Ludlow on A 442) is another ancient market town on the River Severn. The river divides the town in two: The quaint, Italianate High Town is perched on a 200-foot-high sandstone cliff, and Low Town is set on the other side of the river. A steep, winding road, several passageways of steps, and a two-car funicular cliff railway, which climbs a four-in-seven gradient, link the two parts of the town. The remaining wall of a late Norman castle sits at the top of the cliff and leans 17 degrees off the perpendicular (more than the Leaning Tower of Pisa). The more upright, classical **Church of St. Mary Magdalene** is next to it; designed by Thomas Telford in 1794, the church is surrounded by some pleasant gardens.

Just four miles to the west, set in beautiful countryside, is **Upton Cresset Hall**, a lovely Elizabethan manor with a magnificent gatehouse and a 14th-century Great Hall (open Thursday afternoons in summer, or by appointment; Tel: 074-63-13-07). **Dudmaston Hall**, to the southeast at Quatt, is slightly more accessible (open Wednesday and Sunday afternoons in summer). Fine furniture and interesting exhibits fill this 17th-century house. An excellent small hotel to the northeast is the **Old Vicarage Hotel**, in Worfield, which serves fine food in a pleasant, relaxed setting.

Anyone interested in transportation should visit the **Midland Motor Museum**, just south of Bridgnorth, and, if possible, take the **Severn Valley Railway** for a scenic 16-mile journey along the river valley between Bridgnorth and Kidderminster. You can get on or off the trains at any of the stations in between; Bewdley is a good place to start. Trains run daily from mid-May to the end of September and on most weekends for the rest of the year. There are refreshment facilities at most of the stations, and if you take a picnic basket you can stop at the little station of Hampton Loade or Arley and walk down to a picnic spot by the river before catching a train back later in the day. The Bridgnorth Railway Station is home to the largest collection of standard-gauge steam and diesel locomotives in Britain.

GETTING AROUND

This is such a broad area that there is no central point of entry to it. The region is accessible through three major cities: London, Birmingham, and Bristol. Travellers by air will come via London's Gatwick or Heathrow, or through the international airport at Birmingham. Birmingham has direct flights from major European and North American cities and feeder connections to the London airports and other domestic airports. Luxury-coach services by Flightlink (Tel: 021-554-5232) run from all these airports, and National Express (Tel: 021-622-4373) has bus services between all the major towns and cities in the Heart of England. Overseas visitors can also obtain a 30-day Brit-Express Card from National Express, which provides a discount on long-distance travel services.

The area is well served by the railway network, and high-speed trains run every half hour to Coventry, Birmingham, and Wolverhampton from London's Euston Station. The southern part of this region is served by trains running from London's Paddington Station. There are discounted fares for off-peak travel, and overseas visitors can buy BritRail passes, which entitle them to periods of inexpensive, unlimited travel. Visitors to Stratford-upon-Avon can also go via Guide Friday's fast rail/road service from Euston via Coventry to Stratford. Several services operate daily, including a post-theater service.

For those visitors who want to venture away from the

main centers, a car is almost essential. The motorways make the area easily accessible; most points can be reached within two to three hours from London and four or five hours from Dover and Folkestone. The most efficient and attractive point of entry for car drivers travelling from London is across the Severn Bridge to Chepstow via the M 4. You can then explore the Heart of England and return via Stratford and the A 34 or via the A 40 and the Cotswolds—both link up with the M 40 into London. It is also possible to travel around by bus along some beautifully scenic routes, but plan your journey carefully and be sure you are armed with the latest timetables or you might get stranded.

If you are going to Stratford first and want to enjoy the surrounding countryside, Guide Friday Ltd., Civic Hall, Market Place, 14 Rother Street (Tel: 0789-29-44-66), can arrange car rentals through the major national and international companies. Taxis can be very expensive.

As mentioned earlier, **river and canal trips** are an increasingly popular way to explore the area. Two major firms that book these trips, as well as offer cruises along the Thames and other waterways of England, are: **Hoseasons Holidays**, Sunway House, Lowestoft NR32 3LT, Tel: (0502) 50-10-10; Telex: 975189; Fax: (0502) 51-43-98; and **Blake's Holidays**, Wroxham, Norwich NR12 8DH, Tel: (0603) 78-29-11; Fax: (0603) 78-28-71.

ACCOMMODATIONS REFERENCE

▶ **The Angel Inn and Posting House.** High Street, **Pershore** Worcestershire WR10 1AF. Tel: (0386) 55-20-46; Fax: (0386) 55-25-81.

▶ **Arrow Mill. Arrow,** near Alcester, Warwickshire B49 5NL. Tel: (0789) 76-24-19; Fax: (0789) 76-51-70.

▶ **Ashleigh House.** Whitley Hill, **Hemley-in-Arden** B95 5DL. Tel: (0564) 223-15.

▶ **Bell Hotel.** 52 Church Street, **Tewkesbury** GL20 5SA. Tel: (0684) 29-32-93; Telex: 43535; in U.S., (602) 954-7600 or (800) 528-1234.

▶ **Billesley Manor Hotel and Restaurant. Billesley,** Alcester, Warwickshire B49 6NF. Tel: (0789) 40-08-88; Fax: (0789) 76-41-45; in U.S., (212) 696-1323, (212) 535-9530, or (800) 223-5581.

▶ **The Birche. Shelsley Beauchamp,** Worcestershire WR6 6RD. Tel: (0886) 52-51.

▶ **Bredwardine Hall Guest House. Brewardine** HR3 6DB. Tel: (0981) 75-96.

▶ **The Butcher's Arms. Woolhope** HR1 4RF. Tel: (0432) 772-81.

▶ **The Chase Hotel.** Banbury Road, **Ettington,** Stratford-upon-Avon CV37 7NZ. Tel: (0789) 74-00-00.

▶ **Clearwell Castle. Clearwell,** Coleford GL16 8LG. Tel: (0594) 323-20.

▶ **Corse Lawn House Hotel. Corse Lawn,** Gloucestershire GL19 4LZ. Tel: (0452) 784-79; Telex: 437348; Fax: (0452) 788-40.

▶ **Coverdale Private Hotel.** 8 Portland Street, **Royal Leamington Spa** CV32 5HE. Tel: (0926) 33-04-00; Fax: (0926) 83-33-88.

▶ **Croft Country Guest House. Vowchurch** HR2 0QE. Tel: (0981) 55-02-26.

▶ **Dinham Hall Hotel.** Ludlow SY8 1EJ. Tel: (0584) 87-64-64; Fax: (0584) 87-60-19.

▶ **Duke's Hotel.** Payton Street, **Stratford-upon-Avon** CV37 6UA. Tel: (0789) 693-00; Fax: (0789) 41-47-00.

▶ **Ettington Park Hotel.** Alderminster, near **Stratford-upon-Avon** CV37 8BS. Tel: (0789) 74-07-40; Telex: 311825; Fax: (0789) 874-72; in U.S., (212) 661-4540 or (800) 223-1588.

▶ **Evesham Hotel.** Cooper's Lane, off Waterside, **Evesham** WR11 6DA. Tel: (0386) 76-55-66; Telex: 339342; Fax: (0386) 76-54-43; in U.S., (602) 954-7600 or (800) 528-1234.

▶ **The Feathers Hotel.** The Bull Ring, **Ludlow** SY8 1AA. Tel: (0584) 87-52-61; Telex: 35637; Fax: (0584) 87-60-30; in U.S., (312) 251-4110 or (800) 323-5463.

▶ **Feathers Hotel.** High Street, **Ledbury** HR8 1DS. Tel: (0531) 26-00 or (0531) 52-66; Fax: (0531) 20-01.

▶ **Folly Farm Cottage. Ilmington,** near Shipston-on-Stour, Warwickshire CV36 4LJ. Tel: (0608) 824-25.

▶ **Fownes Hotel.** City Walls Road, **Worcester** WR1 2AP. Tel: (0905) 61-31-51; Telex: 335021; Fax: (0905) 237-42.

▶ **Green Dragon Hotel.** Broad Street, **Hereford** HR4 9BG. Tel: (0432) 27-25-06; Telex: 35491; Fax: (0432) 35-21-39.

▶ **Holdfast Cottage Hotel.** Marlbank Road, **Welland,** near Malvern WR13 6NA. Tel: (0684) 31-02-88.

▶ **Hope End Hotel.** Hope End, **Ledbury** HR8 1JQ. Tel: (0531) 36-13.

▶ **King's Head Hotel.** Agincourt Square, **Monmouth,** Gwent NP5 3DY. Tel: (0600) 21-77; Telex: 497294; Fax: (0600) 35-45.

▶ **Lansdowne Hotel.** 87 Clarendon Street, **Royal Leam-**

ington Spa CV32 4PF. Tel: (0926) 45-05-05; Telex: 337556; Fax: (0926) 45-00-83.

▶ **Lion Hotel.** Wyle Cop, **Shrewsbury** SY1 1UY. Tel: (0743) 531-07; Fax: (0743) 527-44; in U.S., (212) 541-4400 or (800) 223-5672.

▶ **Lord Leycester Hotel.** 17 Jury Street, **Warwick** CV34 4EJ. Tel: (0926) 49-14-81; Telex: 41363; in U.S., (212) 714-2323, (800) 522-5568, or (800) 223-6764.

▶ **Mallory Court.** Harbury Lane, **Bishop's Tachbrook,** near Royal Leamington Spa CV33 9QB. Tel: (0926) 33-02-14; Telex: 317294; Fax: (0926) 45-17-14.

▶ **Northleigh House.** Five Ways Road, **Hatton,** near Warwick CV35 7HZ. Tel: (0926) 48-42-03.

▶ **Old Black Lion Inn.** Lion Street, **Hay-on-Wye** HR3 5AD. Tel: (0497) 82-08-41.

▶ **The Old Vicarage. Awre,** near Newnham GL14 1EL. Tel: (0594) 512-82.

▶ **Old Vicarage Hotel. Worfield,** Bridgnorth WV15 5JZ. Tel: (0746) 44-97; Fax: (0746) 45-52.

▶ **One Eight Four.** 184 West Malvern Road, **West Malvern** WR14 4AZ. Tel: (0684) 56-65-44.

▶ **The Park House Hotel.** Park Street, **Shifnal,** Shropshire TF11 9BA. Tel: (0952) 46-01-28; Fax: (0952) 46-16-58.

▶ **Parva Farmhouse. Tintern,** Chepstow, Gwent NP6 6SQ. Tel: (0291) 68-94-11; Fax: (0291) 27-92-98.

▶ **Prince Rupert.** Butcher Row, **Shrewsbury** SY1 1UQ. Tel: (0743) 23-60-00; Telex: 35100; Fax: (0743) 573-06; in U.S., (212) 714-2323, (800) 522-5568, or (800) 223-6764.

▶ **The Redfern Hotel. Cleobury Mortimer** DY14 8AA. Tel: (0299) 27-03-95; Fax: (0299) 27-10-11.

▶ **Royal George Hotel. Tintern** NP6 6SF. Tel: (0291) 68-92-05; Fax: (0291) 68-94-48.

▶ **St. Pierre Hotel.** St. Pierre Park, **Chepstow** NP6 6YA. Tel: (0291) 62-52-61; Fax: (0291) 27-99-75.

▶ **The Shakespeare.** Chapel Street, **Stratford-upon-Avon,** Warwickshire CV37 6ER. Tel: (0789) 29-47-71; Telex: 311181; Fax: (0789) 41-54-11; in U.S., (212) 541-4400 or (800) 223-5672.

▶ **Speech House.** Forest of Dean, **Coleford** GL16 7EL. Tel: (0594) 226-07; Fax: (0594) 236-58; in U.S., (212) 541-4400 or (800) 223-5672.

▶ **Stratford House Hotel and Shepherd's Restaurant.** Sheep Street, **Stratford-upon-Avon** CV37 6EF. Tel: (0789) 682-88; Fax: (0789) 29-55-80.

▶ **Stretton Hall Hotel.** Old Shrewsbury Road, **All Stretton,** Church Stretton SY6 6HG. Tel: (0694) 72-32-24.

▶ **Telford Hotel, Golf and Country Club.** Great Hay, **Sutton Hill**, Telford TF7 4DT. Tel: (0952) 58-56-42; Telex: 35481; Fax: (0952) 58-66-02.

▶ **Tewkesbury Park Hotel, Golf and Country Club.** Lincoln Green Lane, **Tewkesbury** GL20 7DN. Tel: (0684) 29-54-05; Telex: 43563; Fax: (0684) 29-23-86.

▶ **Welcombe Hotel and Golf Course.** Warwick Road, **Stratford-upon-Avon** CV37 0NR. Tel: (0789) 29-52-52; Telex: 31347; Fax: (0789) 41-46-66; in U.S., (212) 684-1820, (800) 221-1074, or (800) 237-1236.

▶ **Westgate Arms.** Bowling Green Street, **Warwick** CV34 4DD. Tel: (0926) 49-23-62; Telex: 311928; Fax: (0926) 504-48.

▶ **White Swan.** Rother Street, **Stratford-upon-Avon** CV37 6NH. Tel: (0789) 29-70-22; Fax: (0789) 687-73; in U.S., (212) 541-4400 or (800) 223-5672.

▶ **Wyndham Arms. Clearwell**, Coleford GL16 8JT. Tel: (0594) 336-66; Fax: (0594) 364-50.

YORK

By Frank Dawes

In no other English city are the strata of history more visible than in York. Its peat-rich soil has preserved, layer upon layer, the buildings and artifacts of almost two millennia of civilization. Every epoch since the Roman occupation has left its mark on York.

Three miles of stout limestone wall, with just a few gaps here and there, encompass an almost theatrically Medieval city dominated by York Minster, the largest Gothic cathedral north of the Alps; its great square towers are visible for miles across the relatively flat countryside. "The antiquity of York," wrote Daniel Defoe in 1724 in *A Tour Thro' the Whole Island of Great Britain,* "showed itself so visibly at a distance that we could not but observe it before we came quite up to the city."

What was remains so today, although York is no museum piece but a thriving commercial and shopping center, the home of chocolate and candy manufacturers, with new-technology coal mines just a short drive away.

It is historic York, of course, that draws two million visitors each year. The people who live and work here cope easily and cheerfully with the tides of tourists. Although on the whole not given to boastfulness (self-mockery is more their style), the folks of York are quietly proud of their city's attractions. Citizens' inquisitive interest in strangers ("Where are tha from? What does tha do?") may embarrass their southern cousins, but most visitors find it engaging.

If you have only a limited time to spend in York, go immediately to the minster—without a doubt the city's most spectacular treasure. After you have explored the cathedral, take a walk, no matter how brief, on the famed city walls. The views they command are spectacular, and they give you a magical taste of what living in a Medieval town was really like. For those who can explore York at a more leisurely pace, choose a tour that takes you all the way around the city walls, beginning with Micklegate Bar and ending at York Minster and the old Medieval city.

MAJOR INTEREST

York Minster (largest English Medieval cathedral,
    with glorious stained glass)
City walls and gates
Medieval streets and buildings
The Shambles
Jorvik Viking Centre

Eboracum

When the invading Roman legions marched north less than 100 years after the death of Christ, they set up a temporary camp at the confluence of the rivers Ouse and Foss. In time, this became a permanent fort, and Eboracum, as the Romans called it, grew into a city of the first importance. Not only was it the headquarters of the Sixth Legion and capital of the province of Lower (that is to say, Northern) Britain, it also flourished as a port served by galleys that were able to navigate the River Ouse 50 miles inland from the North Sea. At its peak, the garrison reached 6,000 men.

A network of arrow-straight Roman roads converged on Eboracum, where Emperor Hadrian made his base. When Constantius Chlorus died here in A.D. 306, his son was proclaimed emperor from York and became, as Constantine the Great, the first Roman emperor to embrace Christianity.

The Romans ruled Britain for three centuries (71–410) until they left to defend their native soil. In York their paved streets lie buried beneath today's thoroughfares— Via Praetoria ran where Stonegate is today and Via Principalis lies under Petergate.

The only tangible evidence of the long Roman occupation is the Multangular Tower in the gardens of the **Yorkshire Museum and Botanical Gardens** on Museum Street. The tower was originally the west-corner tower of a fourth-century fortress, and from the Roman brickwork at the base the eye travels up some 19 feet or so to the

Medieval structure on top. The museum, recently refurbished with new galleries, is concerned mainly with archaeology and natural history, with a strong emphasis on Yorkshire. Roman coffins are displayed here, remnants that together with kitchen utensils, mosaics, jewelry, and the like are being constantly unearthed as archaeologists scrape away at the city's substrata. As recently as the 1960s, during repairs to the central foundations of York Minster, the walls of the Sixth Legion's administrative headquarters, the Principia, were uncovered.

Eoforwic

During what is known as the Anglian period (627–867), Eboracum was known as Eoforwic, the capital of the Saxon kingdom of Northumbria and, under the scholar Alcuin (735–804), the center of learning. (Later, at Charlemagne's court in Aachen, Alcuin was to be the intellectual leader of the Carolingian renaissance.)

The Saxons accepted Christianity in the seventh century when Saint Paulinus converted King Edward, who then appointed Paulinus bishop in 634. The king was baptized in a small wooden chapel said to have been on the site of today's minster.

Jorvik

After the Romans departed, Scandinavian adventurers found it easy to raid and pillage the coasts of Britain, and by the 850s they came in fleets of 300 ships. In the middle of the ninth century the Vikings sailed up the Ouse from the North Sea in their longships and took the city by storm, renaming it Jorvik. Jorvik became the capital of Danelaw, the conquered north and eastern part of England, while Alfred the Great clung to his southern kingdom of Wessex, with its capital at Winchester.

The Vikings brought with them their culture, and even today all over Yorkshire you can find villages with Scandinavian names. Many of York's main thoroughfares are called "gates," from the Norse for "street." (Gates are also confusingly called "bars.") The Vikings repaired and extended Jorvik's old walls and laid out the streets as they remain today. It became one of Europe's major ports, thronged by traders from overseas, its warehouses stuffed with merchandise.

Between 1976 and 1981, the York Archaeological Trust

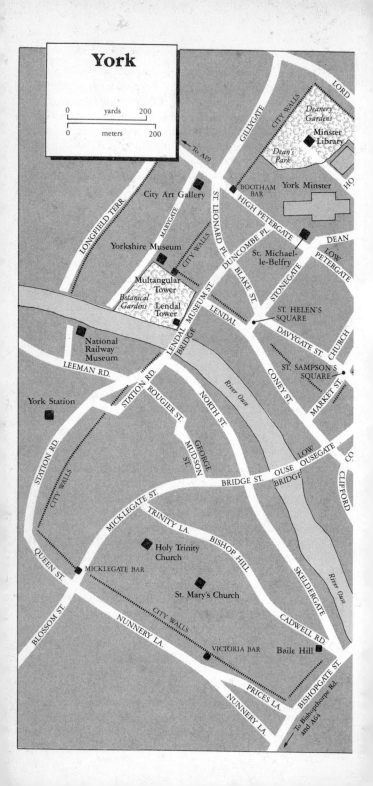

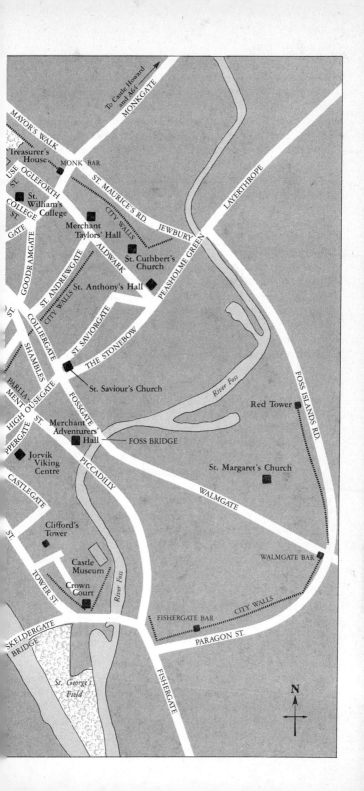

carried out a major dig in Coppergate and discovered one part of the old Viking city: four rows of buildings, deep beneath the foundations of their 20th-century successors. Preserved in the damp peat-rich soil, plant and insect remains as well as those of human beings, along with their everyday tools and implements—even boots and shoes—have been found by archaeologists. At the site of the dig, Heritage Projects, an offshoot of the Trust, built the underground **Jorvik Viking Centre**. The museum displays two rows of reconstructed buildings as they were 1,000 years ago; another two are preserved as they were when found in the late 1970s, deep beneath a shopping mall. Visitors climb aboard "time cars," which carry them back through the years, past the sights and sounds of 30 generations of York citizens, until the clock stops at Coppergate on a late October day in 948. The scene is re-created vividly for all the senses, even smell: A whiff of appetizing stew mingles with the odors of a pigsty and a latrine. Even the diseases and the rudimentary dentistry of our ancestors have been re-created with merciless authenticity.

The Jorvik Viking Centre was a huge success from the moment it opened and almost always has a long line at its doors. If you have the patience to wait, you'll find the experience a rewarding one.

Quieter but hardly less exciting than the Jorvik Viking Centre, the **Archaeological Resource Centre** is in St. Saviour's, a Norman church only 300 yards away. The memorials include a marble tablet for Mary Morris, who was courted by George Washington.

At St. Saviour's you can examine hands-on exhibits of bones, pottery, and other Viking relics, and you can speak with archaeologists about their work. There is a computer database for those seeking specific objects. On display is the Viking-style ship *Tormodson* ("brave son of Thor"), built at the turn of this century in Aafjord, Norway, and saved from destruction by a maritime historian.

Medieval York

The earls of Northumbria took over Jorvik from the departing Danes; 100 years later, in 1066, the Normans invaded England and marched north from the landing beaches of the Channel. They sacked Jorvik, but York rose from this traumatic upheaval to become a powerful Medieval city, except for London the greatest in the land, the civil and ecclesiastical capital of the north, and a thriving port from which ships sailed to Europe with cargoes of corn, wool, hides, and lead. To this day, the archbishop of York has the title Primate of England, second only to the head of the Anglican church, the archbishop of Canterbury, who is called Primate of All England.

The City Walls

The old city, no more than a mile across, is encircled by fortified walls, which are open from dawn to dusk. An almost complete walking circuit can be made on top of the wall, but wear sensible shoes, for there are many breaks in the wall, and its grassy slopes are steep. Given the vagaries of the English climate, as always it is a good idea to carry an umbrella. The circuit can be started at any of the "bars" (gates), which resemble the turreted gateways of Medieval castles, or at the occasional breaks in the wall, where steps lead to the top. In springtime, Wordsworthian "hosts of golden daffodils" adorn the slopes of the moat that runs outside the walls.

The River Ouse divides the wall into two parts. A good way to cover the walls is to start at Lendal Tower north of the river and on the west side of town and go counter-clockwise. From Lendal Tower cross Lendal Bridge, going south past the railway station and the splendidly Victorian **Royal York Hotel**, where despite modernization, gentility will prevail as you linger over tea and crumpets beneath high, ornate ceilings. The Royal York was built more than 100 years ago and, now carefully restored, is a splendid example of the grand Victorian railway hotel. The food is not outstanding, but the 148 bedrooms offer a high standard of comfort with every modern convenience. The immensely popular **National Railway Museum** is west, beyond the station on Leeman Road. The museum tells the story of railways and railway engineering in Britain with period platform tableaux and a recently opened Great Railway Show reached by a tunnel under the road.

Continuing south, you will come to the most important of the four original gates, **Micklegate Bar**, which guarded York from the hostile south. In the Middle Ages, heads of vanquished rebels were often displayed here, among them those of Richard, duke of York, and Sir Henry "Hotspur" Percy, who helped put Henry IV on the throne of England but was executed for later rebelling against him.

From Micklegate, the wall runs parallel to Nunnery Lane between St. Mary's Convent, founded in 1686, and two churches, **Holy Trinity** and **St. Mary's**. The latter has a Saxon tower and is partly constructed of Roman masonry. The former was once the church of a Benedictine priory, and stocks remain in the churchyard.

At **Baile Hill** the wall runs northeast to meet the Ouse at Skeldergate Bridge. Baile Hill was the first of two mounds raised by William the Conqueror, but nothing remains of the castle that once stood upon it.

Across the river, the second of William's man-made hills is topped by **Clifford's Tower**, an imposing stone quatrefoil keep with a gatehouse and chapel, built around 1300 and reached by an exhausting flight of steps. It is named after Roger de Clifford, who was executed here in 1596.

Clifford's Tower was preceded by an earlier wooden Norman castle that burned to the ground on March 16, 1190, after 150 Jews took refuge inside from an anti-Semitic mob. Rather than surrender they committed mass suicide similar to that at Masada in Israel. The head of each household was responsible for killing his own immediate family. The rabbis then killed the remaining men and set fire to the tower, incinerating themselves.

In the shadow of the present stone tower is the **Crest Hotel**. Somehow its light, airy rooms and smart cocktail bars, **Clifford's** and **Turpin's**, don't seem out of place in this historic setting. Many of the 128 bedrooms have a view of the ancient battlements as well as modern creature comforts, such as mini-bars and in-house movies. Three rooms have their own Jacuzzi baths and three are specially fitted for the disabled. An even newer addition to the list of York's hotels is the Grange Hotel, converted from an early 19th-century town house (see below).

Close by Clifford's Tower is the **Assize Court** (now known as the Crown Court), located in a magnificent building designed by John Carr in 1773, and the **Castle Museum**, a former women's prison on Tower Street that today depicts ordinary Yorkshire life from the 18th century onward. It is a leading folk museum, best known for its reconstruction of 18th- and 19th-century city life. For example, Kirkgate, a cobbled street, has an original horse-drawn hansom cab (the invention of a York man, Joseph Hansom, who was born at 114 Micklegate) parked outside the shops of candlemakers and blacksmiths. Half Moon Court is an Edwardian street complete with a gaslit pub. The Castle Museum has the cell in which the infamous highwayman Dick Turpin was held for three months before being hanged in 1739.

Other exhibits in this imaginative museum include policemen's truncheons, old valentines, vintage firearms, musical instruments, and snuffboxes.

South of the Castle Museum is **St. George's Field**; here the citizens of York have ancient rights "to walk, shoot with bows and arrows, and dry linen." Needless to say, the first is the only right that is regularly exercised today. To the northwest of the museum, in Coppergate, is the Jorvik Viking Centre.

Resume your walk along the city walls at **Fishergate Bar**, and continue on east to **Walmgate Bar**, which has its original barbican and portcullis, with inner oak gates and a wicket. Nearby on Walmgate is **St. Margaret's Church**, its Norman porch richly decorated with the signs of the zodiac. This part of the wall turns and ends at the **Red Tower**. Walk north along Foss Islands Road to rejoin the ramparts. En route, you will come to Peasholme Green and the **Black Swan Inn**, built for a merchant in the 16th century. Later, when it became a pub, one of the upstairs rooms was used for illegal cockfighting. Today it is still a pub, but an entirely law-abiding one. **St. Anthony's Hall**, also on Peasholme Green, is a fine, timber-framed guildhall, as is **Merchant Taylors' Hall**, which you will pass as you continue toward the city walls. (The finest and grandest guildhall is the **Merchant Adventurers' Hall**, built in the 14th and 15th centuries by city notables concerned mainly with the export of cloth. It is located to the south, near the Foss Bridge, and it is well worth visiting to see its beautiful Medieval timberwork.)

The City Walls Concluded

At **Monk Bar**, the gate just north of Merchant Taylors' Hall, the most dramatic section of the walls begins, traversing two sides of the Roman city of Eboracum. It is from here that the soaring triple towers of the minster can be seen at their best. Within the enclave are the **Treasurer's House**, the **Minster Library** (with an exhibition hall open to the public), **St. William's College**, and the lawns of the **Deanery Gardens**.

These ancient walls took a terrific battering from Cromwell's cannonballs during the Civil War, when the Royalists were besieged here, having set up a printing press in

St. William's College to wage a war of words against Parliament. In 1644 Prince Rupert arrived with reinforcements for the beleaguered city, but to no avail.

The wall ends at **Bootham Bar**, a bit north of Lendal Tower. Its Norman portcullis remains, as if ready to be lowered at any moment against an invading army.

YORK MINSTER

It is impossible to approach this, the largest and most glorious Medieval cathedral in Britain, without reverence and awe. In 1984 the world was horror-struck when the minster was badly damaged in a fire started by a bolt of lightning, engulfing the 13th-century south transept in flames. After the conflagration, a team of 67 stonemasons, joiners, woodcarvers, scaffolders, and painters rebuilt the roof and the intricately vaulted ceiling using 150 large oak trees, some from the Queen's estates. Carvings illustrate the words of the canticle "Benedicte—all ye works of the Lord, praise ye the Lord." A thousand books of 22-carat gold leaf were used in the new decorations. The restoration, completed a year ahead of schedule, took four years—an infinitesimally small period in the long history of the minster. Twice before the church had been ravaged—in 1829, when a blaze burned out the choir, and in 1840, when a workman accidentally ignited the timber roof of the nave. The noble cathedral has always survived such disasters, just as it has survived wars and sieges through the ages.

The present structure took 250 years to build and was completed in 1480. Many of the masons who labored on it were swept away by the plague, but their magnificent work lives on. The south transept, restored by their 20th-century heirs, is an imposing sight by day or by night, when floodlights dramatically illuminate it. High above the door is the famous **Rose Window**, which was cracked and splintered into 40,000 fragments by the 1984 fire but is now almost miraculously restored. Its red and white roses commemorate the end of the bloody 15th-century feud between the "Red Rose" House of Lancaster and the "White Rose" House of York. This window is only one of the minster's 130 stained-glass windows. The church's chief glory, these priceless examples of English Gothic glass were removed in 1939 to secure them from possible bomb damage. After the war, it took 20 years to reinstall them under the painstaking direction of Dean Milner-White.

The west window's heart-shaped traceries, known as the "Heart of Yorkshire," are particularly beautiful, yet it is the **"Five Sisters" Window** that attracts the most attention. Each lancet of this odd, early English grisaille glass is more than 50 feet tall and 5 feet wide.

Among the startlingly lifelike statues inside the minster are many of past archbishops, including the Purbeck marble effigy of Archbishop Walter de Gray, who began the building.

A more recent memorial is the astronomical clock in the north transept, which is dedicated to the 18,000 men of the Royal Air Force stationed at bases in the northeast who died during World War II.

The main entrance to the cathedral is at the west end, where you will find information on tape. The cathedral is open daily. The octagonal **Chapter House** is noted for its 13th-century vaulting, and the **Foundations Museum** exhibits archaeological finds. In 1967 it was discovered that the church was in imminent danger of collapse due to structural fatigue, erosion, and changes in the water table under the foundations. Repairs in reinforced concrete were quickly begun and are visible in the recently refurbished museum.

THE STREETS OF OLD YORK

The narrow streets and alleys near York Minster are packed with curiosities and are best explored either on foot or in one of the horse-drawn carriages for hire opposite the minster. You can get information from the **Tourist Information Centre** in Rougier Street, off Station Road. If you choose to explore by carriage, you will invariably get a commentary from the driver. He will almost certainly point out the birthplace of Guy Fawkes, the man who hatched the Gunpowder Plot and tried to blow up Parliament in 1605. There is some confusion over the actual place—it may be in Stonegate or in High Petergate—but there is no doubt that Fawkes was born in York.

Young's Hotel in High Petergate lays unsubstantiated claim to being Fawkes's actual birthplace. In any event it offers inexpensive, comfortable rooms and generous meals. There are plenty of hostelries where a pint of the local Theakston's Best Bitter, Old Peculiar, or John Smith's Bitter can be taken in old-fashioned ease without the accompaniment of Muzak. The **Roman Bath** in St. Sampson's Square has the remains of one in its basement, and the **King's Arms** on King's Staith has a board recording the flood level as early warning to its customers. Also by the river, at Acaster Malbis three miles south of the city, the **Ship Inn** has its own moorings and fishing and serves drinks in the garden.

In **Coffee Yard** off Stonegate, the town's oldest print-shop is marked by a carving of a red devil. (Apprentices to what is now the archaic craft of hot-metal printing are still known as "printers' devils.") Boot scrapers can be seen at many doorways, surviving from the days when cobbles were a rarity and mud plentiful—only in 1541, when Henry VIII and Catherine Howard visited York, were the streets "swept, sanded and gravelled" for the first time. The Red House on Duncombe Place has a torch snuffer for the convenience of the linkmen (torchbearers) who used to escort people through the unlit streets, and a former tobacconist's at 76 Petergate displays a gilded horse's head at its door. A gas flame used to spurt from its mouth for anyone wanting a light.

Another curiosity of the old York streets is the "firemark," a plaque mounted on houses before a municipal fire service existed. Fire engines were operated by insurance companies and called only at those houses bearing their company mark, no matter how desperate the blaze.

The best-known York street is **The Shambles**, once the butchers' quarter, with its Medieval timbered gables overhanging so far that it is possible to shake hands across facing upper stories. The Shambles leads to the city's shortest street, which boasts its longest name: **Whip-Ma-Whop-Ma-Gate**. As guides will delight in telling you, this is where petty criminals were flogged.

Northwest of York Minster on Exhibition Square is the **City Art Gallery**, noted for its British paintings and for the Lycett Green Collection of works by old masters.

Shopping in York is not unlike visiting Aladdin's Cave. There is an open-air market in Newgate every day except Sundays, a new pedestrians-only mall in Coppergate, and an array of department stores in Coney Street. **Liberty** and **Laura Ashley** can be found in Davygate. The Medieval lanes and alleys are crammed with shops of all varieties. In The Shambles, **Cox of Northampton** sells sheepskin; for leather go to Walmgate and **Ralph Ellerker's**, which started as a saddlery in 1796. In Goodramgate, **Donald Butler** sells fine china and **Trinity** all manner of dolls. **Spelman's** in Micklegate is the place for antiquarian books, while **The Little Gallery** in Low Petergate ships "all gifts to all countries."

If you need a refreshing cuppa in the midst of all that shopping, **Taylors Tea Rooms** in Stonegate serve not just tea but toast, Earl Grey fruitcake, and a Yorkshire rarebit made with Theakston's ale and roasted ham as well. Its partner is **Bettys Café** in St. Helen's Square. Bakers such as **Yates** in Low Petergate sell parkin and Pontefract cakes as well as fresh bread, and **Scott's**, the pork butcher in the same street, does excellent black puddings, another Northern delight.

Seasonal Events

Just as the Vikings welcomed the approach of spring with "Jolablot" (winter festivities), so York brightens up the otherwise dreary month of February with its annual **Jorvik Viking Festival**. This includes longships racing on the Ouse, Viking battles in the streets, fireworks, and the recitation of sagas. The **York Races** take place every month from May through October, and the Ebor Handicap is in August.

Castle Howard

Fifteen miles northeast of York on A 64, toward the Yorkshire Moors, **Castle Howard**, a Baroque, domed 18th-century mansion stands by a lake on an arrow-straight 5-mile drive. The impressive setting of the television version of Evelyn Waugh's *Brideshead Revisited,* it was designed by Sir John Vanbrugh with the help of Nicholas Hawksmoor for the third earl of Carlisle, Charles Howard, and remains the home of his descendants, although it is open to visitors. The interior, especially the Great Hall under the dome, with its Italianate frescoes and chimneypiece, is richly furnished, and works by Holbein and Van Dyck are displayed in the Long Gallery.

Staying in and around York

In addition to the Crest, the affordable Young's, and the Victorian Royal York mentioned above, the city and its environs abound with hotels and guesthouses to suit every taste and budget, although in peak season accommodations are heavily booked. The classiest place to stay is traditionally **Judge's Lodging** at 9 Lendal, a Georgian house that, as its name suggests, used to be the residence of Assize Court judges. The hefty bill reflects the fact that every bedroom has a four-poster and that the food and wine are French—and French at its best. **Middlethorpe Hall**, on Bishopthorpe Road outside the city by the racecourse, is stately, complete with liveried footman. Game features prominently on the menu, along with roast beef with Yorkshire pudding.

These hotels now have a rival in **The Grange Hotel**. Its transformation from period town house to luxurious 29-room hotel filled with antiques was performed by Christophe Golut, a Swiss designer whose new restaurant at the House of Lords in London has attracted praise. The Grange has two restaurants, one a brasserie.

If you want a view of the minster from your window, the **Viking Hotel** in North Street can offer it from many of its 187 bedrooms. It is built in a totally up-to-date Scandinavian style, yet its restaurant prides itself on English country fare such as apple pie and Wensleydale cheese. Much smaller, with 35 bedrooms, the **Dean Court Hotel** can be found in Duncombe Place beneath the soaring twin towers of the minster's west front. Its atmosphere is reminiscent of Trollope and *Barchester Towers,* yet all bedrooms are equipped with bath, television, and phone. The food is solidly traditional.

Also centrally placed, **St. Williams** in College Street looks more like a monastery refectory than the popular restaurant it is. In summer long trestle tables are set in the courtyard outside a 15th-century building. The food is wholesome and comes in large portions.

GETTING AROUND

The drive to York is north from London on A 1 or M 1, turning onto A 64 through Tadcaster, and totals 193 miles. By train it is two hours from London's King's Cross Station, a considerable improvement on the stagecoach of Defoe's day, which took four days. By bus, via National Express from Victoria Coach Station, it takes four to five hours.

ACCOMMODATIONS REFERENCE

▶ **Crest Hotel.** 1 Tower Street, **York** YO1 1SB. Tel:

(0904) 64-81-11; Telex: 57566; Fax: (0904) 61-03-17; in U.S., (301) 593-6444 or (800) 548-2323.

▶ **Dean Court Hotel**. Duncombe Place, York YO1 2EF. Tel: (0904) 62-50-82; Telex: 57584; Fax: (0904) 62-03-05.

▶ **The Grange Hotel**. Clifton, York YO3 6AA. Tel: (0904) 64-47-44; Telex: 57210; Fax: (0904) 61-24-53.

▶ **Judge's Lodging**. 9 Lendal, York YO1 2AQ. Tel: (0904) 63-87-33; Telex: 57200.

▶ **Middlethorpe Hall**. Bishopthorpe Road, York YO2 1QB. Tel: (0904) 64-12-41; Telex: 57802; Fax: (0904) 62-01-76; in U.S., (212) 535-9530 or (800) 223-5581.

▶ **Royal York Hotel**. Station Road, York YO2 2AA. Tel: (0904) 65-36-81; Telex: 57912; Fax: (0904) 62-35-03; in U.S., (212) 684-1820 or (800) 221-1074.

▶ **Viking Hotel**. North Street, York YO1 1JF. Tel: (0904) 65-98-22; Telex: 57937; Fax: (0904) 64-17-93.

▶ **Young's Hotel**. 25 High Petergate, York YO1 2HP. Tel: (0904) 62-42-29.

THE NORTH COUNTRY

LAKE DISTRICT, NORTH YORKSHIRE MOORS, DURHAM, HADRIAN'S WALL

By Frank Dawes

The North—"Up North" to those who live in the southern parts of Great Britain—is not as it was. If J. B. Priestley were to revisit Bradford, where he was born, he might well imagine himself to be in the Punjab; a whole area here has been colonized by Mirpuris who came to work in the mills in the 1960s and have adhered strictly to their own traditions, customs, and language. Indeed, the traditional idea of the North as a place of flat caps and shawls, warm beer, fish-and-chips, backyard pigeon lofts, and mill chimneys, as portrayed by L. S. Lowry in his paintings and Walter Greenwood in *Love on the Dole,* is now mere nostalgia.

What has *not* changed is the scenery that captured the hearts and imaginations of poets and writers from Wordsworth to the Brontës to Priestley. Within an area defined by what used to be called simply the Great North Road (A 1, up the east side of the North), the Road to the Lakes (M 6, up the west side of the North), and the Scottish border (the area of Hadrian's Wall) lies a beguiling combination of superb scenery—rich in historical

and literary associations—and ample opportunities for
outdoor exercise.

MAJOR INTEREST

The Great North Road
North Yorkshire Moors and Dales
Durham City (castle and cathedral)
Castles: Warkworth, Alnwick, Dunstanburgh, and
    Bamburgh
The Farne Islands for bird-watching
Holy Island (Lindisfarne) castle and ecclesiastical
    ruins

The Road to the Lakes
Spectacular views from the Trough of Bowland
Lake District's Wordsworth sites and atmosphere

Border Country
Carlisle
Border Forest Park
Berwick-upon-Tweed
Hadrian's Wall

Exploring the North of England can take a few days or a
few weeks. It is even possible to sample Yorkshire,
Cumbria, and Northumberland in a single day from London, leaving King's Cross at 7:45 A.M. on one of the
occasional special excursions arranged by British Rail.

Breakfast is served in the Pullman car as **The Hadrian**
speeds through Peterborough, and a couple of hours
later the great cathedrals of York and then Durham are
gliding past (there's a particularly fine view of the latter
from the railway viaduct spanning the valley). The train
skirts the metropolis of Newcastle-upon-Tyne, then deposits passengers at Hexham for a journey by bus along an
arrow-straight Roman military road, followed by a walk
along the wall Hadrian built at the northernmost frontier
of the Roman Empire nearly 2,000 years ago.

Passengers rejoin the train, which has travelled empty
across the narrowest part of England from the Tyne to the
Solway, at a station on the 72-mile "Long Drag" between
Carlisle and Settle, a masterpiece of Victorian railway engineering. The viaducts, tunnels, cuttings, and embankments
were accomplished with dynamite, pick and shovel, and
the sweat—and sometimes the blood—of vast armies of

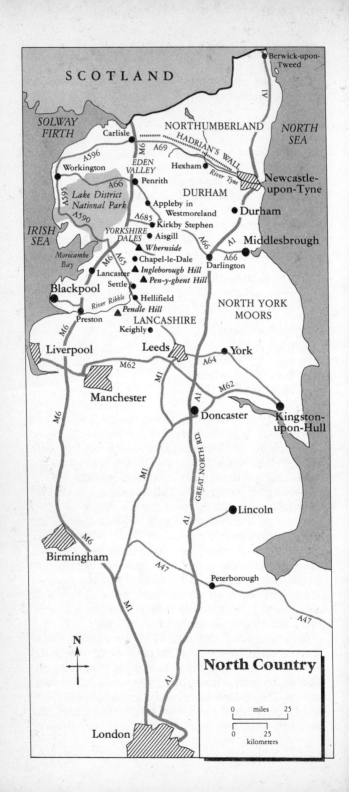

North Country

0   miles   25

0   25
kilometers

"navvies." More than a hundred of them lie buried in the little churchyard at Chapel-le-Dale.

While dinner is served aboard the train, the incomparable scenery of the high Pennines passes the windows: the Eden Valley with its red sandstone bridges, villages, and churches, and the Gorge, famed for its salmon; the Druid temple beside Long Meg Viaduct; Cross Fell; and the hill towns of Appleby and Kirkby Stephen—all glimpsed from high-flying viaducts between the darkness of tunnel after tunnel, carrying the track to its summit at Aisgill, over 1,000 feet above sea level. The train then descends through the upland sheep farms of Garsdale and Dentdale, crossing the head of the River Ribble on a viaduct with 24 arches, a quarter of a mile long and 105 feet high, and passing through the limestone-walled fields of the Yorkshire Dales beneath the three peaks of Pen-y-ghent, Ingleborough, and Whernside to Settle.

From Hellifield you can see Pendle Hill, home of the Lancashire witches, and at Keighley, the Worth Valley line branches into Brontë country. By the time the charlotte russe is served, the train is pausing briefly at Leeds before heading south through Doncaster to rejoin the main line to London, arriving back at King's Cross just after 10:00 P.M. This admittedly long day trip from London traces a triangle explored in more detail in the rest of this chapter.

Our closer look at the most interesting parts of the area roughly covered by this train excursion first heads north through North Yorkshire to Durham and Newcastle-upon-Tyne, then follows England's eastern coast up toward the Scottish border. Next, we explore the Cumbrian Lake District in northwestern England before heading north to the border country above and along Hadrian's Wall.

THE GREAT NORTH ROAD

Heading north through North Yorkshire, the A 1 passes between two national parks: the Yorkshire Dales to the left and the North York Moors to the right. The edge of the moors, reached by A 170, is marked by **Sutton Bank**, a 700-foot escarpment on which a white horse was marked out in the turf by Victorian children under the direction of John Hodgson, the village schoolmaster at Kilburn. A gang of local men then dug out the turf to create a lasting monument 314 feet long and 228 feet high. Kilburn's other claim to fame is the cottage of the "Mouseman," the furniture maker Robert Thompson, who left his unusual trademark on every item he crafted and whose tradition is carried on today by his grandsons. At nearby Coxwold is Shandy Hall, where Laurence Sterne, the author of *Tristram Shandy,* lived as vicar, preaching at the church of St. Michael.

THE YORKSHIRE MOORS
Helmsley

The poet William Wordsworth and his sister Dorothy, on their way from Grasmere to Hackness to visit Wordsworth's future wife, abandoned their carriage in the old market town of Thirsk and decided to negotiate Sutton Bank on foot. They reached Helmsley on the south fringe of the moor (20 miles east of the A 1 on A 170, and due north of York) and stayed the night at the **Black Swan**, on the north side of the town's market square. They stayed there again on their way home, and Dorothy wrote in her diary: "My heart danced at the sight of its cleanly outside, bright yellow walls, casements overshadowed with jasmine and its low, double gavel-ended front."

The Black Swan, which until the railway arrived in the 1870s was a coaching inn from which the "Helmsley Highflyer" ran to Leeds and York, is as welcoming today as it was to the Wordsworths. In the 1960s the train suffered a fate similar to the stagecoach, so the way to get there now is by car or bus—or, like the Wordsworths, on foot. The inn is four distinct buildings (Tudor, Elizabethan, Georgian, and modern) that stand amid apple trees in a walled garden next to the parish church. The dining room, where local and traditional dishes, such as steak in strong ale and mustard in Yorkshire pudding, are served, is presided over by motherly women in white caps and aprons.

Helmsley, with its market cross (where stalls are set out every Friday) and ruined 12th-century Norman castle, is a delightful town and a convenient base for exploring the wild moors.

Rievaulx Abbey

Two miles northwest on B 1257 is Rievaulx Abbey (pronounced Ree-vo), built by the Cistercians in 1131 on the
banks of the River Rye. It fell into disuse 400 years later
during Henry VIII's dissolution of the monasteries, and
now, after another four centuries, it is in ruins. Even so,
the abbey is majestic and moving in its quiet and beautiful
setting amid trees and next to the river. A shrine to Saint
William, the first abbot, who made Rievaulx the leading
Cistercian abbey in Britain, is set in the west wall of the
chapter house. The empty coffin here is said to have been
that of his successor, Saint Aelred, renowned for his
gentleness and patience. In his book, *Christian Friendship*, he wrote: "Wonderful must be he who can afford to
do without friends and without love—more wonderful
assuredly than God himself."

Beyond, to the north and northeast, are the moors,
mile upon mile of heather-covered hills where sheep
roam free and grouse and pheasant start up as you approach. Out on the lonely moor, where tracks are still
marked with stone crosses, roads are few and can be
treacherous in bad weather. Ghostly bells have been
heard ringing out from the ruins of Rievaulx Abbey, and
low bridges crossing the streams can become fords when
the rain lashes down. It is hard to believe, once out
among the heather away from the few main roads, that
this lonely country is part of a small, overcrowded island.
Stone-built farmhouses, let alone villages, are few and far
between and even in peak season it's possible to walk for
hours without seeing any living creature other than
sheep. The now unused "golf ball" structures of the NATO
early-warning station looming out of the mist at
Fylingdales Moor merely emphasize the feeling of nature
in isolation. Masses of daffodils blossom in the green
valleys like **Farndale** in spring, and in August when the
heather blooms on the hills the landscape glows deep
purple. Trails are well marked but it's a good idea to carry
a compass and an Ordnance Survey map in case you stray.

On August 12, the "Glorious Twelfth," the deep valleys
and sharply rising hills echo to the cracks of shotguns as
the grouse-shooting season opens. Scotland may boast
the finest grouse shooting, but when it comes to pheasant
the moors of Helmsley and Ryedale are preeminent; The
Black Swan has a gun room and a drying room next to the
garden lounge.

The 100-mile **Cleveland Way**, a walking route (see Getting Around, below), describes a horseshoe from Helmsley up through the moors and back down along the coast to Filey south of Scarborough. At its northernmost edge is Roseberry Topping, a peak-shaped outcrop that looks down grassy slopes toward the chimneys and iron bridges of industrial Tees-side some 10 miles to the west. Perched high on nearby Easby Moor is a 51-foot monument to Captain James Cook, who attended school in the village of Great Ayton below. The school is now a museum, and there are details of Cook's life and voyages around Australia, New Zealand, and North America near his birthplace at Stewart Park in Marton, just outside Middlesbrough. This town on the northern edge of the moors did not exist in Cook's day, but the steel that came later from its blast furnaces went into railways and bridges around the world, notably, by a nice coincidence, the Sydney Harbour Bridge.

Leaving the moors behind, the Cleveland Way follows the coast along some of the highest cliffs in England. At Staithes, where James Cook was apprenticed to a grocer before running away to sea, a steep road winds down to a tiny harbor where fishing cobles anchor. Whitby, with its wheeling seagulls, steep streets, and ruined abbey, was where Cook first went to sea in colliers and where his ships were later built. In his day, whalers plied out of Whitby; today, only token fishing fleets put out to sea here, but otherwise the moors and coast of North Yorkshire are much as Cook knew them.

THE YORKSHIRE DALES

The green valleys to the west of the A 1, patterned with dry stone walls marking out ancient fields, were sculpted by the melting glaciers of the Ice Age, which also created the rushing rivers and waterfalls that give the Yorkshire Dales their dramatic beauty. Limestone is the material from which the scenery is created, fashioned by centuries of water flowing into the cliffs, gorges, tunnels, caves, and shafts, where "potholers" explore for new underground streams and lakes. Those who prefer to stay above ground can follow way-marked heather tracks: the **Dales Way** and the **Ribble Way**, as well as the tougher **Pennine Way**, which runs from the Peak District in Derbyshire up the back-

bone of England to the Cheviot Hills on the Scottish
border (see Getting Around at end of this chapter).

Some of the loveliest villages in the country are just
north of **Ilkley Moor** (celebrated in the Yorkshire dialect
song "On Ilkley Moor baht 'at," which means, simply, on
Ilkley Moor without a hat) along A 65 in Wharfedale.
Ilkley boasts one of the few Michelin-starred restaurants
in England, the **Box Tree** in Church Street, where local
lamb and vegetables are served in haute cuisine style in
an ornate setting. It is expensive, of course, and advance
booking is essential; Tel: (0943) 60-84-84. **Wood Hall**, a
Georgian mansion overlooking the Valley of the Wharfe
near Wetherby and reached by a mile-long drive through
the estate from the village of Linton, has been turned into
a comfortable and welcoming hotel—with a teddy bear in
every bedroom.

To the south toward the mill chimneys of Bradford are
the somber moors that feature in *Wuthering Heights* and
other novels of the Brontë sisters. The **parsonage** where
the sisters lived from 1820 to 1861 is in the little slate-
roofed, gray stone town of Haworth and is now a museum.

Wensleydale is perhaps the most beautiful of all the
Yorkshire Dales. Just outside Leyburn (north of Leeds and
west of the A 1 on A 684), a lane climbs to **Bolton Castle**,
which has guarded the green folds of hills beside the
River Ure for 600 years. Mary, Queen of Scots, was imprisoned here for six months in 1568. The dining room of
this remarkably preserved fortified Medieval manor is
now a restaurant, efficiently managed by the former butler of Lord Bolton at Bolton Hall. The ruins of the 12th-
century **Jervaulx Abbey**, built by Cistercian monks who
bred excellent horses and sheep and who created
Wensleydale cheese, can be seen on the road south to
Ripon (A 6108).

Possibly the most attractive of all the ecclesiastical ruins
in England lies three miles west of Ripon off B 6265 in the
wooded valley of the River Skell. **Fountains Abbey**, taken
over from the Benedictines by the Cistercians in the 12th
century, preserves the spirit of the monastic life with the
nave and Chapel of the Nine Altars, its cloister, dormito-
ries, refectories and infirmary, cellars and workshops,
which somehow survived total destruction at the hands of
Henry VIII. Its monks played a leading role in developing
the Yorkshire wool industry. A short bit east along the
banks of the little river are the lovely gardens of **Studley**

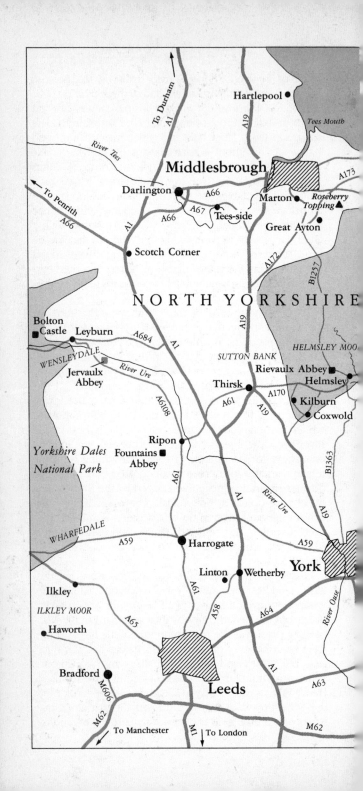

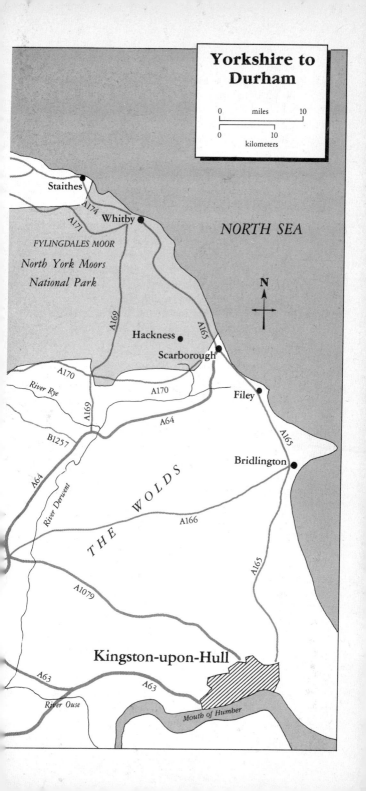

Royal, part of the same National Trust property as the abbey. The gardens were landscaped in formal Dutch style by John Aislabie, Member of Parliament for Ripon and Chancellor of the Exchequer until his involvement in the South Sea Bubble forced him from office in 1720.

DURHAM COUNTY

Going north from Yorkshire, the A 1 and the InterCity rail line cross into the county of Durham, the land of the prince bishops. For centuries the heads of the Christian church ruled here with the power of kings; they commanded their own armies, courts, and coinage. Their bishopric extended from the River Tees to the Scottish border, a kingdom within a kingdom. In more recent times, the countryside was blackened with slag heaps from the coal mines that were a major industry here.

Barnard Castle

At Scotch Corner, the A 66 branches off northeast toward the Pennines, following the route laid down by the Roman legions. Just after it crosses the border with County Durham, an unclassified road splits off from A 66 and meanders its way north across rolling countryside to the River Tees and the town of Barnard Castle, where Charles Dickens came by stagecoach in 1838 to gather background material about the notorious "Yorkshire schools" for his novel *Nicholas Nickleby.* William Shaw and his Bowes Academy, the models for Wackford Squeers and Dotheboys Hall, had been successfully sued by the parents of two children who became blind from untreated infections. The local churchyard contains the graves of 25 boys, as young as seven years, who died in Shaw's care between 1810 and 1834. Dickens, accompanied by the artist "Phiz," travelled under an assumed name and pretended to be in search of a school for the son of a widowed friend. The one-eyed Shaw was suspicious and let them see little; however, they learned everything from a local attorney they met at the **King's Head** pub, which still serves food and drink today. Dickens and "Phiz" also stayed at the George and New Inn at nearby Greta Bridge, where "a rousing fire halfway up the chimney" was more than welcome after a two-day journey from London through raging snowstorms.

One building looks out of place among the Georgian and Victorian stone houses that line the steep streets leading down to the river—a French château set in a formal garden reminiscent of the Tuileries in Paris. This is the **Bowes Museum**, the jewel in Barnard Castle's crown, conceived in 1869 by a son of the earl of Strathmore and packed with lovely things collected from the great houses of Europe: furniture, pottery, and fine paintings by Goya, Tiepolo, and El Greco. There are dollhouses and toys, too, and a magnificent silver swan swimming on a lake of spun glass; at appointed hours, to the minute, an attendant ceremoniously winds it up, and the swan's head twists realistically on its graceful neck before darting down to snatch up and swallow a silver fish.

Teesdale

A winding road (B 6277) between dry stone walls leads northwest up the dale from Barnard Castle and through the former Quaker lead-mining town of Middleton-in-Teesdale to **High Force**, the highest waterfall in England. The water, stained brown from the iron in the rocks, tumbles 70 feet into a wooded gorge filled with wildflowers and ferns. This is very near Cross Fell, where the Tees rises, fed by countless streams furrowing the slopes. It is wild country, with a few whitewashed farmhouses that have been occupied by the same families for generations, and some ancient stone barns where the hardy sheep are sheltered from winter snowdrifts. Three major rivers rise in these high fells of the Pennines: the Tees, the Wear, and the South Tyne.

DURHAM CITY

Back east on the A 1, head north to Durham City. Along with the Grand Canyon, the Great Barrier Reef, the Taj Mahal, the palace of Versailles, and other such places, Durham's magnificent cathedral and castle appear in the list of World Heritage sites. Their towers and battlements dominate a wooded promontory of rock around which the River Wear winds a graceful loop. One of the best views is from a train on the great viaduct that carries the railway line from London to Edinburgh across the deep valley on the western side of the city. Another is from Prebends' Bridge, which bears the verse Sir Walter Scott was inspired to write from it, beginning "Grey towers of Durham . . . " The Great North Road, transformed at this point into a six-lane motorway, bypasses the city to the east.

Secure in their fortress-church—"Half church of God, half castle 'gainst the Scot," as Sir Walter Scott phrased it—the prince bishops were able to repel not only the repeated and ferocious attacks of the Scots but also rebellious Sassenachs.

In addition to its historic castle and cathedral, Durham's university adds a special vitality to the city.

The Cathedral

Arguably the finest Norman cathedral in Europe, Durham was originally the site of a shrine for the miraculously preserved body of Saint Cuthbert, which monks carried from the island of Lindisfarne in 875 to escape marauding Danes. They paused during their flight to rest on this rocky hilltop and then, according to legend, found the coffin impossible to move. In 1020 the remains of the Venerable Bede, who wrote the earliest surviving ecclesiastical history of England, joined those of Saint Cuthbert in the Saxon church that predated the cathedral.

In 1104 Saint Cuthbert's remains were enshrined behind the high altar in the present cathedral, begun 11 years earlier to replace the Saxon church, of which no trace remains, and after another two centuries, the remains of the Venerable Bede were moved to a simple tomb in the Galilee Chapel at the opposite end.

The interior of the cathedral is celebrated for its soaring nave and stout, incised Norman columns. Dr. Johnson was struck by its "rocky solidity and indeterminate duration." The ribbed vaulting of the roof high above is the earliest of its kind in England, and the pointed arches of the nave are thought to be the first example of their use in Europe. A curiosity to visitors is the sanctuary knocker outside, which throughout the Middle Ages offered the protection of Saint Cuthbert to any hunted criminal who grasped its ring.

The Castle

Generations of Durham undergraduates have made their temporary home in this splendid pile, with its Norman gatehouse, tiny chapel in the crypt, and Bishop Cosin's 17th-century "Black Staircase." The 15th-century kitchens, much modernized, still operate to serve the students at the refectory tables in the Norman great hall. When the students are on vacation their rooms (and the refectory) are open to visitors without advance booking at very inexpensive rates, and there is a restaurant serving fresh food at moderate prices. Surprisingly, there are no outstanding hotels or restaurants in Durham City. The largest and most convenient hotel is the **Royal County** in the Old Elvet neighborhood west across the river from the cathedral; the hotel has been extensively renovated.

University life is reflected in the bookshops and pubs along the steep streets and alleys, called "vennels," beneath the castle walls. They lead down to the river, where daffodils crowd the banks in spring and rowboats can be rented. At the **Shakespeare Pub** next door to the tall, dusty offices of the *Northern Echo* pints of Eighty Shillings Ale can be quaffed in small back rooms offering unobtrusive access to the vennel at the side. Durham is a compact city best toured on foot, so leave your automobile at one of the parking lots on the outskirts of the fortified hill.

Washington

North of Durham on the A 1 nearing Newcastle, there are signposts to Washington. This is the place from which George Washington's family took its name, although George himself never came here. Unfortunately, the village green of old Washington, with its sandstone houses and former smithy, has been all but swallowed up by a hideous urban development.

Washington Old Hall was the home of George Washington's direct ancestors for five generations, until they sold it in 1613. George's great-grandfather emigrated to Virginia in 1656, possibly because his father, a Loyalist parson, fell foul of the Roundheads during the Civil War. Three centuries later the house that had been built on the foundations of the old hall was due for demolition, but it was saved by a preservation committee with generous donations from both sides of the Atlantic. It now belongs to the National Trust and is lovingly maintained. The 18th-century gates leading to the hall, just below the church on a wooded hill, were the gift of the Colonial Dames of America.

NEWCASTLE-UPON-TYNE

The Great North Road, skirting the hinterland of Sunderland and the industrialized estuary of the River Wear, dives northward under the Tyne through a toll tunnel. Apart from the Tyne Bridge, the model for the Sydney Harbour Bridge, there are five others spanning this celebrated river and dominating the Geordie capital of the Northeast.

Geordies have a culture and dialect all their own. The latter, with an entirely different set of vowels from standard English, includes phrases such as "wor lass," which means "my wife, daughter, or sister," and "Howay, man!" which from a Southerner would sound more like "I say, you over there!" The lethal local brew—Newcastle Brown Ale—is sometimes referred to as "jawney inter spayus," which means "journey into space."

The **New Castle** that gave the city its name was built in 1080, and a 12th-century keep erected on the site of the earlier fortress survives, together with a stretch of the Medieval walls. **Blackfriars**, built in the 13th century, is a Dominican friary that survived the dissolution of the monasteries.

The town of **Jarrow** on the southern side of the Tyne Tunnel was the home of the Venerable Bede and has a church dating back to A.D. 685. There is also a museum and a reconstructed gate of a Roman fort that once stood there commanding the river. But the name of Jarrow is remembered more for the Hunger Marchers who in 1935 walked almost 350 miles to London to demand work and subsistence; after the cruiser *York* had been launched at Palmers Shipyard in 1931, the gates stayed locked—and Palmers, the town's major employer, *was* Jarrow.

The prosperity of the Tyneside area was based on coal, ships, and the river. It suffered terribly during the Depression, and the novels of Catherine Cookson, who was raised by her grandparents in the docklands of South Shields (to the east of Newcastle at the south side of the river's mouth) reflect the harshness of that period. The South Tyne is now "Catherine Cookson country," and a section of the **South Shields Museum** is devoted to her life and work. Since World War II many of the shipyards and coal mines have closed for good, but there is a new sense of vitality and enterprise about Newcastle. South Shields is only a few stops from the city center on the

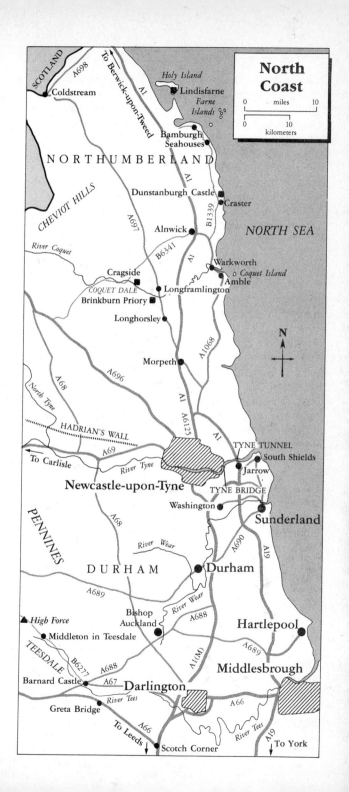

North Coast

miles 0 10
kilometers 0 10

SCOTLAND
A698
Coldstream
To Berwick-upon-Tweed
A1
Holy Island
Lindisfarne
Farne Islands
Bamburgh
Seahouses
NORTHUMBERLAND
CHEVIOT HILLS
A697
Dunstanburgh Castle
Craster
B1339
NORTH SEA
Alnwick
A1
B6341
River Coquet
Cragside
Warkworth
Coquet Island
Amble
COQUET DALE
Longframlington
Brinkburn Priory
Longhorsley
A1068
N
Morpeth
North Tyne
A68
A696
A1
A6125
HADRIAN'S WALL
A69
To Carlisle
River Tyne
TYNE TUNNEL
South Shields
Jarrow
Newcastle-upon-Tyne
TYNE BRIDGE
Washington
Sunderland
PENNINES
A68
River Wear
A690
A19
DURHAM
Durham
A689
River Wear
High Force
Bishop Auckland
A688
Hartlepool
Middleton in Teesdale
A1(M)
TEESDALE
B6277
A688
A67
Middlesbrough
Barnard Castle
Darlington
River Tees
Greta Bridge
A66
River Tees
A19
To Leeds
A66
To York
Scotch Corner

Tyneside Metro, a fast, clean, inexpensive service that makes the London Underground look antediluvian.

The Civic Centre and Eldon Square shopping center in Newcastle, together with the even newer Metro shopping mall on the outskirts, contrast with an older generation of buildings such as the Central Exchange and Arcade and the Grainger Market, which was considered by the Victorians to be "the most spacious and magnificent in Europe." The grandeur of Grey Street, overseen by a 135-foot statue of the prime minister Earl Grey, has been restored by the removal of decades of soot deposits. The Theatre Royal and other classical buildings give Newcastle a sense of style and sophistication sometimes absent in other English provincial cities. Unlike them, Newcastle even provides a nightlife with its discos and clubs, including the *Tuxedo Princess,* a converted ferry moored directly under the Tyne Bridge.

Other good things about Newcastle are Singin' Hinny (hot buttered fruit scones); pease pudding; prize leeks; working men's clubs; and pigeon racing. There is a wide choice of hotels here, including two on Neville Street near the railway station: the **Royal Station** and the recently renovated **County Thistle**, with its elegant Café Mozart. Both of these occupy vast Victorian buildings with wood paneling and ornately decorated plaster ceilings that recall an era when steam was king and everyone travelled by train. Now they have the facilities expected of modern hotels, including parking and easy access to shopping, theaters, and restaurants that offer everything from Madras curry to French nouvelle cuisine. If you want Singin' Hinny or any of the other local delicacies mentioned above, alas, you have to get yourself invited into the homes of real Geordies!

Newcastle is a good base for day trips to the ancient Roman sites along Hadrian's Wall, to the west of the city; if pressed for time you can view the wall from above in a light aircraft (see "Hadrian's Wall" below).

CASTLES ON THE COAST

Between Newcastle and the Scottish border to the north, and lying more or less parallel to the Great North Road, is one of the finest unspoiled stretches of coastline in Great Britain. Mile upon mile of clean, soft sand, fringed by dunes and golf courses, is watched over, as it has been for centuries, by Medieval castles. A few miles north of Morpeth, the A 1 crosses the River Coquet (pronounced cocket), a lovely stream rich in trout and salmon. Upstream in Coquet Dale, reached by B 6341 or B 6344, is **Cragside**, the mansion estate of the Tyneside magnate who invented the rifled cannon and became the first Lord Armstrong. It was the first house in the world to be lit by hydroelectricity, with a system Armstrong designed using artificial lakes and subterranean pipes. In the 900-acre park, he planted literally millions of trees and shrubs, including spectacular rhododendrons, and laid down 40 miles of paths and driveways. The property is owned by the National Trust and is open to visitors.

The Coquet winds its way to the sea, looping around the 12th-century **Brinkburn Priory**, inviting anglers and others to linger in perfect tranquillity on the wooded banks that the Augustinian canons knew. **Embleton Hall**, on the edge of Longframlington on A 697 to Coldstream, is a country house made into a homey hotel by Trevor Thorne and his wife, Judith. It is an early 18th-century stone house with a late Victorian wing, where the Fenwick family lived for two centuries, leaving their family crest on the pediment above the main entrance. The five-acre garden includes a "Ha-ha" (an ornamental sunken fence), a grass tennis court, and a croquet lawn. Nearby in Longframlington, the **Besom Barn** uses locally grown provisions to create imaginative dishes, such as Ewesley Fell lamb baked with root vegetables and rosemary and served with a sauce of Port wine and fresh mint. To the south on A 697 in Longhorsley is **Linden Hall**, a country-house hotel standing in its own park of 300 acres. This is more a stately home than a hotel, with spacious period rooms and a wide range of leisure facilities, all reflected in the price.

Warkworth Castle

Little more than a mile before it reaches the sea, the Coquet forms a horseshoe round the ancient town of Warkworth (on A 1068), with its narrow, humpbacked cobbled bridge alongside the parvenu 1960s structure that usurped its function after six centuries. The town is dominated by what Shakespeare's Henry IV described as a "worm-eaten hold of ragged stone," and three scenes from that play are set at Warkworth Castle, which dates to the 12th century. It is distinguished by its cruciform keep, great hall, chapel, and tower carved with the Percy lion. Upstream, and reached only by a rowboat that operates on weekends, is **Warkworth Hermitage**, a tiny chapel hewn out of the rock. Warkworth was the ancestral home of the Percy family, and it was the third Lord Percy and his son, Harry Hotspur (who rode "as if his spurs were hot"), who placed Henry IV on the throne of England in 1399. Later the Percys conspired against the king, and Hotspur's head ended up on Micklegate Bar in York.

Brightly painted fishing boats called cobles are still made in the Amble boatyard, to the south of Warkworth, in an estuary once busy with colliers but now the domain of yachters (a splendid new marina has been built there) and golfers attracted by the links on the dunes by the sea. One mile offshore is the low-lying Coquet Island, with sandy beaches and a lighthouse, a sanctuary for puffins, terns, eiders, fulmars, and oystercatchers carefully managed by the Royal Society for the Protection of Birds. There are boat trips from Amble Harbour around the island, with commentaries.

Alnwick

North of Warkworth the Great North Road used to squeeze its way through the Hotspur Gate at the heart of this old market town, the seat of the earls of Northumberland. Now A 1 bypasses the town, but the Percy lion still adorns the gate and sits atop the Tenantry Column, erected by grateful tenants after their rents were reduced during a depression in the early 19th century. The Norman **Alnwick Castle** sits elegantly in its pastoral setting, with stone-carved soldiers staring out from the battlements over the meadows beside the River Aln, where horses and cattle graze. This 12th-century structure is the home of the present duke and duchess of Northumberland; inside are a collection of Meissen china and a superb library with second folio editions of Shakespeare. Paintings by Titian, Van Dyck, and Canaletto hang beside modern photographs and greeting cards from various members of the royal family.

The firm of Hardy's, sponsor of the Fishing Tackle Museum in Alnwick, also had its brush with royalty. Soon after King George V came to the throne, the novelist Thomas Hardy attained his 70th birthday, and the king was reminded that it might be a good idea to send a telegram to "old Hardy." The maker of the royal fishing rods at Alnwick was surprised to receive the king's misdirected congratulations on reaching an age he was still far from attaining on a day that was not his birthday.

Hardy Pie (made from fish, of course) is on the menu at the **White Swan** in Bondgate, which is also remarkable for its Olympic Room. In 1911 the *Olympic* and the *Titanic* were the world's biggest steamships. The *Olympic* was broken up at Palmers in Jarrow in 1935, and its first-class lounge was taken out and reassembled at the White Swan. The 43 guest rooms here have all the modern amenities and traditional, comfortable furnishings.

Dunstanburgh Castle

Around the tiny, almost circular harbor of **Craster**, a few miles northeast of Alnwick on B 1339, the stone jetties are strewn with crab and lobster pots. The village is famed, however, for fish that are no longer caught off its shores. The herrings that are smoked in a harborside shed to make Craster kippers are now brought from the west of Scotland. Be that as it may, Craster kippers (not to mention its smoked salmon) are delectable and much sought after.

Beyond the village, on a rock ledge high above the sea, is the commanding bulk of Dunstanburgh Castle. This was the stronghold of John of Gaunt, who as uncle of the boy-king Richard II was the most powerful baron in England. The castle was severely knocked about during the Wars of the Roses, changing hands no fewer than five times. Its impressive ruins can be reached only on foot along a grassy coastal path strewn with boulders and through a wicket gate at the north side of Craster. From there, it is a mile to the great gatehouse, with its two towers and walls several feet thick. The site covers 11 acres, and the path continues beyond the castle around Embleton Bay, skirting golf links and golden sands. At the seaward side of Dunstanburgh, Gull Crag drops sheer to the rocks below. Peer over the edge and you will see innumerable gulls riding the air currents as they come and go from their nests on the cliff ledges, their cries competing with the crash of the waves.

The Farne Islands

Gull Crag's population of seabirds is merely the overspill from the Farnes. Terns, comical puffins, clumsy cormorants, kittiwakes, and eiders are to be found in these 30 rocky outcrops a few miles offshore. This is also one of the main breeding grounds of the gray seal. Like the coastal strip, the islands are owned by the National Trust, but landing is allowed on some of them, and boats sail every day, weather permitting, from the harbor at **Seahouses**. In summer the harbor is often crowded with daytrippers. The cruise around the islands, with an hour ashore, provides magical opportunities to see and photograph at close range nesting birds, Manx shearwaters skimming the waves, or gannets crash-diving on shoals of mackerel and herring.

Bamburgh Castle and Holy Island

There is a memorial to Grace Darling in the churchyard at her home village of **Bamburgh** just north of Seahouses (on B 1342), and a small museum devoted to the gallant rescue she made with her father in 1838 of the crew of the stricken ship *Forfarshire* off the coast here. But her heroics are overshadowed by the pink-walled castle perched atop a 150-foot outcrop. Little survives of the early fortifications of the kings of Northumbria except a deep well. Within the stout walls of the 12th-century keep the ambience is Victorian, reflecting its ownership by the first Lord Armstrong, who lavished the money he made out of armaments on rebuilding it.

On a clear day there are stunning views from the battlements up and down the sandy coast. Another dramatic castle can be seen on the nearby Holy Island, or **Lindisfarne**, which is really only a half-time island—when the tide goes out a causeway emerges (reached via a small road that branches west from A 1 at West Mains). There is a hut on stilts, reached from the causeway by a flight of stairs, for those who fail to get the tide timings right, even though they are clearly displayed on a board.

Colonies of wildfowl and waders feed on the sands and flats as they did when Saint Aidan, journeying from that far-off island of the western shore, the holy Iona, crossed the sands at low tide and founded the monastery of Lindisfarne in the year 634. An illuminated manuscript of the Lindisfarne Gospels survives in the British Museum, although the monastery, which first brought Christianity to these northern parts, was sacked successively by the Vikings and the Danes in the two centuries after the manuscript was written.

As Bishop Lightfoot said, "When Finian built his first church on lonely Lindisfarne, with its wooden walls and thatched roof, it was destined, nevertheless, to be the precursor of stately, imperial Durham."

The red stone walls of the priory church built by Benedictine monks from Durham in the latter part of the 11th century are still standing, and the carved pillars and zigzag-ornamented arches mirror those in Durham Cathedral. Northumberland's historic themes of religion and war are repeated on Holy Island, with the castle perched on its crag near the priory in stark silhouette at sunrise or sunset. Among castles, however, this was a Johnny-come-lately: Built in the mid-16th century to defend Holy Island against the Scots, it was never to loose a single cannonball from its battlements. It was renovated in 1903 in the romantic style of Sir Edwin Lutyens.

THE ROAD TO THE LAKES

The fact that there is superhighway (the M 1 and M 6) for the entire 250 miles from London to the Lake District makes for a speedy journey through the Midlands, which used to be known, and not without reason, as "the Black Country." Just north of the industrialized conurbations of Lancashire (Manchester), due west from Preston on the M 55, however, is Blackpool, a resort town with six miles of beaches, three piers, a "Golden Mile" of fun fairs, and a 518-foot structure aping the Eiffel Tower. But for a more attractive detour, turn off the M 6 at Junction 31 and take the road northeast toward Clitheroe, which accompanies the River Ribble inland from Preston.

Northcote Manor, a Victorian mill owner's aspiration to gentility, now a country hotel, stands foursquare behind stone walls on the outskirts of Langho, just before Clitheroe. You can look out its windows at cows and sheep grazing contentedly in the meadows of the Ribble valley; Pendle Hill, the haunt of such Lancashire witches as Old Demdike, Old Chattox, and Mistress Nutter, looms on the horizon. Northcote Manor serves superb terrines and sweets and imaginative main courses such as lobster in Champagne and dill sauce and breast of wood pigeon (from local shoots) on foie gras, garnished with black grapes. The vegetables are fresh from the kitchen garden.

At Clitheroe, there's the diminutive, 800-year-old **Whalley Abbey**, founded by the Cistercians in the 13th century, and nearby are charming stone-built villages such as Bolton-by-Bowland and Downham with their greens, brooks, and ancient stocks. Toward Lancaster and the Lake District to the northwest lies the **Forest of Bowland**, which now has few trees but stupendous scenery: wave after wave of rocky hills, purple in late summer and autumn when the heather is out. The **Trough of Bowland** is a natural cleft climbing over 1,500 feet from the Ribble valley to provide views on a clear day of the Isle of Man and the distant mountains of North Wales.

Lancaster

The narrow, winding, unclassified road through the Trough of Bowland drops down to Lancaster, which is also on the M 6. **Hornsea Pottery**, on Wyersdale Road, set in 42 acres of landscaped parkland, offers guided factory tours and a wide range of china, earthenware, and glass at reduced prices. A maritime museum in the Georgian **Custom House** on St. George's Quay tells the story of Lancaster's once-thriving trade to the Americas, taking slaves out of Africa and returning with tobacco and cotton, and of the fishing industry based on Morecambe Bay's famous prawns and shrimps. Today both are moribund, but Lancaster remains the administrative center of the county and the home of one of Britain's newer universities.

About ten miles north of Lancaster, a mile to the right off the M 6, 18th-century **Lupton Tower** near Kirkby Lonsdale in Lupton is a guesthouse with a vegetarian restaurant. Its seven bedrooms have views across the River Lune to the fells that John Ruskin described as "the loveliest in England, therefore in the world."

THE SOUTHERN LAKES

Some of Ruskin's watercolors and Turner's *Passage of the St. Gothard* can be seen at **Abbot Hall** in Kendal (22 miles north of Lancaster), as can the work of the portraitist George Romney, who grew up in this market town, then

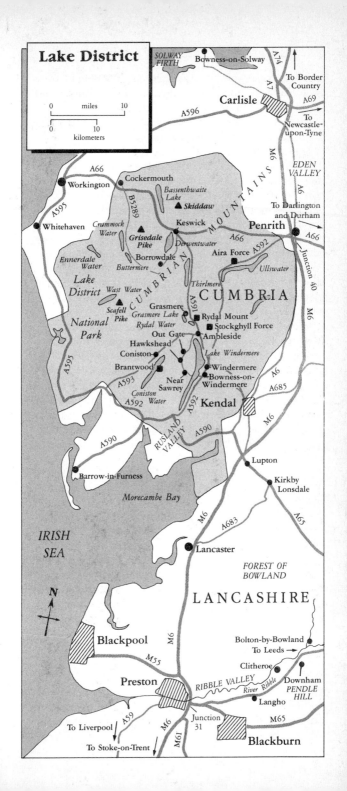

as now the gateway to the southern lakes. Within this tiny area are to be found England's highest mountain and largest lake, but the scale is not grand: Scafell Pike reaches 3,206 feet, and Lake Windermere is ten miles long and just over a mile at its widest.

The landscape, sculpted in the Ice Age, changes with the season: luxuriant broad-leafed woods green in summer and a fire of reds, browns, and golds in fall; snow-covered peaks in winter, and in the spring, yes, daffodils. It is even more beautiful when its waterfalls and glades are lit with sunshine. Hill farming is still a major occupation here. This is an outdoor area that attracts both serious walkers and climbers and casual ramblers—whichever you are, one of Alfred Wainwright's splendid guides should go with you. If walking is too tame, mountain bicycles with fat tires and 15 gears can be rented locally, as can horses.

In his long life, William Wordsworth tramped the fells in all weather and foresaw the need to protect his native countryside by making it a national park, which it is today. In his *Guide through the District of the Lakes,* Wordsworth wrote of the "persons of pure taste throughout the whole island, who, by their visits (often repeated) to the Lakes in the North of England, testify that they deem the district a sort of national property, in which every man has a right and interest who has an eye to perceive and a heart to enjoy."

Despite horrendous motor traffic on the narrow roads, acid rain, fallout scares, nuclear processing plants and power stations on the coast, and the persistent use of the Lake District's contours for games of "chicken" by low-flying combat jets, the natural attractions of the place remain much as they were when they inspired the age of English romanticism. In the woods of the Rusland Valley, between Windermere and Coniston, the charcoal burners who faded away 50 years ago, after Arthur Ransome illustrated their mysterious wigwams in *Swallows and Amazons,* are returning, encouraged by the growing popularity of barbecuing in Britain.

Lake Windermere

The town of Windermere barely existed before the railway came in the mid-19th century—despite the opposition of the then aging Wordsworth. He knew Bowness, also on the lake's eastern shore, and mentions the White

Lion there (now the **Royal Hotel**, with 29 beds and good food) in *The Prelude*. The **Belmont Manor** in Windermere is a comfortable and moderately priced hotel. There are peacocks on its extensive grounds overlooking the lake.

The young Wordsworth used the ferry that still runs across the lake between Ferry Nab and Ferry House, providing a shortcut to Hawkshead, to the west of the lake, where he attended grammar school between 1779 and 1787. (His name is carved into the wood of his old desk there.) The center of Hawkshead is closed to through traffic, which helps greatly toward preserving the character of the poet's "beloved Vale." Eight bedrooms at **Field Head House**, where he was a guest of the artist John Harden, are open to visitors.

Hill Top Farm, two miles south at Near Sawrey, was the home of Beatrix Potter, whose children's books featuring Peter Rabbit, Jemima Puddle-Duck, and others were illustrated with sketches and paintings of the hills and lakes hereabouts. Potter bought local farmlands to save them from developers and left these and her 17th-century farmhouse to the National Trust when she died in 1943. The "New Room," where she did much of her work, is open to visitors and displays her furniture and china. Hill Top Farm is, however, very small in relation to the huge crowds it attracts and should be avoided on weekends and bank holidays. There is a permanent gallery on Main Street in Hawkshead. Formerly the office of Potter's husband, a local attorney, it features a rotating selection of 500 watercolor illustrations from her books.

Coniston Water

John Ruskin lies in the churchyard at Coniston, and a museum in the village is devoted to his life and work as an artist, writer, scientist, critic, and fighter for social justice. He moved here in 1871, long after Wordsworth was dead, yet Ruskin was influenced by the English Romantics. **Brantwood,** his home on the eastern side of the lake, is open to visitors.

Tennyson spent his honeymoon by Coniston Water. Its haunting beauty wreathed in dawn mists is captured by Turner in a painting now in the Tate Gallery in London. The best way to see Coniston Water, which lies west of Lake Windermere, is from the richly upholstered opulence of the steam yacht *Gondola,* launched in 1859 and

now owned and operated by the National Trust; it runs
between Coniston and Park-a-Moor.

Ambleside, Rydal, and Grasmere

To the north of Lake Windermere, in the shadow of the
high fells, the associations with Wordsworth are stronger
than anywhere else in the Lake District. Every wood,
mere, beck, tarn, and fell seems to echo evocative lines.
His visitors here included Sir Walter Scott, Shelley, Keats,
Emerson, Hawthorne, Charlotte Brontë, and Mrs. Gaskell.

At Ambleside, where Stockghyll Force sends its waters
cascading from a height of 70 feet, is **Old Stamp House**,
now a law office, where Wordsworth was the official
distributor of stamps for Westmorland, a county now
merged with Cumberland into Cumbria. **Rydal Mount**, on
the road (A 591) to Keswick, was Wordsworth's home
from 1813 until his death in 1850. Both the house and the
garden he lovingly designed are open to visitors year-
round. The road to Grasmere (A 549) skirts Rydal Water,
one of the smallest of the lakes; the neighboring lake,
Grasmere, measures just one mile by one-half mile and
has a green island in it.

Overlooking its placid waters is **Dove Cottage**, on the
outskirts of **Grasmere**. Wordsworth and his sister Dorothy
lived here in the opening years of the 19th century while
he wrote, among other works, *Michael, Resolution and
Independence,* and *Ode on Intimations of Immortality*
and completed *The Prelude.* The house and museum next
door contain the world's foremost collection of his manuscripts and possessions. After Wordsworth married he
turned the cottage over to his friend Thomas De Quincey,
best known as the author of *Confessions of an English
Opium Eater,* and moved briefly to Allan Bank, planting
the grounds there, and then to the old rectory before
settling finally at Rydal Mount. For a short spell, Wordsworth taught at the Lych Gate school by St. Oswald's
Church, and his son John was a pupil there. It is now
Sarah Nelson's gingerbread shop. The yew trees in the
churchyard at Grasmere were planted by Wordsworth,
and he and his wife Mary are buried here beneath a
simple headstone.

Overlooking Grasmere among the rhododendrons in a
three-acre garden is **Michaels Nook Country House Hotel**, built in 1859 as the summer home of a Lancashire mill

owner who named it after the shepherd in Wordsworth's lines,

> Upon the forest-side at Grasmere Vale
> There dwelt a shepherd, Michael was his name.

In 1969 the house became an 11-room hotel; filled with antiques, it is now patrolled by Jake, a harmless Great Dane. A tempting menu is served by candlelight. Michaels has an arrangement with the nearby **Wordsworth Hotel**, which has 37 rooms, whereby the latter's swimming pool, saunas, and solarium are available to the guests of both establishments.

THE NORTHERN LAKES

The unofficial frontier between the southern and northern lakes is the broad pass of Dunmail Raise, and within a ten-mile radius of Keswick there is a wide variety of lakes. Thirlmere, dammed in 1876, supplies Manchester with water. Buttermere and Crummock Water are quiet places, rarely disturbed by anything more than an occasional rowboat. Bassenthwaite Lake is skirted by a main road, A 66, and is the base of a sailing club, but is nonetheless uncrowded.

Derwentwater, just south of Keswick, is surrounded by perfect picnic spots and is busy with boats of all kinds from a club, a marina, and rental shops as well as canoeists, water-skiers, and wind-surfers. The **Stakis Lodore Swiss Hotel**, large by lakeland standards and impressively sited with views of the lake and the Lodore Falls, offers international cuisine and indoor and outdoor pools, as well as saunas and massage.

Keswick

The town lies on the River Greta in a natural amphitheater, surrounded by the peaks of Skiddaw, Blencathra, Catbells, and Grisedale Pike. Walking the fells here calls for stout shoes and raincoats, and Keswick is a good place to buy them, together with rucksacks, sheepskins, and all kinds of woollens. (The **Sheepskin Warehouse Shop** at the Royal Oak Hotel on Station Road has a wide selection at good prices.) Wordsworth used to walk the 13 miles from Grasmere and back to visit his friends, the other "Lake Poets" Coleridge and Southey, who both lived at

Keswick. He fought against the coming of the railway; now the railway station has been closed and transformed into a year-round leisure center where an indoor pool has a wave-making machine and a simulated tropical climate.

The old **Moot Hall** in the market square, which as recently as 20 years ago was filled with market stalls selling eggs, butter, and flowers, is now a visitors' information center. However, the Saturday market outside continues a six-century tradition, and the clerks in the old-fashioned shops off the marketplace are unfailingly courteous. One of the local traders, Myers of Keswick, has opened a shop in New York City's Greenwich Village to purvey Cumberland sausage, pork pies, and black pudding to expatriates. Keswick is as famous for its pencils as Kendal is for its "mint cake" confection. The Pencil Museum at the Cumberland Pencil Company traces the history of plumbago mining in Borrowdale— the town six miles south of Keswick on B 5289 that penetrates the high fells and offers a stunning view over Derwentwater from Friar's Crag.

Ullswater

The largest of the northern lakes, east of Lake Thirlmere and Derwentwater, is seven and a half miles long, with a main road (A 592) now winding along the shore where Wordsworth once "wandered lonely as a cloud." In April and May the bank is still covered with golden *Narcissus Pseudonarcissus,* but the large pleasure boats, motor cruisers, powerboats, and yachts make the surface of Ullswater almost as busy in the summer as the road around it. Aira Force, the waterfall that inspired Wordsworth's poem *The Somnambulist,* can be reached on foot through the woods on either side of Aira Beck from the National Trust parking lot.

Penrith

It is only a short drive north on A 592 from the head of Ullswater (or east on A 66 from Keswick) to Penrith, the hometown of Wordsworth's parents. Although born near the coast in Cockermouth, the poet, his sister, and his future wife all attended nursery school here in the 1770s. His excursion to Penrith Beacon as a five-year-old is remembered in *The Prelude.* Main roads from all directions, including the A 66 across the Pennines from Durham, meet the **M 6** here. The **North Lakes Gateway Hotel** is next to Junction 40 on M 6 just outside the old town. Surrounded by a new housing development, it offers access to a leisure center with two squash courts, a gym and solarium, indoor pools, and a whirlpool.

THE BORDER COUNTRY

Emperor Hadrian built his wall across the neck of North Britain from Bowness on the Solway Firth, north of Penrith and Carlisle, to Wallsend-on-Tyne in order to forestall the northern barbarians. The present-day frontier separating Scots and Sassenachs runs instead diagonally from Gretna Green, where runaway couples from England used to be married "over the anvil," to just north of Berwick-upon-Tweed. There is no wall now or custom post to mark it, merely signs by lonely roadsides announcing to travellers that they have just entered Scotland.

Carlisle

The cannons of the Citadel, a round, red-stone, crenellated tower outside the railway station, were last fired in anger by the Scots against the duke of Cumberland's forces in 1745. Parts of the city wall survive and can be walked. Mary, Queen of Scots, was a prisoner in the castle, which displays the improvements and modifications of monarchs over eight centuries. **Mary's Tower** now houses the museum of the Border Regiment, whose regimental march "D'ye ken John Peel?" commemorates the huntsman who is buried at Caldbeck, 16 miles southwest of the city.

Carlisle Cathedral is one of the smallest in Britain and has been in its time both a priory and a prison. Its interior is graced by an exquisite 14th-century east window with tracery lights showing the Last Judgment. The canopied choir stalls have misericords carved with beasts, birds, and monsters; paintings of the Apostles and scenes from the lives of Saint Anthony, Saint Cuthbert, and Saint Augus-

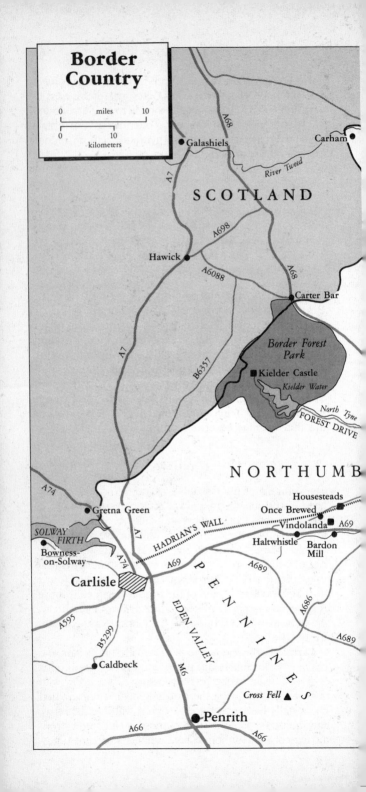

tine decorate the backs. It was in this cathedral that Robert the Bruce was excommunicated with "bell, book, and candle" and that Sir Walter Scott was married in 1797.

The Roman city of fountains and statuary here, its villas kept warm in the inhospitable climate with hot air ducted beneath mosaic-tiled floors, was called Luguvallium. Relics of this lost city are kept in a large museum in **Tullie House** on Castle Street, which has become a national study center for the Romans' border-defense system.

The Border Forest Park

At the heart of the Border Forest Park, northeast of Carlisle, is Kielder Water, one of the largest artificial lakes in Northern Europe. It is used extensively for fishing, windsurfing, canoeing, and other water sports. **Kielder Castle**, built as a shooting lodge by an 18th-century duke, is folded away in the green valley of the North Tyne, 18 miles beyond the market town of Bellingham, from which it is reached on B 6320 and an unclassified road. It marks the start of the Forest Drive, which climbs 12 miles and over 1,500 feet through many picnic areas and walking trails to join the A 68 just south of the Scottish border at Carter Bar. Oh Me Edge, at the middle of the drive, is just one of many curious place names to be found in these remote northern hills; others include Pity Me, Once Brewed, and Wide Open.

Berwick-upon-Tweed

Following the border all the way east to the North Sea, you'll come to Berwick-upon-Tweed. Mighty Tudor walls ten feet thick, with gateways, ramparts, and bastions, encircle this town, which changed hands 13 times between England and Scotland in the Middle Ages and eventually, in 1482, ended up in England, but only just. A two-mile walk around the top of the walls, which are among the best preserved in Europe (York notwithstanding), affords an overall view of the town, the sea, and the River Tweed.

There was a castle here, too, but most of it now lies beneath the railway station built in 1850 at the northern end of Robert Stephenson's Royal Border Bridge. The bridge spans the Tweed Valley on 28 of the most graceful arches to be seen anywhere.

From the 1,333-foot summit of **Halidon Hill** on the outskirts of Berwick a panorama of the Borders unfolds.

To the south Holy Island and the Farnes are visible on a clear day. Landward are the Cheviot Hills and the Scottish Lowlands, between which the castles at Norham, Etal, and Wark are impassive survivors of historic battles on Flodden Field (where the English vanquished the Scots in the 16th century) and at Carham (where in 1018 the victorious Scots claimed all the land between the Tweed and Edinburgh as their spoil). In the distance, above the sleepy town of Wooler, is Humbleton Hill, where Hotspur and his father obliterated the Scots' army led by Lord Douglas. Part I of Shakespeare's *Henry IV* opens with the news of that battle. Halidon Hill itself was the site of another conflict in which the Scots were defeated.

Hadrian's Wall

The ancient wall stretched 73 miles—or 80 Roman miles—from Bowness (Ituna) on the Solway Firth in the west to Wallsend-on-Tyne (Segedunum) in the east. It was originally composed of stone 10 feet thick and 15 feet high, and, in the middle reaches where limestone and mortar were in short supply, of turf 12 feet high on a 20-foot-wide base. The turf construction did not stand up too well to the rigors of the Pennine winters; its builders may have rushed the job and, in any case, were unused to working in such wet and windy conditions. After a mere 60 or 70 years the wall had to be rebuilt and was then executed in stone eight feet wide. It was an enormous construction job, but the Roman Empire, with eight centuries of conquest and colonization behind it when it invaded Britain, was equal to the task.

Every Roman mile (1,620 yards) along the wall a fort, or mile castle, was placed. The auxiliary troops who manned these forts during a 250-year period came from all over the Roman Empire, of which this was the northernmost bastion. As Parnesius, a centurion of the seventh cohort of the 13th Legion, says in *Puck of Pook's Hill* by Rudyard Kipling: "Just when you think you are at the world's end, you see a smoke from East to West as far as the eye can turn, and then, under it, also as far as the eye can stretch, houses and temples, shops and theatres, barracks and granaries, trickling along like dice behind—always behind—one long, low, rising and falling, and hiding and showing line of towers. And that is the Wall!"

A more recent feat of civil engineering, the Tyne Valley railway built in the 1830s, runs between Carlisle and Newcastle alongside Hadrian's Wall. Haltwhistle, Bardon Mill, and Hexham are convenient stops for visiting three of the best-preserved and most interesting Roman sites, which are also easily reached off the main A 69 road. Yet another way of seeing the wall (and Kielder Water or Durham Cathedral as well) is in a Cessna Skylane from Newcastle or Tees-side airports. Tel: (0325) 33-27-52 for details.

Vindolanda (in present-day Chesterholm) was a fort on the Stanegate, or "Stone Way," and it has been excavated and restored to give a vivid impression of garrison life 17 to 19 centuries ago. In the museum, a wood tablet sent to a Roman soldier from a loving relative, perhaps his mother, reads in translation: "I have sent you pairs of socks and from Sattia two pairs of sandals and two pairs of underpants." The poet W. H. Auden put himself into the sandals of a legionnaire on guard when he wrote,

> Over the heather the wet wind blows,
> I've lice in my tunic
> and a cold in my nose.
> The rain comes pattering out of the sky,
> I'm a Wall soldier, I don't know why.

There are full-scale reconstructions of the turf wall, a turret from the stone wall, and a timber gate tower as well as the *vicus,* the civilian settlement near Vindolanda.

Housesteads (Vercovicium), about two miles east, is the best preserved of the forts actually on the wall, which snakes over the green hills and can be walked for a considerable stretch. The fort extended over five acres and housed 1,000 soldiers. Its ruins, dating from A.D. 122 to the end of the fourth century, include walls, gateways, granaries, barracks, and a latrine with a flushing tank.

In a wooded valley half a mile west of Chollerford, between Housesteads and Newcastle, **Chesters Fort** (Cilurnum) contains the best surviving example of a Roman military bathhouse, used by the 500-strong cavalry *ala* that was based here. Stones from the bridge that carried Hadrian's Wall across the North Tyne can be seen on the riverbank opposite the bathhouse.

Dere Street

At Corbridge (junction of A 68 and A 69), Dere Street, the Roman road linking York and the far north, met Stanegate running east to west. This was the site of **Corstopitum**, a supply town for the cohorts guarding the wall. The ruins of their military compounds, temples, storehouses, and granaries survive, and the museum contains an intricately sculpted fountainhead known as the Corbridge Lion.

Dere Street can still be traced north of Scotch Corner on the B 6275, which joins A 68 near Bishop Auckland. The Roman fort of Vinovium stood at Binchester on the River Wear, downriver from the 800-acre park surrounding Auckland Castle, seat of the bishops of Durham. Stones were carried from this fort to build the **Saxon church** at nearby Escomb that is thought to be the earliest complete example of its kind anywhere in Britain. The splendid Roman chancel arch and a stone, upside down with LEG VI (Sixth Legion) carved in it in the north wall, as well as diamond broaching in many other stones, display the antiquity of **Escomb Church**.

At Lanchester, north of Bishop Auckland, a Norman church was again built from stones from the fort of Longovicium, and there is a Roman altar in the porch. North of Corbridge, long, straight stretches of the A 68 retrace the route of Dere Street, which was wide enough to take two lanes of chariots. Stretches were built on embankments raised above the surrounding moor, making it, literally, the High Road to Scotland, which it remains to this day.

GETTING AROUND

Most visitors to Britain from overseas arrive in the southeast, but the distance involved in travelling to the North is not great: 300 miles at the outside. The InterCity trains take three to four hours from London, and express buses using the motorways, five to six hours. There are numerous interconnecting bus and rail services between towns. If time is at a premium, it is possible to fly from Gatwick or Heathrow to regional airports such as Newcastle or Tees-side. They also handle some international flights, but the majority go to either Manchester or Prestwick (Glasgow), both of which are more convenient starting points for touring the North Country than London; car rental can be arranged easily at these airports. There are sea-ferry routes from North Shields on the Tyne to Scandinavia, between Liverpool and Ireland, and between Heysham (Lancaster) and the Isle of Man.

An excellent source of information on North Country walks (the various "ways" referred to in the chapter above) is the Ramblers Association, 1–5 Wandsworth Road, London SW8 2XX; Tel: (071) 582-6878.

ACCOMMODATIONS REFERENCE

▶ **Belmont Manor. Windermere** LA23 1LN. Tel: (0539) 43-33-16.

▶ **Black Swan Hotel.** Market Place, **Helmsley** YO6 5BJ. Tel: (0439) 704-66; Telex: 57538; Fax: (0439) 701-74; in U.S., (212) 541-4400 or (800) 223-5672.

▶ **County Thistle Hotel.** Neville Street, **Newcastle-upon-Tyne** NE99 1AH. Tel: (0912) 32-24-71; Telex: 537873; Fax: (0912) 32-12-85; in U.S., (212) 714-2233, (800) 522-5568, or (800) 223-6764.

▶ **Embleton Hall. Longframlington,** near Morpeth NE65 8DT. Tel: (0665) 702-49.

▶ **Field Head House.** Outgate, **Hawkshead** LA22 0PY. Tel: (0966) 62-40.

▶ **Linden Hall Hotel.** Longhorsley, **Morpeth** NE65 8XG. Tel: (0670) 51-66-11; Telex: 538224; Fax: (0670) 885-44.

▶ **Lodore Swiss Hotel.** Borrowdale, **Keswick** CA12 5UX. Tel: (0596) 842-85; Telex: 64305; Fax: (0596) 843-43; in U.S., (402) 493-4747 or (800) 44-UTELL.

▶ **Lupton Tower. Lupton,** near Kirkby Lonsdale LA6 2PR. Tel: (0448) 74-00.

▶ **Michaels Nook Country House Hotel. Grasmere** LA22 9RP. Tel: (0966) 54-96; Telex: 65329; Fax: (0966) 57-65.

▶ **Northcote Manor.** Northcote Road, **Blackburn** BB6 8BE. Tel: (0254) 405-55; Fax: (0254) 465-68.

▶ **North Lakes Gateway Hotel.** Ullswater Road, **Penrith** CA11 8QT. Tel: (0768) 681-11; Telex: 64257; Fax: (0768) 682-91.

▶ **Royal County Hotel.** Old Elvet, **Durham** DH1 3JN. Tel: (0913) 86-68-21; Telex: 538238; Fax: (0913) 86-07-04.

▶ **Royal Hotel.** Queens Square, **Bowness-on-Windermere** LA23 3DB. Tel: (0966) 230-45; Telex: 65464; Fax: (0966) 224-98; in U.S., (602) 954-7600 or (800) 528-1234.

▶ **Royal Station Hotel.** Neville Street, **Newcastle-upon-Tyne** NE1 5DH. Tel: (0912) 32-07-81; Telex: 53681; Fax: (0912) 22-07-86; in U.S., (212) 684-1820 or (800) 221-1074.

▶ **White Swan Hotel.** Bondgate Within, **Alnwick** NE66 1TD. Tel: (0665) 60-21-09; Telex: 53168; Fax: (0665) 51-04-00.

▶ **Wood Hall. Linton,** near Wetherby LS22 4JA. Tel: (0937) 672-71; Fax: (0937) 643-53.

▶ **Wordsworth Hotel. Grasmere** LA22 9SW. Tel: (096) 655-92; Telex: 65329; Fax: (0966) 57-65.

WALES

By Charlotte Atkins

Formerly the deputy editor of The UK Holiday Guide *and* Family Holidays in Britain *magazines, Charlotte Atkins is now Travel Editor of* Woman's Own *magazine and a regular contributor to* The Sunday Times *of London. She is also the coauthor of* The French Channel Ports.

While the Principality of Wales, that pouch bulging on England's left hip into the Irish Sea, shares the English monarchy and government, it has its own distinct culture. Indeed, Wales is the nearest "foreign" country to England. Yet British subjects don't need a passport to visit, and there's no language barrier—although Wales, of course, has one of the oldest languages and literatures in Europe.

Wales is Celtic from the moment you pass the "*Croeso i Cymru*" ("Welcome to Wales") signs on the border. In fact, some people argue that place names like Llanrhaeadr (the village of the waterfall), Betws-y-Coed (the sanctuary in the wood), and Llangollen (pronounced Lan-goth-lan) were invented to trip the foreign tongue.

The visitor, however, will encounter no problems. Everyone speaks English—although for many it's a second language. In Gwynedd, the most northwesterly county, for example, around 75 percent of the children are monoglot Welsh until they go to school, and in the morning the village streets echo to hails of "*bore da!*" ("good morning"). The most obvious remnants of the Celtic heritage are people's names: At today's christening ceremonies, first names like Angharad, Gareth, Bet, Rhiannon, Thomas, and Megan are coupled with centuries-old surnames like

Jones, Roberts, Evans, Lloyd, and Davies. These are all unmistakably Welsh. And besides its own patron saint, David, honored on March 1, a national flag and emblem (a red dragon on a green and white background), and its own postage stamps, Wales lays claim to the *eisteddfod* (pronounced eye-steth-vod), a festival of music, poetry, and dancing that is a significant part of the country's tradition.

There are several such jamborees held throughout Wales every year, but the two most famous are the National Eisteddfod (the first week in August) and the International Music Eisteddfod (held every July in a field just outside Llangollen).

MAJOR INTEREST

Snowdonia National Park and Snowdon Mountain Railway
Portmeirion Italianate village
Castles, especially Harlech, Conwy, and Caernarfon in North Wales
Isle of Anglesey
International Music Eisteddfod in Llangollen
Ffestiniog Railway
Pembrokeshire Coast National Park
Brecon Beacons National Park
Cardiff

Although there is no geographical north/south divide in Wales, the two areas are different. It's even said that a northerner finds it difficult to understand a southerner—and vice versa—when conversing in Welsh. Rock-solid community spirit runs high in North Wales. When a villager dies, for example, it's not unusual for 500 to turn out for the funeral. The north also has the edge on rural solitude—apart from a pocket of heavy industry on the banks of the River Dee, most of the area is devoted to mountains, lakes, hill farms, rivers, crofts (country cottages), and sheep-farming pastures (Wales grazes a total of six million sheep).

Slate has been a part of everyday life in North Wales for centuries. In the 19th century the industry boomed, and an escalating demand for the product throughout the world led to the development of ports (such as Porthmadog and Dinorwig) and the building of slate-heaving railways (for example, the narrow-gauge Ffestiniog Railway, which runs from Porthmadog to Blaenau Ffestiniog).

With the decline in demand, most of the quarries ceased production, but several, especially those at Blaenau Ffestiniog and Bethesda, have responded to a new demand from visitors who come to pay their respects to the area's industrial archaeology and see demonstrations of the skills that earlier generations had mastered.

The majority of the Welsh population lives in the more heavily industrialized south, particularly around Port Talbot and the capital city, Cardiff. Here steel making and manufacturing have provided most of the employment for as long as anyone can remember, and the once green and peaceful valleys are havens of coal production, which at one time supplied the rest of Britain. In its mid-19th-century heyday, the thriving Welsh coal industry attracted workers from England, Ireland, Italy, Greece, and Spain, but as competition grew the Welsh mines went into steady decline; by the end of World War I many coal-mining villages were silent and deserted.

At just over 8,000 square miles, Wales is so small that the sea is always within easy reach. Seaside towns have obvious appeal to families. To the north, there are the brash and breezy Rhyl, the dignified Victorian resort of Criccieth, dandy Colwyn Bay, and elegant Llandudno. In mid-Wales, there's Aberystwyth, and to the south, Tenby, where massive low-tide sands and gaily painted houses lend an almost Caribbean flavor. Much of the seashore between Harlech and Pwllheli is peppered with recreational vehicles, campsites, and chalets. The rock pools and woody river valleys of the **Gower Peninsula** in the south, the first area in Britain to be designated an Area of Outstanding Natural Beauty, are also popular with vacationers.

Despite its humble proportions, Wales manages to squeeze three of the United Kingdom's ten national parks into its borders, each one an ideal retreat for the touring motorist: Snowdonia, at the top of the map, Brecon Beacons, in the southeast (nudging the border with England at Ross-on-Wye), and Pembrokeshire in the southwest. The designation "national" does not mean that the land is state owned, but there are still plenty of public footpaths to go around.

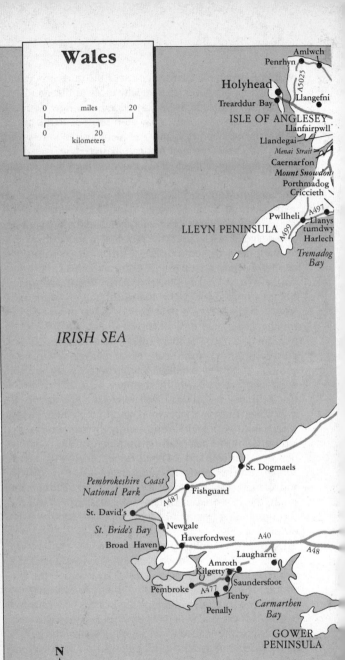

NORTH WALES

Although all of Wales could be tackled in a two-week whip around, it is more sensible to concentrate on one particular part. For first-timers, the north, and particularly Gwynedd in the scenic northwest corner, makes a perfect introduction. In high summer this is the area most popular with British vacationers. The best time to tour is in the spring, when the slopes and fields are covered in daffodils and blossoms, or in autumn, under a crisp blue sky, when the leaves are turning orange brown, sharp frosts turn the bare landscape white, and early-morning mists lend the mountain peaks and river valleys a ghostly air. From October through March most tourist attractions are closed, but the uncluttered landscape more than compensates.

The coast from Prestatyn around to Barmouth is strung with popular holiday towns, and from June through August the broad, shallow, sandy-pebbly beaches are crowded with the bucket-and-spade brigade. The seafronts can generally be relied upon to display all the traditional characteristics of the English seaside: pinball machines along the pier, donkey rides, Punch-and-Judy shows, brightly colored changing huts, Formica-topped café tables, and brass-band stands.

Colwyn Bay has one of the best beaches along the north coast, a sweeping arc of golden sand fringed by a wide promenade built for deck-chair lounging. It's also the haunt of yachtsmen, the clattering of halyards around the jetties competing with the livelier sounds of pedal boats and fairground Wurlitzers. The giant flumes at Rhyl's Leisure Centre, one of the largest amusement parks in Britain, echo to the sounds of frenzied screams.

But **Llandudno** is undoubtedly the grande dame of North Wales's resorts. Her claims to fame are her size (the largest seaside resort in the country) and her literary association with the Reverend Charles Lutwidge Dodgson, a.k.a. Lewis Carroll, the author of *Alice's Adventures in Wonderland,* who lived and wrote here. Don't miss the White Rabbit memorial opposite the Gogarth Abbey Hotel, unveiled in 1933 by David Lloyd George as part of the celebration of Carroll's centenary. Llandudno's other attractions are less cerebral; the wide bay revives childhood beach memories beside the Victorian pier, one of the best such examples in Britain, now lined by postcard, souvenir, and candy stalls. A stroll along the **West Shore** beach affords staggering views of the Conwy Estuary, Puffin Island, and the Menai Strait. Or you can take a walk or a drive, or ride the cable car or tram up to the visitor center at the top of Great Orme Country Park and Nature Reserve. Little Orme, the headland at the opposite end of town, is smaller but significant to naturalists and bird watchers.

Although the seafront is lined with moderately priced Victorian establishments, the best place to stay in Llandudno is **Bodysgallen Hall**, hidden in the woods just south of town. The building's dark oak paneling, chunky drapes and carpets, antiques, stone-mullioned windows, massive fireplaces, and glorious gardens, backed by moody views of Snowdonia, define it as a world apart from the seaside hostelry. Martin James works wonders in the kitchen.

Out of season the only sounds here are the gentle crashing of waves and the screeching of scavenging sea gulls as the towns sink into hibernation, building up energy for the next summer's onslaught.

Snowdonia National Park

A few miles southwest of Colwyn Bay on A 470 lies Parc Cenedlaethol Eryri ("Land of the Eagles"), the Welsh name for the 840 square miles that lie within the boundary of Snowdonia National Park, tucked into Wales's northwest corner. It includes **Snowdon** itself, the "monstrous peak," as Daniel Defoe described it, at 3,560 feet the highest mountain south of the Scottish border, as well as 13 other summits that are more than 2,900 feet high.

The park roughly covers the Medieval kingdom of Gwynedd, a military stronghold ruled by Owain Glyndwr, one of Wales's greatest heroes. It is a fascinating geographical site, studded with glaciated U-shaped valleys, lakes, razor-sharp mountain edges, and other legacies of its Ice Age torment. It is a mecca for lovers of the outdoors—walkers, backpackers, climbers, pony trekkers, and whitewater canoeists—but even the most sedate tourists will find the peaks, forests, lakes, raging streams, and undulating lowland scenery spectacular.

It wasn't long before a quick-thinking entrepreneur established a restaurant, bar, and shop on Snowdon's summit. The Snowdon Mountain Railway, one of the steam-driven, narrow-gauge "Great Little Trains of Wales," will take you on a four-and-a-half-mile run from Llanberis almost to the top of the mountain at half-hour intervals throughout the summer. But it is arguably more pleasant to climb. The easiest route is the Llanberis Path from **Llanberis** itself—it parallels the railroad tracks for five miles and climbs to 3,200 feet. Dolgellau and Betws-y-Coed are excellent starting points for more challenging, spectacular walks through the park itself.

It's no coincidence that it was here that Sir John Hunt's victorious Everest team of 1953 did their training; or that 88 years earlier Edward Whymper chose the same region to prepare for his conquest of the Matterhorn. The best views of Snowdon are from the Llanberis Pass, where it's easy to pull off the road (if you don't mind appearing sedentary as teams of climbers scale the rocks). On the descent to the wooded valley of Nant Gwynant, another site gives views westward over the shimmering lakes of Gwynant and Dinas. But the finest views of Snowdon are from the parking lot in the tiny village of Rhyd-Ddu, where you feel on top of the mountain, rather than overshadowed by it.

Mull over Snowdon's presence from **Y Bristro** restaurant in Llanberis, a longtime favorite as much with locals as visitors. The menu is set price, but there is a choice of five or six dishes per course, including roast rack of lamb in almond and cream sauce, and salmon or prawns, both smoked locally. There's even a Welsh wine on the list.

The one-street town of **Bala**, especially popular with ramblers, is easily outshone by its five-mile-long lake, Llyn Tegid, also known as **Bala Lake**. Access is easy, and it's possible to completely circumnavigate it by road. One of the few hotels in town to raise its head above mediocre modesty is **Fron Feuno Hall**. Built as a hostel for monks in the 16th century, it was later enlarged to become a family house. There are three large bedrooms, each with its own bathroom and views over the gardens, woods, and lake.

If you don't mind driving in and out a few miles from Bala, there are two commendable hotels on the outskirts. **Tyddyn Llan Country House**, a member of the Welsh Rarebits group of prestigious hotels, is a gray stone Georgian property in the Vale of Edeyrnion, on the road to Llangollen. It bulges with antiques and paintings, passions of its owners, Peter and Bridget Kindred, and the superb quality extends to the evening menu, which features lamb, salmon, and other local specialties. It's also very quiet here—birdsong is the only sound from most bedrooms. Just inside Snowdonia's boundaries, high above the River Dee, is **Dewis Cyfarfod**, a less expensive bed-and-breakfast option. The house is run with special touches, from the bottles of mineral water and novels in the bedrooms to the hot lemon pudding on the dinner table.

Betws-y-Coed, at the confluence of the rivers Conwy, Llugwy, and Lledr, is a major gateway to the national park and, as such, is crowded in summer, particularly on week-ends. Among its gray stone buildings are a handful of Welsh woollen and craft shops, such as **Pennant Crafts**, which sells local pottery, with its characteristic white flower pattern on a dark blue background. As a major tourist spot, the town is well served by hotels and guesthouses. It even has its own Fairy Glen, a waterfall one mile from the village on the A 470 road to Dolgellau and reached by a footpath up from the whitewashed **Fairy Glen Hotel**, a cozy 17th-century house overlooking the River Conwy.

The village of **Portmeirion**, situated about 10 miles south of Snowdon on A 498 on a wooded headland near Porthmadog, is best known as the setting for the cult television series "The Prisoner," although it also inspired Noel Coward to write *Blithe Spirit*. The village itself, at the end of a private road, was the fantasy creation of an eccentric architect, Sir Clough Williams-Ellis, who bought the site in 1925; it resembles a stage set more than a popular holiday village. The community's center point is the 14-room **Portmeirion Hotel**; still in the Williams-Ellis family, it was closed by fire in 1981 but reopened in 1988. The hotel's interior is almost as fantastical as the village. Many rooms are decorated thematically: The mirror room, for example, not for the self-conscious, is lined from floor to ceiling with gilt-framed glass. Another relies solely on Indian imports, while others contain antiques shipped from around the globe. Portmeirion itself exhibits Oriental, Indian, and Italian influences. Twenty of the pastel pink, yellow, and blue houses in the village are self-catering units belonging to the hotel, interspersed with the occasional shop, restaurant, and even a town hall, and leading down to a beautiful sweep of beach and a residents' swimming pool.

Llangollen, buried at the heart of the Dee Valley on A 5, makes an important appearance on the international map every July with its **International Music Eisteddfod**. Hotels are booked up months in advance, hardly surprising when festival participants include the likes of the Vienna Boys Choir. One favorite hotel is the **Bryn Howel**, a 19th-century family-run country house. The town also stirs when orange-and-yellow-coated canoeists hold slalom races on the River Dee. But most of the time Llangollen is the quintessential quiet Welsh town, enough of a backwater for the local laundromat to double as the video store. It attracts a small but steady flow of visitors exploring the valley, calling in at the woollen mill or the pottery works, climbing up to the ruins of the 12th-century fortress—Castell Dinas Bran, which towers over the town—or taking a ride on a horse-drawn barge from the wharf along the canal that parallels the river. The Dee flows through town, and the gardens behind several hotels and restaurants end abruptly at its banks. One such is **Gales**, a restaurant and wine bar that also has eight daintily decorated bedrooms on Bridge Street; another is **Caesar's Restaurant**, right beside the bridge.

The 153-year-old **Ffestiniog Railway** follows a route alongside which heaps of slate were once piled from the massive quarries at Blaenau Ffestiniog. Vacationers now trundle the 26-mile round trip that departs every hour or so from Porthmadog's High Street to **Blaenau Ffestiniog**, one of the most famous slate towns in Wales. A small railway museum in the station supplies history and details. The round trip takes approximately two hours.

Blaenau Ffestiniog is popular for the underground floodlit tours (helmets provided) of the **Llechwedd Slate Caverns** and **Gloddfa Ganol Ffestiniog Mountain Centre**, once the world's largest slate mine and now an open-air museum. Tours take in the machinery in the mill, plus a ride by Land Rover through part of the tunnel system and a newly opened Narrow-Gauge Railway Centre, with both locomotives and rolling stock.

One of the largest studio pottery works in rural Wales is down the road, housed in a converted mill that used to grind flour for ships' biscuits. Pottery is for sale, but you can also tour the workshop and watch craftsmen molding, baking, and painting the earthenware—they'll encourage you to make your own with the help (or hindrance) of a potter's wheel. The building can't be missed; its entire outer wall has been painted by Ed Povey with a mural called *Pots,* which includes the figures of Lloyd George and other less famous local personages. Tourist

Information Centres are located in Llanberis, Blaenau Ffestiniog, Harlech, Bala, Conwy, and Dolgellau.

WELSH CASTLES

Some 700 years ago, King Edward I of England built 17 massive castles to dissuade the fiery Celts from challenging his authority. This enormous campaign to Anglicize Wales cost the King dearly, yet the money was well spent: Apart from one major revolt, his castles succeeded in keeping the peace for the next 100 years.

Built by a small army of workers under a French master mason, the castles marked the end of Welsh independence. But Edward's fortresses (Caernarfon, Conwy, Harlech, and Beaumaris, all in North Wales, are the four most noteworthy) are not the only castles Wales has to offer the visitor. Even earlier, after William the Conqueror had sailed from Normandy in 1066 and seized the English throne, the Normans looked westward from their newly acquired position of strength along the English–Welsh border and spotted a country torn apart by civil war and ripe for conquest. They stormed the land, building castles as symbols of their power. At first, these were simple wooden affairs on top of grassy mounds (or "mottes"); later came massive multiwalled buildings that were the last word in military technique.

Today Wales is stocked with an abundance of Norman and Gothic castles, their aged battlements illustrating more than anything else the country's turbulent history. Politics aside, castles are a vital part of both the heritage of Wales and its glorious landscapes. When they were built they became obvious focal points for civilian settlements, giving the rural Welsh their first taste of urban life. In North Wales they are particularly varied and magnificent and constitute the most concentrated group of Medieval castles in Europe. A large proportion of them are now maintained and managed by Cadw, the Welsh equivalent of English Heritage.

"Put yourself in the mind of an attacking force," advises the Welsh Office, the government body that administers the country. "It's the only way to understand just what castles are all about." The hefty, seemingly impenetrable gateways are nowadays the easiest of entrances. In Medieval days there would usually have been a long ramp followed by a drawbridge. You can probably see just where the drawbridge would have hinged into its original pivot holes. The next line of defense was the portcullis, its sliding grooves clearly visible in the castle walls, followed by the stout doorways of the gate passage. All along the journey attackers would have been picked off by archers and would have had boiling water poured on them from aptly named murder holes.

Harlech Castle

Whether you approach the little town of Harlech (off A 496 in Snowdonia) from the north or the south, the view of its castle as you round the last corner is breathtaking. One of Edward's coastal fortresses, Harlech was built in the late 13th century. It commands the most impressive location of all Welsh castles, perched 200 feet above sea level at the foot of a cliff, overlooking the grand sand-duned sweep of Tremadog Bay and the Royal St. David's Golf Course. It was the last Royalist castle to capitulate to the Parliamentarians in 1647 and in Elizabethan times had been a debtors' prison. Its gates are now open to visitors throughout the year.

A walk around the castle's breezy ramparts on a fine day offers a constant change of scenery: the neck of the Llyn Peninsula, the gray rooftops of Harlech's white houses, a fleet of sand dunes, and the bulk of Mount Snowdon. The castle sits on a promontory once lapped by waves; although the immediately surrounding land is now reclaimed, a stairway still plunges down the rock face to a water gate at the bottom.

The walls of Harlech Castle stand sturdy, but the central core, the Inner Ward, is open to the elements. It is a grassy quadrangle strewn with foundations of walls now only knee high. Apart from a 143-step climb to the top of the gatehouse, there's a freestanding exhibition about the Edwardian conquest in one of the few rooms still intact.

One of Wales's grandest country-house hotels lies at the end of a long driveway in Talsarnau, 3 miles to the north of Harlech. The **Hotel Maes-y-Neuadd** (pronounced Mice-er-Nayeth) is the kind of place that, once you discover it, you will want to keep a secret—especially if you have been lucky enough to get a front bedroom overlooking Snowdon and the Traeth Bach estuary. It's run by two families; one family member, Olive Horsfall, heads the kitchen team, preparing a daily menu of such Welsh specialties as lamb in honey, cider, and rosemary; herrings with apple and sage; and Welsh Amber Pudding (apple tart with orange curd and marmalade). Lunch reservations are essential at the popular restaurant (Tel: 0766-78-02-00).

Conwy Castle

The most important room inside all Medieval castles is the Great Hall, and the one at Conwy is a grand example. Although it is now roofless and floorless, it's easy to imagine the three gaping fireplaces in full flame and the fine tracery windows in their prime in the Middle Ages. From the farthest tower, built high on a buttress of rock, the view is spectacular, looking down on streets still laid out on their original Medieval lines and across to the estuary of the foaming River Conwy.

The old town of Conwy itself, on the coast north of Snowdon on A 55, sits wrapped in three quarters of a mile of Medieval stone walls. On a stroll along the crest, no place for acute vertigo sufferers, you will encounter only sea gulls on their battlement perches. In Conwy's High Street an Elizabethan town house, Plas Mawr, now serves as the headquarters for the Royal Cambrian Academy of Art; the Visitor Centre, in Rose Hill Street, has exhibitions, film shows, and a crafts store. Down on the quay, Conwy possesses what is reputed to be the smallest house in Britain, furnished as a mid-Victorian Welsh cottage.

Caernarfon Castle

This "camp on the land opposite Anglesey," as the name translates, shot to modern-day fame with the investiture of the present Prince of Wales in July 1969. On the day of the ceremony 500 million television viewers worldwide tuned in to the castle.

Caernarfon Castle, which is just across the Menai Strait from the Isle of Anglesey in North Wales, looks the part—after all, it was Edward I's royal seat of government for North Wales. Shaped like an hourglass, its interior once housed a 100-foot Great Hall where all of the castle's residents could eat, drink, and be merry—though perhaps their mirth waned when the food arrived stone cold after being carried from the kitchen on the far side of the courtyard (a deliberate segregation because of fire hazards). In the Eagle Tower you can see a Prince of Wales exhibition and trace the royal family tree. And you can see how the crafty Edward made his own son, born in Caernarfon, Prince of Wales after subduing the Welsh princes.

The mammoth Caernarfon Castle and its towering cliff walls are best encompassed from the opposite bank of the River Seiont. Its pretty bands of red sandstone were inspired by the spectacular fifth-century walls at Constantinople, which King Edward had admired on his travels. **Seiont Manor Hotel** in Llanrug east of Caernarfon has taken its name from the salmon-filled waters that flow through its estate. The gardens also contain a traditional millpond, an herb garden, and a lake; the building is the original farmstead of a Georgian manor house.

The town of **Caernarfon**, on the Menai Strait, is small and quiet, little more than a square, a modest handful of stores, the Black Boy Inn, and a castle. Drive directly south on route A 487 and you cross the neck of the Llyn Peninsula. Although on the map it looks as if its landscapes will be flat, on the ground you are in for surprisingly bumpy scenery. This neglected limb of land, the "Land's End of Wales," basks in accolades as an Area of Outstanding Natural Beauty, as well as boasting David Lloyd George's boyhood home at Llanystumdwy. His simple grave on the banks of the River Dwyfor is much visited, as are the stone cottage opposite the Feathers public house that was his home until 1890 and the town museum, which contains many mementos of his political career.

The Llyn Peninsula also boasts one of the best hotels/ restaurants in Wales, Chris Chown's **Plas Bodegroes** (pronounced Bod E Groyce, "the place of rosehips") in Pwllheli. It is small, with only five bedrooms, but very beautiful, surrounded by beech woods and six acres of garden. Food, supplied by a network of locals, includes Welsh black beef, free-range veal, chickens and ducks, and salmon and sea trout fished by the Bangor boats, all served with organically grown vegetables and local wild mushrooms. Five-course menus cost around £20. If you stay the night you'll find that bedrooms are given equally tender loving care—the rooms with four-posters have particularly worthy views.

Other Castles

Criccieth Castle stands above its tiny, timeless seaside town on the Llyn Peninsula's southern flank. It is backed by the mountains of Snowdonia and fronted by the broad sweep of Tremadog Bay. On a clear day you can see Harlech Castle in the distance. Although there's some disagreement about who actually built it, majority opinion seems to support the view that it is a native Welsh castle to which Edward added a few strengthening touches. Its main feature is a twin-towered gatehouse, a rare type of structure, built by Llywelyn the Great. It is certainly a much simpler, more irregularly shaped, and altogether far less sophisticated affair than any of the pure Edwardian castles.

If Dracula had owned a Welsh pied-à-terre it could well have been **Dolwyddelan Castle**, about 5 miles southwest of Betws-y-Coed on A 470. Not that there's anything remotely Gothic about this native Welsh structure, but if you see it wrapped in patches of mist and bathed with eerie shafts of light, its simple solitary square tower is quite awesome. The castle is barely penetrable, even today. Its first line of defense is a five-bar gate, followed by a farmyard full of barking dogs. Next there is a trudge up a steep track, through a siege of chomping Friesian cattle (and a final slosh through mud if there's been any rain), and then a perilous climb up the inside of the tower to its battlements, from where the view over the Lledr valley is, literally, breathtaking. It clearly wasn't weaponry that kept the enemy at bay here—physical exhaustion sufficed.

Rumor has it that Llywelyn was born here, but he wasn't. (It is likely that he was born in a castle built earlier somewhere down in the valley.) It is almost certain, however, that he built Dolwyddelan. The reason may be difficult to fathom, since the castle's isolated position seems to bestow no defensive role whatsoever. But it did, in fact, guard an old road, the Medieval pass from Meirionnydd to the Vale of Conwy. From the battlements, restored by the Victorians, its location makes much more sense.

All of Edward's castles had the sea in common—or at least a river leading to it. Since the English communities were so isolated in the midst of hostile terrain, it was clearly impractical to bring supplies overland across miles of Wales and utterly impossible to reach the castles in times of siege. At **Rhuddlan Castle**, a mile or two inland from Rhyl, an army of diggers worked six days a week for three years to divert the canal, which is still the main artery of the River Clwyd as you see it today.

North Wales contains a number of weird and wonderful 19th-century shams. From the outside, **Penrhyn Castle**, on the A 55 Conwy road 2 miles east of Bangor, looks like an ancient monument, with its insurmountable walls, toothy battlements, turrets, and the castellated like. But its roots date no further back than the 19th century, when the architect Thomas Hopper built the neo-Gothic structure for an army of servants rather than soldiers. It is an utter fake, an extravagance designed to reflect the enormous wealth accumulated by the Douglas Pennants from their sugar interests in the West Indies and later from the nearby slate mines.

Outside, the grassy banks are awash with nodding daffodils throughout the spring, while inside there is hardly an undecorated surface in the entire place. The furniture, wall panelings, and mighty doors were all made specially for the house, mostly from oaks grown on the estate, and carved with motifs that echo those found on the exterior walls. There are highly polished slate fireplaces and even a slate bed, weighing nearly a ton, on which Queen Victoria refused to sleep. The castle also houses a huge collection of dolls. Whether or not the style of Penrhyn is to your taste, one thing is certain: You can't possibly ignore it.

THE ISLAND OF ANGLESEY AND BEAUMARIS CASTLE

It can be snowing in Snowdonia, they say, while daffodils are blooming in Anglesey. Separated from the Llyn Peninsula by the Menai Strait but easily reached on the Menai Suspension Bridge or the neighboring Britannia Bridge, the island of Anglesey has 125 miles of coastline. The clear blue waters at Trearddur Bay in the west are ideal for swimming, sailing, and water-skiing, while the cruising center at Holyhead, the chunk of northwest Anglesey that got away, bursts at the seams every August for the Menai Strait Regatta Fortnight boat races. Away from the water there are five golf courses, sports centers at Amlwch and Llangefni, and a bird-watching reservoir three miles long. And if you thought Snowdonia had the monopoly on heights, you'll think differently after a bracing walk up the main street of Moelfre village.

Anglesey's **Beaumaris Castle**, in the town of Beaumaris, sits right at the end of a street of Georgian houses, making the town one of the prettiest in Wales. It used to be one of the busiest, too, in the days when its ferry was Anglesey's only link to the mainland. Since the construction of bridges, however, Beaumaris has become a peaceful backwater.

The immediately obvious difference between Beaumaris and the rest of Edward's castles is that it doesn't perch on a haughty rock. It stands on a flat, seemingly vulnerable stretch of marshland, so all its barriers had to be constructed. The most perfectly designed concentric castle in Britain, Beaumaris is a highly compact unit—thus defenders on the higher inner walls could fire their missiles over the heads of their fellows on the outer wall. Today the fields are full of passive bowls players and a few gardeners.

Beaumaris, built in the 1290s, was Edward's last Welsh bastion, and it remains unfinished. Edward had competing demands on his resources, and since peace was established in this part of the world at about this time, Beaumaris was no longer a priority.

Ye Olde Bull's Head inn on Castle Street is almost as old as the castle. Details reveal its age (over 500 years): back-breakingly low ceilings, timber beams, and a courtyard where stagecoach horses were once watered. The place is run by Keith Rothwell, David Robertson, and their wives, who will be happy to fill you in on the latest fish catches, the inn's culinary specialty.

As you leave Anglesey, pick up a platform ticket from the railway station in the village of Llanfairpwll. No ordinary ticket this, it contains all 58 letters of the town's proper name: Llanfairpwllgwyngyllgogerychwyrndrobwll-llantysyliogogogoch, which roughly translates as "St. Mary's (church) by the white aspen over the Whirlpool and St. Tysilio's (church) by the red cave."

SOUTH WALES

Pembrokeshire Coast National Park

The smallest of the three national parks in Wales, **Pembrokeshire**'s 225 square miles mainly hug the southwest coast in the form of the **Pembrokeshire Coast Path**. The path follows the ups, downs, ins, and outs of the shoreline of Britain's only coastal national park for 167 miles, from St. Dogmaels in the north to Amroth in the south, taking in the enormous sweep of St. Bride's Bay. The ragged outline and craggy cliffs of Pembrokeshire resemble the coastline of Cornwall, but this beautiful corner of Wales remains far less known and visited. Even during the peak holiday season it feels remote, a wild seascape where you can wander for hours on end without meeting a soul. Come here in the depths of winter and you could be at the very edge of the world.

Apart from the beauty of its landscape, the Pembrokeshire coastline enjoys the year-round presence of beautiful wildflowers and hordes of seabirds, including cormorants, shags, choughs, guillemots, and razorbills. The area is also a favorite haunt of geologists, who come to examine rocks that date back 2,000 million years; even the untrained eye will appreciate the elemental forces that have twisted and folded the land masses and the erosive power of the sea that has created caves, arches, stacks, and other geological features. Although this is now rather a remote, thinly populated region, the coast path abounds in evidence of earlier inhabitants in the flint chippings, left by Stone Age people some 10,000 years ago, and in the Iron Age forts built on several promontories.

There is a halfway point on the Pembrokeshire Coast Path—in culture as well as in miles. The so-called **Landsker Line**, drawn inland at Newgale, marks the northern limits of Norman influence in Wales. To the south are bold, castellated church towers, English village names, and a relatively dense pattern of settlement. To the north the villages are more scattered, the chapels more modest, and the village names Welsh.

The path can be overgrown in places, especially in the season when it is little used. Wear long pants to protect yourself from the gorse and brambles. Because many of the villages are little more than a clutch of cottages, chapel, and pub, accommodation has to be planned carefully, although hot, filling lunches (often based on seafood) can almost always be bought in pubs. Four miles off the path as it passes near Fishguard (an unattractive town whose sole raison d'être is as a departure point for ferries to southern Ireland) is the **Penlan Oleu**, a renovated Welsh farmhouse. It scores high on location, with views over Fishguard Bay, and has everything the weary walker could want—simple rooms, wholesome dinners (often fish from the bay), and huge breakfasts in the morning.

Another nice place to break the wearying journey is the resort of **Tenby**, built on a peninsula and surrounded by sea on three sides. Its pastel pink, yellow, blue, and green houses and seafront hotels have drawn holiday visitors for two centuries with the promise of health-giving sea breezes. Described as one of the most romantic spots in Europe, it has a network of casbah-like alleyways of shops and cafés that echo to the screeches of gulls. **Mangle's Pantry**, serving thick vegetable soups, ploughman's platters, and homemade apple crumble, is a good lunch stop. Overnighters are a three-minute drive away from a wonderful hotel in the village of Penally, Steven and Elleen Warren's **Penally Abbey**. It has been their home for five years, and the personal touch is what makes it so special—there is no reception desk, for example—but the informality disguises a keen, low-key professionalism. The bedrooms are large and very beautiful, with original arched doors and four-posters. There's a small, heated indoor pool for weary feet and the kind of candlelit dinners that would carry anyone through another week's trekking.

The coastal path next passes through **St. David's**, the smallest city in Britain. The modestly sized cathedral (which defines it as a city) and the remains of the Bishop's Palace sit incongruously down in a dip, strategically built there to be hidden from invading Vikings. Although the cathedral now ranks low on Britain's ecclesiastical scale, it was once a vital center of pilgrimage—two visits to St. David's equaled one to Rome or Canterbury. The whitewashed **St. Non's Hotel**, yards from the cathedral, takes its name from the mother of St. David, the country's patron saint. It's not fancy but perfectly comfortable, and the food, though publike, is filling.

St. Bride's Hotel in Saundersfoot, on the edge of the park, is an excellent place to start or finish a trip along the path. Worn out walkers will find a night of modestly priced luxury—perhaps a two-hour soak in a bath. You need to wear something smart for dinner, but it's worth the effort just for the views over Carmarthen Bay.

The Boat House, Dylan Thomas's blue, sea-shaken home from 1949 until his death in 1953, is ten miles east of Saundersfoot in Laugharne (pronounced "Larn"). Built on a rocky breakwater, the house, particularly the wooden hut where Thomas penned *Under Milk Wood* and other works, has stunning views of the estuary. It's now a "house of information," with relics and memoirs of the poet's life. Nearby, fans can down a pint at Thomas's favorite wateringhole, Brown's Hotel; you can also buy copies of his works in the tiny bookshop across the street and visit the churchyard of St. Martin's, where he is buried.

Pembrokeshire Coast National Park Information Centres are at St. David's, Haverfordwest, Pembroke, Tenby, Fishguard, Broad Haven, and Kilgetty.

Brecon Beacons National Park

Wales's third national park is in South Wales north of Cardiff and west of Pembrokeshire. Brecon Beacons's 519 square miles of high hills, crags, and bleak moorland is effectively three distinct areas, namely, the western flank, an empty upland wilderness dominated by the Black Mountain; the shapely Brecon region; and the flat-topped Black Mountains in the east (not to be confused with the singular and solitary Black Mountain). Apart from the park's geographical high points, topped by the 2,907 feet of Pen-y-Fan, the area contains wooded patches, farmlands, lakes, and the gentle valley of the River Usk. In common with its two sisters, it attracts a vast number of outdoor enthusiasts (particularly pony trekkers) as well as people who tour by car.

Good hotels are well spaced. The park's natural focal point is the town of **Brecon**, whose narrow streets and tiny shops are dominated by the massive 13th-century **Priory Church of St. John the Evangelist**, towering high above the River Honddu. **Brecon Castle**, built by William the Conqueror's half brother, is best viewed from the gardens of the **Castle of Brecon Hotel**, suitably high up on Castle Square, with views across the Usk valley and the imposing Brecon Beacons. Or head for the market town of Crickhowell, where the kitchen at the **Bear Hotel**, a family-run 15th-century coaching inn in the center, serves young salmon caught by fishermen in the coracles (traditional small, rounded boats made of intertwined willow and hazel), as well as local lamb, wild duck, and *swein* (an old Welsh word for swine).

Cardiff

Wales is not a country of big cities, as the modest proportions of its capital city (population 277,000) testify. Even the most expensive hotels and restaurants, concentrated around the triangle of roads formed by Westgate Street, Castle Street, and High Street/St. Mary Street, charge prices comparable to those in a provincial English city.

Cardiff, down on the southeastern coast of Wales, is an attractive, green city facing England across the mouth of the Severn, its pleasant aesthetics helped along by the fact that its more prestigious monuments are built in local white Portland stone and are floodlit during civic functions. **Cardiff Castle**, bang in the center of town, is really a three-in-one affair, a stylistic hodgepodge with thick Roman outer walls, a Norman keep, and a 19th-century wing full of richly decorated rooms. But the castle constitutes only one seventh of the Civic Centre—its neighbors, all worthy of attention, are the Law Courts, the City Hall, the Welsh Office, the University College, the Institute of Science and Technology, and the National Museum of Wales. This latter is essential viewing for enthusiasts of all things Welsh, as well as for fans of French Impressionist painting.

Cardiff's covered "arcades" add a dimension of interest to the modern, could-be-anywhere shopping arteries. Their Art Nouveau entrances are heralded by such names as Morgan, Royal, Oxford, and Dominion. Down these narrow alleyways lurk specialist, antiquary, eccentric, and crafts stores, among them **Lear's Bookshop** (the largest in town) in the Royal Arcade and **Castle Welsh Crafts** in Castle Street.

The Royal Hotel on St. Mary's Street is a Cardiff institution with a deservedly faithful clientele. But if you prefer to stay in green-belt country and make occasional forays to the city, a good choice would be the **Celtic Manor**, a 19th-century house with huge bedrooms in Coldra Woods, 12 miles out of town along the M 4 to Newport. Although essentially a businessman's hotel, with traffic roaring below the windows on the M 4, the place has a lot of charm, woodland views, good sports facilities, amd an impressive French restaurant.

GETTING AROUND
Some corners of Britain demand a car; Wales is one of them. The M 4 motorway runs from London to Newport, Cardiff, and Swansea (it takes roughly two and a half hours to Cardiff). Visitors to North Wales can take the M 1 and M 6, and then join the A 5. Apart from the stretch of M 4, which runs well into South Wales just north of the Gower Peninsula, there are no motorways in Wales, although the "A" roads are fast and wide.

Regular InterCity trains run from London to Cardiff (two hours) and Chester, just across the border from North Wales (three hours). Cars can be rented at both stations.

ACCOMMODATIONS REFERENCE

▶ **Bear Hotel.** High Street, **Crickhowell,** Powys NP8 1BW. Tel: (0873) 81-04-08; Fax: (0873) 81-16-96.

▶ **Bodysgallen Hall. Llandudno,** Gwynedd LL30 1RS. Tel: (0492) 58-44-66; Telex: 617163; Fax: (0492) 58-25-19; in U.S., (212) 535-9530 or (800) 223-5581.

▶ **Bryn Howel Hotel and Restaurant. Llangollen,** Clwyd LL20 7UW. Tel: (0978) 86-03-31; Fax: (0978) 86-01-19.

▶ **Castle of Brecon Hotel.** Castle Square, **Brecon,** Powys LD3 9DB. Tel: (0874) 46-11; Telex: 57515; Fax: (0874) 37-37.

▶ **Celtic Manor.** Coldra Woods, **Newport,** Gwent NP6 2YA. Tel: (0633) 41-30-00; Fax: (0633) 41-29-10.

▶ **Dewis Cyfarfod. Llandderfel,** Bala, Gwynedd LL23 7DR. Tel: (0678) 32-43.

▶ **Fairy Glen Hotel. Betws-y-Coed,** Gwynedd LL24 0SH. Tel: (0690) 22-69.

▶ **Fron Feuno Hall. Bala,** Gwynedd LL23 7YF. Tel: (0678) 52-11-15.

▶ **Gales.** 18 Bridge Street, **Llangollen,** Clwyd LL20 8PF. Tel: (0978) 86-00-89; Fax: (0978) 86-13-13.

▶ **Hotel Maes-y-Neuadd. Talsarnau,** Gwynedd LL47 6YA. Tel: (0766) 78-02-00; Fax: (0766) 78-02-11; in U.S., (212) 684-1820 or (800) 221-1074.

▶ **Ye Olde Bull's Head.** Castle Street, **Beaumaris,** Isle of Anglesey, Gwynedd LL58 8AP. Tel: (0248) 81-03-29; Fax: (0248) 81-12-94.

▶ **Penally Abbey. Penally,** near Tenby, Pembrokeshire, Dyfed SA70 7PY. Tel: (0834) 30-33.

▶ **Penlan Oleu. Llanychaer,** Fishguard, Dyfed SA65 9TL. Tel: (0348) 88-13-14.

▶ **Plas Bodegroes Hotel and Restaurant. Pwllheli** LL53 5TH. Tel: (0758) 61-23-63; Fax: (0758) 70-12-47.

▶ **Portmeirion Hotel. Portmeirion,** Gwynedd LL48 6ET. Tel: (0766) 77-02-28; Fax: (0766) 77-13-31.

▶ **The Royal Hotel.** St. Mary's Street, **Cardiff** CF1 1LL. Tel: (0222) 38-33-21; Fax: (0222) 22-22-38; in U.S., (212) 986-4373 or (800) 223-5608.

▶ **St. Bride's Hotel.** St. Bride's Hill, **Saundersfoot,** Dyfed SA69 9NH. Tel: (0834) 81-23-04; Telex: 48350; Fax: (0834) 81-33-03.

▶ **St. Non's Hotel. St. David's,** Haverfordwest, Dyfed SA62 6RJ. Tel: (0437) 72-02-39; Fax: (0437) 72-18-39.

▶ **Seiont Manor Hotel. Llanrug,** Caernarfon, Gwynedd LL55 2AQ. Tel: (0286) 768-87; Fax: (0286) 28-40.

▶ **Tyddyn Llan Country House. Llandrillo,** near Corwen, Clwyd LL21 0ST. Tel: and Fax: (0490) 842-64.

THE INDUSTRIAL HERITAGE

By Anthony Burton

After leaving a career in publishing, Anthony Burton has been writing full-time for the past 22 years. He has concentrated on the industrial and transport history of his native Britain and has written several books and television and radio series on those subjects.

The Industrial Revolution, which began in Britain in the middle of the 18th century, was one of the turning points of history. It also brought in the filth and noise of the first industrial towns, the squalor of slums, and the hard, monotonous, grinding toil of the first factories. But that pain has become a distant memory, and what is left is a story of endeavor, ingenuity, and pioneering spirit. The physical remains of that revolution, most of which are located from the Midlands to the north and in Wales, are as important and fascinating as the Roman ruins or the country estates that have been standard fare on the British tourist menu for generations.

In this chapter we depart from our format of focusing on a defined region because the important sites of the Industrial Revolution are widely dispersed.

It sometimes seems from historical accounts that industry appeared, full-fledged, somewhere around 1760. But recognizable industrial activity dates back far beyond that year, and those who want a truly romantic start to the history of industry cannot do better than to head for the village of **Pumpsaint** in Dyfed, Wales. The Romans came here in search of wealth and found it in what is now the **Dolaucothi gold mine**. It is a vast site where the Roman engineers diverted water from the nearby Rivers Cothi and Annell and used it to wash away the topsoil to expose the rock with its veins of rich ore. Later, the Romans quarried out the stone and dug tunnels deep into the hillside. Centuries after that, Victorian engineers came back to reopen the mines, creating a labyrinth of tunnels and shafts. Mining engineers now take groups into this underground world.

Coal

Coal mines are more commonplace than gold mines, and it was coal that literally fueled the Industrial Revolution. At their peak, British mines were turning out nearly 300 million tons of coal a year, and mining dominated many of the industrial areas. The world of the miner was, however, a mystery to most people—until recently, when the decline in demand for coal closed many pits and some found new life as museums, among them the **Big Pit** at Blaenavon in South Wales. This was a working colliery until 1980, and the aim today is to introduce visitors to the everyday life of the pit. On the surface you will see the changing rooms and pit head baths, the railway, and a reconstructed miner's cottage, but the principal attraction is underground. Fitted out with helmets and cap lamps, you enter the cage and are lowered to the galleries and the coal face, where former miners explain what went on down there.

Miners must go where the coal is, and villages with a strong sense of community grow up around the pit. Both mine and village are fully represented in the large open-air museum of **Beamish**, in the heart of the northeastern coalfield some ten miles northwest of Durham. One of the main features is the pit head with its original steam winding engine, which first began work in 1855. A railway leads from the mine to a row of 19th-century pit cottages, restored to show life at different periods. The Beamish Railway carries a working replica of George Stephenson's early 19th-century steam engine Locomotion, built in 1975 for the 150th anniversary of the Stockton and Darlington Railway. The railway also passes by a re-creation of a typical small-town street of the 1920s. Here are the

Industrial Heritage

```
0        miles        40
0        40
         kilometers
```

Liver

● Llanberis
▲ *Mt. Snowdon*
Porthmadog ● Blaenau
            Ffestiniog
            GWYNEDD

IRISH SEA

● Tywyn

A487

W A L E

River Cothi

■ Dolaucothi
● Pumpsaint

A40

DYFED

GW

Cardi

DEVON

River Tamar

● Sticklepath A30

DARTMOOR

CORNWALL

Tavistock
■ Morwellham
  Quay
● Cotehele

A30

A38

● Plymouth

N

station, a row of houses, the Cooperative store, and the pub. Everything, from shop fittings to the trams that run down the street, is of the period. Add a farm with animals, a transport collection, and a vintage fairground, and you have a museum that reflects every aspect of life in the region.

Iron

The area of Coalbrookdale and Ironbridge in Shropshire has been called the birthplace of the Industrial Revolution. The story began in the early 18th century, when Abraham Darby established his ironworks here using a revolutionary technique of smelting iron ore using coke. The whole area can now be thought of as one giant museum, split up into different sections, some consisting of conventional displays in buildings, others being based on existing features in the industrial landscape, but it is at the Coalbrookdale works that any tour of the area should start. Darby's original furnace is preserved as part of the **Coalbrookdale Museum of Iron and the Old Furnace**. It was from this furnace that iron flowed to be cast into the parts of the first iron bridge, which still spans the River Severn and which gives Ironbridge its name. Between Coalbrookdale and the bridge is another museum in an old warehouse by the Severn, but the major site in the area is **Blists Hill**, higher up the hill above Ironbridge. Blists Hill is still a working industrial complex. There are remains of its giant blast furnaces, and wrought iron is still made in a puddling furnace, a genuine industrial rarity. But there is also a wealth of other exhibits—a miniature town with shops and a pub, a colliery with a steam winding engine, a foundry, a candle factory, print works, and a curious canal where the boats, resting on cradles, were lowered down a steep incline to a lower level of the canal beside the River Severn. Down here, too, is the **Coalport China Works Museum**. There is more than enough of interest in the area to fill a whole day's touring.

Not all the museums of the iron industry are on such a large scale. The little village of Sticklepath, on the edge of Dartmoor, is home to **Finch's Foundry**, where edged tools such as scythes were once made. Here a succession of waterwheels provides the power for the various processes. One wheel moves the bellows that blast air into the furnace where the iron is heated, another powers the mighty hammers used to shape the metal on the anvil, and a third turns the grindstones on which the blades are sharpened. The latter gives literal significance to "keep your nose to the grindstone," for the grinder lies on a platform with his head just above the turning wheel. The same system can be seen at work, on a grander scale, at the **Abbeydale Industrial Hamlet** on the edge of Sheffield. Steel was manufactured on the site, and you can also see the whole range of machinery needed to turn an iron bar into a razor-sharp scythe blade. Elsewhere in the city the story of Sheffield steel is told in more detail—from the overall view presented at the **Industrial Museum** to the specialized work to be seen at **Shepherd Wheel**, a cutlery-grinding establishment.

Wool and Cotton

Historically, Britain's industrial wealth derived from the wool trade: the complex business of taking wool from the sheep, spinning it into yarn, and weaving that yarn into cloth. At first, this depended on individual spinners and weavers working in their own homes. Memories of those days are preserved in the **Colne Valley Museum** at Golcar in West Yorkshire, housed in a restored group of weavers' cottages. Here the women and children worked on the lower floors turning the wool into yarn, which then went to the men working at the hand looms on the upper floors. Spinning and weaving are still practiced here as they have been for centuries. Originally, the cloth would have been taken by the weavers or their masters to sell at one of the major trading centers. A magnificent example, the **Piece Hall**, built in 1775, has survived in nearby Halifax. Two floors of offices, joined by a colonnaded walkway, surround a central courtyard. The old offices now contain shops; a new industrial museum is also part of the complex.

Before being used, the cloth from the loom needed to be "fulled"—pounded in water by giant hammers—so that the fibers shrank and matted together. A water-powered fulling mill has survived at Helmshore in Lancashire. A cotton spinning mill was added to the Helmshore complex in the middle of the 19th century, and this has now become home to the **Museum of the Lancashire Textile Industry**. Displays tell the story of cotton, but the real attraction here is the old mill itself and its machinery, notably its spinning mules. The mules each spin 714 strands of yarn by means of whirring spindles on a moving carriage, which trundles back and forth across the mill floor. The mule, first devised at the end of the 18th century and for many decades the mainstay of the cotton industry, is fascinating to watch.

The first successful cotton mill, using the power of the waterwheel to turn many spindles, was built by Richard Arkwright at **Cromford** in Derbyshire in 1771. It was here that the factory age was born, and the village that Arkwright built to house the new work force was, in effect, the first mill town. The old mill still stands, though it is now little more than an empty shell. But the village still has much of its old atmosphere. North Street, in particular, shows the quality of Arkwright's houses. The long windows on the upper floors mark the workshops where the men wove while the women and children went off to the mill. A better-preserved example of an early Arkwright mill can be seen nearby at Matlock Bath. Cromford established a pattern—a water-powered spinning mill was built, then a village housing the work force grew up around it.

A fine example of the system is to be seen in the perfectly preserved complex at **Styal** in Cheshire. The mill at Styal was begun in 1784, was gradually expanded over the years, and remained at work for nearly two centuries. At first it relied entirely on waterwheels, but later steam power was added and power looms joined the spinning machinery. The atmosphere of this country mill in a delightful setting is very different from that of the crowded textile towns farther to the north. The mill is now in the care of the National Trust, and its original character has been preserved. Styal's importance, however, lies largely in the story it tells of the mill workers. Like the mill itself, the little village has remained virtually unchanged. The most poignant reminder of the old days is the apprentice house, which was home to more than 100 poor and orphaned children who worked 12 hours and more each day in the mill.

By the beginning of the 20th century, steam engines in mills had reached a monstrous size. Trencherfield Mill at Wigan had one of the biggest. Four huge cylinders were fed by steam to turn the enormous flywheel, around which ropes were wrapped to transfer the drive to all parts of the mill and set more than 80,000 spindles turning. The mill is now part of a new museum complex at **Wigan Pier**—there really was a Wigan Pier—a stop on the Leeds and Liverpool

Canal marked by old warehouses that now contain industrial exhibits. Local citizens have even forgiven George Orwell for his less-than-flattering portrayal of the town in his book *The Road to Wigan Pier* and have named the new pub after him. The museum is designed to tell the story of the area, and the past is brought to life by actors. Children can sit in the schoolroom furnished with slates and chalk and be shouted at by a suitably stern disciplinarian. The canal, which runs through the center of the site, can be explored on foot along a towpath or by boat (there is a regular water-bus service).

Canals

Canals fed the industries of Britain from the 1760s through to the 1820s, when the railway first became established. A complex network of more than 1,000 miles of waterway was constructed across Britain, and most of it is still in use—no longer to carry cargo but for the pleasure of boaters. Even a short trip on a canal is a good introduction to industrial Britain. But most canals also contain long, quiet rural stretches: The Leeds and Liverpool Canal, for example, once clear of the mill towns, runs through a landscape of moorland and rough fells. For those who are interested in history, there are excellent museums along the canals.

The **Boat Museum** at Ellesmere Port in Cheshire occupies what was once a major inland port complex that grew up where the Shropshire Union Canal met the River Mersey. The port and warehouses, designed by the engineer Thomas Telford, gained new importance with the construction of the Manchester Ship Canal at the end of the 19th century. Some of the original structures remain, including the steam engine used for the hydraulic system of the docks. But the principal interest lies in a collection of boats that once plied the inland waterways. Pride of place here belongs to the narrowboats, crafts approximately 70 feet long and 7 feet wide that were once in use on many of England's canals. One of the museum's prize exhibits is *Friendship,* the last privately owned horse-drawn narrowboat to work on the system. The tiny back cabin, where the family who operated the boat once lived, is perfectly preserved. Not all canals and rivers had the same size locks, so other boats were also in use, and the museum also has a collection of wide boats and short boats. Preserved cottages, a working forge, and the boat horses in their stable block complete the busy scene here.

A new **National Waterways Museum** opened in 1988 at The Docks in Gloucester, at the end of the Gloucester and Sharpness Canal. It is sited in a magnificent Victorian warehouse and has three floors of displays and exhibits telling the story of Britain's canals. Outside on the water are historic craft of all kinds, including a massive steam dredger. This is a splendid museum in a beautiful setting in the heart of the city.

The **Black Country Museum** at Dudley (some ten miles west of Birmingham) is a large open-air museum similar to those of Beamish and Ironbridge but firmly based on its canal location. The old canal basin, with its limekilns and workshops, has been preserved. The principal attraction here, though, is the narrow Dudley Tunnel, which links vast caverns where limestone was once quarried. The Dudley Canal Trust runs trips by electric narrowboat into the tunnel. In one of the narrowest sections, passengers are encouraged to try "legging." There was never a towpath in Dudley Tunnel, so the boatmen lay on their backs, put their feet against the tunnel wall, and walked the boat along. Thomas Newcomen constructed one of the first steam engines in Dudley in 1712, and a working replica is on display in the museum. Other Black Country industries, from chain making to coal mining, are also represented here, and there is a full range of buildings, from a Methodist chapel to a town pub.

Ports

The canal system joined the industries to the ports, and so to the rest of the world. Some of the early ports were a good way inland on navigable rivers and were often built to serve particular local needs. The River Tamar, which divides Cornwall from Devon, runs through the heart of a countryside rich in copper mines and tin mines. Small ports line the riverbanks, among them the one at **Cotehele**, where a typical Tamar sailing barge is preserved. Although the vessel looks romantic, it spent its trading days carrying manure. Farther upstream is a much greater port, **Morwellham**, whose wharves were connected to the local canal system and the mines by a complex railway that carried trucks high above the quays on wooden trestles. The workshops and houses that grew up around the quays form the basis of the open-air museum, and you can combine a visit there with a train ride into the heart of a hill to visit one of the old mines. Even in its heyday Morwellham could hardly claim to be a major port—though it could, with some justice, claim to have a beautiful setting.

If you want to see a port that is a true child of the Industrial Revolution, the place to go is **Liverpool**. Manchester was the commercial heartland of the Lancashire cotton industry, but it was through the port of Liverpool that the raw cotton came in from America and the finished products went out to the world. A new cargo was added in the 19th century—emigrants, many from Ireland, heading for a new life across the Atlantic. The **Merseyside Maritime Museum**, on the docks near the heart of the city, includes a superb example of Victorian industrial design, the Albert Dock. This is a closed dock ringed by warehouses, some now converted into housing, others to shops, and one block to the museum. There is an air of nobility about these buildings on giant iron pillars that lift them above the cobbled quay. Iron is the keynote here; even the classical façade on the office building at the entrance to the dock is iron. The museum has two aspects: the docks themselves, where ships such as the Mersey pilot cutter are displayed and dockside machinery is demonstrated; and the displays inside the various buildings. The most ambitious, and one of the most popular, is "Emigrants to a New World," where actors help re-create the story of European emigration from 1830 to 1930. Other exhibits vary in scale from full-size ships to miniature ones, and an expert shows just how to put a ship in a bottle. In 1988, Albert Dock also became home to the **Tate Gallery Liverpool**, which, like the original gallery in London, specializes in the best of modern art.

Shipbuilding

The story of British shipping is seen with greatest clarity in **Portsmouth**, where you can trace warships from the 16th to the 20th centuries. The story begins with the raising of Henry VIII's warship *Mary Rose* from the waters of the Solent in 1982. The vessel is by no means complete, but enough remains to give a clear picture of how she was built and how she would have looked. Experts are now at work in Portsmouth conserving the ancient timbers and replacing others. The remarkable salvage operation on the *Mary Rose* did more than reveal the remnants of the old structure—it also brought to life the different artifacts carried on board, from the bows and arrows of the military to the more mundane articles of everyday use. All these are displayed in a special museum alongside the old ship in the naval dockyard at Portsmouth, under the shadow of Admiral Nelson's flagship. The *Victory* is now restored, so what is seen today is the vessel very much as she was when she achieved her finest hour at the Battle of Trafalgar in 1805. She was a first-rate ship—which is not to say that she was excellent, but merely to define her as a ship bearing at least 100 guns. By the time of Nelson's great battle she was already old fashioned, work having started on her in 1759—something like fighting a World War II engagement with a Victorian battleship. The *Victory* represents the end of a long tradition of wooden ships moved by sails and engaging the enemy by firing broadsides from cannon set in lines all down the sides of the boat. The end it might have been, but it was a glorious end for *Victory*.

A new generation of warships appeared in the 19th century as the cannonball was replaced by the explosive shell and sails gradually gave way to steam. In 1861, the frigate *Warrior* was launched and the new age arrived. Everything about her was new: The old muzzle-loaded cannon had given way to breech-loaded guns with rifled bores; the steam engine supplemented the sail; and most important, she was armor-plated. Her hull consists of a sandwich, with iron as the filling and wood on the outsides. She was faster, more maneuverable, better protected, and better armed than any ship of Nelson's navy. Now that she is restored, it is possible to see just what a very fine ship she is. The *Warrior* is berthed at the quay just inside the dockyard gates.

The story of warships at Portsmouth does not end here, for at neighboring Gosport is the **Royal Navy Submarine Museum**, based on the World War II submarine HMS *Alliance*. This sleekly functional craft seems very far removed from the ancient timbers of the *Mary Rose*.

Railways

By far the most important change in transport took place not at sea but on land, with the arrival of the steam locomotive running on iron rails. Academics debate over which railway first began the modern age, but the designation generally goes to George Stephenson's Stockton and Darlington line, opened in 1825. The locomotive works were established at **Shildon** in Durham under the supervision of Timothy Hackworth. Here you can see something of the original line, parts of the works, and the Hackworth museum, based in the house where he lived and telling the story of his life and achievements. Here, too, is a working replica of Hackworth's most famous engine, Sans Pareil, which he built to compete in the Rainhill Trials of 1829, tests devised so that a locomotive could be chosen for the new Liverpool and Manchester Railway. The winner was Stephenson's Rocket, but Sans Pareil put up a brave fight.

Those who want a view of Britain's railway heritage from the earliest days to the most modern innovations should make their way to the **National Railway Museum** in York. Here is a vast range of locomotives covering the whole story of steam. The world record holder for steam locomotives, Mallard, is here, as is the last to be built for British Rail, Evening Star. The story is then continued into the age of diesel and electric trains. Locomotives represent only a part of train history, for rolling stock, too, has changed over the years: Compare the Bodmin and Wadebridge coach of the 1830s, little better than a cattle truck, with the splendor of Queen Victoria's coach of 1869. Around these main features are displayed railway paraphernalia, from signals to posters.

For many enthusiasts, however, the railways come to life only when the old engines have fire in their bellies. There is no shortage of preserved railways in Britain, though the movement began only in 1950 when a group of enthusiasts got together to try to save the little seven-and-a-quarter-mile-long **Talyllyn Railway** in Wales. It is little only in the sense of being narrow gauge, with the rails a mere two feet, three inches apart, but it makes a giant effort, climbing from sea level high into the hills using engines up to a century old. The magnificent scenery is accompanied by the sound of the locomotives struggling to take you there. The steam railway is perhaps better typified by the main lines and their innumerable lesser branches, and no railway has ever won more hearts than the G.W.R., prosaically the Great Western Railway, but to its thousands of enthusiasts, God's Wonderful Railway. The **Severn Valley Railway**, once a part of that great railway empire, runs for 16 miles from Kidderminster to Bridgnorth and is dedicated to keeping the G.W.R. tradition alive. Stations have been restored to look just as they did half a century ago and carriages are vintage stock, but the chief attractions are the old steam engines, everything from main-line locomotives to diminutive tank engines.

It is easy to lose sight of the importance of railways when indulging in nostalgia, so a useful corrective is to visit a line originally built for the process of hauling goods, not passengers. The 13½-mile-long **Ffestiniog Railway** was originally intended to take slate from Blaenau Ffestiniog to the port of Porthmadog. It just happened to pass through some of the most beautiful mountain scenery in Wales along the way, and scenery is part of the lure that draws the crowds today. But it also has a special place in the affections of railway enthusiasts. This was the first narrow-gauge railway to carry steam locomotives, and it still runs double-ended Fairlies, extraordinary contraptions that look like two conventional engines that have backed into each other and become permanently stuck together. It is a railway in which all the best elements of railroading come together, and to add to its appeal, it takes visitors to the heart of the most Welsh of Welsh industrial centers.

Slate

Blaenau Ffestiniog is the slate capital of Wales. Here people have quarried and mined to dig out the stones that would roof millions of houses. The town seems overwhelmed by slate, mountains of it all over the valley, great mounds that after rain gleam like jewels in the sun. The **Gloddfa Ganol Slate Mine** is more than just a mine, certainly more than just a museum: It is a mountain of slate into which miners have burrowed to create tunnels and caverns. The scale is spectacular. There are 30 different levels to the mine—the lowest some 500 feet below the town and the highest 1,600 feet above sea level. Visitors see deep into the workings of a slate mine and also catch a glimpse of the life and craft of the slate workers. Those who find themselves fascinated by this industry can find out more by visiting the **Welsh Slate Museum** at Llanberis, under the shadow of Snowdon and the Snowdon Mountain Railway.

The preceding, of course, is just a brief glimpse of Britain's industrial heritage. Nearly 100 railway museums and preserved railways go unmentioned here, and entire industries have been left untouched. One or two, however, are so well served by museums that you should add them to your itinerary. The **Gladstone Pottery Museum** at Longton, near Stoke-on-Trent, is one such place. Like many of the best industrial museums, it is based on an old working site. Gladstone was never one of the great names like Wedgwood or Spode, and that is perhaps part of its appeal. It is plain, honest, no-nonsense pottery, proving that true beauty exists in the commonplace. There are the wonderful sinuous shapes of the tall bottle ovens where the pots were fired, matched by the beauty of the pots on display. Here visitors can see every step of pottery making, from the shaping of the clay to the addition of the final decorative touches.

All this dashing about from steam engine to furnace is warm work, so what could be a more appropriate way to finish than with a cooling draught? Brewing must surely rank among the great British trades, and the story of beer is told in loving detail with opportunities for sampling at the brewing capital of England, Burton-upon-Trent. The **Bass Museum** occupies only a part of what is still a major working brewery—which is very much a part of the Industrial Revolution. It has its own steam engine (on show), it was built near a canal, and it has its own railway system. The brewery differs from most factories in that few industrial processes can boast such a palatable end product.

CHRONOLOGY
OF THE HISTORY OF
ENGLAND & WALES

The aim of this chronology is to give a quick guide to the historic context of the towns, buildings, and monuments that visitors will see on their travels through England and Wales. The time bands are unevenly spaced, reflecting the fact that the further back in time you go, the less you will find preserved today. Although the human race first came to Britain around half a million years ago, and there is ample evidence of the life of cave dwellers, there is little to see beyond stone axes preserved in museums. So, this chronology begins at the period when people first began to leave significant monuments on the landscape.

The Neolithic Age

The Neolithic Age, or New Stone Age (c. 4000 B.C. to 2000 B.C.), was the age of forest clearance and settlement, crop growing, and stock raising. Tools were manufactured from the hard stones, especially flints, the latter sometimes coming from deep mines, such as those of Grimes Graves, Norfolk. The dead were buried in communal burial places, either long barrows, great mounds surrounded by ditches, or stone chambers. The most striking memorials of the age are the henge monuments, the rings of bank and ditch of which Avebury and Stonehenge are the finest examples.

The Bronze Age

The Bronze Age (c. 2000 B.C. to 500 B.C.) saw the arrival of metal tools and weapons, and, as with the Neolithic Age, we know it now from its burial mounds and strange, mysterious monuments. The round barrows are familiar marks in the landscape, hemispherical humps that dot the tops of ridges. But the most impressive features are the stone rings and standing stones, such as the Rollright Stones in Oxfordshire.

The Iron Age

The end of prehistory is marked by a sophisticated Celtic culture in Britain (c. 500 B.C. to 50 B.C.). There is ample evidence of a settled way of life in such villages as Chysauster in Cornwall. Defense was a prime concern, however, resulting in the typical hill forts of the period. Maiden Castle near Dorchester in Dorset—an area of 45 acres surrounded by earth ramparts and ditches—is a fine example, while nearby South Cadbury hill fort is said to be the site of King Arthur's Camelot.

The Romans

The Romans (55 B.C. to A.D. 409) founded many of Britain's cities, among them London, York, and Lincoln, and joined them together by a network of roads, many of which survive in the routes that modern roads follow. Surviving villas with decorated pavements, central heating, and elaborate baths point to a rich, highly civilized lifestyle. Forts, fortifications, and military roads serve as reminders that the Romans came as military conquerors.

- **55–54 B.C.:** Caesar's expedition.
- **A.D. 43–47:** Claudian invasion and conquest of southern England.
- **50:** Foundation of London (Londinium).
- **61:** Revolt of Queen Boadicea.
- **122:** Hadrian's Wall begun.
- **c. 340–369:** Barbarian raids in Britain.
- **409:** Revolt against Constantine III and the end of Roman rule in Britain.

The Dark Ages and the Anglo-Saxons

With the end of the Roman Empire came invading armies of Saxons, Angles, and Jutes. They brought with them Norse religion and culture, still remembered in our days of the week: "Tiw's day," "Woden's day," and "Thor's day." In time, the country became divided between the Anglo-

Saxon kingdoms of what is now England and the Celtic realms of Wales. It was not a peaceful time, and the kingdoms were soon to be invaded by the Vikings from Scandinavia, who eventually established the Danelaw of North and East England. Christian missionaries arrived in the country, and their success can be seen in the early churches and crosses.

This period saw the establishment of many of the towns that are still important in Britain today. Some were simply developments of Roman centers, but others, such as Southampton, were essentially new Saxon towns. The Saxons also established "burhs," fortified towns, such as Oxford. The Norse established their own capital at York. The arts were represented by rich ornamental work such as that found in the Sutton Hoo burial ship, now in the British Museum, and by epic poems such as *Beowulf.* The period's finest accomplishment is to be seen in the beautiful illuminated manuscripts of the Christian church.

- **429**: Saint Germanus comes to Britain.
- **c. 450**: Saxon settlements in Kent.
- **477–495**: Saxon settlement of Sussex and Wessex.
- **c. 500**: British princes, said to include Arthur, establish peace at the battle of Mons Badonicus.
- **597**: Saint Augustine's mission arrives in Kent.
- **664**: Synod of Whitby establishes a unified church in England.
- **731**: Bede's ecclesiastical history completed.
- **757**: Offa becomes king of Mercia and begins fortifying the Welsh border by building the so-called Offa's Dyke.
- **793**: First Danish raids.
- **865**: The "Great Army" of Danes invades England.
- **871**: Alfred the Great becomes king.
- **878**: Alfred defeats the Danes.
- **919**: Foundation of Norse kingdom at York.
- **c. 940**: Monasteries founded at Glastonbury and Abingdon.
- **979**: Ethelred the Unready crowned.
- **1003**: Danes invade.
- **1014**: Danes elect Canute as king.
- **1016**: Ethelred dies and Canute becomes king of all England.
- **1037**: Harold becomes king.

- **1066**: Danes defeated at Battle of Stamford Bridge; English under Harold then defeated by William of Normandy at Battle of Hastings.

Normans and Plantagenets

The conquering Normans had one overriding priority: to establish their own rule. Consequently, the first and most important contribution they made to the English landscape was the castle. In its simplest form, the castle consisted of the motte and bailey—a motte, or mound, with a wooden tower on top, surrounded by a bailey, or courtyard, protected by a moat. Soon, the wooden tower was replaced by the stone keep, a daunting fortress of which the great White Tower of London is a particularly impressive example. The Medieval castle reached its ultimate expression with Edward I's conquest of Wales, when he promptly set about defending his newly won land with a string of border fortresses.

The Normans also brought with them elaborate Church rituals that required large churches, cathedrals, abbeys, and monasteries. The local churches remained comparatively simple in form but were often richly decorated with wall paintings explaining the scriptures to a largely illiterate populace. Architectural change came with the building of Durham Cathedral, begun in 1093, where the introduction of ribbed vaulting led to the full flowering of the Gothic style. The period also saw the establishment of the great religious houses, the monasteries and abbeys with their fine churches and extensive lands. The Medieval Church had a power to match that of the monarchy itself, a power that can still readily be seen in ruins such as those of Tintern and Fountains abbeys. Learning, too, was advanced with the establishment of universities at Oxford (1249) and Cambridge (1281).

The feudal society of the Normans was based on the lord of the manor, who gathered his wealth from the work of the villagers who plowed the fields and tended the stock. It was a land of contrasts but seldom a land at peace. Discontent between peasant and lord, between church and state, and between lord and lord, and the wider issues of international wars, including the Crusades in the Holy Land, combined to make this a period of seemingly endless turmoil.

- **1086**: The Domesday survey.
- **1087**: Accession of William II.
- **1100**: Accession of Henry I.
- **1135**: Accession of Stephen.
- **1139–1153**: Civil War as Stephen is challenged by Geoffrey and Matilda of Anjou.
- **1154**: Accession of Henry II.
- **1162**: Thomas à Becket appointed archbishop of Canterbury.
- **1170**: Becket murdered in Canterbury Cathedral.
- **1189**: Accession of Richard I.
- **1190**: Start of Richard I's crusades, which end in his imprisonment in Germany.
- **1199**: Accession of John.
- **1215**: Signing of Magna Carta.
- **1264**: Simon de Montfort's rebellion begins.
- **1272**: Accession of Edward I.
- **1276–1283**: Wars with Wales, culminating in the conquest of the principality.
- **1296**: Edward I invades Scotland.
- **1306**: Rebellion of Robert the Bruce.
- **1314**: Scots defeat the English at the Battle of Bannockburn.
- **1327**: Deposition of Edward II in favor of his son Edward III.

The Late Middle Ages

This period—which received its most notable, if not always its most accurate, chronicling in the plays of William Shakespeare—was dominated by war: the Hundred Years War between England and France and the seemingly endless civil wars between the houses of York and Lancaster (Wars of the Roses). Wars abroad cost a great deal of money, and taxation was resisted, most violently in the Peasants Revolt. To this bloodshed that washed over the country was added the horror of the Black Death, which reduced Britain's population by a third. Yet this period showed a fine, exuberant flowering of many arts. In architecture, the Gothic achieved its greatest expression in majestic cathedrals with tall spires, complex tracery windows, pointed arches, and elaborate decoration. Even today, the strong, sweeping curves of, say, Wells Cathedral seem almost incredibly bold. Perhaps the principal feature of the age was the birth of a truly English literature. It was a literature based in part on the high romance and chivalry of courtly life and in part on the experience of the rougher world of ordinary men and women. Its first masterpiece was Langland's *Piers Plowman,* but that was soon surpassed by Geoffrey Chaucer's *Canterbury Tales.* Another great work of the time is Malory's *Morte d'Arthur.* Literature was given a further boost at the end of the period with the arrival of William Caxton's printing press.

- **1337**: Start of the Hundred Years War.
- **1346**: Battle of Crécy.
- **1348**: Beginning of the Black Death.
- **1356**: Battle of Poitiers.
- **1362**: First version of *Piers Plowman.*
- **1377**: Accession of Richard II.
- **c. 1386**: *The Canterbury Tales.*
- **1399**: Accession of Henry IV.
- **1400–1410**: Rebellion of Owen Glendower of Wales.
- **1413**: Accession of Henry V.
- **1415**: Battle of Agincourt.
- **1422**: Accession of Henry VI.
- **1450**: Jack Cade's rebellion.
- **1470**: *Le Morte d'Arthur* completed.
- **1475**: Accession of Edward IV.
- **1477**: Caxton's first book printed in England.
- **1483**: Death of Edward IV and Edward V and accession of Richard III.
- **1485**: The Battle of Bosworth and the death of Richard III marks the end of the Wars of the Roses.
- **1492**: Columbus in the New World.

The Tudors

The accession of Henry Tudor brought an end to the apparently endless struggle of the Wars of the Roses. Peace at home was also marked by a new prosperity founded, in good measure, on the wool trade, while at the same time the country was looking increasingly to its overseas connections with the Americas and the Far East. This was an age of discoveries and innovations. Britain built up a navy under Henry VIII that was to prove its worth with the defeat of the Spanish Armada. The arts flourished, particularly architecture. The wealthy no longer needed to concentrate on grim castles for defense but could turn to exuberantly decorated homes instead—houses such as Burghley and Hardwick Hall. The Gothic style also reached its climax, typified by the extraordinary fan-vaulted ceiling of King's College Chapel, Cambridge. The old religious houses were less fortunate, reduced to ruin by Henry VIII's dissolution of the monasteries and the break with Roman Catholicism. Other arts, however, thrived. Painters such as Holbein depicted the famous, while the English miniaturist Nicholas Hilliard provided the most telling images of the age. British music found a distinctive voice in the works of William Byrd. But it was in literature that the period reached its peak of achievement—first with the poems of Edmund Spenser, then with the plays of Christopher Marlowe, and finally with the genius of William Shakespeare.

- **1509**: Accession of Henry VIII.
- **1515**: Cardinal Wolsey appointed lord chancellor.
- **1517**: Martin Luther's 95 theses posted at Wittenberg.
- **1533**: Henry VIII marries Anne Boleyn.
- **1536**: The union of England and Wales and dissolution of the monasteries; publication of the first English-language Bible.
- **1545**: Sinking of Henry VIII's ship *Mary Rose*.
- **1552**: Birth of Edmund Spenser.
- **1553**: Accession of Mary.
- **1558**: Accession of Elizabeth I.
- **1562**: Sir John Hawkins's first voyage transporting slaves from Africa to America.
- **1564**: Births of Christopher Marlowe and William Shakespeare.
- **1587**: Execution of Mary Stuart.
- **1588**: Defeat of the Spanish Armada.
- **1603**: Death of Elizabeth I.

The 17th Century

This century of contrasts saw the Stuart dynasty take the throne, lose it in the Civil War, and regain it at the Restoration. It ended with the firm establishment of Protestant domination with the accession of William of Orange in the English Revolution. The period saw the flamboyance of the Restoration and the austerity of Puritanism. It was above all a century of religious conflict, which appeared in such diverse forms as the Catholic Gunpowder Plot to blow up Parliament and the departure of many Puritans to look for a new and better life in America. These differences spilled over into other areas, notably literature and the world of ideas. On one side there was the metaphysics of the poet John Donne and on the other the austere majesty of Milton and the plainer allegory of Bunyan. The world was viewed in different lights, colored by the philosophical thoughts of Thomas Hobbes and the scientific discoveries of Isaac Newton. In architecture, there were new themes to explore in the styles of the Baroque and the Classical. Christopher Wren, the master of the Baroque, set his mark on London following the Great Fire, while Inigo Jones produced such formal masterpieces as Somerset House in London. The outstanding composer of the age was Henry Purcell.

- **1603**: James VI of Scotland becomes James I of England and Wales.
- **1605**: The Gunpowder Plot.
- **1611**: Authorized Version of the Bible published.
- **1616**: Death of Shakespeare.
- **1620**: Pilgrims set sail from Plymouth.
- **1625**: Accession of Charles I.
- **1642**: Civil War begins.
- **1649**: Execution of Charles I.
- **1651**: Thomas Hobbes, in *Leviathan,* develops a pessimistic rationalism.
- **1653**: Oliver Cromwell becomes lord protector.
- **1660**: Charles II restored.
- **1666**: Great Fire of London.
- **1667**: Publication of *Paradise Lost.*
- **1685**: Accession of James II; Edict of Nantes revoked; thousands of French Protestants arrive in England.
- **1687**: Publication of Newton's *Principia Mathematica.*
- **1688**: Accession of William of Orange and Mary.
- **1690**: John Locke completes his *Essay Concerning Human Understanding.*

The 18th Century

The period tends to be associated with the name "Georgian," for George I came to the throne in 1714 and George III was still alive when the century ended. Britain did not experience the political revolutions that convulsed Continental Europe, yet there were profound changes. Britain lost one colony in the American Revolution, but at the same time a new empire was being built in India. This age presented two faces to the world. One showed an urbane, cleanly classical aspect, epitomized in the architecture of Bath; the other was a dirtier, rougher visage, representing the new and exciting age of industrial development. These divisions were fundamental. On the one hand were the arts, notably architecture, where a severe Classicism ruled, where a dining room by Robert Adam would be furnished by Sheraton or Chippendale and the food would be eaten off plates by Wedgwood, possibly to the accompaniment of music by the fashionable composer of the day, Handel. The other side appeared in the rush toward industrialization— canal building, the construction of the first factories, and the appearance of the steam engine. Literature showed an equally lively sense of innovation: The novel was born with the work of Richardson, Fielding, and Sterne, while others, led by the poets William Blake and William Wordsworth, turned away from the aggressive industrial world. This was also a period when changes in agriculture produced the pattern of neat fields and farms that now seem typical of the attractive British landscape.

- **1702**: Accession of Queen Anne.
- **1712**: Thomas Newcomen builds a steam engine at Dudley.
- **1714**: Accession of George I.
- **1726**: *Gulliver's Travels* published.
- **1727**: Accession of George II.
- **1735**: William Hogarth's *The Rake's Progress*.
- **1738**: John Wesley founds Methodism.
- **1740**: David Hume finishes *A Treatise of Human Nature*.
- **1745**: Bonnie Prince Charlie leads unsuccessful Jacobite Rebellion.
- **1760**: Accession of George III; construction of Britain's first true canal.
- **1771**: First powered cotton mill opens.
- **1773**: The Boston Tea Party.
- **1776**: American Declaration of Independence.
- **1776**: Adam Smith's *An Inquiry into the Nature and Causes of the Wealth of Nations* published.
- **1779**: Completion of the world's first iron bridge.
- **1785**: Start of the French Revolution.
- **1791**: Thomas Paine's *Rights of Man*.

The 19th Century

The 19th century can be split into two periods: the Georgian age shading off into the Regency, and the Victorian age. In terms of the arts the distinction has some validity, but as regards the development of society as a whole, there is no such division. The new world of industry and trade went on expanding: Factories continued developing, the steam engine appeared on rails as a steam locomotive, and a new generation of industrial cities grew up. But while engineers such as Isambard Brunel looked for new forms for their bridges, ships, and railway stations, architects increasingly turned back to the older styles of the Gothic for churches, town halls, and mansions. In the arts, the Romantic movement that had begun with Wordsworth and his contemporaries was extended by artists such as Turner, the poets Keats and Shelley, and such novelists as the Brontë sisters. Increasingly, however, there was a growing concern with social questions, and changes can be seen most clearly in the novel. At the beginning of the century, Jane Austen conducted her minute dissections of an enclosed society, and at the end Charles Dickens created his loud, teeming world.

- **1804**: The first steam locomotive runs on rails.
- **1805**: Battle of Trafalgar.
- **1815**: Battle of Waterloo.
- **1820**: Accession of George IV.
- **1832**: The Great Reform Bill extends the franchise.
- **1836**: Dickens's *Pickwick Papers*.
- **1837**: Accession of Queen Victoria.
- **1838**: First steamship crosses the Atlantic.
- **1851**: The Great Exhibition.
- **1854**: Start of Crimean War.
- **1859**: Charles Darwin's *Origin of Species*.
- **1869**: Opening of Suez Canal.
- **1876**: Victoria declared empress of India.
- **1880**: Start of Boer Wars.

The 20th Century

In the 19th century Britain was one of the great powers of the world, with a huge empire and a manufacturing industry that earned it the title "workshop of the world." That structure has slipped and crumbled in the 20th century.

One by one, the old colonies have achieved independence, and industrial innovation has largely become the provenance of other countries. Britain has been a participant, rather than an innovator, in the major developments of the age—the motor car, the airplane, and the computer. The process has been accelerated by two world wars, and the bombings of the second necessitated major rebuilding in many towns and cities. The confidence that produced the Gothic extravaganzas of the Victorian age has evaporated, however, so that there has been little new development to warrant more than modest praise. In the arts, literature has continued to be the most innovative and successful medium, though music, not historically one of Britain's stronger arts, has thrived, covering a wide range from Benjamin Britten to the most successful of popular musicians, the Beatles. Much of the character of modern Britain derives from a long history; it remains to be seen whether that character will be preserved, adapted, or simply lost.

- **1901**: Death of Victoria, accession of Edward VII.
- **1910**: Accession of George V.
- **1914–1918**: World War I.
- **1918**: Women win the vote.
- **1922**: Formation of BBC.
- **1924**: First Labour government.
- **1936**: Death of George V, abdication of Edward VIII, and accession of George VI.
- **1939–1945**: World War II.
- **1947**: India given independence.
- **1952**: Accession of Elizabeth II.
- **1973**: Britain enters the European Economic Community.
- **1979**: Margaret Thatcher is the first woman to become prime minister.
- **1982**: War in the Falklands.

—Anthony Burton

INDEX

FOR THE BEST IN PAPERBACKS, LOOK FOR THE

In every corner of the world, on every subject under the sun, Penguin represents quality and variety—the very best in publishing today.

For complete information about books available from Penguin—including Pelicans, Puffins, Peregrines, and Penguin Classics—and how to order them, write to us at the appropriate address below. Please note that for copyright reasons the selection of books varies from country to country.

WHEN TRAVELLING, PACK

WHEN TRAVELLING, PACK

All the Penguin Travel Guides offer you the selective and up-to-date information you need to plan and enjoy your vacations. Written by travel writers who really know the areas they cover, The Penguin Travel Guides are lively, reliable, and easy to use. So remember, when travelling, pack a Penguin.